THE VIKING AGE: IRELAND AND THE WEST

The Viking Age:
Ireland and the West

*Papers from the Proceedings of the Fifteenth
Viking Congress, Cork, 18–27 August 2005*

John Sheehan & Donnchadh Ó Corráin
EDITORS

Shannon Lewis-Simpson
EDITORIAL ASSISTANT

FOUR COURTS PRESS

Typeset in 10.5 pt on 12.5 pt Ehrhardt by
Carrigboy Typesetting Services for
FOUR COURTS PRESS LTD
7 Malpas Street, Dublin 8, Ireland
www.fourcourtspress.ie
and in North America for
FOUR COURTS PRESS
c/o ISBS, 920 NE 58th Avenue, Suite 300, Portland, OR 97213.

A catalogue record for this title is available
from the British Library.

ISBN 978–1–84682–101–1

Printed in England
by MPG Books, Bodmin, Cornwall.

Contents

Illustrations

Colour plates, between pp 308 and 309

Contributors

LESLEY ABRAMS is a Fellow of Balliol College and a member of the History Faculty of the University of Oxford.

MICHAEL P. BARNES is Emeritus Professor of Scandinavian Studies in University College London.

DOUGLAS B. BORTHWICK is a researcher in the Department of Geography and Environment, University of Aberdeen.

KRISTIN BORNHOLDT COLLINS, University of Cambridge.

PAUL C. BUCKLAND, Crosspool, Sheffield.

HOWARD B. CLARKE is a former Associate Professor in the School of History, University College Dublin.

KEVIN J. EDWARDS is Professor of Geography and Environment at the University of Aberdeen.

COLMÁN ETCHINGHAM is a Lecturer in the Department of History, National University of Ireland, Maynooth.

GILLIAN FELLOWS-JENSEN is a former Associate Professor at the Institute of Name Research, University of Copenhagen.

CLAUS FEVEILE is Curator at Den Antikvariske Samling, Ribe.

IAN FISHER is an Honorary Research Fellow with the Department of Celtic, University of Glasgow and was formerly a field-investigator with Royal Commission on the Ancient and Historical Monuments of Scotland.

ANNE-SOFIE GRÄSLUND is Emeritus Professor in the Department of Archaeology and Ancient History, Uppsala University.

JAN RAGNAR HAGLAND is Professor of Scandinavian Languages at the Norwegian University of Science and Technology, Trondheim.

ANDREW HALPIN is an Assistant Keeper in the Irish Antiquities Division of the National Museum of Ireland.

STEPHEN H. HARRISON is Principal Researcher at the Irish Viking Graves Project at the National Museum of Ireland.

PERNILLE HERMANN is an Assistant Professor at the Scandinavian Institute at the University of Aarhus.

VOLKER HILBERG is a Curator at the Archäologisches Landesmuseum Schleswig and is a member of the scientific staff of the Forschungsprojekt Haithabu.

MAURICE F. HURLEY, formerly Senior Archaeologist in Waterford City, was City Archaeologist in Cork from 1991 to 2005.

JUDITH JESCH is Professor of Viking Studies at the University of Nottingham.

SVEN KALMRING is a Curator at the Archäologisches Landesmuseum Schleswig and is a member of the scientific staff of the Forschungsprojekt Haithabu.

EAMONN P. KELLY is Keeper of Irish Antiquities at the National Museum of Ireland.

JAMES E. KNIRK, Professor, is Director of Runic Archives, Museum of Cultural History, University of Oslo.

RAYMOND LAMB, the former Orkney Archaeologist, lectures in Orkney College, University of the Highlands and Islands.

ALAN M. LANE is Senior Lecturer in the School of History & Archaeology, Cardiff University.

SHANNON LEWIS-SIMPSON is a Lecturer in the Department of English, St John's, Memorial University of Newfoundland.

THOMAS LINDKVIST is Professor of Medieval History at the University of Göteborg.

NIELS LUND is Professor of History at the University of Copenhagen.

THOMAS H. McGOVERN is Professor of Anthropology, Hunter College, City University of New York.

ELSE MUNDAL is Professor of Old Norse Philology at the Centre for Medieval Studies, University of Bergen.

JOHN NAYLOR is a post-doctoral Research Assistant on the VASLE project, University of York.

SÆBJØRG WALAKER NORDEIDE is a Researcher at the Centre for Medieval Studies, University of Bergen.

TOMÁS Ó CARRAGÁIN is a Lecturer in the Department of Archaeology, University College Cork.

BARRA O'DONNABHAIN is a Lecturer in the Department of Archaeology, University College Cork.

GUÐMUNDUR ÓLAFSSON is Head of Archaeology at the National Museum of Iceland.

INGVILD ØYE is Professor of Medieval Archaeology at the University of Bergen.

ANNE PEDERSEN is Curator and Senior Researcher at the National Museum of Denmark.

EMER PURCELL is a Research Associate on CELT (Corpus of Electronic Texts), Department of History, University College Cork.

JULIAN D. RICHARDS is Professor of Archaeology at the University of York.

ELSE ROESDAHL is Professor of Medieval Archaeology at the University of Aarhus.

DANIEL SÄVBORG is a Lecturer in the Department of Literature, Uppsala University.

JOACHIM SCHULTZE is a Curator at the Archäologisches Landesmuseum Schleswig and is a member of the scientific staff of the Forschungsprojekt Haithabu.

BERIT J. SELLEVOLD is a Senior Researcher at the Norwegian Institute for Cultural Heritage Research (NIKU).

JOHN SHEEHAN is a Senior Lecturer in the Department of Archaeology, University College Cork.

SVAVAR SIGMUNDSSON is Assistant Professor at the Árni Magnússon Institute for Icelandic Studies.

MAEVE SIKORA is an Assistant Keeper in the Irish Antiquities Division of the National Museum of Ireland.

LINZI SIMPSON is a Senior Consultant Archaeologist with MGLARC Ltd, Dublin.

SØREN M. SINDBÆK is a Lecturer in the Department of Archaeology, University of York.

KEVIN P. SMITH is Deputy Director of the Haffenreffer Museum of Anthropology, Brown University, Providence, Rhode Island.

ÞÓRGUNNUR SNÆDAL is a Senior Executive Officer at the National Heritage Board in Stockholm.

ANNE STALSBERG is Associate Professor in the Museum of Natural History and Archaeology, the Norwegian University of Science and Technology, Trondheim.

STEFFEN STUMMANN HANSEN formerly served with Føroya Fornminnissavn, Faroe Islands.

OLOF SUNDQVIST is a Senior Lecturer in the Department of Humanistics and Social Sciences, University of Gävle, Sweden.

GUÐRÚN SVEINBJARNARDÓTTIR is a Research Fellow at the Institute of Archaeology, University College London.

ORRI VÉSTEINSSON is a Lecturer in the Department of History and Archaeology, University of Iceland.

CLAUS VON CARNAP-BORNHEIM, Professor, is Director of the Archäologisches Landesmuseum and Director of the Archäologisches Landesamt Schleswig-Holstein.

PATRICK F. WALLACE is Director of the National Museum of Ireland and Adjunct Professor in the Department of Archaeology, University College Cork.

DOREEN WAUGH is a Research Fellow at the School of Celtic and Scottish Studies, University of Edinburgh.

ELIZABETH WINCOTT HECKETT is a Research Associate at the Department of Archaeology, University College Cork.

The Fifteenth Viking Congress
Cork, 2005

PATRON

Her Excellency Mary McAleese, Uachtarán na hÉireann

ORGANIZING COMMITTEE

Donnchadh Ó Corráin, Department of History, University College Cork
John Sheehan, Department of Archaeology, University College Cork
Patrick F. Wallace, National Museum of Ireland

STUDENT ASSISTANTS

Emer Purcell, Department of History
Griffin Murray, Department of Archaeology

Members & Associates

Denmark
Jan Bill, Gillian Fellows-Jensen, Claus Feveile, Pernille Hermann, Poul Holm (accompanied by Dorthe Uldall and Kristoffer Holm), Michael Lerche Nielsen, Niels Lund, Anne Pedersen, Else Roesdahl, Jens Peter Schjødt, Søren Michael Sindbæk.

England
Lesley Abrams, Michael Barnes, Mark Blackburn, Paul Buckland, Jayne Carroll, James Graham-Campbell, Richard Hall, Judith Jesch, David Parsons, Julian Richards, Leslie Webster, Gareth Williams.

Faroe Islands
Steffen Stummann Hansen

Greenland
Jette Arneborg

Iceland
Anton Holt, Guðmundur Ólafsson, Vésteinn Ólason (accompanied by Unnur Alexandra Jónsdóttir), Svavar Sigmundsson (accompanied by Thorgerdur Arnadóttir), þórgunnur Snædal, Gísli Sigurðsson, Guðrún Sveinbjarnardóttir, Orri Vésteinsson.

Ireland
Kristin Bornholdt Collins (accompanied by Guy J.D. Collins and Lyra Bornholdt Collins), Howard Clarke, Michael Connolly, Colmán Etchingham (accompanied by Cathy Swift), Andy Halpin, Stephen H. Harrison, Maurice Hurley, Jørgen H. Jørgensen, Eamonn P. Kelly, Anne-Christine Larsen, Thomas Martin, Finbar McCormick, Máire Ní Mhaonaigh, Tomás Ó Carragáin, Donnchadh Ó Corráin, Barra O'Donnabhain, Raghnall Ó Floinn, Dáire O'Rourke, John Sheehan, Maeve Sikora, Linzi Simpson, William J. Smyth, Patrick F. Wallace, Niamh Whitfield.

Norway
Sverre Bagge, Signe Horn Fuglesang, Jan Ragnar Hagland, Sigrid Kaland, James E. Knirk (accompanied by Kari Egeland), Else Mundal, Berit Sellevold, Dagfinn Skre, Anne Stalsberg, Sæbjørg Walaker Nordeide, Ingvild Øye.

Scotland
James Barrett, Colleen Batey, Clare Downham (accompanied by David Dumville), Kevin Edwards, Ian Fisher, David Griffiths, Arne Kruse, Raymond Lamb, Olwyn Owen, Caroline Paterson, Doreen Waugh, Alex Woolf.

Sweden
Stefan Brink, Anne-Sofie Gräslund, Helmer Gustavson, Thomas Lindkvist, Rune Palm, Neil Price, Daniel Sävborg, Olof Sundqvist, Claus von Carnap-Bornheim.

Wales
Nancy Edwards, John Hines, Alan Lane.

Student Delegates
Andres Dobat (Denmark), Hildur Gestsdóttir (Iceland), Gunhild Hovik Hansen (Wales), Shannon Lewis-Simpson (England), John Maas (Ireland), Mogens Skaaning Høegsberg (Denmark), Griffin Murray (Ireland), Ole-Magne Nøttveit (Norway), Emer Purcell (Ireland), Jonas Wellendorf (Norway).

Congress Diary

Delegates arrived at University College Cork on Wednesday, 17 August 2005. Formal proceedings began next morning with a welcome by the College President, Professor Gerard Wrixon. This was followed by a busy day of lectures on the main Congress theme, Viking-Age Ireland. Before dinner that evening many delegates enjoyed a walking tour of UCC's campus. Later they attended a reception in the Staff Common Room, hosted by the Department of Archaeology and the Department of History. Here an important new work on the earliest Viking activity in the south-west, *Underworld: Death and Burial in Cloghermore Cave, Co. Kerry*, by Michael Connolly and Frank Coyne, was launched.

Friday morning was devoted to papers on the second theme of the Congress, the Development of Urbanism. Following lunch, the members of the Congress visited the poster sessions hosted by the student delegates. That evening they attended a reception where they were joined by many members of Munster's archaeological and historical societies. After the reception, Donnchadh Ó Corráin gave a public lecture on 'Irish and Vikings in the North Atlantic'. A vote of thanks was proposed by James Graham-Campbell.

Saturday was entirely devoted to a coach excursion to Limerick and Clare, conducted by Patrick F. Wallace. The first stop was Killaloe, a pre-Norman borough and early capital of the Dál Cais kings. Here, too, Magnus Barelegs spent a winter as the guest of Muirchertach Ó Briain, king of Munster. The delegates visited St Flannan's Cathedral and examined its rune-inscribed stone and twelfth-century high cross. They also visited nearby Béal Boru, a fortress commanding the passage up and down the river Shannon, the Viking highway to the Irish midlands. Following lunch in the Medieval Inn, Limerick, there was a tour of the thirteenth-century King John's Castle in the heart of the medieval city. This included a visit to its in situ remains of Viking-age houses. A mayoral reception for the Congress delegates was hosted in the castle by the Right Worshipful Councillor Dermot Scully. This was followed by a visit to the nearby St Mary's Cathedral, hosted by the Very Reverend the Dean of Limerick, Dr Maurice Sirr. On the return journey to Cork the delegates enjoyed a splendid dinner in Springfort Hall and a post-prandial stroll in its tranquil gardens.

On Sunday the Congress returned to its main theme and devoted the full day to Viking-Age Ireland. Following dinner that evening, the delegates bravely undertook a walking tour of Viking and Medieval Cork (or, as it turned out, part of it) in pouring rain. This was led by Maurice Hurley, City Archaeologist, and included visits to St Fin Barre's Cathedral and South Main Street, the latter being the core of Viking Cork. The tour was followed by a much needed and generous reception hosted by Beamish and Crawford in their historic brewery. A memorable vote of thanks to our hosts was proposed by Jørgen H. Jørgensen.

On Monday the delegates spent the day on a coach excursion to Waterford, organized by Eamonn McEneaney and Dáire O'Rourke. This began with a visit to the newly-discovered and very important Viking site at Woodstown, on the banks of the River Suir, above Waterford. Following lunch, delegates took part in a seminar on the Woodstown site, chaired by Patrick F. Wallace. This included short presentations by Dáire O'Rourke and Maurice Hurley. Afterwards there was a tour of the Waterford Treasures exhibition, led by Orla Scully, and a reception hosted by Waterford City Council in Reginald's Tower, the oldest civic urban structure in Ireland, the precursor of which may have been Dundory, a tenth-century Viking fortification. On the return journey to Cork delegates dined well at Aherne's Seafood Restaurant and the Coach House Restaurant, at Youghal. The Vikings had a settlement at Youghal in the ninth century, as the delegates were reminded.

On Tuesday the Congress addressed a third theme, Scandinavia and the Continent. Following afternoon tea, the congress photograph was taken in the President's Garden at University College Cork, and the day's formal academic proceedings ended. There followed the meeting of the Congress Council. This was chaired by Donnchadh Ó Corráin, and it was unanimously agreed that the next Congress, that of 2009, should be held in Iceland. That evening the XVth Viking Congress Banquet, with a 'Viking' menu, took place at Hayfield Manor Hotel, beside the University. It was a memorable occasion, made poignant by the members' recollections of those distinguished scholars who had died since the notable Congress of 2001 on the Faroe Islands.

Wednesday 24 August, the final day of the main Congress, was devoted to papers on the last theme of the Congress, Weapons and Warfare. Some delegates departed that evening; others prepared for the post-Congress tours.

The first post-Congress tour, a coach trip to Co. Tipperary, took place next morning. Led by Tomás Ó Carragáin, it began with an extended visit to one of Ireland's best-known monuments, the Rock of Cashel. This was the royal centre of the kingdom of Munster before it became its ecclesiastical capital and seat of its archbishop. Its kings played a notable role in the Viking wars. The delegates inspected several important monuments, including the round tower and the twelfth-century high cross. They visited Cormac's Chapel, a very early example of Irish Romanesque, which has a sarcophagus ornamented in the Urnes style. During lunch in nearby Brú Boru, delegates were treated to a performance of traditional Irish song and dance. In the afternoon a trip was made to the Glen of Aherlow, where the ecclesiastical sites of Toureen Peakaun, raided by the Vikings in 830, and Berrihert's Kyle, named after Berechert, the Anglo–Saxon saint, were visited.

Next day, Friday, delegates rose well before dawn to set out in darkness by coach to the westernmost part of Co. Kerry, the Iveragh Peninsula. Dawn had broken over the mountains of Kerry when they reached Killarney, the heartland of the kingdom of the Eoganacht of Loch Léin who had fought, with some success, against their Viking attackers in the early ninth century. The coach travelled west along the valley of the Laune, the Vikings' access route to Eoganacht of Loch Léin, and then along the north shore of the Iveragh Peninsula, where one overlooks Dingle Bay, the site of much ninth-century Viking activity. Refreshed by plentiful mugs of tea and thick slices of porter cake at O'Keeffe's Bar on the pier at Portmagee, they boarded the three half-deckers for the twelve-kilometre Atlantic journey to Skellig Michael. The sea was rough (as it should be) and the sea legs (and indeed much else besides) of many notable Viking scholars were put to the test. None failed. The skill of the boatmen and the derring-do of the delegates (especially at the landing-stage) prevailed. Led by John Sheehan, they climbed the steep steps to the summit and spent hours in bright sunshine inspecting Ireland's most dramatically situated early medieval monastery and its marine environment. This unique site, which contains the best-preserved oratories and beehive huts in Ireland, was raided by the Vikings several times. Just before leaving, the delegates toasted in Irish whiskey the memory of Abbot Étgal who died as a prisoner of the Vikings in the course of a raid on Skellig in 824. It was eirenically agreed that he had died by misadventure, namely, because of cultural misunderstanding.

The final day of the post-Congress tour, in glorious weather, was led by Donnchadh Ó Corráin. It began with a leisurely boat cruise down the River Lee to Cork Harbour, where there are several sites of Scandinavian origin as well as some Norse place-names, notably Foaty and Dunkettle. The delegates disembarked at Cóbh, the old transatlantic liner port and took lunch in a restaurant overlooking the harbour. Then they transferred to a coach to visit important sites in east Cork and west Waterford. They went first to Ardmore, a rich monastic site with a panoramic view of the ocean. It has ogham stones, a very well-preserved round tower and an important Romanesque frieze. The tour then turned inland and followed the heavily wooded valley of the Blackwater northwards to the great medieval ecclesiastical sites of Molana and Lismore. Molana is famous as a riverside monastery that had a distinguished school of early medieval canon law. Lismore was the greatest and richest ecclesiastical centre in the east of the kingdom of Munster, and notable for its learning. Both were raided several times by the Vikings. The tour returned to Cork city inland through the lush farmlands of Waterford and Cork. Following dinner at University College Cork that evening, the delegates retired for final farewell drinks at the Kingsley Hotel. *Haec olim meminisse juvabit.*

* * *

We acknowledge, with thanks, the generous support given the Congress by the Heritage Council, its principal sponsor, and by the following: Beamish and Crawford Ltd; Four Courts Press; Limerick City Council; Midleton Distillery Ltd; the National Museum of Ireland; Shannon Heritage Ltd; UCC Arts Faculty Conference Fund; UCC Department of Archaeology; UCC Department of History; Waterford City Council; and Wordwell Ltd.

Finally, it gives the Organizing Committee great pleasure to acknowledge the unfailing enthusiasm, energy and courtesy of its assistants: Emer Purcell, Department of History, and Griffin Murray, Department of Archaeology.

Conversion and the Church in Viking-Age Ireland

LESLEY ABRAMS

Something of great interest happened between 'the burning of Rechru by the heathens', recorded in the Annals of Ulster under the year 795, and the visit to Rome by the king of Dublin, Sihtric Silkenbeard (Sigtryggr silkiskegg), in 1028. In the intervening two hundred and thirty-three years, the Scandinavian foreigners in Ireland – like so many others throughout the first millennium – made the transition from a traditional pagan religion to Christianity. The conversion of the Hiberno-Scandinavians is, however, a transition that has to some degree been taken for granted and not extensively explored. This is not really surprising, for any attempt to clarify how it might have occurred raises difficult, but fundamental, questions about the nature of interaction between the native population and those who arrived from overseas. Also at issue is the political and ecclesiastical character both of the society that the Scandinavian incomers found in Ireland and of the society they created for themselves. I have examined the conversion of Ireland's Scandinavians in the past, focussing particularly on questions of evidence (Abrams 1997), but I would like to take the opportunity offered by the Viking Congress in Cork to return to the issue more generally, posing some questions about the nature of the process.

The fundamental issue of definition dogs any discussion of conversion (see Abrams 2000). Conversion is a problematic concept, and the term has meant different things to those who have used it, both now and in the past. A population can be considered converted when it is baptized, for example, or when it adopts Christian practice, when it has absorbed Christian belief, or when an institutional Church has been established. The choice of definition will condition perception (not to mention identification and dating) of the process. Two fundamental models have been applied. In the classic top-down model, churchmen target kings, and kings impose the new religion on their people through a variety of means, from brute force to the passing of laws. The bottom-up model, on the other hand, imagines a more organic conversion – by osmosis or peer pressure from friends and neighbours – where assimilation into an existing Christian population (if there is one) takes place without any directing authority. Top-down conversion is often seen in terms of political communities and group identities, whereas bottom-up is necessarily more individual.

Conversion marked a crucial stage of development in the encounter between incomer and native in the Scandinavian settlements established overseas. Ireland in the ninth and tenth centuries was a land with entrenched Christian institutions, where society had long been defined by Christian custom. By 980, Amlaíb Cuarán (Óláfr Kvaran), king of Dublin, was sufficiently connected to the Christian establishment to be buried at the Hebridean monastery of Iona. The absence of source material has nevertheless meant that both date and method of the transition to Christianity of his fellow countrymen remain obscure. It is, of course, impossible to give a specific date to a process, especially if it is drawn out over time. But historians, using different criteria, have nonetheless suggested conflicting dates for the conversion of the Scandinavians in Ireland. These range from the second half of the ninth century (as soon as Vikings began to stay on a permanent basis) to the early eleventh (when a diocese was founded in Dublin and its king went on pilgrimage to Rome). Disagreement may be inevitable under the circumstances. In any case, differences between men and women, elite and non-elite, military men and craftworkers, occupants of *longphuirt*, townspeople, and hinterland-dwellers from region to region may have meant that Scandinavians in Ireland became Christians at different times. If we are to begin to understand *how* conversion happened, however, as well as when, we must ask not just how religious establishments may have drawn in the new Christians, but how Hiberno-Scandinavian society worked: was collective political identity the most relevant force when it came to religious change, for example, or might individuals have been able to operate on their own initiative?

Answers to such questions are not easy to come by. Archaeological evidence of religious identity is sparse, although Thor's hammers and furnished burials at least reflect the practice of contemporary – pagan – Scandinavia (Johnson 2004, 88). In any event, the way in which material remains relate to religious change is complex and controversial, and uncertainties of dating also complicate the application of physical evidence to a narrative of conversion. Monumental sculpture which combines Christian and Scandinavian mythological imagery is found in Scandinavian settlements in northern England and south-western Scotland, but none has so far been discovered in Ireland, where sculpture from the settlement period with any Scandinavian connection is difficult to identify. Hogbacks, characterized as 'Viking colonial monuments' by James Lang, are found in substantial clusters in areas of Scandinavian settlement in England and Scotland but are represented in Ireland by a lone example at Castledermot (Co. Kildare). According to Lang, its patron may have 'misunderstood' the real thing in producing his imitation (Lang 1971, 155). As far as I know, only the Rathdown slabs, in the region south of the Liffey, have in addition been associated with Hiberno-Scandinavian Christians (Clarke 2000, 36–7, fig. 3), and their repertoire of motifs – though unlike contemporary Irish sculpture – bears no relation to Scandinavian art elsewhere. The runic inscription in Old Norse on a standing cross at Killaloe (Co. Clare) which reads 'Thorgrim raised this cross' is a rare manifestation of explicitly Scandinavian Christianity in Ireland (Barnes et al. 1997, 53–6). It seems to belong to late in the period (perhaps the eleventh century) and tells us unfortunately little about the context of its construction – nothing about how long Thorgrim or his family had been Christian (assuming he was of Scandinavian ancestry), and how he (and/or they) had become so – though it is noteworthy that a matching ogham inscription proclaims Thorgrim's Christianity in Irish as well as Scandinavian form.

Written sources occasionally mention apparently pagan cult objects (i.e., *ATIG* 994), but there are no surviving accounts, contemporary or retrospective, of missionary campaigns targeting the Scandinavian immigrants. Annals offer the best written evidence (though only indirectly) that pagan Vikings became Christian. Of the two main names for Scandinavians used in the Irish annals, *geinte* ('heathens') and *Gaill* ('foreigners'), the former identifies the Vikings in religious terms, very much as The Other, whereas the latter gives them a national name in the local Irish context. Both are used in the ninth century. On the other hand, as David Dumville, among others, has observed, the increasing use of *Gaill* in preference to *geinte* must be significant, and the decline of *geinte* after the 940s surely says something about the Scandinavians' conversion (Dumville 1997, 37). It also helps if we look beyond Irish sources, as the baptism or confirmation of two (perhaps three) Viking kings of Dublin is recorded in the Anglo-Saxon Chronicle. The ambitions of these kings to control York along with Dublin had brought them into conflict with the West Saxons, themselves struggling to dominate the north of England. First Sihtric and then his son Olaf (Amlaíb Cuarán) and nephew Ragnall seem to have formally accepted Christianity following political agreements with, respectively, the Anglo-Saxon kings Athelstan and Edmund (*ASC* 926 and 943). Therefore, if we believe the Anglo-Saxon Chronicle, the formal conversion of at least the Dublin royal family can be attributed to English political initiatives and to Hiberno-Scandinavian involvement in northern Britain in the second quarter of the tenth century (Abrams 1997).

What this suggests, if it is not a trick of the sources, is that the ruling dynasty in Dublin had up to this late point not formally accepted the Christian religion, though it says nothing about the religious identity of the rest of the Scandinavian population. It is possible that the rulers of Dublin had already been Christian in a way that Anglo-Saxon kings (or chroniclers) did not recognize, but, if so, that Christianity remains elusive. The Irish annals make it clear that there had been much interaction between Viking and native and therefore plenty of opportunity for cultural exchange long before the mid-tenth century. While Vikings killed Irish secular and ecclesiastical leaders, as the annals repeatedly attest, they also allied with them and married their sisters and daughters. Amlaíb, king of the Foreigners in the mid-ninth century (Óláfr inn hviti, Olaf the White), is said in the Fragmentary Annals to have married the daughter of the overking of the Northern Uí Néill (Radner 1978, 112). Several daughters of Cerball of Osraige appear in *Landnámabók* as ancestors of Icelandic settlers (tabulated in Todd

1867, 297–302). There is no evidence that conversion was a pre-requisite of these early alliances, and little evidence either way of the religious consequences.[1]

Diplomatic conversions by English and continental kings in their dealings with Vikings are well known, and not just in tenth-century Northumbria: from Louis the Pious and the Danish king Harald Klak in the 820s to Æthelred and the Norwegian Ólafr Tryggvason in the 990s (Sawyer et al. 1987), Christian rulers bound pagan Vikings to them through the imposition of baptism in order to limit Scandinavian attacks, establish peace, or tie the foreigners more firmly into their hegemonies – and Christian writers scored these as royal successes. But not, apparently, in Ireland. One explanation could be that Irish kings did indeed successfully exert pressure to convert in the ninth century, but that their efforts and agreements simply went unrecorded by annal writers with other interests. The apparent paganism of the Dublin Viking leaders in the second quarter of the tenth century suggests otherwise. Perhaps this family had a particular attachment to a traditional warrior ideology. Or perhaps Irish kings, unlike their Frankish and Anglo-Saxon contemporaries, just did not *do* that kind of thing. Although churches and kings worked 'in tandem, each [...] content to boost the pretensions of the other' (Ó Corráin 1981, 327), there does seem to be a general contrast to be drawn between the behaviour of Irish kings and their Viking-Age counterparts in Anglo-Saxon England and Francia. There, kings could play a central role in the religious programme of their kingdoms, appointing bishops, setting Christian policy, and 'running' the Church – in other words, taking the lead in matters of ecclesiastical policy. The extent to which this was the case in Ireland is very unclear (the ninth-century bishop-kings of Munster are obviously exceptional, being both kings and bishops); but if kings did not play these roles in Church affairs, they may not have seen it as their business to bring pagan Vikings to the font. There is better evidence from the mid-eleventh century of kings and churchmen working together (Holland 2002), and by the early twelfth century, Archbishop Anselm's letters indicate his expectation that kings correct both social and ecclesiastical abuses (Fröhlich 1994, 214–16; Schmitt 1946–61, V: 373–4).

If converting pagans was not the business of Irish kings, we might expect it to be the business of the Irish Church. Máire Ní Mhaonaigh (1998) has shown that the Viking stereotype was alive and well in Irish literature of the period, but the Viking convert is more elusive. In England there were Scandinavians in the episcopate as early as the 920s, and material signs of Scandinavian integration and cultural influence on Christian expression in the form of sculpture from at least the early tenth century. In Ireland, as I understand it, Scandinavian art styles did not make a serious impact until the eleventh century, at which time they influenced secular and religious art alike (Ó Floinn 2001, 91–7). In the later

---

[1] For a son of Olaf the White with a Christian name (Carlus), see *AFM* 866.

tenth century, there is evidence from personal names, as some Scandinavians adopted Irish names that declared their Christianity – especially those with the prefixes *Gilla* ('servant') and *Mael* ('tonsured one, devotee'), such as *Gilla Pátraicc m. Imhair* ('servant of Patrick, son of Ímar') (*AU* 983). Also in the late tenth century, Scandinavian rulers can occasionally be associated (peacefully) with churches: Amlaíb Cuarán with the religious house at Skreen, for example (Bhreathnach 1996), and the dynasty that ruled Limerick with the church at Inis Cathaig (Scattery Island) in the Shannon estuary, where ecclesiastical life continued without apparent disruption (*AFM* 972 and 975).

Alfred Smyth has explained the absence of evidence of early absorption of Scandinavians into the Irish Church by citing the strength of monasticism. Although religious communities which had Scandinavian political allies were able to survive, 'no compromise was possible on a religious level', he argued, and 'hostility between Irish monastic rulers and the Norsemen's repressed missionary endeavour' (Smyth 1975–9, II: 260–1). The Church, turned inwards, may have dedicated itself to opposing the Viking threat through prayer and reform rather than evangelizing it. Howard Clarke, on the other hand, has argued that there was continuity of ecclesiastical provision in ninth- and tenth-century Dublin. At the religious sites of Dublinn and nearby Kilmainham, groups of male burials with weapons may indicate that Vikings took over and occupied the monastic enclosure, as they did at Repton in Derbyshire (*ASC* 874). But Clarke has argued that 'ordinary churches' could have continued to operate around Dublin, and that 'episcopal functions were maintained at major church sites in the vicinity, such as Clondalkin' (2000, 34). No churches have as yet been shown to have had a continuous existence in the Hiberno-Scandinavian town, but on the basis of its mixed material culture, Clarke has envisaged a population of 'cohabiting Irish and Scandinavians', combining Christianity with 'elements of pagan belief if not overt practice' (2000, 31 and 38). In particular, he argued that the town's female inhabitants would have been Christian and practised Christian burial, though the royal dynasty probably buried its dead in the burial mounds across the Poddle estuary, near the Thingmount (Clarke 2000, 32–4; 2002, 3). Clarke conceived of 'the great majority of [Dublin's] local population [being] Irish as well as Christian' (2000, 33), a situation which would have required ecclesiastical provision in the Scandinavian town for one sector of its population, but not the other.

How Scandinavian takeover affected pre-existing ecclesiastical geography and religious provision is obscured by the paucity of sources. As conceived by Clarke, in political terms Dublin would have been under Scandinavian political leadership, but subject to Irish episcopal jurisdiction. This is difficult to accommodate within the characterization of the Irish Church as a collection of political units, 'ecclesiastical states' (Sharpe 1984, 269), where bishoprics were coterminous with kingdoms. Colmán Etchingham's model of episcopal government has portrayed the domains of bishops as co-extensive with defined polities, their authority being bound up with the kings who patronized them (1999, 187). If that was the case in the tenth century, it is hard to imagine how overlapping powers within Dublin could have been managed. When dioceses came to be created for the Scandinavian towns, they appear to have been defined territorially, based on political units in the Irish way. The tiny diocese of Waterford, for example, occupied only the area immediately around the Hiberno-Scandinavian town. It was not absorbed into the Irish ecclesiastical unit that surrounded it.

Of course churchmen from outside Ireland could have been active in the Hiberno-Scandinavian towns, especially from regions where the kings of Dublin had relationships of patronage or clientage. Though tenth-century Iona increasingly faced away from Ireland after the early ninth-century raids (Herbert 1988, 78–87), Doherty has argued for its influence in Dublin (1998, 299–301), and Jennings (1998) has assumed that it was busy among the Scandinavian populations throughout the Irish Sea and Atlantic zones (see also Abrams 2007). In the tenth century, Scandinavian kings of York returning to Dublin were not generally on friendly terms with the West Saxons, so it may be unlikely that they were accompanied by churchmen from southern England. Relations with the Northumbrian Church may have been better. More certain is the substantial ecclesiastical contact between Ireland and England in the eleventh century, and some have argued that the establishment of the diocese in Dublin belonged to Knútr's hegemonic activities (Gwynn 1955, 3–6; Hudson 1994). This may not survive scrutiny, but other influences from the wider Scandinavian world should not be discounted. By the eleventh century, Norway, Denmark and Wales (ruled by a family with close personal ties to the Dublin kings) may have been sources of Christian influence. Churches in Dublin and Waterford were dedicated to St Olaf, whose *uestimentum* was said to have been donated to Dublin's cathedral by the first bishop (Todd 1844, 3 and 141; Clarke 2004, 144). Dedications to St Werburgh, associated with Chester, and St Audoen, potentially a connection with Rouen, presumably reflect Dublin's links with churches outside Ireland. These dedications are unfortunately difficult to tie to a date of foundation.

Amlaíb Cuarán may have returned to Dublin in the 950s and patronized Irish poets and Columban religious houses in the region (Bhreathnach 1996), but he was buried on Iona, and a Dublin diocese was not heard of until late in the reign of his son, Sihtric Silkenbeard (989–1036) (Gwynn 1992, 50–67). Clarke has suggested a date of *c.*1030 for its foundation (2000, 34). It is curious that Amlaíb did not establish an episcopal centre in his kingdom of Dublin.[2] Although the origins of the see remain obscure, it does not appear to have been an Irish

2 Alex Woolf has reminded me, however, that Dublin may have been only one part of a much larger polity until the very end of the tenth century. The formation of a diocese may have followed on from the redefinition of political units.

initiative. Alex Woolf has even suggested that the first bishop, Dúnan, *ardespoc Gall* ('high-bishop of the Foreigners'), may have been a bishop for Scandinavians in the Irish Sea zone, and that a diocese was not fixed at Dublin until after his death in 1074 (*AU* 1074; Woolf 2003, 171–2). The second bishop of Dublin, Gilla Pátraic, was sent for consecration to Canterbury by the Irish king of Munster and the Scandinavian king of Dublin. Some have taken this to suggest that the diocese was a Canterbury-sponsored foundation from the start. Dioceses in other Hiberno-Scandinavian towns were similarly late. Although a son of the king of Waterford also bore the Christian name Gilla Pátraic when he died in the 980s (*AU* 983), the first bishop of Waterford was not consecrated until 1096 (also in Canterbury) (Gwynn 1942). The first bishop of Limerick does not appear in the record until *c.*1107 (Gwynn 1992, 112–13).

How far the conversion of a king affected the rest of the population is unclear. If there was a Viking ideology centred on religious cult, it may have had staying power among military men, distinguishing them from the town's other inhabitants. The top-down model of conversion stresses the importance of royal influence, but towns might have been able to make independent decisions, and town-dwellers might even have had something like individual choice. If this were so, conversion through interaction and personal decision-making is conceivable, though local pastoral care would have had to be already on hand. In Sihtric's reign, royal patronage was directed at the cathedral church. Numerous other churches, first attested in the twelfth century, may have been established in the eleventh. Clarke has noted that many were dedicated to non-Irish saints, several of which (such as John the Baptist or Paul) might have particularly appealed to recent converts (2004, 147–57). He has argued that many were *Eigenkirchen*, reflections of the piety of the Hiberno-Scandinavian population.

The creation of dioceses for the towns, though a reflection of Christianized populations, hardly indicates integration of the Hiberno-Scandinavians, as the configuration of the dioceses exemplified the towns' continuing political independence. Thanks to the wealth of archaeological evidence uncovered in recent excavations, there has been a change in the perception of relations between natives and Foreigners. Clarke's vision of a Dublin occupied by 'cohabiting Irish and Scandinavians' (2001, 31), for example, represents a shift from ideas of isolated urban enclaves towards a model of more integrated populations, whether in the urban hinterlands (Bradley 1988) or rural way-stations (Sheehan et al. 2001). On the other hand, despite this mixed material culture and written evidence of constant political interaction, Scandinavians and Irish did not assimilate, even after the major Scandinavian defeats of 980 and 1015 increased Irish control of Dublin. The towns retained their separate identities and were not integrated politically into the larger units of Irish life, even if they came under Irish control; and the Hiberno-Scandinavian dioceses remained outside the formal structure of the Irish Church until the creation of a provincial system under the impetus of reform in the early twelfth century. Only in 1111, at the synod of Ráth Bressail, was Dublin incorporated into the neighbouring Irish diocese (Gwynn 1992).

In some respects, therefore, there seems to have been a continuing divide between Hiberno-Scandinavians and Irish. Norse was still spoken in the eleventh century, and Scandinavian dynasties continued to signal their identity with Norse personal names. The rulers of Dublin led Viking-style expeditions and were called kings of the Foreigners. While the earliest extant instances of 'Ostman', apparently derived from ON *austmaðr* ('east-man'), and the place-name Oxmantown or Ostmanby (*Houstmanebi*) date to after the Anglo-Norman invasion, they indicate that there was still a perception of an ethnic dimension to the Dublin settlement (Purcell 2003–4, 276–7). This reflects a distinction between Hiberno-Scandinavians and Irish found in eleventh-century sources (Duffy 1995, 382–3), which continued to be recognized long after the late twelfth century (Curtis 1908; Purcell 2003–4).

The Irish in the early Middle Ages were notable evangelists, but that famous early zeal was bound up with exile. It would have been a different matter having heathens in your own backyard. Smyth has pointed out (1975–9, II: 260–1) that Bede provides a precedent for a Church holding itself aloof from an unloved neighbour, racially defined: 'The Britons would not proclaim to the English the knowledge of Christian faith which they had' (*HE* v. 22). In the Viking Age, religious separatism, the absence of a unitary state, and in particular the cellular nature of Irish political and ecclesiastical institutions may have combined to keep Irish and Scandinavians apart. It was a complex situation, and religion's role in negotiations between the two societies is unfortunately obscure.

ACKNOWLEDGMENTS

I should like to thank Clare Downham for drawing Inis Cathaig to my attention, Ruth Johnson for information on Thor's hammers in Dublin, and Alex Woolf for reading a draft version of the paper.

BIBLIOGRAPHY

Abrams, L. 1997. 'The conversion of the Scandinavians of Dublin', *Anglo-Norman Studies*, 20, 1–29.
Abrams, L. 2000. 'Conversion and assimilation' in D.M. Hadley & J.D. Richards (eds), *Cultures in contact: Scandinavian settlement in England in the ninth and tenth centuries* (Turnhout), pp 135–53.
Abrams, L. 2007. 'Conversion and the Church in the Western Isles in the Viking Age: "A very difficult thing indeed"' in B. Ballin Smith et al. (eds), *West Over Sea: studies in Scandinavian sea-borne expansion and settlement* (Leiden), pp 169–93.

AFM = O'Donovan, J. (ed. and trans.). 1856. *Annála Ríoghachta Éireann. Annals of the Kingdom of Ireland by the Four Masters*, 2nd ed. (Dublin).

ASC = Plummer, C., and J. Earle (ed. and trans.). 1892 [1952]. *Two of the Saxon Chronicles Parallel* (Oxford).

ATIG = Stokes, W. 1895. 'The Annals of Tigernach', *Revue Celtique*, 16, 374–420.

AU = Mac Airt, S. & G. Mac Niocaill (ed. and trans.). 1983. *The Annals of Ulster* (Dublin).

Barnes, M.P., J.R. Hagland & R.I. Page. 1997. *The runic inscriptions of Viking Age Dublin* (Dublin).

Bhreathnach, E. 1996. 'The documentary evidence for pre-Norman Skreen, County Meath', *Ríocht na Midhe*, 9, 37–45.

Bradley, J. 1988. 'The interpretation of Scandinavian settlement in Ireland' in J. Bradley (ed.), *Settlement and society in Medieval Ireland: studies presented to F.X. Martin, osa* (Kilkenny), pp 49–78.

Clarke, H.B. 2000. 'Conversion, church and cathedral: the diocese of Dublin to 1152' in J. Kelly & D. Keogh (eds), *History of the catholic diocese of Dublin* (Dublin), pp 19–50.

Clarke, H.B. 2002. *Dublin, Part I, to 1610*, Irish Historic Towns Atlas (Dublin).

Clarke, H.B. 2004. 'Christian cults and cult centres in Hiberno-Norse Dublin and its hinterland' in A. MacShamhráin (ed.), *The Island of St Patrick: church and ruling dynasties in Fingal and Meath, 400–1148* (Dublin), pp 140–58.

Clarke, H.B., M. Ní Mhaonaigh & R. Ó Floinn (eds). 1998. *Ireland and Scandinavia in the Early Viking Age* (Dublin).

Curtis, E. 1908. 'The English and the Ostmen in Ireland', *English Historical Review*, 23, 209–19.

Doherty, C. 1998. 'The Vikings in Ireland: a review' in H.B. Clarke et al. (eds), *Ireland and Scandinavia* (Dublin), pp 288–330.

Duffy, S. 1995. 'Ostmen, Irish and Welsh in the eleventh century', *Peritia*, 9, 378–96.

Dumville, D.N. 1997. *The churches of north Britain in the first Viking-Age* (Whithorn).

Etchingham. C. 1999. *Church organization in Ireland, A.D. 650 to 1000* (Maynooth).

Fröhlich, W. (trans.). 1994. *The letters of Saint Anselm of Canterbury*, 3 (Kalamazoo).

Gwynn, A. 1942. 'The origins of the diocese of Waterford', *Irish Ecclesiastical Record*, 59, 289–96.

Gwynn, A. 1955. 'The first bishops of Dublin', *Repertorium Novum: Dublin Diocesan Historical Record*, 1, 1–26.

Gwynn, A. 1992. 'The synod of Rath Breasail' in G. O'Brien (ed.), *The Irish church in the eleventh and twelfth centuries* (Dublin), pp 180–92.

HE = Colgrave, B., and R.A.B. Mynors (ed. and trans.). 1969. *Bede's Ecclesiastical History of the English People* (Oxford).

Herbert, M. 1988. *Iona, Kells and Derry: the history and hagiography of the monastic familia of Columba* (Oxford).

Holland, M. 2002. 'The synod of Dublin' in S. Duffy (ed.), *Medieval Dublin III* (Dublin), pp 81–94.

Hudson, B. 1994. 'Knútr and Viking Dublin', *Scandinavian Studies*, 46, 319–35.

Jennings, A. 1998. 'Iona and the Vikings: survival and continuity', *Northern Studies*, 33, 37–54.

Johnson, R. 2004. *Viking Age Dublin* (Dublin).

Lang, J.T. 1971. 'The Castledermot hogback', *Journal of the Royal Society of Antiquaries of Ireland*, 101, 154–8.

Ní Mhaonaigh, M. 1998. 'Friend and foe: Vikings in ninth- and tenth-century Irish literature' in H.B. Clarke et al. (eds), *Ireland and Scandinavia* (Dublin), pp 381–402.

Ó Corráin, D. 1981. 'The early Irish church: some aspects of organization' in D. Ó Corráin (ed.), *Irish Antiquity: essays and studies presented to Professor M.J. O'Kelly* (Dublin), pp 327–41.

Ó Floinn, R. 2001. 'Irish and Scandinavian art in the Early Medieval period' in A.C. Larsen (ed.), *The Vikings in Ireland* (Roskilde), pp 87–97.

Purcell, E. 2003–4. 'The expulsion of the Ostmen, 1169–71: the documentary evidence', *Peritia*, 17–18, 276–94.

Radner, J.N. 1978. *Fragmentary Annals of Ireland* (Dublin).

Sawyer, B. & P. Sawyer 1987. *The Christianization of Scandinavia* (Alingsås).

Schmitt, F.S. (ed.). 1946–61. *S. Anselmi Cantuariensis Archiepiscopi Opera Omnia*, 6 vols (Edinburgh).

Sharpe, R. 1984. 'Some problems concerning the organization of the Church in Early Medieval Ireland', *Peritia*, 3, 230–70.

Sheehan, J., S. Stummann Hansen & D. Ó Corráin. 2001. 'A Viking Age maritime haven: a reassessment of the island settlement at Beginish, Co. Kerry', *Journal of Irish Archaeology*, 10, 93–119.

Smyth, A.P. 1974–9. *Scandinavian York and Dublin*, 2 vols (Dublin).

Todd, J.H. 1844. *The Book of Obits and Martyrology of the Cathedral Church of the Holy Trinity* (Dublin).

Todd, J.H. 1867. *Cogadh Gaedel Re Gallaibh: The War of the Gaedhil with the Gaill* (London).

Woolf, A. 2003. 'The Diocese of the Sudreyar' in S. Imsen (ed.), *Ecclesia Nidrosiensis 1153–1537* (Oslo), pp 171–81.

Runic inscriptions and Viking-Age Ireland

MICHAEL BARNES & JAN RAGNAR HAGLAND

Runes and runic inscriptions have for obvious reasons been a recurring theme in the long series of Viking Congresses – sometimes, as for instance at the Ninth Congress on the Isle of Man in 1981, even a major theme. The Irish inscriptions have, although in a less prominent way, been on the agenda at some of the more recent congresses. Until 1997, when *The Runic Inscriptions of Viking Age Dublin* by Barnes, Hagland and Page was published (launched at the Thirteenth Viking Congress in Nottingham that year), only three Irish inscriptions had been edited – all three, it seems, from the very end of the period we call the Viking Age. After the 1997 publication (which contains the runic material discovered during the Medieval Dublin Excavations 1962–81, plus the Roosky bracelet and the three items known from earlier finds), the total number of runic inscriptions from Ireland available to the scholarly world had risen to sixteen. Some of the Dublin inscriptions had been briefly mentioned in earlier work, but not given the full runological treatment. Even at sixteen, the amount of text conveyed by the corpus of Irish runes is not great.

Nor is the general picture greatly altered by the discovery of a new inscription in 1996 during the Temple Bar West excavations carried out by Linzi Simpson (Fig. 2.1). Nevertheless, since this runic artefact is relatively unknown and seems to contain one or two items of interest, we offer a brief account of it below.

So, can the Irish runic inscriptions add anything to our understanding of Viking-Age Ireland? This question cannot be answered in terms of a simple yes or no. The meaningful content of the inscriptions *per se* does not appear to add very much to what can be deduced from the sum of archaeological evidence relating to Vikings and Viking activity in Ireland. To judge the significance of the runic finds to the study of Viking-Age Ireland we need, of course, first of all to know their time of origin as precisely as possible. This, as always, is one of the difficult problems in runology. Nonetheless, the entire corpus of runic inscriptions from Ireland seems datable in the period *c.*950–1125, that is to say in the late Viking Age or shortly thereafter. That is certainly true of the Dublin inscriptions (Barnes, Hagland and Page 1997, 13). It should, however, be stressed that the dating of the Dublin material derives from the archaeological strata in which the inscribed objects were found. As we all know, that does not necessarily give the exact date of individual artefacts. The four inscriptions found outside Dublin (IR 1, 2, 3 and 15) all seem to belong in the period 950–1125 too – though the usual uncertainty about exact dating applies. IR1, the Greenmount

11

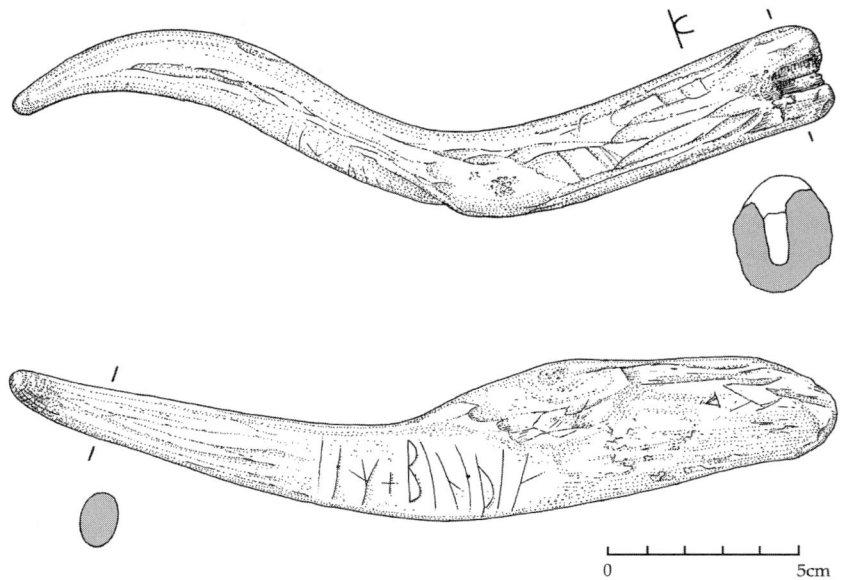

0   5cm

2.1 Rune-inscribed handle, of deer antler, from Temple Bar West, Dublin (96E246:3000:18)
(© National Museum of Ireland. Drawing: John Murray).

inscription, Co. Louth, is inscribed on an object with 'interlaced pattern of inlaid silver wires flanked by niello' of a type found on pieces of metalwork of about 1100 (Barnes, Hagland and Page 1997, 50). IR 2, the Killaloe cross, and IR 3, the Beginish stone, are dated to approximately the same time, Killaloe only very tentatively (Barnes, Hagland and Page 1997, 56, 58). IR 15, a single-rune inscription from Roosky, Co. Donegal, is carved on an arm-ring or bracelet of a type current in the period 850–950 (Barnes, Hagland and Page 1997, 60). This is, then, possibly the oldest of the runic inscriptions found in Ireland so far.

As for the source value of the Irish runic inscriptions, it seems pertinent here as a start to confront our 1997 edition with the optimistic intentions expressed in a brief report on the project, by one of the present authors, at the Twelfth Viking Congress at Hässelby, Stockholm in 1993 (Hagland 1994). In this report the runological as well as the linguistic aims of the project were enunciated. The intention was to provide a survey of the runic forms found in the Irish Sea area – the range of graphs with specific reference to diagnostic forms – ordered geographically as well as chronologically. On the linguistic level, questions pertaining to language contact and Scandinavian origin were to be asked and discussed. We are, of course, not the ones to judge how far these aims have been achieved. Nonetheless, we think it is fair to say that the questions were given reasonable coverage in the edition. And in the course of the discussion some general answers concerning the importance of the runic inscriptions for aspects of the history of Viking-Age Ireland were suggested. There is no reason to reiterate all those points here. A couple, though, may be briefly reformulated, and it is worth reopening one question touched upon in the edition – that of runes and literacy in Viking-Age Dublin.

Before we do so, it should be pointed out that the 1993 presentation, rather too optimistically, stated (with the text there garbled by a page-setting error) that

> The archaeological context of the Dublin runes will have to be discussed in such terms as: What sorts of sites are involved? What does the archaeological evidence reveal about habitation, possible commercial activities, manufactures? Indeed, anything that may contribute to the understanding of the inscriptions (Hagland 1994, 302).

Unfortunately, the kind of archaeological analyses needed to illuminate such discussions were not available at the time we were compiling the edition. It is possible that a detailed contextual analysis of each individual runic inscription from Dublin would provide us with further insights into the corpus as a whole and its role in Viking-Age society. But that is for the future.

One factor worth emphasizing is the very existence of a group of runic inscriptions from Dublin. Comparison may, of course, be made with various Scandinavian towns, but by and large the material from Bergen, Trondheim, Lödöse etc., is of a later date. Viking-Age York, in contrast to Dublin, has not so far yielded a single indubitably Scandinavian runic inscription. This might have to do with the age of Scandinavian ascendancy in the two towns, but early Viking-Age Hedeby has its share of runic artefacts, including runic sticks not unlike those that characterize the medieval urban environment. But then we have no idea who made the Dublin inscriptions – local residents or passers-by. The appearance of runes in Dublin and their absence from York may tell us about the culture of those who visited the towns rather than those who lived there.

A further point of interest is what the Irish inscriptions in general can tell us about developments in runic writing in the Scandinavian-speaking world. A striking feature of four of them (IR 1, 2, 9 and 12) is the occurrence of dotted runes (on this feature, see Haugen 1976 and Knirk, this volume). The practice of dotting certain characters seems to have begun around the year 1000, and its place of origin has generally been identified as Denmark. The appearance of three ᛁs (dotted ᛁs) in both IR 1 Greenmount and IR 9 Christchurch Place, and of a ᛔ (dotted ᛔ) in IR 2 Killaloe would not disturb this view, for IR 9 is dated in the mid-eleventh century and IR 1 and 2 somewhat later. IR 12 Fishamble Street, on the other hand, which sports a clear ᚼ (dotted ᚾ), is given a date of *c.*1000, roughly the time at which dotting is supposed to have originated in Denmark. Recently, Page and Hagland have suggested on the basis of evidence from *runica manuscripta* that dotting may 'have been created in Scandinavian communities, perhaps in Danish-influenced areas, of the British Isles [...] and exported from there to Scandinavia' (1998, 68). And they postulate the existence of a full inventory of dotted graphs 'no later than, say, 1050'. The ⋔ of IR 12 and, to a lesser extent, the dotted runes of IR 1, 2 and 9, might be thought to offer some support to these untraditional ideas about developments in Scandinavian runic writing in the late Viking Age. And third, it may be of some value within the framework of a Viking Congress in Ireland to reopen briefly the question of literacy among the Vikings in Ireland, in Dublin in particular. It is appropriate to quote here once more the opinion expressed by John Ryan (1990, 126) about the general culture of the Norse citizens of Dublin.

> It seems to be an historical fact that they produced absolutely no literature. Not a single Dublin writer in prose or poetry is known between the settlement at Áth Cliath in the middle of the ninth century and the coming of the Normans. The same is true of the Northmen all over Ireland. A few runic inscriptions alone bear witness to any knowledge, even rudimentary, of letters.

This is evidently a reiteration of views expressed as early as 1949 ('It seems to be a historical fact that they produced no literature'; Ryan 1949, 82). The statement must, of course, be seen in the context of the extended discussion of what Theodore M. Andersson once termed 'the Irish Hypothesis' (Andersson 1964, 56–61). As far as the alleged literary achievements of the Norse population are concerned, the discussion probably reached its climax with Sophus Bugge's suggestion (1908) that a *Brjáns saga* – a saga which was later incorporated into *Brennu-Njáls saga* – was written in the Norse colony of Dublin shortly after the Battle of Clontarf in 1014, a view which seems to have gained little support. Here is not the place to go into the history of this debate or the question of Irish influence on Icelandic literature in general, a fairly recent survey of which is given by Gísli Sigurðsson (1988). It may be, however, that Ryan's picture of a virtually illiterate Viking-Age Norse Dublin needs to be modified. The extent of runic writing known in the present state of research is not, of course, dramatically different from that available to scholarship in 1990. Nonetheless, as pointed out by Barnes, Hagland and Page (1997, 11–13), there is in pre-Norman Dublin faint evidence of the epigraphic use of other scripts than runes. There is a single ogam text (on a comb found in excavations at Dublin Castle), apparently a personal name (Old Norse *Áki*), and there are several inscriptions in varieties of the Latin alphabet. How far this adds up to anything that could be called 'literacy' depends greatly, of course, on one's definition of the term. In our opinion, however, it is reasonable to assume that the scant evidence we have of what Ryan calls 'a rudimentary knowledge of letters' is but the tip of the iceberg.

At least, it would be strange if it represented the sum total of runic and other kinds of writing used in Viking-Age Dublin. To be sure, this is no more than an assumption. But whatever the truth of the matter, the fragmentary evidence we have demonstrates clearly enough that the code of writing was cracked. The Norse population of pre-Norman Dublin was, in consequence, not living in a totally illiterate society.

The extent and the importance of runic literacy in this context cannot easily be fathomed. But it was demonstrably present – even to the extent of being used for apparently trivial purposes. A slightly disconcerting feature, though, is the number of Dublin inscriptions that defy interpretation. Possibly we have not been clever enough to discern the messages. Conceivably some kind of cipher or code has been used. But it is perhaps as likely that sequences of runes with no apparent linguistic meaning testify precisely to the 'rudimentary knowledge of letters' that Ryan invokes – that we have here the products of people who knew the runic characters, but not how to employ them to write language. On the other hand, as we have seen, the population of Dublin was not only exposed to runic script. Ogam and Roman were known to some. Whether that included the Norsemen – visitors or residents – we shall probably never know for sure. The ogam-inscribed comb from Dublin Castle and the two-script and bilingual Killaloe stone do, however, suggest that this may sometimes have been the case.

IR 17

In conclusion, we offer a brief presentation of the newly discovered Temple Bar West inscription, which, in accordance with our established practice (Barnes, Hagland and Page 1997, 1), we number IR 17. The inscribed piece – a handle made from deer antler – of dimensions roughly 20 x 3.5 x 2cm was excavated in 1996 by Linzi Simpson (museum no. 96E245:3000:18). Simpson states the following about the archaeological context of the find:

> The handle was found in a clearance level (F3000) which I think probably dates to the early twelfth century, but was badly contaminated by post-medieval material – however it also produced earlier material in the form of metal and bone pins – the area of habitation was scarped sometime in the Anglo-Norman period, but scarped right down to late eleventh-/early twelfth-century levels (pers. comm.).

The inscription is 51mm long, the height of the runes varying from 9 to 18mm. The runes stand at a safe distance from either end of the handle so nothing has been lost. Cutting marks can be seen over most of the surface, presumably from when the object was shaped.

The text reads:
ᛁᛏᛣ + ᛒᛁᚼᛏᛒᛁᚴ
*ïm + b i n ï þ i k
        5   10

The runes are well-preserved and appear to have been cut with a sharp tool. Of the ten graphs, only nine are clearly identified as runes, the first (counted as rune 1 above for convenience) being somewhat shorter and fainter than the rest. Runes 2 and 7 have an indentation about half way down the vertical, presumably intentional – the one on rune 7 placed slightly to its right. The vertical of rune 3 may have been cut in two strokes; it changes direction at the meeting point of branches and vertical giving it a 'broken' appearance. Between runes 3 and 4 there is a small cross, presumably a separator. A faint, ascending line cuts across the lower part of rune 7's vertical and almost reaches the following character. The verticals of runes 8–10 slope to the right, that of rune 10 markedly so.

Forms diagnostic of fuþark type are: ᚽ **n**, ᛒ **b**; of age ᛏ **ï**.

Interpretation
The presence of the dotted ï suggests a date hardly earlier than the eleventh century – which seems to agree well with the archaeological context of the find.

The inscription was reported by Simpson (1999), who includes a drawing of the inscribed object. She states briefly: 'An unusual find was a handle made from deer antler with a "long-branch" runic inscription, tentatively identified as reading "owns me/binds me"' (Simpson 1999, 32, 34). This is in part repeated by Johnson (2004, 85) who adds a dating of the archaeological context in which it was found: 'An inscription on an antler knife handle from tenth-century level at Temple Bar West reads "owns me or binds me", perhaps as a deterrent to would-be thieves'. Somewhat confusingly, this piece of information is illustrated by a drawing of IR 9 – an inscribed cattle scapula from Christchurch Place, Dublin (cf. Barnes, Hagland and Page 1997, 31). As indicated above, the inscription seems to belong in a later context than the tenth century. And while ᛒ is normally counted a long-branch rune, ᚽ is short-twig, while ᛏ belongs to the medieval expanded *fuþark*.

The initial graph of the inscription is not certainly a rune. It occurs at about the same level as the small cross between runes 3 and 4 and may simply mark the opening of the text. If so, several interpretations seem possible. The sequence **ïm+binïþik** can be divided into discrete units that each gives good sense on its own. Thus the first two runes may be taken as *em* ('am': 1st person singular present tense of *vesa* or *vera* '[to] be'). After the separation mark we have **bin** and **þik** which could give *bein* (n. 'bone') and *þik* (personal pronoun 2nd singular accusative 'you'). However, the three words which emerge make little sense when combined.

The sequence **binïþik** might represent an unusual spelling of the personal name *Benedict(us)* (with þ denoting spirant pronunciation of Latin *d*, as often in medieval Scandinavian runic writing), though the precise form seems to be unparalleled in runic inscriptions or Norse manuscripts. The name *Benedictus* – in various forms – was introduced into Norwegian and Icelandic anthroponymy during the course of the twelfth century and became quite popular in the Late Middle Ages. It seems to be unknown in Irish, however (Erich Poppe, pers. comm.), and must be considered uncertain as an interpretation of the present inscription. Equally doubtful is the syntactic construction *em Beneþik* ('[I] am Benedict').

Another possibility is that we have here a garbled fragment of the *Ave Maria*: ([…]*e M Beneþik* […]), but there is no way of demonstrating the correctness or otherwise of this idea.

Alternatively, the initial graph of the inscription may be taken as a rune rather than a text introducer. It might in that case be an over-extended ı **s** – a phenomenon amply evidenced in the corpus of medieval Norwegian inscriptions (cf. *NIyR* V, 119, n. 2). This allows for an interpretation which makes linguistic sense: *sem píni þik* ('which may punish you' or 'torment you'). Runologically this implies that rune 4 (ß) represents the unvoiced bilabial stop /p/, which is not at all uncommon, even in the Middle Ages after ß or Ҡ had been introduced as symbols for /p/. Grammatically, this solution postulates a relative clause with an implicit antecedent (the referent possibly being the object on which the inscription is written). A verb in the 3rd singular present subjunctive would suggest a type of relative clause well-attested in Old Norse: one used to express a requirement, a wish to be fulfilled, etc. (cf. Haugen 1993, 17.6.2). On the handle of a tool – most likely a knife – a sentence like this may seem not implausible. There are, however, difficulties that cannot easily be disregarded. First the relative particle *sem* rather than *es* or *er* would be unexpected in a relatively early inscription such as this. Then there is the elaborate syntactic construction with an implicit antecedent – unusual, possibly even unprecedented, in a simple runic inscription like the present one.

What is clear enough is that the runes of IR 17 are incompatible with the interpretations 'owns me' or 'binds me' suggested in the initial reports. 'Owns me' is in Old Norse *á mik*, likely to be written **amik** in runes. 'Binds me' would be not **binïþik** but **bintrmik** or something very similar, with the dental stop of *binda* ('bind') denoted and first singular **mik** ('me') rather than second person þik ('you').

Here we have been able to do no more than illustrate some of the possibilities and impossibilities. Our conclusion thus far is that content-wise IR 17 is as problematic as the majority of the Dublin inscriptions we know already.

BIBLIOGRAPHY

Andersson, T.M. 1964. *The problem of Icelandic saga origins: a historical survey* (New Haven).

Barnes, M.P., J.R. Hagland, & R.I. Page. 1997. *The runic inscriptions of Viking-Age Dublin*, Medieval Dublin Excavations 1962–81, Ser. B, 5 (Dublin).

Bugge, S. 1908. *Norsk sagaskrivning og sagafortælling i Irland* (Kristiania).

Gísli Sigurðsson. 1988. *Gaelic influence in Iceland: historical and literary contacts: a survey of research*, Studia Islandica, 46 (Reykjavík).

Hagland, J.R. 1994. 'The Dublin runes' in B. Ambrosiani & H. Clarke (eds), *Developments around the Baltic and the North Sea in the Viking Age*, Birka Studies, 3 (Stockholm), pp 302–4.

Haugen, E. 1976. 'The dotted runes: from parsimony to plenitude' in B. Almqvist & D. Greene (eds), *Proceedings of the Seventh Viking Congress, Dublin, 15–21 August 1973* (Dublin), pp 83–92.

Haugen, O.E. 1993. *Grunnbok i norrønt språk* (Oslo).

Johnson, R. 2004. *Viking Age Dublin* (Dublin).

NIyR = Olsen, M. et al. 1941 (in progress). *Norges innskrifter med de yngre runer*, 6 vols (Oslo).

Page, R.I. & J.R. Hagland. 1998. '*Runica manuscripta* and runic dating: the expansion of the younger fuþąrk' in A. Dybdahl & J.R. Hagland (eds), *Innskrifter og datering/ Dating inscriptions*, Senter for middelalderstudier, 8 (Trondheim), pp 55–71.

Ryan, J. 1949. 'Pre-Norman Dublin', *Journal of the Royal Society of Antiquaries of Ireland*, 79, 64–83.

Ryan, J. 1990. 'Pre-Norman Dublin' in H. Clarke (ed.), *Medieval Dublin: the making of a metropolis* (Dublin), pp 110–27.

Simpson, L. 1999. *Director's findings: Temple Bar West* (Dublin).

The Dunmore Cave [2] hoard and the role of coins in the tenth-century Hiberno-Scandinavian economy

KRISTIN BORNHOLDT COLLINS

Dunmore Cave, in Mohil, Co. Kilkenny, just north of Kilkenny City and east of the boundary between Munster and Leinster, was centrally located in the ancient kingdom of Ossory, along prime stomping ground between Dublin, Limerick and Waterford (Fig. 3.1). Not only was *Dearc Fearna* the site of a ghastly assault in AD930 (*AU* 930.1), but its deep, dark caverns have also produced two mixed hoards dating to different decades of the tenth century. These hoards speak to us about the role of coins at a formative stage in Ireland, when they occupied a decidedly 'grey area' in terms of their popular perception and mechanics for use. In the ninth century and first quarter of the tenth century, coins would have been weighed out and perhaps fragmented and melted down, and they generally masqueraded as bullion in a metal-weight economy (Dolley 1966, 23, 30). By the mid-tenth century onwards, still decades before the institution of a mint in Dublin (*c*.995), foreign coins circulated as coin (Dolley 1966, 31), at least nominally, and would have been regarded as something 'more than bullion' (Stevenson 1966, xvi) in what has been described elsewhere as a 'dual economy' (Blackburn 2001, 135; Graham-Campbell 2001).

The hoards from Dunmore Cave were probably purses – true 'emergency hoards' containing relatively accurate reflections of the currency of the day (Grierson 1975, 131) – and provide precious testimony to this economy in transition. The earlier hoard was lost around 930 (Dolley 1975; Blackburn and Pagan 1986, no. 111; Dolley's '*c*.928' was informed by the traditionally accepted date of the massacre and should be adjusted to *c*.930, which is equally well supported by the numismatic evidence) and may reasonably be associated in some way with the infamous bloodbath, which should be viewed in the context of contemporary rivalries between Limerick and Dublin (e.g. Downham 2004, 85). The more recent find came to light in November 1999 and has an entirely separate historical context, having been deposited *c*.965 or soon after. The find is multifaceted and extraordinary, comprising the remains of a sumptuous garment, complete with ornate belt, purse and other valuables. The find includes forty-three (+) objects of silver and bronze, as well as a glass bead and remnants of leather and textile. In anticipation of the comprehensive final report (Halpin forthcoming), this article records the coin element only (Appendix I), which is of particular interest to the numismatic community at large. It will also consider what we can learn from Dunmore Cave [2] regarding the role of coins in a mixed

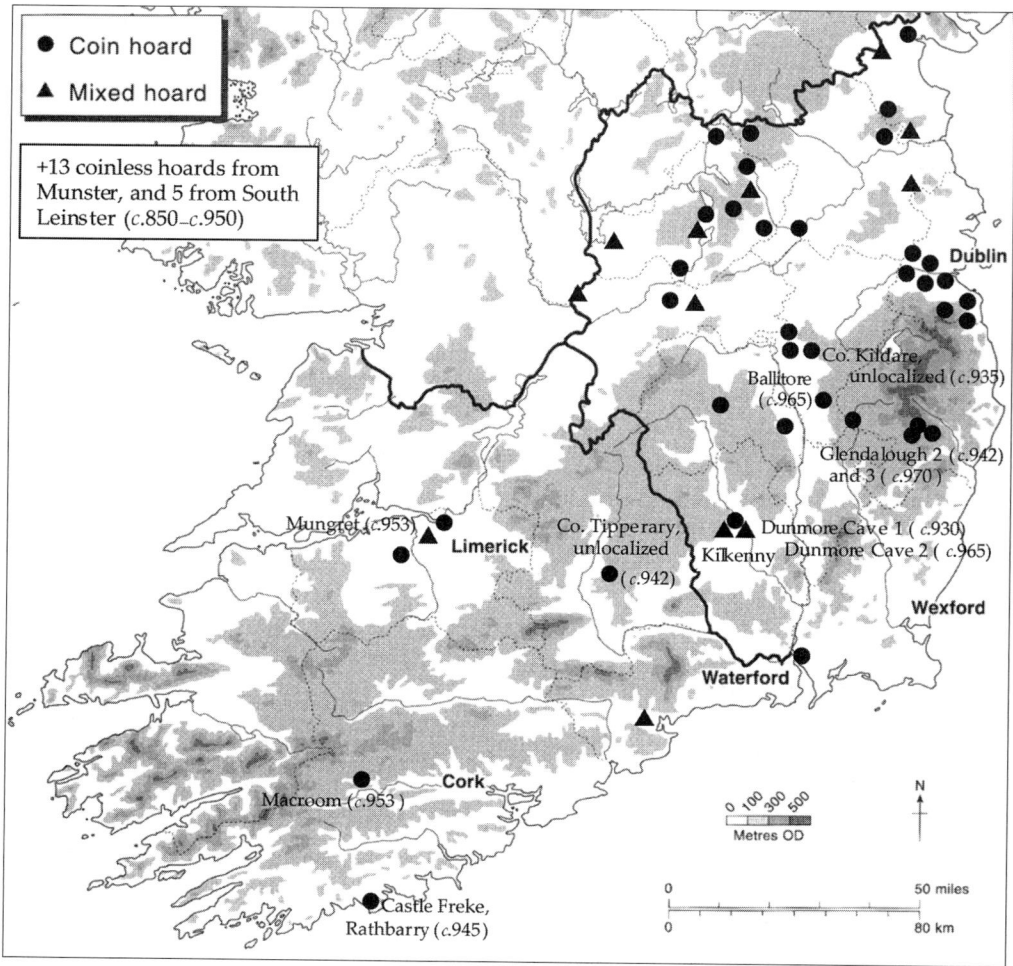

● Coin hoard
▲ Mixed hoard

+13 coinless hoards from
Munster, and 5 from South
Leinster (*c*.850–*c*.950)

Dublin

Co. Kildare,
Ballitore   unlocalized (*c*.935)
(*c*.965)

Glendalough 2 (*c*.942)
and 3 (*c*.970)

Mungret (*c*.953)   Co. Tipperary,   Dunmore Cave 1 (*c*.930)
Limerick   unlocalized   Kilkenny   Dunmore Cave 2 (*c*.965)
(*c*.942)

Wexford

Waterford

Cork

Macroom (*c*.953)

N

Metres OD

Castle Freke,
Rathbarry (*c*.945)

50 miles

80 km

3.1 Distribution of tenth-century pre-reform coin hoards from Munster and South Leinster
(cos Kilkenny, Laois, Kildare, Carlow, Wicklow and Wexford), with other coin hoards from
Munster (all) and Leinster (deposited after *c*.950) (based on Sheehan 1998b, fig. 15.5).

or dual economy, and make some preliminary observations about the wider
context of the deposit and what this might contribute to the interpretation of the
find as a whole.

BACKGROUND: THE IRISH HOARDS

Anyone investigating Viking-Age silver hoards from Ireland will appreciate the
tremendous debt owed to several exceptional scholars who have produced the
essential literature for this subject, not least of whom is Michael Dolley (see full

bibliography in Thompson 1986; see also Hall 1974; Graham-Campbell 1976; Kenny 1987; Sheehan 1998a; 1998b; 2000a). Most recently, John Sheehan has taken a broad and rigorous approach to the hoards, with a particular emphasis on the non-numismatic material, subjecting them to detailed and systematic analyses. Although the approach has in some ways obscured the significance of the coins, Sheehan's seminal work has effectively delineated the basic patterns of chronology, composition and structure, and geographical distribution, and this solid foundation provides a general context in which to view the Dunmore Cave finds.

The Irish hoards (*c*.800–*c*.1100) consist of three basic deposit types: coinless; mixed; and coin hoards – like contemporary hoards elsewhere in the Viking world. In total, there are more than 130 silver hoards of Scandinavian character on record from Ireland (Sheehan 1998a, Appendix, check-list to AD1000; 1998b, 147–8; hoards with coins are listed by Blackburn and Pagan (1986), which should be consulted alongside the updated online check-list at www.fitzmuseum. cam.ac.uk/dept/coins/projects/hoards/). Of these, no less than fifty-two are coinless; eighteen are mixed, that is, coins with ingots or ornaments (Hiberno-Scandinavian, Irish or imported objects from Scotland, Scandinavia or the Baltic, e.g. Sheehan 1998a, 177–97; 2000a, 51–3), either whole or fragmented into hack-silver (to Sheehan's sixteen hoards of this category (1998b) should be added a find from before 1987 from Ladestown (Rushy Island), Co. Westmeath, deposited in the 980s or 990s, and the 1999 Dunmore Cave [2] hoard); and over sixty hoards contain coins only. The coins found in Ireland are predominantly Anglo-Saxon pennies in the tenth-century finds and Hiberno-Scandinavian coins from Dublin in the eleventh, but also represented are coins from the Continent, Kufic dirhems, and rare issues of the Viking rulers from Northumbria and East Anglia: testaments to a far-reaching web of trading networks and political contacts.

Regarding basic hoard types, two primary spheres of silver circulation are evident (see maps: Sheehan 1998a, 174; 2000, 59). Coinless hoards are earliest, dating broadly from *c*.850 to *c*.950 (Sheehan 2000a, 53), and are well distributed across the country, though there are few in the northwest (where few hoards of any kind are found) or central midlands/north Leinster. Mixed hoards date almost exclusively to the early and middle decades of the tenth century, remaining a significant presence into the 980s. Approximately 75 per cent of hoards consisting exclusively of coins were deposited after *c*.940 (Sheehan 1998a, 170–1; 1998b, 148), while coin hoards dominate the scene by the 990s, coinciding with the establishment of Sigtryggr's mint in Dublin just before the millennium, and are subsequently the primary hoard-type in the eleventh century. The hoards with coins only concentrate in Dublin, the northeast coast and the central midlands, predominantly falling into a 'great arc between 30 and 70 miles from Dublin' (Kenny 1987, 514). Some mixed hoards, mainly those with whole ornaments or ingots (Sheehan 2000a, Classes 2 and 3), also occur within this arc, as well as in the south of Ireland alongside coinless deposits, mainly those with hack-silver (ibid., Classes 4 and 5), hence mixed hoards straddle both traditions to a limited extent, or one might say even bridge them. However, as demonstrated by Sheehan (2000a), it is the specific bullion composition that enables further inter-pretation of the nature of these finds, and whether they are economically 'passive' and therefore essentially socially-motivated (Class 1); 'potentially active' (Classes 2 and 3) and correlating in distribution and function with coin depositions; or 'active' with varying degrees of social and economic complexity and little overlap with the coin-dominated region (Classes 4 and 5). The Dunmore Cave hoards fall into the last category and by virtue of their coin and hack-silver elements were indisputably commercially inspired, albeit deposited away from the main area of coin circulation. This is not to say that the coins, particularly in the later find, had necessarily lost their significance as coin, for the distinction by this stage was more a matter of general emphasis than exclusion, and by the 960s foreign coins would have represented one possible means of payment across Ireland.

In terms of sheer quantity and intrinsic value, the coinless hoards are by far the richest category of material, while coin hoards are relatively plentiful, but almost insignificant in terms of their value by weight (Kenny 1987, 517–18). While it has quite reasonably been suggested that all silver hoards should be viewed together to comprehend the remarkable total wealth involved (Graham-Campbell 1976, 39–40; Kenny 1987, 518), this obscures another important point, namely that regarding an emerging coin mentality. Naturally, the phase involving coins required smaller quantities of silver, a function of their practicality for everyday transactions, and this needs to be appreciated as an equally significant (and quite separate) phenomenon. Had the coins been regarded simply as bullion they would not exist today, for they would have been melted down and fashioned into ingots, arm-rings or other ornaments, like their predecessors, or randomly fragmented beyond recognition (e.g. Dysart 4, Lough Ennell, Co. Westmeath, deposited *c*.907). The fact that whole and occasionally deliberately halved and quartered coins (which could also circulate by tale) exist at all from this intermediate period is further evidence of strides toward regular coin use. Ironically, it is the small but numerous coin-hoards – too often misconstrued as a 'lack' of material – that signal increasing commercial activity and a major turning point in the tenth-century Irish economy; their individual or pooled value is irrelevant, and presumably only the tip of the iceberg.

As the coin hoards from *c*.940 onwards demonstrate, trusted foreign coins had become a convenient medium of exchange even before a mint in Ireland, particularly in Dublin and its hinterland. For some this is hard to comprehend, as coinage 'should' have a political dimension, which can only be meaningful within a mint's intended area of jurisdiction. However, this aspect of coinage is not essential to its basic economic function, as seen for example in Anglo-Saxon

England in the late sixth and early seventh centuries when gold tremisses from Merovingian France circulated prior to, and during the early stages of, local coin production, first as jewellery and then with a limited monetary capacity (e.g. Grierson and Blackburn 1986, 157). A more recent example of foreign coins substituting for a local currency is Colonial America, where settlers employed a variety of foreign currencies including Spanish silver 8-reales, which were in such popular demand that they remained legal tender in the USA until 1857 (Cribb et al. 1999, 266). China also had a period in the nineteenth and early twentieth centuries when it struggled to produce a trusted coinage, resulting in a preference for imported coin – first Spanish and Mexican silver dollars, and later currency from the USA, Japan and Hong Kong, and France and Britain (Cribb et al. 1999, 204–5). Both the need and preference for foreign coin, which can arise amongst neophytes as well as established coin-users, testifies to a fundamental commercial motivation behind coinage. The adoption of good Anglo-Saxon coins in Ireland prior to a locally-produced coinage therefore fits well with what we know of human nature and economic adaptation.

To summarize, two fundamentally different types of economy are indicated: that represented by Class 1 hoards, and to some extent Classes 4 and 5, which is in essence the manifestation of the social function of wealth, where large quantities of silver were required to establish bonds, alliances and certain kinds of transactions (Sheehan 2000a, 60); the other represented by hoards with ingots and hack-silver (Classes 2–5) and hoards with coins, reflecting purely commercial developments, and a shift toward regular coin use in Ireland. Mixed hoards like those from Dunmore Cave are least numerous, but they provide the key for understanding the whole picture, for it is where the two traditions intersect that one begins to appreciate the dynamic driving this economic transformation. That is, the dominating idea of coinage was itself a force in eroding traditional perceptions of silver, replacing its symbolic aspect with something less personal, more prescribed and utilitarian. Indeed, the distribution of finds with coins compared with those with hack-silver suggests that it was exposure to imported coin, not a linear 'evolutionary' stage involving the generation of hack-silver, that ultimately led to coin-production in Ireland (Sheehan 2000a, 62). The spread of consciousness of coin as coin, and the concomitant decline of silver as a transmitter of social messages, are therefore main features of the tenth-century Irish economy. Tracking these developments through the chronological and geographical distinctions in the Irish evidence helps to identify the point at which the idea of coinage began to be embraced. Although mixed hoards first appear earlier, the crucial watershed, as noted by Sheehan, may be identified where coin hoards intensify, *c.*940, followed by a period of adjusting and over-lapping economies, represented by the mixed hoards of the 950s to the 980s.

Interestingly, one of the hoards from Dunmore Cave falls just before the watershed, and the other towards the end of the period of overlap. Although the hoards contain only a small sample of the 'currency of the day', each identifies a little more strongly with the economic milieu in which it was created. That is, the eclectic and highly fragmentary nature of the earlier hoard suggests a predominantly bullion-minded owner, whereas the comparatively homogeneous later hoard, with bent whole pennies bearing incontrovertible signs of circulation by tale and a purposely cut halfpenny, was clearly assembled by a coin-user who also thought, as occasion demanded, in bullion terms.

MIXED HOARDS AND A DUAL ECONOMY

As noted above, mixed hoards like Dunmore Cave [2], are tangible, quantifiable manifestations of a shifting economic mindset in Ireland, but the concept is not straightforward and the interpretation of a mixed hoard still requires some clarification. This is in part because such complex amalgamations have traditionally been regarded as part of the coinless/bullion camp, simply because it is apparent that part of the composition indicates a metal-weight mentality. However, these hoards are products of a more flexible economic environment where coins 'as coin', not just random lumps of bullion, had a role in and of themselves. They could be weighed out if necessary, and may have been treated by some with a degree of suspicion or contempt, but they were also sometimes accepted and counted by tale, which was certainly the most convenient method of reckoning, as long as good silver was involved. Sometimes this was checked, and testing the quality of the alloy (or for forgeries) could be done by stabbing the coin with a knife, bending it or even by biting the coin, leaving marks which are tell-tale signs of circulation. During the mixed hoard interlude, 950s–980s, and perhaps for some time before and after, one would have been thinking and reckoning in *both* terms. Blackburn identified a comparable development in the Danelaw in the later ninth and early tenth centuries, where 'for the first forty or fifty years of Scandinavian presence […] there were two co-existing types of economy' (2001, 135). This situation arose despite the fact that the Scandinavian settlers began minting their own coins in East Anglia and the East Midlands from the mid-880s. Coin and bullion were not mutually exclusive. In other words, just as one may be bilingual, one can also be 'bi-economic', which is precisely the mindset implied by the term 'dual economy'.

The fact that ingots, ornaments or hack-silver might occupy the same purse therefore does not reveal a strictly bullion-minded owner, but suggests that not all people accepted, or not all kinds or size of transaction were suited to, exchange in the medium of coin. In this situation of economic flux, as well as vigorous 'international' and cross-cultural trade, it was necessary to maintain a variety of payment options. Although not an exact parallel, it can be instructive to consider the diversity of payment alternatives within your own wallet, with some actual cash present – perhaps in multiple currencies – in addition to virtual money, e.g. plastic cards, cheques, tokens and store vouchers or coupons. These alternatives provide convenience – not confusion – to one's economic life. It is therefore important to recognize Ireland's tenth-century dual economy, reflect on the 'mechanics', and to accept that the various means of payment and modes of reckoning could – and did – coincide without causing undue chaos.

DUNMORE CAVE [2]: HOARD CONTENTS AND CONNECTIONS

In addition to the remains of fourteen or fifteen coins, the latest of which is a single pre-reform coin of Edgar (see below), the mixed purse-element of the Dunmore Cave [2] find included: three cut fragments of small silver ingots; a small hammered disc-shaped piece of silver; a cut and folded fragment of a decorated silver brooch pin; a looped rod of silver; two long, folded ingots of copper or copper alloy; and one whole, plain penannular silver arm-ring of the type associated with Scandinavian Scotland (Graham-Campbell 1995, 38–40, 57–9). A detailed consideration of the bullion component awaits expert attention and the final hoard report, but a few preliminary comments may be made. While the ingots are not culturally diagnostic (Sheehan 1998b, 148), the arm-ring is distinctive, with a distribution that places its origin in Scotland, where over ninety complete examples of 'ring-money' are known (Graham-Campbell 1995, 57–9). The recent reprovenancing to the Isle of Man of a group of four such rings in the National Museum of Ireland (Graham-Campbell and Sheehan 2007) means that no less than twenty-four are also known from Man, while only seventeen are recorded from all of Ireland (nine from four hoards plus eight single-finds: John Sheehan, pers. comm.). These rings relate, if loosely, to a 24g/ounce weight standard (*c*.24.0g +/– 0.8g: Warner 1975–6) and functioned as a highly practical and adaptable alternative currency dating broadly *c*.925–*c*.1075, and mainly from 950–1050 (Graham-Campbell 1983, 63), perhaps even administered and produced on an official basis as a 'state currency' in Scotland (Crawford 1987, 133–4). The presence of ring-money in the Dunmore Cave [2] hoard hints strongly at some sort of connection with Scandinavian Scotland or the Irish Sea region.

Also present in the assemblage were items relating to a man's attire, including a remarkably well-preserved set of ornate copper-alloy belt-fittings (a hinged buckle and two strap-ends), as well as a large decorated glass bead and small fragments of leather and textile with traces of green pigment (probably malachite), apparently silk from the east Mediterranean. Finally, there was a most intriguing collection of sixteen hollow cone-shaped objects made of woven silver wire in three sizes (seven large, six medium, three small), at least one with delicate spiral extensions, which appear to have been associated with fragments of a loosely knitted ornament of silver-wire coils. It remains unclear how the cones were worn and whether they had a practical function, for example as some kind of fasteners, or were purely decorative, perhaps as large studs or part of a fringe with dangling tassels or bobbles; either way, this was an eye-catching (even downright flashy), high-value article of clothing – not the cloak of a local shepherd or farm-hand.

While no exact parallels regarding shape and size have been found for the conical ornaments, a single object of similar general construction was unearthed in Patrick Wallace's excavations in Dublin (E172:11170, from Level 1 of Fishamble Street, Plot 2, dating to *c.*920s: Graham-Campbell 2002, 89). Graham-Campbell has also noted a group of three related silver-wire objects from a tenth-century male grave in Iceland, and possibly a fourth of gold wire from a separate grave (Graham-Campbell 2002, 89). Finally, woven silver-wire ornaments are also known from the Isle of Man, where delicate 'balls' were present in two (of the seven) tenth-century graves from St Patrick's Isle, Peel (Grave II 84.16/1 (420) and Grave III 85.60/L (595): Freke 2002, 66–73, pl. 20, fig. 21; Graham-Campbell 2002, 88–9). Based on their placement in the graves, these have been interpreted as fringe ornaments adorning garments that had probably been used as shrouds. While uncoffined Grave III contained only four balls and no associated objects, Grave II, an adult (probably male) lintel grave, contained no less than eighteen, as well as larger tubular wires which could have been sewn down to form part of the decoration (possibly similar to the coils from Dunmore Cave?). The same grave also had a polyhedral-headed ringed pin, an insular interlace-decorated copper-alloy buckle, and a coin of Edmund (939–46), confirming a post-940s date for the grave assemblage. A more detailed investigation of the size, form and function of these objects alongside the cone-shaped ones from Dunmore Cave could prove instructive.

Like the buckle in the Manx burial described above, the bossed and incised hinged buckle and zoomorphic strap-ends from Dunmore Cave fall into the corpus of ninth- to tenth-century Insular belt- and equestrian-equipment known primarily from the Western Isles of Scotland, Man and Ireland. This material has been expertly considered by Caroline Paterson (2001), but awaits a more comprehensive assessment, particularly in the light of the growing number of stratified finds from Dublin and, not least, the coin-dated material from Dunmore Cave. It is hoped that such an investigation will establish regional variations in types and styles and likely centres of production (Dublin and Man are main contenders), as well as a chronology for distinguishing 'early' and 'late' examples. Other Manx examples include a buckle and strap-end from one of the uncoffined adult burials at Peel (84.16/L [629]) and closely-related mounts from Ballateare, as well as a variety of material from the famous mound burials at Knock y Doonee, Balladoole and Cronk Mooar (Bersu and Wilson 1966). Other buckle finds include a fragmentary decorated D-ring buckle from Whithorn from rubble in Phase 2, which was dated in part by a coin of Edgar (Hill 1997, 195–6, 199, 371 [BZ18.4]); another buckle from a late ninth- or early tenth-century male grave at Kildonnan, Eigg (Paterson 2001, 127–9); and another from Bishop's Lough, Co. Westmeath (Paterson 2001, 128). The harness-equipment from the late ninth-century male inhumation at Kiloran Bay, Colonsay, is also related to this group (Graham-Campbell and Batey 1998, 118–22) and has been compared to a mount found at Freestone Hill, Co. Kilkenny (Downham 2004, 91), as is that from a tenth-century grave from Norway (Kolset, Mære parish, Nord-Trøndelag: Petersen 1940, 67–8), while a ninth-century date has been assigned to a buckle from a woman's grave near Kaupang (Blindheim 1976, 23–4). Double-sided, perforated strap-ends (ultimately derived from a ninth-century Anglo-Saxon variety) are more common, with over thirty on record (Paterson 2001, 129), including at least seven or eight from tenth-century levels at Dublin (Ó Ríordáin 1976, pl. 17; Paterson 2001, 129). Another Dublin strap-end find (with a harness-mount) is from Temple Bar West, from a level sealed by early tenth-century houses, making it one of the few securely dated ninth-century examples (Simpson 1999, 26). Importantly, however, this class of material is absent from the graves of the earliest Scandinavian settlers in Ireland at Kilmainham/Islandbridge. The metalwork therefore appears to have been produced over an extended period, probably beginning sometime in the later ninth century and reaching its height of popularity in the tenth century. That it remained fashionable until at least the 960s is demonstrated by the 'late' examples in the Dunmore Cave [2] hoard.

More specifically, with its billeted roundels, interlace panel, boss-capped rivets and zoomorphic detail, the buckle from Dunmore Cave looks similar to examples from Kildonnan, Eigg and Bishop's Lough, Co. Westmeath, yet differs in its construction (a single solid casting rather than a composite form with a cast upper plate riveted to sheet-metal backing). The double-sided 'perforated' strap-end is immediately recognizable as this well-known type, yet it is curious in not actually being perforated. One explanation may be that it was copied from earlier examples, the 'hole' having become vestigial and incorporated for aesthetic effect. Clearly this class of material still holds many secrets. Nonetheless, it points not just to Dublin, but to ports beyond, giving the non-coin element of the Dunmore Cave [2] assemblage a distinctly Irish Sea flavour.

Coins
In contrast to the first Dunmore Cave find, the coin element derives entirely from Anglo-Saxon England (Appendix I) and includes one coin of Athelstan (924–39), two of Edmund (939–46), six from the reign of Eadred (946–55), two 'irregular' pennies, probably struck during the reign of Eadred or soon after, one of Eadwig (king of England 955–7; Wessex only 957–9), and one of Edgar (king of Mercia 957–9; all England 959–75), with two additional fragments that are too

small to identify. The hoard was deposited before Edgar's reform of the Anglo-Saxon coinage (*c*.973) – a Rubicon in Anglo-Saxon monetary history – after which, among other changes, all coins bore a standard design with the moneyer and mint named in every reverse legend (e.g. see Blackburn 1991, 157–60, note 3 and refs). A more or less regular system of periodic recoinages subsequently became a revenue-producing feature of the new coinage, further ensuring the homogeneity of the currency pool in England, which continued to contrast sharply with that in and around Ireland and the Irish Sea.

It is unfortunate that the objects of the hoard were removed from their resting place in a rock crevice upon discovery and the site was only later investigated and excavated by archaeologists. While valuable information was undoubtedly lost regarding the precise context, it appears that all associated material has been recovered. Assuming this is the case, the hoard contained fourteen or fifteen distinct coins, of which nine are whole (or near whole), one is a cut halfpenny, and five are small, broken fragments. The small size is not atypical for Irish coin hoards, where approximately 35 per cent consist of 'practical sums' between four and nineteen coins, and is certainly consistent with the premise that this is a purse, or everyday currency 'caught out' of active circulation.

While it is apparent that the fragments were not broken recently, such as during recovery of the find, it is unclear whether they deteriorated in the assemblage over time or were hoarded as such. However, unlike a true savings hoard, one might expect to see some smaller denominations in a purse find, and it seems almost more than coincidence that the weight of the five fragments (0.74 g) plus the cut halfpenny equals the weight of the latest whole coin in the hoard (1.37 g). This hints at the possibility that they represent 'small denominations' and may have been acquired as part of a payment equivalent in bullion value to the most current penny, creating a round sum. If this were the case, the purse contained the equivalent of ten pennies (or as many as fourteen and a half). As a penny had a relatively high value (say, *c*.€20 to *c*.€30), this was significantly more than 'lunch money'. A rough idea of the spending value of the coin element of Dunmore Cave [2] in an Anglo-Saxon context can be approximated from a tenth-century law code, VI Athelstan, 6.2 (Whitelock 1979, 424, no. 37), where the compensation price for one sheep was 5*d*. In other words, the purse contained enough coined-money to purchase two (or perhaps three) sheep in tenth-century terms. Obviously, the total value including the bullion component would have been significantly higher.

Noteworthy additions
The coin element includes some pristine examples of several better known and well-represented moneyers and mints (e.g. Hunred, Theodmar, Wulfgar, Heriger) with die-links to other Irish and Irish Sea hoards. There are also some important new additions to the corpus of tenth-century pre-reform coins (see

CTCE), namely a coin of Edmund by the north-eastern moneyer Landuc (Appendix I: 2), who was previously only known from the preceding reign. Also, there is an entirely new variation on the *Horizontal Trefoil* type of Eadred, with a pellet on either side of the upper trefoil on the reverse (Appendix I: 4). The latter is also from a new moneyer for this reign, Byrhtelm. A moneyer by the same name struck at Langport and 'Weardburh' for Athelstan (*Circumscription Cross* type), but it would be a stretch to suggest this was the same man. However, a 'Berhtelm' is also attested under Edmund (also *Horizontal Trefoil* I type), where the single example (*SCBI BM* 289) has a distinctive obverse legend with widely spaced letters, similar to the Dunmore Cave [2] legend, but interspersed with pellets. Extra pellets are the distinguishing feature of the Eadred *Horizontal Trefoil* I variant, albeit more 'restrained' and on the reverse, and the overall style suggests that this might be a product of the same moneyer.

Composition
A hoard's 'anatomy' may also be considered in terms of its age- and mint-structures, while specific features within a find, such as secondary treatment, can also be revealing. In Ireland and the Irish Sea context it is typical for a range of reigns and mints to be represented in tenth-century deposits, reflecting the character of the Irish Sea currency pool generally (Metcalf 1986, 144–51; 1992), and even the local pool from which coins were drawn (Bornholdt-Collins 2003, chapter 5.5). English hoards of the pre-reform period are far fewer in number, but were generally restricted to the current reign and type, since coins were periodically reissued, leaving only the most recent as legal tender. Though there are only a few hoards to demonstrate it, hoards from England also tend to be dominated by local issues, suggesting that coins circulated within a limited geographical area, near their mint of origin (e.g. Metcalf 1992, 100; Jonsson 2006). Outside England, however, the well-respected Anglo-Saxon coins remained in circulation much longer, sometimes even for decades, and there is extensive mixing of mints, reflecting a period of vigorous circulation after leaving England. It is therefore interesting to plot and compare the age- and mint-structures of the Anglo-Saxon coin element in Irish hoards, which can help to pin-point the approximate date of deposit, possible location where the hoard was assembled, as well as anomalies or features that might relate to attitudes toward coin use, wider trends or local circulation patterns.

Age-structure and approximate date of deposit
When the age-structure of the Dunmore Cave [2] hoard is depicted in a bar chart (percentage of coins in the hoard converted into rates per year, reign by reign), a distinct bell curve is produced (Fig. 3.2). It demonstrates that this is not a savings hoard that was added to sporadically over time, or there would be gaps and peaks in the chronology, and that it is an adequate sample (if not the

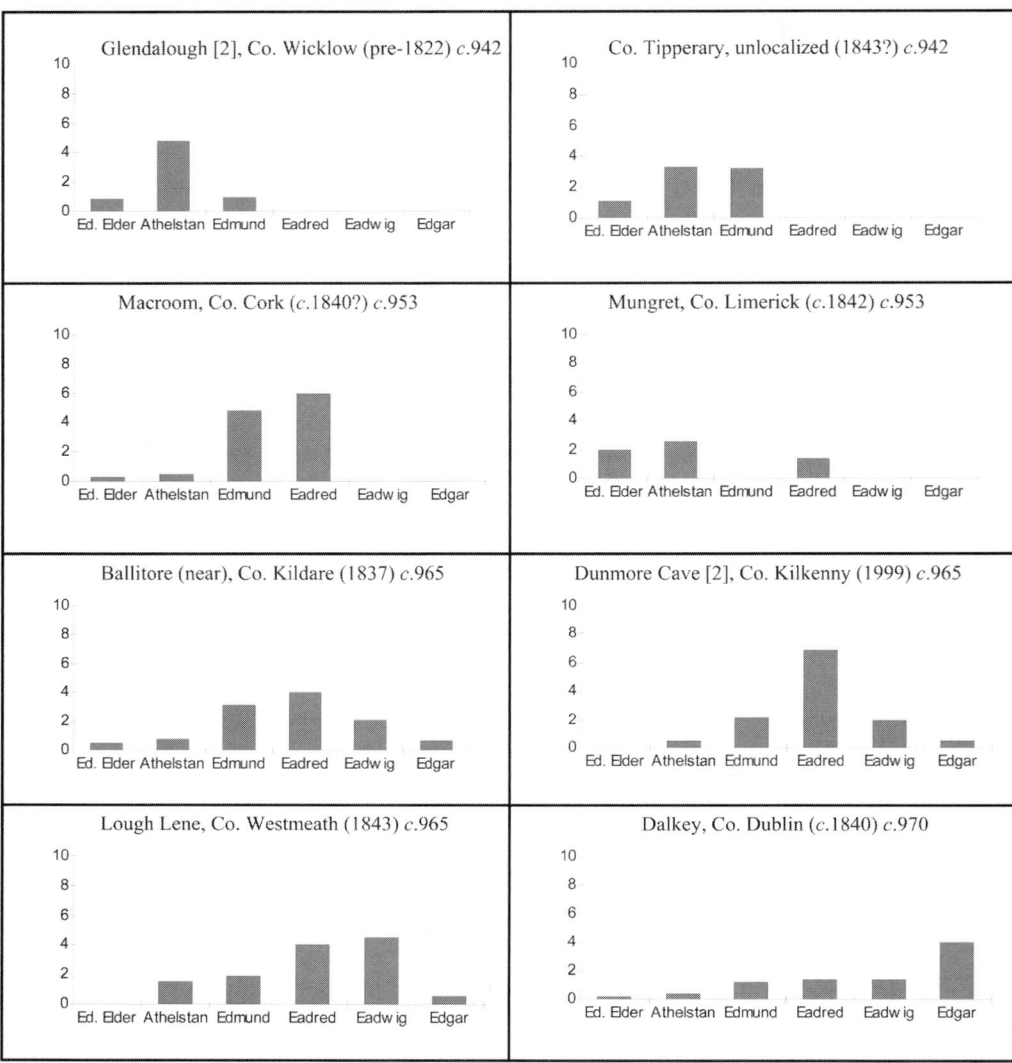

3.2 Age-structure of Dunmore Cave [2] and selected Irish coin hoards (percentage of Anglo-Saxon coins in the hoard converted into rate per year, reign by reign).

whole find), unlike the find from Mungret, Co. Limerick (Blackburn and Pagan 1986, no. 135), which produces patchy results since it is only partially known. Normally one might expect a gradual 'wastage rate', with the latest reign being either least or best represented, depending on whether the hoard was put together earlier or later in a reign (e.g. fig. 3.2: Glendalough [2], Co. Wicklow, and Lough Lene, Co. Westmeath vs. Macroom, Co. Cork, and Dalkey, Co. Dublin), so this peculiar distribution requires some other interpretation. On the one hand, the age-structure suggests that the money came together quite early in Edgar's reign, before Edgar's coinage flooded the available currency pool, and so an approximate date of deposit should be somewhat earlier than Edgar-dominated hoards, such as Dalkey, Co. Dublin, and Derrykeighan, Co. Antrim (Blackburn and Pagan 1986, nos 163–4), and on this basis an approximate deposit date of *c.*965 is proposed here. However, assuming that wastage occurred at a steady rate, one might reasonably have expected coins of Eadwig to be better represented than those of Eadred, since the reign was more recent, albeit shorter, than that of Eadred.

The age-structure of Dunmore Cave [2] is therefore somewhat enigmatic, but interestingly it finds its closest parallel with another South Leinster find, that from near Ballitore, Co. Kildare (Blackburn and Pagan 1986, no. 142). The idiosyncratic age-structures appear to be a function of the circulation pool in which these assemblages came together. It may be relevant that the Munster finds from Macroom, Co. Cork, and Mungret, Co. Limerick (Blackburn and Pagan 1986, nos 132, 135), also both had Eadred components, having been deposited in that reign. Also noteworthy are two more distant finds from north-west Leinster, which could have been drawn in part from the same currency pool before being deposited elsewhere in Ireland: Kilkenny West, Co. Westmeath, pre-1824, *c.*970 (Blackburn and Pagan 1986, no. 170; see Sheehan, this volume) which, based on the reconstruction by Dolley and Martin (1959), has a very slight, but nevertheless anomalous, surge under Eadred, and Mullingar [1], Co. Westmeath, *c.*986 (Blackburn and Pagan 1986, no. 179), which contained mainly coins of Æthelred, but is of peculiar interest in preserving at least one coin of Eadred, and none of Eadwig or Edgar. This suggests that the hoard was drawn from a currency pool so dominated by coins from the reign of Eadred that some survived even several decades later. This simply is not observed in most contemporary large and well-documented hoards from the Dublin vicinity or from Man. Nor are coins of Eadred 'over-represented' in the National Museum of Ireland's collection as a whole, suggesting that this is a relatively isolated and significant phenomenon. It is interesting to note, however, that the finds from Oldcastle, Co. Meath, *c.*958, and Lough Lene, Co. Westmeath, *c.*965 (Blackburn and Pagan 1986, nos 139, 146), also seem to have notable Eadred elements, even if they do not dominate in the same way, and a possibility is that each contains a parcel from the Eadred-dominated currency pool in addition to coins acquired elsewhere.

Although it can only be proposed tentatively based on such limited evidence, the suggestion is that the coins available in South Leinster, and perhaps Munster, in the middle decades of the tenth century, had a distinctive character created by an influx of coins of Eadred into the local economy. It suggests that coins did not just mix in one centre, i.e. Dublin, before redistribution, but that they entered through different ports, creating distinct circulation areas within Ireland. As such, it is also a further demonstration of coin use prior to the introduction of the Hiberno-Scandinavian coinage. Finally, that there should be a detectable influx of coins of Eadred is in itself interesting, his reign having coincided with the end of Viking rule at York in *c*.954.

Mint-structure

'Mint-structure' here refers to the proportions of coins from different parts of Anglo-Saxon England, reduced very broadly to general 'minting regions': north-west England, north-east England and the midlands/south (e.g. see Metcalf 1995, 17–18, fig. 12). Mints from eastern England (as well as 'uncertain' ones) were omitted, because they produced only minor results which do not vary significantly from region to region. The data and detailed explanation of the method formed a part of my doctoral thesis with a comprehensive analysis of the mint compositions from hoards of five coins or more from the Irish Sea region from *c*.950 to *c*.973 (Bornholdt-Collins 2003, chapter 5.5, appendix iv). From this analysis it was possible to suggest what, theoretically speaking, a 'typical' Irish, Scottish or Manx hoard should look like in terms of its proportions of mints (Fig. 3.3). That each region is so distinctive demonstrates that the Irish Sea was not one big 'mixing bowl' (or the hoards would look homogeneous across the board), but that local economies were subject to individual economic and political stimuli. It is also unequivocal evidence that the coins entering the Irish Sea zone were not 'just loot', but were in active circulation, indicative of some degree of normal monetary circulation prior to local minting. Finally, in terms of its practical application, the method has produced a basic measuring stick (Fig. 3A) with which to assess the composition of actual hoards, and from this one can discern the likely origin of other deposits, for assemblages were not necessarily put together in the place they were found. It is not a straightforward science, since hoards may consist of multiple parcels from multiple regions, but patterns emerge. For example, the Irish hoards depicted in Fig. 3B consist of coins drawn from entirely different currency pools. The proportions of mint regions represented in the hoard from Dalkey, Co. Dublin, are typical of Ireland, whereas the hoard from Smarmore, Co. Louth, appears to have been assembled in Man, and, unsurprisingly, the hoard from Derrykeighan, Co. Antrim, from the very north of Ireland, was drawn from currency circulating in Scotland.

When Dunmore Cave [2] is dissected in this way, it emerges that about half of the coins derive from north-west England, with a significant proportion also from the north-east and only a small component from the south (Fig. 3C). In other words, it looks like a typical 'Irish' hoard, not like one put together in Man or Scotland, despite other elements in the assemblage pointing toward influences from this direction.

Secondary treatment

Dunmore Cave [2] is extraordinary in providing a secure sample of coins bearing physical signs of a 'circulation history'. Not only was this a practical sum

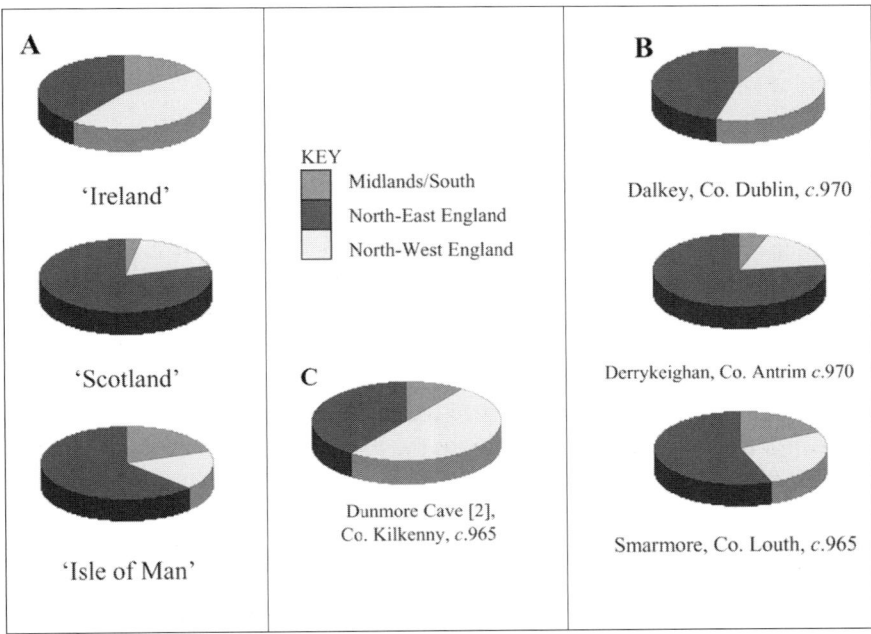

3.3 Mint-structure of (a) theoretical coin hoards per region; (b) actual selected hoards from Ireland; and (c) Dunmore Cave [2].

including small change, but the fact that all but the latest whole coin display signs of bending (e.g. Appendix I: 3, 5, 6, 12 compared with 13) demonstrates that the coins changed hands, presumably on numerous occasions, in the course of being used. Specifically, the fineness and quality of the silver alloy has been tested by gently bending, not mutilating, the coins. In one case, it is apparent that a tooth or other instrument was employed (Appendix I: 8), which conveniently illustrates that they were not bent during post-depositional processes, but in normal marketplace activity. Furthermore, it is too much of a coincidence that the only un-bent coin is also the most recent coin in the hoard. The coin of Edgar had not been in circulation long enough to acquire such signs of circulation, and/or it was familiar enough to be trusted at face value. Apparently it was not the norm to test every coin in a transaction, and older coins will simply have had more opportunities for being tested. What we glimpse in Dunmore Cave [2] is a textbook example of coin use 'in action' in tenth-century Ireland, and it provides a rare baseline for assessing this prominent and revealing secondary feature in past and future finds.

While Scandinavian numismatists have a long tradition of recording secondary treatment such as pecking and bending (e.g. Welin 1956; *CNS* series; Kilger 2006), the subject has only gained appreciation in numismatic circles in Britain and Ireland over the last two decades – indeed, it has sometimes been accepted practice to heat and flatten coins in an attempt to return them to their former glory – and systematic data is not yet available (Archibald 1990; Bornholdt-Collins 2003, chapter 6.4). Nevertheless, preliminary work demonstrates that pecking was never as widespread or intensive in Britain and Ireland as it was in Scandinavia in the later tenth and eleventh centuries, where peck-marked coins appear from the 970s onwards, intensify in the 990s, and are prevalent through the eleventh century (e.g. Malmer 1985, 51; Jonsson 1995, 165). Low-level testing spanned a much broader period in Britain and Ireland. In the period when testing was most pronounced, from the end of the ninth century until the 920s, it appears that random samples of coins were tested by pecking and bending, while unfamiliar or exotic coins (e.g. Kufic dirhems or Carolingian deniers, or halfpennies) were also more likely to be singled out (Archibald 1990, 15). Based mainly on the sample in the British Museum, Archibald observed that mid-tenth-century hoards from England rarely include pecked coins, while there is a strong tendency for bending in contemporary hoards from surrounding Scandinavian spheres; a general increase in bending (and occasional pecking) is then found in England in the eleventh century, despite it being a patently coin-using society. In fact, while pecking is infrequent by the later eleventh century, bending continued right through the Norman Conquest and, although it is rarer, it is still a regular feature of English hoards from the first half of the twelfth century (Archibald 1990, 20–1). This suggests that bending (and sporadic pecking) could be a matter of 'fashion' and marketplace ritual, perhaps inspired at times by a concern for forgeries, and is not to be interpreted as a sign of disregard for the coin as coin. Pecking is also exceedingly rare amongst the Manx finds (*c.*955–*c.*1070), where a mere 2 per cent of the Manx National Heritage collection bear peck-marks, while approximately 20 per cent are bent (Bornholdt-Collins 2003, 324), supporting Archibald's observation that the practice was more typical of the Scandinavian milieu in the mid-tenth century. Bending among the finds from Britain and Ireland is clearly much more common than previously appreciated, and numismatists must work towards assessing the true extent and significance of it with help from finds like Dunmore Cave [2].

Cut halfpenny
It is a widely accepted assumption that small denominations are uncommon in hoard contexts, since there is a natural tendency to discriminate against light or low-value coins in a 'savings' context, so the cut halfpenny in Dunmore Cave [2] immediately stands out. One is less surprised to see a small denomination in a purse-find, but the halfpenny is nevertheless remarkable since pre-reform cut coins are exceedingly rare across the board for tenth-century coinage, including stray finds. To date, there are thirty-five Anglo-Saxon pre-reform cut fractions on record, of which twenty-five have secure provenances in Britain and Ireland

(Bornholdt-Collins 2003, chapter 6.2, appendix v); (three further possible cut halfpennies have come to light as metal-detector finds in England since 2004 (*British Numismatic Journal*, Coin Register 2005, 169; 2006, 206, 211), although these have not yet been examined to confirm whether they are actually cut or simply broken). Of these only six are from Ireland, from two hoards (Mungret, Co. Limerick, and Dunmore Cave [2], Co. Kilkenny) and one excavation find (Knowth, Co. Meath). Three examples derive from the Chester (Castle Esplanade) 1950 hoard from north-west England, and there is one single-find from York, while no pre-reform cut fractions are confirmed from Wales or Scotland. The remaining fifteen derive from a handful of hoards and one single-find from the Isle of Man. Thus more than half of the provenanced examples come from 0.2% of the total area. While some low-level cutting might be expected generally, this fact led to the conclusion that cut halfpennies, which signal the need for lower value currency and therefore 'a money economy better adapted to small, everyday transactions' (Metcalf 1998, 76), are likely in this period to have been a distinctive characteristic of the Manx currency in the mid-tenth century. Despite the small sample, the proportions are such that examples in non-Manx contexts have a high probability of having been drawn from the currency pool in Man. What is more difficult to say is whether the halfpenny in the Dunmore Cave [2] hoard was brought directly from Man or if it was acquired in southern Ireland following an influx of coins from Man (such as a single very large payment) that was then dispersed through the local economy; either seems reasonable and is supported by the historical record. Based largely on the cut fraction component, I have suggested that the Mungret hoard from Co. Limerick may have been assembled in or near Man (see below), and one might suppose the same of Dunmore Cave [2], except that, intriguingly, the overall mint-structure is more typical of Ireland (see above).

WIDER CONTEXT: HOARDS AND HISTORY

In terms of placing the coin element in its local context, there is only a handful of potentially relevant hoards with coins from the surrounding region. Appendix II comprises a check-list (with references) of those hoards from 'south Leinster' (counties Kilkenny, Laois, Kildare, Carlow, Wicklow and Wexford) – the area immediately surrounding Dunmore Cave – and Munster (see also Fig. 3.1). Unfortunately, all but the Dunmore Cave hoards are old discoveries, and the coins are either dispersed or details relating to them are incomplete. It is hoped that the information might be useful to anyone investigating either hoard from Dunmore Cave, or indeed pre-reform tenth-century coin hoards from the south of Ireland – hence a broad view is presented. Nevertheless, one is forced to look beyond the region for adequate comparisons, both due to the limited source material and the nature of the evidence, which was as mobile as the people using it. Accepting these limitations, some useful comparisons and observations may still be made which assist in viewing the Dunmore Cave [2] hoard in a wider context.

Firstly, there are few contemporary deposits of immediate relevance, although Ballitore, Co. Kildare, stands out, while it is unfortunate that no particulars are known for Glendalough [3], Co. Wicklow; nevertheless, neither is recorded as having had a bullion element, and therefore each fundamentally differs from Dunmore Cave [2]. Secondly, there are only four mixed hoards from south Leinster and Munster, each dating to a different decade. Three – the two from Dunmore Cave and that from Mungret – are on virtually the same latitude, all on a Limerick trajectory, while the fourth, Knockmaon – Co. Waterford, *c.*1000 – was deposited nearer the south coast (between Waterford and Cork) several decades later. Though late, Knockmaon is interesting in having a pre-reform parcel – including fragments of ring-money – alongside Dublin-minted coins from the turn of the millennium. There are a few possibilities to explain this: it could be a true savings hoard, collected locally, through contacts with traders from the Irish Sea and France, and added to over time; or, since currency could remain in circulation for an extended period, it may represent money in active circulation, the varied purse of a cosmopolitan trader. The 'bottom line' is that, even after minting began in Ireland, bullion and foreign currency could still mix in one's purse or savings, and the transition from a dual economy, especially outside Dublin, was gradual; furthermore, the ring-money, whether old at the time of deposit or culled from active duty, adds further weight to the supposition that there were direct links between southern Ireland and the Hebrides or Irish Sea zone in the later tenth century. The find of three arm-rings from the River Shannon (Co. Clare) is yet another example of this Scoto-Norse material, which is otherwise rare in Ireland, from Munster (Sheehan 2000b). Finally, I have observed elsewhere that, although only partially recorded, the hoard from Mungret, Co. Limerick, dating to about a decade before Dunmore Cave [2] and therefore the closest mixed hoard parallel, is also anomalous for Munster and is likely to have been assembled elsewhere – and quite possibly in the Isle of Man – rather than drawn from the local currency (Bornholdt-Collins 2003, 59, 293).

While Limerick seems a long way from the Irish Sea, the connection has a plausible historical basis through the activities of the Limerick branch of the great dynasty of Ívarr (Downham 2003; 2007, 35–42, 53–5). That is, Maccus and Guðrøðr, the sons of Haraldr of Limerick (d. 940), are known to have operated in the Irish Sea region in the 970s and 980s (e.g. Davies 1990, 48–60; Etchingham 2001, 171–83; Hudson 2005, chapter 3; Downham categorically refutes Hudson's 2005 suggestion of a Normandy-based lineage for the sons of Haraldr), perhaps beginning in the later 960s following increasing pressure from the Irish Dál Cais (*AU* 967.5: Davies 1990, 58). The Mungret hoard, and perhaps also the insular harness-mount from Co. Kilkenny, might be early indicators of such ties forming between Munster and Man and the Isles. Welsh and Irish annals together reveal the Haraldssons' domination of the region in the 970s, and of Man specifically by the 980s, while there is also evidence of continuing ties with home and ambitions to reclaim authority there. For example, in 974 Maccus, with a retinue from the Isles, raided Inishcathy (Scattery Island on the Shannon at Kilrush, Co. Clare), and captured Limerick's king, Ívarr (*AFM* 972.10 and *AI* 974.2), if only temporarily. The long-distance relationship continued into the next decade, despite the fall of Limerick to Brian Bóroma, with whom an alliance to oppose Leinster and Dublin was made at Waterford in 984 (*AI* 984.2) (Downham 2003, 42–3 and 2004, 86); apparently it was more efficacious to ally with the overking of Munster than oppose his growing power. A notice in the *Annals of Inisfallen* stating that 'foreign mercenaries' were banned from Munster in 972 (*AI* 972.1) might also refer to Irish Sea 'trouble-makers' like the sons of Haraldr and their followers. Intriguingly, another concrete link between Munster and Man is seen several decades later, when Røgnvaldr, the grandson of Haraldr of Limerick and king of Man and the Isles, died in Munster in 1005 (*AU* 1005.1), suggesting that the ties ran deep and were sustained over time. Of course, the hoard from Knockmaon, Co. Waterford, also provides material evidence of an ongoing connection between the geographical regions. While it is generally unwise to connect finds with specific events or people, there is good reason to expect some tangible signs of Irish Sea culture in Munster and particularly en route to Limerick, and finds such as the Dunmore Cave [2] hoard should be interpreted with this general historical context in mind.

CONCLUSION

Though located away from major Hiberno–Scandinavian centres, the River Nore – which converges with two other major navigable rivers, the Barrow and Suir, at Waterford Harbour – ensured that Dunmore Cave was hardly off the beaten track in tenth-century Ireland. These river routes would have been well-travelled by traders and political operators alike. The economic influence and shifting rivalries between Limerick, Waterford and Dublin would have been felt across Munster and south Leinster, compounded in the second half of the tenth century by Irish ambitions to dominate the region and all its resources (Downham 2004). The historically-attested link between Munster and the Irish Sea through the displaced sons of Haraldr of Limerick seems particularly significant in the light of the second find from Dunmore Cave. Finds of such astounding quality and preservation are exceedingly rare, but we should not be too surprised to find the occasional 'bread crumb' of evidence for the political tensions and wide-ranging influences radiating across the region.

While the final report is eagerly awaited and there is still much to be learnt from the Dunmore Cave [2], Co. Kilkenny, find, it is clear that the ensemble as a whole exudes wealth and far-flung interests, and must have belonged to a powerful individual. The owner appears to have been a male traveller from, or with close connections to, the Irish Sea region. His rich garment of imported fabric with fine insular metalwork commanded respect, and he was equipped for financial dealings in a dual economy, carrying an assortment of wealth acquired en route from Scotland, Man and the Isles, and Ireland. The composite assemblage therefore ranges from Irish Sea to 'Irish', including a group of coins that appear in the main to have been collected in Ireland and whose composition might even be described as distinctively 'South Leinster/Munster?' in character. Obviously, we will never discover the actual identity or affiliations of the owner, but the find is probably best viewed in the context of the situation created by the ambitious Haraldssons, who would have introduced Irish Sea material culture to the region, whether directly or indirectly, through their influence and network of contacts.

ACKNOWLEDGMENTS

This paper stems from an ongoing project funded by the British Academy in which the National Museum of Ireland's coin collection is being catalogued for publication in the *Sylloge of Coins of the British Isles* series. I am deeply grateful to both institutions, and to Mark Blackburn and Michael Kenny, for the privilege of working with this material. Sincere thanks go to Patrick Wallace, Raghnall Ó Floinn and especially to Michael Kenny for providing access to the coins, for their hospitality and time during several visits to Dublin, and for the generous financial support that enabled me to attend the Viking Congress in Cork. I am most grateful to Andy Halpin for supplying information about Dunmore Cave [2], as well as permission to discuss it in advance of its official publication. Many thanks also go to John Sheehan for providing details on Irish finds, including the newly appreciated location of the Kilkenny West, Co. Westmeath (not Co. Kilkenny) hoard; and to John Sheehan and James Graham-Campbell for allowing me to read and cite their important 'ring-money' paper prior to its publication. This paper also benefited from the expertise of Stewart Lyon, Hugh Pagan, Elina Screen and Clare Downham, whose kind help I wish to acknowledge. I am grateful to Clare Downham for bringing the *AI* 973 reference to my attention, and for the information that the annal has been mistranslated as 'foreign officials', for the Irish word is *suaitrech*, a Norse loanword *svartleggja*, or 'blackleg, mercenary'. The interpretations and any errors in the text and appendices are entirely my own. Finally, I have drawn on original research from my doctoral dissertation at the University of Cambridge (2003), for which I remain indebted both to Manx National Heritage for substantial funding, and to my supervisors, Catherine Hills, Department of Archaeology, and Mark Blackburn, Keeper of Coins and Medals, Fitzwilliam Museum, Cambridge.

BIBLIOGRAPHY

AFM = O'Donovan, J. (ed. and trans.). 1990 [1856]. *Annála Ríoghachta Éireann: Annals of the Kingdom of Ireland by the Four Masters*, 2nd ed. (Dublin).

AI = Mac Airt, S. (ed. and trans.). 1951. *The Annals of Inisfallen (MS. Rawlinson B. 503)* (Dublin).

Almqvist, B. & D. Greene (eds). 1976. *Proceedings of the Seventh Viking Congress, Dublin. 15–21 August 1973* (Dublin).

Archibald, M. 1990. 'Pecking and bending: the evidence of British finds' in K. Jonsson & B. Malmer (eds), *Sigtuna Papers* (London), pp 11–24.

AU = Mac Airt, S. & G. Mac Niocaill (ed. and trans.). 1983. *The Annals of Ulster (to AD 1131)* Part I. (Dublin).

Bersu, G. & D.M. Wilson. 1966. *Three Viking graves in the Isle of Man*, Society for Medieval Archaeology Monograph Series, 1 (London).

Blackburn, M.A.S. (ed.). 1986. *Anglo-Saxon monetary history: essays in memory of Michael Dolley* (Leicester).

Blackburn, M. 1991. 'Æthelred's coinage and the payment of tribute' in D.G. Scragg (ed.), *The battle of Malden, AD991* (Oxford), pp 156–69.

Blackburn, M.A.S. 2001. 'Expansion and control: aspects of Anglo-Scandinavian minting south of the Humber' in J. Graham-Campbell, R. Hall, J. Jesch & D.N. Parsons (eds), *Vikings in the Danelaw: select papers from the proceedings of the Thirteenth Viking Congress, Nottingham and York, 21–30 August 1997* (Oxford), pp 125–42.

Blackburn, M.A.S. & H. Pagan. 1986. 'A revised check-list of coin hoards from the British Isles, *c*.500–1100' in M.A.S. Blackburn (ed.), *Anglo-Saxon monetary history*, pp 291–313. A revised, updated and extended version (*c*.450–1180) is available online at <http://www.fitzmuseum.cam.ac.uk/dept/coins/projects/hoards/>

Blindheim, C. 1976. 'A collection of Celtic(?) bronze objects found at Kaupang (Skiringssal), Vestfold, Norway' in B. Almqvist & D. Greene (eds), *Proceedings of the Seventh Viking Congress*, pp 9–27.

Bornholdt-Collins, K. 2003. 'Viking-Age coin finds from the Isle of Man: a study of coin circulation, production and concepts of wealth' (PhD thesis, University of Cambridge).

Cook, B. & G. Williams (eds), *Coinage and history in the North Sea World*, c.*AD500–1250: essays in honour of Marion Archibald* (Leiden).

Crawford, B.E. 1987. *Scandinavian Scotland* (Leicester).

Cribb J., I. Carradine & J. Flower. 1999. *The coin atlas: a comprehensive view of the coins of the world throughout history* (London).

CNS series = Malmer, B. (ed.). 1975–1987. *Corpus Nummorum Saeculorum IX–XI qui in Suecia reperti sunt: catalogue of coins from the 9th–11th centuries found in Sweden* (Stockholm).

CTCE = Blunt, C.E. et al. 1989. *Coinage in tenth-century England, from Edward the Elder to Edgar's reform* (Oxford).

Davies, W. 1990. *Patterns of power in early Wales* (Oxford).

Dolley, M. 1970. 'A supplementary note on the Macroom find of tenth-century English pence', *Seaby's Coin and Medal Bulletin*, June 1970, 199–200.

Dolley, M. 1975. 'The 1973 Viking-Age coin-find from Dunmore Cave', *Journal of the Kilkenny Archaeological Society*, New Series 1 no. 2, 70–9.

Dolley, R.H.M. 1960a. 'Some new light on the Viking-Age silver hoard from Mungret', *North Munster Antiquarian Journal*, 8/3, 116–33.

Dolley, R.H.M. 1960b. 'A hoard of tenth-century Anglo-Saxon coins from Glendalough', *Journal of the Royal Society of Antiquaries of Ireland*, 90/1, 41–7.

Dolley, R.H.M. 1962a. 'The 1843(?) find of Viking-Age silver coins from Co. Tipperary', *Journal of the Cork Historical and Archaeological Society*, 67/205, 41–7.

Dolley, R.H.M. 1962b. 'New light on the 1837 Viking-Age hoard from Ballitore', *Journal of the Royal Society of Antiquaries of Ireland* 92:2, 175–86.

Dolley, R.H.M. 1966. *Sylloge of coins of the British Isles 8: the Hiberno-Norse coins in the British Museum* (London).

Dolley, R.H.M. & H. Pagan. 1964. 'A half-forgotten Viking-Age coin hoard from Glendalough', *Spink's Numismatic Circular*, 72:1, 1–2.

Dolley, R.H.M. & J.S. Martin. 1959. 'New light on a tenth-century find from the west of the county Kilkenny', *Numismatic Chronicle*, 19, 175–82.

Dolley, R.H.M. & K.F. Morrison. 1963. 'Finds of Carolingian coins from Great Britain and Ireland', *British Numismatic Journal*, 32, 75–87.

Downham, C.E. 2003. 'Britain and Scandinavian Ireland: the dynasty of Ívarr and pan-Insular politics to 1014' (PhD thesis, University of Cambridge).

Downham, C.E. 2004. 'The historical importance of Viking-Age Waterford', *Journal of Celtic Studies*, 4, 71–96.

Downham, C.E. 2007. *Viking kings of Britain and Ireland: the dynasty of Ívarr to AD1014*, Edinburgh.

Dumas, F. 1979. 'Les monnaies normandes (X^e–XIIe siècles) avec un repertoire des trouvailles', *Revue Numismatique*, 6:21, 84–140.

Etchingham, C. 2001. 'North Wales, Ireland and the Isles: the Insular Viking zone', *Peritia*, 15, 145–87.

Freke, D. 2002. *Excavations on St Patrick's Isle, Peel, Isle of Man, 1982–88: Prehistoric, Viking, Medieval and later*, Centre for Manx Studies Monographs, 2 (Liverpool).

Graham-Campbell, J. 1976. 'The Viking-Age silver hoards of Ireland' in B. Almqvist & D. Greene (eds), *Proceedings of the Seventh Viking Congress*, pp 39–74.

Graham-Campbell, J. 1983. 'The Viking-Age silver hoards of the Isle of Man' in C. Fell, P. Foote, J. Graham-Campbell & R. Thomson (eds), *The Viking Age in the Isle of Man: select papers from the Ninth Viking Congress, Isle of Man, 4–14 July 1981* (London), pp 53–80.

Graham-Campbell, J. 1995. *The Viking-Age gold and silver of Scotland (AD850–1100)* (Edinburgh).

Graham-Campbell, J. 2001. 'The dual economy of the Danelaw: the Howard Linecar memorial lecture 2001', *British Numismatic Journal*, 71, 49–59.

Graham-Campbell, J. 2002. 'Tenth-century graves: the Viking-Age artefacts and their significance' in D. Freke, *Excavations on St Patrick's Isle*, pp 83–98.

Graham-Campbell, J. & C.E. Batey. 1998. *Vikings in Scotland: an archaeological survey*, (Edinburgh).

Graham-Campbell, J. & J. Sheehan. 2007. 'A Viking-Age silver hoard of "ring-money" from the Isle of Man rediscovered', *Proceedings of the Isle of Man Natural History and Antiquarian Society*, 11:4, 527–40.

Grierson, P. 1975. *Numismatics* (Oxford).

Grierson, P. & M. Blackburn. 1986. *Medieval European coinage: the Early Middle Ages (5th–10th centuries)*, I (Cambridge).

Hall, R.A. 1974. 'A check-list of Viking-Age coin finds from Ireland', *Ulster Journal of Archaeology*, 36–7, 71–86.

Hill, P. 1997. *Whithorn and St Ninian: the excavations of a monastic town, 1984–91* (Stroud).

Hudson, B. 2005. *Viking pirates and Christian princes: dynasty, religion and empire in the North Atlantic* (Oxford).

Jonsson, K. 1995. 'Numismatics', *Current Swedish Archaeology*, 3, 163–71.

Jonsson, K. 2006. 'The pre-reform coinage of Edgar: the legacy of the Anglo-Saxon kingdoms' in B. Cook & G. Williams (eds), *Coinage and history in the North Sea World*, pp 325–46.

Kenny, M. 1987. 'The geographical distribution of Irish Viking-Age coin hoards', *Proceedings of the Royal Irish Academy*, 87, 507–25.

Kilger, C. 2006. 'Silver-handling traditions during the Viking Age: some observations and thoughts on the phenomenon of pecking and bending' in B. Cook & G. Williams (eds), *Coinage and history in the North Sea world*, pp 449–66.

Malmer, B. 1985. 'Some thoughts on the secondary treatment of Viking-Age coins found on Gotland and in Poland', *Nummus et Historia* (Warsaw), 49–56.

McCarthy, J.P. & M. Dolley. 1977. 'The Castle Freke (Rathbarry, Co. Cork) find of tenth-century Anglo-Saxon coins', *Spink's Numismatic Circular*, 8:11, 488–90.

Metcalf, M. 1986. 'The monetary history of England in the tenth century, viewed in the perspective of the eleventh century' in M.A.S. Blackburn (ed.), *Anglo-Saxon monetary history: essays in memory of Michael Dolley* (Leicester), pp 133–57.

Metcalf, M. 1992. 'The monetary economy of the Irish Sea Province' in J. Graham-Campbell (ed.), *Viking treasure from the north-west: the Cuerdale hoard in its context* (Liverpool), pp 89–106.

Metcalf, M. 1995. 'The monetary significance of Scottish Viking-Age coin hoards, with a short commentary' in J. Graham-Campbell, *The Viking-Age gold and silver of Scotland*, pp 16–25.

Ó Ríordáin, B. 1976. 'The High Street excavations' in B. Almquist and D. Greene (eds), *Proceedings of the Seventh Viking Congress*, pp 135–40.

Pagan, H.E. 1974. 'An Anglo-Saxon coin hoard from the west of Country Cork', *Journal of the Cork Historical and Archaeological Society*, 79, 62–3.

Paterson, C. 2001. 'Insular belt-fittings from the pagan Norse graves of Scotland: a reappraisal in the light of scientific and stylistic analysis' in M. Redknap, N. Edwards, S. Youngs, A. Lane & J. Knight (eds), *Pattern and purpose in Insular art* (Oxford), pp 125–32.

Petersen, J. 1940. *British antiquities of the Viking period found in Norway*, vol. 5 in H. Shetelig (ed.), *Viking antiquities in Great Britain and Ireland* (1940–54) (Oslo).

SCBI BM = Archibald, M.M. & C.E. Blunt. 1986. *Sylloge of coins of the British Isles 34: Anglo-Saxon coins V, Æthelstan to the reform of Eadgar, 924–c.973* (London).

Sheehan, J. 1998a. 'Early Viking-Age silver hoards from Ireland and their Scandinavian elements' in H.B. Clarke, M. Ní Mhaonaigh & R. Ó Floinn (eds), *Ireland and Scandinavia in the Early Viking Age* (Dublin), pp 166–202.

Sheehan, J. 1998b. 'Viking-Age hoards from Munster: a regional tradition?' in M.A. Monk & J. Sheehan (eds), *Early Medieval Munster: archaeology, history and society* (Cork), pp 147–63.

Sheehan, J. 2000a. 'Ireland's early Viking-Age silver hoards: components, structure and classification', *Acta Archaeologica*, 71, 49–63.

Sheehan, J. 2000b. 'Viking-Age silver and gold from county Clare' in Ó Murchadha, C. (ed.), *County Clare Studies* (Ennis).

Simpson, L. 1999. *Director's findings: Temple Bar West* (Dublin).

Stevenson, R.B.K. 1966. *Sylloge of coins of the British Isles 6: National Museum of Antiquities of Scotland, Edinburgh part I, Anglo-Saxon coins (with associated foreign coins* (London).

Thompson, R.H. 1986. 'The published writings of Michael Dolley, 1944–1983' in M.A.S. Blackburn (ed.), *Anglo-Saxon monetary history*, pp 315–60.

Warner, R. 1975–6. 'Scottish silver arm-rings: an analysis of weights', *Proceedings of the Society of Antiquaries of Scotland*, 107, 136–43.

Welin, U.S.L. 1956. 'Graffiti on Oriental coins in Swedish Viking-Age hoards', *Kungliga Humanistiska Vetenskapssamfundets i Lund Årsberättelse*, 149–71.

Whitelock, D. (ed.). 1979. *English historical documents c.500–1042*, 2nd ed. (Oxford).

APPENDIX I: CATALOGUE OF COINS

Dunmore Cave [2], Co. Kilkenny (1999), *c*.965
NMI:1999.260–73

Obverse	Reverse	Reign and description
1.		**Athelstan (924–39)** *CC* (or *CR*?) 0.41g, fragment (with smaller fragment attached, no. 15) Almost certainly a Chester coin, based on the form of 'Ð' with the cross bar on the curve rather than the upright.
+ÆÐ[ ]R [ ]ON[ ]		Possibly the same reverse die as *SCBI* Copenhagen 695 (*CC*, Chester/Paul [PAVELS]), noted by Hugh Pagan.
2. 		**Edmund (939–46)** *HT 1-NE 1*, Landuc 1.47g, 0° – cracked, bent (x 2) Large lettering; reverse is double-struck.
+EADMVNDREX LAND/VCMO		This moneyer is previously unknown for Edmund, but Landuc struck *NE 1* coins for Athelstan.

3.

+E[AD]MVNDRE+   OĐELRI/CESMOT

Edmund (939–46)
HR 1, Othelric(es)
1.29g, 70° – large fragment, bent (x 2)
CTCE, p. 128: 215, Derby?

Struck from the same dies as *SCBI BM* 440 (ex Chester 1950 hoard).

4.

+EADREDRE+   BYRHT/ELΠΠΟ

Eadred (946–55)
HT 1 var., Byrhtelm
1.55g, 100° – whole, bent (x 2)

This is a new *HT* variety and moneyer for this reign. The type locates it away from Mercia. There was a moneyer Byrhtelm at Langport and 'Weardburh' in Athelstan's *CC* type, and Berhtelm was an *HT 1* moneyer for Edmund (*CTCE*, p. 123: 16, 'Langport??').

5.

+EADREDREX⁻   HVNR/EDHO

Eadred (946–55)
HT 1 North-Eastern, Hunred
1.26g, 240° – slightly chipped, bent (x 2)
CTCE, p. 141: 96

Hunred was a prolific moneyer under Eadred (minor after), who probably struck at a substitute mint south of the Humber while York was in Scandinavian hands; Hunred may have moved back to York upon its recovery. Hunred's first die is believed to have come from Derby, but he was later supplied by a York-influenced engraver. Same dies as *SCBI Edinburgh* 229 (ex Iona hoard).

6.

+·E·AD·RE[ ]EX·   ĐEODM/AERM

Eadred (946–55)
HT 1 North-Eastern, Theodmaer
1.50g, 10° – bent (x 2)
CTCE, p. 141: 98

Like Hunred, Theodmaer struck coins at an alternative mint south of the Humber, in north-eastern Mercia, while York was controlled by Scandinavians. He struck only in *HT 1* and in this reign, and his name is always spelt '-AER' (not '-ÆR'. Pellets (etc.) in the obverse legend are a characteristically north-eastern feature, also seen in coins of Hunred. Same reverse as *SCBI BM* 580 (ex Kintbury hoard).

7.

[ ]E[A   ]   ÐV[   ]/[   ]

Eadred (946–55)
HR 1, Thurmod
0.22g, fragment
CTCE, p. 143: 176, north midlands

Thurmod struck at Chester under Edgar. Same dies as *SCBI BM* 635 (ex Tiree hoard) and *SCBI Edinburgh 287* (ex Iona hoard).

8.

+EADREDREX   PVLFGA/RESMOT

Eadred (946–55)
HR 1, Wulfgar(es)
1.33g, 50° – chipped and bent (x 2)
CTCE, p. 143: 185, north midlands

Wulfgar struck at Chester during Athelstan's and Edgar's reigns. Mark from bending instrument or tooth(?) visible under initial cross on obverse.

9.

+E[   ]   +[T]

A/S penny fragment, probably a *BC* coin of **Eadred**
0.10g
Initial cross and spidery 'E' visible on obverse; cross-bar of 'T' (from MONET[A]) and initial cross visible on reverse.

See *SCBI BM* 711 reverse (Saraward, 'Lincoln') for similar punch used for initial cross, as noted by Stewart Lyon.

10.

+EA[D]RE
= retrograde

REGD/[R]M[Z   ] =
'REEDT/RMSE'?

Cross bar of D can be
read as upright of
upside down T, as on
halfpenny below.

Irregular, from the reign of **Eadred**
HR 1, Regther(es)
1.12g, 340° – retrograde obverse

Possibly same dies as Clonterbrook Trust sale (1974) 39 (first coin) ex Lockett (1960) 3699, presumably ex Carlyon-Britton (1918) 1698 (c) ex Sir John Evans ex Killyon Manor hoard (no. 20 in the publication of the KM hoard in *NC*) as noted by Hugh Pagan; not documented in photographs taken of the Lockett coins before their dispersal.

11.

+E[A   ]D+   REIMOT/[   ]
                       'MOT' upside down

Irregular, probably from the reign of **Eadred**
HR 1, retrograde obverse
0.63g, 180°? – bent (x 1)
cut halfpenny

Style of 'M' suggests that it is directly copied from an *HR 1* coin of a Derby moneyer, e.g. Regther(es) or Wulfgar(es).

12.

+EADVVIGERE   VVILS/IGMO

Eadwig (955–9)
HR 3, Wilsig
1.50g, 90° – bent (x 2)
CTCE, p. 156: 134, north-west Mercia, probably Chester

Letters NE in middle row are a continuation of 'MO' for MONETA, not the mint name. A mule demonstrates that the *HR 3* type was struck late in Eadwig's reign, and was issued right up to the introduction of Edgar's coinage (see *CTCE*, p. 151). Same obverse die as *SCBI BM* 843 & 841 (Thurmod).

13.

+EADG˜A˜RREX   HERIG/ERMO

Edgar (957/9–75)
HT 1 '*York*', Heriger
1.37g, 200° – whole and un-bent
CTCE, p. 166: 79, York

14.

Anglo-Saxon penny fragment, too small to identify, but not visibly associated with any other coin in the find.
0.01g

Part of triangle wedge and outer rim visible.

15.

not available

Anglo-Saxon penny fragment stuck to the fragment of Athelstan (no. 1 above), but evidently not from the same coin. Image not to scale.

It appears to be of the *HC* type, reign and details uncertain.

For explanation of types refer to *Coinage in tenth-century England* [*CTCE*] by C.E. Blunt, B.H.I.H. Stewart and C.S.S. Lyon (Oxford, 1989).

APPENDIX II: CHECK-LIST OF TENTH-CENTURY COIN HOARDS
(pre-reform, or with pre-reform element) from south Leinster and Munster

Provenance	Contents	Date of deposit	Principal references
Dunmore Cave [1], Co. Kilkenny, 1973	Total: 9 coins, many fragmentary, and hack-silver. Edward the Elder (2), Athelstan (1), Vikings of Northumbria (3), Vikings of Lincoln (1); Kufic (2); cut piece of a small silver ingot (1).	c.930	Dolley 1975; Hall 1974, 73; Blackburn and Pagan, 111.
Co. Kildare, unlocalized, 1840	Total: 11 coins, some fragmentary. Edward the Elder (4), Athelstan (2), plus fragments of four other Anglo-Saxon coins of the same period; Kufic (1).	c.935	Hall 1974, 74; Blackburn and Pagan, 114.
Glendalough [2], Co. Wicklow, pre-1822	Total: c.50 coins, including Edward the Elder (10), Athelstan (34, including one irregular with a double obverse), Edmund (3).	c.942	Dolley and Pagan 1964; Hall 1974, 74; Blackburn and Pagan, 124.
Co. Tipperary, unlocalized, c.1843	Total: 19 coins. Edward the Elder (6); Athelstan (9, including 1 irregular); Edmund (4)	c.942	Dolley 1962a; Hall 1974, 74; Blackburn and Pagan, 125.
Castle Freke, Rathbarry, Co. Cork, 1785–99	Total: unknown, believed to be all of Athelstan and Edmund.	c.945	Pagan 1974; McCarthy and Dolley 1977; Hall 1974, 74; Blackburn and Pagan, 127.
Macroom, Co. Cork, c.1840	Total: a 'large' find, of which 15 coins are recorded (the rest were allegedly melted down). Edward the Elder (1), Athelstan (1), Edmund (5), Eadred (8).	c.953	Dolley 1970; Hall 1974, 75; Blackburn and Pagan, 132.
Mungret, Co. Limerick, c.1842	Total: 'a considerable number' and ingots, of which 9 coins and 7 ingots were recorded. Edward the Elder (4), Athelstan (3), Eadred (1), Vikings of Northumbria (1); small silver ingots, whole (7).	c.953	Dolley 1960a; Hall 1974, 75; Blackburn and Pagan, 135.
Ballitore, near Co. Kildare, 1837	Total: 38 coins, dispersed by Sotheby, June/July 1842 and substantially reconstructed by Dolley. Edward the Elder (4), Athelstan (4), Edmund (8), Eadred (13), Eadwig (3), Edgar (4), Vikings of Northumbria (2).	c.965	Dolley 1962b; Hall 1974, 76; Blackburn and Pagan 142.
Dunmore Cave [2], Co. Kilkenny, 1999	Total: 15 coins (including a tiny fragment), some fragmentary, and hack-silver, and other items associated with a fine garment. Athelstan (1), Edmund (2), Eadred (8, including two irregular), Eadwig (1), Edgar (1), plus two fragments not identified; also, cut pieces of small silver ingots (3); a small hammered disc-shaped piece of silver (1); a cut and folded piece of silver brooch pin (1); a looped rod of silver (1); long, folded copper alloy ingots (2); a whole, plain penannular silver 'ring-money' arm-ring (1).	c.965	Blackburn and Pagan, 151b; Halpin (ed.), forthcoming.
Glendalough [3], Co. Wicklow, c.1835/6	Total: 'a small parcel', all Anglo-Saxon, details uncertain, but included 'a number' of Edmund, Eadred and Eadwig (without portrait), and Edgar (3).	c.970	Dolley 1960b; Hall 1974, 78; Blackburn and Pagan, 166.
Knockmaon Co. Waterford, 1912	Total: 14+ coins, with a pre-reform component and hack-silver. Anglo-Saxon [Edgar] (4); Continental (7); Hiberno-Scandinavian [*Crux* & *Long Cross*] (3+); 'ring-money' fragments (3).	c.1000	Dolley and Morrison 1963, no. 23; Hall 1974, 79; Dumas 1979, no. 3; Blackburn and Pagan 195.

Ragnarök and the stones of York

PAUL C. BUCKLAND

INTRODUCTION

To anyone approaching the medieval churches of the Humber Basin of eastern England with a geologist's eye, the frequency of non-local materials in their structures is particularly striking. In some cases, this largely reflects the lack of availability of good local stone for those parts of the structure for which ashlar was required, principally quoins, imposts and arches, but even here the choice of materials is often surprising. Why, for example, does the well-known late Anglo-Saxon church at Barton-on-Humber in Lincolnshire (Rodwell and Rodwell 1982) utilize Millstone Grit for its decorative and structural features, when it sits a few kilometres from the fine freestones of the Middle Jurassic of the Lincolnshire Limestone, or across the estuary, the Cave Oolite? Later building throughout the region is dominated by sources on the Lower Magnesian Limestone, 60km to the west, where the scale of working and ease of transport down the rivers of the basin gave these sources economic advantages (Gee 1981) over smaller more local sources, although wall stone, in coursed or random rubble, was often locally derived either from beach or field cobbles or from local borrow pits. Even here, however, the approach was not always apparently logical, and far-travelled material ended up as rubble walling on sites where other stone was more locally available. Other factors are therefore at work. Some of the smaller material is likely to have moved as ballast (Buckland and Sadler 1990; Hoare et al. 2002), but the problem extends outside of the floodplain settlements of the Vale of York and the Humber. In the heart of the Yorkshire Wolds at Kirby Grindalythe, the early Norman lower stages of the tower are largely in the most suitable local stone, the Birdsall Grit, but the north wall is in a regularly coursed oolitic limestone, probably from the Malton Oolite, and the quoins incorporate large blocks of Millstone Grit (Fig. 4.1).

The several coarse felspathic sandstones which occur in the Upper Carboniferous Millstone Grit series provide the scarps which make up the central Pennines, and north of Leeds, the overlying Coal Measures are wholly cut out with the Lower Magnesian Limestone lying directly on the sandstones and shales of the Millstone Grit. At Ledsham, on the boundary between Coal Measures and Limestone, to the south of this unconformity, the Anglo-Saxon church (Faull 1986), adjacent to the medieval limestone quarries of Thevesdale (Gee 1981), is largely built of large blocks of Millstone Grit. At Bramham, further to the east, where much of the village appears to sit on the benches of a

4.1 The base of the tower at Kirby Grindalythe, East Yorkshire, from the north-west. The north wall with its small ashlars of Malton Oolite and its white bonding courses contrasts with the quoins, largely of Millstone Grit, and the later Norman work in the Birdsall Grit (photo: Paul Buckland).

former quarry in the Lower Magnesian Limestone, the church incorporates much Millstone Grit. The several sandstones which make up the outcrop of the Millstone Grit are virtually indistinguishable. Therefore, attempts to identify the material in Hemingbrough church, situated near the Ouse downstream of Selby, as either Bramley Fall, near Leeds, or Plumpton Rocks near Knaresbrough (Burton 1888), or the material in Thomas of Bayeaux's cathedral at York as 'Pateley Bridge' (Phillips 1985, 196) are perhaps overly optimistic. The problems of sourcing have been discussed by Buckland and Gaunt (Buckland 1988; Gaunt and Buckland 2002), but this is largely a secondary aspect with regard to medieval use of the stone away from the outcrop (Fig. 4.2). Examination of other rock types, including the Permian Lower Magnesian Limestone and Jurassic limestones and sandstones, incorporated into churches, indicates similar origins: much of the material is clearly re-used from substantial Roman structures, most of which in the Humber Basin must have originated in York (Buckland 1987; 1988). Lewis holes, cramp and butterfly clamp holes are evident on many of the blocks which have not been re-cut. Skipwith, near Selby, incorporates gritstone demi-column drums end-on in the west face of the tower. At Hemingbrough, in the northeast angle of the original nave, behind the present pulpit, a gritstone

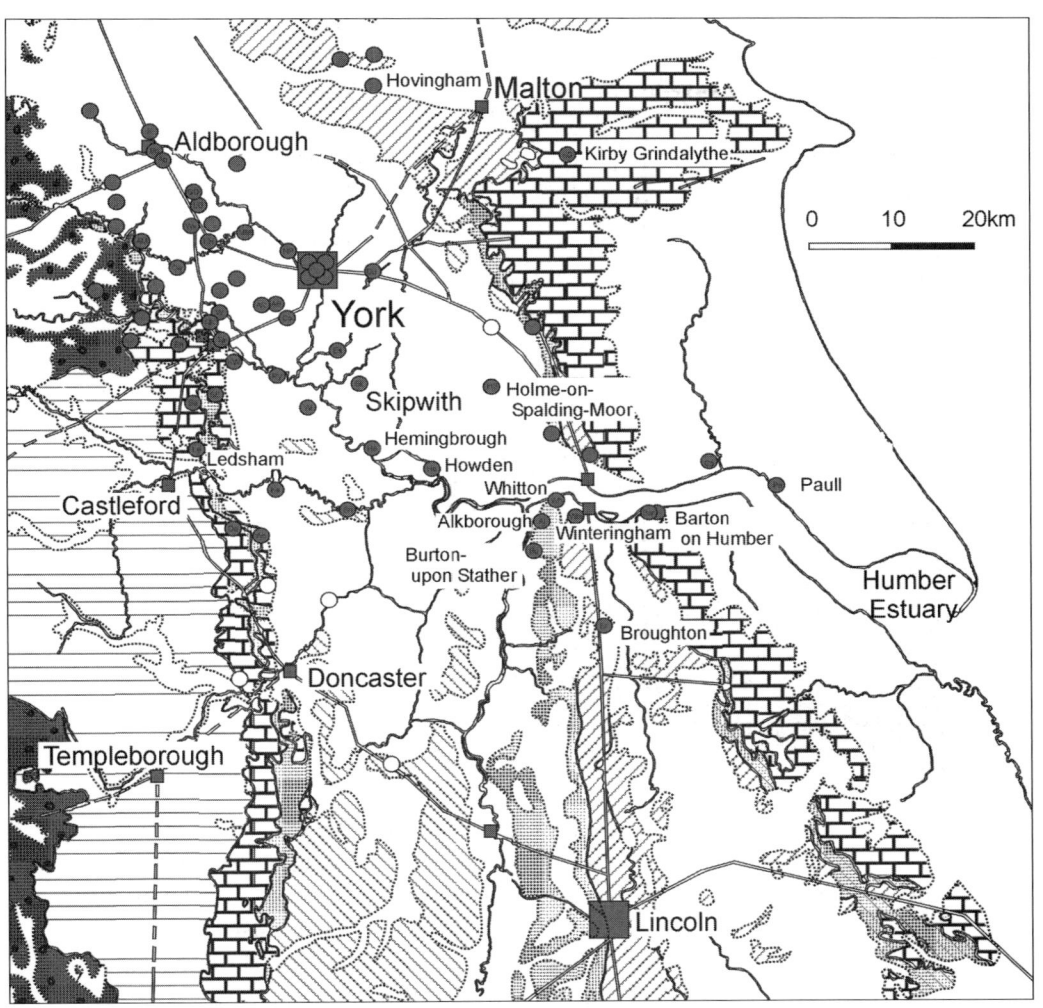

4.2 Distribution of Millstone Grit in the churches of the Humber Basin. Roman sites are denoted by squares, and churches with gritstone by circles. The Millstone Grit outcrop is the deeply shaded area on the left of the map, the Coal Measures are horizontally lined, and the Lower Magnesian Limestone is the left-hand brick pattern; the Chalk is the right-hand brickwork and the unshaded areas denote Quaternary (Drift) deposits. Other units consist of Triassic and Jurassic rocks. Sites mentioned in the text are indicated.

block has a Latin inscription, probably of third-century date (Hassall and Tomlin 1992), cut through and re-used upside down as a masonry block. Whilst other rock types have been traced, the most useful and easily recognized starting point is the use of Millstone Grit, and Figure 4.2 provides a plot of the stone's re-use in churches in the Humber Basin. What require discussion are the dates and social context of the re-use of Roman material.

4.3 The south-west corner of the nave at Alkborough, Lincolnshire, showing the use of re-cut blocks of Millstone Grit for quoins (photo: Paul Buckland).

THE ARCHITECTURAL EVIDENCE

The Lincolnshire group of Romanesque church towers has recently been subject to detailed study by David Stocker and Paul Everson (2006). They conclude that the construction of towers was a post-Conquest phenomenon, relating to changes in the burial ritual introduced by the Conqueror's Archbishop of Canterbury, Lanfranc. In several places, including churches incorporating significant amounts of Millstone Grit at Alkborough and Whitton on the Humber, they note that towers have been added to pre-existing naves. In both cases, it is probable that the gritstone relates to the earlier structure on the site. At Alkborough, the quoins of the west corners of the nave, evident between the tower and modern buttresses, are largely of gritstone (Fig. 4.3), although it is impossible to ascertain the duration of the interval between the construction of a simple two-cell nave and small chancel and the addition of a tower. A similar pattern is evident in the church at Skipwith (Taylor and Taylor 1965). In most cases, however, the evidence for an earlier structure on the site, for example at Winteringham on the Lincolnshire side of the Humber, Paull on the north side and Howden (Bilson 1913; see Fig. 4.2), rests on the incorporation of distinctively alien rock types,

4.4 Ragnarök, as depicted in the graffito on a re-used block of Lower Magnesian Limestone on the inside of the tower at Skipwith, East Yorkshire (3-D scan taken with a Minolta VI-900 by Jeremy Pile, School of Conservation Sciences, Bournemouth University).

often extensively re-trimmed, in later fabrics. In the medieval period, until the massive redistribution of materials occasioned by the Reformation, the costs of transport dictated that once stone arrived on a site, it was rarely moved off, and even rubble was extensively recycled (cf. Stocker 1990; Stocker and Eversham 1990).

THE SKIPWITH RAGNARÖK

St Helen's Church at Skipwith was visited by the Fourth Viking Congress in 1961, when the late Harold Taylor discussed its architectural sequence. His description in the congress volume (Taylor 1965) does not differ substantially from that in Taylor and Taylor (1965). He did not, however, comment upon the building materials, or upon what is perhaps the most interesting element of the building. Low down in the north wall, inside the tower, is a large block of Lower

Magnesian Limestone, in a wall otherwise largely of re-cut Millstone Grit blocks. The block was first noted in 1886, and Collingwood (1911) describes it as 'grotesque figures and beast, incised with chisel', apparently regarding it as post-Conquest work. It was probably exposed when the floor in the church was lowered during refurbishment in 1877; when the stone lay previously above ground level any carving is likely to have been obscured by plaster. The block (Fig. 4.4, Pl. 1) measures roughly 63cm wide by 36cm in height, and its lower edge, built into the wall and partly obscured by modern cement, has curves suggesting a previous use, perhaps as a sculptural element. Cut into the surface of the stone is a rather confused scene in which a central maned or collared quadruped is biting at the foot of a figure in a conical cap or helmet. To the right, a similar slightly smaller figure advances to the left whilst another in a rounded helmet flees to the right. The head and arms of another individual, with the right arm drawn back in a similar position to the arms of the figures above, are evident below the quadruped. Beneath the tail of the animal, which has a transverse rectangular end, appears the head and left arm of a further figure in a rounded helmet with prominent nose-guard. Above this figure, and using the contour of the tail and back of the quadruped as its ventral surface and the lower side of the left arm of a large figure in a conical helmet for its dorsal surface, is a large snake with its head facing downwards; the eye with its pupil is particularly evident. The large figure on the left has outstretched arms, and a series of vertical lines above the eyebrow indicate either hair or part of the helmet, whilst lines below the nose may suggest a full face-guard or cheek-pieces. There is also some suggestion that this individual is wearing a tunic, cut off at the shoulders, with a belt around the waist and toggle at the neck. Over the right shoulder of this warrior, a triangle containing a lozenge-shaped eye indicates a further figure. Between the large figure and the one with his foot in the mouth of the quadruped, the stone is partly effaced but there appear to be a number of upward and outward curving lines. The economy of line, utilizing a single cut to define two surfaces, makes the image difficult to interpret in detail, but it has long been agreed that what is depicted is Ragnarök, although the description and interpretation by the late Jim Lang (1991) in the *Corpus of Anglo-Saxon Stone Sculpture* needs some revision. Although it inevitably conflates events in the myth, the scene is remarkably close to the account in Snorri's Prose Edda. The central beast is the wolf Fenrir and the warrior with his foot on the wolf's lower jaw is Viðarr, son of Oðinn (*contra* Lang 1991), who avenged his father's death. The adjacent figure is perhaps Viðarr's brother, Váli. This allows the suggestion that the prominent figure on the left of the slab is intended to be Oðinn. The expanded shaft and clavate end of the wolf's tail is curious until it is realized that it here doubles as Thor's hammer, with the god himself, perhaps dead, being depicted beneath the tail, the upper contour of his left arm and back of his head being also the edge of the right rear leg of the animal. Along the wolf's back and tail/Thor's hammer, lies the Miðgarðsormr, the Midgard serpent, Jörmungandr, whose poisonous breath results in Thor's death immediately after he has killed it; its head is formed by the angle beneath the left arm of the large warrior figure and the angle of the hammer. The few lines in the centre are difficult to interpret, but it is possible that the serpent wraps around the sacred ash Yggdrasill. If the large figure with the more elaborate helmet is intended to be Oðinn, then the sharply triangular head over his shoulder could be intended to be one of his ravens rather than another warrior. There is no trace, however, of another of his attributes, a spear, and both hands appear open flat, with the fingers defined. Whilst Lang (1991) refers to the figures as 'squatting', it is more probable that the graffitist is trying to portray movement, which would also explain the rather awkward position of the arms of three of the figures. Lang was also non-committal over Bailey's (1980, 234) identification of helmets on several of the warriors. Close examination under varied lighting conditions makes it plain that the putative head of Thor is wearing a close-fitting helmet with cheek-pieces and a prominent nose-guard, although it is equally possible that it is a full-face visor. Similar problems attend the interpretation of the head of the larger figure. What at first appears as hair below a small conical cap is better seen as the over-emphasized eyebrows on a helmet, the actual eyebrow being indicated by a line above the eye. The lines either side of the nose would form a guard and the lines curving down from the end of this and running beneath the eye would then reflect the cheek-guards of the helmet, although either a drooping moustache or the skeumorph of such on a full face guard is also possible. Such an interpretation is not out of place in the context of Vendel pieces, or for that matter helmets from Anglo-Saxon contexts. Most recently both groups have been discussed with regard to the helmet from Coppergate in York (Tweddle 1992), and whilst it might be seen as going beyond the evidence available in what is after all a very crude sketch at Skipwith, the presence of both rounded and pointed helmet types in the graffito could be taken to support a late date, closer to AD1000 than the middle of the ninth century, when York first fell to the Great Army.

Both Lang (1991) and Pevsner and Neave (1995) suggest that the carving was done whilst the block was *in situ* in the tower, but close examination of the angles of the lines, cut with a knife, rather than the chisel suggested by Collingwood (1911), into the soft, almost lithographic stone, shows that the block was likely to have been either at head height or slightly above when the graffito was made. This indicates that the block was probably part of a standing structure when Ragnarök was sketched onto it; the question is where did this occur? There can be little doubt that the stone derives from Roman York. Column sections, as well as lewis holes and dovetail-shaped clamp holes, are evident on several blocks and a sculptured block incorporated in the south wall of the tower appears to represent a three-dimensional carving of a boar. The Lower Magnesian Limestone is not the preferred stone for large dimensional blocks in York, where

Millstone Grit predominates in load-bearing and structural situations (Gaunt and Buckland 2002), but it was used for inscriptions, including the Trajanic one from over the fortress gate in King's Square at the end of Petergate, and for water-holding structures like the small fountain or cistern from Bishophill in the Colonia (RCHMYI 1962, pl. 21).

Unlike the closest parallel in terms of the mix of materials, St Mary Bishophill Junior in York, Skipwith shows a logical pattern of larger blocks at the base giving way to smaller material higher up, and the size of many of the smaller blocks of Lower Magnesian Limestone, as in St Mary's, suggests that they originate in Roman *Saxa quadrata*. Buckland (1987) has put forward the hypothesis that the materials for the construction of the tower of St Mary Bishophill closely reflect a source in a length of Colonia wall, built in Lower Magnesian Limestone, its footing course in massive Millstone Grit blocks and an added external bastion or internal tower in Jurassic oolite, a pattern similar to that seen in the so-called Anglian Tower and adjacent length of fortress wall (Buckland 1984).

DISCUSSION

Archaeologists tend to lapse into the vernacular and talk about stone-robbing, but whilst this undoubtedly did occur, the norm would be that everything is owned and that the quantities required to make even a simple two-celled church would not be acquired by subterfuge from the ruins of Roman York. Eburacum disappears into its Anglo-Scandinavian hinterland by the process of gift of building materials and often that process of gift may leave the recipient with more expense than the local acquisition of stone. Many sites lie adjacent to once navigable waterways, but even in the stone-free area of the Foulness valley, there were easier and closer sources than the massive re-used blocks of Millstone Grit apparent in the later medieval fabric of the hilltop church of All Saints, Holme-on-Spalding-Moor. It seems even more likely that the land-locked community at Kirby Grindalythe – a free translation of this Scandinavian name ('the church farm on the valley slope with cranes') conjures up its remoteness – would not have entered lightly into an agreement which required the movement of several hundred blocks, each weighing up to a tonne, over 45km by the most direct route via Roman road, if still useable, or by river, over 90km down the Ouse and up the Derwent to Malton, with a final portage overland of 15km, unless there was a commitment, either in terms of spirituality or loyalty, other than simple acquisition of raw materials. It is probable that Kirby had been involved in an earlier case of the re-use of stone. All that survives of the medieval church is the tower, the lower part of the north wall of which uses small oolite ashlars with levelling courses in a whiter, more thin-bedded limestone (Fig. 4.1). Both are from the local Jurassic, although the outcrop lies a few kilometres to the north of the more convenient Birdsall Grit employed in the Norman work in the tower. In terms of stone size, insofar as a sample of the possible source is available, this wall probably reflects the gift of a section of the enceinte of the Roman fort at Malton, the tower's use of contrasting stone colour in its bonding courses mirroring a common Roman practice, familiar in the use of brick in the Multangular Tower in York (RCHMY1 1962, pl. 2). It is uncertain whether the Millstone Grit quoins formed part of the primary stone structure on the site. A similar pattern of re-use of Malton and York material is perhaps apparent in the tower of Hovingham Church, to the west of Malton, although it is uncertain whether the gritstone in this tower originates in the Middle Jurassic of the North York Moors, rather than the Millstone Grit of the Pennines.

The fort at Malton was excavated by Corder during the 1920s (Corder 1928), and his sections through the eastern defences show a large ditch cutting across the site of the gate. His fixation with Rome meant that he interpreted this as a Late Roman re-defence of the enclosure, but it is apparent from his sections that the ditch can only have been cut after the fort wall had been almost entirely removed down to its foundations, and it is more probable that the re-defence, essentially what is evident in the morphology of the site at the present day, pre-dates the construction of the Norman castle in the west corner of the enclosure, and is sufficiently post-Roman for use to have already been found for most of the fort's stone. The mostly likely context is in a first wave of church construction in Malton's hinterland, perhaps in the Anglian period, with the refortification, which may not run around the entire enclosure, occurring at some time during the Anglo-Scandinavian period. There are several historical contexts and as in the case of Roman Malton, the less the stratigraphic constraint, the greater the possibilities (cf. Buckland 1982) but the *burh*, if such it is, may have acted as a focus for the encircling farms, founded by the remnants of the Great Army or later settlers. Malton is not unique in this pattern of refortification. At Doncaster in South Yorkshire, Buckland and Magilton have argued that the two phases of re-defence of the late Roman fort enclosure, the latter taking place after much of the fort wall had been robbed out and before the construction of the Norman castle in the north-east corner of the site, may relate to Anglian or Mercian activities in this frontier zone, followed by the imposition of an Anglo-Scandinavian focus at the head of navigation, again circled by a ring of Scandinavian place-names (in Buckland, Magilton and Hayfield 1989, fig. 4). It is perhaps ironic, however, that the one site with a rich Viking burial in the region, that at Adwick-le-Street (Speed and Walton Rogers 2004), is from a settlement with a firmly Anglo-Saxon name. Tracking the small ashlars of Lower Magnesian Limestone from Doncaster has proved difficult and the only evidence for the use of sandstone from the Coal Measures in a Roman structure is in a finely tooled fragment which perhaps once formed part of an inscription (Buckland and

Magilton 1986). Several churches in the Doncaster region sited on or adjacent to the Magnesian Limestone outcrop include significant quantities of Carboniferous sandstones, and at Bolton-on-Dearne, north of the River Don, on the outcrop of the Darfield Rock, the quoins and jambs of the Mercian-style nave use, or rather re-use a different Carboniferous source, probably recycled from the Roman fort at Templeborough, near Rotherham, which had been abandoned in the early third century. Thomas May's excavations on this site do not show any clear evidence of post-Roman refortification (1922), but the pattern of apparently illogical dispersal of stone beyond its hinterland is equally apparent. To the north, at Castleford, a probable ditch cutting through the earlier Roman deposits has been interpreted as late Roman work (Abramson et al. 1999; Rush et al. 2000), but Buckland (2002) has questioned the paucity of late Roman finds and suggested that it might be later. If not another Viking strongpoint at the head of navigation (and the structure is less convincing than the Malton and Doncaster evidence), a historical context could be sought in the confrontation between King Eadred's West Saxon army and Eiríkr blóðøx's Northumbrians in AD948, after the former's burning of Ripon (Rollason 2002), although one should be reluctant to seek close historical contexts for such poorly dated structures, something which has bedevilled study of the defences of York (cf. Buckland 1984; Ottaway 2004).

Gift exchange is a two-way process. It is possible that what is acquired along with the stones is simply the sense of *Romanitas*, the acquisition of a material part of Rome, of which the Church was the successor. In discussing Anglo–Saxon and Anglo-Scandinavian sculpture in Yorkshire, David Stocker has suggested that the remains of Roman York formed part of the patrimony of the Archbishop of York (2000). It is tempting to see the archbishop's hand in the redistribution of its remains at a time when there were changes in land ownership, or at least tenure, and a need to extend the web of patronage out from the city. It is too easy to see York as a continually populous settlement when the reality is much more likely to have been something akin to what Piranesi's drawings of mid-eighteenth-century Rome project (Ficacci 2001), a series of shifting foci around churches, elite halls and wharfage amidst the ruins of grandeur, which only late in the Anglo-Scandinavian period started to coalesce into something approaching an entity. On the contentious ground of Lindsey, York stone only seems to have penetrated as far south as Burton-upon-Stather on the cliff above the Trent and Broughton on Ermine Street. Roman Lincoln is much more difficult to track, not least because limestone is more likely to be re-used as lime than stone, but the mix of materials at Alkborough, above Trent Falls, the confluence of the rivers Trent, Don and Ouse, is instructive (see Fig. 4.2). The first traceable stone church uses Millstone Grit, whereas the tower arch is clearly a re-set Roman arch in a fine Jurassic limestone, its source further emphasized by a piece of Roman diagonal lattice sculpture in its footings (Stocker and Everson 2006, fig. 4.4). The nature of the land-holding at Alkborough when Domesday was compiled is complex, and the statement that Thorold, Sheriff of Lincoln, gave the church to Spalding Priory in 1051 by *Pseudo-Ingulphus* has been regarded as a post-Conquest forgery (Stocker and Everson 2006, 97). In the absence of a bishop in Lincoln, however, was Thorold in a position to grant some of its stone to a community which previously saw itself as within the purview of York? There is much to be made from a close examination of stone distribution and the slim, often untrustworthy documentary record.

CONCLUSION

With the Skipwith graffito we enter the world of the individual, not the commissioned world of the elite, where one man's Sigurðr battling with a dragon was another's Thor and the world serpent, or St Michael at the mouth of Hell, or where the apparently pagan symbolism was purely heraldic. Parts of Ragnarök appear on crosses in Cumbria (Collingwood 1927), although Bailey (2000) is doubtful over the interpretation of most other than Gosforth. At Kirk Andreas in the Isle of Man, the figure with his foot in a canine quadruped's mouth is clearly Oðinn, complete with raven and spear (Kermode 1907), but the casual nature of the Skipwith piece sets it apart. In this twilight world, when Kveld-Úlfr might espouse Christianity but sacrifice to Thor in a storm, or his grandson write a poem in York to save his own neck, a bored Viking warrior, a barbarian inside the gates, scratched his own vision of one end of the World onto a stone in a decaying Roman building. That stone then became caught up in a cascade of building materials which spread the connection with Rome from the edge of the Pennines to the mouth of the Humber. It deserves to be better known, and indeed better looked after.

ACKNOWLEDGMENTS

This paper has a curious beginning in that it started with a comment from Peter Addyman with regard to the Roman sewer in Church Street, York, 'You're a geologist, you sort it out'. Forty years later, I am still trying to sort it out, but wish to thank Peter for his initial suggestion. The stone distribution work began as part of a project in Sheffield by Pat Foster, funded by a grant from the University Hossein-Farmy Award; Pat has gracefully passed all his primary data over to me, and I have revisited every relevant building. Discussion with Geoff Gaunt, formerly with the British Geological Survey, continues to be particularly useful, and in York the work of Patrick Ottaway and Toby Kendall, the latter including new work on the tower at Skipwith, is acknowledged. This research has been much longer in gestation than birth, and I am grateful to Eva Panagiotakopulu and Kevin Edwards for pointing out the lapses in logic and to Eva's brother Tassos for sorting out my rough distribution maps. My wife, Joan, has also stood in many cold churchyards.

BIBLIOGRAPHY

Abramson, P., D.S. Berg & M.R. Fossick. 1999. *Roman Castleford: excavations 1974–85, II, the structural and environmental evidence* (Leeds).

Bailey, R.N. 1980. *Viking-Age sculpture in Northern England* (London).

Bailey, R.N. 2000. 'Scandinavian myth on Viking-period stone sculpture in England' in G. Barnes & M. Clunies Ross (eds), *Old Norse myths, literature and society: Proceedings of the 11th International Saga Conference, 2–7 July 2000, University of Sydney* (Sydney), pp 15–23.

Bilson, J. 1913. 'Howden church: some notes on its architectural history', *Yorkshire Archaeological Journal*, 22, 159–65.

Buckland, P.C. 1982. 'The Malton burnt grain: a cautionary tale', *Yorkshire Archaeological Journal*, 54, 53–61.

Buckland, P.C. 1984. 'The Anglian tower and the use of Jurassic Limestone in York' in P.V. Addyman & V.E. Black (eds), *Archaeological papers from York presented to M.W. Barley* (York), pp 51–7.

Buckland, P.C. 1987. 'The building stones: petrological analysis' in L.P. Wenham, R.A. Hall, C.M. Briden & D.A. Stocker, *St Mary Bishophill Junior and St Mary Castlegate*, Archaeology of York, 8:2, pp 110–15.

Buckland, P.C. 1988. 'The stones of Roman York: building materials in Roman Yorkshire' in J. Price & P. Wilson (eds), *Recent research in Roman Yorkshire* (Oxford), pp 237–88.

Buckland, P.C. 2002. 'Review of P. Rush et al. 2000. *Roman Castleford: excavations 1974–85. III. The Pottery* (Leeds)', *Britannia*, 33, 399–401.

Buckland, P.C. & J.R. Magilton. 1986. *The archaeology of Doncaster, vol. 1: the Roman civil settlement* (Oxford).

Buckland, P.C., J.R. Magilton & C.L. Hayfield. 1989. *The archaeology of Doncaster, vol. 2: the medieval and later town* (Oxford).

Buckland, P.C. & J. Sadler. 1990. 'Ballast and building stone: a discussion' in D. Parsons (ed.), *Stone quarrying and building in England AD43–1525* (Chichester), pp 114–25.

Burton, T. 1888. *The history and antiquities of the parish of Hemingbrough in the county of York* (York).

Collingwood, W.G. 1911. 'Anglian and Anglo-Danish sculpture in the East Riding, with addenda to the North Riding', *Yorkshire Archaeological Journal*, 21, 254–302.

Collingwood, W.G. 1927. *Northumbrian crosses of the pre-Norman Age* (London).

Corder, P. 1928. *The defences of the Roman fort at Malton* (Leeds).

Faull, M.L. 1986. 'The decoration of the south doorway of Ledsham church tower', *Journal of the British Archaeological Association*, 139, 143–7.

Ficacci, L. 2001. *Giovanni Battista Piranesi: selected etchings* (Cologne).

Gaunt, G.D. & P.C. Buckland. 2002. 'Sources of building material in Roman York' in P. Wilson & J. Price (eds), *Aspects of industry in Roman Yorkshire and the North* (Oxford), pp 133–44.

Gee, E. 1981. 'Stone from the medieval limestone quarries of South Yorkshire' in A. Detsicas (ed.), *Collecteana historica: essays in memory of Stuart Rigold* (Maidstone), pp 247–55.

Hassall, M.W.C. & R.S.O. Tomlin. 1992. 'Inscriptions' in 'Roman Britain in 1991', *Britannia*, 23, 309–24.

Hoare, P.G., R. Vinx, C.R. Stevenson & J. Ehlers. 2002. 'Re-used bedrock ballast in King's Lynn's "Town Wall" and the Norfolk port's medieval trading links', *Medieval Archaeology*, 46, 91–106.

Kermode, P.M.C. 1907. *Manx crosses* (London).

Lang, J. 1991. *Corpus of Anglo-Saxon stone sculpture III: York and eastern Yorkshire* (London).

May, T. 1922. *The Roman forts of Templebrough near Rotherham* (Rotherham).

Ottaway, P. 2004. *Roman York* (Stroud).

Pevsner, N. & D. Neave. 1995. *The buildings of England: Yorkshire: York and the East Riding* (Harmondsworth).

Phillips, D. 1985. *Excavations at York Minster 2: the cathedral of Archbishop Thomas of Bayeaux* (London).

RCHMYI 1962. *Royal Commission on Historical Monuments: the City of York I. Eburacum: Roman York* (London).

Rodwell, W.J. & K.A. Rodwell. 1982. 'St. Peter's Church, Barton-on-Humber: excavation and structural study, 1978–81', *Antiquaries Journal*, 62, 283–315.

Rollason, D. 2002. *Northumbria, 500–1100: creation and destruction of a kingdom.* (Cambridge).

Stocker, D.A. 1990. 'The archaeology of the Reformation in Lincoln: a case-study in the redistribution of materials in the mid sixteenth century', *Lincolnshire History and Archaeology*, 25, 18–32.

Stocker, D. 2000. 'Monuments and merchants: irregularities in the distribution of stone sculpture in Lincolnshire and Yorkshire in the tenth century' in D.M. Hadley & J.D. Richards (eds), *Cultures in contact: Scandinavian settlement in England in the ninth and tenth centuries* (Turnhout), pp 179–212.

Stocker, D. & Everson, P. 1990. 'Rubbish recycled: a study of the reuse of stone in Lincolnshire' in D. Parsons (ed.), *Stone: quarrying and building in England AD43– 1525* (Chichester), pp 83–101.

Stocker, D.A. & P. Everson. 2006. *Summoning St Michael: early Romanesque towers in Lincolnshire* (Oxford).

Taylor, H.M. 1965. 'Anglo-Saxon churches in Yorkshire' in A. Small (ed.) *Proceedings of the Fourth Viking Congress, York 1961* (Edinburgh), pp 56–66.

Taylor, H.M. & J. Taylor. 1965. *Anglo-Saxon architecture II* (Cambridge).

Tweddle, D. 1992. 'The Anglian helmet from Coppergate', *Archaeology of York*, 17:8, 851–1201.

Unsung heroes: the Irish and the Viking wars

HOWARD B. CLARKE

Chapter 39 of Asser's Life of King Alfred of Wessex, composed ostensibly in 893, expresses a striking sentiment in relation to the battle of Ashdown. This was one of a number of military engagements fought between the West Saxons and Danish Vikings in the winter of 870–1. At that time Asser, a Welshman, was presumably at home in Wales. He did not witness this event in person, though (as he tells us) he had been shown the solitary thorn-tree round which the battle had raged. Evidently former battlefields were tourist attractions already in the ninth century! In the course of his description of this West Saxon victory, Asser comments as follows: 'one side [the Danes] acting wrongfully and the other side [the West Saxons] set to fight for life, loved ones and country' (*pro vita et dilectis atque patria*) (Stephenson 1959, 30; Keynes and Lapidge 1983, 79–80). Much later, generations of Englishmen would fight for 'king and country', but Asser is here articulating a sentiment that pre-dated by far the emergence of the nation state. Such expressions of sentiment are not common in Viking-Age contexts, but there is no reason to suppose that it was not genuine even if, as Alfred Smyth argued, the text is an early eleventh-century forgery applying therefore to the so-called Second Viking Age (Smyth 1995, 149–367). It prompts the question: what motivated Englishmen, Franks, Irishmen or Welshmen to risk life and limb in doing battle with Vikings?

Standard accounts by modern scholars of Viking raids and of Viking warfare tend to build up a picture of inexorability and invincibility. Raid is piled on raid and victory is piled on victory: the terrorists are on a winning streak. Of course, we all recognize that Viking armies could be defeated, sometimes spectacularly so, but nevertheless an impression is created of Scandinavian supermen. This in turn is reinforced by maps with large arrows indicating directions of attack, without any corresponding sign of whether such attacks were opposed, and, if so, who won. With that in mind, I made a study some years ago of the outcome of raiding by Dublin-based Vikings and of warfare between them and the native Irish (Clarke 1990–2). In broad terms, the Irish annals contain an impressive amount of detail about the Viking wars. Sometimes an annalist specifies 'the foreigners of Áth Cliath'; on other occasions one has to reach a judgment about the identity of particular Viking armies. Dublin was the most important and the most powerful Scandinavian settlement in the country and its military forces – land-based and sea-based – would have posed the greatest challenge to the natives. How effectively did the Irish meet that challenge?

The analysis was divided into two phases, 841–902 and 917–1014. The first phase is associated with a settlement described by the annalists as a naval encampment (*longphort*); the second phase with a stronghold (*dún*). In between these two phases the settlers and especially their war-leaders were exiled to various parts of Britain. In both phases, as one would expect, it was the adjoining provinces of Brega to the north and Leinster to the south that bore the brunt of the raids. The number of recorded, successful plundering raids by Dublin-based Vikings during the *longphort* phase is small (Clarke 1990–2, 95). Even in this early phase of warfare, the Irish won most of their battles with Dublin Vikings. For the latter the one major victory came in 888, when Flann Sinna led a large combination of native forces to defeat, the dead including the king of Connacht, the bishop of Kildare and the abbot of Kildalkey (*AU, s.a.* 887). In 902, a Brega-Leinster coalition drove out the foreigners 'from Ireland' (*AU, s.a.* 901). After their return to Dublin, the main target areas for periodic plundering were the same as before, though the intensity increased down to the middle of the tenth century (Clarke 1990–2, 103). In the period 917–1014 at least twenty-five military engagements took place between Irish armies and Dublin ones, the latter sometimes containing native allies. Of these, the purely Irish forces won fifteen, most notably the battle of Tara in 980, after which King Amlaíb Cúarán retired, or was obliged to retire, to Iona in Scotland (*AU, s.a.* 979; Clarke 1990–2, 105–7). In addition, between 936 and 1013 there were at least thirteen military assaults by Irish armies on Dublin itself, most of them successful (Clarke 1990–2, 108–13). The leaders of these attacking forces were usually reigning kings of Tara (high-kings), sometimes assisted by allies. Here the trendsetter was Donnchad Donn mac Flainn of the Southern Uí Néill, who burnt Dublin in 936 (*AFM, s.a.* 934). By the end of the tenth century, Dublin – then a town of some size and importance – had been brought to heel, to start with by Máel Sechnaill mac Domnaill, the king of Mide. Rarely thereafter did Dublin warriors take a military initiative overland in Ireland without native allies.

The capacity of the Irish to defeat Viking armies more often than not may have a bearing on a quite different question – that of the extent and nature of Scandinavian rural settlement in Ireland. The traditional view of the impact of the Vikings on this country tended to emphasize the trading and urban dimensions. Over the last generation, some archaeologists and historians have been countering the accuracy of this interpretation. The alternative case was stated broadly in 1988 by John Bradley, who was influenced to some degree by Alfred Smyth's path-breaking study of the historical geography of the province of Leinster in the Middle Ages (Bradley 1988; Smyth 1982, 149). Bradley's Dyflinnarskíri (Dublinshire) was reconstructed largely on the basis of twelfth-century evidence, while his references to 'the cantreds of the Ostmen' date mainly from the thirteenth century (Bradley 1988, 62–5). In much of the text, the terms 'Viking' and 'Hiberno-Scandinavian' are used interchangeably, while the caption to the map seems to equate 'control' (= overlordship) with 'settlement'. Towards the end, however, a distinction is drawn between two phases of Scandinavian settlement in Ireland: the first characterized by isolated coastal settlements established in the ninth century at places such as Annagassan, Dublin, Larne and Strangford; and the second, beginning in the second decade of the tenth century, characterized by towns, exploitable hinterlands, economic transformation and rapid cultural integration (Bradley 1988, 68). This chrono-logical dimension is to be welcomed, particularly in view of the tendency of archaeologists in Ireland to label the entire period extending from the first recorded raids in 795 to the capture of Waterford and Dublin in 1170 as 'Viking'.

There are very few purely Norse place-names in the Dublin area (Bradley 1988, 55; Clarke 1998, 336). Of these, some were given to small islands (Dalkey, Ireland's Eye and Lambay) and one to a headland (Howth). Leixlip upstream on the Liffey may have been no more than a natural feature where salmon negotiated a rise in the bed of the river in order to spawn. A side-stream, the Stein(e), took its name from the Long Stone – a territorial marker erected by Vikings at an unknown date. Bullock denoted a small harbour on the south side of Dublin Bay, while Windgate acquired its name from a gap in the hills leading towards Wicklow. Virtually all of the evidence cited by Bradley is likely to reflect processes that were taking place in the eleventh and twelfth centuries, at a time when Dublin was under the control of a long succession of native rulers. Down to the 1030s, despite periods of weakness, the traditional provincial rulers of Leinster, Uí Dúnlainge, remained as a relatively effective power. As tribute-takers from the whole province, they were probably able to limit permanent territorial expansion by the Northmen, though not to prevent periodic raiding. North of Dublin, rulers of Brega continued to be a force to be reckoned with. In an expressive phrase, Gille Mo Chonna (d. 1013) is said to have 'yoked the foreigners to the plough', while as late as 1146 the men of southern Brega defeated the (under-) king of Dublin, Raghnall mac Torcaill, and his Leinster allies (*AU*, *s.a.* 1012; *ATig*, *s.a.* 1146). The Gunnhildr, Gunnar, Ólafr and Thorkell of the hybrid place-names could represent no more than the result of outward migration from the territorial core of the kingdom of Dublin at a relatively late stage in the eleventh and twelfth centuries. It is very much to be doubted whether they mark the boundaries of Hiberno-Scandinavian overlord-ship or control in the way that Smyth and Bradley envisaged.

A few years ago I tried a different approach to the problem of defining the territorial limits of the Dublin-based Scandinavians. The accompanying map highlighted two features, one of them mentioned in Bradley's discussion. This is a class of grave-slabs of a particular type, named after a local concentration in the barony of Rathdown. Their distribution is entirely a Leinster one (in a Viking-Age context) and they are believed to date from the late tenth to the twelfth century (Clarke 2000, 36–7, fig. 3). In other words, they represent

Hiberno-Scandinavian Christian belief and practice. The other feature is the early endowment of Christ Church Cathedral, co-founded *c*.1030 by King Sitriuc Silkbeard. The geographical distribution of these lands is strikingly similar, apart from a couple of grants north of the Liffey (Clarke 2000, 35–6, fig. 3). When the Vikings first settled at Dublin in 841, therefore, they probably took over the small kingdom of a minor Uí Dúnlainge sub-dynasty, Uí Fergusa, together with the northern part of the kingdom of Uí Briúin Cualann and the south-eastern lands of Uí Dúnchada. Some early settlement appears to have taken place on the northern bank of the Liffey, where a few isolated burials have been discovered, and for a time the River Tolka may have functioned as an approximate boundary on the Brega side (Ó Floinn 1998, 139; Stout and Stout 1992, 15). In combination, these districts could have constituted the heartland of the original Fine Gall, and the ninth-century Scandinavian farm of which traces have been found at Cherrywood is in exactly the right place (Ó Néill 2006, 86). The term 'Fine Gall' is first documented in 1013, in a context a short distance north of the Liffey at Drinan, south-east of Swords (*Ann. Inisf.*, *s.a.* 1013). In the following year, clerics from Armagh, having journeyed south to take back the body of the slain Brian Bórama, took possession at Swords, then on the northern border of a historically credible Dyflinnarskíri (*AU*, *s.a.* 1014). A century later, when the northern boundary of the combined diocese of Glendalough and Dublin came to be defined, the locations cited are Greenoge on the Broad Meadow Water and Lambay Island (Comyn and Dinneen 1902–14, III: 306–7).

What all this suggests, it seems to me, is that the rulers of Brega and of Leinster, despite the vicissitudes of the Viking Age, were successful in limiting by military means the territorial expansion of the Dublin Vikings and their Hiberno-Norse descendants. There are occasional hints of expansionism, such as Amlaíb Cúarán's interest in Skreen, near Tara, for a brief period in the 970s (Bhreatnach 1996, 40–2). In his case, however, the crushing defeat in 980 would have put paid to such ambitions. The heroes of that hour were Máel Sechnaill mac Domnaill and the men of Mide, which brings me to my last point – the one hinted at in the main title – unsung heroes. Most of the Irishmen who fought against Vikings, losing life and limb in many instances, are unknown to us and were probably uncelebrated by contemporary writers. Yet praise-poetry, as among the Scandinavians, was alive and well as a socio-political medium. The individuals whose praises were sung in this genre tend, unsurprisingly, to be high-status men and sometimes women. Máel Finnia, for example, the king of Brega whose forces helped to evict the Dublin Vikings in 902, died in the following year and was commemorated as 'a stout hero, very noble and warlike' (*héo ruadh rogorm roglach*: *AU*, *s.a.* 902). His ally in that memorable enterprise, Cerball mac Muiricán, was described on the occasion of his death six years later as 'king of Leinster of the troops of heroes' (*ri Laighean límbh laechradh*: *AFM*, *s.a.* 904). Other redoubtable fighters against Vikings include Niall Glúndub and Muirchertach of the Leather Cloaks, who were both killed by Dublin Vikings and in whose honour verses were likewise composed (*AU, s.a.* 918, 942; *AFM, s.a.* 917, 941). Lorcán of Leinster's exploits in 943 were celebrated in a poem, as was Congalach Cnogba's thoroughgoing destruction of Dublin in the following year (*AFM, s.a.* 941, 942). The latter's killing of King Blacair is said to have taken place 'at Áth Cliath [in] a conflict of heroes' (*i nÁth Cliath* [...] *cuinscle laoch*: *AFM, s.a.* 946). A poem celebrating the killing of Ragnall mac Ímair in 994 praises an Irish king for having 'routed the heathen hordes as far as the Boyne' (Ní Mhaonaigh 1998, 398, n. 89).

Thus, when Vikings came to Ireland, they encountered a people who had long been accustomed to waging war. After all, 'to fight was an obligation of status' (Charles-Edwards 1996, 26). During the Viking Age, the Irish continued to fight one another as well as against the foreigners. The precise causes of these wars are unknown or can only be guessed at, but the men who fought in them – whether in brief skirmishes or in pitched battles, together with periodic sieges of Dublin in particular – were pursuing economic and political interests and fulfilling legal and social obligations that stemmed from their home circumstances. It is not unreasonable to suppose that at least some Irishmen, like their West Saxon counterparts in the winter of 870–1, were fighting against Vikings *pro vita et dilectis atque patria*. As I have commented elsewhere, Vikings 'brought untold misery, injury, and death to tens of thousands of men, women, and children' (Clarke 1999, 58). Heroes and heroines, sung or unsung, should never be forgotten.

BIBLIOGRAPHY

AFM. O'Donovan, J. (ed.). 1851. *Annála Ríoghachta Éireann: Annals of the kingdom of Ireland by the Four Masters, from the earliest period to the year 1616*, 7 vols (Dublin).
Ann. Inisf. Mac Airt, S. (ed.). 1951. *The Annals of Inisfallen (MS Rawlinson B 503)* (Dublin).
ATig Stokes, W. (ed.). 1993. *The Annals of Tigernach*, 2 vols (Llanerch).
AU. Mac Airt, S. & G. Mac Niocaill (eds). 1983. *The Annals of Ulster (to AD1131)*, Part 1, *text and translation* (Dublin).
Bhreathnach, E. 1996. 'The documentary evidence for pre-Norman Skreen, County Meath', *Ríocht na Midhe*, 9:2, 37–45.
Bradley, J. 1988. 'The interpretation of Scandinavian settlement in Ireland' in J. Bradley (ed.), *Settlement and society in medieval Ireland: studies presented to F.X. Martin, O.S.A.* (Kilkenny), pp 49–78.
Charles-Edwards, T.M. 1996. 'Irish warfare before 1100' in T. Bartlett & K. Jeffery (eds), *A military history of Ireland* (Cambridge), pp 26–51.
Clarke, H.B. 1990–2. 'The bloodied eagle: the Vikings and the development of Dublin, 841–1014', *The Irish Sword*, 18, 91–119.

Clarke, H.B., M. Ní Mhaonaigh & R. Ó Floinn (eds). 1998, *Ireland and Scandinavia in the Early Viking Age* (Dublin).

Clarke, H.B. 1998. 'Proto-towns and towns in Ireland and Britain in the ninth and tenth centuries' in H.B. Clarke et al. (eds), *Ireland and Scandinavia*, pp 331–80.

Clarke, H.B. 1999. 'The Vikings' in M. Keen (ed.), *Medieval warfare: a history* (Oxford), pp 36–58.

Clarke, H.B. 2000. 'Conversion, church and cathedral: the diocese of Dublin to 1152' in J. Kelly & D. Keogh (eds), *History of the Catholic diocese of Dublin* (Dublin), pp 19–50.

Comyn, D. & P.S. Dinneen (eds). 1902–14. *The History of Ireland by Geoffrey Keating, D.D.*, 4 vols (London).

Keynes, S. & M. Lapidge (trans.). 1983. *Alfred the Great: Asser's 'Life of King Alfred' and other contemporary sources* (London).

Ní Mhaonaigh, M. 1998. 'Friend and foe: Vikings in ninth- and tenth-century Irish literature' in H.B. Clarke et al. (eds), *Ireland and Scandinavia*, 381–402.

Ó Floinn, R. 1998. 'The archaeology of the Early Viking Age in Ireland' in H.B. Clarke et al., *Ireland and Scandinavia*, 131–65.

Ó Néill, J. 2006. 'Excavation of pre-Norman structures on the site of an enclosed early Christian cemetery at Cherrywood, county Dublin' in S. Duffy (ed.), *Medieval Dublin VII: proceedings of the Friends of Medieval Dublin symposium 2005* (Dublin), pp 66–88.

Smyth, A.P. 1982. *Celtic Leinster: towards an historical geography of early Irish civilization AD500–1600* (Blackrock, Co. Dublin).

Smyth, A.P. 1995. *King Alfred the Great* (Oxford).

Stevenson, W.H. (ed.). 1959. *Asser's Life of King Alfred, together with the Annals of Saint Neots erroneously ascribed to Asser*, new impression (Oxford).

Stout, G. & M. Stout. 1992. 'Patterns in the past: county Dublin 5000BC–1000AD' in F.H.A. Aalen & K. Whelan (eds), *Dublin city and county, from prehistory to present: studies in honour of J.H. Andrews* (Dublin), pp 5–42.

Peaceful wars and scientific invaders: Irishmen, Vikings and palynological evidence for the earliest settlement of the Faroe Islands

KEVIN J. EDWARDS & DOUGLAS B. BORTHWICK

INTRODUCTION

The peaceful two-fronted academic war between historians and archaeologists was spoilt some years ago when a third intruder invaded the field; the natural scientist, embodied in the botanist (Debes 1993, 460). There is no doubt that the Faroe Islands shared in the Norse diaspora westwards across the North Atlantic, and this is shown most clearly by language and archaeology (Mortensen and Arge 2005). The islands are also implicated in the contested view, long and popularly held, that Irish monks, the *papar*, were even earlier settlers (Debes 1993). Indeed, one palaeobotanist inferred that the Irish hermits were preceded in the archipelago by prehistoric visitors (Jóhansen 1986–7). This paper offers a commentary on some of the multiple strands of evidence evinced in the quest to uncover the human foundation of the Faroes, and presents recent pollen-analytical findings which add materially to the debate.

BEGINNINGS

The *Navigatio Sancti Brendani Abbatis* (Selmer 1959) might suggest that St Brendan made a North Atlantic voyage in a skin boat (sixth century AD), or that someone did before the *Navigatio* was first set down, perhaps in the seventh or eighth century (Dumville 1988). The 'Island of Sheep' has been equated with the Faroes, and the 'Paradise of Birds' with the islands of Mykines or Vagar (Fig. 6.1). As to whether the *Navigatio* 'provides evidence that monastic navigators reached the Faroes, Iceland, Greenland, and America?', Dumville (2002, 126) concluded with an emphatic 'No, no, no, and no!'. He preferred to see it as a celebration of monastic life and not a historical narrative, although the geographical allusions were barely addressed.

More reliance has been placed upon *Liber de mensura orbis terrae*, written at the Frankish court around AD825 by the Irish monk Dicuil (Tierney 1967). Dicuil noted a group of islands some two days' and nights' sailing north of the British Isles. He went on to record another set of small islands, previously unoccupied, that for a century had been settled by Irish hermits until the islands

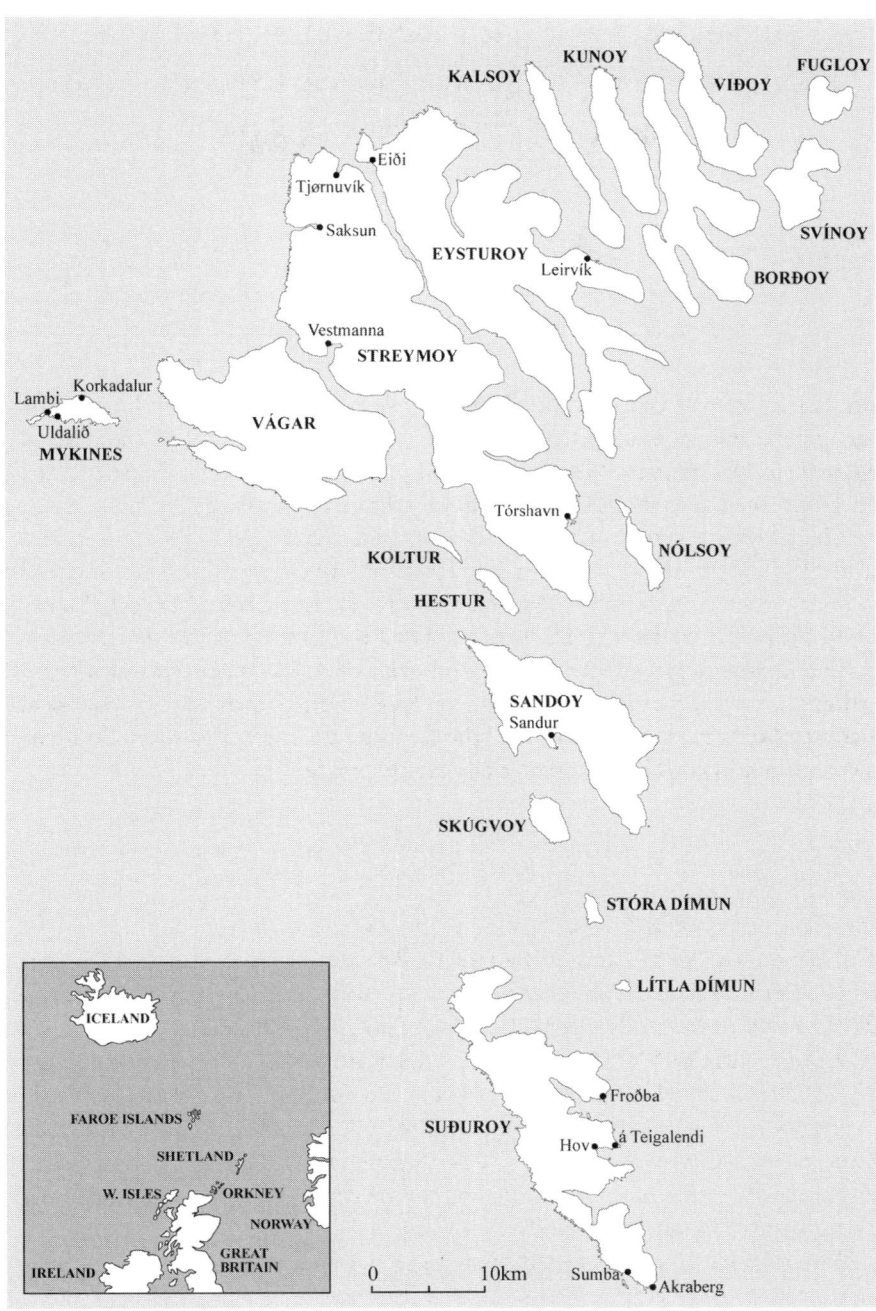

6.1 The Faroe Islands showing places mentioned in the text. The inset map shows the location of the Faroe Islands in the eastern North Atlantic area.

had been emptied by Norse pirates – these were now full of countless sheep and many types of seabirds. Although the Faroes have enjoyed most support as Dicuil's settled islands, as opposed to Shetland or the coastal islands of Norway, both of which had prior occupants, an alternative interpretation has been advanced. Thorsteinsson (2005) contended that the order in which the island groups are described – from Thule (Iceland?) southwards – means that the Faroes best represent the first group and Shetland the second. The supposed pre-anchorite emptiness of the second group of islands is dismissed by Thorsteinsson as simply Dicuil being preoccupied with the seafaring achievements of clerics. Given the references to 'Picts' in Roman and early medieval sources, including comments from such clerics as Gildas, Adomnan and Bede (Gourlay 1993), this seems unlikely. Even if it is argued that such observers were not geographically precise, it is perhaps being particularist to make the claim that the order in which proximal island groups were described is relevant, or necessarily so – Dicuil, for instance, in contrast to his possible south to north ordering of islands, discussed Africa before Ireland. Lamb (1995, 13) also saw an ambiguity in Dicuil's description which could signify that both groups are one and the same (that is, the Faroes). While it is easy to agree with Thorsteinsson that Dicuil's position is not 'solid documentation of a pre-Viking settlement of Irish monks in the Faroes' (2005, 42), it has never been seen as such.

ROUTES, GENETICS AND LANGUAGE

The routes of Norse colonization – whether directly from Scandinavia, and probably Norway, and/or via the Northern and Western Isles of Britain and from the Irish settlements – are generally accepted. This has been reinforced by genetic evidence which suggests that 87 per cent of male settlers in the Faroes, and possibly more, were of Scandinavian descent, while up to 13 per cent were of British and/or Irish ancestry (Jorgensen et al. 2004; Goodacre et al. 2005). For females, however, it is estimated that 83 per cent came from the British Isles and 17 per cent were of Scandinavian descent (Als et al. 2006). The population of the Faroe Islands has greater levels of such Scandinavian versus British Isles assymetry than are found in either the Northern Isles of Scotland or in Iceland (Agnar Helgason et al. 2000; 2001). It seems that unlike areas closer to Scandinavia, such as Shetland and Orkney, the Faroes were less strongly settled by Scandinavian family groups. Presumably, Scandinavian males took indigenous British Isles female partners with them to the Faroe Islands. Some of the British Isles males could have been partners of Scandinavian women and a proportion of the British and Irish contingent would have been slaves.

For the moment, the genetic evidence is unlikely to be useful regarding an earlier presence of Irish ecclesiastics, assuming their presumed celibacy and an absence of females greeting their arrival in the Faroes! It is conceivable, perhaps, that the *papar* took males and females with them to assist domestically or agriculturally, though this might be considered to run counter to notions of isolation and the contemplative idyll.

Linguistic evidence, of course, overwhelmingly demonstrates the Scandinavian influence of the successful colonizers (Arge et al. 2005 and references therein). According to *Færeyinga saga*, the islands were settled from Norway, but some settlers who were of Norse origin came from the Hebrides. For instance, the place-name Mykines may be derived from the Celtic *muc(c)inis* ('hog' or 'pig island'), and the Mykines place-name Korkadalur means 'oats valley' (Matras 1981). Matras also pointed out that the first element of the Streymoy place-names Papurshalsur (in Saksun) and Paparøkur (near Vestmanna) could be *papar* names, found commonly in the Western and Northern Isles of Scotland. These could, however, have been brought with the Norse settlers who came to the Faroes from these areas and therefore have nothing to do with an earlier occupation. This could also apply to the element *ærgi*, referring to shieling activity and thought to have been adopted into the Norse language from Gaelic perhaps at an early stage during the Norse settlement (Fellows-Jensen 2002; Matras et al. 2003). Indeed, the frequency of the word (there are eighteen known *ærgi* names (Arge et al. 2005)) may stem from the Irish or British women who could well have been the primary workers in Faroese shielings.

ARCHAEOLOGY AND CHRONOLOGY

In the absence of proven pre-Norse archaeological sites or finds, the timing for a first human landfall by immigrants involves the early Norse habitation site of Toftanes, Leirvík (Vickers et al. 2005) and the midden at Undir Junkarisfløtti, Sandur (Arge 2001; Church et al. 2005). The oldest radiocarbon dates at each site calibrate dendrochronologically (two standard deviations and rounded to the nearest ten years using the computer program Calib v.5.0.2 (2007), and plotted in OxCal (2007)) to cal. AD690–890 and 690–970 respectively (Fig. 6.2). These age estimates are statistically indistinguishable and they are not inconsistent with the suggested Norse date of arrival on historical grounds of about AD800 (Debes 1993, 458).

The inscribed cross-slabs from the graveyard at Ólandsgarður, Skúvoy, have been used as supporting evidence for an early Irish hermetical presence in the Faroes (Dahl 1968). The dating evidence is far from diagnostic however (Arge 1991). According to Fisher (2005), it is probable that, whatever the date, this group of stones is an 'Irish' link, and they may indicate a Hebridean contribution to the Norse conversion of the islands.

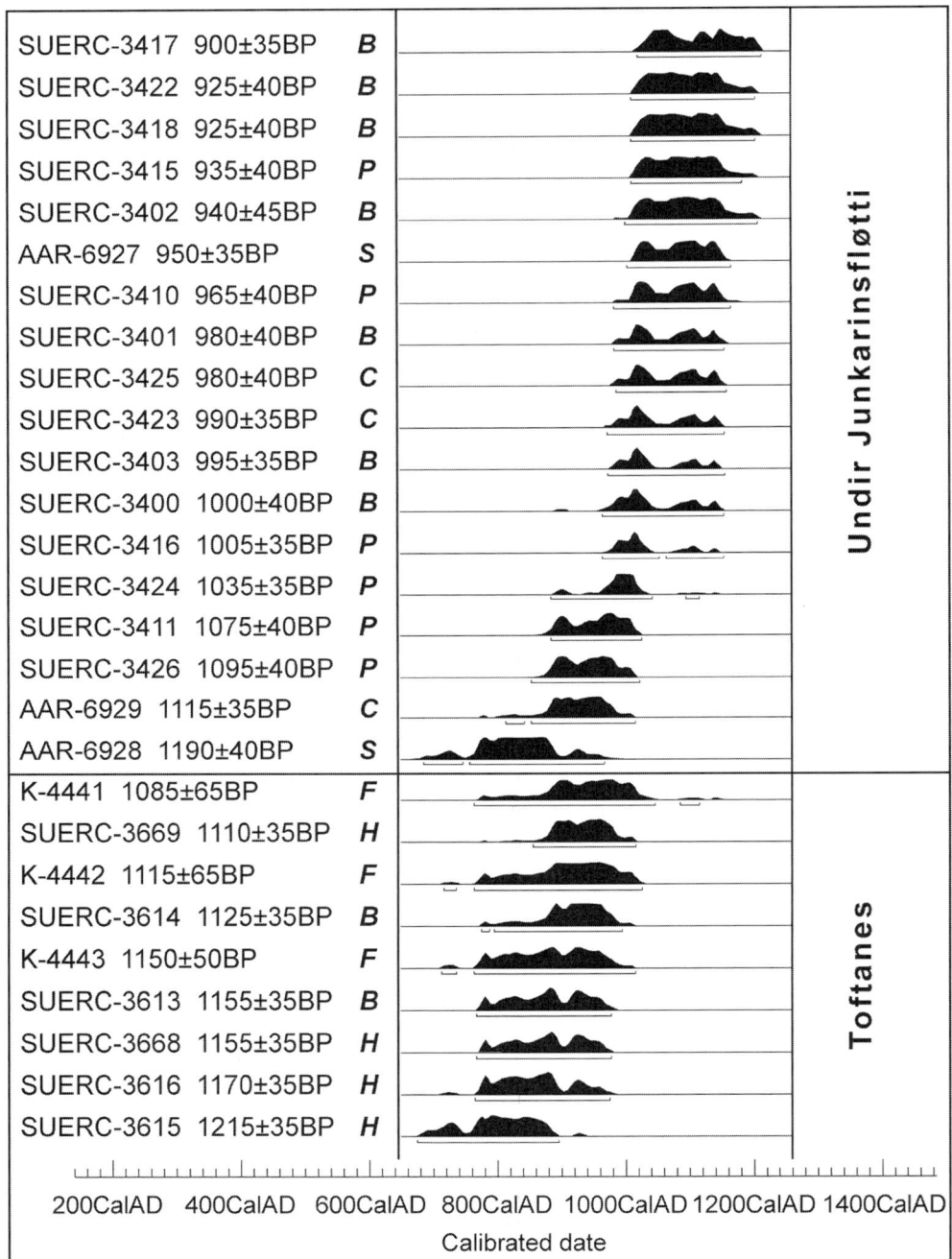

6.2 Radiocarbon dates for the settlement site of Toftanes, Streymoy and the midden at Undir Junkarinsfløtti, Sandur, Sandoy (see text for calibration details).

THE 'ANCIENT' FIELDS

Of particular emphasis for earlier periods has been the so-called ancient (or Irish, Celtic or Frisian: Brandt and Guttesen 1981) fields, championed by the influential state archaeologist Sverri Dahl, who had seen similarities with field systems on the west coast of Ireland (Dahl 1968). The form of the Faroese fields varies considerably, although they tend to be found on steep (up to 50°), south-facing slopes. They may have had origins as diverse as fields for cereal cultivation (Jóhansen 1978) or as relict areas used for turf-stripping (P.C. Buckland, quoted in Edwards 2005). Símun Arge (1991) has suggested that they were perhaps the forerunners of the ubiquitous relict *reinævelta* systems. If this were so, the ancient field-forms might be expected to be more widespread and not restricted to their currently known distribution (Edwards 2005, fig. 2). It is unlikely that they would all be hidden beneath modern fields, although ridged field boundaries within the now fenced infield of Sumba, Suðuroy, close to the impressive 'ancient' field system of Akraberg (*akur* = '(cereal)field'), are certainly intriguing.

It can be very difficult to date field systems and those in the Faroes are, in truth, of uncertain age. For the system at Lambi on the island of Mykines, Jóhansen (1978) had suggested a date of around AD600 on the basis of comparison with the nearby radiocarbon-dated profile of Uldalíð. This research has been questioned on palynological, palaeoentomological and chronostratigraphic grounds (Buckland et al. 1998) – although it does not disprove Jóhansen's assertions. The identification of cereal-type pollen at Lambi has since been replicated in continuing research at other supposed ancient field sites (Froðba, Akraberg and á Teigalendi on Suðuroy; authors unpublished) and this will be discussed elsewhere. Thorsteinsson (1979) showed that the fields named *Ruddstaðir* near Sandur are mentioned in a document of AD1412 as belonging to the church; there is no additional indication of their antiquity.

PALYNOLOGY

Background

Johannes Jóhansen (1986–7) saw the pollen grains of the weed *Plantago lanceolata* (ribwort plantain) as indicating a prehistoric human presence as long ago as 2300BC. No palynologists bothered to respond to this claim because they were either unfamiliar with or disinterested in the Faroese archaeological and botanical scenes, or because the interpretation of the findings seemed so patently improbable. Two non-palynologists took up the gauntlet and showed that the plant had equally been in Iceland long before Norse settlement (Hansom and Briggs 1989–90). To Jóhansen's credit, he accepted this paper whilst editor of *Fróðskaparrit*, the journal in which the criticism appeared.

It was Dahl who had encouraged Jóhansen (1978, 103) to look for signs of early vegetational impact in his pollen diagrams. This he had done at Lambi, and prior to that, at Tjørnuvík, Streymoy, the site of the pagan graves of Yviri í Trøð (Dahl and Rasmussen 1956; Jóhansen 1971). The site at Lambi is riddled with puffin burrows, which casts doubt on its suitability for detailed study. The valley peat at Tjørnuvík might also be considered sub-optimal given the steep slopes adjacent to it and the likelihood of erosion substantiated by the minerogenic content of the deposits. Pollen and radiocarbon data from Tjørnuvík revealed cereal-type pollen grains in sediments dated to around 1290 ± 100BP (cal. AD590–970 at 2σ). Even though the site has every likelihood of contamination from soil inputs containing old carbon, a re-investigation by Hannon et al. (1998) and Hannon and Bradshaw (2000) not only found early cereal-type pollen grains, but was able to further constrain the chronology by radiocarbon (1270 ± 60BP or cal. AD660–890 at 2σ on seeds from a 0.3cm thick stratum) and by tephrochronology. The latter allowed detection of volcanically derived tephra shards originating from Icelandic production of the *landnám* tephra of $AD871\pm2$. This microtephra was deposited after initial finds of cereal-type pollen, thus supporting the early radiocarbon dates and overcoming difficulties associated with the existence of a radiocarbon 'plateau' at this time (see below). The antiquity argument is not fully resolved, however, as AD871 is still many decades later than the possible Norse settlement date of AD800 (Debes 1993).

Tephrochronology may have been used similarly at Heimavatn, Eiði, Eysturoy (Hannon et al. 2001), although it is not mentioned in the site publication (Hannon et al. 2005). The first cultivation at Heimavatn is estimated at *c.*AD570 by extrapolation between radiocabon dates. The site of Korkadalur, Mykines (Hannon and Bradshaw 2000; Hannon et al. 2001) – the name already indicated as meaning oats valley – produced cereal-type pollen at a date of 1355 ± 60BP (cal. AD570–800 at 2σ).

Double landnám

In his consideration of Jóhansen's pollen data, Debes (1993, 461) addressed the question of the number and nature of *landnám* episodes in the pollen records. Debes is only able to accept a gap between the Irish (AD600–700) and a later identifiable Norse *landnám* (AD850–900) if an intervening Norse *landnám* also occurred *c.*AD800, and is represented by the continued cultivation of oats by Viking incomers. He did not feel that there would have been land available for a second Norse colonization. Leaving aside the question of whether it is reasonable to extrapolate from two sites to the whole of the Faroe Islands, this topic is taken up in part by Stummann Hansen (2003, 59). He noted that none of the pollen diagrams from the Faroes provided evidence of two *landnám* horizons, but rather one from *c.*AD600 or one from *c.*AD800.

From a palynological perspective, the demands for two or more *landnám* events in pollen diagrams may be a tall order when it comes to Faroese vegetation

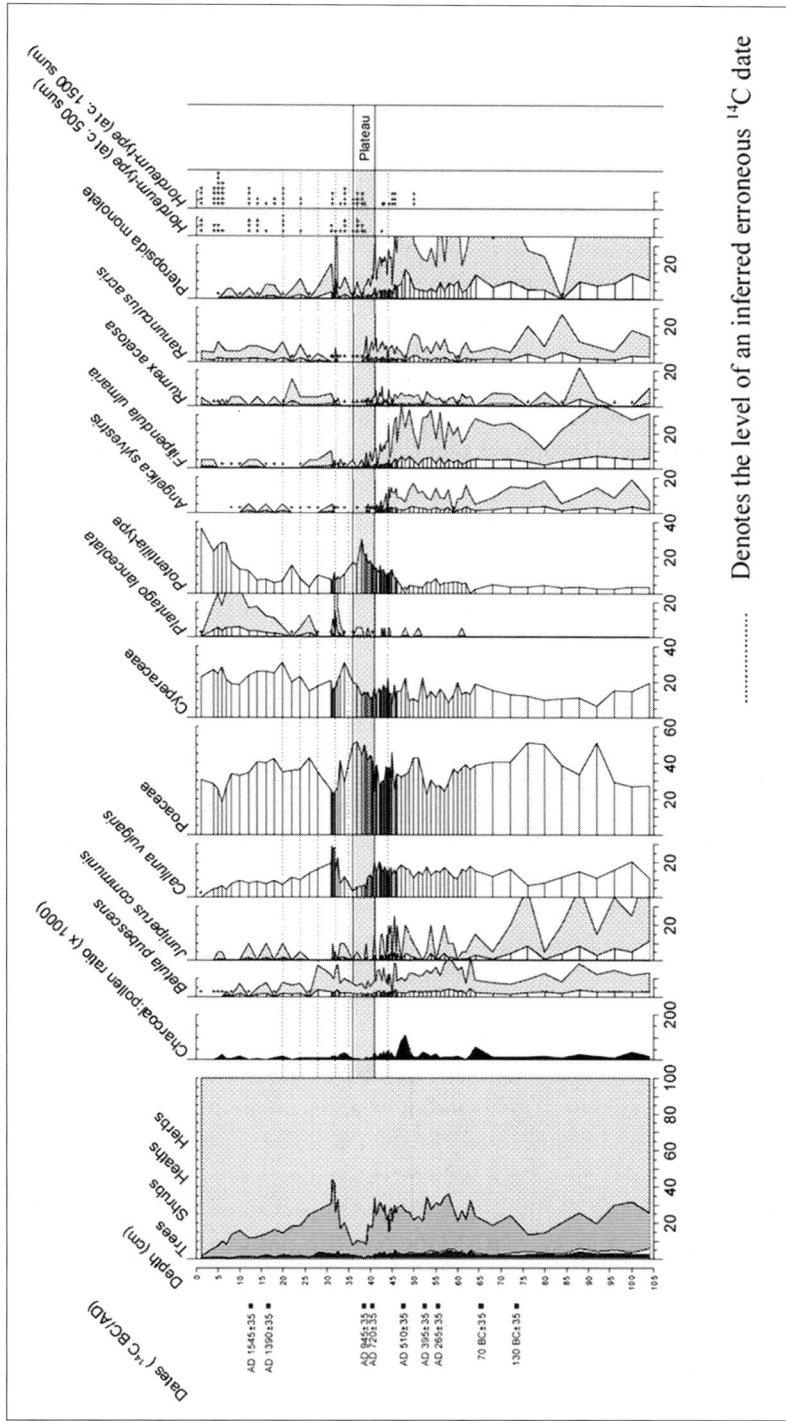

6.3 Selected pollen and charcoal data from Hov, Suðuroy. The BC/AD age-estimates will have associated errors (note the 1 standard deviation errors shown with their equivalent BP dates). The radiocarbon plateau area encloses the conventional *landnám* period.

········· Denotes the level of an inferred erroneous ¹⁴C date

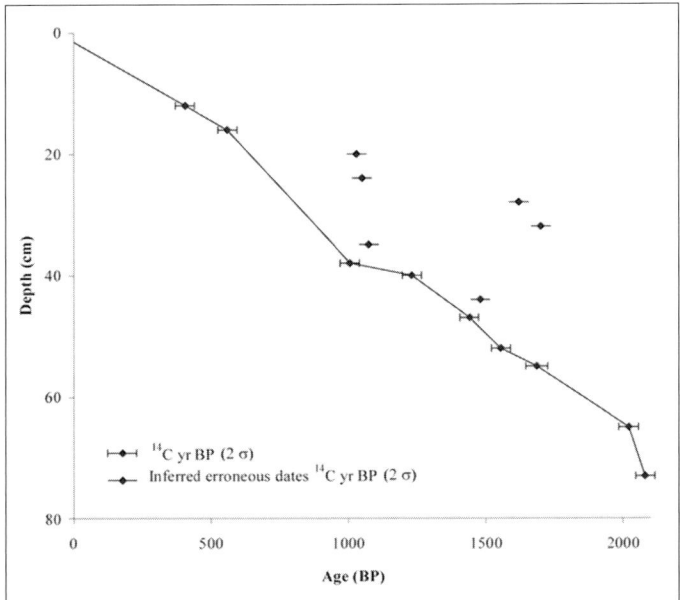

6.4 Radiocarbon dates and age–depth curve for the Hov profile.

history. The woodland pollen record for the archipelago is always muted as a consequence of the restricted arboreal cover in such an exposed, isolated area (it is often the tree and shrub pollen in more continental areas which reflects anthropogenic and other environmental impacts most sensitively). Furthermore, once diminished, an already sparse woodland flora is unlikely to fare well against the depredations of grazing animals, people and an inimical climate.

A new investigation at Hov

The infield valley mire at Hov, Suðuroy, investigated by Jóhansen (1981, 1985) produced a pollen sequence indicating pastoralism and cultivation from *c.*AD850–900. The site was re-investigated (Edwards et al. 2005a; Borthwick 2007) using high-resolution pollen sampling and a comprehensive programme of small-sample radiocarbon-dating.

The conventional period of human impact (that is, from about AD800 and within a plateau of the radiocarbon calibration curve: Fig. 6.3) corresponds with reductions in the meagre woodland records for downy birch (*Betula pubescens*) and juniper (*Juniperus communis*) along with those for heather (*Calluna vulgaris*), tall-herbs such as wild angelica (*Angelica sylvestris*), meadowsweet (*Filipendula ulmaria*) and undifferentiated ferns (*Pteropsida* monolete indet.), together with buttercup (*Ranunculus acris*) and common sorrel (*Rumex acetosa*). These declines probably reflect increased grazing pressures. Grasses (*Poaceae*) and sedges (*Cyperaceae*), much as in the modern Faroese environment, are dominant vegetation types. The later expansion of herb taxa often associated with human impact (but not solely), most notably ribwort plantain (*Plantago lanceolata*), common sorrel and buttercup, probably represents the development of improved grassland habitats. Tormentil (*Potentilla*-type) may have occupied damper grassland. The incidence and pattern of microscopic charcoal is too low to infer that fires were used for anything other than heating and cooking.

Using the routine pollen count of 500 total land pollen (TLP) at Hov, cereal-type pollen, barley (*Hordeum*) type, made its first appearance at *c.*AD730. This is slightly before the otherwise palynologically inferred *landnám* phase, but the date could be within the radiocarbon error band of supposed Norse settlement. The application of rapid scanning techniques (Edwards and McIntosh 1988; Edwards et al. 2005b), where searches for the large cereal-type grains are intensified to produce effective counts of around 1500 TLP for contiguous samples of sediment, revealed barley-type grains extending back to perhaps as early as AD540. The latter date at least precedes the period of radiocarbon dating imprecision generated by the plateau in the calibration curve over the period *c.*AD770–880 (Arny Sveinbjörnsdóttir et al. 2004; Dugmore et al. 2005), which unfortunately complicates chronological assessments around the time of *landnám*.

A total of fifteen radiocarbon dates were obtained from the Hov peat monolith, six of which produced inversions in the age–depth model (Fig. 6.4). One of these inversions followed a peak in charcoal concentrations and the presence of cereal-type pollen, and occurred prior to the conventional *landnám* period. The remaining dates inferred to be erroneous, were probably generated in the post-*landnám* environment, occurring later than *c.*AD1010 (Fig. 6.3). It may be hypothesized that these inversions are the result of older carbon in soils eroded and moved downslope or blown-in to the accumulating mire as a consequence of human activity at or close to the site (cf. Ashmore et al. 2000). When considered as a whole, this evidence may be used to suggest two phases of land-use intensification, albeit without specifying precise locations. Thus, there appears to have an earlier phase of activity associated with erosion, the first date inversion and a peak in charcoal values, and a later, sustained phase with more consistent evidence of cultivation and pastoral activity. Whether this reflects a double *landnám* of Irish and then Norse settlers cannot be resolved by palynology, but the evidence certainly adds to the corpus of Faroese pollen sites suggesting an early settlement date as well as associated environmental impacts.

CONCLUSIONS

Science, in the form of genetics, radiometric dating and palynology, is contributing immensely to the settlement history of the Faroe Islands. Findings from other natural science approaches could also have been presented, including those involving soils, insects, plant micro- and macrofossils (e.g. Buckland 1992; Edwards et al. 1998; 2005a; Hannon et al. 2005; Church et al. 2005).

Regarding the possible early settlers at Tjørnuvík and Mykines, Jóhansen (1985, 58) observed that 'it is most likely that they were Irish monks or hermits. One might, however, some day turn up new evidence showing that other people [...] made these settlements, but that is a task for historians and archaeologists'. It might be suggested that Scandinavian settlers visited the Faroe Islands prior to the normal *landnám* time of *c.*AD800, with the intention of leaving a viable population of sheep to reproduce sufficiently to sustain later immigrant colonizers before their crops and settlements became established. Assuming that untended sheep could survive successions of winters prior to the Medieval Warm Period proper (Hughes and Diaz 1994), the palynological data suggest that subsequent human visits may not have occurred for perhaps two centuries.

Stummann Hansen (2003, 59) noted that, despite the growing number of pollen records indicating a pre-ninth century date for human activity, conclusive archaeological proof of a Celtic or pre-Viking presence was still lacking. Such caution finds an echo in the failure to find a Mesolithic archaeological presence in the Scottish Outer Hebrides and Northern Isles, despite pollen evidence to the contrary (Edwards 1996; in press). In both areas, that archaeological evidence would now appear to be available (Melton and Nicholson 2004; Gregory et al. 2005). Just as the Outer Hebrides in particular had their own problems of survival and discovery – sites hidden beneath peat, sand and sea, bones destroyed by acid soil, and too few people looking for evidence – the challenge may be issued to those interested in the archaeology of the Faroe Islands to search more assiduously for potential sites, whether they be Celtic, Scandinavian or something else.

ACKNOWLEDGMENTS

The Leverhulme Trust is thanked for financial support. Alison Sandison and Ed Schofield kindly assisted with the production of artwork. Símun Arge, Paul Buckland, Anne-Christine Larsen and Steffen Stummann Hansen freely gave of advice and Paul Buckland is additionally thanked for commenting on an earlier draft of the paper.

BIBLIOGRAPHY

Als, T.D., T.H. Jorgensen, A.D. Børglum, P.A. Petersen, O. Mors & A.G. Wang. 2006. 'Highly discrepant proportions of female and male Scandinavian and British Isles ancestry within the isolated population of the Faroe Islands', *European Journal of Human Genetics*, 14, 497–504.

Arge, S.V. 1991. 'The *landnam* in the Faroes', *Arctic Anthropology*, 28, 101–20.

Arge, S.V. 2001. 'Forn búsetning heima á Sandi', *Frøði*, 2, 5–13.

Arge, S.V., G. Sveinbjarnardottir, K.J. Edwards & P.C. Buckland. 2005. 'Viking and medieval settlement in the Faroes: people, place and environment', *Human Ecology*, 33, 597–620.

Ashmore, P., B.A. Brayshay, K.J. Edwards, D. Gilbertson, J. Grattan, M. Kent, K. Pratt, & R. Weaver. 2000. 'Allochthonous and autochthonous mire deposits in relation to slope instability: palaeoenvironmental investigations in the Borve Valley, Barra, Outer Hebrides, Scotland', *The Holocene*, 10, 97–108.

Batey, C.E., J. Jesch & C.D. Morris (eds), *The Viking Age in Caithness, Orkney and the North Atlantic: select papers from the proceedings of the Eleventh Viking Congress, Thurso and Kirkwall, 1989* (Edinburgh).

Sveinbjörnsdottir, A.E., J. Heinemeier & G. Gudmundsson. 2004. '14C dating of the settlement of Iceland', *Radiocarbon*, 46, 387–94.

Borthwick, D.B. 2007. 'The timing and impact of the Norse *landnám* on the vegetation of Hovsdalur, Faroe Islands' (PhD, University of Aberdeen).

Brandt, J. & R. Guttesen. 1981. 'Changes of the rural landscape on the Faroe Islands in the Middle Ages' in V. Hansen (ed.), *Collected papers presented at the permanent European conference for the study of the rural landscape, Roskilde 1979* (Copenhagen), pp 17–24.

Buckland, P.C. 1992. 'Insects, man and the earliest settlement of the Faroe Islands: a case not proven', *Fróðskaparrit*, 38–9, 107–13.

Buckland, P.C., K.J. Edwards, J.P. Sadler, & M.H. Dinnin. 1998. 'Late holocene insect faunas from Mykines, Faroe Islands, with observations on associated pollen and early settlement records', *Fróðskaparrit*, 46, 287–96.

Calib v.5.02html. 2007. <http://calib.qub.ac.uk/calib/> [23 April 2007].

Church, M.J., S.V. Arge, S. Brewington, T.H. McGovern, J. Woollett, S. Perdikaris, I.T. Lawson, G.T. Cook, C. Amundsen, R. Harrison, K. Krivogorskaya & E. Dunbar. 2005. 'Puffins, pigs, cod, and barley: palaeoeconomy at Undir Junkarinsfløtti, Sandoy, Faroe Islands', *Environmental Archaeology*, 10, 179–97.

Dahl, S. 1968. 'Fortidsminder', *Trap Danmark*, 5th ed. (Copenhagen), 13, 188–211.

Dahl, S. & J. Rasmussen. 1956. 'Víkingaaldargrøv í Tjørnuvík', *Fróðskaparrit*, 5, 153–67.

Debes, H.J. 1993. 'Problems concerning the earliest settlement in the Faroe Islands' in C.E. Batey et al. (eds), *The Viking Age in Caithness, Orkney and the North Atlantic*, pp 454–64.

Dugmore, A.J., M.J. Church, P.C. Buckland, K.J. Edwards, I. Lawson, T.H. McGovern, E. Panagiotakopulu, I.A. Simpson, P. Skidmore & G. Sveinbjarnardóttir. 2005. 'The Norse *landnám* on the North Atlantic islands: an environmental impact assessment', *Polar Record*, 41, 21–37.

Dumville, D.N. 1988. 'Two approaches to the dating of *Navigatio Sancti Brendani*', *Studi medievali*, 3rd ser., 29, 87–102.

Dumville, D.N. 2002. 'The North Atlantic monastic thalassocracy: sailing to the desert in early mediaeval Insular spirituality' in B.E. Crawford (ed.), *The papar in the North Atlantic: environment and history* St John's House Papers, 10 (St Andrews), pp 121–31.

Edwards, K.J. 1996. 'A Mesolithic of the Western and Northern Isles of Scotland? Evidence from pollen and charcoal' in T. Pollard & A. Morrison (eds), *The early prehistory of Scotland* (Edinburgh), pp 23–38.

Edwards, K.J. 2005. 'On the windy edge of nothing: a historical human ecology of the Faroe Islands', *Human Ecology*, 33, 585–96.

Edwards, K.J. in press. 'The development and historiography of pollen studies in the Mesolithic of the Scottish islands' in S.B. McCartan et al. (eds), Mesolithic Horizons: papers presented at the seventh international conference on the Mesolithic in Europe, Belfast 2005 (Oxford).

Edwards, K.J & C.J. McIntosh. 1988. 'Improving the detection rate of cereal-type pollen grains from *ulmus* decline and earlier deposits from Scotland', *Pollen et Spores*, 30, 179–88.

Edwards, K.J., P.C. Buckland, R. Craigie, E. Panagiotakopulu & S. Stummann Hansen. 1998. 'Landscapes at *landnám*: palynological and palaeoentomological evidence from Toftanes, Faroe Islands', *Fróðskaparrit*, 48, 229–44.

Edwards, K.J., D. Borthwick, G. Cook, A. Dugmore, K-A. Mairs, M. Church, I. Simpson & W. Adderley. 2005a. 'A hypothesis-based approach to landscape change in Suðuroy, Faroe Islands', *Human Ecology*, 33, 621–50.

Edwards, K.J., G. Whittington, M. Robinson & D. Richter. 2005b. 'Palaeoenvironments, the archaeological record and cereal pollen detection at Clickimin, Shetland, Scotland', *Journal of Archaeological Science*, 32, 1741–56.

Fellows-Jensen, G. 2002. 'Old Faroese *ærgi* yet again' in A. Johansen (ed.), *Eivindarmál: heiðursrit til Eivind Weyhe á seksti ára hansara 25 april 2002, Annales Societatis Scientiarum Færoensis Supplementum*, 32 (Tórshavn), 89–96.

Fisher, I. 2005. 'Cross-currents in North Atlantic sculpture' in A. Mortensen & S.V. Arge (eds), *Viking and Norse in the North Atlantic*, pp 160–6.

Færeyinga saga = Ólafur Halldórsson (ed.). 1987. *Færeyinga saga*. Stofnun Árna Magnússonar á Íslandi, Reykjavík.

Goodacre, S., A. Helgason, J. Nicholson, L. Southam, L. Ferguson, E. Hickey, E. Vega, K. Stefánsson, R. Ward & B. Sykes. 2005. 'Genetic evidence for a family-based Scandinavian settlement of Shetland and Orkney during the Viking period', *Heredity*, 95, 129–35.

Gourlay, R.B. 1993. 'Before the Vikings: the pre-Norse background in Caithness' in C.E. Batey et al. (eds), *The Viking Age in Caithness, Orkney and the North Atlantic*, pp 111–19.

Gregory, R.A., E.M. Murphy, M.J. Church, K.J. Edwards, E.B. Guttmann & D.D.A. Simpson. 2005. 'Archaeological evidence for the first Mesolithic occupation of the Western Isles of Scotland', *The Holocene*, 15, 944–50.

Hannon, G.E. & R.H.W. Bradshaw. 2000. 'Impacts and timing of the first human settlement on vegetation of the Faroe Islands', *Quaternary Research*, 54, 404–13.

Hannon, G.E., M. Hermanns-Auardóttir & S. Wastegård, S. 1998. 'Human impact at Tjørnuvík in the Faroe Islands', *Fróðskaparrit*, 46, 215–28.

Hannon, G.E., S. Wastegård, E. Bradshaw & R.H.W. Bradshaw. 2001. 'Human impact and landscape degradation on the Faroe Islands', *Proceedings of the Royal Irish Academy*, 101B, 129–39.

Hannon, G.E., R.H.W. Bradshaw, E. Bradshaw, I. Snowball & S. Wastegård. 2005. 'Climatic change and human settlement as drivers of late-holocene vegetational change in the Faroe Islands', *The Holocene*, 15, 639–47.

Hansom, J.D. & D.J. Briggs. 1989–90. 'Pre-landnam *plantago lanceolata* in north-west Iceland', *Fróðskaparrit*, 38–9, 69–75.

Helgason, A., S. Sigurðardóttir, J. Nicholson, B. Sykes, E.W. Hill, D.G. Bradley, V. Bosnes, J.R. Gulcher, R. Ward & K. Stefánsson. 2000. 'Estimating Scandinavian and Gaelic ancestry in the male settlers of Iceland', *American Journal of Human Genetics*, 67, 697–717.

Helgason, A., E. Hickey, S. Goodacre, V. Bosnes, K. Stefánsson, R.Ward & B. Sykes. 2001. 'mtDNA and the islands of the North Atlantic: estimating the proportions of Norse and Gaelic ancestry', *American Journal of Human Genetics*, 68, 723–37.

Hughes, M.K. & H.F. Diaz. 1994. 'Was there a "medieval warm period", and if so, where and when?', *Climatic Change*, 26, 109–42.

Jóhansen, J. 1971. 'A palaeobotanical study indicating a pre-Viking settlement in Tjørnuvík, Faroe Islands', *Fróðskaparrit*, 19, 147–57.

Jóhansen, J. 1978. 'Cereal cultivation in Mykines, Faroe Islands, AD600', *Danmarks Geologiske Årbog 1978*, 93–103.

Jóhansen, J. 1981. 'Vegetational development in the Faroes from 10000BP to the present', *Danmarks Geoogiske Undersøgelse Årbog 1981*, 111–36.

Jóhansen, J. 1985. *Studies in the vegetational history of the Faroe and Shetland Islands*, Annales Societatis Scientiarum Færoensis Supplementum, 11 (Tórshavn).

Jóhansen, J. 1986–7. 'Joansokugras (*plantago lanceolata*) og forsogulig buseting i Foroyum (*Plantago lanceolata* in the Faroe Islands and its significance as indicator of prehistoric settlement)', *Fróðskaparrit*, 34–5, 68–75.

Jorgensen, T.H., H.N. Buttenschön, A.G. Wang, T.D. Als, A.D. Børglum & H. Ewald. 2004. 'The origin of the isolated population of the Faroe Islands investigated using Y-chromosomal markers', *Human Genetics*, 115, 19–28.

Lamb, R. 1995. 'Papil, Picts and Papar' in B. Crawford (ed.), *Northern Isles connections: essays from Orkney and Shetland presented to Per Sveaas Andersen* (Kirkwall), pp 9–27.

Matras, A.K., H. Andreasen, & S. Stummann Hansen. 2003. 'A Viking-Age shieling in Skarðsvík, Fugloy, Faroe Islands', *Fróðskaparrit*, 51, 200–1.

Matras, C. 1981. 'Korkadalur', *Fróðskaparrit*, 28–9, 78–80.

Melton, N.D. & R.A. Nicholson. 2004. 'The Mesolithic in the Northern Isles: the preliminary evaluation of an oyster midden at West Voe, Sumburgh, Shetland, UK, *Antiquity* 78, Project Gallery <http://antiquity.ac.uk/ProjGall/nicholson/> [23 April 2007].

Mortensen, A. & S.V. Arge (eds). 2005. *Viking and Norse North Atlantic: select papers from the proceedings of the Fourteenth Viking Congress, Tórshavn, 19–30 July 2001*, Annales Societatis Scientiarum Færoensis Supplementum, 44 (Tórshavn).

OxCal (2007). < http://c14.arch.ox.ac.uk/oxcal/OxCalPlot.html> [23 April 2007].

Selmer, C. (ed.). 1959. *Navigatio sancti brendani abbatis* (Notre Dame, IL).

Stummann Hansen, S. 2003. 'The early settlement of the Faroe Islands: the creation of cultural identity' in J.H. Barrett (ed.), *Contact, continuity, and collapse* (Turnhout), pp 33–71.

Thorsteinsson, A. 1979. 'Ruddstaðir í brukkum – ein muturgøla frá 1412', *Mondul*, 1, 14–21.

Thorsteinsson A. 2005. 'There is another set of small islands' in A. Mortensen & S.V. Arge (eds), *Viking and Norse in the North Atlantic*, pp 39–42.

Tierney, J.J. 1967. *Dicuilus: liber de mensura orbis terrae*, Scriptores Latini Hiberniae (Dublin).

Vickers, K., J. Bending, P.C. Buckland, K.J. Edwards, S. Stummann Hansen & G. Cook. 2005. 'Toftanes: the palaeoecology of a Faroese *landnám* farm', *Human Ecology*, 685–710.

Laithlinn, 'Fair Foreigners' and 'Dark Foreigners': the identity and provenance of Vikings in ninth-century Ireland

COLMÁN ETCHINGHAM

Thirty years ago, the philologist David Greene commented on the term *Laithlinn* or *Lothlind* in the *Proceedings of the Seventh Viking Congress*, held in Dublin. The name occurs four times in ninth-century Irish sources to designate a Viking polity. Greene stated that 'none of the examples necessarily mean "Norway" or "Scandinavia"; all we can extract from them is that they refer to some maritime centre of Viking power'. He added 'it is at least possible that the original *Lothlind* was [...] perhaps in Gaelic-speaking Man or Western Scotland' (1976, 76–7). Donnchadh Ó Corráin was more emphatic that 'there is, then, no good historical or linguistic evidence to link *Lothlend/ Laithlind* with Norway', that '*Laithlinn* was the name of Viking Scotland', and that this was the place of origin of the Dublin and York dynasty (1998, 296–7, 306). Coinciding with Greene's paper, Alfred Smyth argued that 'Fair Foreigners' (*Finngaill*) and 'Dark Foreigners' (*Dubgaill*) in the Irish annals denote, respectively, the Norwegian Vikings of Dublin and Danish Vikings of York (1975–6). Recently, David Dumville approved Smyth's non-literal translation of the elements *finn* and *dub* in these names as 'old' and 'new', respectively, but denied that the names are ethnonyms designating 'the Norwegians of Dublin and the Danes of York'. Dumville cast them as family or dynastic names, 'Dark Foreigner' meaning the 'family of New Dubliners' whose descendants controlled Dublin for centuries (2005, 83–4).

The present writer discussed, more fully than is possible here, the location of *Laithlinn* (Etchingham 2007) and the distinction between 'Fair Foreigners' and 'Dark Foreigners' (Etchingham forthcoming). Since the issues are related, the subject merits reconsideration for the proceedings of the Fifteenth Congress, the first in Ireland since that in which Greene participated.

THE LOCATION OF *LAITHLINN*

The most extensive discussion of *Laithlinn/ Lothlind* is that of Ó Corráin (1998), who, like others, assumed it was a variant of the more common *Lochla(i)nn*. Previously, Greene made the same assumption, but appreciated the priority of

Laithlinn/Lothlind, with four ninth-century examples, whereas the annals first register *Lochla(i)nn* only in the eleventh century. Carl Marstrander's derivation of *Lochla(i)nn* from Rogaland in southwest Norway (1911, 250–1) was withdrawn when he realized it could not account for *Laithlinn/Lothlind* (1915, 56–7). Explaining *Laithlinn/Lothlind* is crucial, as Greene realized. The present writer would also suggest that *Laithlinn/Lothlind* is not necessarily the same Viking polity as *Lochla(i)nn*. Accounting for *Lochla(i)nn*, as a real, historical entity, is relatively straightforward. We shall review the evidence briefly, before considering *Laithlinn/Lothlind*. Two references to Magnús berfœttr ('barelegs') of Norway, in *AU* for 1102 and *ATIG* for 1103, describe him as *rí Lochlainni/rí Lochland* ('king of *Lochla(i)nn*'), undoubtedly referring to Norway. Mention here also of the Isle of Man and the Scottish Isles distinguishes these components of the Insular Viking zone from *Lochla(i)nn*. *ATIG* for 1058 describes Magnús, son of Haraldr harðráði, as 'son of the king of *Lochland*', where *Lochla(i)nn* plainly means Norway, and is distinguished from the Orkneys, the Hebrides and Dublin. A poem of 1072, highlighted by Ó Corráin, calls Haraldr harðráði himself *rí Lochlainne* (1998, 318). *Lochla(i)nn* is not diagnostic in Irish annalistic accounts of the battle of Clontarf in 1014. Numerous literary examples of *Lochla(i)nn* refer more loosely to the Viking world in general, or a supernatural otherworld. In Irish annals, already by the mid-eleventh century, however, *Lochla(i)nn* means the kingdom of Norway. Elsewhere, the present writer rejects Ó Corráin's case for identifying *Lochla(i)nn* with Scandinavian Scotland (Etchingham 2007; Etchingham 2001, 151–3).

What of earlier *Laithlinn*? Two mid-ninth-century annals are crucial. *AU* for 848 has: 'A battle won by Ólchobur, king of Munster, and by Lorcán son of Cellach, with the Leinstermen, against heathens, at Scíath Nechtain, in which fell Jarl Þórir, deputy of the king of *Laithlinn* and 1200 with him'. *AU* for 853 has: 'Áleifr, son of the king of *Laithlinn*, came to Ireland, and the Foreigners of Ireland submitted to him, and tribute (was rendered) by the Irish'. *Laithlinn* denotes a Viking political entity, ruled by a king, the superior of a *jarl*. An oft-quoted verse on the Vikings, generally dated to the mid-ninth century (Ó Corráin 1998, 302–3), mentions the threat posed 'by the fierce warriors of *Lothlind*' (Stokes and Strachan 1903, 290). Finally, a recently publicized poem, on a battle of 868, mentions 'a keen host from fierce *Laithlind*' (Ó Corráin 1998, 304). These four mid-ninth-century instances of *Laithlinn/Lothlind* (with *-th-*) are clearly distinct from the apparently later *Lochla(i)nn*. Ó Corráin's recent, emphatic advocacy of an Insular location for *Laithlinn* and *Lochla(i)nn* (1998) focused on the better documented *Lochla(i)nn*, but also embraced *Laithlinn*, which he took to be synonymous. As detailed elsewhere (Etchingham 2007), Ó Corráin's argument was logically flawed, being circular. He proceeded from premise (both terms denote Scandinavian Scotland) to conclusion (ditto), via a series of untested assertions, and failed to consider alternative interpretations.

He is readily refuted as regards *Lochla(i)nn* which, as we have seen, means Norway in eleventh- and twelfth-century annals. His case for ninth-century *Laithlinn* is also insecure. The 'historical record', of which Ó Corráin regarded his as 'the most plausible and economical interpretation' (1998, 296), is conspicuously absent for Scotland, where he located *Laithlinn*, and for Norway, where he insisted it was not, in the mid-ninth century. For both countries, Ó Corráin's is an argument from silence.

Consider the argument regarding Norwegian kingship. Ó Corráin endorsed Claus Krag's and Peter Sawyer's rejection of later literary accounts of the Ynglings of Vestfold and Norwegian unification (1998, 297–9). From Knut Helle he deduced 'in the early Viking Age there were no kings of Norway' (1998, 299–300). There follows a logical non sequitur: 'the kings and sons of kings mentioned in the Irish annals cannot, therefore, be linked to any Norwegian dynasty, regional or otherwise' (1998, 300; cf. 337). Absence of evidence precludes demonstrating a link, certainly, but it cannot be ruled out on the premises stated. Ó Corráin invoked the historical opinions of Greene, the philologist: 'there is no strong evidence that the Irish learned much about Scandinavia proper; this need not surprise us, since the connections of the Vikings of Ireland were predominantly with the Atlantic area rather than with the homeland' (Greene 1976, 77). Ó Corráin deduced: 'There is, then, no good historical or linguistic evidence to link *Lothlend/Laithlind* with Norway' (1998, 306). Greene's untested claim becomes a supporting block for Ó Corráin's convictions.

If scepticism about the Inglings and ninth-century unification of Norway be justified – as rigorous source-criticism suggests – *Laithlinn* is hardly an earlier form of *Lochla(i)nn* ('Norway'). Why should we assume they were the same? After all, the words are different, even if the latter replaces the former in linguistically modernized annals (*AFM* and *FA*). They occur in annals of distinct periods. It does not follow, however, that *Laithlinn* cannot be in Norway. Ó Corráin invoked the 'logistical problem' of large fleets coming from Norway to raid Ireland after 820. Accordingly, they probably came from the 'Isles of Scotland' (1998, 324). No case is made for this. In fact, the hardest part of an expedition from Norway to Ireland would be the 400km leg across the North Sea to Shetland, but which might take only twenty-four hours with favourable winds (Crawford 1987, 12–13). This completed, Orkney, mainland Scotland, the Hebrides and Ireland were readily accessible. Is it plausible that Vikings from Norway, established in the Scottish Isles by about 820, had a logistical capacity lacking in Norway itself? We cannot argue from silence that early Viking Norway did not mount great expeditions to the west.

Egon Wamers rightly asked: 'Why should we invent a "maritime centre" on an island in the west for which there is neither historical, literary nor archaeological evidence?' (1998, 66). To do so rests on an argument from silence on the double. Norway is dismissed, in the absence of contemporary ninth-century sources, while comparative documentary silence prompts a speculative history of Viking-Age Scotland. Limited evidence for Scotland in Irish annals, however, belies the speculative construct: *Laithlinn* (or, indeed, *Lochla(i)nn*) is never demonstrably located in Scotland, and is distinguished from Hebridean and Northern Isles components of Viking Scotland. Only the eye of faith can locate *Laithlinn* of the sources in Scotland. Scotland lacks the substantial Norwegian archaeological reflexes of raiding in Ireland. Significant settlement and a powerful Viking kingdom in Scotland, by about 850, as postulated by Ó Corráin, are not evident archaeologically (Graham-Campbell and Batey 1998). The silence of archaeology, like documentation, is not conclusive, but supports Wamers's point about the absence of evidence for an Insular *Laithlinn/Lochla(i)nn*. It is quite possible, then, that mid-ninth-century *Laithlinn* was in Norway. Here, by contrast with Scotland, abundant Viking-Age grave-deposits indicate Viking raiding in Ireland, chiefly from western Norway. West Norwegian grave deposits of Irish origin do not decline around 825, when Ó Corráin's 'Viking Scotland' supposedly took over raiding in Ireland, but continue into the tenth century (Wamers 1985, 1998). Helle, Krag and Wamers held that the Vestfold Ingling 'tradition' of Haraldr hárfagri is an overlay, barely disguising the primarily Oppland and west Norwegian focus of his activities in the literature. Of course, a 'western' Haraldr hárfagri, shorn of Vestfold accretions, need not be a historical figure. However, if early Viking raiding of Ireland emanated from western Norway, why cannot this be the region whose royal authority – in Irish annals *rí Laithlinne* – had representatives in Ireland in 848 and 853?

Wamers tentatively suggested Hlaðir in Trøndelag may be *Laithlinn* (1998, 66, n. 84). Hlaðir, in saga-literature and skaldic poetry, supported Haraldr hárfagri's putative drive for Norwegian unification in the later ninth century, and continued to feature in tenth-century Norwegian 'history'. The jarls of Hlaðir are portrayed as effectively rulers of Norway in the tenth century. Hákon Sigurðarson, jarl of Hlaðir, supposedly acknowledged the overlordship of Haraldr blátann of Denmark in the later tenth century. Jarls of Hlaðir were subsequently agents of Knútr in the early eleventh century. These literary sources are silent about Hlaðir before the later ninth century. This region was, however, more fertile, and perhaps richer and more strategically significant than those further south, in western and southwestern Norway (see, e.g., Foote and Wilson 1970, 41–4, 46; Andersen 1977, 75–101). Trondheimsfjord and the Trøndelag region have Viking-Age graves with Irish ecclesiastical metalwork, although not in the immediate vicinity of Trondheim/ Hlaðir itself (Wamers 1998, 66). Derivation of *Laith* from Hlaðir is linguistically feasible, with loss of the Old Norse case ending *-ir* (-i-stem nominative plural?) in composition. The second element *linn*, given the invariably palatal *-l-* in Irish sources, hardly derives from Norse *land*, giving *-lann*, as in the apparently later *Lochla(i)nn*. Perhaps it is simply Irish *linn* ('pool, lake'), denoting the indented waterway of the Trondheimsfjord.

In any event, we cannot deny categorically direct contact between Ireland and Norway in the ninth century, or that *Laithlinn* may be an Irish reflex of ninth-century Norwegian politics. After all, Norwegian expeditions of the eleventh and twelfth centuries did recruit support in an old-established network of settlements in the west. Comparable expeditions might have been mounted in the ninth century, even if serious historians must be sceptical about literary 'traditions' from a later era. Could it be that the contemporary Irish annals afford a glimpse of ninth-century Scandinavian history that is more reliable than the Icelandic sagas, albeit one that is fleeting, tantalizing and capable only of tentative interpretation?

'FAIR FOREIGNERS' AND 'DARK FOREIGNERS'

Another such insight may be the Irish annalistic distinction between two Viking groups, one termed *finn* ('white/bright/fair') and the other *dub* ('black/dark'), much discussed by historians. There are seventeen instances of *Dubgenti* ('Black/Dark Pagans'), or *Dubgaill* ('Black/Dark Foreigners'), juxtaposed six times with *Finngenti* ('White/Bright/Fair pagans'), or *Finngaill* ('White/Bright/ Fair Foreigners'), between 851 (when *Laithlinn* was current in the annals) and 941. Smyth suggested that *dub* and *finn* mean 'new' and 'old' respectively, referring to the 'newness' of mid-ninth-century 'Danish' Viking arrivals in Ireland, and the 'oldness' of 'Norwegians', present for two generations (1975–6). As noted, Dumville endorsed Smyth's retranslation of *dub* and *finn*, while claiming that they denote not York 'Danes' and Dublin 'Norwegians', but 'families who [...] turned into dynasties' (2005, 83, 91). One must beware of confusing literal translation with interpretation. We will return to this, having first considered the evidence.

AU for 851 reports newly arrived *Dubgenti* at Dublin, who inflicted 'a great slaughter of *Finngaill*', evidently the incumbents. *Dubgenti* also plundered Linn Duachaill (on the east coast north of Dublin), but suffered 'a great slaughter'. Large numbers of casualties show that *Finngaill* and *Dubgenti* describe not merely 'families' or 'dynasties', but warrior-bands, or even distinct communities. Likewise, *AU* for 852 reports the arrival of 'the crews of 160 ships of *Finngenti*' at Carlingford Lough, Co. Louth, and their defeat by *Dubgenti* after a three-day battle. *Dubgenti/Dubgaill* subsequently appear in the ninth-century annals in 856, 867, 870, 875, 877x2 (once in conflict with *Finngenti*) and 893 (*AU*). In the tenth century, the title 'king of the *Dubgaill*' or 'king of the *Dubgaill* and *Finngaill*' refers to the linked kingship of Dublin and York, in 917, 918, 921, 927 (all *AU*) and 941 (*CS*).

Two of the above were encounters between *Dubgenti/Dubgaill* and the Welsh king Rhodri Mawr, in 856 and 877, and the meagre Welsh chronicles – wholly overlooked by Smyth and incompletely consulted by Dumville – notice what corresponds to *Dubgenti*. The Latin *Annales Cambriae* (*AC*) for 853 report devastation of Anglesey *a Gentilibus Nigris* ('by Black Pagans'), corresponding to *Kenedloed Duon* ('Black Pagans') of the later vernacular *Brut y Tywysogyon* (*BT*). York was devastated in 867 by *Dub Gint* ('Black Pagans': *AC*) – corresponding to the Irish annals' *Dubgaill*. In 987, Welsh annals report 2,000 captives taken from Anglesey by Guðrøðr Haraldsson with *Nigris Gentilibus* (*AC*) / *Llu Du* (*BT*) ('Black Pagans/Host'). In 989, Meredith ap Owain redeemed the captives from *Gentilibus Nigris* (*AC*)/ *Kenedloed Duon* (*BT*). These references of the 980s, overlooked by Smyth and Dumville alike, corroborate and supplement Irish references to *Danair*, 'Danes', in 986, 987 and 990. Crucially, *AU* for 987 records an alliance of Mac Arailt (Haraldsson) with *Danair*, corresponding to the Welsh annals' alliance of Haraldsson with *Nigri Gentiles*. In sum, Irish and Welsh annalists in the mid-ninth century referred to 'black' Vikings: *Dubgenti, Dubgaill, Gentiles Nigri, Kenedloed Duon, Llu Du*. The Irish continued to do so until 941, while the Welsh again did so in the 980s, describing as 'Black Pagans' an element the Irish called 'Danes' and which English sources also suggest were Danish, as argued elsewhere (Etchingham 2001, 171–83; Etchingham forthcoming).

The hypothesis that 'black' consistently identifies primarily Danish Vikings through 140 years is reasonable, if unprovable, on the evidence. Most telling is that 'black' Vikings are frequently, though not exclusively, associated with Britain (England, Pictland and Wales) in Irish and Welsh annals. *Finngenti* and *Finngaill*, by contrast, occur only in Irish annals, only in an Irish context and almost invariably in juxtaposition to intrusive *Dubgenti/Dubgaill*. *Rí Finngall 7 Dubgall* applied in 921, 927 and 941 only to kings linked with both York and Dublin. As argued elsewhere (Etchingham forthcoming), Smyth seems justified in detecting a distinction between Dublin-focused 'Norwegian' Vikings and York-focused 'Danish' Vikings. In this respect, Dumville appears mistaken, as he certainly is in endorsing Smyth's re-translation of *dub* as 'new'. This epithet is rightly interpreted as denoting new Viking arrivals in Ireland in 851, but interpretation is not translation and there is no warrant in Irish or Welsh for translating *dub/du* as 'new'. Literal connotations of colour apart – which Smyth seems right to reject (1975–6, 103–7) – the figurative meanings in both languages are 'bitter, dire, gloomy, melancholy, wicked'. These reflect an essentially negative perception of newcomers who first appeared in Ireland in 851, by contrast with old-established Vikings. The defining epithet in *Finngenti/Finngaill* has the figurative meanings 'white, bright, lustrous, fair, handsome, blessed, just, true, clear'. The *dub/finn* dichotomy may stem from a mid-ninth-century perception that some Vikings were more acceptable than others, on the 'devil you know' principle (Etchingham forthcoming).

In any event, *Dubgenti/Dubgaill* undoubtedly refers in Ireland to a secondary Viking group and, it seems, to one of primarily Danish origin. If so, Danes were a distinctive element of the Irish Vikings. Insular metalwork in Viking-Age Scandinavian graves includes a small corpus of material in Denmark, alongside the predominantly west Norwegian concentration (Wamers 1985, 46, 48, 66–7; 1998, 48–51). If we accept that *Dubgenti/Dubgaill* of 851 were primarily Danish, the previously established *Finngenti/Finngaill* were not Danish and, therefore, presumably, were primarily Norwegian. Here we return to the connotations of *Laithlinn*.

'FAIR FOREIGNERS', 'DARK FOREIGNERS' AND *LAITHLINN*

The sequence of events in 848–53 can be interpreted as identifying the *Finngenti/Finngaill*, who resisted the *Dubgenti/Dubgaill*, with *Laithlinn*. Events begin with the battle of 848, wherein 'Jarl Þórir, deputy of the king of *Laithlinn*' was defeated and killed by Irish forces (*AU*). It was, perhaps, this slaying of a Scandinavian royal that prompted Frankish notice of a great victory by the *Scotti* ('Irish') over the *Nordmanni* ('Northmen') in 848 (MGHS 1, 442). In 849, 140 ships *di muinntir rígh Gall* ('of the followers of the king of the Foreigners') subjugated the Foreigners already in Ireland, throwing the country into chaos (*AU*). In 851, *Dubgenti* arrived and defeated the *Finngaill* at Dublin, while *Dubgenti* defeated *Finngenti* in a major naval encounter in 852 (*AU*). Finally, in 853, there arrived Amlaíb (Áleifr) 'son of the king of *Laithlinn* [...] and the Foreigners of Ireland submitted to him, and tribute (was rendered) by the Irish' (*AU*). This inaugurated a twenty-year period when Amlaíb and his associate (brother?) Ímar (Ívarr) dominated Dublin-based Viking activity in Ireland and Britain. This terminated with Amlaíb's disappearance from the annals after 871 and the death of Ímar 'king of the Northmen (*rex Nordmannorum*) of all Ireland and Britain' in 873 (*AU*). The beginning of Amlaíb's and Ímar's regime, in 853, involved restoration of a hegemony identified with *Laithlinn*. This had been interrupted by the killing of Þórir in 848, and was restored at the expense of the *Dubgenti*, briefly triumphant in 851–2.

Dumville, however, saw the triumphs of *Dubgenti* in 851 and 852 as inaugurating the takeover of Dublin by Amlaíb and Ímar. He added '*Dubgenti* and *Dubgaill* continued to be used in relation to the leaders of the Dubliners, and exclusively so as far as I can see, until the early 940s'. These leaders he dubbed the 'family of New Dubliners', in deference to Smyth's retranslation of *dub* (2005, 83–4). The evidence belies this interpretation, however. Amlaíb and Ímar are not associated with the *Dubgenti* in 851–2, Amlaíb arriving on the scene only in 853. This could just as well be a reversal of the *Dubgenti*'s triumphs. Amlaíb is called 'son of the king of *Laithlinn*', a polity whose previously recorded royal was killed by the Irish in 848. *Laithlinn* denotes a pre-*Dubgenti* Viking hegemony in Ireland and Amlaíb's arrival seems best interpreted as restoration of that hegemony. A careful reading of annals and annalistic material in the twelfth-century literary compendium *CGG* shows that *Dubgenti/Dubgaill* is not used of the Dublin leadership after 853. The evidence is detailed fully elsewhere (Etchingham forthcoming), but some examples may suffice.

Horm (Ormr), 'chief of the *Dubgenti*', killed by Rhodri Mawr in 856 (*AU*), was not apparently of Dublin, but was a leader of the *Dubgenti* at Carlingford Lough in 852 (*FA* §235). The *Dubgaill* (*AU*) /*Dub Gint* (*AC*) who took York in 867, are to be identified primarily with the Danish conquerors of Northumbria, as are the *Dubgaill* who slaughtered the Picts in 875 (*AU*). In the same year, Oistín (Eysteinn), son of Amlaíb *regis Norddmannorum* ('king of the Northmen'), was treacherously slain *ab Alband* ('by Hálfdanr': *AU*), an attack by the apparent leader of the York Vikings (*ASC*, 72–5) on Amlaíb and Ímar's successor-regime at Dublin. In 877, *AU* reports a battle in northeastern Ireland 'between *Finngenti* and *Dubgenti*, in which Hálfdanr, chief of the *Dubgenti*, fell'. *Finngenti* are here adversaries of the man who killed Oistín son of Amlaíb of Dublin two years earlier, and so avenged him upon the *Dubgenti*. *CGG* §25 plausibly identifies the *Finngenti* leader as Bárith (Bárðr/Bárøðr), elsewhere identified as *mac Ímair* (Ívarsson: *CS* for 881, i.e. son of Ímar of Dublin, d. 873). Until the mid-870s, then, the Dublin regime is that of the sons of Amlaíb and Ímar, one of whom was slain by *Dubgenti* in 875, after which Bárith son of Ímar, an adversary of *Dubgenti*, ruled until 881 (*AU*). With the return of the 'grandsons/ descendants of Ímar' to Ireland after 914, their first leader Ragnall (Ragnaldr) is called 'king of the *Dubgaill*' in 917 and 918 (*AU*). He never ruled at Dublin, but is called 'king of the *Finngaill* and *Dubgaill*', on dying at York in 921 (*AU*) – a title subsequently used of Ragnall's kinsmen Sitriuc (Sigtryggr) ua hÍmair (grandson of Ívarr: *AU* for 927) and Amlaíb (Áleifr) son of Gothfrith (Guðrøðr: *CS* for 941), both of whom graduated from Dublin to York.

Pace Dumville, the terms *Dubgenti/Dubgaill* are not used of the Dublin leadership in the era of Amlaíb and Ímar and their successors. They commonly designate Vikings active in Britain, or who intervened in Ireland in 851–2 and occasionally thereafter, and who, in the 870s, were hostile to the regime of Amlaíb's and Ímar's sons. *Dubgaill* in the royal titles of tenth-century Vikings seemingly denotes primarily the Danish Vikings they ruled from York. The Dublin leadership after 851–2 is identified in 853 with *Laithlinn*, linking it with the pre-*Dubgenti* order of 848. It is likely that Amlaíb restored to power the *Finngenti/Finngaill* of 851–2. *Finngaill*, in the titles of tenth-century kings descended from Ímar, seems to distinguish the Dublin-based and predominantly Norwegian portion of their domain. It was those so designated and apparently associated with *Laithlinn*, and not the *Dubgaill/Dubgenti*, who prevailed at Dublin after the conflict of 851–2.

BIBLIOGRAPHY

AC = Phillimore, E. (ed.). 1888. 'The *Annales Cambriae* and Old Welsh genealogies', *Y Cymmrodor*, 9, 141–83.
AFM = O'Donovan, J. (ed. and trans.). 1856. *Annála Ríoghachta Éireann: annals of the kingdom of Ireland by the Four Masters*, 2nd ed. (Dublin).
Andersen, P.S. 1977. *Samlingen av Norge og kristningen av landet 800–1130* (Bergen).
ASC = Garmonsway, G.N. (ed.). 1954. *The Anglo-Saxon Chronicle*, 2nd ed. (London).
ATIG = Stokes, W. (ed.). 1896–7. 'The Annals of Tigernach: fourth fragment AD973–1088/The Annals of Tigernach: the continuation AD1088–1178', *Revue Celtique*, 17, 337–420; 18, 9–59, 150–97, 268–303, repr. in *The Annals of Tigernach ii* (Felinfach, 1993).
AU = Mac Airt, S. and G. Mac Niocaill (eds). 1983. *The Annals of Ulster (to AD1131)* (Dublin).
BT = Jones, T. (ed.). 1955. *Brut y Tywysogyon or the Chronicle of the princes (Red Book of Hergest version)* (Cardiff).
CGG = Todd, J.H. (ed.). 1867. *Cogadh Gaedhel re Gallaibh* (London).
Crawford, B. 1987. *Scandinavian Scotland* (Leicester).
CS = Hennessy, W.M. (ed.). 1866. *Chronicum Scotorum* (London).
Dumville, D. 2005. 'Old Dubliners and new Dubliners in Ireland and Britain: a Viking-Age story' in S. Duffy (ed.), *Medieval Dublin*, 6, pp 78–93.
Etchingham, C. 2001. 'North Wales, Ireland and the Isles: the Insular Viking zone', *Peritia*, 15, 145–87.
Etchingham, C. 2007. 'The location of historical *Laithlinn/Lochlainn*: Scotland or Scandinavia?' in M. Ó Flaithearta (ed.), *Studia Celtica Upsaliensia: Proceedings of a Symposium of the Societas Celtologica Nordica, Uppsala, 2004* (Uppsala), pp 11–31.
Etchingham, C. forthcoming. 'Names for Vikings in the Irish annals' in Jon-Viðar Sigurdsson et al. (eds), Proceedings of the Irish Sea Conference, Oslo November 2005.
FA = Radner, J.N. (ed.). 1978. *Fragmentary Annals of Ireland* (Dublin).
Foote, P. & D. Wilson. 1970. *The Viking achievement* (London).
Graham-Campbell, J. & C. Batey. 1998. *Vikings in Scotland: an archaeological survey* (Edinburgh).
Greene, D. 1976. 'The influence of Scandinavian on Irish' in B. Almqvist & D. Greene (eds), *Proceeding of the Seventh Viking Congress, Dublin, 1973* (Dublin), pp 75–82.
Marstrander, C. 1911. 'Lochlainn', *Ériu*, 5, 250–1.
Marstrander, C. 1915. *Bidrag til det norske sprogs historie i Irland* (Kristiania).
MGHS = *Monumenta Germaniae Historica Scriptores.*
Ó Corráin, D. 1998. 'The Vikings in Scotland and Ireland in the ninth century', *Peritia*, 12, 296–339.
Smyth, A. 1975–6. 'The *black* foreigners of York and the *white* foreigners of Dublin', *Saga-Book of the Viking Society*, 19, 101–17.
Stokes, W. & J. Strachan (eds). 1903. *Thesaurus Palaeohibernicus*, 2 (Cambridge).
Wamers, E. 1985. *Insularer metallschmuck in wikingerzeitlichen gräbern nordeuropas* (Neumünster).
Wamers, E. 1998. 'Insular finds in Viking-Age Scandinavia and the state formation of Norway' in H.B. Clarke, M. Ní Mhaonaigh & R. Ó Floinn (eds), *Ireland and Scandinavia in the Early Viking Age* (Dublin), pp 37–72.

Place-names as evidence for urban settlements in Britain in the Viking period

GILLIAN FELLOWS-JENSEN

While most of the Scandinavian place-names in Britain are borne by habitative sites or natural features in rural areas, there are some names which point to the existence of towns or urbanized settlements. Not surprisingly, these tend to be found in the areas where urban settlements are known to have existed in Roman Britain, although continuity of site does not of course necessarily imply continuity of settlement. The comparatively numerous Roman towns in Britain would seem to have been abandoned soon after AD410 and it is uncertain how many inhabitants they are likely to have had in the immediately succeeding centuries.

I have argued earlier that it was probably the arrival of the Danes in England which was responsible for the intensification of urbanization there. The Danish army is known to have frequently taken up its winter-quarters in old Roman settlements, where the walls could still afford some form of defence against attack, while the English, under King Alfred and his children, retaliated by establishing many fortified settlements in the southern and western parts of England, the so-called *burh*s, often exploiting old Roman towns or forts for this purpose.

Within these fortified areas, both the Danes and the English began to organize urban settlements with a network of streets, sometimes retaining certain elements of the Roman town-plans, particularly the gates, but ignoring many of the others. Specialized areas were undoubtedly developed for craftsmen and tradesmen, who have often left traces of their employment in the form of archaeological evidence. It is my aim here to try to exploit a different kind of evidence for urbanization, namely that provided by street-names. It should not be forgotten however, that most street-names in English towns are only recorded in sources dating from well after the Viking period, and the formation of the names themselves cannot be dated closely.

The oldest surviving records of post-Roman street-names in England come from tenth-century Winchester (Biddle and Keene 1976, 234–5). There is an Old English (OE) charter from 909 reading *on þa ceap stræt* ('in the market street': now High Street) and *on þa stræt midde* ('in the middle street': not located), while one from 996 reads *andlang flæsmangara stræte* ('along the meat-sellers' street': now Parchment Street) and *to Scyldwyrtana stræte* ('to the shield-wrights' street': now Upper Brook Street). A late transcript of a document from 990 refers to *on Tænnerestret* ('in the tanners' street': now Tanner Street). These five records combine to suggest that the most common generic occurring in old street-names in Winchester was OE *stræt*, a loanword from Latin (*via*) *strata*, meaning 'a Roman road or a paved street'. The specifics of three of the Winchester names are occupational terms and that of a fourth name denotes a market, while the fifth name points to the fact that the street lies somewhere in the middle, presumably between two other streets.

Specialized areas were also reserved for craftsmen in other English towns in the post-Roman period. In London this was probably originally in the part of the city now generally referred to as *Lundenwic*, where a trading town would seem to have existed to the west of the Roman city in the seventh to ninth centuries (Clark 1989, 12–13). Later, however, there was a movement back to within the Roman walls so that a fortified town could be established there (Vince 1990, 17–27). One of the early streets to be established here was probably *Candelwrichstrete* (1180x1187) ('the street of the candle-wrights or chandlers': now Cannon Street). Other specialized streets are the old street-markets *Westceap* ('the west market'); *Eastceap* ('the east market': now Cheapside and East Cheap); *Corueiserstrate* ('the cordwainers' street') from Middle English (ME) *corviser* from Old French *corveisier* (now Cordwainer Street); and *Roperestrete* ('the ropers' street' from OE *rap* 'rope': now part of Thames Street; Ekwall 1954, 79–80, 182–5). On the whole, however, it would seem to be more characteristic for old streets in London containing occupational terms as their specific to bear names containing the OE generic *lane* ('lane'), a word denoting narrow roads in both urban and rural areas in England.

Nowhere in the street-names of London or Winchester, however, do we find an example of an old name containing the Danish generic *gata* ('street in a town') even though both these cities did come into contact with the Danes in the Viking period. London played a major role in the struggle against the Danes in the late tenth and eleventh centuries, but the defences would seem to have been in good order. Although the citizens ultimately had to submit to Svein Forkbeard in 1013, Svein died before he could consolidate his hold on the kingdom. While the rivalry between Svein's son Knut and Æthelred's son Edmund continued, they eventually came to terms and the citizens of London bought peace with the Danes, who took up their winter-quarters in the city. After the deaths of Svein and Edmund, Knut the Great was chosen as king, but London does not seem to have played a major role as a royal seat in his reign or in those of his sons, and Knut was in fact buried in Winchester, where he had taken up residence with a large following. That there are no Danish street-names in London or Winchester in spite of their history suggests that both cities were well established as administrative and commercial centres with English street-names before the Danes moved in (Fellows-Jensen 2004, 358).

To find street-name evidence for a Danish presence in England we have to turn to the Danelaw, where names containing *gata* frequently denote streets in urbanized areas, most noticeably in the city of York, which was conquered by the

Danes for the first time in 866 and settled by them in connection with the first of the great partitions of land in 876. The York Viking kingdom survived until 954, when the last Danish ruler, Eric Bloodaxe, was expelled by the English king Eadred. There are at least thirty-six old street-names in *-gata* here.

There are also many such names in the Five Boroughs, where the second major Danish partition of land took place in the East Midlands in 877 but where the boroughs are assumed to have been regained by the English in the campaigns led by King Alfred's daughter Æthelflæd in 917 and 918. Little is known for certain about the history of the boroughs in the period, however, except that they are all stated by the *Anglo-Saxon Chronicle* to have been in the hands of the English by 942 (Hall 1989, 177). In Lincoln there are thirty-six streets with names in *-gata*, in Nottingham twenty-five, in Leicester twenty-three, in Stamford eleven but in Derby only four.

The third major partition of land among the Danes was that made of East Anglia in 880. Unlike York and the Five Boroughs, Norwich does not owe its status as an important city to an origin as a Roman fortress. The development of the city would seem to have resulted from the merging of a number of separate settlements between about 850 and 925, presumably under the Danes, who had begun their attacks there in 865 and continued to rule the city until 917 (Ayers 1987). Here, too, Danish influence is reflected in the twenty-eight street-names in *-gata*.

It is not only in the boroughs where Danish influence was known to have been at work that place-names in *-gata* are to be found. They occur in many urbanized settlements throughout the Danelaw and in other parts of northern England. In all of these towns, however, the majority of the old street-names which survive are of English origin, and it would seem unlikely to me that it was the Danes who were the first to coin street-names here, partly because the English names that survive in towns in northern and eastern England are similar in type to the old street-names in Winchester and London and partly because the specifics of many or most of the names in *-gata* are of English origin. What is immediately clear, however, is that it is first and foremost in York that the names in *-gata* also tend to have Scandinavian specifics. No fewer than twenty of the thirty-six street-names in *-gata* there have defining elements that are either certainly or possibly of Danish origin. The specifics in question are: a personal name, either feminine *Guðrún* or masculine *Guðþormr*, in Goodramgate; the Danish place-name **launhlið* ('hidden gateway') in Lounlithgate; occupational terms such as *barkari* ('tanner') in Berkergate, *fiskari* ('fisherman') in Fishergate, *heymangari* ('hay merchant') in Haymongergate, *kjötmangari* ('meat-seller') in Ketmangeregate, *koppari* ('turner, cup-maker') in Coppergate, *plógsveinn* ('ploughman') in Ploxwangate, *skjaldari* ('shield-maker') in Skeldergate; nationalities in the form of *Brettar* ('Britons') in two different Bretgates; terms for animals such as *hafr* ('he-goat') in Havergate, *hjörtr* ('hart, stag') in Herteregate, *hundr* ('hound') in

Hungate; topographical terms such as *kjarr* ('marsh') in Cargate, *nes* ('promontory') in Nessgate; *steinn* ('stone') in Stonegate; and adjectives such as *holr* ('hollow') in Holgate, *lítill* ('little') in Lytlegate, and *mikill* ('great') in Micklegate. It is important to note, however, that it is only the Danish personal name and place-name, and the words *barkari*, *kjötmangari*, *koppari*, *plógsveinn*, *hafr*, *hjörtr*, *kjarr* and *steinn* that certainly betray evidence of Danish linguistic influence, several of the other elements listed have close English cognates.

If we also look at the other towns where old street-names in *-gata* occur frequently, we find that there are even fewer of these with specifics that are certainly or possibly of Danish origin. In Lincoln, for example, there is the personal name *Brandr* in the lost Brauncegate; the place-name **languað* (Langworth in Horncastle wapentake) in Langworthgate; the occupational term *skinnari* ('skinner') in Skynnergate; the animal term *hundr* ('hound') in two Hungates; the plant term *þorn* ('thorn') in Thorngate; the topographical terms *klif* ('cliff') in *Clifgat(e)* and *steinn* in Staynegate; the cultural feature *bryggja* ('bridge') in Briggegate; and the adjectives *danskr* ('Danish') in Danesgate, *holr* ('hollow') in Holegate, *mikill* ('great') in Mikelgate. This is twelve names in all but only the personal name and place-name and the words *steinn* and *dansk* must necessarily be Danish.

In Norwich we find the Danish personal name *Koli* in Colgate; the occupational terms *fiskari* ('fisherman') in Fishergate, and *sútari* ('shoemaker') in Souteregate; the animal term *hundr* ('hound') in two Hundegates; the topographical term *sandr* in Sandgate; the cultural feature *skeið* ('flat track, race-course') in Skeydegate; and the adjectives *holr* ('hollow') in two Hollegates, and *smalr* ('little') in two Smalegates. This makes a total of ten names but it is significant that the specifics in all these names except *skeið* might conceivably be of English origin.

In Nottingham there are only five names in *-gata* that have specifics of certainly or possibly Danish origin. These are the place-name Derby in Derbigate; the occupational terms *barkari* ('tanner') in Barker Gate, and *fiskari* ('fisherman') in Fisher Gate; the animal term *hundr* in Hounds Gate, and the adjective *holr* ('hollow') in Hologate. This makes a total of five names in which only Derby and *barkari* are specifics that are certainly of Danish origin.

There are also only five names in *-gata* in Leicester whose specifics may be of Danish origin. These are the place-name Thirnby in Thurnby Gate; and the adjectives *holr* ('hollow') in Holegate, *norðr* in Northgate Street, *súðr* in Southgate Street and *vestr* in West Gate. Of the five names only *Thurnby Gate* has a specific that is certainly of Danish origin. None of the four old names in *-gata* recorded in Derby has a Danish specific.

At this stage in my investigation I have convinced myself that all that is certain about the Danish contribution to urban settlement in England is the use of the word *gata* to denote an urban street, together with some vocabulary that was considered suitable as specifics for such names. In addition, I would argue that it must have been York that formed the model for the street-names of the Danelaw. This is partly because there are many more purely Scandinavian names in *-gata* in York than in the other Danelaw towns and partly because *gata* is not the only Scandinavian street-name generic to occur in York. The other Scandinavian generics in use there are four isolated instances: *bogi* ('bow') in le Staynbowe (1276), Old Norwegian *búð* ('tent, booth') in Bootham (*c.*1150), *steinn* ('stone') in Divelinestaynes (1233x1239) (now Dublinstones), and *toft* ('building plot') in Kingestoftes 1227 (now Toft Green). These are found together with two elements which make more frequent appearances.

There are several instances of names in *-geil*, a typically Norwegian word meaning 'narrow alley' that occurs more frequently than *gata* in medieval Norwegian to describe roads bounded by fences, and probably points to Norwegian influence in York. There are occasional instances in this city of *geil* alternating with other street-name generics. For example, the earliest occurrence of the widespread name Finkle Street is in the form *Finclegayle* (1361), although all the other instances of that street-name contain *-stræt*. There are a few names in *-geil* containing animal terms as specifics, for example *Noutegail* (1405) containing *naut* ('cattle'), *Swyngaille* (1276) containing *svín* ('pig'), and *fesegayl* (1299) containing *féhús* ('cow-house'). Other specifics in names in *-geil* refer to other living creatures, for example *Fothlousgayl* (1218x1220), containing an adjective denoting 'footless' or 'legless' and referring to the presence of cripples. Two names in *-geil* contain the Scandinavian word *þurs* meaning 'troll or giant', and there are three names in *-geil* containing the occupational terms ME **feltere* ('felt-maker') in *Feltergayl* (*c.*1280) (now Fetter Lane), and ME *glovere* ('glover') in *Glovergail* (*c.*1250) (later *Girdlergate*, now Church Street), while *trichur* in *Trichurgail* (1301) is a loanword in ME from Old French *tricheor* ('trickster'). Two other street-names are related to occupations, namely *Bacusgail* (1312) containing OE **bæchus* ('bake-house'), and *Funtaynesgayle* (*c.*1277) containing Old French *fontein* ('spring, fountain'), probably associated with the activities of the bleachers in nearby Blake Street (**bleikja-stræt*).

Another street-name generic with several instances occurring in York is one with a specialized meaning, namely *lending* ('place where one can land from a vessel'). It is found in five street-names with early records, all borne by small lanes running down to the Ouse, namely *Sancti Martini Lending* (*c.*1170x1199); *Saynt Lenard Lendyng* (1391); *fischelending* thirteenth century; *Sywinlending* (1300); and *le Lymelendyng* (1375). It seems likely that some or all of these staithes were developed for use in the Scandinavian period. It is interesting to note that about 20km further downstream the River Ouse at Selby there are other staithes with names in *-lending*, namely *le Lendyng* (1525); *le Houthwaitelendyng* (1525), whose specific is a Danish place-name in *-þveit*; *Gatelending* (twelfth century), containing the Danish animal term *geit* 'she-goat'; and *Knarlending*

(1320), containing the Danish term for a merchant ship *knarr* (Smith 1961a, 32). These names in Selby seem to be analogical formations based on the four names in York, although they may well all date from the Viking period.

It is clear that many of the names in *-gata* must also be analogical names, not only some of the younger names in *-gata* in York itself, for example Davygate, probably named after the David who was the son of John le Lardiner of York to whom the land had been granted in 1137, Whipmawhopmagate, which can hardly be older than its first occurrence in 1505, and Deangate, which is known to have been given to a road constructed in 1903 to ease the traffic flow around York Minster, but probably also many, perhaps most, of the street-names in *-gata* in the Five Boroughs. It certainly seems likely that many of the street-names in *-gata* in towns elsewhere in Yorkshire are also analogical formations based on the names in York. This is certainly the case with some of the towns of comparatively recent growth that have no really ancient street-names. George Redmonds has recently argued convincingly that a name such as Kirkgate in Huddersfield must simply be a transferred name, an analogical name one may say, for it was first recorded in about 1800 (Redmonds 2004, 174). This follows the fashion current in more ancient towns in the neighbourhood, for example Wakefield, where a Kirkgate dates back to 1298, and Leeds where there was a Kirkgate in 1320, even though the Wakefield street-name probably originated as a **kjarr-gata* ('road to the marsh') to judge from the earliest record in the form *Kergate* 1275, an exact parallel of *Cargate*, earlier *Kergathe* (now King Street in York).

Some of the more rural examples of names in *-gata* in Northern England certainly seem to have developed from Scandinavian *gata*, but in a secondary sense, referring to a track through the country and also apparently to a 'cattle walk or pasture'. This must be the sense of the word that is found in the name of a road running through the parish of Askwith in West Yorkshire on its way between Blubberhouses and Otley and recorded as Psalter Gate, with its specific an obvious example of a folk-etymological reshaping of the term salter or salt-merchant. There is a reference to a part of this road in a charter dated 1190×1208 in the form *Saltgate* (Farrer 1914, no. 54; Smith 1961b, 62). *Salt(er)gate* was presumably used as a regular route by salters, although in the charter the place-name would seem to refer to a plot of pasture land. Tracks referred to as Saltgate and Saltergate in the Danelaw occur fairly frequently, for example in Lincoln.

A different type of analogical *gata*-name is represented across the northern Pennines in towns in Cumberland and Westmorland. Here we find *gata* in several street-names but there are comparatively few of these instances with Scandinavian specifics. Among the nine street-names in *-gata* in Carlisle, ten in Penrith and five in Kendal, there are no names whose specifics must necessarily be Scandinavian. More significant is the fact that the specifics of two of the names in Carlisle were originally borne by gates in the city wall and that the same personal names occur in settlement names in *-bý* in the city, namely Botcherby and Rickerby. These names certainly reflect the capture of the city by William Rufus in 1092 and his plantation there of peasant settlers. Together with several other personal names of Norman origin in *-bý* in the neighbourhood of Carlisle, *Bochard* and *Richard* point to an intensification of settlement here after the Norman Conquest and analogical naming on the model of a type of name familiar from the Danelaw (Fellows-Jensen 1985, 21–4).

All that can be said with certainty, thus, is that the urbanized settlements in Northern England reflect the same kind of development as that seen outside the Danelaw. It is only the occurrence of purely Scandinavian street-names in *-gata*, *-geil* and *-lending* that certainly betrays Danish influence, while the analogical examples of *gata*-names reflect a more general spread of Danelaw toponymy, transcending to some extent the chronological and geographical limitations.

Note

Early forms of street-names in the present paper are taken from the following sources:

York: Palliser, D.M. 1978. 'The medieval street-names of York', *York Historian*, 2, 2–16.

Raine, A. 1955. *Medieval York: a topographical survey based on original sources* (London).

Smith, A.H. 1937. *The place-names of the East Riding of Yorkshire and York*, English Place-Name Society, 5 (Cambridge).

The Five Boroughs: Cameron, K. 1959. *The place-names of Derbyshire*, Part 2, English Place-Name Society, 28 (Cambridge), 447–53.

Cameron, K. 1985. *The place-names of Lincolnshire*, Part 1, English Place-Name Society, 58 (Cambridge).

Cox, B. 1998. *The place-names of Leicestershire*, Part 1, English Place-Name Society, 75 (Cambridge).

Gover, J.E.B., A. Mawer & F.M. Stenton. 1940. *The place-names of Nottinghamshire*, English Place-Name Society, 17 (Cambridge).

Norfolk: Sandred, K.I. & B. Lindström. 1989. *The place-names of the City of Norwich*, Part 1, English Place-Name Society, 61 (Cambridge).

BIBLIOGRAPHY

Ayers, B. 1987. *English Heritage book of Norwich* (London).

Biddle, M. & D.J. Keene. 1976. 'The early place-names of Winchester: Winchester in the eleventh and twelfth century, general survey and conclusions' in M. Biddle (ed.), *Winchester in the Early Middle Ages*, Winchester Studies, 1 (Oxford), pp 231–508.

Clark, J. 1989. *Saxon and Norman London* (London).

Ekwall, E. 1954. *Street-names of the city of London* (Oxford).

Farrer, W. 1914. *Early Yorkshire charters*, 1 (Edinburgh).

Fellows Jensen, G. 1981. 'Scandinavian settlement in the Danelaw in the light of the place-names of Denmark' in H. Bekker-Nielsen, P. Foote & O. Olsen. (eds), *Proceedings of the Eighth Viking Congress, Århus, 24–31 August 1977* (Odense), pp 133–45.

Fellows-Jensen, G. 1985. *Scandinavian settlement names in the north-west* (Copenhagen).

Fellows-Jensen, G. 2004. 'The Anglo-Scandinavian street-names of York' in R.A. Hall (ed.), *Aspects of Anglo-Scandinavian York*, The Archaeology of York, Anglo-Scandinavian York, 8:4 (York), pp 357–71.

Hall, R.A. 1989. 'The five boroughs of the Danelaw: a review of present knowledge', *Anglo-Saxon England*, 18, 149–206.

Redmonds, G. 2004. *Names and history: people, places and things* (London).

Smith, A.H. 1961a. *The place-names of the West Riding of Yorkshire*, Part 4, English Place-Name Society, 33 (Cambridge).

Smith, A.H. 1961b. *The place-names of the West Riding of Yorkshire*, Part 5, English Place-Name Society, 34 (Cambridge).

Vince, A. 1990. *Saxon London: an archaeological investigation* (London).

Ribe: continuity or discontinuity from the eighth to the twelfth century?

CLAUS FEVEILE

INTRODUCTION

The archaeological evidence for an active and impressive eighth- and ninth-century marketplace in Ribe is overwhelming. Likewise, there can be no doubt about the appearance of a medieval town there at the end of the eleventh century. But, there is almost no definite archaeological evidence of a settlement there in the intervening period. Consequently, the impression of Ribe as a well-established urban society (Jensen 1991), existing from the beginning of the eighth century throughout the Viking Age and into the medieval period, has to be revised (Feveile 2006b; Sindbæk 2005, 166).

Written sources concerning Viking-Age Ribe are few (Skovgaard-Petersen 1981). It is mentioned for the first time in the Frankish annals in the 850s, when the Danish King Horik the Younger gives the missionary Ansgar a piece of land there for the erection of a church as well as permission for a priest to take up permanent residence. Mention is made of Bishop Leofdag of Ribe (*Liopdago Ripensis ecclesiae episcopo*) as being among the participants at the synod in Ingelheim in 948. In 965 and 988 Ribe is also referred to as an episcopal residence. Finally, the town is noted in Adam of Bremen's *Gesta*, dating from the 1070s, in which it is described as being 'surrounded by a river streaming in from the ocean and through which the ships steer towards Friesland or at any rate to England and our Saxony' (Skovgaard-Petersen 1981, 51).

The first archaeological attempts to locate ancient Ribe were made in the 1950s and took place in the area around the present cathedral on the southwest bank of Ribe River. Here, however, the layers do not date any earlier than the late eleventh century. In the 1960s, the archaeological search led to excavations outside the town, e.g., Dankirke and Okholm (Hansen 1990; Feveile 2001). The final breakthrough came in the 1970s, when an excavation campaign of several years duration was carried out on the northeast bank of the river. Here, the remains of the market place, as well as an inhumation grave dating from the eighth century, were discovered. The process of publishing these excavations, which extended from 1970 to 1976, is underway; five volumes have been published and one is currently in preparation (Bencard 1981; 1984; Bencard et al. 1990; 1991; 2004). During the period between 1984 and 2000, over twenty further excavations were conducted on the north and east bank of the river. A number of provisional results and surveys have been published (Frandsen and Jensen 1988; 1990; Feveile 1994; Feveile et al. 1992; Feveile and Jensen 2000), while a more comprehensive series, *Ribe Studier*, dealing with the results from these excavations, has been launched (Feveile 2006a).

This paper outlines the conclusions from *Ribe Studier*. The picture emerges of a town which does not go through a continuous, gradual development from a seasonal market place into a medieval episcopal residence and trading town. On the contrary, the evidence indicates an unstable situation with profound changes. Today, and in future research, the most interesting questions are what did Ribe look like in the tenth and eleventh centuries, and where was it located?

EIGHTH TO TWELFTH CENTURY

The oldest part of Ribe was situated on the north and east bank of the River Ribe (Fig. 9.1), while by the end of the eleventh century, the town had spread to both sides of the river, with its centre on the southwest bank. Recent geological research has demonstrated the existence of a layer of drifting sand, $c.6000m^2$ in area, covering a plough-layer with traces of furrow (ard marks) from the pre-Roman Iron Age or earlier (Dalsgaard 2006; Aaby 2006). Subsequently, the eighth-century market place was established on top of this natural sand bank and not, as has previously been stated, on a man-made layer of sand (Jensen 1991; Feveile 1994).

In this riverside area, $c.200m$ long and 80m wide, solid culture layers up to $c.2m$ in depth have been investigated. These consist of workshop floors, fireplaces and waste layers containing tens of thousands of archaeological objects. The latter evidence extensive craft production (bead making, bronze casting, amber polishing, comb manufacturing, shoe making, potting), as well as the importation and trade of goods (including raw materials for craftsmen and ready-made goods, such as Frankish ceramics and glass, volcanic basalt, Scandinavian soapstone, whetstones of slate, whalebones and glass beads from the Middle East). The oldest culture layers, which can be dated to the period $c.704$–10, derive from market-place activity, the organization of which is not precisely known. After a few years, the market place was organized in a row of plots, $c.6$–8m wide and probably up to 20–30m in length, placed at right angles to the river. The individual plots, which numbered up to 40 or 50, are separated by shallow, narrow ditches, with wattle work preserved along their edges in places. This basic structure existed unaltered for the next 150 years or so, with only small adjustments to the plot boundaries. Until $c.770$–80, the use of the market place appears to have been seasonal and, as a consequence, no houses are found on the plots, with only a few pit-houses, wells and what appear to have been shelters occurring. From this period onwards, however, the evidence

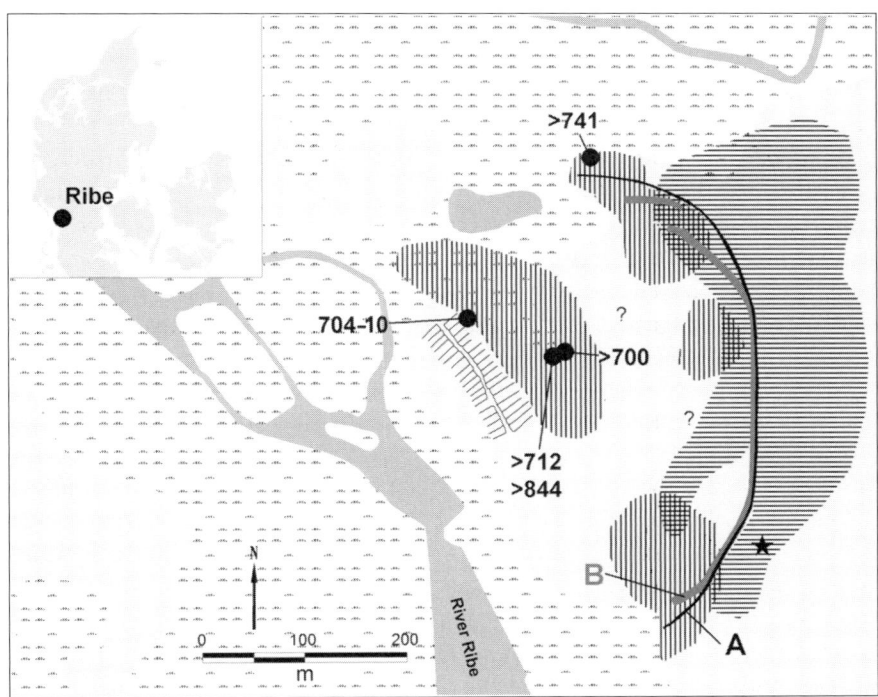

9.1 Simplified map of eighth- and ninth-century Ribe. The background map shows low-lying areas (grass turf), higher dry areas (light grey) and the modern River Ribe. The main elements are: the market place divided into plots (thin black lines); settled areas (vertical hatching); graveyards (horizontal hatching); the Ribelund graveyard (black star); the town's ditch (A); and the moat (B). Finally, the dendro-dated wells are marked (black dots).

indicates that the plots were used throughout the year. The excavations have not revealed the form and size of these houses, though it may be assumed that they were similar to the buildings known from other contemporary market places in Scandinavia, such as Hedeby, Birka and Kaupang. The course of the river in the eighth and ninth centuries is not precisely known and, consequently, no archaeological investigations have been carried out in order to investigate the outline of the harbour area. The growth of these Ribe culture layers stops around the middle or second half of the ninth century, for unknown reasons, and the next finds made in the market place area are traces of buildings from the High Middle Ages, the twelfth and thirteenth centuries.

Behind the area with the workshop plots, traces of settlements in the form of pit houses, post-built houses, wells, fences and road systems have been found during many small- and large-scale excavations. It is important to note that culture layers are not preserved to any great degree outside the market place area where, consequently, we are dealing with areas where only the features buried in the ground have been preserved. Among the best-documented features are some post-built houses dating from the second half of the eighth and the beginning of the ninth century; these are of the same shape and size as houses known from contemporary rural settlements in Jutland. The overall extent of the excavated area, however, is so small that no clear evidence exists concerning how the settlement was organized, and whether it had a farm-like structure or a more dense urban layout. The material found in the settlement clearly indicates a connection with the market place, as to a certain degree traces of craft production and trade are also found in the majority of the excavations outside the area with the workshop plots.

It must be emphasized that no definite permanent settlement dating from the first half of the eighth century has been found, however early settlement might be represented in a number of undated settlement zones. At the same time, it is also important to note that there are only a few objects dating from the tenth century and most of the eleventh century, and there are no real structures, such as houses or wells, for example, that are assignable to this period

About forty-seven graves have been investigated in Ribe, dating from the eighth to eleventh centuries, all situated in a large borderline area to the east and the north of the settlement. These have been investigated in five separate excavations, but there is hardly any doubt that originally they formed part of one or several large graveyards. The majority of the graves – about thirty-three – can be dated to the eighth and ninth centuries. Apart from two examples – both child inhumation burials – all of the graves are poorly equipped cremations. The majority are without grave-goods, but in some examples there are a few finds in the form of glass beads and various iron items. One eighth-century cremation grave contained riding equipment, while another ninth-century example contained a Frankish sword-mount of gilded silver. The remaining fourteen burials are inhumations and probably date to the tenth and eleventh centuries.

At the beginning of the ninth century, a ditch was dug around Ribe, *c.*2m wide and 1m deep (Fig. 9.1). Several excavations have revealed that this feature forms a border between an internal developed area and an external undeveloped area or graveyard. The ditch is so slight that it cannot have served as a fortification. Instead, it was symbolic and marked the town limits. It demarcates an area of *c.*12ha and is well-defined towards the east, while its northern and possible western courses are unknown. Consequently, it is not known whether it turns back towards the river, forming a semi-circle, or stops at the low-lying, wet area to the north of the market place. During the second half of the ninth century, or at the latest around the beginning of the tenth century, this ditch was substituted by a flat-bottomed moat, 6–7m wide and 1m deep, with traces of an internal bank. During the twelfth century, when the town was re-established, its area covered more than 50ha on both sides of the River Ribe (Fig. 9.2). A moat, 10–12m wide and 2m deep, with a bank, was established to the south-east. This construction should be viewed in connection with other fortifications on the southern side of the river.

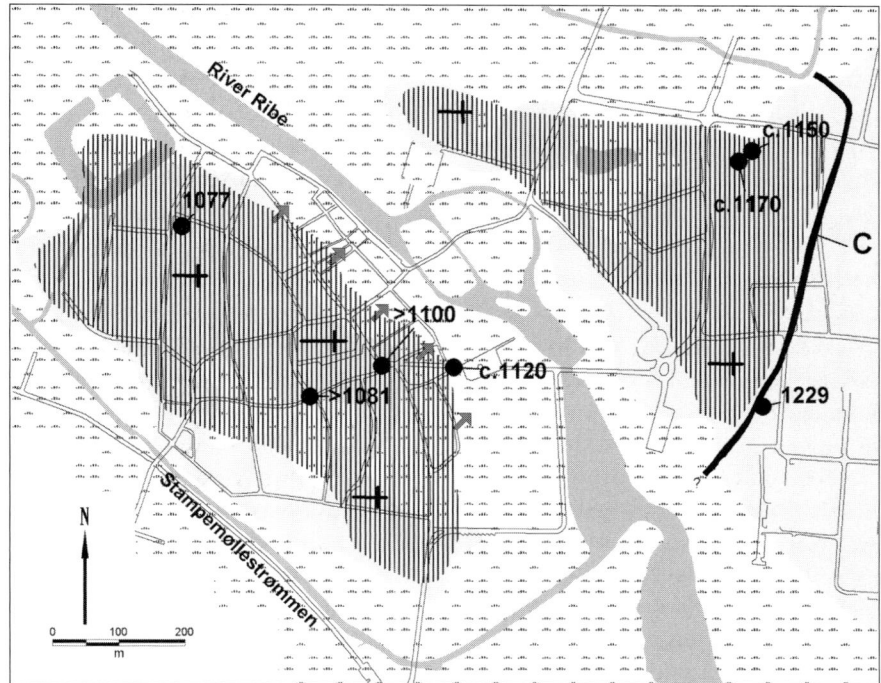

9.2 Simplified map of twelfth-century Ribe superimposed on a modern roadmap. Settled areas (vertical hatching); churches (small cross); Cathedral (large cross); moat (C). Finally a selection of dendro-dated wells and other structures are marked (black dots).

Ever since the first excavations on the site of the market place, sceattas have been recovered at regular intervals in Ribe, so that in all 204 examples are now on record (Feveile 2006c). These are scattered, single-finds, dropped in connection with trade. The predominant type is the Wodan/Monster (85 per cent), followed by Porcupine (11 per cent) and Continental Runic (2 per cent) types, as well as single examples of a few other types. The coins are not only found in layers dating from the first half of the eighth century, but their loss – and thereby also their circulation – continues until the beginning of the ninth century. While Metcalf has argued that the examples of Wodan/Monster-type were minted in Ribe or south-western Denmark (Metcalf 1993), other researchers believe that they were minted somewhere in the Frisian area before *c.*755 (see Malmer 2002).

TENTH AND ELEVENTH CENTURIES

Among the extensive material from Ribe, the only datable finds from the tenth or eleventh centuries are two coins, occurring as single-finds. One is a tenth-century Danish copy of a Dorestad coin (Feveile 2006a, 1.1, 300), which was recovered from the top of an older pit-house; the second can be attributed to King Hardeknut (1035–42) (type: Hauberg 44var) (Feveile 2006a, 1.2, 89; tavle 33:4) and was excavated in a culture layer together with local ceramics, which does not allow for a dating closer than the eleventh or twelfth century. This latter type of coin is occasionally found in hoards from the late twelfth century. It may thus have been lost in connection with the settlement remains from this period that were excavated in the same area.

At Ribelund, a total of fifteen inhumation and two cremation graves have been investigated. While the latter contained grave-goods, all of the inhumation graves were unfurnished. These may be divided into two groups, based on their orientation. It is not possible to conclude whether there is continuity or otherwise between the two types of burial rite, or between the two groups of inhumation graves. Carbon-14 dating of two of the inhumation graves resulted in a date-range extending from the tenth to the early eleventh centuries.

If Ribe covered a sizeable area and had even a moderate level of activity during this period, it is strange that there have been so few conclusively dated tenth- and eleventh-century finds recovered following fifty years of archaeological investigation on both sides of the river. Moat A was constructed in the middle or late ninth century and Moat B was not built until the twelfth century, but there are virtually no significant finds or structures from the intervening period. When one looks at the extent and scale of the town during the centuries before and after this period, it would be unreasonable to imagine that this apparent gap is accidental. Indeed, it has been suggested that the layers and structures from this period have basically been dug away by later activities (Jensen et al. 1983, 162). The only important exception may be the burial place at Ribelund, where two radiocarbon dates suggest activity during this period.

It should be noted that currently there is no proof that the settlement had expanded or completely moved to the south side of the River Ribe by the tenth or early eleventh century. The earliest datable structure on this side is a well that is dendrochronologically dated to 1077, and intensive activity here did not apparently take place until the end of the eleventh or early twelfth century (Madsen 1997, 472; 1999, 81; Søvsø 2006). This leaves us with the situation that Ribe cannot be documented by archaeological sources in a convincing way from between the late ninth century/early tenth century and the end of the eleventh century. The archaeological sources, thus, do not match the written ones, in which Ribe is mentioned in various contexts – predominantly ecclesiastical – during the course of the tenth and eleventh centuries. However, Adam of Bremen's reference to Ribe at the end of the eleventh century can possibly be linked with the earliest medieval finds from both sides of the river.

There are a few coin types, struck under Knud the Great (1018–35), Hardeknut (1040–2) and Svend Estridsen (1047–4), that are traditionally associated with Ribe, and the town has also been identified by Moesgård (2003,

10) as a possible place of origin of a hitherto unknown coin group from Knud the Holy (1080–6). The basis for ascribing coins from Knud the Great to Ribe is fragile, however, and rests only on the similarity between the town name that occurs on them (RIHBIIR, RINHE, RICYEBII and RIE…II) to Ribe. While it has been argued that these coins could have been minted in England, the most recent research indicates that they were almost certainly struck in southern Scandinavia. Malmer, who has recently dealt with the extensive coin material as a whole, refers to Ribe as one of the place-names found on the coins and thus accepts the above-mentioned spellings as signifying Ribe. She is cautious, however, about placing the various stamp chains, since chains 151 and 152, which are the specific ones on which these names are found, are only located in the geographical area labelled 'South', that is, southern Scandinavia (Malmer 1997, 53). It should also be noted that the coins with these names number less than 30, and that none of these were found in Jutland.

As has been made clear, the sources for Ribe are very scarce and equivocal where the tenth and eleventh centuries are concerned. The few archaeological finds may be regarded as showing that Ribe – on a certain scale – did exist, in support of the historical and numismatic evidence. Conversely, it would not be reasonable to overlook the almost total lack of actual structures and finds dating from this period. It lies beyond the scope of this paper to embark on a detailed discussion of the causes and consequences of these observations, but essentially there are three scenarios on which future work should be based. The first possibility is that the absence of more substantial finds and structures is partly due to unfortunate circumstances. That is, we have simply chosen the wrong places to locate the many excavations so far, and there may be methodological problems in the categorization and dating of the more ordinary types of artefact. In this scenario, it is merely a question of further excavation and research before the apparently absent phases of Ribe can be located physically.

The second possibility is that Ribe either disappeared or moved. Ever since the discovery of the early town, its transfer or expansion from the north to the south side of the river has been compared with Birka's removal to Sigtuna and Hedeby's to Schleswig. It should therefore be considered whether the massive resurrection of Ribe, dating to no later than 1100, is the result of its transfer from a location outside the present town area. In this scenario, Ribe, situated on the north side of the river in the eighth-ninth centuries, disappears or moves to another unknown location before being re-established on a site occupying both sides of the river around 1100.

Finally, it is conceivable that the majority of the functions that were focused on Ribe – trade, craft, the King's representative – were transferred elsewhere at some point during the late ninth/early tenth century, perhaps to one or several of the large farm-estates in the area. In this context, it is the ecclesiastical function that is important if the written sources are to be given weight. If it is correct that a church was physically founded, with a later bishopric associated with it, its archaeological traces would not necessarily be very extensive and it is possible that the investigations on both the north and the south side of the river would not have encountered them.

SUMMARY

The development of Ribe from the early eighth century until the twelfth century cannot be described as a continuous and gradual development towards increasingly complex conditions. On the contrary, a number of radical changes took place in relation to the function and the physical extent of the place during its initial centuries.

In the early eighth century, a marketplace was founded, being divided into small individual plots within a few years. On the basis of the existing archaeological evidence, the use of these plots appears to have been seasonal, with no permanent structures having been found in them. However, from the occurrence of graves dating from the first half of the eighth century, it can be assumed that people stayed there on a more permanent basis. Permanent buildings dating to the second half of this century are found on the plots, just as is the case outside the plotted area. During the first half of the ninth century, a ditch was dug around Ribe, and this appears to have been replaced by a regular moat quite soon afterwards – possibly by the middle of the century, but hardly later than 900.

The following period of *c*.150–200 years offers almost no archaeological evidence of human activity on either side of the river. The most important traces are fourteen inhumation graves which, on the basis of radiocarbon dating, can be dated to the tenth-eleventh centuries. This general lack of archaeological evidence contrasts with the written sources, which mention either Ribe or institutions/persons that were presumably based in it during this period.

In the late eleventh century, the settlement was re-established. It has not been possible to conclude on which side of the river the initial re-establishment took place, but over a few decades many hectares on both sides of the river became included in the town. The south side rapidly becomes the centre of this settlement. During the twelfth century, an extensive fortification, Moat C on the northern side of the river and Stampemøllestrømmen on its southern side, is constructed. Presumably Moat D can be dated to the same period.

BIBLIOGRAPHY

Aaby, B. 2006. 'Pollenanalyser fra markedspladsen i Ribe, ASR 9 Posthuset og ASR 951 Plejehjemmet Riberhus' in C. Feveile (ed.), *Ribe studier*, 1.1, pp 133–45.
Bencard, M. 1981. *Ribe excavations 1970–76*, 1 (Esbjerg).

Bencard, M. 1984. *Ribe excavations 1970–76*, 2 (Esbjerg).

Bencard, M., L.B. Jørgensen & H.B. Madsen (eds). 1990. *Ribe excavations 1970–76*, 4 (Esbjerg).

Bencard, M., L.B. Jørgensen & H.B. Madsen (eds). 1991. *Ribe excavations 1970–76*, 3 (Esbjerg).

Bencard, M., A.K. Rasmussen & H.B. Madsen (eds). 2004. *Ribe excavations 1970–76*, 5 (Århus).

Birkebæk, F. & H.C. Vorting. 1979. 'Sven Grathes vold og grav omkring Roskilde', *Historisk Årbog fra Roskilde amt*, 1979.

Dalsgaard, K. 2006. 'Fygesandsaflejringer ved Ribe' in C. Feveile (ed.), *Ribe studier*, 1.1, pp 93–105.

Feveile, C. 1994. 'The latest news from Viking-Age Ribe: archaeological excavations 1993' in B. Ambrosiani & H. Clarke (eds), *Developments around the Baltic and the North Sea in the Viking Age: Proceedings the Twelfth Viking Congress, Hässelby slott, 1993*, Birka Studies 3 (Stockholm), pp 91–9.

Feveile, C. 2001. 'Okholm, en plads med håndværksspor og grubehuse fra 8.–9. århundrede', *By, marsk og geest*, 13, 5–32.

Feveile, C. (ed.). 2006a. *Ribe studier: det ældste Ribe, udgravninger på nordsiden af Ribe å 1984–2000*, 1.1 & 1.2 (Aarhus).

Feveile, C. 2006b. 'Ribe on the north side of the river, 8th–12th century: overview and interpretation' in C. Feveile (ed.), *Ribe studier*, 1.1, pp 13–91.

Feveile, C. 2006c. 'Mønterne fra det ældste Ribe' in C. Feveile (ed.), *Ribe studier*, 1.1, pp 279–312.

Feveile, C., S. Jensen & K. Ljungberg. 1992. 'Endlich gefunden: Ansgars Ribe, ein bericht über die ausgrabungen 1989 in der Rosenallé in Ribe', *Offa*, 47, 209–34.

Frandsen, L.B. & S. Jensen. 1988. 'Pre-Viking and early Viking-Age Ribe: excavations at Nicolajgade 8, 1985–86', *Journal of Danish Archaeology*, 6, 175–89.

Frandsen, L.B. & S. Jensen. 1990. 'The dating of Ribe's earliest culture layers', *Journal of Danish Archaeology*, 7, 228–31.

Hansen, H.J. 1990. 'Dankirke: jernalderboplads og rigdomscenter, oversigt over udgravningerne 1965–70', *Kuml*, 1988–9 (1990), 201–48.

Hjermind, J. & H.K. Kristensen. 1987. 'Svend Grathes vold', *Museerne i Viborg Amt*, 14, 84–9.

Jensen, S. 1990. 'Ribes befæstning i vikingetiden' *Mark og Montre*, 1990, 69–73.

Jensen, S. 1991. *The Vikings of Ribe* (Ribe).

Jensen, S. 1993. 'Early towns' in S. Hvass & B. Storgaard (eds), *Digging into the past: 25 years of archaeology in Denmark* (Copenhagen), pp 202–5.

Jensen, S., Madsen, P.K. & O. Schiørring. 1983. 'Excavations in Ribe, 1979–82', *Journal of Danish Archaeology*, 2, 156–70.

Kolstrup, E. 1991. 'Mikroskopiske levn fra Ansgars Ribe: 800– og 900-tallets plantevækst belyst ved pollenanalyser', *By, marsk og geest*, 3, 44–51.

Madsen, P.K. 1999. 'Middelalderkeramik fra syv udgravninger i Ribe 1980–84 – kronologi, datering og bytopografi' in P.K. Madsen (ed.), *Middelalderkeramik fra Ribe: byarkæologiske undersøgelser 1980–87* (Aarhus), pp 11–88.

Malmer, B. 1997. *The Anglo-Scandinavian coinage c.995–1020*, Commentationes de nummis Saeculorum IX–XI, in Suecia repertis, n.s., 9 (Stockholm).

Malmer, B. 2002. 'Münzprägung und frühe stadtbildung in Nordeuropa' in K. Brandt, M. Müller-Wille & C. Radtke (eds), *Haithabu und die frühe stadtentwicklung im nördlichen Europa* (Neumünster), 117–32.

Metcalf, D.M. 1993. *Thrymsas and sceattas in the Asmolean Museum Oxford*, 2 (London).

Moesgaard, J.C. 2003. 'Danelund-skatten', *By, marsk og geest*, 15, 7–16.

Sindbæk, S.M. 2005. *Ruter og rutinisering: vikingetidens fjernhandel i Nordeuropa* (Copenhagen).

Skovgaard-Petersen, I. 1981. 'The written sources' in M. Bencard (ed.), *Ribe Excavations 1970–76*, 1, 21–62.

Søvsø, M. 2006. 'Arkæologiske undersøgelser i Sønderportsgade: Ribes hovedgade gennem 900 år', *By, marsk og geest*, 18, 5–33.

Norwegian Crosses in the Hebrides and Shetland?

IAN FISHER

The free-standing crosses of Western Norway include some which still stand in dramatic coastal and fjord landscapes, although others survive only as fragments in the museum stores of Bergen and Stavanger. Yet these impressive monuments are little known to scholars elsewhere, for the literature is almost exclusively in Norwegian. Some were illustrated as early as the 1620s by Jon Skonvig and other artists working on Ole Worm's runic project and they recorded folk-traditions, often associating the crosses with King Óláfr Haraldsson, 'the Saint' (Moltke 1956). The first comprehensive survey was published in 1842 by the distinguished patriot and antiquarian, W.F.K. Christie, and this was followed in 1973 by a detailed monograph by Bishop Fridtjov Birkeli. His work has recently been modified by two Bergen University dissertations, one analyzing the locations of the crosses and the status of those who erected them (Gabrielsen 2002; 2005), and the other examining their petrology as part of a study of the quarrying industry of Hyllestad, Sogn og Fjordane (Baug 2002; 2005). Birkeli's study was 'a contribution to elucidate the transition from heathen Norse religion to Christianity', with an extended discussion of the 'mission-period' (Birkeli 1973; Kaland 1995; Krag 2005, 138–59). It is generally accepted that public monuments such as large crosses would not be earlier than the reign of Håkon the Good, 'Athelstan's foster-son' (d. 961), whose abortive mission involved clerics from Anglo-Saxon England where he had been educated. There is also a widespread perception in the West, commonly expressed on internet pages, of a longer and more symbiotic process of 'Celtic' conversion, symbolized by St Sunniva's companions, the 'Selja-men'.

Little positive archaeological evidence for this Celtic conversion has been cited, as opposed to the negative testimony of the decline in pagan burial rites. However, it is worth drawing attention to two small cross-marked stones in Rogaland, both at major power-centres, which if found in western Britain or Ireland would be dated to the ninth century or earlier. Birkeli (1973, 86–7) illustrated one roughly-incised cross on a standing-stone beside a pilgrim-route at Akre, Hedmark, but even in its weathered state the cross at Sola, Rogaland, is far more sophisticated. Incised on a small pillar believed to have been used as a *gappestok* ('pillory'), it is a Latin cross with barred terminals, 170mm high by 110mm in span. At Avaldsnes on Karmøy, a small almost equal-armed cross with slightly bowed arms and neat triangular terminals is carved on a slab, now used as a headstone, whose less deeply incised initials and '1711' date are surely additions. Without extensive knowledge of Norwegian churchyards, it cannot be asserted that these crosses do not belong, like some simple carvings in Ireland, to the post-medieval period. The same is true of a recumbent slab with small relief cross at Hyllestad old churchyard and the sunken Latin cross on the 'troll-stone' at Kabelvåg in Lofoten. However, the published volumes of *Norges Kirker* and a recent work on churchyards (Klingberg et al. 2005) provide no comparisons to deny early medieval dates for these carvings.

A more clear-cut case of an early eleventh-century stone showing Insular influence, published by Sæbjorg Walaker Nordeide, is a massive slab discovered in the 1950s during grave-digging at Hustad, Nord-Trondelag (Nordeide 2005). It bears in outline a large and typically Nordic cross with curving wedged arms and below it a worn face-mask. Misidentification of this as Óðinn led to the stone being consigned to a small dark hut where Nordeide was unable to inspect its back. Examination by the present writer revealed the shattering effects of the dynamite used by the grave-digger to move the heavy slab, but identified clear traces of a second cross of similar form. The stone was therefore not a recumbent slab but a rare double-faced cross-slab, of Insular type although Scandinavian in ornament.

Returning to the free-standing crosses, it must be noted that Birkeli's total of sixty, quoted on information panels throughout western Norway, includes about twenty lost examples for which he considered documentary evidence or tradition to be reliable. Almost all of the crosses are spread over 350km of western Norway from Rogaland to the Nordfjord, but with none close to Bergen. About half of the survivors remain at or near their original sites, a precious few intact and others represented by fragments in churches, such as that on the outlying island of Kinn. The largest crosses, at Kvitsøy, Gard and Korssund, are up to 4m high and are prominently sited beside the *leia*, the sheltered sailing-channel that runs up much of the west coast. It has been suggested that these were erected by potentates or high ecclesiastics (Gabrielsen 2005), while the two fine crosses at Eivindvik, seat of the Gulating assembly, also served an obvious public function. Many of more moderate size were probably erected by landowning families, and several were associated with pre-Christian burial mounds, sanctifying or giving protection against the spirits of the ancestors. A distribution map by Kaland (1995, 14) excludes crosses less than 1m in height, but Birkeli includes a few below that threshold, including three from Numedal in Buskerud (Birkeli 1973, 128–30), and there are others in the southern county of Vest-Agder (*ex inf* F-A Stylegar). These small cruciform stones are often referred to as 'churchyard crosses' and groups of them, not recorded by Birkeli, survive at Hyllestad and at the church of Guddal in the same area.

One distinguished art-historian lamented at the Cork Viking Congress that 'these crosses have no typology', and ornamental features are indeed few – mainly the shapes of arms and armpits, and central holes in a few cases. Where there is so little evidence, the treatment of minor features such as bevelled edges may become significant. The crosses in the southern area around Sola and Stavanger often have wedge-shaped arms, sometimes with rounded ends, and continental metalwork may have been an influence. Some of this group have central crosslets and *V-spisser* ('V-arrows'), incised or in relief, extending down into the shaft. This feature also seems to occur on the much-damaged fragment from Lirhus, Voss, 180km to the north, which when seen by Birkeli was inverted and not recognizable. The most remarkable of these carvings, and the only dateable point in the Norwegian series, is the apparently anthropomorphic cross at Stavanger, 3.85m in visible height (Birkeli 1973, 151–7). Its long runic inscription commemorates Erlingr Skjálgssunr, 'Erling of Sola' as he is styled in *Agrip*, who was murdered in 1028 by one of Óláfr Haraldsson's retainers.

Birkeli assigned several of the crosses to 'Anglian' and 'Celtic' groups, the former with elegant wide-curving armpits as on Svanøy and at the Gulating site of Eivindvik. The 'Celtic' type was defined by straight arms and narrow semicircular armpits, in crosses at Loen at the head of the Nordfjord and at Eivindvik churchyard. While there are indeed parallels for these contrasting forms in the different ethnic areas of Britain and Ireland, it must be stressed that knowledge of early medieval Insular sculpture has advanced greatly since 1973. Furthermore, petrological examination of the crosses has shown that over twenty of them, including examples of both of Birkeli's types, were taken from the long-established quernstone quarries at Hyllestad (Baug 2002; 2005). Indeed, the cross at the entrance to Eivindvik churchyard shows the impression of a quernstone previously cut from the layer above. This garnet-mica-schist (*granatglimmerskift*), although unresponsive for ornamental carving, was of remarkable strength and allowed the creation of large crosses such as that on Kvitsøy, over 4m in height by 1.8m in span but only 0.17m in thickness. There is some evidence that crosses were being carved at the fjord-side quarries which were ideal for transport.

Birkeli, who had numerous scholarly contacts in Britain and Ireland, discussed several areas in seeking models for the Norwegian crosses. He considered the Outer Hebrides but rejected their small crosses as too insignificant and, as with those on the North Yorkshire Moors, he did not allow for the possibility of reciprocal influence from Norway itself. In a few examples in the Hebrides and Shetland, however, a case can be made for such 'colonial' influence. The churchyard of Kilbar on the island of Barra is known for its cross-slab with the runic inscription to Þorgerðu, the most significant ornamented and inscribed carving in the Hebrides (Fisher 2001, 107–8; Barnes and Page 2006, 221–32, 346). Birkeli (1973, 228) was the first to mention two small cruciform stones in the same churchyard, described in more detail by the present writer (Fisher 2001, 107). One of these has armpits of irregular and varying outline, a feature of some Norwegian crosses, with chamfered ends to the arms and a central crosslet. Three of the armpits have distinct bevels and this is most conspicuous in the narrowest one, which exhibits what the writer has called a 'channelled armpit'. The other stone is decidedly uneven in form, with its shaft tapering asymmetrically to the cross-head, short wedge-shaped arms and a cylindrical top arm. Most of its edges have deep rounded bevels and the armpits are channelled, while both faces of the cross-head bear equal-armed crosslets, one with a curved shaft. Similar irregularity is a feature of several Norwegian crosses, and the deep bevels and channelled armpits can be found in some of the crosses in the Sola area and at Vereide in the Gloppen district on the Nordfjord.

The largest group of early medieval carvings in the Outer Hebrides is found in the north-west coastal area of North Uist and its adjacent tidal island of Vallay (Fisher 2001, 109–11), a district characterized by numerous place-names of Scandinavian origin. They include several cruciform stones with tight bevelled armpits, almost (or in one cross from Vallay completely) enclosed. The largest of the group, at Cille Pheadair, 1.5m in visible height by 0.83m in span, is remarkable for its almost horizontal alignment of two relief bosses in the cross-head. A damaged cross at Hougharry bears a single boss and the pierced armpits on the cross from Vallay are enclosed by mouldings, but otherwise the tight bevelled armpits are the only ornamental feature of the group. They occur on two fragmentary cruciform stones on Iona, and geological identification as hornblende-schist confirms that these also are from North Uist, perhaps sent as grave-markers with a body destined for burial in Reilig Odhráin.

The closest Norwegian comparison for this North Uist group is the cross at Grindheim in the fertile Etne district of South Hordaland, near the southeast shore of Hardangerfjord. Now situated in a churchyard and adjoining a tall runestone, it is believed to have stood originally on one of the numerous nearby pre-Christian burial-mounds (Birkeli 1973, 169–74; Gabrielsen 2002, 67–9). It measures 1.95m in visible height by 1.12m in span, but its present appearance as a tau-cross, coincidentally resembling the more complete of the Iona fragments, is due to the removal of its top arm some time after it was drawn for Skonvig about 1626 (Moltke 1956, I: 167). The almost enclosed bevelled armpits closely resemble those of the Uist group, and while the influence could run in either direction, it is probable that this well-proportioned cross provided a model for the smaller and less regular Hebridean ones.

Early medieval sculpture in the Shetland Islands shows various Scandinavian links. A recent addition to this corpus is a group of small carved slabs associated with cist-burials excavated in 2000 near the chapel on St Ninian's Isle. Radicarbon dates of the burials are centred on the tenth century (Barrowman and Forsyth forthcoming). While one of the carvings bears an irregular linear cross, two of them are plaited ribbon-crosses with double transoms (Fisher forthcoming). This cross-type with multiple plaited transoms remained popular in Scandinavia, and an interesting parallel is found on a runestone from Holm in the Swedish province of Halland (Moltke 1956, I: 104). Another, of the thirteenth century and with ringed junctions, is an architectural carving on the exterior of the stone church of Kinsarvik, Hordaland (Christie and Svarstad 1963, 7–8).

The remarkable group of about forty cruciform stones in the northern islands of Unst and Yell was briefly described and illustrated previously by the author (Fisher 2005). While they vary considerably in form, all are of the small type that in Norway would be described as 'churchyard crosses'. The most sophisticated ones on Unst, at Norwick and on the offshore island of Uyea, share features with the Sola-Stavanger group including concave upper shafts and wedge-shaped top arms with asymmetrically rounded ends. The latter feature is also found on stones at Framgord and Lundawick. Some of these carvings also have convex-sided 'swollen' shafts, for which there is a close parallel in the 2.2m-high cross at Rygg in the fertile district of Gloppen on the south side of Nordfjord (Birkeli 1973, 200–2). This also displays the short, straight side-arms and tall, asymmetrically-ended top arm that are found in several of the Unst carvings.

One of the most remarkable of the Unst cruciform stones is in the ancient churchyard of Framgord, situated on a low promontory above the north end of Sandwick beach. This area is notable for the excavation of Norse buildings by Stummen Hansen and of later structures by Bigelow. The stone has a swollen shaft like the Rygg cross, and carved in relief in the cross-head there is a small Latin cross with a shaft of similar form. Parallels for the relief cross are found on the hillside cross at Eivindvik and on small wheel-crosses of steatite, probably of the thirteenth century, at Rollag and Svene in Numedal, Buskerud (Christie 1981, I: 301–2, 351). The Framgord churchyard also preserves a rare group of tapered medieval grave-covers, known locally as 'keel-stanes', from their sloping or concave sides and narrow flat ridges. A close parallel, with deep concave sides and head- and foot-stones, is preserved at the stone church of Støle in Etne. The significance of the type is indicated by the excavation of seventeenth-century wooden coffins of similar form at Kinsarvik church, also in Hordaland (Christie and Svarstad 1963, 12, 17, 34; Klingberg et al. 2005, 18).

Chronological uncertainties make it impossible to demonstrate influence from Norway to Scotland in any individual case, but the comparisons brought together here may reveal an unacknowledged debt. If so, it is appropriate that models of Christian art should come from the rich fields of Sola, Etne and Gloppen, where so many treasures of Insular church craftsmanship had been buried centuries earlier.

ACKNOWLEDGMENTS

I am grateful to many friends in Norway for hospitality and practical assistance during fieldwork and research. Irene Baug and Kristine Holme Gabrielsen kindly gave copies of their dissertations and discussed their material.

BIBLIOGRAPHY

Barnes, M.P. & R.I. Page. 2006. *The Scandinavian runic inscriptions of Britain*, Runrön, 19 (Uppsala).
Barrowman, R. & K. Forsyth (eds) (forthcoming). The chapel and burial ground on St Ninian's Isle, Shetland: excavations past and present, Society for Medieval Archaeology Monograph.
Baug, I. 2002. *Kvernsteinsbrota i Hyllestad*, Norsk Bergverksmuseums skriftserie, 22 (Kongsberg).
Baug, I. 2005. 'Frå kvernstein til steinkross: produksjon og distribusjon' in F.B. Førsund (ed.), *Steinkrossane på Vestlandet*, Hyllestadseminaret, 2004 (Hyllestad), pp 6–12.
Birkeli, F. 1973. *Norske steinkors i tidlig middelalder: et bidrag til belysning av overgangen fra norrøn religion til kristendom*, Skrifter utgitt av det Norske Videnskaps-Akademi i Oslo, II, Hist.-filos. Klasse, n.s., 10 (Oslo).
Christie, H. & C. Svarstad. 1963. *Kinsarvik Kirke*, Fortidsminner, 46 (Oslo).
Christie, S. & H. Christie, 1981. *Norges kirker: Buskerud*, Norske minnesmerker, utgitt av Riksantikvaren (Oslo).
Fisher, I. 2001. *Early medieval sculpture in the West Highlands and Islands*, RCAHMS and Society of Antiquaries of Scotland, Monograph series, 1 (Edinburgh).
Fisher, I. 2005. 'Cross-currents in North Atlantic sculpture' in A. Mortensen & S.V. Arge (eds), *Vikings and Norse in the North Atlantic: Select Papers from the Proceedings of the Fourteenth Viking Congress, Tórshavn, 19–30 July 2001* (Tórshavn), pp 160–6.
Fisher, I. forthcoming. 'The carved stones' in R. Barrowman & K. Forsyth (eds) (forthcoming), The chapel and burial ground on St Ninian's Isle, Shetland: excavations past and present, Society for Medieval Archaeology Monograph.
Førsund, F.B. (ed.). 2005. *Steinkrossane på Vestlandet*, Hyllestadseminaret, 2004 (Hyllestad).
Gabrielsen, K.H. 2002. 'Vestlandets steinkors: monumentalisme i brytningen mellom hedendom og kristendom' (Master's thesis, Universitetet i Bergen).
Gabrielsen, K.H. 2005. 'Korsreiserne: hvem lot reise steinkors?' in F.B. Førsund (ed.), *Steinkrossane på Vestlandet*, Hyllestadseminaret, 2004 (Hyllestad), pp 40–50.
Kaland, S.H.H. 1995. 'Fra hedensk til kristen religion', *Arkeo* (1995), 1, 12–16.
Klingberg, H. et al. (eds). 2005. *Kirkegården: et levende kulturminne* (Oslo).
Krag, C. 2005. *Vikingtid og rikssamling, 800–1130*, Aschehougs Norges Historie, 2 (Oslo).
Moltke, E. 1956. *Jon Skonvig og de andre runetegnere: et bidrag til runologiens historie i Danmark og Norge*, Bibliotheca Arnemagnaeana, supplementum, 1 (Copenhagen).
Nordeide, S.W. 2005. 'Fra Odin til Kvitekrist', *Spor*, 39:1, 18–21.

Late Viking-Age runestones in Uppland:
some gender aspects

ANNE-SOFIE GRÄSLUND

The old, much-debated question of whether rune-stones are located by road-ways or at grave-fields seems to have no simple answer; a combination of the two ideas seems reasonable, since grave-fields are often located along roadways. Having dealt earlier with rune-stones at grave-fields (Gräslund 1987), my starting point in this paper will be some stones connected to communication systems. In a project on rune-stones in and around Sigtuna, the oldest town in the heart of Uppland (Gräslund et al. forthcoming), we have studied a number of stones that are of relevance to this question. The main purpose of the project was to investigate whether the stones reflected urban-rural relations, i.e. whether there are differences or similarities between the stones in the town and those in the hinterland. However, in this respect we have found no great differences between the town and the hinterland, and instead, our conclusion is that the early medieval town of Sigtuna should not be seen as separate from its hinterland. From the point of view of runic monuments, at least, the two seem to be one unit. On the other hand, a comparison between the Sigtuna area and another very rich rune-stone area, that of Täby-Vallentuna, famous *inter alia* for its many stones raised by the Jarlabanke family, shows clear differences.

My point of departure is some rune-stones in the Sigtuna area indicating communication routes, by sea and by land. There are several stones in the neighbourhood with such a location, but as four of these are among the tallest and most beautiful rune-stones in Uppland, I have selected them to illustrate my hypothesis (Figs 11.1–4). Two of the stones face Garnsviken, which today is a shallow inlet (U460, U463). In the Viking Age, it was *c.* 5m deeper than today and in all probability served as an important water route to Uppsala; it would have been a short-cut compared to the water route used today. A place-name north of Garnsviken, Edeby, seems to indicate that ships were rolled over land for one part of the road, before reaching Lake Mälaren again. Two other stones are located facing the land roads north and north-east of Sigtuna (U455, U462). We might suppose that the north-east road was the last part of a route connected to the so-called Långhundraleden, a very important water route going from the Baltic to Uppsala. The inscriptions on these stones are as follows:

U460, Skråmsta, Haga parish: *Ingefast had the stone raised in memory of Olev, his father, and Öd in memory of her husband.*

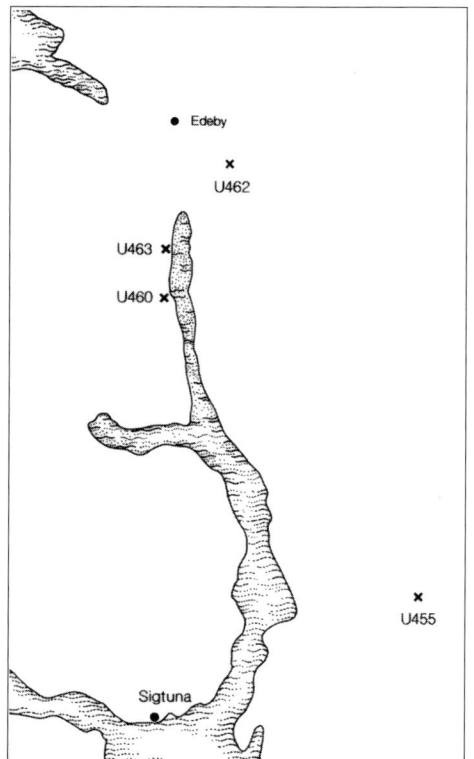

11.1 Map of the Garnsviken area north of Sigtuna, with the location of the rune-stones in Fig. 11.2 marked (drawing: Alicja Grenberger).

U463, Ala, Vassunda parish: *Vädralde and Vige had the stone raised in memory of Holmsten, their father and Holmfrid in memory of her husband.*

U462, The vicarage, Vassunda parish: *Djärv and Gunnar and Gullö had the stone raised and the bridge built in memory of Halvdan their father, Holmfrid in memory of her husband.*

U455, Näsby, Odensala parish: *Ingefast had this stone raised in memory of Torkel, his father and Gunnhild, his mother. Both of them drowned.*

In each of these cases, at least one woman is mentioned, either among the raisers of the monument or among those commemorated in its inscription. One popular opinion about the rune-stones is that they are raised in memory of Vikings who died abroad. This is certainly valid for several of the rune-stones, but not for the majority. As I have shown in an earlier publication, women are often involved in raising rune-stones (Gräslund 1989, 225), and this is also demonstrated in the cases of the stones mentioned above. Each of these four stones has the same kind of ornamentation, and in my suggested chronological system they belong to group Pr 4, that is to the final quarter of the eleventh century (Gräslund 1994).

It has been argued that women were not active in raising rune-stones in the early phases, but this is a claim that must be rejected. So also must the suggestion that bridge-stones, which are generally seen as Christian, were raised at a late stage. This can be exemplified by the following inscriptions (Figs 11.5–7), probably carved around the year 1000 or during the first quarter of the eleventh century:

U69, Eggeby, Spånga parish: *Ragnälv had this bridge made in memory of Anund her noble son. May God help his spirit and soul better than he deserved. No memorials will be greater. The mother made it for her only son.*

U617, Bro church: *Ginnlög, Holmger's daughter, sister of Sigröd and of Göt, she had this stone raised and this bridge made in memory of Assur, her husband, son of Håkon Jarl. He kept watch against Vikings with Geter. May God now help his spirit and soul.*

Sö101, Ramsundsberget, Jäder parish: *Sigrid, mother of Alrik, daughter of Orm, made the bridge for Holmger's soul, her husband, Sigröd's father.*

U328, Lundby, Markim parish: *Gyrid and Gudlög they had this stone raised in memory of Onäm their father and of Assur her husband. Read these runes!*

In two of these inscriptions it is quite obvious that kinship on the maternal side is important. This importance is stressed by the fact that both Ginnlög and Sigrid are presented as daughters, of Holmger and Orm respectively. When discussing kinship and oral culture, reference should be made to two rune-stones, one from Hälsingland in northern Sweden and the other from Småland in southern Sweden. Apparently, it was very important to be able to enumerate one's forefathers, something that has been regarded as being of the highest relevance in rural societies up to modern times.

Let us start with the stone from Småland, Norra Sandsjö (Sm71), where six generations are cited:

11.2 Runestone at Skråmsta, Haga parish, U460 (after *Upplands runinskrifter*).

11.3 Runestones at Ala, Vassunda parish, U463 (left) and the Vicarage, Vassunda parish, U462 (right) (after *Upplands runinskrifter*).

Ärnvad had this stone raised in memory of Hägge, his father, and of Hära, his father, and Karl his father, and Hära, his father, and Tegn his father, and in memory of these five forefathers.

Here, only the fathers are mentioned, but in the second inscription, from Malsta (Hs14), we also meet a mother and even another woman (although we do not know her place in the family, since parts of the inscription are lost):

*Romund raised this stone in memory of Hä-Gylve, Bräses's son. And Bräse was Line's son and Line was Unn's son, and Unn was Ofeg's son and Ofeg was Tore's son. Groa was Hä-Gylvae's mother, and then **barlaf** ... and then Gudrun. Romund, Hä-Gylve's son, cut these runes. We fetched this block of stone in Balsten. Gylve acquired this district and also three estates farther north. He also acquired **lanakr** and afterwards Färdsjö* (for the new reading of the names by Lena Peterson, see Brink 1994, 152).

The two above-mentioned bridge-stones from the Lake Mälaren area are good examples of the importance of also claiming kinship on the maternal side. More than twenty inscriptions from Uppland could be added to this group, on stones

11.4 Runestone at Näsby, Odensala parish, U455 (after *Upplands runinskrifter*).

which were raised in memory of fathers-in-law or mothers-in-law. It is even more pronounced on an inscription from Knivsta, north of Sigtuna (U472), where Gillög presents herself as Ekenäv's daughter and had the stone raised in memory of Dragmal, her maternal grandfather.

The historian Christer Winberg, in his study of land ownership and kinship systems in Sweden from the Middle Ages up to the eighteenth century, refers to the background evidence of statements in the Viking-Age runic inscriptions (1985, 26). The rune-stones were normally raised by the closest family members, but in some cases there are relationships evident that are impossible to explain in a patrilinear system. These include stones raised by men in memory of their brothers-in-law, or by men in memory of their sister's daughters, or by a man in memory of his father-in-law. Winberg's conclusion is that the system of bilateral kindred goes back at least to the Viking Age.

The Canadian historian Alexander Murray has studied the Germanic kinship structure, using Tacitus' *Germanica*, Late Roman evidence and the Frankish legal collection *Lex Salica* (Murray 1976). His conclusions are that the earlier historiographic view of a unilinear clan basis to society before the Middle Ages should not be accepted. He writes:

> 'Any comprehensive view of the development of kinship structure, nevertheless, should be based upon the notion of the bilateral kindred as

11.5 Runestones at Eggeby, Spånga parish, U69 (left) and Bro church
(right) (after *Upplands runinskrifter*).

the basic kin group of society and upon the recognition of the antiquity
and vitality of cognation. [...] It has permitted the reinterpretation of
important texts, which illustrates the ancient world's view of barbarian
society, and aspects of association, property-holding, inheritance and the
legal rights of women [...it] has allowed us to recognize the persistence of
ancient social forms into the society of the early Middle Ages' (Murray
1976, 223).

The system of a bilateral kindred organization implies close bonds between an
individual and his mother's family (1976, 60). One example, with relevance for the
runic inscriptions, is the special relation between nephew and maternal uncles
mentioned already by Tacitus. There are some rune-stones raised in memory of a
maternal uncle (for example Ög 81, Ög 207, Sö 296 and Sm 121). The inscription
on Ög 209 should also be mentioned, as it is made in memory of a nephew.

The importance of maternal kinship is also evident through the occurrence
of metronymica. The best-known Viking-Age example is Sven Estridsen, the
Danish king, whose father was Ulf Jarl and whose mother was Estrid, daughter
of Sven Forkbeard. As she was of royal blood, the son got her name. There are
several examples of metronymica in the Icelandic sagas, such as in *Egils saga* and
in *Laxdaela saga*, sometimes because the father had died at an early age. But they
also occur when the father was still living and well known (Kvaran 1996, 38). In
fact, there are also some runic inscriptions where the raiser introduces himself

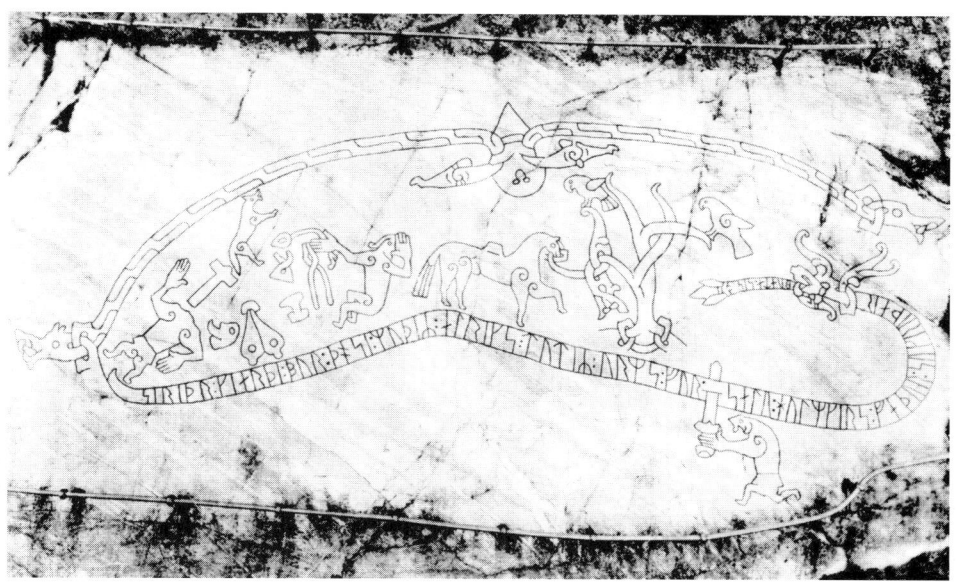

11.6 Runestone at Ramsundsberget, Jäder parish, Sö 101 (after *Södermanlands runinskrifter*).

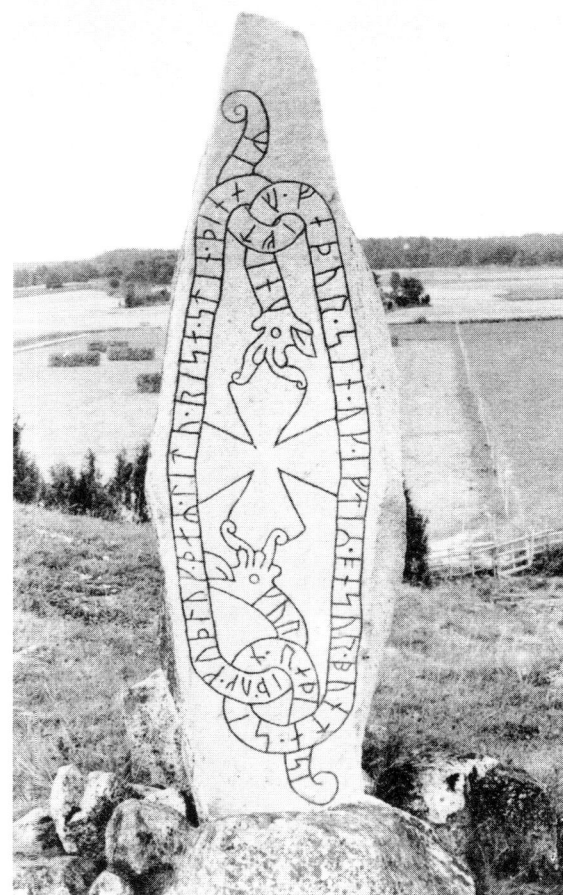

11.7 Runestone at Lundby, Markim parish, U328 (after *Upplands runinskrifter*).

as his mother's son, for example a carving in today's Uppsala, U897: *Sigvid, Gillög's son, raised the runes in memory of Ragnälv, his mother-in-law*. We know of several metronymica among the Swedish aristocracy in the thirteenth century, knights such as Magnus Marinason from Södermanland and Magnus Kristinason from Västergötland (*Äldre svenska frälsesläkter*, vols 1 and 3).

Nineteen rune-stones are identified as belonging to the Jarlabanke family, the earliest with ornamentation in Pr 2, the latest in Pr 5. Many women are mentioned in these inscriptions, although always as wives or mothers. One of the carvings, in style Pr 4, on an earthbound rock in Täby (U143), is inscribed: *Jorun had bridges made in memory of her husband, and Häming and Jarlabanke in memory of Ingefast, Estrid in memory of Ingvar a very good young man*.

Jorun was Jarlabanke's mother and Estrid his grandmother. It is surprising that no sisters or daughters are mentioned in the Jarlabanke inscriptions, as there are many sisters, daughters and even step-daughters and mothers-in-law mentioned on other stones in Uppland. In this respect, if we examine the inscriptions of another large group – the Ingvar stones – we find mentions of women as mothers, as well as one example of a daughter. However, women are not present here to the same degree as in the Jarlabanke inscriptions. There are other obvious differences between the Jarlabanke stones and the Ingvar ones. The former extend over a long time-span, several generations from the beginning of the eleventh to the beginning of the twelfth century. The Ingvar stones, on the other hand, were probably raised within a fairly short period following the Ingvar expedition, which probably took place at the beginning of the 1040s. Only one of the Jarlabanke stones mentions travelling abroad, with the remainder giving more of an impression of stability at home. They are also, to a very high degree, explicitly Christian, with crosses and/or prayers. Concerning their ornamentation, practically all Ingvar stones are carved in the birds-eye-view style, while the heads of the rune-bearing animals on the Jarlabanke stones are portrayed in profile. Regarding gender, women are mentioned in most of the Jarlabanke inscriptions (with the exception of the stones that Jarlabanke raised in memory of himself), while they are of less common occurrence in the Ingvar inscriptions. Another major difference concerns distribution: while the Jarlabanke stones are restricted to the Attundaland, the Ingvar stones are distributed over a large part of the Lake Mälaren region, especially in Södermanland and the western part of Uppland. The interesting fact that their areas of distribution do not overlap might show the different power-bases of these two families (Gräslund 2004).

In an innovative article on re-reading the rune-stones, Anders Andrén has claimed that the complex interplay between images and text on the stones must be taken into account for a new type of interpretation to emerge (Andrén 2000). For example, he postulates that if the layout of the design is composed using one rune animal, this may indicate that one family is involved; if the layout contains two rune animals, this may indicate that two or more families are involved, and so on. He provides some examples in accordance with this idea, but unfortunately he concludes that 'in some instances, especially in Uppland, there is no such correlation between image and text' (2000, 23). Andrén mentions the seven stones raised by Jarlabanke in memory of himself (or more correctly, the seven inscriptions on six stones, as U212 has inscriptions on two sides); only one person, and thereby one family, is mentioned, but they are all composed using two rune animals. His explanation is that 'these extraordinary actions by Jarlabanke can be regarded as nearly desperate ways for him to claim property and other rights. By composing the stones with two snakes, he alluded that these rights came from another family, most plausibly as an inheritance from his wife' (2000, 23). Concerning other stones with two rune animals, he argues that:

> Although the stones are composed of two snakes, only two or more persons are mentioned as sponsors, usually two or more children. If we want to maintain that snakes generally speaking represented different families, the only possible solution of these compositions is that the sponsors were half-brothers and half-sisters, although that was not mentioned in the texts (2000, 23).

In my view, this forces the interpretation too far. The inscriptions on the four stones in the Sigtuna area, used as the starting point in this article, are all limited to one family each. Two of the stones show one rune animal and the other two have two animals each. Thus, for these stones, Andrén's hypothesis is not valid.

As a consequence of his argument concerning half-brothers and -sisters, Andrén claims that polygamy was common in eleventh-century central Sweden, illustrating this with two runic inscriptions, one from Södermanland and one from Uppland:

> Sö297, Uppinge, Grödinge parish: *Amoda and Moda had this stone laid after Sigrev, their husband and Sigsten's and Holmsten's brother.*
> U1039, Bräcksta, Tensta parish: *Stodbjörn and Östen raised the stone in memory of their father Gulle. Mercy has Christ, give relief to his soul. Kjule carved these runes. Kättilög was his wife called and Viälv.*

These two inscriptions may, perhaps, be seen as evidence of polygamy. However, bearing in mind that Uppland has more than 1300 Viking-Age runic inscriptions, and that women are mentioned in 39 per cent of those which have at least one name or word of determinate sex (for Södermanland, the figures are in excess of 400 inscriptions with women mentioned in 30 per cent of them), these must be regarded as exclusive exceptions. However, it should be noted that the editors of *Sveriges Runinskrifter* consider the possibility that the similar names (variation:

Amoda and Moda) on the Grödinge stone may represent a mother and her daughter. Andrén also refers to Adam of Bremen's text in support of his argument:

> The idea of common polygamy can be further supported by the writings of Adam of Bremen in the 1070s. According to him, many powerful and rich men among the Svear had several wives, and all the children in these polygamous families had equal rights of inheritance (Adam IV, 21). Adam, in other words, seems to describe a kind of official polygamy among the Svear, which was partly different from the usual custom of concubines among powerful men (Andrén 2000, 24).

The question is whether Adam's text is reliable or not in this respect. Do we trust him when in chapters 19 and 25 he writes about the cynocephali, human beings with their heads at their chests? Regarding Adam's information on polygamy, it is worth noting that the commentators of the latest Swedish translation comment: 'Adams information about extensive and systematic polygamy (or polygyny) within Scandinavian magnate families does not find any support in *Heimskringla*, where concubinage is not concealed, however' (Adam 1984, 287). Referring to Adam's text, another comment is that polygamy was possible, but a luxury that few men could allow themselves (Hedberg 1976, 492). This seems to be in accordance with the anthropological view: in a society with about equal numbers of men and women, for demographic reasons polygamy is only possible for a very restricted stratum. The occurrence of concubinage in the Scandinavian Middle Ages was, following the historical evidence, limited to the uppermost layer of society, the royal families and the finest aristocracy. Thus, the statement that polygamy was *common* in Viking-Age society must be rejected.

However, no one denies that many women took part in the enterprise to create memorial monuments to deceased family members. Raising rune-stones was a very public act – the stones were meant to be visible to and were probably intended to be read by as many as possible. Thus, in my view, the women who commissioned these stones have crossed the border of the private sphere and succeeded in what Augustus Emperor called raising a memorial more lasting and durable than copper!

BIBLIOGRAPHY

Adam = Svenberg, E. (ed.). 1984. *Adam av Bremen: historien om Hamburgstiftet och dess biskopar*, with commentary by C.F. Hallencreutz, K. Johannesson, T. Nyberg & A. Pilz (Stockholm).
Andrén, A. 2000. 'Re-reading embodied texts: an interpretation of rune-stones', *Current Swedish Archaeology*, 8, 7–32.

Brink, S. 1994. 'En vikingatida storbonde i södra Norrland', *Tor*, 26, 145–62.

Gräslund, A-S. 1987. 'Runstenar, bygd och gravar', *Tor*, 21, 241–62.

Gräslund, A-S. 1989. '"Gud hjälpe nu väl hennes själ": om runstenskvinnorna, deras roll vid kristnandet och deras plats i familj och samhälle', *Tor*, 22, 223–44.

Gräslund, A-S. 1994. 'Rune-stones: on ornamentation and chronology' in B. Ambrosiani & H. Clarke (eds), *Developments around the Baltic and the North Sea in the Viking Age: Proceedings the Twelfth Viking Congress, Hässelby slott, 1993*, Birka Studies 3 (Stockholm), pp 117–31.

Gräslund, A-S. 2004. 'Om identitet: några vikingatida exempel' in *Saga och Sed: Kungliga Gustav Adolfs Akademiens årsbok* 2004 (Uppsala), 23–37.

Gräslund, A-S. et al. forthcoming. 'Similar and not different: a project on the rune-stones in and around Sigtuna as reflecting the urban-rural relations'.

Hedberg, G. 1976. 'Aegteskab', *Kulturhistoriskt lexikon för nordisk medeltid och renässans*, XX: 486–93.

Kvaran, G. 1996. 'Islandske metronymika', *Studia Anthropologica Scandinavica*, 14, 37–41.

Murray, A.C. 1976. *Germanic kinship structure: studies in law and society in antiquity and the early Middle Ages* (Toronto).

Ög = Brate, E. (ed.). 1911–18. *Östergötlands runinskrifter, Sveriges Runinskrifter*, 2 (Stockholm), www.nordiska.uu.se/forskn/samnord/htm.

Sm = Kinander, R. 1935–61. *Smålands runinskrifter, Sveriges Runinskrifter*, 4 (Stockholm), www.nordiska.uu.se/forskn/samnord/htm.

Sö = Brate, E. & E. Wéssen (eds). 1924–36. *Södermanlands runinskrifter, Sveriges Runinskrifter*, 3 (Stockholm), www.nordiska.uu.se/forskn/samnord/htm.

U = Wéssen, E. & S.B.F. Jansson (eds). 1940–58. *Upplands runinskrifter, Sveriges Runinskrifter*, 6–9 (Stockholm), www.nordiska.uu.se/forskn/samnord/htm.

Winberg, C. 1985. *Grenverket: studier rörande jord, släktskapssystem och ståndsprivilegier*, Rättshistoriskt bibliotek, 38 (Stockholm).

Äldre svenska frälsesläkter: ättartavlor utgivna av Riddarhusdirektionen, 1 Stockholm 1957, 3 Stockholm 1989.

Weapons and warfare in Viking-Age Ireland

ANDREW HALPIN

INTRODUCTION

The common view of the Viking impact on warfare and weaponry in Ireland stresses the utterly inferior military technology and organization of an Irish society that had not faced any significant external threat in centuries. The contrast between the two cultures, in military terms, is typified by comparisons such as that between a typical 'Viking' sword and an Irish 'crannog' type sword (e.g. Mallory 1981, 108, fig. 2). This view, best argued over forty years ago by Etienne Rynne (1966), undoubtedly retains a great deal of truth, but it is in need of reassessment. Such a reassessment will probably require more archaeological evidence than is currently available and certainly more sustained research than has to date been carried out, but I hope here to offer some observations on various aspects of warfare and weaponry in the four centuries after the arrival of the Vikings, which may at least highlight issues to be addressed.

PRE-VIKING IRELAND

Fairly plentiful historical sources – which will be considered below – elucidate many aspects of the Viking impact on Irish warfare. Assessing the impact on weaponry, however, can be more difficult because it is largely a matter of archaeological, rather than historical inquiry, and is beset with various problems of source material and the progress of research. We must begin with a consideration of the state of Irish military technology on the eve of the Viking period. Historical sources clearly indicate that the armoury of Irish warriors of the eighth century, as in previous centuries, consisted of swords, spears and shields for defence (for a full discussion of this evidence see Halpin 1999, 19–31). These are also the items represented in the archaeological record but, primarily because of the lack of furnished burials, this record is rather meagre and is particularly lacking in examples from well-dated contexts. Thus, while we have some spearheads and shield bosses datable to the seventh and eighth centuries, such as those from Lagore (Hencken 1950–1, 94–9, figs 29–33), one can at this point do little more than mention them, as little serious analysis has been carried out (Rynne's 1956 thesis contains some discussion, but remains unpublished).

Rynne (1981) has produced a classification of pre-Viking swords, of which the latest type – his so-called 'crannog' swords – is thought to have been current at the time of the earliest Viking raids, leading to the unflattering comparisons noted earlier. There is, however, no firm basis for dating these swords any later than the seventh century, and it is purely an assumption that they were still in use when the Viking attacks began. In the absence of any evidence for swords of any other types being used in Ireland at the end of the eighth century, it might not be considered an unreasonable assumption that 'crannog' swords were still the current form. But could there have been other types of swords in use by the time of the Viking raids? Peirce (2002, 28–9) recently suggested that a very fine sword from near Askeaton, Co. Limerick (NMI, registration no. Wk25), usually considered as of 'Viking' form, should be classified as a variant of Petersen's (1919) Type A and be dated to the eighth century. If this is correct, it raises the possibility that the sword could have reached Ireland before the Viking raids began – and, indeed, there is no reason why some Irish warriors could not have obtained state-of-the-art weapons from England or continental Europe during the eighth century. The technological quality of Irish weapons of the pre-Viking period has also been questioned, but such metallographic studies as have been carried out are not entirely damning. While some of these weapons are undoubtedly technologically inferior, others were found to be of reasonable quality, with quite effective carburized and heat-treated cutting edges (Scott 1990, 108–46, 146–7). Moreover, the idea of overwhelming Viking military superiority is hardly borne out in the historical record. As Clarke (1990–2, 97, 105–8) put it, 'the most striking feature of the recorded battles [between the Vikings and the Irish] is that the Vikings lost most of them'. I would not seek to deny initial Viking military superiority, but one must be careful not to overstate this and to bear in mind that such superiority could have been compensated for relatively quickly by the more powerful Irish kings. Military technology is always an area in which rapid responses to new influences can be expected.

THE VIKING IMPACT

Nevertheless, the appearance in ninth-century Ireland of very fine weapons, such as those found in the Viking graves at Kilmainham and Islandbridge, Dublin (see, for example, Bøe 1940, 12–38, 61–4, 82–91; Walsh 1998; Pierce 2002, 39, 42–3, 56–9, 66–7), almost certainly represents a significant new development in military technology, at least in quantitative terms if not qualitative. We still await the publication of a long-promised study of Irish Viking swords, and discussing the impact of these weapons on the Irish is difficult because they tend to occur either in graves, which are automatically (albeit no doubt correctly) assumed to be Viking, or in culturally-neutral settings such as rivers. Were these swords widely adopted or imitated by Irish warriors? It is surely likely that they were to some extent, but the extent of this borrowing remains unknown. Indeed, if there is some uncertainty about the form of swords used by Irish warriors in the eighth century, there is if anything even less certainty about the forms of swords used in the ninth century. Potentially, the best example of adoption of Viking swords by Irish warriors is the famous sword from Ballinderry crannog, Co. Westmeath (NMI, registration number 1928:382; Bøe 1940, 77–9, Pierce 2002, 63–5), a ninth-century sword found in a probable tenth-century context on a classic Irish site. As I will argue later, however, there are grounds for thinking that Ballinderry is exceptional, rather than typical, in its weaponry assemblage.

There is one clear example of the adoption of Viking weaponry by the Irish. The axe was unknown as a weapon in pre-Viking Ireland and was clearly introduced by the Vikings, probably in the ninth century (Halpin 1999, 47). Thereafter, it was widely adopted by the Irish as a cheaper substitute for the sword, and axes are referred to with great frequency in sources of the eleventh and twelfth centuries as used both by Scandinavians and Irish. By the late twelfth century, Giraldus Cambrensis, the chronicler of the English conquest, depicts it as a veritable national weapon of the Irish. He stated that the Irish used:

> *three types of weapons – short spears, two darts […] and big axes well and carefully forged, which they have taken over from the Norwegians and the Ostmen […]. They are quicker and more expert than any other people in throwing, when everything else fails, stones as missiles, and such stones do great damage to the enemy in an engagement.* (O'Meara 1982, 101)

I will return later to the 'short spears and darts', but for now it should be noted that Giraldus was surprisingly well-informed in knowing that the Irish had adopted the axe from the Norse – a point confirmed by archaeology, since all known battle axes of this period are derived from Scandinavian forms, particularly Petersen's (1919) Type M. Such axes are relatively common in Ireland and generally dated to about the eleventh century (Halpin 2005, 362–3, pl. 3), but there is evidence for a development from the classic Scandinavian forms, characterized by a broadening of the neck of the axehead and a progressively more upward-splaying blade. This process finds its fullest expression in late medieval axeheads dating probably to the thirteenth century, or perhaps later (e.g. Halpin 2005, pls 1, 2, 5), but it can already be seen in two probable twelfth-century examples, one from the River Corrib near Galway (Halpin 2005, pl. 4), and the other from Winetavern Street in Dublin (Fig. 12.1).

EXCAVATED HIBERNO–NORSE WEAPONRY

My research to date has focused primarily on the weaponry found on excavated sites of this period, particularly the National Museum of Ireland's excavations

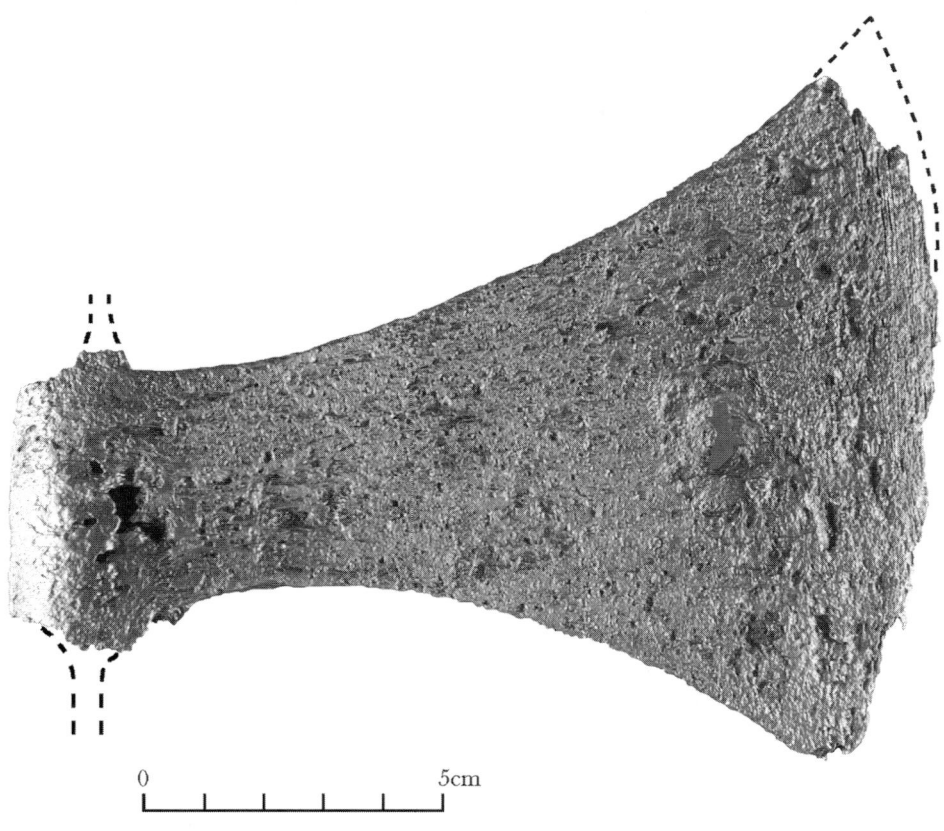

12.1 Twelfth-century iron axehead from Winetavern Street, Dublin (NMI: E81:2428)
(© National Museum of Ireland).

in Dublin (shortly to appear in the *Medieval Dublin Excavations, 1962–81* series),
but including other sites such as Waterford (Halpin 1997). These sites have
produced a substantial assemblage of weaponry, but it is of a quite distinctive
character, since it effectively represents material lost or discarded within the
Hiberno-Norse towns. This is seen by comparing the weaponry assemblage from
the National Museum's excavations in the Hiberno-Norse settlement of Dublin
with that from the nearby and only slightly earlier cemeteries at Kilmainham and
Islandbridge (see table, Fig. 12.2). The latter is characterized by an abundance
of the larger, more prestigious weapons, especially swords, but these are rare on
the settlement sites, where the assemblage is dominated by the humble
arrowhead. The very different profiles of these two weapon assemblages are the
result of different biases operating in the processes both of deposition and (at
least in the case of the cemeteries) of recovery.

Spearheads

Before turning to archery material, I want firstly to look at the next most common weapon type in the settlement site assemblage – spearheads, of which there are over twenty examples from Hiberno-Norse contexts in Dublin. It can be argued that the spear was the most important weapon in medieval warfare, in the sense that it was the most widely used, at all periods and by all social grades. In Ireland, this is surely reflected in the fact that at least twelve different Irish terms for spears occur in early medieval sources (Halpin 1999, 43–5). Attempts to define the differences between these terms, much less reconcile them with an archaeological typology, tend to prove futile, but the terminological diversity clearly points to a corresponding range of forms and functions, especially relating to distinctions between spears intended for throwing, and those intended for use in hand-to-hand fighting. The most striking feature of the spearheads from the excavations in Dublin is their size (Fig. 12.3). Only two of them could even be described as of moderate dimensions, yet they dwarf the other, more typical Dublin spearheads. The longest (NMI, E43:1958), is 35.6cm in length and of Petersen's Type K or Solberg's (1985, 86–87) Type VII.2B. The other large spearhead (NMI, E172:14661) is 29.2cm in length and is a good example of Petersen's Type H, or Solberg's (1985, 122–3) Type IX.3, with a relatively sophisticated pattern-welded blade. When the blade lengths of all the Dublin spearheads are plotted on a histogram (see table, Fig. 12.4), we see that 90 per cent of them are less than 15cm in length and 50 per cent are under 10cm.

Clearly, there are depositional biases at work here – larger spearheads are less likely to be lost or discarded – but I am not aware of any other sites in the Viking world which have produced such a preponderance of small spearheads. This suggests that cultural factors may also be in operation, and at this point we must return to Giraldus's statement about the Irish using small spears and darts – a statement fully confirmed by other documentary sources of the eleventh and twelfth centuries. An emphasis on small, light spears, presumably intended for throwing rather than for hand-to-hand combat, is perfectly understandable in the context of medieval Irish warfare which, for reasons best explained by Simms (1975–6), was characterized by mobility rather than solidity, and by fast-moving skirmishes rather than pitched battles. There is good historical evidence that the Hiberno-Norse adapted to these patterns of warfare, at least on occasion (Halpin 1999, 30–1, 48–53). Are we seeing, in the Dublin spearheads, evidence that they also adapted to Irish weapon standards?

Archery material

It is archery, however, which provides the vast bulk of the weapon assemblage from excavated sites of this period, in Dublin and elsewhere. At the beginning of the Viking period, the bow and arrow had been effectively unknown in Ireland for at least a thousand years, and the Vikings must be credited with the

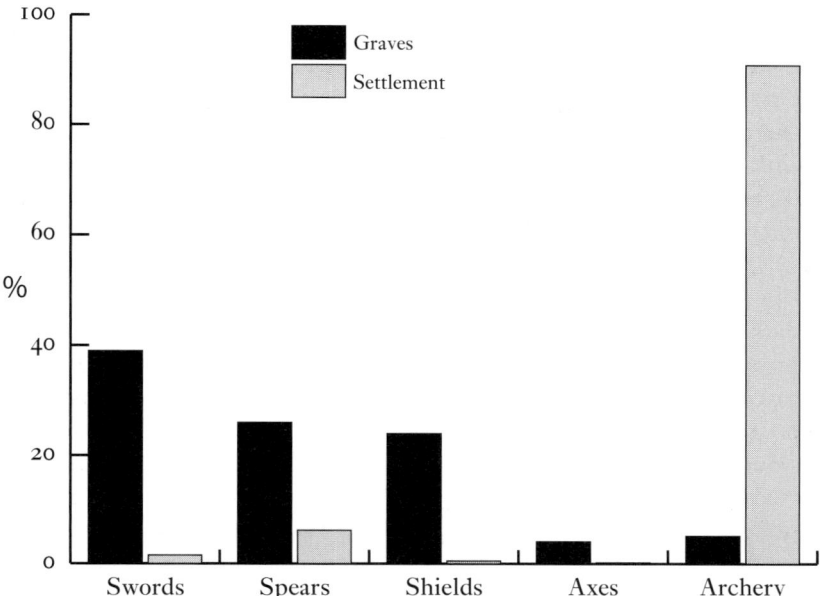

12.2 Table showing proportions of weapon types recovered from Kilmainham/Islandbridge cemeteries ('Graves') and excavated sites in Dublin ('Settlement').

reintroduction of archery. Hiberno-Norse urban sites, particularly in Dublin, have produced many hundreds of iron arrowheads and, while the size of this assemblage may give a misleading picture of the importance of archery in Viking warfare, it does allow us to address statistical and chronological issues in a way that is not possible for other weapon types.

The typology of these arrowheads (Fig. 12.5) breaks down into two main groups: firstly, broad-bladed arrowheads, which can be either leaf-shaped, shouldered or triangular, and secondly, bodkin-bladed arrowheads, with narrow, spike-like blades designed for only one purpose, to penetrate mail armour. These armour-piercing arrowheads make up a substantial majority of the assemblage as a whole – almost 70 per cent – and this underlines the most important feature of this material, its essentially military nature. At least 80 per cent of the Hiberno-Norse arrowhead assemblage can fairly confidently be identified as being military in function, while no more than 5 per cent was definitely intended for hunting. The remainder cannot be categorized with certainty, but I would argue that most of these were likely to have been for military use also.

Both broad blades and bodkin blades occur in tanged and socketed forms. The tanged types are typically Scandinavian and are precisely what one might expect to find in the Hiberno-Norse towns. But the assemblage also includes a range of socketed types which, to my knowledge, are not common in Scandinavia at this

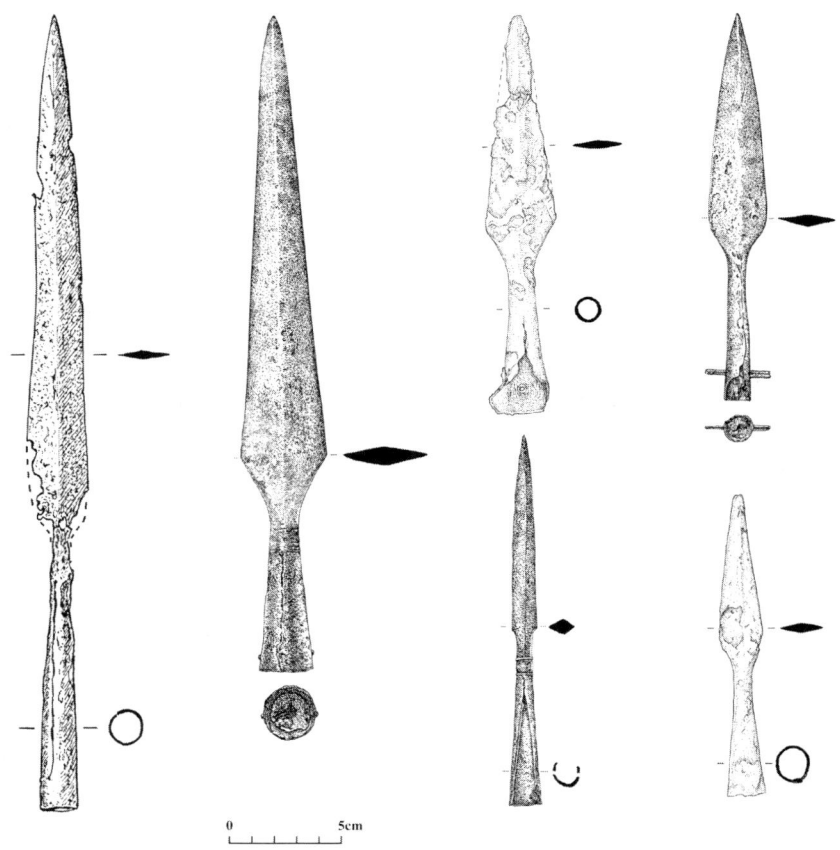

12.3 Spearheads from Hiberno-Norse Dublin.

date. In fact, from the mid-tenth century onwards the popularity of tanged types in Dublin declines rapidly. Could it be that this trend (see table, Fig. 12.6) is in some sense a mirror of the declining Scandinavian character of Dublin and the other Hiberno-Norse towns?

The socketed types are clearly in the majority from the mid-tenth century onward, but their origins represent something of a conundrum if, as currently seems to be the case, these cannot be sought in Scandinavia at this date. It is clear that they are not borrowed from the Irish, because despite the continuous tradition of Viking archery from the early ninth century, there is no evidence for any serious use of the bow by the Irish, at least for military purposes, before the thirteenth century. The entire corpus of arrowheads known from native Irish sites prior to the thirteenth century consists of a total of four arrowheads: two from the Dunbell raths, Co. Kilkenny; and one each from Cahercommaun, Co. Clare and Lagore crannog, Co. Meath (Halpin 1999, 96–7). All are of

Millimetres

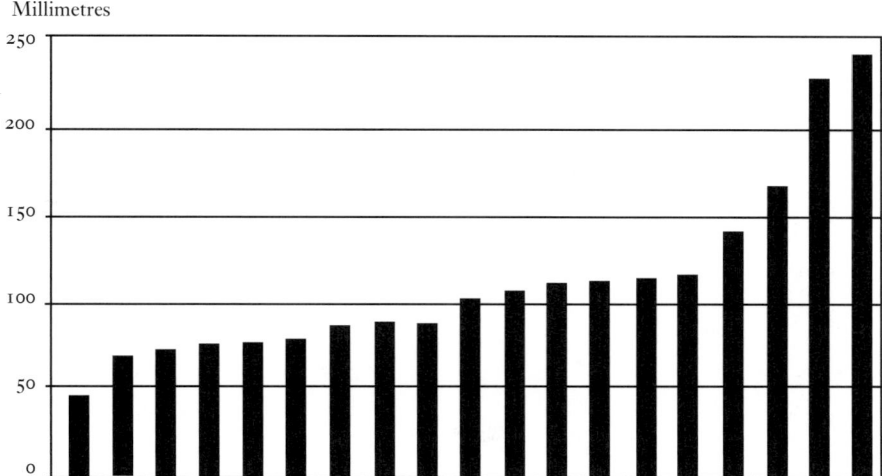

12.4 Table showing blade-lengths of spearheads from Hiberno-Norse contexts in Dublin.

Scandinavian tanged form (Type 1 in Fig. 12.3) and it is extremely doubtful if they can be interpreted as reflecting the activities of the actual inhabitants of these sites. There is, however, one exceptional discovery relevant to this discussion. One of Europe's finest medieval bows was found in a probable tenth-century context at Ballinderry crannog, Co. Westmeath (Hencken 1935–7, 139, 214, 225–6, fig. 8:D). This was no isolated find, for Ballinderry produced a veritable arsenal of 'classic' Viking weaponry: apart from the sword mentioned earlier, a battleaxe, two spearheads and a socketed knife were also found (Hencken 1935–7, 127, 138–9, 143, 156, figs 5:A, C, D, 25:A). Is Ballinderry the outstanding example of the extent to which Viking weaponry was being adopted by the Irish in the tenth century? This may be so, but in view of the lack of any other evidence for Irish archery, the presence of the bow suggests that something atypical was happening at Ballinderry, whatever that may have been.

Finally, I wish to turn my attention the largest group of Hiberno-Norse arrowheads, the armour-piercing types. These first appear in quantity around the middle of the tenth century, in both tanged and socketed forms, and they quickly become dominant in the arrowhead assemblage, accounting for 60 per cent of the total by the eleventh century and rising to over 70 per cent of the total by the early twelfth century. The presence in such large numbers of arrowheads which are designed purely for use against armoured opponents (and which are actually less effective against unarmoured opponents than traditional broad-bladed arrowheads) clearly says something about the prevalence of armour at this period. This seems to make perfect sense in the context of Irish historical sources of the eleventh and twelfth centuries, which consistently indicate the widespread

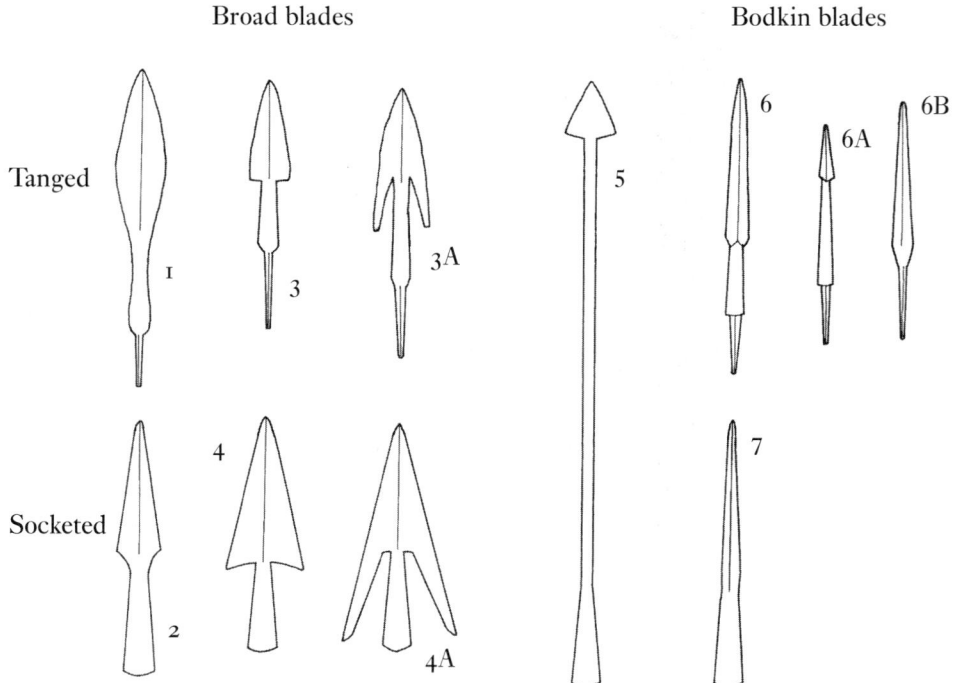

12.5 Typology of Hiberno-Norse arrowheads.

use of armour by Viking and Hiberno-Norse warriors (Halpin 1999, 37–42). However, these same sources are equally adamant that the Irish did not wear armour – indeed, on occasion Irish defeats are explicitly explained in terms of the ineffectiveness of Irish weapons against Viking armour (see, for example, Todd 1867, 53, 67–9; Bugge 1905, 65–6, 101–2). This is at best an overstatement, if not a deliberate distortion of the facts, but there is certainly no evidence for the widespread use of armour by Irish forces and this raises questions about how to interpret the predominance of armour-piercing arrowheads in the Hiberno-Norse towns. Could it be, for instance, that the warriors of Dublin (at least) were mainly concerned to equip themselves for theatres of war outside of Ireland?

Similar patterns have been noted elsewhere. The predominance of armour-piercing arrowheads at the Slavic fortress of Starigard/Oldenburg, on the Baltic coast, was interpreted by Kempke (1988, 301–2) as a response to the emergence of armoured, mounted aristocratic warriors in the Baltic area during the tenth century. In the wider European context, this can be seen as a manifestation of the rise of the *miles*, the armoured, mounted warrior who was such an important

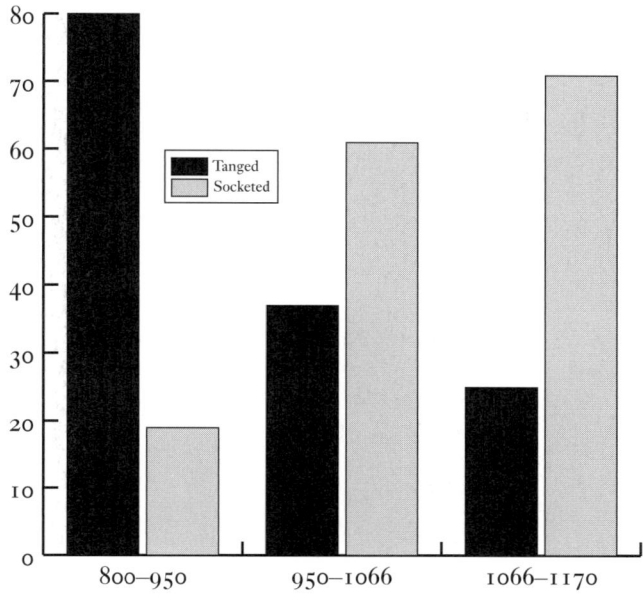

12.6 Table showing relative proportions of tanged and socketed arrowheads in Dublin, by period.

part of the feudal package developing in the tenth century. Kempke also seems to suggest that there was an eastward progression in the shift to armour-piercing arrowheads. Thus, whereas armour-piercing forms are already in the majority in the arrowhead assemblage at Trelleborg in the late tenth century (Nørlund 1948, 137–9), they do not predominate at Starigard until the eleventh century, while further east, at Opole in Poland and Novgorod in Russia, armour-piercing forms are not in the majority until the twelfth century (Kempke 1988, 301–2; table 1). There is no comparable archaeological evidence in Britain, but Brooks (1978, 87–93) has argued from historical sources that it is precisely in the later tenth century that most Anglo-Saxon warriors begin to wear mail armour, apparently at the deliberate encouragement of Aethelred II.

Dublin is apparently in the vanguard of these developments, as 60 per cent of all arrowheads dating to the second half of the tenth century are armour-piercing. Can this be interpreted in the way it has been interpreted further east? Traditionally, Irish historians have tended to argue that feudalism did not reach Ireland until after the English conquest in the late twelfth century, but more recently historians such as Byrne (1987, 10–12) have spoken about the 'feudalization' of Irish society in the two centuries prior to this, the effects of which were particularly noticeable in warfare. Kings now commanded significant numbers of well-equipped full-time and mercenary troops, and had the resources to undertake prolonged campaigns, on water as well as on land, and to fortify their kingdoms with castles. Byrne sees implicit evidence for the existence of a quasi-feudal military class of noble warriors, who increasingly operated on horseback (Byrne 1987, 11). Regardless of whether this should be interpreted in terms of feudalism, it clearly amounts to a radical transformation of Irish warfare, and the Vikings and Hiberno-Norse must be seen as prime agents in this. This can be viewed both in terms of their direct military impact and indirectly, in their opening up of Irish societies to developments elsewhere, and their creation of the wealth necessary for Irish kings to partake of these developments. Thus, despite their very mixed military record in Ireland, the Vikings and their descendants had a profound effect, not just on weaponry, but on Irish military and political development.

BIBLIOGRAPHY

Brooks, N.P. 1978. 'Arms, status and warfare in Late-Saxon England' in D. Hill (ed.) *Ethelred the Unready*. British Archaeological Reports (British Series), 59 (Oxford), 81–103.
Bugge, A. (ed.). 1905. *Caithreim Cellachain Caisil* (Oslo).
Byrne, F.J. 1987. 'The trembling sod: Ireland in 1169' in A. Cosgrove (ed.), *Medieval Ireland, 1169–1534*. New History of Ireland, 2 (Dublin), pp 1–42.
Clarke, H.B. 1990–2. 'The bloodied eagle: the Vikings and the development of Dublin, 841–1014', *Irish Sword*, 18, 91–119.
Graham-Campbell, J. 1980. *Viking artefacts: a select catalogue* (London).
Halpin, A. 1997. 'Archery material' in M.F. Hurley & O.B.M. Scully with S.J. McCutcheon (eds), *Late Viking-Age and Medieval Waterford: excavations, 1986–1992* (Waterford), pp 538–52.
Halpin, A. 1999. 'Archery and warfare in medieval Ireland: a historical and archaeological study' (PhD thesis, University of Dublin).
Halpin, A. 2005. 'The *galloglach* axe revisited' in T. Condit & C. Corlett (eds), *Above and beyond: essays in memory of Leo Swan* (Bray), pp 361–72.
Hencken, H. O'N. 1935–7. 'Ballinderry crannog no.1', *Proceedings of the Royal Irish Academy*, 43C, 103–238.
Kempke, T. 1988. 'Zur überregionalen verbreitung der pfeilspitzentypen des 8–12 jahrhunderts aus Starigard/Oldenberg', *Bericht der Römisch-Germanischen Kommission*, 69, 292–306.
Mallory, J.P. 1981. 'The sword of the Ulster Cycle' in B.G. Scott (ed.), *Studies on early Ireland*, pp 99–114.
Nørlund, P. 1948. *Trelleborg*, Nordiske Fortidsminde, 4:1 (Copenhagen).
O'Meara, J.J. (trans.). 1982. *Gerald of Wales: the history and topography of Ireland* (London).
Peirce, I. 2002. *Swords of the Viking-Age* (Woodbridge).

Petersen, J. 1919. *De Norske vikingesverd: en typologisk-kronologisk studie over vikingetidens vaaben* (Oslo).

Rynne, E. 1956. 'Irish iron weapons of pre-Norman times' (MA thesis, National University of Ireland).

Rynne, E. 1966. 'The impact of the Vikings on Irish weapons', *Atti del VI Congresso Internazionale delle Scienze Preistoriche e Protostoriche*, 3 (Rome), 181–5.

Rynne, E. 1981. 'A classification of pre-Viking Irish iron swords' in B.G. Scott (ed.), *Studies on early Ireland: essays in honour of M.V. Duignan*, pp 93–7.

Scott, A.B. & F.X. Martin (eds). 1978. *Giraldus Cambrensis: Expugnatio Hibernica* (Dublin).

Scott, B.G. (ed.), 1981 *Studies on early Ireland: essays in honour of M.V. Duignan* (Belfast).

Scott, B.G. 1990. *Early Irish ironworking* (Belfast).

Simms, K. 1975–6. 'Warfare in the medieval Gaelic lordships', *Irish Sword*, 12, 98–108.

Solberg, B. 1985. 'Norwegian spearheads from the Merovingian and Viking Periods' (PhD thesis, University of Bergen).

Todd, J.H. (ed.). 1867. *Cogadh Gaedhel re Gallaibh* (London).

Walsh, A. 1998. 'A summary classification of Viking-Age swords in Ireland' in H.B. Clarke, M. Ní Mhaonaigh & R. Ó Floinn (eds), *Ireland and Scandinavia in the Early Viking Age* (Dublin), pp 222–35.

The Suffolk Street sword: further notes on the College Green cemetery, Dublin

STEPHEN H. HARRISON

The last volume of the *Proceedings of the Viking Congress* included a paper (Harrison 2005) on a neglected group of 'Viking' graves from Dublin that had been reassessed as part of the Irish Viking Graves Project, based at the National Museum of Ireland (hereafter NMI). These graves, found at College Green (NGR O 159 341), form part of a remarkable concentration of Viking-Age furnished burial sites in the Dublin area (Ó Floinn 1998, 131–43), of which Kilmainham and Islandbridge/Inchicore are perhaps the best known (e.g. O'Brien 1998). The modern College Green is the last remnant of much larger open area situated to the east of the Poddle, a small tributary of the Liffey which marked the eastern limit of enclosed settlement of Dublin from at least the tenth century onwards (Gowan with Scally 1996, 11–14). In the Middle Ages, this open area was called Hoggen Green, a name clearly derived from ON *haugr* or 'mound', the largest of which, the 'Hogges', was situated some 400m east of the Poddle, between the modern College Green and Suffolk Street (Clarke 2002, 3; Harrison 2005, 330, 336). Haliday (1881, 162–6), who first drew attention to this monument, used a late seventeenth-century survey to estimate its circumference at 240ft (giving a diameter of *c.*22m) and its height at 40ft (12.2m). This very substantial mound would have dominated the surrounding, flat landscape and provided excellent views across the Liffey estuary and the inner part of Dublin Bay. Indeed, the earliest record of it, preserved in the Norman French *Deeds of the Normans in Ireland* (also known as the *Song of Dermot and the Earl*), describes Domnall Mac Gilla Mo-Cholmóc standing on '*la Hogges*' to witness a battle between Anglo-Norman and Hiberno-Norse forces at the east gate of Dublin in 1171 (Orpen 1892, 170–1; Mullally 2002, 112). Haliday (1881, 169–71) was also the first to suggest that this mound was the 'Thingmotte', the formal assembly site of Dublin's *Þing*, an interpretation that has been followed by several other commentators, who have compared the mound's stepped profile, shown in a surviving document, to Tynwald Hill, a stepped mound traditionally associated with the Manx parliament (Harrison 2005, 334), and perhaps also the similar (destroyed) mound called Doomster Hill at Govan, on the Clyde (Ritchie 1999, 19). Duffy (1998, 82–5), on the other hand, has dismissed this idea, arguing that while 'Thingmotte' was a suburb of Dublin, there is no evidence that the name was ever applied to 'the Hogges'. The 'motte' of Thingmotte is derived from the ON *mót* or 'meeting', and has none of the connotations of a 'mound' associated with the Norman French or Latin *mota*, as Haliday assumed. Nonetheless, artificial mounds are frequently found at early medieval assembly grounds in both England and Ireland, and it remains entirely possible that the 'Hogges' had similar associations with Dublin's Viking-Age assembly (Harrison 2005, 335).

It has sometimes been suggested that the Hogges was originally a burial mound, but despite its considerable scale (Ó Floinn 1998, 136), there are no records of any graves having been disturbed during its demolition, which took place in 1685 (Haliday 1881, 163). In 1647, however, when a rather smaller mound 'near Trinity College' was levelled, what appears to have been a long cist with some form of 'pillar stones' at its corners and a standing stone at its head or foot was discovered (Ware 1658, 348–50; Harrison 2005, 330–1). Although no artefacts were found and its date is uncertain, the monument has parallels with some early medieval Scottish graves (Alcock 1992, 127–8: Close-Brooks 1980, 327–30) and is likely to have been of similar, if not specifically Viking-Age, date. More certain evidence for 'Viking' (i.e. 'ninth-tenth-century furnished') burial at College Green is provided by a group of eight artefacts found immediately to the east of the Hogges, at the site of the Royal Arcade, presumably during its construction in 1819. These artefacts – two swords, four spearheads, a shield boss and a tinned copper-alloy and amber buckle – were acquired by the Royal Irish Academy (hereafter RIA) as part of the Sirr collection in 1844 (NMI/RIA Archive) and were discussed in the previous article, the swords indicating a minimum of two graves, although the spearheads suggest that the original total may have been a little higher (Harrison 2005, 331–4).

The present paper focuses on another group of graves which were found about thirty years after the Royal Arcade examples, on the south rather than the east side of the Hogges, in the modern Suffolk Street. Haliday (1881, 155) had provided a slightly confused account of a 'recently exhumed' skeleton with a metal (presumably rust) stained skull 'supposed to be a helmet', which had been found there, 'in the same locality' as a 'valuable Danish sword' and an 'urn', but he did not provide a source for this information (Harrison 2005, 333–4). However, recent research has uncovered further information about these burials and has led to the identification of what is almost certainly Haliday's 'Danish sword' within the NMI collection.

THE SUFFOLK STREET BURIALS

Although Haliday's ground-breaking *Scandinavian Kingdom of Dublin* was published in 1881, it should be remembered that this was some fifteen years after his death in 1866, and that much of his research seems to have taken place at an earlier date again, between *c.*1850 and *c.*1856 (Predergast 1866, xlvi, xcix, c). There is very little evidence to suggest that J.P. Predergast, his editor, made any substantial changes to his original text, and consequently it would seem that Haliday's 'recent' discoveries are more likely to have occurred around the 1850s rather than the 1870s. Between 1830 and 1863, number 3, Suffolk Street, was occupied by one Richard Glennon, an individual variously described as a 'preserver of birds and beasts', 'dealer in mineralogy, shells &c.', 'antique coins', 'mining agent', 'bird stuffer', and from 1856 onwards 'dealer in antiquities' (Anon 1830, 75; 1840, 448; 1856, 1062; 1863, 1389). Briggs (1978, 147), who cited a reference to the premises as 'the queerest little shop in Dublin', published excerpts of a letter and note from Glennon and his wife, which has been preserved among the Bateman papers in the Sheffield City Museum. Attempting to sell a 'Celtic' skull to the antiquarian Thomas Bateman, Glennon noted that it had been found

> … in sinking a shore opposite our house in Suffolk Street it was 10 feet from the surface some years ago there was found (about 10 yards from where the skull dug up [*sic*]) a skeleton of a Man of enormous size with a complete suit of armour ornamented with gold and a Gold hilted sword [*sic*]. They are in Trinity College, Dublin. The skull is supposed to be that of a Warrior from the numbers of deep cuts on his forehead and top of head, some of which had healed up while he was living.

Dated 22 May 1855, the letter describes a discovery that may well have been 'recent' when Haliday was compiling his notes. Glennon also seems to have acquired further material at approximately this time, notably two bronze axes, which were acquired by the Dublin antiquarian, Thomas Ray, and eventually passed to the NMI. A transcript of a label written by Glennon himself is preserved in the RIA/NMI 'New Register' (1906:435–6), stating that these artefacts were found 'when sinking [the] main sewer opposite No. 3 Suffolk St Dublin in May 1857 *near* a skeleton of a man lying North and South. A clay urn full of bones was found about the same time …' Two sources refer to a 'shore' or 'sewer', two refer to the discovery of a gold hilted sword, all refer to a skeleton (with two emphasizing its skull), two record the presence of a nearby 'urn', and two date the discovery to May. If it is assumed that the 'New Register' year is a transcription error, the coincidence of detail in these accounts is striking. Correlating Glennon and Haliday's accounts, the sword accompanied an inhumation burial, *allegedly* of a large individual, which had been found 'some years' before 1855 (perhaps *c.*1850) and *c.*9m from the point where a second inhumation burial was later found (probably in May 1855). While the first skeleton is unlikely to have had 'armour', a composite (gilt?) copper-alloy and iron artefact or artefacts may well have been placed in the grave with the sword. Both Haliday and Glennon emphasized the second skeleton's skull, the first because it was 'metal stained' and the second because of its 'wounds', with the

Ray label indicating that what was presumably the same skeleton was orientated north-south. Modern commentators would suggest that the 'helmet' suggested by Haliday is more likely to have been a shield boss (Ó Floinn 1998, 136), an interpretation which has also been applied to an early nineteenth-century account of a grave at Parnell Square on the opposite side of the Liffey estuary (Walker 1818, 131fn; Bøe 1940, 67). Three metres, the recorded depth of this second skeleton, is unusually deep for a Viking grave, but at 13½ft (4.1m), the bronze axes were also located well below the surface (RIA/NMI archive), and it seems likely that part of the Hogges may have been spread over this area during its demolition. It is certainly believed that material from the mound was used to raise the level of Nassau Street, the eastern continuation of Suffolk Street (Haliday 1881, 161).

THE SUFFOLK STREET SWORD

Unlike the second burial, the depth and precise recovery circumstances of the first skeleton (*c.*1850) remain uncertain. However, Glennon's note to Bateman clearly states that the sword (and indeed the 'armour') which accompanied it were in Trinity College, Dublin. A detailed history of the College's nineteenth-century museums (for there were several) is beyond the capacity of the present paper (see Crooke 2000, 101), but the mid-1840s saw the employment of Robert Ball as Director of the Dublin University Museum, who spent several years struggling to organize and record its diverse collections, which included geology, mineralogy, zoology, botany and 'ethnological science' as well as 'antiquities' (Ball 1846, 1847, 1848). Surviving acquisition records stretch from *c.*1845 to the end of 1848, but contain no references to anything that might be considered a 'Viking sword', even though one of Ball's early aims was the creation of an 'armoury' that would include chronological exhibits of European weapons (1846, 2). Nonetheless, when the Museum's archaeological material was presented to the RIA in 1882, this assemblage included a single Viking Age sword (RIA/NMI archive). As Ball's death in 1857 (Jellet 1858, 30) presumably marked the end of the University's active acquisition of 'antiquities', this sword must have been acquired between 1849 and 1857, a period for which no surviving records can be found at present. While a small number of graves at Kilmainham were found in this period (specifically in 1847, 1848, 1849 and 1851), the RIA's close relationship with the Young family seems to have resulted in their acquisition of this material in its entirety (IVGP forthcoming). The Suffolk Street sword is the only other example from Dublin known to have been found in this period, and is also the only one specifically stated to have been in Trinity College. Furthermore, this statement was made by an individual who lived a short walk from its main gate, and who, as a taxidermist, may have had direct links with its Museum through its extensive zoological collection. Thus, it seems almost certain that the 'Trinity College' sword is that from Suffolk Street.

Although the Trinity College material, as part of the RIA collection, passed to the Dublin Museum of Science and Art (now the NMI) following the latter's establishment at the end of the nineteenth century (Crooke 2000, 121), it has proved difficult to identify the sword within its modern collection. Unfortunately, several Viking-Age swords have almost identical lengths and these were confused when William Wakeman first catalogued them in the 1890s. The Trinity College sword was confused with another example acquired in 1872, and (as Wk32) was incorrectly provenanced to Dollymount, Dublin (NMI archive). However, this sword has an older label (1882:153), clearly identifying it as part of the Trinity College group, and corresponds precisely with the relevant 'New Register' entry. Consequently, Wakeman's provenance cannot be correct and the sword now known as Wk32/1882:153 is definitely that from the Dublin University Museum, not Dollymount, and thus almost certainly that from Suffolk Street.

Today, this 54cm long double-edged sword has an intact, if corroded, hilt, but most of its lower blade has broken away, and more unusually a hole has been punched through the blade a short distance below the guard. All of this damage had already occurred in 1882. While it is tempting to suggest that the hole was created for display purposes, it is perhaps more likely to have occurred during its recovery. If it formed part of the deposition ritual, on the other hand, it would apparently be entirely unique. The sword's patina is entirely different to that of the artefacts from the Royal Arcade (Harrison 2005, 331–4), but this seems to be the result of intensive cleaning, which has also affected the hilt. The upper and lower guards, both rectangular with rounded ends, have no surviving decoration, but fragments of twisted wire are visible on one side of the pommel, which seems originally to have been lobed. Sceptics may argue that this is hardly the gold hilt described by Glennon, let alone what Haliday (1881:155) called 'one of the most valuable Danish swords discovered in Ireland, the gold ornaments of the handle having been sold for £70', but it is clear that the latter account in particular is highly exaggerated. None of the elaborately hilted swords found at Islandbridge (Wilde 1866) were valued at more than a pound each in 1866 (RIA/NMI archive). Haliday's comment can, however, be compared to those of J. Huband Smith, who believed that a labourer who discovered a Viking grave at Kilmainham *c.*1836 had secreted 'some ornaments of gold of considerable value … [the effects of which became] speedily apparent in a well-stocked shop, which he afterwards opened in a village not ten miles distant from Dublin (Smith 1841, 44)'. Clearly, the city's antiquarians were suspicious of the morals of Dublin's labourers, although they remained perfectly happy to negotiate with them under different circum-stances. In reality, few Viking-Age artefacts have any bullion value, although if, as seems likely, this sword is an example of Petersen's Type K, it may well have been decorated with silver and copper-alloy wire originally (Walsh 1998, 230–2), and have looked rather more impressive when first recovered.

DISCUSSION

If this classification is correct (and the damaged pommel makes it difficult to be absolutely certain), this is the second sword of this type known from College Green, the other (Sirr 261) coming from the Royal Arcade. Although both can be dated to the ninth century, the latter example is single-edged and therefore potentially slightly earlier. The third (extant) sword from the site (Sirr 260) is of Petersen's Type H, and could be of ninth- or tenth-century date, but while the possibility of a later burial cannot be entirely ruled out, it seems that the College Green cemetery is broadly contemporary with the overwhelming majority of burials from Dublin, and of ninth-century date (Ó Floinn 1998, 137–8).

While the cemetery's date remains unchanged by this new evidence, it confirms a pattern of burial whereby graves occur at the eastern and southern edges of the Hogges, rather than within the mound itself. This strongly suggests that the mound pre-dates at least the majority of the Viking-Age graves surrounding it, and adds weight to the theory that it has a prehistoric (or at least pre-Viking Age) origin. The re-use of extant mounds for 'Viking' burial is not uncommon, particularly in Scotland, but these 'secondary' burials are normally placed in the mounds' upper levels, as at Boiden, Argyll & Bute (Stewart 1854) and Tote, Skye (Lethbridge 1920). There are, however, some instances of graves placed at the edges of mounds, perhaps most notably in the antiquarian records of Pierowall, Orkney (Thorsteinsson 1968, 168–9). It is also interesting to note that at least two Viking-Age burials have been found close to Tynwald Hill (Wilson 1974, 20), albeit slightly further from it than those at College Green. While the absence of reliable excavation records for either area makes detailed comparison problematic, it is also interesting to note that both mounds occur in areas that were clearly foci for prehistoric ritual activity. At Tynwald Hill, a Bronze Age cist has been found a short distance from the mound (Cubbon 1973, 33), and the (lost) 'urn' noted by both Haliday and Glennon (above) was presumably of similar date, with the surviving bronze axes providing further evidence for Bronze-Age ritual activity at College Green (Harrison 2005, 331).

While it is perhaps uncertain that the Hiberno-Norse community were aware of this (subterranean) material, it should be pointed out that as many as 20 per cent of 'Viking' burial sites occur in places which also have evidence for prehistoric activity, a figure that can hardly be coincidental (Harrison 2007, 197). College Green is, however, the only burial site at Dublin with prehistoric associations, although several other sites occur at contemporary Christian, or at least indigenous, burial grounds, notably St Michael le Pole (Simpson 2000, 17–19), Donnybrook (O'Brien 1992), and of course Kilmainham and Islandbridge/Inchicore (O'Brien 1998, 40–1), as well as the recent discovery at Finglas (Sikora, this volume). Again, this reflects broader trends across Britain and Ireland, where no less than 29 per cent of Viking-Age burial sites have similar associations, with the phenomenon being most common in the area south of the North Channel (Harrison 2007, 195). While detailed discussion of these two forms of site re-use is beyond the current paper, it should be pointed out that both can be considered as attempts to associate the graves of newcomers with older, more local burial traditions, perhaps in the interests of strengthening the authority of their successors (ibid., 198).

In the case of College Green in particular, it may not be entirely unreasonable to suggest that the deposition of what were clearly high-status graves around the base of the Hogges may also have further enhanced the prestige of this monument among the emergent Hiberno-Norse community. At the very least, the burial evidence confirms that the site, which was clearly significant in the twelfth century, was also important in the ninth. While this does not necessarily demonstrate direct continuity, and the relationship between the burials and the later assembly ground remains uncertain, it does demonstrate the symbolic importance of the site in both the earlier and later periods of Dublin's development as an Hiberno-Norse city. Although scholars are only beginning to give Hoggen Green, the Hogges, and (the) Thingmotte some of the attention which they clearly deserve, it is hoped that future research, both historical and archaeological, will improve our understanding of what is perhaps the least understood of Dublin's early suburbs.

ACKNOWLEDGMENTS

As on previous occasions, much of this paper has been based on work carried out as part of the Irish Viking Graves Project. I am grateful to the IVGP, particularly Raghnall Ó Floinn, Head of Collections at the NMI, for permission to publish this material in advance of the forthcoming Catalogue. Any errors, particularly those relating to the interpretation of this new evidence, are entirely my own.

BIBLIOGRAPHY

Alcock, E. 1992. 'Burials and cemeteries in Scotland' in N. Edwards & R. Lane (eds), *The Early Church in Wales and the West*, Oxbow Monograph 16 (Oxford), pp 125–9.
Anon. 1830. *The treble almanac of the year 1830* (Dublin).
Anon. 1840. *The Dublin almanac, and general register of Ireland* (Dublin).
Anon. 1856 & 1863. *Thom's Irish almanac and official directory of the United Kingdom of Great Britain and Ireland* (Dublin).
Ball, R. 1846. *First report on the progress of the Dublin University Museum, January 1846* (Dublin).
Ball, R. 1847. *Second report on the progress of the Dublin University Museum, June 1847* (Dublin).
Ball, R. 1848. *Third report on the progress of the Dublin University Museum, December 1848* (Dublin).

Briggs, S. 1978. 'Dealing with antiquities in nineteenth-century Dublin', *Irish Historical Record*, 31.4, 146–8.

Bøe, J. 1940. 'Norse antiquities in Ireland' in H. Shetelig (ed.), *Viking antiquities in Great Britain and Ireland* 3 (Oslo).

Clarke, H.B., M. Ní Mhaonaigh & R. Ó Floinn (eds). 1998. *Ireland and Scandinavia in the Early Viking Age* (Dublin).

Close-Brooks, J. 1980. 'Excavations at the Dairy Park, Dunrobin, Sutherland, 1977', *Proceedings of the Society of Antiquaries of Scotland*, 110, 327–80

Crooke, E. 2000. *Politics, archaeology and the creation of a National Museum of Ireland: an expression of national life* (Dublin).

Cubbon, A.M. 1973. *The ancient and historic monuments of the Isle of Man* (Douglas).

Duffy, S. 1998. 'Ireland's Hastings: the Anglo-Norman conquest of Dublin' in C. Harper-Bill (ed.) *Anglo-Norman Studies*, 20, pp 69–86

Gowan, M. with G. Scally, 1996. *A summary report of excavations at Exchange Street Upper / Parliament Street, Dublin: Temple Bar Archaeological Report*, 4 (Dublin).

Haliday, C. 1881 (reprint. 1961). *The Scandinavian kingdom of Dublin* (Dublin; reprint Shannon).

Harrison, S.H. 2005. 'College Green: a neglected 'Viking' cemetery at Dublin' in A. Mortensen & S.V. Arge (eds), *Viking and Norse in the North Atlantic: select papers from the proceedings of the Fourteenth Viking Congress, Tórshavn, 19–30 July 2001* (Tórshavn), pp 329–39.

Harrison, S.H. 2007. 'Separated from the foaming maelstrom: landscapes of Insular "Viking" Burial' in S. Semple & H. Williams (eds), *Anglo-Saxon Studies in Archaeology and History*, 14, 194–201.

Jellett, J.J. 1858. 'Council report', *Proceedings of the Royal Irish Academy*, 7, 29–31

Lethbridge, T.C. 1920. 'A burial of the 'Viking Age' in Skye', *The Archaeological Journal*, 77, 135–6.

Mullally, E. 2002. *The deeds of the Normans in Ireland:* la geste des Engleis en Yrlande (Dublin).

O'Brien, E. 1992. 'A reassessment of the 'great sepulchral mound' containing a Viking burial at Donnybrook, Dublin', *Medieval Archaeology*, 36, 170–3.

O'Brien, E. 1998. 'A reconsideration of the location and context of Viking burials at Kilmainham / Islandbridge, Dublin' in C. Manning (ed.) *Dublin and beyond the Pale: studies in honour of Patrick Healy* (Dublin), pp 35–44.

Ó Floinn, R. 1998. 'The archaeology of the early Viking Age in Ireland' in H.B. Clarke et al. (eds), *Ireland and Scandinavia*, pp 131–65.

Orpen, G.H. (ed.). 1892, *The Song of Dermot and the Earl* (Oxford).

Prendergast, J.P. 1866 (reprint 1961). 'Some notice of the life of Charles Haliday' in C. Haliday, *The Scandinavian Kingdom of Dublin* (Dublin; reprint Shannon), iii–cxiii.

Ritchie, A. 1999. *Govan and its carved stones* (Balgavies).

Walker, J.C. 1818 (2nd ed.). *Historical memoirs of the Irish bards: an historical essay on the dress of the ancient and modern Irish, addressed to the Rt. Hon. Earl of Charlemont to which is subjoined a memoir of the armour and weapons of the Irish* (Dublin).

Smith, J.H. 1841. 'An account of the discovery, in the month of November last, of a human skeleton, accompanied with weapons, ornaments, &c., interred on the sea shore, in the vicinity of Larne, in the county of Antrim', *Proceedings of the Royal Irish Academy*, 2, 40–6.

Simpson, L. 2000. 'Forty years a-digging: a preliminary synthesis of archaeological investigations in Medieval Dublin' in S. Duffy (ed.) *Medieval Dublin 1* (Dublin), pp 11–68.

Stewart, H.J., 'Notice on the discovery of some ancient arms and armour, near Glenfruin, on the estate of Sir James Colquhoun of Luss, Baronet' *Proceedings of the Society of Antiquaries of Scotland*, 1 (1854), pp 142–5.

Thorsteinsson, A. 1968. 'The Viking burial place at Pierowall, Westray, Orkney' in B. Niclasen (ed.), *Proceedings of the Fifth Viking Congress, Tórshavn, July 1965*, (Tórshavn, 1968), pp 150–73.

Walsh, A. 1998. 'A summary classification of Viking-Age swords in Ireland' in Clarke et al. (eds), *Ireland and Scandinavia*, pp 222–35.

Ware, J. 1658 (2nd ed.). *De Hibernia et antiquitatibus eius, disquisitiones* (London).

Wilde, W. 1866, 'On the Scandinavian antiquities lately discovered at Islandbridge, near Dublin', *Proceedings of the Royal Irish Academy*, 10, 13–22.

Wilson, D.M. 1974. *The Viking Age in the Isle of Man: the archaeological evidence* (Odense).

Who were the *Papar*? Typological structures in *Íslendingabók*

PERNILLE HERMANN

According to *Íslendingabók* (1122–33), there were Christians called *papar* (monks, priests) in Iceland before the Norse settlement. These *papar* were believed to be Irish, which was evident from the books, bells and croziers they left behind:

> *Í þann tíð vas Ísland viði vaxit á miðli fjalls ok fjöru. Þá váru hér menn kristnir, þeir es Norðmenn kalla papa, en þeir fóru síðan á braut, af því at þeir vildu eigi vesa hér við heiðna menn, ok létu eptir bækr írskar ok bjöllur !! ok bagla; af því mátti skilja, at þeir váru menn írskir.* (*Íslendingabók*, 5)

'At that time Iceland was covered with forests between mountains and seashore. Then Christian men whom the Norsemen call monks were here. But they went away, because they did not wish to live here together with heathen men, and they left behind Irish books, bells and croziers, from this it could be seen that they were Irishmen'.

Another Old-Icelandic work, *Landnámabók*, also mentions the presence of *papar* in Iceland. It describes them in almost the same way as does *Íslendingabók*: the *papar* were believed to have come from the West, and again books, bells and croziers are mentioned as evidence that they were Irish (*Landnámabók*, 31–2). The *papar* in the North Atlantic have been widely studied in recent years, especially in the Papar Project, begun in 2001 by Barbara Crawford. The project investigates locations associated with *papar* names in the North Atlantic to get a better understanding of the underlying geographical, environmental and cultural factors. As regards to Iceland, archaeological investigations are not conclusive on the question of pre-Norse activity (Guðrún Sveinbjarnardóttir 2002, 101–6; Kristján Ahronson 2002; cf. Crawford 2002, 9–10). Crawford points to an important aspect of the somehow inconclusive results of archaeology: 'But what else can one expect? Small bands of Irish monastic explorers and ascetics were not going to leave large amounts of material evidence for future archaeologists to discover and analyse' (2002, 10). Nor does the study of place-names provide firm conclusions. Place-names are not easy to date, and it remains an open question whether the Icelandic *papar* names belong to the eighth century or whether the Norse settlers (who could have known *papar* traditions from elsewhere in the North Atlantic) brought the names with them to Iceland and applied them to specific locations (Guðrún Sveinbjarnardóttir 2002, 101–6; MacDonald 2002, 21–2).

What of the Old-Icelandic works, *Íslendingabók* and *Landnámabók*? Can they be taken as evidence for the existence of *papar* in Iceland? Most scholars believe that the information about *papar* in *Landnámabók* derives from *Íslendingabók* (cf. Jakob Benediktson 1968, 32): this makes *Íslendingabók* the only Icelandic text that refers independently to the presence of *papar* in Iceland. It has been argued that Ari Þorgilsson, the author of *Íslendingabók*, got his information about the *papar* from an earlier non-Icelandic work, *De mensura orbis terrae* (*c.*825), written by the Irish monk Dícuil (Helgi Gudmundsson 1997). Dícuil mentions that monks had lived in islands north of Britain, and one of these, Thule, is (as stated by many, and among them Raymond Lamb) 'reasonably identifiable as Iceland' (Lamb 1995, 13). Guðrún Sveinbjarnardóttir, however, reminds us that, taken at face value, the proposed textual relationship leaves Dícuil's work as the only independent written source for *papar* in Iceland and, since Dícuil does not explicitly mention Iceland, the presence of *papar* there cannot be proved from his work alone (Guðrún Sveinbjarnardóttir 2002, 99).

Of course, the fact that it has not been finally proved that *papar* were in Iceland does not mean that they were absent. In this paper, I will draw no firm conclusions about this question. My principal concern is not to elucidate an eighth-century reality but to discuss a twelfth-century tradition. In effect, this will be done through an analysis of *Íslendingabók*, the Old-Icelandic work that records that, regardless of what happened before the Norse settlement, there existed in the twelfth century a tradition about *papar* which was considered worth including in the first piece of Icelandic historiography. Here I will not try to prove or disprove what lies behind the notice of the *papar* and their appurtenances, nor will I discuss their possible communities and religious affiliations. Instead, the *papar* will be interpreted within their immediate literary context, *Íslendingabók*.

However, before I move on to this matter, a few words should be said about twelfth-century tradition. Aidan MacDonald has emphasized four aspects that are inherent in the *papar* phenomenon. Of these, one is a memory of and creative reflection on actual encounters between Norsemen and *papar* in the North Atlantic, and the tradition that developed about such a background. MacDonald writes:

> [A] tradition develops, originally oral, eventually written, which possibly both influences and is influenced by similar traditions, native and foreign: those fashioned by the Norse themselves out of the stuff of their explorations of the North Atlantic and its coasts and islands; and those received by them from others during their interaction, more or less prolonged, with its various peoples and cultures (2002, 21).

Here, MacDonald points out that the tradition was open to assimilating new elements depending upon its geographical and social setting; and consequently variants of the *papar* tradition may have existed. The creative background of the *papar* tradition could also be formulated in terms of the concept of 'cultural memory', a concept introduced by Jan Assmann, which has to do with a culture's continuous construction of narratives of the past to give meaning to the shifting needs of the present (Assmann 1992). This concept invokes a constructive and functionalist view on history, namely, that preoccupation with the past has to do not only with recording the past as such but with establishing its meaning at the time of writing. Another aspect (also mentioned by MacDonald) is how elements associated with the *papar*, such as place-names, when first established, subsequently seem to have contributed to a 'learned rationalization' of tradition (2002, 21). MacDonald emphasizes Iceland in this connection (rightly, I believe), and it seems relevant to discuss the possibility of a learned rationalization of tradition in Iceland. Could it not be that in integrating the *papar* in the Icelandic history, *Íslendingabók* contributed to a learned rationalization of the tradition? Ari, the author of *Íslendingabók*, lived in the Christian world and looked back on a pagan one. A challenge for him, as the first to write the history of Iceland, was how to combine pagan and Christian material and how to treat of such different periods as integral parts of the same history. One solution is to impose a learned interpretation on the Icelandic past. Typology and allegory were learned strategies that could be used to give meaning to past events, pagan and Christian (cf. McCone 1990, 56). Interpreted typologically or allegorically, an event from pagan time could be transposed from an otherwise pre-Christian and ahistorical context to meaningful history, one could make the irrational rational. Through such interpretative strategies or organizing principles, past events that could otherwise be dismissed as unedifying may be seen as significant in the history of salvation. Here, I suggest that the description of the settlement is an essential and integral part of what may be called *Íslendingabók*'s typological structure, and that the *papar* can be understood as a meaningful element within that structure. Seen in this light, the structure of events in *Íslendingabók* may be taken to be indebted to learned medieval typological paradigms and to salvation history (Hermann 2007).

How, then, is the settlement described in *Íslendingabók*? A Norwegian called Ingólfr is said to have been the first man to settle in Iceland. We are told where he first went ashore and where he settled. Both places are mapped through place-names. We are told that at the time of his settlement, Iceland was covered with forests from mountain to shore. This description gives the impression of wild nature and an empty land. The place-names connected to Ingólfr, Ingólfshöfði and Ingólfsfell, impose a structure to that landscape, since these new places differentiate and relativize the landscape. In this way, orientation is established, and the land is no longer empty. Thus place-names give meaning to an empty land, and directly connect the first settler to the new place.

But the land is not really as empty as one is led to believe. Following the description of the landscape, we are told that *papar* were already there. The reference to the *papar* conveys two central messages: firstly, Christian clerics were on the island at the time of settlement and, secondly, they left when the Norwegian settlers came. What follows is based on the premise that the indication of the presence of the clerics is as important as their leaving.

The *departure* of the *papar* makes it possible to consider the new land uninhabited and allows one to construct the history of the Icelanders as a *creatio ex nihilo*, as a whole new culture built from the bottom up. Because the land is empty, the settlement can be understood in terms of a cultural paradigm that involves neither war nor the assimilation of an earlier population. There is a single cultural paradigm, 'the emigration from Norway' (cf. Lindow 1997, 456; Glauser 2000). As I have said, the place-names connected to the first settler, Ingólfr, establish new places that constitute bases of authority and points of reference within this cultural paradigm. Inasmuch as they establish an identity between person and land, the Norse settlement is inscribed on the landscape.

The *presence* of the *papar*, on the other hand, is significant inasmuch as it imposes a certain meaning on the empty land; even if the land was at first sight empty, it was not *terra nullius*. Together with the material objects – the bells, books and croziers, which are Christian symbols – the presence of the *papar* defines the specific character of the land. They and their religious objects give grounds for considering the apparently wild nature and empty land as *Christiana terrena*, as consecrated ground, and thus this land may be viewed as the Lord's. Seen in this light, a promised-land motif, representing the newly discovered landscape as ideal (Frakes 2001, 170), may be implicit in Ari's image of Iceland. Margaret Clunies Ross has tied the statement that the land was covered with forests to ideas of fertility and, according to her, the spiritual force associated with the *papar* and their religious objects, together with such fertility, convey a sense of paradisiacal land (Clunies Ross 1998, 145). The Christian character of the land is emphasized, if only by contrast, in the description of another settlement in *Íslendingabók*, namely that of Greenland (*Íslendingabók*, 13–14). This follows the same pattern as Ingólfr's settlement in Iceland. Firstly, the description of Greenland includes a place-name, Eiríksfjǫrðr, connected to the discoverer, Eiríkr inn rauði, and, secondly, the Icelandic discoverers of Greenland also make finds revealing that other people had been there earlier. In the case of Greenland, however, the objects revealing the presence of these others are not, as in Iceland, Christian symbols but fragments of boats and stone tools. Within *Íslendingabók*, the finds serve to assign significance to a given place: unlike Iceland with its Christian symbols, Greenland's boats and stone tools do not make it consecrated ground. *Íslendingabók*'s description of the settlement in Greenland has been discussed by John Lindow, who argues that the material objects situate Iceland within the Christian world and Greenland outside it

(Lindow 1997, 460). Recently, Shannon Lewis-Simpson has written of the contrast in *Íslendingabók* between Iceland and Greenland and the consequences of this for the image of Greenland and its inhabitants in later writings (Lewis-Simpson 2006).

Let me turn to how the pagan and Christian periods are united in *Íslendingabók* and to the available strategies that, in principle, can unite these entities that are fundamentally different from a religious point of view. In other words, are the pagan and Christian periods set forth as opposites or are they recounted as a continuum? *Íslendingabók* can be divided in two parts. The first, chapters 1–6, treats of the pagan period, and the second, chapters 7–10, of the Christian period. In the first, the empty land is imbued with meaning; it is partly characterized as empty, partly as spiritual, and the Norwegian settlers are pagans. Apart from the settlement, the bringing of the law and the establishment of the *Alþingi* are central themes. In the second part, Christianity is introduced, eventually accepted, and the Icelandic dioceses are established. It seems to me that *Íslendingabók* removes the dichotomy between the pagan and Christian periods, and establishes continuity between the differing parts: pre-Christian elements continue to exist after the change of faith. This continuity is seen (among other things) from the fact that the line of law speakers does not end with the acceptance of Christianity, not even when the succession of bishops had been established. Continuity is also to be deduced from the way the two parts of the work relate to each other. The second part, which treats of the Christian period, neither breaks with, nor changes, what is established in the first part, which treats of the pagan period. The religious change introduces new themes, but none-theless the second part retails a genuine continuation of profane events from pagan times. For instance, a pagan, Úlfljótr, brings the law to Iceland and establishes the legal institution, the *Alþingi*, which in the course of time become the locus of the acceptance of Christianity. The very decision that Icelanders should become Christian was thus made at the *Alþingi*, the political centre inherited from pagan times and by the pagan law speaker, Þorgeirr. Important events, viz., that the Norwegian missionary, Thangbrand, does not succeed in his effort to convert the Icelanders (*Íslendingabók*, ch. 7) and that Þorgeirr eventually decides that all Icelanders should be under the same law, show that that Christianization is not articulated as a clear-cut Christian achievement, but one in which there is, so to speak, a synthesis of the pagan and the Christian.

This relation between the two parts may be called as the typology of *Íslendingabók*. This has to do with the circumstance that Christianity is accepted on the basis of pre-existing pagan institutions that fulfil their purpose precisely through the act of christianization. The two parts relate to each other as basis and fulfilment rather than as opposites and, understood in this way, the pagan past is linked to the Christian present, rather as in biblical exegesis the Old Testament is linked to the New.

Such a typological structure is supported by the interpretation of the *papar* and their religious appurtenances as meaningful, not in the sense of possible historical realities, but rather as spiritually significant and as signs pointing to the land as consecrated prior to settlement. If the island was consecrated ground when the settlers settled it, then Christianity was, in a sense, latent in the pagan period – existing, but not yet, nor for a period active. It would manifest itself when the time was right.

Gerd Weber has argued that a Christian author did not have to reject the pagan period, inasmuch as pagans possessed a divine gift, a *ratio* that could help them understand nature (Weber 1987, 120). In *Íslendingabók*, the pagan settlers are described more than once as wise, and pagan names given to persons are linked to the essential elements of the pagan past: Ingólfr is the founding father, Úlfljótr is the lawbringer, and Þorgeirr is the bringer of the new faith. Consonant with the description of the pagans as wise, their decisions turn out to be central to Christian matters. That pagans may be in possession of a divine gift may also have to do with the point of view represented, among many others, by Hugh of St Victor, viz., that pagans were under God's protection even if unaware of it, and even if not devoted to Christ (Southern 1971). The departure of the *papar* from the island marks a contrast between Christian clerics and pagan settlers, a contrast that underlines the idea that the settlers themselves were capable of cultivating the island and of making the wise decision that Icelanders should become Christians, even though they were pagans when that decision was made. That the *papar* had gone by then emphasizes that significant and correct judgments were made from within the pagan community.

There does not seem to be a qualitative difference in the treatment of pagans and Christians. This indicates that *Islendingabók* does not set them wholly apart. It has been argued by Old Norse scholars that Old Norse-Icelandic literature in the twelfth and thirteenth centuries in general considered past and present as a meaningful continuum (Clunies Ross 1998, 85), and that pagans and Christians were not viewed in black and white terms (Lönnroth 1969, 2; Torfi Tulinius 2002, 292). In *Íslendingabók*, it seems as if past and present are assimilated through the available Christian typological strategies.

Íslendingabók's typological structure may be further elaborated. In an effort to unite the pagan and Christian periods as integral parts of the same history, the author makes use of an existing formal pattern taken from the Bible. Thus, the Bible forms the basis on which *Íslendingabók* models Icelandic history, and the typological structure of *Íslendingabók* may be understood in terms of biblical texts. In his Epistle to the Romans (5.12–16), Paul divides history into three phases personified by Adam, Moses and Christ. The first, *ante legem*, stretches from Adam to the giving of the law to Moses, and here mankind lived according to natural law. The second phase, *sub lege*, stretches from Moses to Christ, and here mankind lived according to written law. In the last phase, *sub gratia*, which stretches from Christ to the end of the world, mankind lives in God's grace (Staines 1983, 152; for reference to natural law see Ó Corráin 1984, 391–4; Weber 1981).

Like Paul, the author of *Íslendingabók* divides history into three phases, and specific persons serve as transitional figures. The first phase is the taking of the land, personified by Ingólfr; the second, the constitution of the law, personified by Úlfljótr; and the third is the acceptance of Christianity, personified by Þorgeirr. Furthermore, in his (2.14), Paul defends natural law, and *Íslendingabók* takes up a Pauline understanding, in that the pagan settlers are described as being under natural law. Within this system the settlers move from a position outside Christianity where they are not quite lost to a propitious position under written law. In the text this movement is in three phases determined by three main themes – settlement, the bringing of the law, and Christianity.

Efforts that combine pagan past and Christian present, such as 'typological structures', 'three-phase systems' and 'the law of nature', are not only to be found in Old-Icelandic literature, but also, for instance, in early Irish literature. McCone writes:

> At the more abstract level of theory, this construct [the law of nature] made it possible to develop a 'native' historical typology in which Christianity represented the natural or logical fulfilment of pre-existing trends and traits in Irish history and society rather than a rude intrusion from outside. The potentially uncomfortable break between the pre-Christian past and the Christian present could thus be minimized and the integration of both phases into an essentially unitary mytho-historical model facilitated (1990, 106).

Further discussion of Irish and Old Norse material and analogies is not possible within this short presentation.

In summary, one essential thing for the Christian author writing the history of Iceland was to articulate the change of faith and to show how Iceland could become part of world history and of salvation history. The ultimate significance ascribed to Christianization in *Íslendingabók* is, for instance, seen from the way the author organizes his material: chapter 7, the account of Christianization, is by far the longest. Besides, both the narrative and style change in this chapter. Nonetheless, the author constructs a history in which the pagan period is not qualitatively different from the Christian one, and pagans are not really lost but possessed of a certain *ratio* and natural law. The equality is articulated by making Christianity a fulfilment of what already existed in the pagan period and something that was promised even before the Norse settlement. It seems, however, that the pagan period cannot fully legitimize itself. The very mention of the *papar* and their appurtenances makes Iceland *Christiana terra* and already a part of world history. However, a movement from the pagan period as past to the Christian period as present is unavoidable. This enables the Icelanders to choose Christianity actively and voluntarily and to be considered part of salvation history. But despite the movement from pagan to Christian, the vision of history in *Íslendingabók* seems to be static: at least the *papar* and the typological structure indicate that whatever happens is within God's control. With regard to the *papar*, it may be as relevant to ask *what* they were in twelfth-century tradition rather than *who* they were in eighth-century reality. Even if they were in Iceland before the time of settlement, these reflections on the typology and the three-phase view of history suggest that description of the settlement and the information about the *papar* can be understood according to a learned, basically literary, interpretation that seeks to represent and explain Iceland's position in world history.

ACKNOWLEDGMENTS

I thank Donnchadh Ó Corráin, Raymond Lamb and Guðrún Sveinbjarnardóttir for commenting on my paper at the Congress and for giving me useful references.

BIBLIOGRAPHY

Assmann, J. 1992. *Das kulturelle gedächtnis: schrift, erinnerung, und politische identität in frühen Hochkulturen* (Münster).
Clunies Ross, M. 1998. *Prolonged echoes: old Norse myths in medieval northern society*, 2 (Odense).
Crawford, B.E. (ed.), *The Papar in the North Atlantic: environment and history* (St Andrews).
Crawford, B.E. 2002. 'Preface' in B.E. Crawford (ed.), *The Papar in the North Atlantic*, pp 7–11.
Frakes, J.C. 2001. 'Vikings, Vinland and the discourse of Eurocentrism', *Journal of English and Germanic Philology*, April, 157–99.
Glauser, J. 2000. 'Sagas of Icelanders (*Íslendinga sögur*) and *þættir* as the literary representation of a new social space' in M. Clunies Ross (ed.), *Old Icelandic literature and society* (Cambridge), pp 203–20.
Guðrún Sveinbjarnardóttir. 2002. 'The question of *papar* in Iceland' in B.E. Crawford (ed.), *The 'Papar' in the North Atlantic*, pp 97–106.
Helgi Guðmundsson. 1997. *Um haf innan: Vestrænir menn og íslenzk menning á miðöldum* (Reykjavik).
Hermann, P. 2007. '*Íslendingabók* and history' in P. Hermann, J.P. Schjødt & R. Tranum Kristensen (eds), *Reflections on Old Norse myths* (Brepols), pp 17–32.
Íslendingabók = Jakob Benediktsson (ed.). 1968. *Íslendingabók. Landnámabók*, Íslenzk fornrit, 1 (Reykjavik).

Lamb, R. 1995. 'Papil, Picts and Papar' in B.E. Crawford (ed.), *Northern Isles connections: essays from Orkney and Shetland presented to Per Sveaas Anderson* (Kirkwall), pp 9–27.

Landnámabók = Jakob Benediktsson (ed.). 1968. *Íslendingabók. Landnámabók*, Íslenzk fornrit, 1 (Reykjavik).

Lewis-Simpson, S. 2006. 'The role of material culture in the literary presentation of Greenland' in J. McKinnell, D. Ashurst & D. Kick (eds), *The fantastic in Old Norse Icelandic literature: sagas and the British Isles. Pre-prints of the 13th International Saga Conference, Durham and York August 2006*, 2 (Durham), pp 575–82.

Lindow, J. 1997. '*Íslendingabók* and Myth', *Scandinavian Studies*, 69:4, 454–64.

Lönnroth, L. 1969. 'The noble heathen: a theme in the Sagas', *Scandinavian Studies*, 41:1, 1–29.

MacDonald, A. 2002. 'The *papar* and some problems: a brief review' in B.E.Crawford (ed.), *The 'Papar' in the North Atlantic*, pp 13–29.

McCone, K. 1990. *Pagan past and Christian present in early Irish literature* (Maynooth).

Ó Corráin, D. 1984. 'The laws of the Irish', *Peritia*, 3, 382–438.

Southern, R.W. 1971. 'Aspects of the European tradition of historical writing. 2. Hugh of St Victor and the idea of historical development', *Transactions of the Royal Historical Society*, 21, 159–79.

Staines, D. 1983. 'The holistic vision of Hugh of Saint Victor' in E. Cook, C. Hosek, J. Macpherson, P. Parker & J. Patrick (eds), *Centre and labyrinth: essays in honour of Northorp Frye* (Toronto), pp 147–61.

Torfi Tulinius. 2002. *The matter of the north: the rise of literary fiction in thirteenth-century Iceland* (Odense).

Weber, G.W. 1981. 'Irreligiosität und heldenzeitalter: zum mythencharakter der altisländischen literatur' in U. Dronke, G.P. Helgadottir, G.W. Weber & H. Bekker-Nielsen (eds), *Speculum Norroenum: norse studies in memory of Gabriel Turville-Petre* (Odense), pp 474–505.

Weber, G.W. 1987. '*Intellegere historiam*: typological perspectives of Nordic pre-history' in K. Hastrup & P. Meulengracht Sørensen (eds), *Tradition og historieskrivning: kilderne til Nordens ældste historie* (Aarhus), pp 95–141.

Viking elements in Irish towns:
Cork and Waterford

MAURICE F. HURLEY

The purpose of this paper is to set out some elements uncovered in the archaeological excavations in the cities of Waterford and Cork that are definitively of Viking origin or display strong Viking influence in their form, morphology or aesthetic. All of the port cities, Dublin, Waterford, Cork and Limerick, and some of the towns on the east and south of Ireland including Wexford, Arklow, Youghal and Kinsale trace their origin to the Vikings. In particular Dublin, Wexford, Waterford, Cork and to some extent Limerick have been shown to contain archaeological strata to support claims previously based on scant historical records, place-names and the occurrence of stray finds. To date, there is no evidence for ninth-, tenth- or early eleventh-century strata in any city except Dublin, where archaeological evidence for ninth- and tenth-century settlement is abundant beneath the contemporary fabric of the urban area. Perhaps this situation reflects the location, number and extent of excavations, but as the corpus of urban excavation grows, the contrast between the extensive early urban development of Dublin and later development of the other cities has become more pronounced.

The earliest evidence for urban development in Waterford dates from the early to mid-eleventh century and in Cork from the late eleventh to early twelfth century. The character of the settlement, the layout, the house-types and the material assemblage in both towns is, however, so similar to that of tenth- and eleventh-century Dublin (Wallace 1992) as to defy any suggestion that their cultural milieux was significantly different from Dublin or that either town was much different from the other. Historical evidence places the establishment of a settlement at Cork in the mid-ninth century and at Waterford in the early tenth century. The assumption is that the initial *longphort* or *dún* formed the nucleus of the settlements that grew and expanded over the years (Hurley 1997a; 2003; 2005). There is of course no particular reason to assume that these early landfall sites were in the same location as the urban settlements of the eleventh century, however, it is as likely as not that they were. Relocating a settlement requires a very good reason and a considerable amount of will. There are no known examples of a settlement being abandoned and re-founded in a new location because it had thrived to such an extent that it outgrew its allotted space. Abandonment of settlements signifies failure, succumbing to the hostility of others, changing patterns of nature, disease or declining social and economic

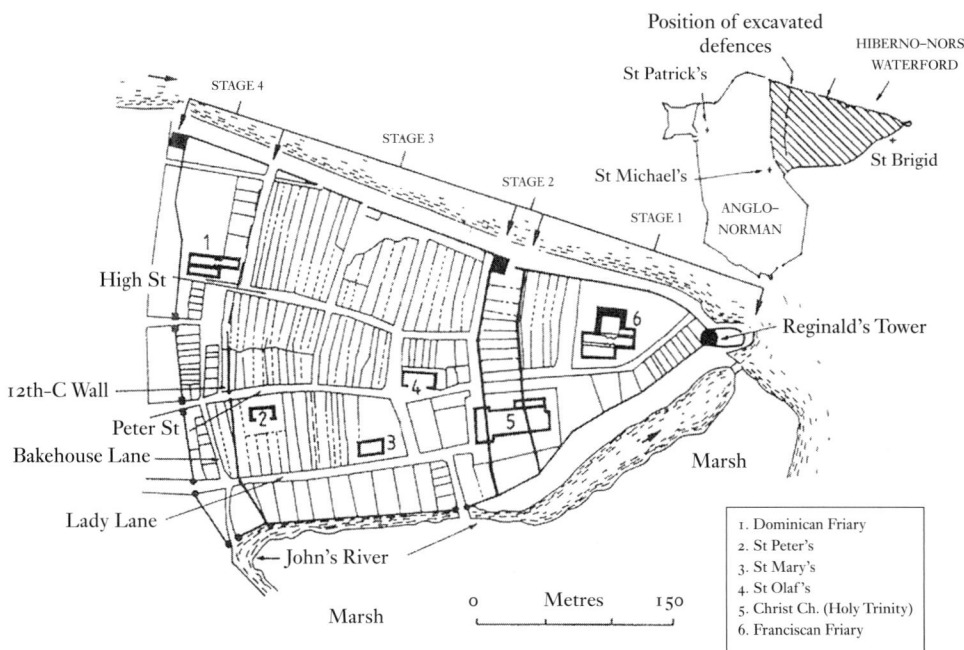

15.1 Suggested stages of topographical development of Hiberno-Norse Waterford, including church locations and burgage plots, superimposed on the street plan recorded by Phillips (1635) (after Bradley & Halpin 1992).

conditions. These are the sorts of events that tend to be recorded in historical records. There is no known historical reference to the re-founding or relocation of Waterford in the first half of the eleventh century or for that matter to the re-founding or relocation of Cork in the late eleventh century. If both these cities were founded anew, or laid out on new sites in the eleventh century, nothing was recorded about the event or the process. In the absence of archaeological evidence for the late ninth, tenth and early eleventh centuries in Waterford, a model of phased expansion based on a concept of sustained growth was put forward (Hurley 1997a). The hypothesis was not solely devised in an attempt to reconcile the discrepancy between the archaeological and historical evidence but also sought to rationalize certain idiosyncrasies in the town layout (Fig. 15.1). Even after sixteen years, since the large-scale Waterford city-centre excavations came to an end (Hurley et al. 1997), subsequent smaller scale excavations have not produced evidence to definitively support or refute the hypothesis. The discovery of a ditch and a ringed-pin in an excavation at Baileys New Street (O'Donnell 2000) is perhaps the only evidence to come close to supporting the hypothesis. Only one of the ditches was excavated: it was *c.* 5.7m wide and at least 1.3m deep, while the other was only subject to limited excavation. The ditches occurred within the suggested primary citadel (see Fig. 15.1, stage 1) – the area subsequently referred to in the historical record as 'Dundory'. The ringed-pin has a broad date-range of the tenth and eleventh centuries (Scully 2004, 24), but it is earlier than the stick-pins, a type found exclusively in the city-centre excavations, with a date-range extending from the mid-eleventh to late thirteenth centuries (Scully 1997a, 438–48).

A similar suggestion for the area likely to contain the earliest settlement in Cork was also proposed (Hurley 1998). This was based on numerous elements pointing to the primacy of the south island as the Viking core of the town from whence it gradually grew and expanded. The primacy of the area is since attested by several archaeological excavations (Ní Loingsigh, Excavation No: 03E1170, in prep.; Kelleher, Excavation No: 04E0031, in prep.), though where stratigraphy from the late eleventh and early twelfth centuries is well preserved not a scintilla of evidence for material of earlier date has come to light. Comparable material was excavated on the south bank of the River Lee (Lane and Sutton 2003), but again nothing of earlier date was evident. The possibility remains that the key to the emergence of Waterford and Cork in the eleventh century lies outside the historic city cores. To date, archaeological work in Cork offers no clue to alternative locations. At Waterford, however, the possibility of a relocated settlement has received credence from the discoveries at Woodstown, 6km upstream from the historic city centre, where a ninth- and tenth-century Viking settlement was excavated in 2004 (O'Brien and Russell 2004; 2005; O'Brien et al. 2005; McNamara 2005). Further excavation on the site should be interesting for many reasons, particularly with regards to the continuity or discontinuity of occupation and the reasons for failure and desertion.

WHAT ARE THE ELEMENTS?

The actual elements identified as Viking or Viking-influenced in the Hiberno-Norse milieu that prevailed in the eleventh century are: the form of the towns, including property layout; the house types; and the artefactual assemblage, including economy, trade, lifestyle, cultural affinities and the prevailing aesthetic. Detailed accounts of many aspects mentioned here are published, especially for Waterford (Hurley 1992; Hurley et al. 1997) and for Cork in several excavation reports (Cleary et al. 1997; Cleary and Hurley 2003). Sites excavated in Cork since 2000 remain unpublished, but the evidence from them has informed recent publications (Hurley 2005). Only selected items are used here to illustrate the points.

Location and layout
Waterford was located on a triangular promontory. It was flanked on one side by the River Suir and on the other by marshy ground surrounding the mouth of St John's River, while the third side was landward and therefore required some form

15.2 A wooden laneway in the backyard of a house fronting South Main Street, Cork, of probable early twelfth-century date (awaiting dendrochronological dates) (photo: Hilary Kelleher, Archaeological Services Unit, UCC).

of man-made protection from the outset in order to capitalize on the naturally defensive properties of the site (Fig. 15.1). The crest of the ridge was at most 6–7m higher than tide level at the waterfront, the ridge attaining a maximum height of 9.3m OD, while the modern quays and surrounding streets (e.g. The Mall) are 2.9m OD. A central main street may have led for *c*.150m from the apex of the triangle towards the west, where it branched to form two main streets. Peter Street ran along the central spine of the ridge, while High Street was on its northern side at a slightly lower level, but following the line of the break in slope. It is likely, therefore, that this street attained the prominence implied by its name because the residents on the northern side would have had unrestricted access to the river, the most ideal location for merchants. A lesser street, Lady Lane, developed parallel to Peter Street on the southern side, but appears not to have attained any prominence during this period. It is not known for sure if any of the interconnecting north/south streets existed in the eleventh–twelfth centuries, or in what period or circumstances they emerged. The areas between the streets were laid out in plots, each a long narrow rectangle lying at right angles to the main streets. The plots became longer as one moved westwards and the divergence of the streets became greater, reflecting the widening of the promontory.

The location and topography of Cork also fundamentally influenced the layout of the settlement. The late eleventh-century settlement was located in estuarine islands in a river valley with steep hills rising on either side at a point where the River Lee began to broaden into a sheltered tidal harbour. The location was evidently favoured because of the protection afforded by a site surrounded by water and an intractable swamp. Perhaps of equal consideration was the critical location at the lowest fording point of the river close to the head of navigable waters. St Finbarre's monastery had long stood nearby on the south bank of the river, consequently the advantages of the location were already an established fact. The surprising discovery made by recent archaeological excavations (O'Donnell 2003; Kelleher 2002) is that the 'island' whereon the settlement stood was not dry ground but a series of reed beds interspersed by braided streams. The reed beds were artificially raised in height by up to 1.5m by clay dug from the marsh. Wooden revetments were built to retain the introduced clay and then houses were built on top of these man-made platforms. It is unclear if the central spinal main street was a feature from the outset of the settlement, though it seems likely that it was, as the bridge on the south end would have connected with roughly contemporary settlement on the south bank of the river (Lane and Sutton 2003). The opportunity to ford the river at this point could only have been exploited by the construction of three bridges and a connecting trackway, for either one without the others would have been pointless (Hurley 2005, 59–60). The bridges were probably wooden and a wooden trackway appears to have been the primary street surface. The evidence for the street itself is sparse, but substantial round-wood trackways leading through the plots offer a good indication of its likely appearance (Fig. 15.2). The plots, positioned at right angles to the line of the main street, were defined by wattle fences, some of which followed the line of the natural water channels of braided streams. Within the plots, the backyards were progressively raised by dumping of dung and domestic refuse, thereby reclaiming ground and creating the familiar long rectangular plots.

The houses
In the eleventh and early twelfth centuries, the houses of both Waterford and Cork were built in an architectural style and to a ground plan derived from a prototype of Scandinavian origin. The houses of Dublin have been the subject of in-depth analysis (Wallace 1992), where the complexity of the cultural influences is analyzed. Wallace's typology of these houses has been used to describe the houses at Waterford (Hurley 1992; Scully and McCutcheon 1997; Hurley 2001) and Cork (Hurley 2003). The rectangular wattle-walled houses (Type 1) were essentially tripartite in plan, with doorways located central to the end walls, giving access to the street and backyard. The tripartite form was dictated by the location of the internal roof supports, which probably formed a trestle carrying the roof. A central kerbed hearth, set in a clay-floored central space, was flanked by side aisles used as sitting benches and beds, while small chambers or paved areas for standing water/milk storage etc. frequently

occurred at either side of the back door. A path leading from the back door was common, and a second house frequently stood at one side of the path, close by the back door of the street-fronting house. The secondary houses (Type 2) were generally more compact, sub-rectangular or square with rounded corners, and of less elaborate ground plan than the Type 1 examples. They generally had only one doorway, frequently no hearth site, and where hearths did occur they were less elaborately paved than those in the street-fronting houses.

When analyzing houses, we are wittingly or un-wittingly influenced by our concept of the contemporary nuclear family home. It is difficult to visualize the extent to which craft, trade and public access was permissible within the house and what form of family grouping constituted a single home. For example, in addition to a nuclear family, how many members of the extended family, servants, slaves, animals etc occupied a single dwelling? What concepts of privacy, if any, existed? We are relatively certain that the street-fronting houses were the main homes and also, in many cases, workshops. The Type 2 subsidiary houses, frequently with insulated double walls, 'convey an impression of greater comfort' (Wallace 1988, 140) or snugness and were conceivably intended as private bed-chambers or, alternatively, additional sleeping accommodation for a surplus of extended family, children, servants, slaves etc (Hurley 2001, 18). The matter of interpreting the function of an increasingly elaborate range of buildings in late eleventh- and early twelfth-century Waterford emphasizes the limitations of a simplistic model of domestic life. In early to mid-eleventh-century Waterford and late eleventh- to mid-twelfth-century Cork the houses were located almost exclusively at the street frontages. In the late eleventh or early twelfth century, sunken buildings (Walsh 1997, 45–53; McCutcheon 1997a, 137–41; McCutcheon 1997b, 141–9) were constructed in Waterford in what was defined as the 'insulae', i.e. towards the centre of the blocks. Only one of the five sunken buildings occurred at the street frontage. This method of presenting the information probably belies the true relationship of the buildings which appear to have been located towards the rear of the street-fronting plots and were probably built by merchants in addition to their pre-existing street-fronting houses. Ascribing buildings in the central part of the blocks to specific street-fronting properties was hampered by the absence of clear division representing the rear end of the plots; in particular the division between the High Street to Peter Street properties, never became apparent. The interpretation of the centre of the blocks was also hampered by the removal of archaeological evidence for the High Street frontage by eighteenth-century cellars and to some extent by an underlying assumption that each house represented an individual property ownership. The question of access to the houses in the centre of the blocks was never sufficiently addressed in the context of the street frontage and the plot layout. The key to the interpretation lies in the development in early twelfth-century Waterford of large rectangular buildings in a new architectural style – the so-called 'sill-beam houses', in the centre of the blocks. More accurately, they formed rows of houses with each building probably catering for a specific function. These new large buildings were possibly constructed as halls by wealthy merchants primarily for dining, entertaining etc, in response to increased prosperity, while the street-fronting houses became more exclusively trade premises.

The artefactual assemblage

Of the many artefacts and environmental evidence indicating lifestyle, trade, cultural affinities and prevailing aesthetic, only a few examples can be given here. By the eleventh century, clearly Scandinavian cultural affinities had become diluted and, in this regard alone, the use of the term Hiberno-Norse is more appropriate. Many items within the artefactual assemblages of Waterford and Cork might be cited as 'ultimately of Viking inspiration' or perhaps 'Scandinavian influenced', but in reality, Ireland of the eleventh and early twelfth centuries remained in what might best be called a post-Viking cultural residue. Influences on social, cultural and aesthetic preferences remain perhaps the most clearly diagnostic of Scandinavian influence.

The evidence indicates an urban people living close to the produce of the rural hinterland and keeping animals within the urban area. It is likely that pigs were kept within the town (McCormick 1997, 830) and it is possible that live cattle, sheep/goats and horses were corralled or housed within the town for short periods in certain circumstances. We cannot be sure if the urban dwellers maintained their own animals on land in the vicinity of the town, as seems likely, though it is evident that the food demand of towns the size of eleventh- and twelfth-century Waterford and Cork could not be met from such an economy, and the purchase of food from a much broader hinterland is implied by sheer number of animal bones recovered (McCormick 1997, 819–53). The sustenance of a largely urban population must, therefore, have been met by the availability of trade items. Consequently, mercantile and military activities were intrinsic to the survival of these essentially non-agricultural settlements.

In addition to food, raw materials such as wood, reeds, wool, hides etc, had to be obtained from the hinterland. Fishing on both the estuaries and open seas was a significant component of the economy (McCormick 1997; McCarthy 1997; 2003). Materials such silver, amber, jet, walrus ivory, boxwood, cork etc, were imported, but all of these items are only present in small quantities in Waterford and Cork. As such, a trade and craft emporium without direct control of the raw materials could not survive. We must assume, therefore, that an affiliated population dwelled in the hinterland (Bradley 1988), that the citizens possessed expertise in certain critical trades, monopolized access to essential raw material from abroad and, above all else, that towns wielded sufficient military power to hold sway over the region. All of these elements were essential to the sustain-ability of the Viking urban centres. With regard to the boat timbers from

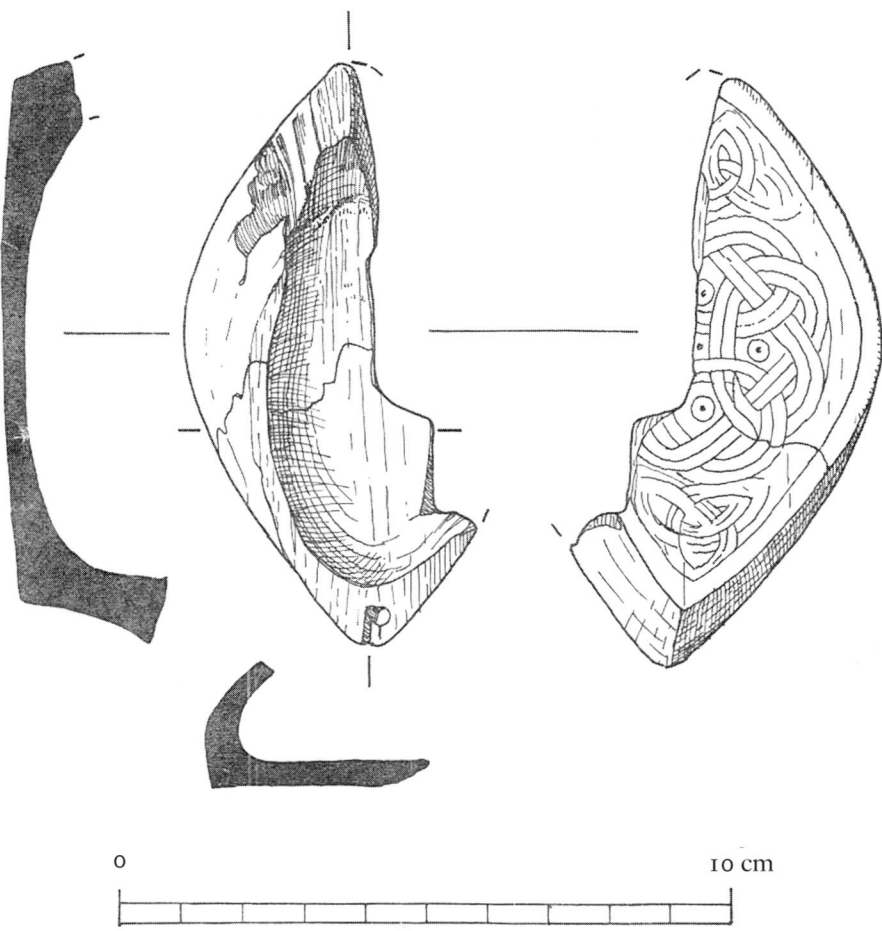

15.3 Decorated toy boat from South Main Street, Cork; early twelfth century (drawing: Rhoda Cronin, courtesy of Moira Ní Loingsigh, Sheila Lane and Associates).

Waterford, seven of the nine timbers analyzed are from boats built in the Norse tradition, thus demonstrating 'the continuation into post-Viking-times of the Viking boat-building tradition' (McGrail 1997, 640).

Of the four bone motif-pieces from Waterford, one from a late eleventh- or early twelfth-century context (Plate 2) displays the strongest elements of Scandinavian design and layout (O'Meadhra 1997, 699–701). The closest parallels to this decoration are to be found in Dublin motif-pieces. The Waterford motif-piece is 'Irish work [...] with ribbons of equal width without the anatomical expansions of their Scandinavian equivalents' (ibid., 701). Influences from the Anglo-Scandinavian world of south-east England are also evident (O'Meadhra 1997, 701–2). While the motif-pieces are likely to be goldsmith's sketches and trials, there are even fewer examples of actual execution in precious metals. A single item from Waterford, however, personifies the Hiberno-Norse style, a silver kite-brooch with gold filigree ornament. It was found in a layer dated to the early twelfth century and has parallels from Ballinderry and Dublin, indicating that the form was in use at least from the mid to late tenth century to the early twelfth century. However, 'when art-historical arguments are taken into account the kite-brooch as a type can be pushed back to the ninth or tenth century and may be earlier' (Whitfield 1997, 506). In typological terms, the Waterford kite-brooch 'shows characteristics which are consistent' with the twelfth-century date of its find spot (Whitfield 1997, 514), emphasizing the longevity of tradition and the incorporation of Viking influences into an increasingly Hibernicized material.

More un-diagnostic and less spectacular than the work of artists and goldsmiths were many items of everyday use; for example, a mid-twelfth-century gaming board from Waterford (Hurley and McCutcheon 1997, 592–4), closely paralleled by the justifiably famous board from Ballinderry (Hencken 1936, 135, 175–90). The Waterford board is undecorated but would have provided a suitable surface for five counters of domed hemispherical form with flat base and central pegs (Hurley 1997b, 666–9). All might have been used for the game of *hnefatafal* – a game probably introduced to Ireland by the Vikings and certainly played in the Viking period. A single item from Cork must serve to illustrate the Hiberno-Norse tradition. It comes from an early twelfth-century house floor at South Main Street (Ní Loingsigh, in prep.), and typifies a culture where even a child's toy boat received a careful decorative execution (Fig. 15.3).

BIBLIOGRAPHY

AFM = O'Donovan, J. (ed.). 1856. *Annála Ríoghachta Éireann: Annals of the kingdom of Ireland by the Four Masters*, 7 vols (Dublin).
Bradley, J. 1988. 'The interpretation of Scandinavian settlement in Ireland' in J. Bradley (ed.), *Settlement and society in medieval Ireland: studies presented to F.X. Martin, O.S.A.* (Kilkenny), pp 49–78.
Bradley, J. & A. Halpin. 1992. 'The topographical development of Scandinavian and Anglo-Norman Waterford city' in W. Nolan & T.P. Power (eds), *Waterford history and society* (Dublin), pp 105–29.
Cleary, R.M., M.F. Hurley, & E. Shee Twohig (eds). 1997. *Skiddy's Castle & Christ Church Cork: excavations 1974–1977 by D.C. Twohig* (Cork).
Cleary, R.M. & M.F. Hurley (eds). 2003. *Excavations in Cork City, 1984–2000* (Cork).
Hencken, H.O'N. 1936. 'Ballinderry crannog No. I', *Proceedings of the Royal Irish Academy*, 43C, 103–239.
Hurley, M.F. 1992. 'Late Viking-Age settlement in Waterford city' in W. Nolan & T.P. Power (eds), *Waterford history and society* (Dublin), pp 49–72.

Hurley, M.F. 1997a. 'Topography and development' in M.F. Hurley et al. (eds), *Late Viking-Age and Medieval Waterford* (Waterford), pp 7–11.

Hurley, M.F. 1997b. 'Artefacts of skeletal material' in M.F. Hurley et al. (eds), *Late Viking-Age and Medieval Waterford* (Waterford), pp 650–98.

Hurley, M.F. 1998. 'Viking-Age towns: archaeological evidence from Waterford and Cork' in M.A. Monk & J. Sheehan (eds), *Early Medieval Munster: archaeology, history and society* (Cork), pp 164–77.

Hurley, M.F. 2001. 'Domestic architecture in medieval Cork and Waterford' in M. Gläser (ed.), *Lübecker Kolloquium zur Stadtarchäologie im Hanseraum III: Der Hausbau* (Lübeck), pp 15–34.

Hurley, M.F. 2003. 'The defences' in R.M. Cleary & M.F. Hurley (eds), *Excavations in Cork city, 1984–2000* (Cork), pp 171–81.

Hurley, M.F. 2005. 'Urban beginnings and the Vikings' in J. Crowley, R. Devoy, D. Linehan & P. O'Flanagan (eds), *Atlas of Cork City* (Cork), pp 56–63.

Hurley, M.F. & O.B.M. Scully with S.J. McCutcheon (eds). 1997. *Late Viking-Age and Medieval Waterford: excavations 1986–1992* (Waterford).

Hurley, M.F. & S.W.J. McCutcheon. 1997. 'Wooden artefacts' in M.F. Hurley et al. (eds), *Late Viking-Age and Medieval Waterford* (Waterford), pp 553–633.

Kelleher, H. 2004. 'Washington Street, Cork' in I. Bennett (ed.), *Excavations 2002: summary accounts of archaeological excavations in Ireland* (Dublin), 73.

Kelleher, H. In prep. 'South Main Street, Cork. Excavation No: 04E0371'.

Lane, S. & D. Sutton. 2003 '3 and 5 Barrack Street' in R.M. Cleary and M.F. Hurley (eds), *Excavations in Cork City, 1984–2000* (Cork), pp 5–12.

McCarthy, M. 1997. 'Faunal remains: Christ Church' in R.M. Cleary et al. (eds), *Skiddy's Castle & Christ Church Cork: excavations 1974–1977 by D.C. Twohig* (Cork), pp 349–60.

McCarthy, M. 2003. 'The faunal remains' in R.M. Cleary & M.F. Hurley (eds), *Excavations in Cork City, 1984–2000* (Cork), pp 375–90.

McCutcheon, S.W.J. 1997a. 'Catalogue of houses: Olaf Street, High Street and Arundel Square' in M.F. Hurley et al. (eds), *Late Viking-Age and Medieval Waterford* (Waterford), pp 53–136.

McCutcheon, S.W.J. 1997b. 'Catalogue of houses: Insula North' in M.F. Hurley et al. (eds), *Late Viking-Age and Medieval Waterford* (Waterford), pp 154–63.

McCormick, F. 1997. 'The animal bones' in M.F. Hurley et al. (eds), *Late Viking-Age and Medieval Waterford* (Waterford), pp 819–53.

McGrail, S. 1997. 'The boat timbers' in M.F. Hurley et al. (eds), *Late Viking-Age and Medieval Waterford* (Waterford), pp 636–43.

McNamara, S. 'Woodstown 6: the finds' in J. O'Sullivan & M. Stanley (eds), *Recent archaeological discoveries on National Road Schemes 2004*, Archaeology and the National Roads Authority Monograph, 2 (Dublin), pp 111–24.

Ní Loingsigh, M. In prep. 'Citi Carpark, Cork, Excavation No: 03E1170'.

O'Brien, R. & I. Russell. 2004. 'Preliminary note on the archaeological site of Woodstown 6, Co. Waterford', *Decies*, 60, 65–70.

O'Brien, R. & I. Russell. 2005. 'The Hiberno-Scandinavian site at Woodstown 6, County Waterford' in J. O'Sullivan & M. Stanley (eds), *Recent archaeological discoveries on National Road Schemes 2004*, Archaeology and the National Roads Authority Monograph, 2 (Dublin), pp 111–24.

O'Brien, R., P. Quinney, & I. Russell. 2005. 'Preliminary report on the archaeological excavation and find retrieval strategy of the Hiberno-Scandinavian site of Woodstown 6, Co. Waterford', *Decies*, 61, 13–122.

O'Donnell, M. 2000. 'Bailey's New Street, Waterford' in I. Bennett (ed.), *Excavations 1999: summary accounts of archaeological excavations in Ireland* (Dublin), 294–5.

O'Donnell, M. 2003. 'Tuckey Street, Cork' in R.M. Cleary and M.F. Hurley (eds), *Excavations in Cork City, 1984–2000* (Cork), pp 13–28.

O'Meadhra, U. 1997. 'Motif-pieces and other decorated bone and antler work' in M.F. Hurley et al. (eds), *Late Viking-Age and Medieval Waterford* (Waterford), pp 699–703.

Scully, O.M.B. 1997. 'Metal artefacts' in M.F. Hurley et al. (eds), *Late Viking-Age and Medieval Waterford* (Waterford), pp 428–89.

Scully, O.M.B. 2004. 'Ringed pin' in E. McEneany & R. Ryan (eds), *Waterford Treasures: a guide to historical and archaeological treasures of Waterford city* (Waterford), 24.

Wallace, P.F. 1988. 'Archaeology and the emergence of Dublin as the principal town of Ireland' in J. Bradley (ed.), *Settlement and society in medieval Ireland: studies presented to F.X. Martin, O.S.A.* (Kilkenny), pp 123–60.

Wallace, P.F. 1992. *The Viking-Age buildings of Dublin: Medieval Dublin excavations, 1962–81, Series A*, 2 vols (Dublin).

Walsh, C. 1997. 'Sunken buildings' in M.F. Hurley et al. (eds), *Late Viking-Age and Medieval Waterford* (Waterford), pp 45–52.

Whitfield, N. 1997. 'The Waterford kite-brooch and its place in Irish metalwork' in M.F. Hurley et al. (eds), *Late Viking-Age and Medieval Waterford* (Waterford), pp 490–518.

The warrior ideal in the Late Viking Age

JUDITH JESCH

THE WARRIOR IDEAL

Contemporary evidence for the warrior ideal of the late Viking Age is found in a few runic inscriptions, some of which have poetic form, and which emanate from an identifiable warrior milieu. There is a richer body of evidence in skaldic verse, in which the poet's praise of the military leader expresses the warrior ideal for those who would later be called on to live up to it, for those who were to be united in an effective troop which would have to perform future military actions.

The Sjörup stone from Skåne (*DR*, no. 279) illustrates how a warrior was expected to behave in a military situation. There we hear of a certain Ásbjǫrn that *Sá fló eigi at Uppsǫlum, en vá með hann vápn hafði* ('he fled not at Uppsala, but struck while he had a weapon').[1] Unfortunately, we know little about this Ásbjǫrn, and where and why he fought so bravely. It is often said that this was the famous battle between Eiríkr the Victorious and his nephew Styrbjǫrn that took place some time in the 980s at Fýrisvellir, just outside Uppsala (for example, Jansson 1987, 87), though this is difficult to demonstrate – we know far too little about tenth-century history to be able to link the inscription to a particular event.

Inscriptions like Sjörup, which give an insight into how the warrior's role and the warrior ideal were understood in the Viking Age, are rare. A group of inscriptions from Hällestad in Skåne may refer to the same battle. One of these (*DR*, no. 295) uses the same expression *Sá fló eigi at Uppsǫlum* ('he fled not at Uppsala') of Tóki, a leader who is being commemorated by his comrades. Otherwise, although there are many thousands of memorial inscriptions on rune-stones, remarkably few of them would actually reveal to the uninitiated that it was a period renowned for violence and martial behaviour.

Skaldic verse, on the other hand, has much more to say about war. The inscriptions from Skåne can be compared with two *lausavísur* ('free-standing verses') by an otherwise unknown Icelander, Þorvaldr Hjaltason (*Skjd* BI:111), apparently referring to the same battle at Fýrisvellir and composed in praise of Eiríkr. The motif of fleeing appears in the second of these stanzas, in which it is said of Styrbjǫrn's troop that *þat eitt lifir þeira [...] es rann undan* ('only those who ran away are still alive'). Naturally, this is not intended as praise; quite the

---

1 While references are given to the corpus editions for runic inscriptions, their normalized texts are taken from the *Samnordisk runtextdatabas* and translations are my own.

opposite, especially when the same stanza tells us that Styrbjǫrn's men *hǫfðu lið fleira* ('had a bigger troop') than the victorious Eiríkr.

The first of Þorvaldr's stanzas names the place of the battle and illustrates another motif to be explored in this paper:

> Farið til Fýrisvallar,
> folka tungls, hverr's hungrar,
> vǫrðr, at virkis garði
> vestr kveldriðu hesta;
> þar hefr hreggdrauga hǫggvit
> (hóllaust es þat) sólar
> elfar skíðs fyr ulfa
> Eiríkr í dyn geira.

> Guardian of the moon of the army [shield > warrior], each horse of the evening-rider [troll-woman > wolf], which is hungry, can come west to Fýrisvellir to the fortified enclosure; there Eiríkr has cut down trees of the storm of the sun of the river-ski [ship > shield > battle > warriors] in din of spears [battle] for wolves. That is no exaggeration.

This stanza praises the victorious Eiríkr for feeding wolves, one of the three carrion-eating 'beasts of battle'. Conventionally, the beasts of battle are two birds, the raven and the eagle, and one mammal, the wolf, and they are often interchangeable in the literary context. There is one runic example of the motif, this time involving the eagle, from the late Viking Age, on the Gripsholm stone (*Sö*, no. 179):

> Þeir fóru drengila
> fjarri at gulli
> ok austarla
> erni gáfu,
> dóu sunnarla
> á Serklandi.

> They travelled in a warrior-like fashion, far for gold, and in the east gave the eagle (food), died in the south, in Serkland.

The stanza is in praise of a certain Haraldr, who went on the renowned expedition to Serkland with his brother Ingvarr; an expedition which undoubtedly had a military element, though it is hard to say what form it took.

These two motifs represent the two main ways of praising the successful and heroic warrior in the late Viking Age, a negative one in which he is said not to have fled from the enemy, and a positive one in which he is said to have given copious food to the beasts of battle. They sum up the warrior ideal of the late

Viking Age, as expressed in poetry and memorial, and give us an insight into the conceptual world of the warrior groups of that period. The runic inscriptions provide undisputably contemporary evidence for the currency of these ideas in the Viking Age, for which the skaldic corpus provides much more extensive evidence, which is also arguably contemporary (Jesch 2001, 15–33). Both motifs have a clear basis in reality: it is not possible to win if one runs away, and the many corpses on a battlefield will undoubtedly attract carrion-eaters. But the motifs should not be taken completely literally, either in the runic inscriptions or in the skaldic verse. Viking-Age texts about war and battle are mostly symbolic and eulogistic rather than realistic and descriptive. Their praise for the hero's actions is almost always indirect, and almost always uses these two motifs and only these two motifs. It is here that we find the key to understanding the warrior ideal of the Viking Age: not only how society understood what warriors did, but also how the warrior ideal was developed to encourage and train the warrior collective.

FUNCTIONS OF THE WARRIOR IDEAL

'He fled not' is an unusual form for praise, in that it is negative. It was clearly not the custom to praise someone by saying 'he fought bravely', rather it is said that he did not run from the fight, that he was not cowardly, that he held firm under attack, that he defended himself and his comrades. This is *litotes* or understatement, in which something positive is expressed by using a negative form of a word or phrase which means the opposite. The effect of this kind of expression is that it draws attention to the alternative. This alternative must have been real: it was quite likely that the warrior might actually run away, as the cowards do in the Old English *Battle of Maldon* (*ASPR* VI:7–16, lines 185–201). Looked at in this way, the statement of not fleeing is not really negative, rather it becomes implicitly a positive expression of heroic courage. It must mean: 'he could have, even should have, fled, but he chose not to.' It is this choice which is heroic, especially if there is an implied contrast with warriors who did flee (Moltke 1985, 295).

There is a runic inscription which shows the result when some warriors do flee (*Sö*, no. 174), commemorating a certain Bjǫrn who was killed in Gotland and *Þý lét fjǫr sitt, flýðu gengir* ('lost his life because his companions fled'). Presumably this actually happened more often than the surviving texts suggest. This reference is unique in runic inscriptions, and when there are references to fleeing cowards in praise poems, it is always to the enemy, as in Þorvaldr Hjaltason's stanzas. This reveals an important difference between the runic inscription and skaldic verse. The rune stone was raised by Bjǫrn's father, who was not a member of the warrior band, and as an outsider could admit that things did not go as they should have, that some of Bjǫrn's comrades betrayed him by fleeing. But in the official poetry of the chieftain and the warrior band, their propaganda, the poems which were to preserve their deeds for the future, such things could not be admitted.

The use of 'he fled not' is thus restricted in skaldic verse. Unlike the *Battle of Maldon*, the skaldic praise poems concentrate on the leader's successes. It would be absurd to say of the victor that he did not flee from the battlefield, so a skald had only two possibilities for using this motif in a praise poem. He could, as in Þorvaldr's stanzas, praise the victor for making his opponent flee. As Þjóðólfr Arnórsson says, in a poem about King Magnús of Norway, his opponent Sveinn *flýði [...] af auðu skipi sínu* ('fled from his empty ship') after the battle of Helganes (*Skjd* BI:337). Such statements strengthen the impression of the victor's success, but do not make him especially heroic. It cannot be said that they construct an ideal against which others can be measured.

However, the motif of not fleeing is heroic, and is especially effective, when used in posthumous eulogies, about kings who have suffered defeat. This is how it is used in Hallfreðr's *Erfidrápa* (memorial poem) about Óláfr Tryggvason's final defeat at Svǫlðr (*Skjd* BI:150–7). In the very first words of the poem the skald calls the king *flugþverrir* ('flight-diminisher': st. 1) and later *flugstyggr* ('flight-shy': st. 19). St Óláfr, also defeated and killed in battle, is similarly called *fljóttskjarr* ('flight-shy') by his chief skald Sighvatr in his *Erfidrápa* (*Skjd* BI:239–45, st. 22). The motif is little used of anyone other than a king or chieftain: I have found only one example, when Óttarr the Black notes that king Knútr is followed to England by Jutlanders who were *flugar trauðir* ('reluctant to flee': *Skjd* BI:272–5, st. 2). But that it applied equally to the lower ranks, at least in Knútr's time, is clear from the English laws of that king (*GA* I:364), which prescribe a harsh punishment for *se man, þe ætfleo fram his hlaforde oððe fram his geferan for his yrhðe, si hit on scipfyrde, si hit on landfyrde* ('the man who flees from his lord or from his companions because of his cowardice, whether in a naval force or one on land'). Although this law has been interpreted in a more restricted context of the developing eleventh-century 'ideal of men dying with their lord' (Frank 1991, 100), the inclusion of 'companions' as well as a lord makes it clear that the provision actually has a broader application.

From the military point of view, there must have been many occasions when troops found it strategically advisable to draw back, and were even instructed to do so by their leader. Yet the praise poems do not acknowledge the possibility of tactical retreat: if a warrior leaves the battlefield it is because he has already been defeated – he has 'fled'. The statement is therefore ideological rather than realistic; its function must be, like the English law just cited, to indoctrinate the young warrior, to prepare him for doing that which most people find it unnatural to do. 'Indeed, the history of warfare can be seen as a history of increasingly more effective mechanisms for enabling and conditioning men to overcome their innate resistance to killing their fellow human beings' (Grossman 1995, 13). Modern warfare has developed various means of conditioning to overcome this resistance (ibid., 177–9). Important aspects of this conditioning include establishing the authority of the leader and enforcing group solidarity (ibid., 141–55). In the Viking Age, poetry was an obvious and public means of doing these things.

In skaldic verse, the leader who does not flee is thus a role model, showing the young warrior listening to the poem how to behave in future battles. And when battle is imminent, the leader's duty is to remind his warriors that flight is not allowed. This is illustrated in a stanza from Hallfreðr's *Erfidrápa* about Óláfr Tryggvason, which claims to reproduce the words that Óláfr himself used before his final battle at Svǫlðr (*Skjd* BI:150, st. 2):

> Geta skal máls, þess's mæla
> menn at vápna sennu
> dolga fangs við drengi
> dáðǫflgan bǫr kvǫðu;
> baða hertryggðar hyggja
> hnekkir sína rekka
> (þess lifa þjóðar sessa
> þróttar orð) á flotta.

> The speech shall be mentioned, which men said the deed-strong tree of battle-tunic [mail-coat > warrior] spoke to his comrades at the flyting of weapons [battle]; the destroyer of the army's security told his men not to think of flight; the powerful words of this people's bench-mate will live.

Óláfr's words will live because they are locked in this stanza and the skald is the guarantee for the fact that they will be remembered. Just as Óláfr Tryggvason encouraged his warriors before the battle, so the skald's job was to encourage future warriors through his poetry.

One of the reasons a warrior might wish to flee from a battlefield is that it is an unpleasant place, with a lot of blood, and a lot of wounded and dead people. A part of the unpleasantness has to do with the carrion-eaters that are attracted to the site by the dead bodies. The very extensive use of the 'beasts of battle' motif in skaldic verse has its origins in this unpleasantness, but it also shows how poetry was used in the Viking Age to confront and overcome natural feelings of fear and distaste. In poetry, the beasts of battle motif becomes something positive, it becomes the ultimate expression of the warrior's courage. The beasts of battle motif is found not only in skaldic verse but also in Eddic poetry, and in other literary traditions too, notably the Anglo-Saxon. But it is noteworthy how extensively, and how differently, it is used in skaldic verse. I have written about this elsewhere (Jesch 2001, 247–52; 2002) and it is sufficient here to summarize.

Earlier scholars tended to see the beasts of battle motif as an ancient, heathen and Germanic relic. But of more importance than the antiquity or otherwise of the motif is how it is used in different ways in the different literary traditions. Old English poetry, for instance, is mainly narrative, it tells a story. There, the beasts of battle motif is used to create expectation and atmosphere, a feeling of unease in connection with a narrative of war and battle (Griffith 1993). The motif is not directly linked to warriors, neither the winners nor the losers, but it can be used to arouse sympathy for those who are defeated, as for instance in lines 104–7 of *The Battle of Maldon*, where it is used at the beginning of the battle, anticipating the defeat of the English (*ASPR* VI:9–10). In Old English poetry, the motif is not generally used in any especially detailed or varied way, the examples are conventional and very similar to each other, and we never see the macabre but realistic picture of the beasts of battle actually eating the dead. In Eddic poetry we have some of the same elegiac tone on the few occasions when the motif is used.

Skaldic verse is quite different. Here, the motif is highly developed and often appears in connection with the praise of the hero. The motif is directly connected to the individual who is being praised, rather than just used to create a general atmosphere as in the Old English poetry. The motif of the beasts of battle is found in over 100 stanzas of skaldic verse from the period 950–1100 (and of course, in some earlier than that, see Jesch 2002). In all of these stanzas, the motif is used according to a fixed pattern, as it is always found in one of three forms:

(1) the warrior is called a feeder of eagles, ravens or wolves;
(2) there is a statement that the warrior fed eagles, ravens or wolves;
(3) there is a statement that eagles, ravens or wolves consumed their food.

The use of the motif is predominantly positive. It is clearly considered a good thing for the warrior to provide the eagle, raven and wolf with carrion, in complete contrast to the unpleasant atmosphere with which the motif is associated in Old English poetry.

The beasts of battle motif is closely associated with the description of and the praise of the hero and his deeds. Thus, it often occurs in subordinate clauses, or appositive phrases, or hidden in kennings. But two skalds in the middle of the eleventh century, Grani and Arnórr, could develop the motif through a whole stanza (*Skjd* BI:357, 313):

> Dǫglingr fekk at drekka
> danskt blóð ara jóði
> (hirð hykk hilmis gerðu
> hugins jól) við nes Þjólar;

ætt spornaði arnar
allvítt of valfalli,
hold át vargr sem vildi
(vel njóti þess) Jóta.

The prince caused the child of eagles to drink Danish blood at Þjólarnes,
I believe the leader's retinue provided the raven's yule-feast; the offspring
of the eagle trampled far and wide across the fallen corpses, the wolf ate
the flesh of the Jutes at will, may he relish this.

Vann, þás Vinðr of minnir
vápnhríð konungr, síðan;
sveið ófám at Jómi
illvirkja hræ stillir;
búk dró bráðla steikðan
blóðugr vargr af glóðum;
rann á óskírð enni
allfrekr bani hallar.

The king then fought [won] a weapon-storm [battle] which the Wends will
remember; the leader scorched not a few corpses of evil-doers at Jóm; the
bloody wolf drew a quickly-roasted torso from the coals; the very greedy
destroyer of the hall [flame] played on unbaptized foreheads.

Both of these seem macabre, but it is likely that they were also intended, at least
in part, to be funny: Grani's stanza presents battle as a Yuletide feast for greedy
children, while Arnórr's shows it more as a barbecue.

There is clearly something psychological, even therapeutic, in this
lighthearted use of the motif. Soldiers have always had to learn to laugh about
killing other human beings. They have to distance themselves from that which
they have to do, in order to be able to do it at all (Grossman 1995, 156–70). The
elegiac type of poetry (the Old English, or the Eddic) emphasizes the fear and
the distaste. In contrast, the upbeat tone of skaldic verse reflects the training of
warriors to suppress these feelings of fear and distaste, in order to become more
effective. And it is the poet's duty to train them, as can be seen in another stanza
by Arnórr (*Skjd* BI:309):

Hefnir, fenguð yrkisefni,
Áleifs; gervik slíkt at mólum;
hlakkar lætr þú hrælǫg drekka
hauka; nú mun kvæði aukask;

Óláfr's avenger, you provided the stuff of poetry. I turn it into language.
You cause the hawks of Hlǫkk [valkyrie > eagle/raven] to drink the liquid
of corpses [blood]. Now the ode will increase.

The heroic deeds of the king, in this case Magnús the Good, create material for the poet, who processes the experience for his audience. War becomes poetry. By this means one can forget how unpleasant it really was and be psychologically prepared for the next time.

The beasts of battle motif is central to skaldic verse. In other literary traditions, such as the Old English, or the Eddic poems, its function is primarily aesthetic. In skaldic praise poetry it has other functions, because this poetry is more intimately associated with the active war-band. Here, the motif has a social function, that of giving prominence to the hero's, the leader's, status and achievements. But if the aim was only to praise the leader, then this could have been done in many other ways. The beasts of battle motif is chosen over other possibilities because it also has a psychological, conditioning function for the audience: the continual use of the motif prepares all warriors for the distasteful side of their profession, alienates them from what happens on the battlefield and enables them to suppress their desire to flee from it. This preparation happens when the warrior band is gathered to hear the skald recite his poem in the collective and celebratory milieu of the feast. The skald is a key figure, not just in the propaganda apparatus of the chieftain, but also in the effective functioning of the whole warrior group.[2]

CONCLUSION

Skaldic verse is indispensable evidence for the study of the conceptual world of the Viking Age. Such texts are not just 'literature', but had important social and psychological functions. Precisely because of their public nature and these functions they are important sources for understanding war in the Viking Age, and what it was that made Vikings 'brave and resourceful fighters' (Clarke 1999, 58). The poems are well enough known to students of the period, but too little used – here I have tried to show how they can be used. For it is only by reading skaldic verse that we can discover what it felt like to be a warrior, and how warriors were prepared for this profession, at least on the psychological level, by the public performance of poetry about past battles.

BIBLIOGRAPHY

ASPR = Krapp, G.P. & E.V.K. Dobbie (eds). 1931–53. *The Anglo-Saxon poetic records* (New York).
Carroll, J. 2005. 'Narrative and direct address in skaldic verse' in A. Mortensen & S.V. Arge (eds), *Viking and Norse in the North Atlantic: select papers from the Fourteenth Viking Congress* (Tórshavn), pp 427–45.

2 On some of the ways in which the poetic text can reveal the relationship between the skald and his audience, see Carroll 2005.

Clarke, H.B. 1999. 'The Vikings' in M. Keen (ed.), *Medieval warfare* (London), pp 38–58.

DR = Jacobsen, L. & E. Moltke (eds). 1941–2. *Danmarks runeindskrifter* (Copenhagen).

Frank, R. 1991. 'The ideal of men dying with their lord in *The Battle of Maldon*: anachronism or *nouvelle vague*' in I. Wood & N. Lund (eds), *People and places in Northern Europe, 500–1600: essays in honour of Peter Sawyer* (Woodbridge), pp 95–106.

GA = Liebermann, F. (ed.). 1903–12. *Die Gesetze der Angelsachsen* (Halle).

Griffith, M.S. 1993. 'Convention and originality in the Old English "Beasts of Battle" typescene', *Anglo-Saxon England*, 22, 179–99.

Grossman, D. 1995. *On killing: the psychological cost of learning to kill in war and society* (Boston, MA).

Jansson, S.B.F. 1987. *Runes in Sweden* (Stockholm).

Jesch, J. 2001. *Ships and men in the Late Viking Age: the vocabulary of runic inscriptions and skaldic verse* (Woodbridge).

Jesch, J. 2002. 'Eagles, ravens and wolves: beasts of battle, symbols of victory and death' in J. Jesch (ed.), *Scandinavians from the Vendel period to the tenth century* (Woodbridge), 251–71.

Samnordisk runtextdatabas. 2004. <http://www.nordiska.uu.se/forskn/samnord.htm>.

Skjd = Finnur Jónsson (ed.). 1912–15. *Den norsk-islandske skjaldedigtning* (Copenhagen).

Sö = Brate, E. & E. Wessén (eds). 1924–36. *Södermanlands runinskrifter* (Stockholm).

U = Wessén, E. & S.B.F. Jansson (eds). 1940–58. *Upplands runinskrifter* (Stockholm).

Vs = Jansson, S.B.F. (ed.). 1974. *Västmanlands runinskrifter* (Stockholm).

The Vikings in Connemara

EAMONN KELLY

INTRODUCTION

The Connemara coastline of Co. Galway, on Ireland's west coast, consists of a number of peninsulas that are separated by broad bays or narrow inlets (Fig. 17.1). In places, the coast is fringed with sand-based grassland, known as *machair*, and offshore islands abound, some of which are inhabited. Examination of a recently compiled database of archaeological finds from Co. Galway (Gibbons 2004) indicates that the coastal region was settled from prehistoric times onwards, with a good deal of Neolithic and Bronze Age material present. With the advent of Christianity, small monastic settlements were founded throughout this region (Gosling 1993, 89–115), possibly on relatively unoccupied lands (Bradley 1988, 67). There appears to be a relatively low incidence of early medieval stray finds of pre Viking-Age date from the region, other than those associated with ecclesiastical sites (Gibbons 2004), and there is an almost total absence of ringforts that elsewhere in the country are associated with early medieval settlement (McCormick et al. 1996, 84; Gosling 1993, 36–43).

By contrast, there are a number of midden sites in various places along the coastline that have produced Viking-Age finds, in addition to others that have not yielded any artefacts but which have been radiocarbon-dated to the Viking Age. Such middens occur at Eyrephort, on Omey Island, around False Bay, Doonloughan Bay, Mannin Bay and Ballyconneely Bay, in the vicinity of Slyne Head and in the Roundstone area. All of the sites share the common factor of being located in immediate proximity to good landing beaches.

There is growing archaeological evidence to support the proposal that an influx of Viking settlers into the region may have been largely responsible for the creation of these middens, and this is supported by historical and place-name evidence.

THE COMING OF THE VIKINGS

According to the Annals of Inisfallen, one of the earliest Viking raids on Ireland took place in 795 when Inishbofin, off the Connemara coast, was struck, following earlier attacks on Iona and Inishmurray (Mac Airt 1988, 119). More than a decade elapsed before the next recorded attack on a monastery in the area. This was the raid of 807 that targeted Roscam, near Oranmore, overlooking

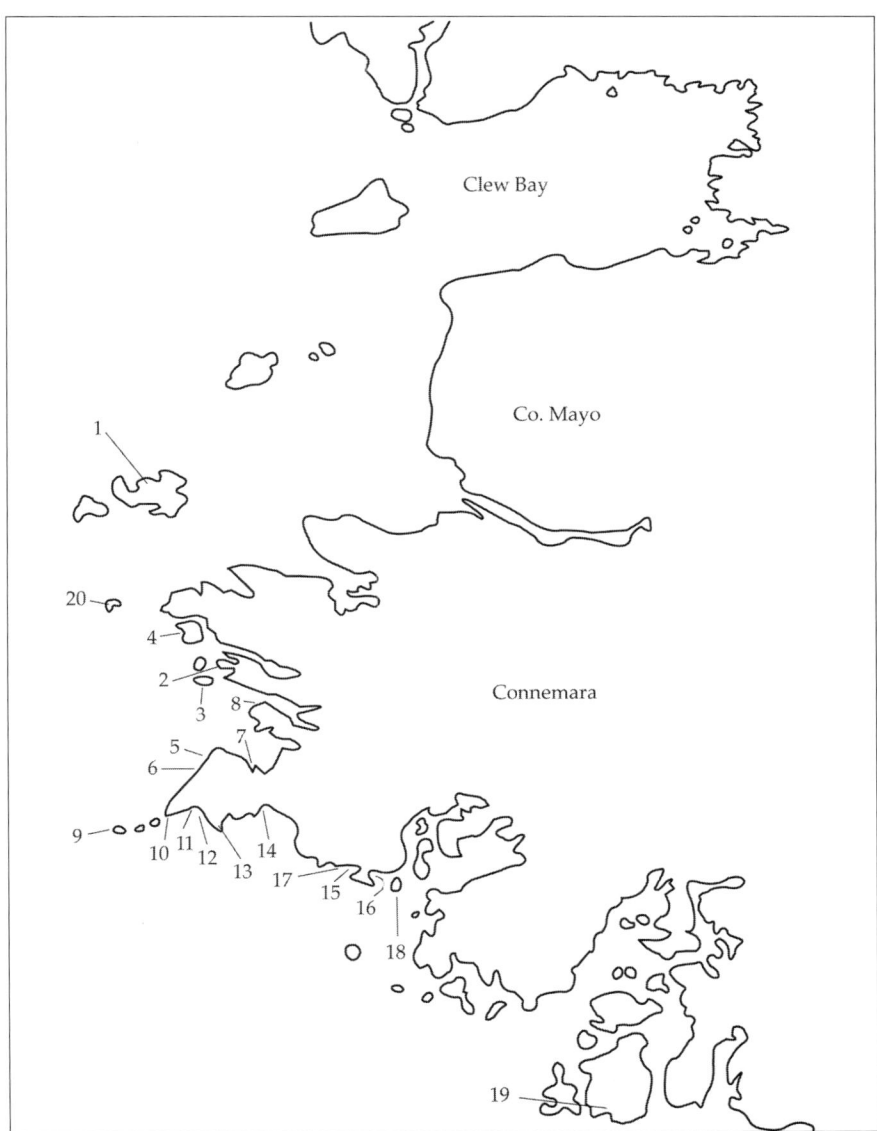

17.1 Map of Connemara and south Mayo, showing places referred to in the text:
1: Inishbofin; 2: Eyrephort; 3: Turbot Island; 4: Omey Island; 5: False Bay, Truska;
6: Doonloughan Bay; 7: Ship Harbour, Mannin Bay; 8: Boat Harbour; 9: Slyne Head;
10: Ballinleama; 11: Silverhill; 12: Creggoduff; 13: Aillebrack; 14: Ballyconneely Bay; 15: Dogs
Bay; 16: Gorteen Bay; 17: Murvey; 18: Inishlackan; 19: Maumeen; 20: High Island.

Galway Bay (Ó Corráin, 1996, 236), having earlier struck Inishmurray (O'Donovan
1856, 413). Not surprisingly, the annalistic accounts highlight the attacks on
Inishbofin, Inishmurray and Roscam. However, raiding monasteries may not

have been the sole purpose, or perhaps even the primary purpose, of the Viking incursion into the area. The attacks on Inishbofin and Roscam have all the hallmarks of being opportunistic raids by fleets that may have come from Norway or Scotland to explore the west coast of Ireland in order to assess the settlement potential of the region.

Following the raid on Roscam, no further mention is made in the annals of attacks on coastal monasteries in the area. This deficiency may be the result of failure to record such events, but it may also suggest that the coastal areas of Connemara came quickly under Scandinavian control.

SECOND PHASE OF VIKING ACTIVITY

Following what we might regard as initial exploratory expeditions, there appears to have been a change in the nature of Viking activity in the area. This may have begun in the second decade of the ninth century, when there appear to have been attempts by the Vikings to secure bases along the Connemara coast and the adjoining coastal areas of south Mayo. Under the year 812, the annals record that 'A slaughter was made of the foreigners by the men of Umhall' in the Clew Bay area of Mayo, and this is followed by 'A slaughter is made of the Conmaicne by the foreigner' (O'Donovan 1856, 419). The Conmaicne Mara were the people who controlled Connemara during the early medieval period, and from whom the modern name of the region derives. For the year 813, the annals once more record a battle between the men of Umhall and the foreigners, in which the Vikings emerged triumphant (O'Donovan 1856, 419).

The annalistic accounts of Irish resistance demonstrate that Viking settlement was only achievable at some cost to the invaders. The potential rewards to be obtained from raiding the relatively impoverished coastal monasteries would hardly justify the cost to the Vikings of establishing bases on the Galway and Mayo coasts. It seems more likely that what lay behind the warfare of 812–13 was a desire by them to establish farming settlements on the machair grasslands that were suitable for grazing animals and for cereal production. What may also have attracted them were opportunities to exploit the rich marine resources of the area, a bounty that appears to have been under-utilized by the natives. That this was the case is suggested by the pattern of recorded activity on the eastern seaboard, where, having secured the coastal areas of Counties Louth and Meath in 827, the Vikings engaged in a great slaughter of marine mammals in the following year (Kelly and Maas 1999, 149, n. 4).

EYREPHORT BURIAL

The name Eyrephort (from the Irish *Iarphort*, 'the western port') may be an abbreviated form of *Iarlongphort*, a name that would indicate a Viking base.

Eyrephort is located at the tip of a long rocky peninsula, the end of which is low-lying with expanses of machair and sand dunes and a small sheltered cove with a gently sloping sandy beach. Offshore islands and rocky shoals help to protect Eyrephort from the worst excesses of Atlantic storms, while the high rocky peninsula offers security from the landward side.

Close to the beach, a ninth-century Viking warrior burial was discovered, containing a sword, a shield and a spear, the broken head of which Raftery mistook for a dagger (Raftery 1960–1, 3–6). Raftery interpreted the burial as the isolated grave of a man who died at sea; however, other scholars believe that the grave may have been associated with wider Scandinavian coastal settlement of the area (Bradley 1988, 67; Sheehan 1987–8, 70; Gibbons and Kelly 2003, 28–32).

TURBOT ISLAND

Offshore from Eyrephort is Turbot Island, for which the Irish name is Inis Tairbeart. The place-name element *tairbeart* is indicative of a place where the portage of boats occurred, an activity associated with Viking mariners. At the eastern end of Turbot Island, there is a low narrow isthmus, flanked by beaches that would have provided options to land in varying wind and tidal conditions and where portages could have been effected easily. Midden deposits of an unknown age have been noted on the isthmus (Robinson 1990, 55).

OMEY ISLAND

Low-lying and machair-covered, Omey is a tidal island to the north of Turbot Island. Towards its north-eastern corner, in the townland of Cartoorbeg, a kidney-ringed polyhedral pin (Fig. 17.3; NMI 2002:20) was found protruding from midden deposits that have been radiocarbon-dated to between AD890 and 1050. The shells present are predominantly cockle, but razor shells, periwinkles and limpets also occur; animal, fish and bird bones are also present. As one proceeds westward along the coast from the midden in question, other middens are present in Cartoorbeg and the adjoining townland of Sturrakeen, but these have yielded no artefacts. Beyond that, in Gooreen townland, there is the site of a monastery founded by St Feicin, where burials and occupation horizons have been excavated (O'Keeffe 1994, 14–17). A second kidney-ringed polyhedral pin from the island is recorded as having been found in a sand dune near this church (Fig. 17.3; NMI 1935:170). However, this vague provenance may mean that it is from one of the Cartoorbeg or Sturrakeen sites, rather than from the church site itself (NMI topographical files). At the southern end of the island, there is an extensive midden at Gooreenatinny and, although artefacts have not been recorded in association with it, it has yielded a calibrated radiocarbon date of 1000–1150, obtained from charcoal (Gosling 1993, 86).

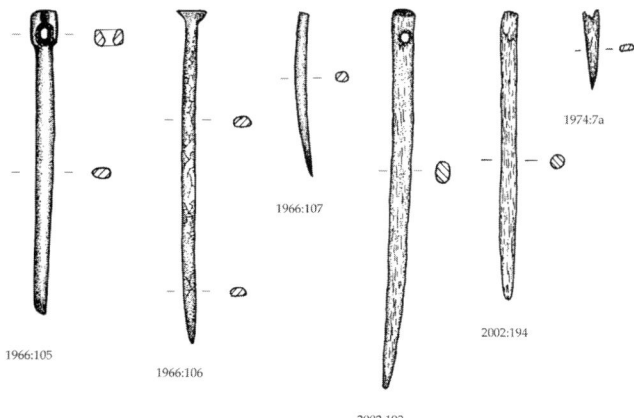

17.2 Bone and antler objects. Aillebrack (1966: 105–7), Ballyconneely (2002: 193–4), Doonloughan (1974: 7a), Truska (1999: 201; 1986: 81), Gorteen Bay (Errisbeg East) (1961: 82).

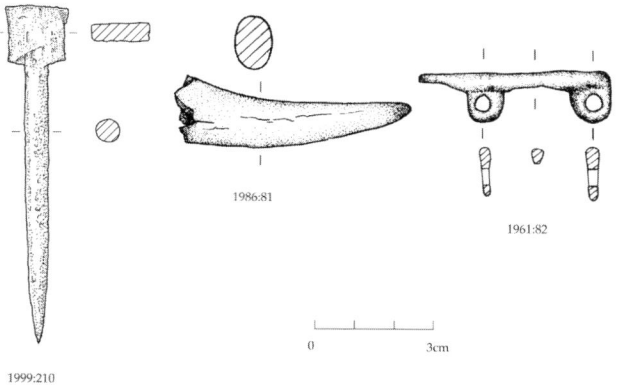

HOUSE SITE, BURIALS AND MIDDEN DEPOSITS AT TRUSKA, FALSE BAY

The place-name Truska may derive from the Old Norse word for a codfish, a name that may have been suggested by the shape of a high dune overlooking False Bay. Near the highest elevation of the dune, human remains and an associated Viking-Age house were discovered in recent years (Gibbons and Kelly 2003, 28–32). Built of stone, the house was rectangular in plan with rounded corners. It was of sunken form, with a gable entrance accessed by a ramp. Erosion has destroyed much of the structure, but it measured approximately 4m by 2.5m internally. It is similar in form to early tenth-century, small, un-aisled examples from Fishamble Street, Dublin, and late ninth-century examples from Essex Street (Simpson 2000, 22–3). Like the Truska house, these are sunken, with gabled and ramped entrances, although the walls are made of wattle as opposed to being stone-built (Simpson 1999, 13–17, fig. 3). A stone-built sunken house of Viking-Age date at Beginish, Co. Kerry, is also of similar form, although it is a more substantial structure (Sheehan et al. 2001, 93–119).

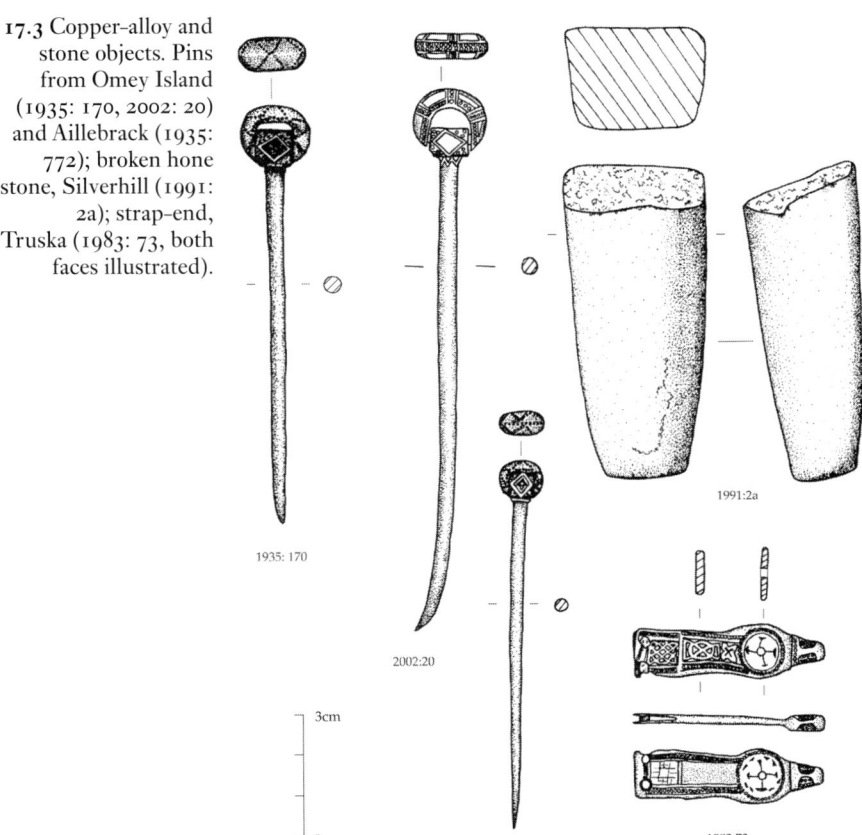

17.3 Copper-alloy and stone objects. Pins from Omey Island (1935: 170, 2002: 20) and Aillebrack (1935: 772); broken hone stone, Silverhill (1991: 2a); strap-end, Truska (1983: 73, both faces illustrated).

1935: 170

2002:20

3cm

0

1935:772

1991:2a

1983:73

A grave dug into the entrance ramp of the Truska house contained the extended skeletons of two young adult males, orientated roughly east-to-west, with the heads to the east. This orientation is the direct opposite to what is found in most Irish Christian burials of the period, where the head is normally to the west. A layer of stones was used to cover the grave and these appear to have been taken from the wall of the house, which clearly pre-dates the burials. Calibrated radiocarbon dates of AD680–890 and AD660–870 were obtained for the skeletons, which post-date the house and appear to coincide with its abandonment. On this evidence, the house could not date any later than the late ninth century. The dates obtained for the burials compare well with a date of between AD700 and 900 obtained from midden material at Truska (Gosling 1993, 85). However, it is not clear from which midden deposit this date was obtained.

A fragment of a decorated antler comb was found on the floor of the Truska house (Gibbons and Kelly 2003, 29). In its general size and decoration the comb compares most closely to an early tenth-century example from Fishamble Street, Dublin (Ian Riddler, pers. comm.) and to a comb fragment from Carraig Aille II,

Co. Limerick (Ó Ríordáin 1948–50, 80, fig. 13, 10.I), a site that also produced a hoard of Viking silver.

A fragment of the upper stone of a rotary quern, carbonized cereal grains, the bones of cattle, sheep, pig, and possibly horse, together with quantities of shells and fish bones, suggest that the occupants of the Truska house engaged in mixed farming and fishing. Stray finds from Truska may relate to the excavated house or may indicate that it is part of a larger settlement. These finds include an antler pin of a type that occurs in Viking-Age Dublin (Fig. 17.2; NMI 1999:210) and a cut antler tine, perhaps left over from the making of combs and pins (Fig. 17.2; NMI 1986:81). Also in the townland of Truska, but to the south of False Bay, a strap-tag of tenth-century date was found in a midden overlooking Doonloughan Bay (Fig. 17.3; NMI 1983:73). Towards the northern end of the beach in the same area, there are three middens, designated as DL2–DL4. Charcoal from collapsed burnt wickerwork on DL3 produced a calibrated date-range of AD779–881 (McCormick et al. 1996, fig. 1, 77, 81). The broken shank of a bone pin, recorded as being from Doonloughan, was probably found in the same complex of middens (Fig. 17.2; NMI 1974:7a).

SHIP HARBOUR, MANNIN BAY

The place-names 'Ship Harbour', located on Mannin Bay, and 'Boat Harbour', at the extreme tip of the Errislannin peninsula, may both be relatively modern translations into English of the Gaelic place-name *longphort*, a name that may indicate the former presence of a Viking base (Gibbons and Kelly 2003, 32). Middens around Ship Harbour in Mannin More townland have produced antler tines (NMI 2007:6) that may have been associated with the production of combs and pins. The bones of cattle and sheep/goat, representing food debris, were also found. There have also been three separate finds of glass and amber beads (Fig. 17.4), some of which can be paralleled among the grave finds from Birka and from Viking-Age Dublin.

MIDDENS AND SETTLEMENTS AROUND SLYNE HEAD

To the south-west of Ship Harbour and Truska extends a peninsula that terminates in a small archipelago at Slyne Head. The twelfth-century Icelandic text *Landnámabók* refers to a place in Ireland, named *Jolduhlaup* ('Mare's Leap'), as being a five-day sail from Reykjanes in Iceland. *Léim Lára* meaning 'Mare's Leap' was the Irish name for Slyne Head and the Old Norse name is considered to be a direct translation of it (Ó Tuathail 1948–52, 155–6). The occurrence of the place-name clearly indicates that the Icelanders had a strong familiarity with the west coast of Ireland, and with the Connemara coast in particular.

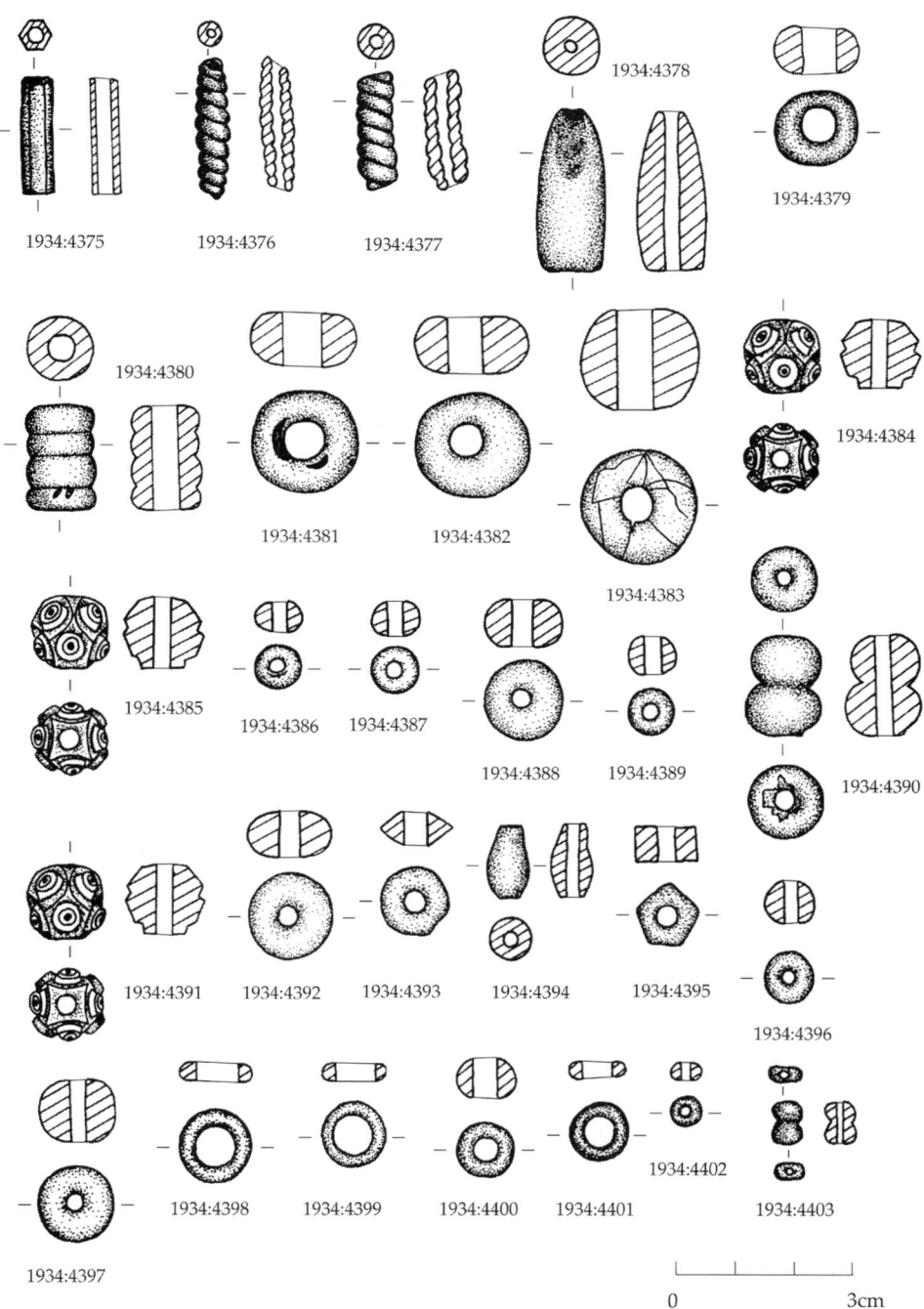

17.4 Glass, amber and stone beads from middens in the vicinity of Ship Harbour, Mannin Bay (acquired in three discrete groups – 1934: 4375–8; 1934: 4379–87; 1934: 4388–402).

In the vicinity of Slyne Head there are middens at Ballinaleama, where they are found in association with field walls and a possible house-site (Gosling 1993, 84; NMI topographical files); other midden sites are located close by in the townlands of Silverhill (ibid., 88), Aillebrack (ibid., 84) and Creggoduff (ibid., 85). A bronze kidney-ringed polyhedral pin of the same type as those found on Omey Island was discovered in a layer of limpet shells in a midden at Aillebrack (Fig. 17.3; NMI 1935:772). At least two other ringed pins and a bone pin (all of unknown type) were also found in the same area, but they were unfortunately lost without having been recorded (NMI topographical files). However, three bone pins from Aillebrack were acquired by the National Museum and they are of forms comparable to the Viking Dublin assemblage (Fig. 17.2; NMI 1966:105–7).

A midden at Silverhill yielded a broken hone of Viking-Age type (Fig. 17.3; NMI 1991:2a) as well as shells and animal bones. Human remains were also found in the area, but they are of unknown date (Gosling 1993, 88). The Irish form of the place-name is *Cnocán an Airgid* – 'the small hill of the silver' (Robinson, 1990, 67), perhaps relating to the former discovery of silver objects there. Two Viking-Age silver hoards have been found in Co. Galway, one from the vicinity of Galway City and the other unprovenanced (Briggs 1981–2, 79–82). No finds have been recorded from the midden deposits at Creggoduff, but a radiocarbon date produced a date-range of between AD1000 and 1200 (Gosling 1993, 85). Ballyconneely Bay lies to the east of the Slyne Head group of middens and close to the shoreline. On the west side of the bay there is a midden (ibid., 84) that has yielded two bone pins (Fig. 17.2; NMI 2002:193–4).

MIDDENS IN THE ROUNDSTONE AREA

Near the village of Roundstone in south Connemara there is a classic tombolo that forms a sandy isthmus, flanked by beaches, separating Dogs Bay from Gorteen Bay. The position of the beaches means that boats can land on the isthmus in varying wind conditions. The Irish name for Gorteen Bay is *Port na Feadóige* ('the harbour of the plovers') and the use of the term *port* ('a built or fortified harbour') rather than *cuan* ('a natural harbour') may be significant.

Midden deposits on the isthmus have yielded a number of Viking-Age antiquities. Two bramble-headed stickpins of a type that has a date-range of between *c.*AD 975 and 1075 are recorded as having been found at Gorteen Bay (NMI topographical files) and a bone object, possibly for net-making (Fig. 17.2; NMI 1961:82) was found in a midden in Errisbeg East, close to the northwest shore of the bay.

At Dogs Bay, in the townland of Errisbeg West, two crucibles of Hiberno-Norse type (Fig. 17.5; NMI 1989:3–4) were found close to where an excavation

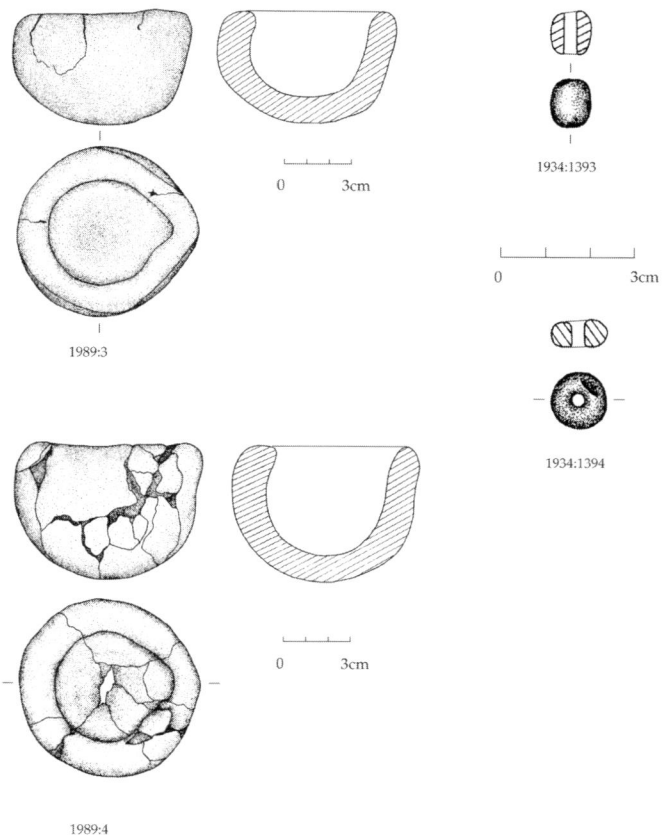

17.5 Two crucibles (1989: 3–4) and two amber beads (1934: 1393–4), Dogs Bay middens.

uncovered a corn-drying kiln, carbonized grain, shells, fish and animal bones (Gibbons 1992, 19–20). The crucibles are of a type found in Dublin that appears to have been used to smelt silver (Justine Bayley, pers. comm.). Also in the Dogs Bay middens were found three amber beads (one now missing) that may be of Viking-Age date (Fig. 17.5; NMI 1934:1393–4). Flanking the north shore of the bay, further middens occur to the west, in Murvey townland; these, however, have produced no diagnostic finds and remain undated. Offshore of Gorteen Bay, to the east, is the island of Inishlackan, where midden deposits occur close to the shore in association with undated burials (Gosling 1993, 86, 143).

At Maumeen, also in south Connemara, two radiocarbon dates were obtained for the earliest habitation associated with a midden deposit. These yielded date ranges of AD870–1020 and 880–1040 respectively. However, no diagnostic finds were made (Erin Gibbons, pers. comm.).

DISCUSSION

During the seventeenth century, cereal cultivation and cattle, particularly milk-cows that were taken to the uplands in summer, were the mainstays of the local agrarian economy in Connemara (O'Flaherty 1684, 15–17) and this pattern may reflect that of earlier times. An influx of Scandinavian settlers to the coastal zone may not have significantly threatened the established way of life of the native Conmaicne Mara. Scandinavian settlers would have brought with them useful maritime technology and knowledge that may have included boat-building, deep-sea fishing, the skills to hunt marine mammals, fish-processing and preservation techniques as well as long-distance trading activities. All of these could have provided a major boost to the local economy. The model proposed by Sheehan of Scandinavian settlers intermarrying with the native Irish and accepting local Irish overlordship may accurately reflect what occurred in Connemara (Sheehan 1987–8, 70).

The presence in the Connemara middens of pins, a strap-tag, beads and crucibles that all appear to have originated in Viking-Age Dublin must be considered further. There are three ringed pins of the kidney-ringed polyhedral class present (two from Omey Island and one from Aillebrack, Slyne Head). This form emerged in the mid- to late tenth century and continued in use throughout the eleventh century. Most ringed pins of this class have been found in Dublin, from where thirty examples are on record, of which twenty come from Fishamble Street within contexts dated *c.*AD975–1000 (Fanning 1994, 38). Outside of Dublin, the type occurs in the midlands, reflecting commercial and political links between Dublin and the kingdom of Míde. The pins in question from Aillebrack and Omey Island are almost certainly from a Dublin workshop, and this small cluster of finds on the west coast must be regarded as significant.

Although the type may have originated elsewhere (O'Rahilly 1998, 32), the two bramble-headed stickpins of late tenth- and eleventh-century date from the Gorteen Bay middens may also be imports from Dublin. The bone and antler pins from Truska, Doonloughan, Ballyconneely and Aillebrack share the same cultural background as the various bronze pins and they are of forms that were in contemporary use in Dublin, as were some of the beads found around Ship Harbour and in the Dogs Bay area. The presence of objects of Dublin work-manship, such as the strap-tag from Truska and the two crucibles from Dogs Bay, makes a strong argument for direct contacts between the coastal settlements of Connemara and Dublin, the main Viking town on the eastern seaboard.

One possible explanation is that the sites were way-stations for vessels travelling in an anticlockwise direction around the coast from Dublin to Limerick, and for sea traffic into Limerick from places like Iceland, Scotland and Scandinavia that would also have moved along the Connemara coast. Such way-stations could have provided safe beaches where ships could land to shelter from storms as well as take on water and provisions and make repairs. It is also possible that the Connemara settlements were involved in the production of food for sale to the growing Viking towns, especially Dublin and Limerick.

There has been no systematic examination of the Connemara middens from the standpoint of identifying the species represented by the discarded shells and fish bones. It is clear, however, that many of the sites appear to be the remains of bait middens in which limpet and periwinkle shells predominate. The bait was used for line-fishing that could have caught inshore species, as well as deep-water species such as cod and ling that were present in large numbers offshore (O'Flaherty 1684, 11–12). If quantities of fish were dried, cured or salted, they would have provided a valuable commodity, the sale of which could explain the presence in Connemara of consumer items manufactured in Viking Dublin.

The Viking town of Limerick may also have provided a ready market for such produce. In 923, a leading Limerick Viking named Tomrar, son of Tomralt, attacked the Conmaicne Mara and they killed him in the ensuing fighting. This may have been an attempt by Tomrar to gain control over the economically valuable resources of Connemara, as well as strategic control over the northern sea-route into Limerick. By the early eleventh century, Limerick was under the control of Brian Bóruma, king of Munster, at a time when the Conmaicne Mara were threatened by more powerful Connacht neighbours (ibid., 366). O'Flaherty claims that a contingent of the Conmaicne Mara fought for Brian Bóruma at the battle of Clontarf, where their chief, Murtagh O'Cadhla, met his death (ibid., 366–7), which suggests that the Conmaicne Mara may have formed a protective alliance with the Munster king. Brian Bóruma may even have visited Connemara, where there is a well named after him on High Island (White Marshall and Rourke 2000, 30).

A coin found during excavations at the High Island monastery may provide concrete evidence of connections between Limerick and Connemara during the eleventh century. It is a rare silver penny that is based on an English penny of Edward the Confessor, dating to between *c.*1050 and 1100 (identified by Michael Kenny, NMI). Only one similar coin is known to exist, and this is a specimen published by H.A. Parsons, who proposed that it was the product of a Limerick mint (1920–1, 59–71).

The High Island excavations also revealed the grave of an adult male who was buried within the by now abandoned church sometime between 1169 and 1221 (White Marshall and Rourke 2000, 92). Unusually, the grave contained grave-goods in the form of a hone-stone and a fishing weight (Scally 1997, fig. 13). Although located within a Christian church, the form of the burial reflects pagan Scandinavian traditions, and it is probable that the burial goods were imbued with important symbolism concerning the deceased. The hone-stone may indicate that he was a man of high status and the weight suggests that he played an important role in the local fishing industry.

CONCLUSION

The overall evidence seems to suggest that there was a substantial Viking settlement in the coastal areas of Connemara. The recent reassessment of the Beginish settlement in Kerry (Sheehan et al. 2001), together with the incidence of Viking-Age finds along the Mayo, Sligo and Donegal coastlines, suggest that there may have been a Scandinavian presence all along the Atlantic coast of Ireland. One of the most enduring legacies of the Vikings may have been their shipbuilding technology that endured into the high medieval period, in the vessels used for trade, piracy and warfare by the O'Malleys (descendants of the men of Umhall) and the O'Flahertys (who came to dominate Connemara in the early second millennium AD). In the late sixteenth century, when Grace O'Malley gained renown for her daring maritime exploits (Chambers 2003), it is probable that many of the mariners who served her were themselves the descendants of Vikings who had settled on the west coast of Ireland.

ACKNOWLEDGMENT

Recent fieldwork and research into Viking-Age sites in the west of Ireland has been undertaken in collaboration with Erin Gibbons, whose invaluable contribution is gratefully acknowledged.

BIBLIOGRAPHY

Bradley, J. 1988. 'The interpretation of Scandinavian settlement in Ireland' in J. Bradley (ed.), *Settlement and society in medieval Ireland: studies presented to F.X. Martin, O.S.A.* (Kilkenny), pp 49–78.

Briggs, S.C. 1981–2. 'On the Viking-Age silver hoards from Co. Galway', *Journal of the Galway Archaeological and Historical Society*, 38, 79–82.

Chambers, A. 2003. *Granuaile, Ireland's pirate queen: Grace O'Malley, c.1530–1603* (Dublin).

Fanning, T. 1994. *Viking-Age ringed pins from Dublin*, National Museum of Ireland Medieval Dublin Excavations 1962–81, Royal Irish Academy Ser. B, vol. 4 (Dublin).

Gibbons, E. 1992. 'Iorras Beag Thiar, Port na Feadoige (Dogs Bay) settlement site' in I. Bennet (ed.), *Excavations: summary report of archaeological excavations 1991*, no. 56, 19–20.

Gibbons, E.K. 2004. 'List of archaeological finds from Co. Galway' in E. Gibbons, S. O'Connell & A. Sherwood, *Galway County Museum Service Feasibility Study* (for Orna Hanley Architects, on behalf of Galway County Council), appendix.

Gibbons, E.K. & E.P. Kelly. 2003. 'A Viking-Age farmstead in Connemara', *Archaeology Ireland*, 17:1, 28–32.

Gosling, P. 1993. *Archaeological inventory of county Galway, Vol. 1: West Galway* (Dublin).

Kelly, E.P. & J. Maas. 1999. 'The Vikings and the kingdom of Laois' in P.G. Lane & W. Nolan (eds), *Laois history and society: interdisciplinary essays on the history of an Irish county* (Dublin), pp 123–59.

Mac Airt, S. (ed.). 1988. *The Annals of Inisfallen* (Dublin).

McCormick, F., M. Gibbons, F.G. McCormac & J. Moore. 1996. 'Bronze Age to medieval coastal shell middens near Ballyconneely, Co. Galway', *Journal of Irish Archaeology*, 7, 77–84.

Ó Corráin, D. 1996. 'Vikings II: Ros Camm', *Peritia*, 10, 236.

O'Donovan, J. (ed.). 1856. *Annála ríoghachta Éireann: Annals of the kingdom of Ireland by the Four Masters from the earliest period to the year 1616*, vol. 1 (Dublin).

O'Flaherty, R. 1684. *A chorographical description of West or H-Iar Connaught, Written A.D. 1684, By Roderic O'Flaherty, Esq.*, ed. J. Hardiman (Dublin, 1846).

O'Keeffe, T. 1994. 'Omey and the sands of time', *Archaeology Ireland*, 8:2, 14–17.

O'Rahilly, C. 1998. 'A classification of bronze stick-pins from the Dublin excavations 1962–72' in C. Manning (ed.), *Dublin and beyond the Pale: studies in honour of Patrick Healy*, (Bray), pp 23–33.

Ó Ríordáin, S.P. 1948–50. 'Lough Gur excavations: Carrig Aille and the "Spectacles"', *Proceedings of the Royal Irish Academy*, 52C, 39–111.

Ó Tuathail, E. 1948–52. 'Léim Lára', *Éigse*, 6, 155–6.

Parsons, H.A. 1921–2. 'An Irish eleventh-century coin of the Southern O'Neil', *British Numismatic Journal*, 16, 59–71.

Raftery, J. 1960–1. 'A Viking burial in Co. Galway', *Journal of the Galway Archaeological and Historical Society*, 29, 3–6.

Robinson, T. 1990. *Connemara: Part 1: introduction and gazetteer; Part 2: a one-inch map*, Roundstone, Co. Galway.

Scally, G. 1997. High Island, Co. Galway: stratigraphical report for 1996 (unpublished report).

Sheehan, J. 1987–8. 'A reassessment of the Viking burial from Eyrephort, Co. Galway', *Journal of the Galway Archaeological and Historical Society*, 41, 60–72.

Sheehan, J., S. Stummann Hansen & D. Ó Corráin. 2001. 'A Viking-Age maritime haven: a reassessment of the island settlement at Beginish, Co. Kerry', *Journal of Irish Archaeology*, 10, 93–119.

Simpson, L. 1999. *Director's findings: Temple Bar West*, Temple Bar Archaeological Report, 5 (Dublin).

Simpson, L. 2000. 'Forty years a-digging: a preliminary synthesis of archaeological investigations in medieval Dublin', *Medieval Dublin I: Proceedings of the Friends of Medieval Dublin Symposium 1999* (Dublin), pp 11–68.

White Marshall, J. & G.D. Rourke. 2000. *High Island: an Irish monastery in the Atlantic* (Dublin).

Dotted runes: where did they come from?

JAMES E. KNIRK

The question posed here concerns the source of the late Viking-Age and medieval dotted runes – that is, characters with a diacritical dot – as a part of the inventory of signs in Scandinavian inscriptions. This can be understood as two inter-related questions: (1) where did the idea of the dot come from? and (2) where was the system developed?

BACKGROUND

Runic script changed dramatically around the dawn of the Viking Age. The older futhark, with twenty-four runes, was replaced by the younger futhark, with only sixteen symbols. This probably happened in the early 700s, since the Ribe cranium-fragment, now fixed to 725–60 (Bencard 2004, 10–15), bears the earliest archaeologically dated inscription where the sixteen-rune futhark is employed (Stoklund 1996; 2007).

The older futhark had already undergone gradual changes through the centuries (Knirk 2002, 638–40; cf. Schulte 2006a): a few infrequent runes were apparently no longer used in inscriptions (for example ï/ë and p); some had assumed new sound-values (for example j in an altered form stood for a); and several individual signs had come to represent two or more distinct sounds in the language. This representational ambiguity was mainly due to the phonological processes of i- and u-mutation (umlaut), whereby new vowel sounds had arisen, which, in conjunction with the loss of short unstressed vowels (syncope), were transformed from positional variants into distinguishing sounds. New signs were not created for these novel phonemes, and the traditional forms had then to signify both original sound and innovation. The developments mentioned above were generally results of the phonological revolution that occurred in the late Proto-Nordic language during this transitional period. Changes also affected consonants with a radical alteration in the distribution of stops and spirants. By the early 700s, the Viking-Age and medieval language of Scandinavia was more or less established.

The term 'reform' ('alphabet reform' or the like) is frequently used to describe the establishment of the sixteen-rune futhark. The linguistic changes presented above provide a background, but the sudden emergence of a well-ordered new system in all of Scandinavia (with some variation, however) out of

f u þ a r k h n i a s t b m l R   f u þ a r k h n i a s t b m l R

18.1 Examples of short-twig (left) and long-branch Viking-Age runes (after Knirk 2002, 641).

the more chaotic conditions of the transitional period seems to require the will of a reformer. The concept of a 'reform' has been challenged (for example recently by Schulte 2006b; 2006c), but the concept still seems necessary to describe the full change. There is otherwise no explanation for the apparently deliberate removal of the older *d*- and *g*-runes from the runic inventory. In addition, the forms of the younger runes, particularly in the short-twig variant (see below), indicate clearly a systematic restructuring of the shapes into a consistent graphematic system (Loman 1965). The new short-twig forms simply could not have developed gradually from the older shapes; a 'reformer' was necessary for these graphic innovations, one who also could have carried out the systematic restructurings of the sixteen-rune futhark that cannot be explained by gradual developments.

The two major variants of the younger futhark, termed the short-twig and long-branch runes, are illustrated in Figure 18.1. Many of the short-twig runes are graphically simpler than the long-branch variants, and they represent a more compact system with several pairs showing minimal distinctions. Traditionally, the relationship between the two variants has been viewed as a two-stage simplification: (a) the row of older runes was shortened to sixteen and several individual shapes were somewhat simplified, thus giving rise to the long-branch forms; (b) the long-branch forms were soon thereafter further simplified to the short-twig runes. Aslak Liestøl, however, challenged this scenario (1981a; 1981b), arguing for the primacy of the short-twig runes. His suggestion produced a simpler model for the reform that led to the younger runes: a one-step reform with all changes of shortening and simplification resulting in the short-twig runes, and then a mixture of this result with various antiquated older runes to produce the long-branch variant. Liestøl has received some support (Barnes 1987; Barnes 2000; Knirk 2002, 640–2).

It is interesting that in England and Friesland, where many phonological changes occurred similar to those in Scandinavia, as well as some specifically Anglo-Frisian developments, the inventory of runes was not curtailed, as in Scandinavia, but rather expanded from the original twenty-four to twenty-six in Friesland and twenty-eight in England (eventually thirty-one), with new runic shapes being created to represent the new distinct sounds in the language (Page 1999, 38–48; cf. Parsons 1999). The graphematic solutions to linguistic changes were entirely different from those in Scandinavia.

Although the younger futhark was clearly easier for rune-carvers to use (forms were often simpler, and the system more compact), the task of decoding – reading – must have been more difficult due to ambiguity concerning which sound several of the characters represented. The shortcomings of the younger runes were exacerbated by the fact that of the sixteen signs, two were variants of *a* and two were variants of *r*.

The writing system apparently served the Scandinavians satisfactorily, but its limitations must have been apparent, and toward the end of the Viking Age, attempts were made at extending the inventory of runes. The solution at this time was to add diacritical marks to characters, such as putting a dot in the angle of the *k*-rune between stave and branch, thus producing ᛕ. The dot indicated that the altered sign stood specifically for one of the variant sounds represented by the rune, in this case *g*. A graphic variant of dotting was crossing or barring; thus the *e*-rune could be either dotted or barred **i** (ᛁ or ᛂ).

The generally accepted chronology of the Viking-Age dotted runes, based on epigraphic occurrences particularly in Denmark, is as follows (DR, cols 999–1003; cf. Lagman 1990, 140–51): (a) dotted **i** (for **e**), dotted **k** (for **g**), dotted **u** (for **y**) all appear *c*.980–1000 in Denmark and perhaps about simultaneously in Sweden (there is a dearth of material in Norway); (b) dotted **t** (for **d**) and dotted **b** (for **p**) appear on Sven Estridsen's coins *c*.1065–75. Dotted runes were used only sporadically initially, and it took time before usage is consistent enough that one can consider the dotted runes to be an integral part of the writing system. They are more widely used from the late 1100s onward as a system, but they are still not employed entirely consistently.

Another procedure for expanding the inventory of runic symbols, introduced in the early Scandinavian Middle Ages, depended on the existence of variant forms. Short-twig and long-branch runes constituted inventories from which individual carvers in some ways could pick and choose, and gradually mixed rune-rows evolved. By combining alternative short-twig and long-branch forms in the same selection, but assigning each of the variants unambiguous or less ambiguous sound-values, the inventory could be expanded and representational ambiguity reduced. Thus the short-twig **a** became the standard representation for *a* in medieval Norway, whereas the long-branch **a** was assigned the sound-value *æ*.

The result of the two procedures for expansion – dotting and functional division between variant signs (as well as a small number of ad hoc constructs) – was that finally, in the Scandinavian High Middle Ages, a general one-to-one correspondence between writing symbol and distinct sound in the language was achieved, or indeed overachieved, with characters being created even for Latin letters superfluous for recording the vernacular.

SOURCE AND DEVELOPMENT OF THE DOTTED RUNES

As the source of the dot itself, Otto von Friesen (for example 1933, 172) pointed to the Anglo-Saxon innovation of the *y*-rune. In the Anglo-Saxon futhorc the *i*-rune was inscribed within the *u*-rune (ᚢ), and the resulting rune represented the *i*-mutation of *u*, namely *y*. The short inscribed vertical could lose its length and become a dot, and the dotted u (ᚢ) was considered to be the model behind dotting in Scandinavia. In *Danmarks runeindskrifter*, Lis Jacobsen (DR, cols 999–1000) soundly rejects this suggestion, mainly on chronological grounds.

At the Viking Congress in Dublin in 1973, Einar Haugen suggested the Carolingian roman-letter 'y' as the source (1976, 88–9). In Carolingian script, also in England and Scandinavia, the letter 'y' had, as a rule, a dot above it as a diacritic to distinguish it from other similar letters (insular 'w', and 'u' or 'v'). Although interesting, this suggestion and Haugen's further speculations on dotting have not met with general acceptance (cf. Lagman 1990, 22). This topic will be returned to later.

In 1997 at a conference on dating inscriptions in Trondheim, R.I. Page presented a joint paper (Page and Hagland 1998) on *runica manuscripta* and the expansion of the younger futhark. Building on the work from 1954 of René Derolez and on David Parsons's conference paper from 1995 (1998), they discuss some interesting Scandinavian rune-rows (in futhark order) and alphabets found in eleventh- and twelfth-century English manuscripts, particularly listings including dotted runes. The manuscripts are St John's College, Oxford, MS 17 (henceforth J: cf. Derolez 1954, 26–34; Page 1999, 60–1), fol. 5v, and British Museum (now British Library) Cotton Galba A.2 (henceforth C: cf. Derolez 1954, 34–52). J is firmly dated to *c*.1110, whereas C was probably from *c*.1150, and although the latter was destroyed in fires in 1731 and 1865, its runes are preserved in engravings in Hickes's *Thesaurus* (1703–5, I/3: tab. vi). The rune-rows of most interest are those with several expansions, specifically J5 and C3 (Page and Hagland's designations), whose long-branch runes clearly represent renderings of the same material (Fig. 18.2).

The detailed discussion by Page and Hagland cannot be presented here. The important point is that several dotted runes are added after the basic sixteen younger runes:

(no. 17) dotted u, called w (*wynn*), although it did not usually have the sound-value *w* in Scandinavia, but rather *y* or *ø* (and more rarely *o*);
(no. 18) barred c, called k, and (no. 19) dotted c, called g (note that the Scandinavian *k*-rune is called *con*, thus c);
(no. 20) barred i, called e;
(no. 21) an *æ*-rune (whose form will be discussed below);
(no. 22) barred t, called d;
(no. 23) dotted b, called p in J5 (only ellipse notation in C3).

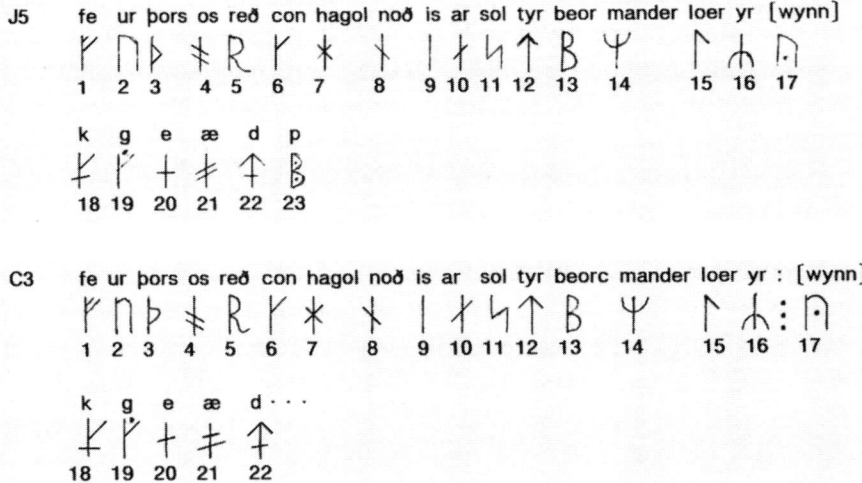

18.2 Schematic drawing of two of the Scandinavian rune-rows, J5 and C3
(after Page & Hagland 1998, 65).

In the other rune-rows discussed by Page and Hagland, C1 contains merely dotted **k** for **g** (with dotting in the angle between stave and branch), whereas C7 is an alphabet including dotted **t** for **d**, dotted **i** for **e**, dotted **k** for **g** (with dotting on the stave), dotted **b** for **p**, dotted **k** for **q** (with dotting in the angle), redundantly dotted short-twig **s**, and other extra symbols but without dotting.

When considering the contents of the listing in J, Parsons employed the received chronology for dotted runes, not uncritically, and maintained that the expanded Scandinavian rune-rows could not in that form derive from Byrhtferth of Ramsey, who flourished around 1010, even though most of the rest of the alphabet material in that manuscript did derive from his work. Page and Hagland set up a sequence of events and chronological frame for the Scandinavian runic material in J and C (1998, 67–8):

> (i) six or seven dotted or crossed runes were added to Scandinavian usage;
> (ii) they all became part of a formal futhark (placed at the end);
> (iii) this information reached England and was put in manuscript form;
> (iv) it was incorporated into a group of other rune-rows in a manuscript; and
> (v) these were copied in J by 1113, and in C by perhaps 1150.

Calling the Scandinavian *k*-rune *con* probably reflects Anglo-Norman writing practices and would mean that stage iv should be placed after 1066. Page and Hagland proceed then with a point of great significance (1998, 68):

> It has been assumed that the dotted runes were first developed somewhere in Scandinavia. We can see no reason why they should not have been created in Scandinavian communities, perhaps in Danish-influenced areas, of the British Isles (though indeed few epigraphical runes survive from them) and exported from there to Scandinavia [...]. One could postulate that the close acquaintance with the Latin alphabet, which at this time was a feature of England in contrast to Scandinavia, was the spur to the expansion of the runic writing system, to making it more representative of the variety of sounds it must denote.

This statement is extremely speculative, and there are reasons why this most likely was not the case. First off: if the system of dotted runes – as the complete system evidenced in these manuscripts – was indeed invented in the British Isles or Ireland and exported to Scandinavia, such that it appears *c*.980–1000 there, it must have developed earlier in tenth-century Britain/Ireland. The problem is the corpus of Scandinavian runic inscriptions from the British Isles (and Ireland), a catch tucked away parenthetically in the statement by Page and Hagland. A glance at the epigraphic evidence reveals quickly what a great difficulty this is: not only are there relatively few runic inscriptions preserved from the Scandinavian communities of the British Isles and Ireland, but the known inscriptions provide no support for any such development. The Scandinavian inscriptions have been published in several corpus editions (Page 1983; Barnes, Hagland and Page 1997; Barnes and Page 2006; Barnes and Hagland, this volume; the Maeshowe corpus is too late, mid-1100s, to have any bearing on this topic: Barnes 1994). These publications provide a corpus of 104 Scandinavian runic inscriptions from the British Isles, 137 when Maeshowe is included.

Combing this corpus, one finds few epigraphic examples of dotted runes, and these are as a rule not from as early as the 900s. There are dots on some Manx stones, which as a corpus are dated to *c*.930–*c*.1020: dotted **i** for **e** on German (Peel) II, Kirk Michael III, Maughold IV, and Onchan, and dotted **u** for **y** on Kirk Michael III. Maughold IV is the youngest of these, art-historically dated to after 1020 (Wilson 1983, 185), and Kirk Michael III is perhaps the oldest, possibly dating to the 900s. The Irish material provides the following examples: IR1 Greenmount with dotted **i** for **e**, dated as 'early medieval'; IR2 Killaloe with dotted **k** for **g**, end of the Viking Age; IR12 Fishamble St., with dotted **u** for *y*/*o*, dated to *c*.1000 (soon after the first examples in Scandinavia); and the new inscription IR17 Temple Bar West (Barnes and Hagland, this volume) with dotted **i** for **e** and from the 1000s. Of the fifty-seven runic inscriptions from the rest of Britain and Ireland, seven show merely dotting of **i** for **e**: SH6 Eshaness II; OR3 Orkney; SC3 Holy Island I; SC10 Inchmarnock; E2 London, St Paul's; E8 Skelton-in-Cleveland; and E9 Pennington. The dotted **i** was perhaps the earliest dotted form in Scandinavia, as far as one can see, and none of the British

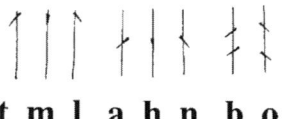

18.3 Liestøl's suggestion for some of the 'original' younger rune-forms (1973, 111).

t m l a h n b o

inscriptions pre-date the earliest Scandinavian examples, though a few may be approximately simultaneous (OR3, SC10, E2 and E8). Although dotting is used as one of the runological criteria for dating inscriptions, the danger of circular reasoning is minimized through the care exercised by Barnes and Page in this area. The following also occur: one inscription with dotted **k** for *k*, OR10 Orphir I, twice in the word *kirkja*, dated to the 1100s; one with dotted **k** for *g*, SC7 Holy Island VIII, in the name *Vigleikr*, dated to the mid-1200s and containing also dotted **i** for *e*; and two with dotted **t** for **d**: SC6 Holy Island IV, with the name *Amundr* written **amundar** (with an epenthetic vowel) and dated probably to the mid-1200s; and E11 Conishead, with the name **dotbrt**, dated to the late 1200s. Basically then, from the entire known corpus, no examples demonstrate the extensive set-up of dotted runes which, as a complete system, is postulated to have developed in the British Isles or Ireland, neither at the necessarily early date for this to be the case, nor later. This is an argument ex silentio, but the lack of any attestations greatly weakens the hypothesis.

Alternative solutions to the problems presented by the origin and development of the system of dotted runes can be suggested. Concerning the dot itself: in an article on the Hedeby inscriptions, Aslak Liestøl (1973, 110–13) discussed how short-twig runes in the early Viking Age were made on the Hedeby I and III rune-sticks (Haddeby stick 2 and 1), dated to the 800s (or 900s), and could have been made on other rune-sticks at that time. The branches and marks were made by pushing in the point of the knife, at different heights and with different orientations of the blade, and also in certain cases multiple times. The blade gives each of the incisions the same general length (Fig. 18.3). Liestøl feels that these may represent the 'original' younger runic forms.

Although the distinctive forms are all short-twig, the branches are put right on the stave with those at an angle crossing the stave, such that **a**, **n** and **o** could be viewed as long-branch variants. Note particularly that the *m*-rune and the *h*-rune consist of an indentation or a dot at the top of the stave and in the middle of the stave respectively. They illustrate that dotting – using the point of the knife to make a distinct form – was a procedure within runic carving. The writing tool – the knife – and the medium – wood – probably give a good indication of where dotting came from: it was part of the runic system (it could also be mentioned that punctuation to separate words usually consisted of one or two dots, that is, a raised period or a colon, made with the point of the knife. A dot could also be added superfluously at the bottom of the short-twig *s*-rune to mark its end). One does not need to look to an Anglo-Saxon *u*-rune with an inscribed **i** that can be shortened to a dot, or to the

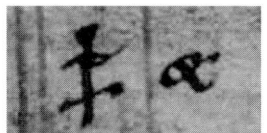 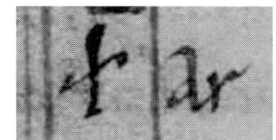 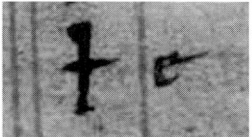

18.4 The *æ*-rune as a barred long-branch *a*-rune in J5 (cf. the *a*-rune and the barring of the *e*-rune).

Carolingian 'y' (with a diacritical dot over) to find a good source for the dot as a diacritic with Scandinavian runes.

As far as the traditional understanding of the chronology and development of dotting in Scandinavia is concerned, it is important to remember how haphazardly the dots were apparently used in the early stages and how long it took before the system was completely established. It does not seem reasonable that a complete system of dotted runes developed in the British Isles or Ireland, but was only applied piecemeal in Scandinavia, as the development seems to be.

A re-evaluation of the runic material in the manuscripts J and C is called for. There are at any rate two problems with dotted runes not addressed adequately by Page and Hagland:

> 1. The *k*-rune is called **c**, the dotted form **g**, and the crossed or barred form **k**. The crossed or barred form of the *k*-rune for **k** is unknown epigraphically, and is described by Page and Hagland as motivated solely by 'orthographic patterning' (1998, 66) (OR10 Orphir I with dotted **k** for *k* is close). This gives the impression of a learned construct – is that what is meant by 'orthographic patterning'? – whereby the essence of dotting has given rise to a system in manuscripts with no basis in epigraphy.
> 2. The form of the *æ*-rune is suspect, and the drawings by Page and Hagland are inaccurate. From the general shape (reflected in their schematic drawing), the *æ*-rune resembles a medieval *o*-rune, but in detail it does not really have that form. It is rather a barred long-branch *a*-rune (see the forms from J5 in Fig. 18.4; the shapes are the same in C3). The employment of a dotted or barred *a*-rune for **æ** is epigraphically unattested, and most certainly an ad hoc learned construct.

CONCLUSIONS

As a summary, the following points can be made:

1. Dotting as a phenomenon was an integral part of the younger runic system, both as punctuation/word-separator and as a 'diacritical mark' on two runes: at the top of the stave of the *m*-rune in the short-twig variant and in the middle of the stave of the short-twig *h*-rune. Therefore, one does not need to seek an

external source for the concept of dotting as a diacritical mark with runes. The concept has its most obvious source within the runic system, particularly in connection with the carving of runes with a knife on wood, where pressing the point of the knife into the wood could produce runic twigs or branches.

2. There is no support in the corpus of Scandinavian runic inscriptions from the British Isles and Ireland for the hypothesis that the system of dotted runes could have been developed there and then exported to Scandinavia. There are early attestations mainly of dotted **i** for **e**, which apparently was the most widespread and earliest dotted rune to be adopted in Scandinavia. If the source for this rune is perhaps the short-twig *h*-rune (ⱡ), whose form became super-fluous when in the later Viking Age the long-branch form became universal, that would explain the early date and prevalence of this dotted rune.

3. In the epigraphic occurrences, the system of dotted runes in Scandinavia appears to be developing gradually. It does not appear to have been imported wholesale as a complete system (cf. Haugen 1976, 86).

4. Exposure to or knowledge of the Latin alphabet might perhaps have acted as a spur in the development of the dotted runes, but the assumption of such exposure is unnecessary. The readers of late Viking-Age runic inscriptions must have seen clearly the shortcomings of the sixteen-rune futhark. In fact, knowledge of the Latin alphabet would probably have led to solutions similar to those in the Anglo-Saxon futhorc, or to the Scandinavian early medieval functional distribution between variant forms and the high medieval ad hoc construction of new forms, not to the use of a diacritic dot, for which there is no obvious source in the Latin tradition (cf. Haugen 1976, 84–5).

5. There are problems connected with the interpretation of the dotted runes in J5 and C3. The *æ*-rune is not a rune with two parallel branches, but rather a barred long-branch *a*-rune, a form for which there are no epigraphic registrations. It appears that the extensive dotted futharks presented in J5 and C3 are at least in part learned constructs based on rudimentary dotted runes, such as those in use in Scandinavia at the end of the 900s. It is clear that knowledge of Scandinavian dotted runes made its way to the British Isles and Ireland in the late 900s (as witnessed by, for example Kirk Michael III and IR12 Fishamble St.), and it is possible that the knowledge of this embryonic system led to the formation of the (partially) learned construct witnessed in J5 and C3.

6. Stages i and ii in the five-point sequence of events leading to J5 and C3 as outlined in Page and Hagland (1998, 67) do not seem to be correct: six or seven dotted or crossed runes were not necessarily all added to Scandinavian usage, and they had scarcely became part of a formal futhark, placed at the end, before information about dotting reached England and was put in manuscript form, at least partially as a learned construct.

BIBLIOGRAPHY

Barnes, M.P. 1987. 'The origins of the younger *fuþark* – a reappraisal', in *Runor och runinskrifter* (Stockholm), 29–45.

Barnes, M.P. 1994. The runic inscriptions of Maeshowe, Orkney (Uppsala).

Barnes, M.P. 2000. 'The Hedeby inscriptions, the short-twig runes, and the question of early Scandinavian dialect markers' in K. Düwel, E. Marold & C. Zimmermann (eds), *Von Thorsberg nach Schleswig* (Berlin), pp 101–9.

Barnes, M.P., J.R. Hagland & R.I. Page. 1997. *The runic inscriptions of Viking-Age Dublin* (Dublin).

Barnes, M.P. & R.I. Page 2006. *The Scandinavian runic inscriptions of Britain* (Uppsala).

Bencard, M. 2004. 'Introduction' in M. Bencard, A.K. Rasmussen & H. Brinch Madsen (eds), *Ribe Excavations, 1970–76* (Højbjerg), V:7–18.

Derolez, R. 1954. *Runica manuscripta: the English tradition* (Brugge).

DR = Jacobsen, L. & E. Moltke. 1941–2. *Danmarks runeindskrifter* (Copenhagen).

von Friesen, O. 1933. 'De svenska runinskrifterna' in O. von Friesen (ed.), *Runorna*, Nordisk kultur, 6 (Stockholm), pp 145–248.

Haugen, E. 1976. 'The dotted runes: from parsimony to plenitude' in B. Almqvist & D. Greene (eds), *Proceedings of the Seventh Viking Congress, Dublin 15–21 August 1973* (Dublin), pp 83–92.

Hickes, G. 1703–5. *Linguarum Vett. Septentrionalium Thesaurus Grammatico-Criticus et Archæologicus*, I, pt. 3: *Grammaticæ Islandicæ Rudimenta* (Oxford).

Knirk, J.E. 2002. 'Runes: origin, development of the futhark, functions, applications and methodological considerations' in O. Bandle, K. Braunmuller, E.H. Jahr, A. Karker, H.P. Naumann & U. Teleman (eds), *The nordic languages: an international handbook of the history of the North Germanic languages* (Berlin), I, pp 634–48.

Lagman, S. 1990. *De stungna runorna användning och ljudvärden i runsvenska steninskrifter* (Uppsala).

Liestøl, A. 1973. 'Runenstäbe aus Haithabu-Hedeby', *Berichte über die Ausgrabungen in Haithabu*, 6: *Das archäologische Fundmaterial II* (Neumünster), 96–119.

Liestøl, A. 1981a. 'The emergence of the Viking runes', *Michigan Germanic Studies*, 7:1, 107–18.fjgkvj`

Liestøl, A. 1981b. 'The Viking runes: the transition from the older to the younger *fuþark*', *Saga-Book*, 20:4, 247–66.

Loman, B. 1965. 'Rökrunorna som grafematiskt system', *Arkiv för nordisk filologi*, 80, 1–60.

Page, R.I. 1983. 'The Manx rune-stones' in C.E. Fell, P. Foote, J. Graham-Campbell & R. Thomson (eds), *The Viking Age in the Isle of Man: select papers from the Ninth Viking Congress, Isle of Man, 4–14 July 1981* (London), pp 133–46. (repr. 1995 in his *Runes and runic inscriptions* (Woodbridge), pp 225–44).

Page, R.I. 1999. *An introduction to English runes*, 2nd ed. (Woodbridge).

Page, R.I. & J.R. Hagland. 1998. '*Runica manuscripta* and runic dating: the expansion of the younger *fuþąrk*' in A. Dybdahl & J.R. Hagland (eds), *Innskrifter og datering/ Dating inscriptions* (Trondheim), pp 55–71.

Parsons, D.N. 1998. 'Byrhtferth and the runes of Oxford, St John's College, Manuscript 17' in K. Düwel (ed.), *Runeninschriften als Quellen interdisziplinärer Forschung* (Berlin), pp 439–47.

Parsons, D.N. 1999. *Recasting the runes: the reform of the Anglo-Saxon* futhorc (Uppsala).

Schulte, M. 2006a. 'Älteres und jüngeres fuþark – phonologische aspekte der reduktion des runenalphabets' in A. Bammesberger & G. Waxenberger (eds), *Das fuþark und seine einzelsprachlichen Weiterentwicklungen* (Berlin), pp 414–33.

Schulte, M. 2006b. 'Die bedeutung des schädelfragments von Ribe für die kürzung der älteren runenreihe' in H. Perridon & A. Quak (eds), *Oppa Swänzsko oc Oppa Dansko*, Amsterdamer Beiträge zur älteren Germanistik, 62 (Amsterdam), pp 3–24.

Schulte, M. 2006c. 'The transformation of the older *fuþark*: number-magic, graphological or linguistic principles?', *Arkiv för nordisk filologi*, 121, 41–74.

Stoklund, M. 1996. 'The Ribe cranium inscription and the Scandinavian transition to the younger reduced futhark' in T. Looijenga & A. Quak (eds), *Frisian runes and neighbouring traditions*, Amsterdamer Beiträge zur älteren Germanistik, 45 (Amsterdam), pp 199–209.

Stoklund, M. 2007. 'The Danish inscriptions of the early Viking Age and the transition to the younger futhark' in J.O. Askedal et al. (eds), Zentrale Probleme bei der Erforschung der älteren Runen (Frankfurt), forthcoming.

Wilson, D.M. 1983. 'The art of the Manx crosses of the Viking Age' in C.E. Fell, P. Foote, J. Graham-Campbell & R. Thomson (eds), *The Viking Age in the Isle of Man: select papers from the Ninth Viking Congress, Isle of Man, 4–14 July 1981* (London), pp 175–87.

Kirkwall revisited

RAYMOND LAMB

Vikings last were collectively present in Kirkwall in 1989 for the Eleventh Congress (Batey et al. 1993). They made their inevitable descents upon St Magnus Cathedral, the Bishop's Palace and Tankerness House Museum, and an attempt was made to show them how these monuments related to the wider townscape. At that time it could be claimed, on the basis of hints in the sagas, that Kirkwall probably had quite an early, and interesting, origin, but it had to be admitted that there had been 'little archaeological research in the town' (Lamb 1993, 45). Much of what had been learned derived from the writer's watching, in 1986, of extensive drainage works under the roads in the vicinity of the cathedral, which indicated the position of the original shoreline in that part of the burgh.

In the years between the Eleventh and Fifteenth Congresses, the observation of fortuitous holes in the roads – watching briefs – was put on a more regular footing, augmented here and there by some exploratory excavations. Individually, the watching-brief reports (including those of 1986) were judged not to justify regular publication, but were written-up for deposition in the Orkney Archaeological Sites and Monuments Record (Orkney College, Kirkwall) and the National Monuments Record of Scotland. Although theoretically available for public consultation, this accumulating archive was known to few people, so in 2005 an initiative was taken to bring it together and to publish a synthesis, augmented by summaries of all the excavations and watching-briefs of which records were held – that is to say, work extending back to the 1970s (for details and references, see Lamb and Robertson 2005). As background to this exercise, the opportunity also was taken to review the references to Kirkwall in the sagas on the assumption not that the references were historically valid, but that they might be; and the expanded archaeological consciousness might allow them to be tested. Such is the situation with the fundamental question of how the town originated.

Orkneyinga saga (ch. 29) relates events in connection with the ousting of Þorfinnr Sigurðarson at the hands of the usurper, Rögnvaldr Brúsason. Taylor (1938, 183) places the events in the winter of 1046. Rögnvaldr planned to spend that winter in Kirkwall, where he had laid in a great store of provisions wherewith to regale his followers through that winter. A task that remained was the vitally important one of going to the island of Papa Stronsay, which produced the best-quality malt for the special Yuletide strong ale. Surely as a self-conscious, theatrical gesture, Rögnvaldr in person led the expedition to secure this most symbolically precious cargo; but while he was on Papa Stronsay overnight, Þorfinnr staged a surprise attack, killed Rögnvaldr and the men who were with him, and re-established himself as the sole ruling earl.

This story relates to the period where it is difficult to assess how much sound 'history' lies in the saga narrative. The emphasis on the unstintingly lavish provision of hospitality for his followers – specifically, for his personal warband – is an insistence on 'Dark-Age' heroic values. The lord expects the loyalty and self-sacrificing bravery in battle of the select warriors of his warband, and in return regales them with lavish presents of jewellery, fine clothes and horses, and with luxurious eating and drinking within the feasting-hall. Such a value-system is readily seen as the heart of the heroic society revealed in *Y Gododdin* (Jackson 1969, 33–7). Rögnvaldr's grand gesture in personally seeing to the supply of that special Yuletide malt, surely is meant to be seen as mock-heroic? The saga-writer is contrasting Rögnvaldr's hale-and-hearty 'Dark-Age' values, with his assessment of the latter years of the restored Þorfinnr's reign, in which the emphasis is on the giving-up of aggressive warfare to allow attention to be turned to the establishment of good government at home, and the fostering of the Church (*Orkneyinga saga*, ch. 31).

The saga-writer then, had a literary agenda to contrast the 'Dark-Age' Rögnvaldr with Þorfinnr, precociously a wise king of the High Middle Ages. From that writer's perspective from Iceland, *c.*1200, a reasoned judgment of events in Orkney a century and a half earlier, is likely to have been neither possible nor attractive. The extreme generosity of the provisions laid in at Kirkwall in 1046 unfortunately is just the sort of detail that fitted the saga-writer's agenda, but if it happened to be true, it would carry interesting implications about the scale of the earl's establishment there. There was, however, no ulterior motive to locate Rögnvaldr Brúsason's establishment at Kirkwall rather than at any other place; this incidental detail, that Kirkwall was an accustomed seat of an earl before the middle of the eleventh century, therefore is at least plausible.

There is of course no suggestion that mid-eleventh-century Kirkwall was urban. Birsay was the successful Þorfinnr's accustomed seat (*Orkneyinga saga*, ch. 31) and Kirkwall is likely to have resembled Birsay in its rural character. This does not mean that an earl lived in one place all the time; the saga says that Thorfinn lived 'most often' (*jafnan*) in Birsay, which implies that he spent some time, albeit a minority of his time, at one or more other places (ch. 31). Rural centres of royal or lordly power are, of course, a feature of other early medieval societies – we may think of Pictish Forteviot, or the Northumbrian Yeavering (Alcock 2003, 229–33, 244–54). These places normally did not become transformed into towns. Kirkwall will be uncommonly interesting if indeed it were one of these rural power-centres which, exceptionally, acquired urban characteristics and made the transition into a town.

We get the next hint of that transition being made, as a casual sideline to the saga's account of the usurpation of the earldom by Rögnvaldr kali Kolsson in 1136. A preparation of the ground for this was the translation of relics of St Magnus from the established episcopal seat at Birsay, into an existing (but unnamed) church at Kirkwall. This may have happened at any time from 1128, although a date closer to Rögnvaldr's coup is usually assumed. The interesting circumstance is that Kirkwall is assumed by now to be a market-place (*kaupstaðr*). *Orkneyinga saga* makes the qualifying statement that the place as yet was not much built-up (*lítt húsaðr*: ch. 57), while *Magnúss saga skemmri* (from a viewpoint in Iceland, *c.*1200) adds 'since then it has grown a lot' (*ok hefir hann mjök siðan eflzk*). The church to which the relics were taken is assumed to be that of St Olaf, in the part of the town known as 'the Burgh' and especially associated with the earls. We note that on some occasion between the demise of Rögnvaldr Brúsason, *c.*1046, and the arrival of Rögnvald Kolsson, in 1136, the place had become a recognized market; which must mean that some earl, whether Rögnvaldr Brúsason or one of his successors, had declared and authorized it to be a market. We may note also that a church – that of St Olaf, or initially perhaps a precursor to it – was an expected adjunct to a market. Kirkwall is an obviously more central location within Orkney than Birsay, and the presence (whether permanently or intermittently) of an earl there, guaranteeing a demand for exotic commodities, would encourage merchants to use that market once it was declared.

Until recently we had little factual basis on which to assess the chances of survival of archaeological deposits in 'the Burgh'. At the extreme of optimism, there could be traces of a feasting-hall and ancillary buildings of the establishment in which the mid-eleventh-century Rögnvaldr Brúsason proposed to entertain his warband. This same area also is the inevitable place to look for the residence of Rögnvaldr Kolsson, nearly a century later; the sagas do not mention any such place in Kirkwall but it would be highly unlikely that he did not live here. Closely associated, on the original waterfront (which still needs to be defined) should be the locations of the earliest merchants' booths. The question we were unable to answer was whether the levels in the area ever had been scraped down, removing much of the archaeology, or had deposits accumulated, preserving early material at levels below disturbance from later buildings? We still do not have any excavations within the Burgh to tell us definitively, but explorations in adjacent areas have indicated substantial depths of deposits, of which the lower parts are waterlogged. We have every hope that these conditions extend into the Burgh itself.

'The Burgh' is at the northern end of the town as it now exists. Southward from it extends a district formerly known as Midtown, continuing the waterfront from the Burgh, but suspected to be of later medieval origin. It led towards the cathedral close. At this southern end of Midtown, and provocatively pressing up against the cathedral precinct, is the site of the castle built *c.*1380 by the St Clair earls, the last upstanding remnant of which was demolished in 1865. It stood on the waterfront, its western side probably rising from the harbour and using the harbour as a moat. The waterfront continued southwards, past the cathedral, and onwards into a district formerly called the Laverock, a mercantile quarter controlled by the bishops. East and uphill from here stood the Bishop's Palace.

At the time of the 1989 Congress it already was suspected that the building-up of Midtown had not progressed far by the end of the Middle Ages, and this assumption was incorporated into the tentative reconstruction-plan showing Kirkwall in 1500, prepared by Karen Wood for use in local history teaching in schools, and reproduced in the Congress publication (Lamb 1993, 44–8). We suspected especially that there had been no building on the western (harbour) side of the Midtown street, and subsequent watching-briefs have borne this out. The eastern, upslope side of Midtown, however, was built up, although probably not yet to its full southward extent as of today, but where, at the end nearest the Burgh, there had been development this extended more than 50m back from the Midtown street frontage, with deposits exceeding 1.3m in depth, indicating a sequence of buildings, and with the lowest layers waterlogged and preserving organic materials. But at the southern end of Midtown, it looks unlikely that the construction of the St Clair castle necessitated the demolition of any pre-existing houses – the 1380 castle was built on a previously unoccupied site.

South from the castle site, the 1986 drain-laying provided the line of the medieval waterfront where this passes the west front of the Cathedral. Immediately in line with the Cathedral's west door, a wharf had been created by cutting back the flagstone bedrock to create a vertical face. Local tradition suggests that a flight of steps led from the landing-place up to the Cathedral door. Continuing south into Laverock, the story appears much the same as in Midtown: buildings on the eastern, upslope side of the street probably going for the full length of that street as it exists today, but the western, harbour side remaining open, possibly as late as the early nineteenth century.

Some useful insights were gained into the extent and quality of the Cathedral close. Particularly rewarding were exploratory trenches dug at Historic Scotland's instigation in an area confined by the eastern side of the seventeenth-century Earl's Palace, but in the Middle Ages within the curtilege of the Bishop's Palace. Medieval deposits here went down in excess of 3m (the deposits, waterlogged in their lower levels, were not bottomed). The area appeared to have been used for the working of log timbers imported from Norway.

The most striking perception to have arisen from the co-ordination exercise is the extreme separation of the secular (earls') from the ecclesiastical (bishops') quarters of the town. The old rivalry between the two quarters of Burgh and Laverock has endured in popular tradition, as that between the 'Doonies' (the earl's men) and the 'Uppies' (bishop's men) which is played out in a game of street football ('the Ba') every Christmas Day and New Year's Day. Rather than as two districts of one town, the medieval situation was two, widely separated towns, with a considerable tract of open space between them.

Archaeologically, the experience throughout the town is that deposits are rich, with waterlogging and preservation of organic materials occurring even some way upslope from the former harbour front. That harbour front is low-lying and must always have been wet, encouraging people regularly to bring in materials with which to raise up the levels, creating rich archaeological sequences. These enhanced perceptions should make possible a well-informed response to future development proposals in Kirkwall; the archaeologically crucial Burgh area in particular has become run-down, and is in need of regeneration.

ACKNOWLEDGMENT

The support of UHI Millennium Institute, for attending the 2005 Cork Congress, is gratefully acknowledged.

BIBLIOGRAPHY

Alcock, L. 2003. *Kings and warriors: craftsmen and priests*, Society of Antiquaries of Scotland Monograph Series, 24 (Edinburgh).

Batey, C.E., J. Jesch & C.D. Morris (eds), *The Viking Age in Caithness, Orkney and the North Atlantic: select papers from the proceedings of the Eleventh Viking Congress, Thurso and Kirkwall, 1989* (Edinburgh).

Jackson, K.H. 1969. *The Gododdin: the oldest Scottish poem* (Edinburgh).

Lamb, R.G. 1993. 'Notes on field excursions' in Batey et al., *The Viking Age in Caithness, Orkney and the North Atlantic*, pp 44–51.

Lamb, R.G. & Robertson, J. 2005. 'Kirkwall: saga, history, archaeology' in O. Owen (ed.), *The world of Orkneyinga Saga: the broad-cloth Viking trip* (Kirkwall), pp 160–91.

Orkneyinga saga = Finnbogi Guðmundsson (ed.). 1965. *Orkneyinga saga: Legenda de Sancto Magno; Magnúss saga skemmri; Magnúss saga lengri; Helga Þáttr og Úlfs*, Íslenzk fornrit, 34 (Reykjavík).

Taylor, A.B. 1938. *The Orkneyinga Saga: a new translation with introduction and notes* (Edinburgh).

Viking-Age and Norse pottery in the Hebrides

ALAN M. LANE

In a paper published in the fourteenth Viking Congress volume, *Viking and Norse in the North Atlantic* (Mortensen and Arge 2005), Jennings and Kruse revisited the debates about the impact of Viking raiding and Scandinavian settlement in the Hebrides (2005). A central part of their assessment referred to the evidence for the use of pottery on Viking sites in the Western Isles and the implications this has for the relationship between Scandinavian incomers and the native population. Their ceramic information was based on work published in 1990, which has now been modified by more recent excavations, and it is the purpose of the present paper to draw this evidence to the attention of a wider audience and to consider what effect this has on Jennings and Kruse's argument.

It is unfortunate that current discussions of the ceramic evidence from the Western Isles are still hampered by lack of publication (cf. Lane 1990). Iain Crawford's Udal, North Uist, site remains unpublished, with only brief interim statements available (Crawford and Switsur 1977; Crawford nd). The recently excavated sites at Barvas (Graham-Campbell and Batey 1998, 75) and Bostadh, Lewis (Neighbour and Burgess 1997), Cille Pheadair (Parker Pearson et al. 2004b) and Bornais (Sharples 2004), South Uist, have only interim statements or partial publication so far. Jennings and Kruse cite this new archaeological work in the Western Isles, and, in particular, quote Sharples and Parker Pearson (1999) as claiming clear continuity between the pre-Viking and Viking-Age societies of the area. However, the views advanced by Sharples and Parker Pearson have been partially superseded by further post-excavation work on their sites as well as continuing excavation at Bornais.

The absence of publication of early Viking or immediately pre-Viking Hebridean sites does severely hinder discussion of the effect of Scandinavian settlement. At present, the only body of material where we have detailed analysis of pre-Viking and Viking assemblages is pottery. My 1983 study, briefly summarized in 1990, showed the presence of distinctive pottery assemblages on pre-Viking and Viking/Late Norse sites throughout the Outer Hebrides (Lane 1983; 1990). This work, based on the excavated assemblage at the Udal, was using provisional stratigraphic data from the excavator, but the absence of definitive publication has meant that the detail of the evidence has not been available. Now new excavations of Viking and pre-Viking sites are beginning to provide further chronological resolution to the sequence and we can see where more chronological resolution is necessary.

The finds from the Udal remain central to our understanding of the pottery sequence although the newer excavated sites in some cases challenge or modify aspects of the evidence. I used the Udal stratified sequence to define the wider Hebridean sequence and recognize material from other sites of similar date. Pottery is plentiful in the Udal Late Iron-Age horizons with some 40,000 sherds in the best stratified deposits associated with cellular buildings in the native pre-Viking tradition (Lane 1990, 117). My work showed a phase of flat-bottomed undecorated bucket and shouldered jar forms with long flaring rims. All of it is handmade, built up from slab coils which, when low fired, often leave clear 'tongue and groove' joining marks (Fig. 20.1). This material, unimaginatively termed 'Plain Style' (by me), dates to the major pre-Viking phases on the site which were thought to run from *c.*AD 350 to 850 (Crawford and Switsur 1977; Lane 1990). The contexts above this contain the remains of rectangular structures which appear to represent the arrival of an incoming population of Scandinavian character (Crawford and Switsur 1977, 130–1). These horizons also contain substantial quantities of coarse handmade pottery – 6,500 sherds in the initial Viking layer X, and 12,000 sherds in the secondary Viking level IXc (Lane 1983, 170–87). Some of the pottery in level X is in the preceding native Plain Style, but both Viking levels produce new material – distinctive sagging and flat-based open bowls and cups as well as flat circular pottery discs or platters.

My analysis of the Udal Viking and pre-Viking ceramics allowed me to identify similar material throughout the Outer Hebrides and to identify a zone of early medieval ceramic use running from the north of Lewis to the islands of Coll and Tiree in the Southern Hebrides. I was able to suggest some fifteen sites which seemed to have pottery of the Udal Plain Style, though the difficulty in distinguishing simple undecorated bucket forms from pottery of other dates is considerable (Lane 1990). The Viking-period style had not been recognized before, but by 1981 I was able to locate some twenty-nine sites with diagnostic Viking-Age pottery throughout the Hebridean ceramic zone (Lane 1990, figs 7.7–7.8). This evidence suggests long-lived patterns of cultural behaviour which divide the Outer Hebrides from the southern islands and Argyll with perhaps important implications for the varying nature of Viking impact.

The importance of the recognition of these two consecutive ceramic styles lay not only in their importance for the cultural history of the area, for example the adoption of new cooking and eating behaviours, but in their potential for the dating of old site assemblages and the recognition of new settlement sites which could be investigated with modern techniques (for example Sharples and Parker Pearson 1999, 43).

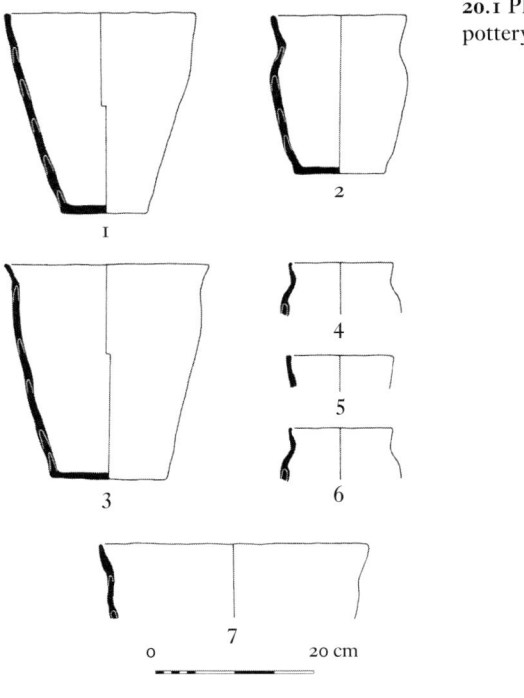

20.1 Plain Style pottery (© Alan Lane).

NEW SITES

In the mid-1980s, a fresh series of excavations began in the Hebrides with researchers from Edinburgh, Sheffield and Cardiff taking an active role in locating and investigating new sites. Of these, Bostadh, Bornais and Cille Pheadair have all seen extensive excavation (Fig. 20.2). Bornais is a complicated multi-period site with Late Iron Age to medieval occupation including both a large single Norse-style longhouse and a substantial medieval settlement cluster (Sharples 2004). Bostadh has important pre-Viking deposits and a short Viking phase (Harding 2004, 268–70), while Cille Pheadair seems to be a single Norse-style farmstead occupied from the eleventh to the early thirteenth century (Parker Pearson et al. 2004b). These new sites have good stratified sequences and multiple radiocarbon dates and allow us to reconsider my sequence based on the Udal and to refine its chronology.

PRE-VIKING POTTERY

My 1983 study of the Udal pottery and related material in the Hebrides accepted *c.*AD400–800 as the likely approximate date-range for the Plain Style. However, the Udal radiocarbon dates have very large standard deviations, and the currently available evidence from the site does not precisely date either the start of the Plain Style or the beginning of the Viking style (Lane 1990, 122). So, what date is the Udal Plain Style? Large shouldered bucket forms decorated with cordons, known as Dun Cuier ware, seem to be its immediate precursors, and two sites, Bornais and Eilean Olabhat, give us multiple radiocarbon dates of the fifth/sixth century AD for this pottery phase (Lane forthcoming). The precise date of inception of the Plain Style is uncertain and indeed it probably reflects a gradual abandonment of decoration over some decades, but a date of *c.*AD550–600 seems an appropriate estimate on present evidence. Two substantial Plain Style assemblages at Beirgh and Bostadh, Lewis, have seventh-/eighth-century dates associated with well-preserved native cellular structures (Harding 2004, 268–70), so it seems to have continued at least up to the beginning of the Viking Age. Its terminal date is uncertain and has been difficult to evaluate given the scarcity of published early Viking contexts in the Hebrides.

VIKING POTTERY

Young's 1966 pottery survey seemed unaware of the possibility of Viking-period pottery in the area and Drimore, the only Viking settlement recognized in the Hebrides prior to the 1970s, produced only five non-diagnostic sherds. The Udal was the first Viking site in the Hebrides to see substantial modern excavation. Here, Iain Crawford reported Viking rectangular buildings stratified between the Late Iron-Age settlement, with its characteristic cellular structures, and well-preserved medieval and late medieval buildings. The pottery in the two Viking levels included both some indistinguishable from the pre-Viking Plain Style and the new Viking style.

This new style of pottery was still made from local clays though with some superficial differences in texture and colour. However, vessel shape and manufacturing technique change quite radically. Rather than the tall buckets and jars of the previous style, we have open bowls and small cups (Fig. 20.3). Some of these have sagging, slightly rounded bases in contrast to the previous exclusive use of flat bases, which had been a characteristic of the Hebridean sequence since at least the Middle Bronze Age. The characteristic pot-building method with clear slabs joined in the 'tongue and groove' manner found in the Plain Style and Dun Cueir ware is replaced by smaller coils pressed together in angled, or flat, joins. The Viking-Age vessels are generally smaller. Particularly characteristic of the Viking levels is the occurrence of flat baking plates or platters. Much of the Viking assemblage, including the platters, is grassmarked, that is, it shows the impressions of grass on the outer basal surfaces of the vessels. This is quite different from the use of grass- or chaff-temper which occurs at various times and places in northern Europe including late Norse/medieval contexts in the

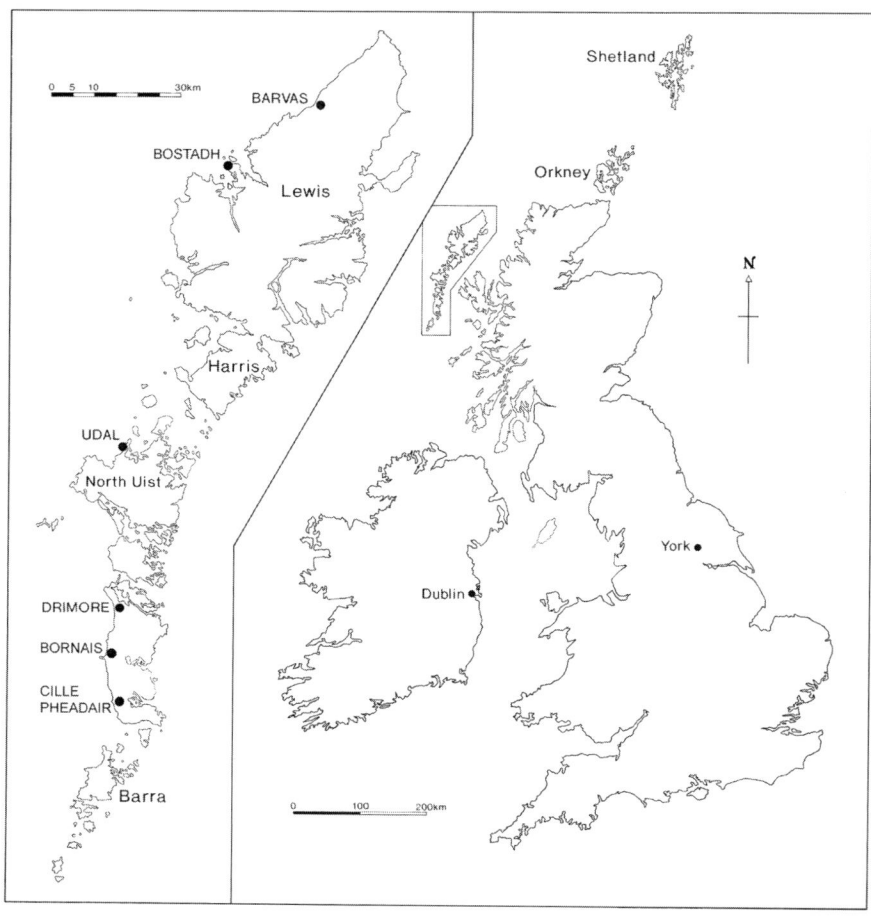

20.2 Map of Hebrides with named sites (© Alan Lane).

Northern Isles and Caithness. In contrast, regular grassmarking, as opposed to the occasional presence of random grass stalk-impressions, seems unrecognized elsewhere in Scotland and appears to be a diagnostic feature of Viking/late Norse pottery in the Hebrides (Lane 1983, 237–9, 249–50; Lane 1990, 123).

As noted already, there are sherds of Plain Style pottery present in the Udal primary Viking layer X. In fact, the majority of diagnostic sherds attributed to level X clearly belong to the pre-Viking Plain Style. The difficulty is in knowing whether this is residual material turning up in a later context, or stratigraphic error in the excavation, or the genuine continuation of the native tradition after the construction of rectangular buildings on the site. Definitive publication of the site with a finalized stratigraphy may make evaluation of those options possible but, for the present, uncertainty must remain. The presence of the new

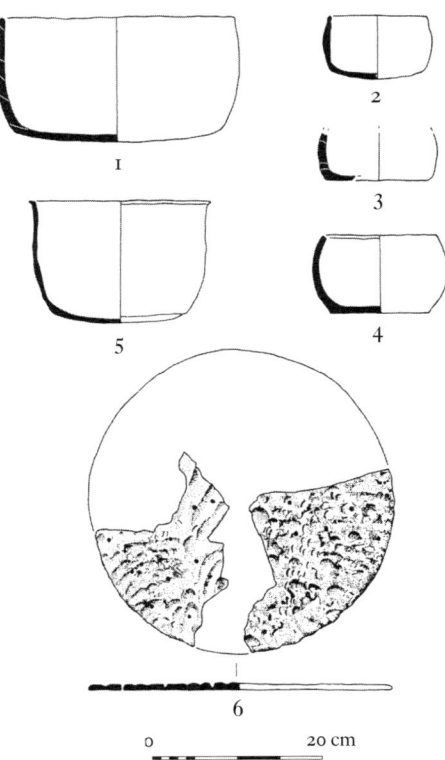

20.3 Viking-style pottery from the Hebrides (© Alan Lane).

style material is perhaps more certain. This includes cups and bowls with sagging and flattish bases and grassmarking. The adoption of the new pot building methods and the abandonment of the long-lived 'tongue and groove' technique are particularly important. Visually, the pottery is slightly different – in some cases thinner and more micaceous – though still with Lewisian gneiss inclusions, but it is not clear whether this indicates the adoption of a different clay source or a slightly different production process. A few sherds of the Viking disc platters are found in level X.

The second Viking level IXc confirms the features of the new Viking style. Open bowls and cups, sagging and flat bases, grassmarking and platters now dominate the recovered pottery attributed to this level by the excavator. Only a few sherds seem likely to be residual Plain Style pottery, re-deposited in the Viking contexts.

The chronology of these two 'Viking' levels depends on their position between the Late Iron Age and medieval deposits. The excavator suggested that they should be dated mid-ninth/tenth century and tenth/late eleventh century respectively (Crawford and Switsur 1977, 131). Level X has a radiocarbon date of AD859±40, calibrated to AD880–1020, but unfortunately this is from whale bone and therefore subject to the marine reservoir effect. Level IXc has two radiocarbon dates calibrated 780–1390 and 1040–1260 (Lane 1990, 119). Though a mid-eleventh-century Norwegian coin may support the excavator's original eleventh-century dating, his subsequent publication suggests that this phase may last into the twelfth century (Crawford nd, 13–14). Again, full publication of the rich bone and metal assemblages is required before any final confirmation of the dating will be possible.

The Viking levels are sealed by a destruction layer and then a series of buildings, including one very well-preserved compartmented long house thought to be twelfth or thirteenth century in date and with appropriate medieval artefacts including English coins (Crawford and Switsur 1977, 132; Crawford nd, 14; Selkirk and Selkirk 1996, 86–7). Pottery continues to be plentiful until the late seventeenth- or eighteenth-century abandonment of the site, but unfortunately it was not possible for me to study this later material and no further study of the medieval assemblage has been possible. Clearly, this raised issues about how closely diagnostic the Viking assemblage is and whether its forms and methods continued in use in the medieval centuries. The excavator was of the view that the platters were confined to the Viking phase and so could be used as a chronological indicator but, as we shall see below, this confidence seems to have been misplaced. The emergence of decoration and changes in vessel form may be traceable in the medieval and later assemblage, but yet again definitive publication is required (Lane 1990, 123; Parker Pearson et al. 2004a, 160–1; Lane 2005).

As noted already, I was originally able to identify twenty-nine sites with Viking pottery from Lewis in the north to Tiree in the south. Grassmarking and sagging bases seem fairly diagnostic, but it is the platter sherds which are an extremely useful assemblage indicator. These 'platters' are thin, flat pottery discs with finger-marks and occasional stab-marks on their upper surfaces and grass-marking on their basal surfaces. With a uniformly light colour, they can be recognized from quite small fragments. Using this evidence, field survey work on South Uist in the 1990s identified twenty-one sites with Viking/Late Norse pottery from eroding surface deposits (Sharples and Parker Pearson 1999, 46, fig. 3) where previously from museum collections I had only located four. Two sites were selected from these for further exploration which led to the large-scale excavation of Cille Pheadair (Parker Pearson et al. 2004b) and Bornais (Sharples 2005). However, the excavation of these two settlements has raised questions about the date of the Viking ceramics and in particular of the platter discs. Both sites show continued use of 'Viking pottery' into the medieval period. Some doubt had already been cast on the date of the platters as the Norwegian steatite baking plates, which it was thought the platters might be copying, are not known prior to their appearance at Oslo about 1100 (Lane 2005). So how secure is the Hebridean dating?

DATING THE VIKING POTTERY

Crawford originally believed that the platters were confined to his secondary Viking level IXc, which he believed was tenth and eleventh century in date (Crawford and Switsur 1977, 131). My analysis showed small quantities of platter sherds (less than one per cent) in the primary Viking layer X at the Udal, whereas there was *c.*12 per cent in the secondary Viking layer IXc (Lane 1983, 182, 204). At Cille Pheadair, the evidence apparently shows that platters were used throughout the occupation, which is radiocarbon dated *c.*1020–1220. However, at Bornais, one part of the site which has been fully published seems to show that ceramic platters continued in use as late as the fourteenth century (Lane 2005, 194–5). In addition, they do not appear to be present in the earlier timber longhouse phase at Bornais, which may be tenth century in date (Sharples 2004, 269), while another new site, Bostadh, Lewis, apparently has early Viking pottery of possible ninth- or tenth-century date, again without platter (Johnson 2005; pers. comm.; Neighbour and Burgess 1997). The date at which the ceramic platters emerged is consequently important. It seems likely that the Hebridean platters are skeuomorphs of the steatite bakestones known from sites in Orkney, Shetland and Norway. Though Weber (1999, 137–8) has suggested dates for these in the Northern Isles from *c.*1100, more recent work by Forster indicates that steatite baking plates may have been in use in the area in the early Viking Age (Forster 2004, 182–98; Forster pers. comm.).

Consequently, the initial date for the use of platter in the Hebrides is currently uncertain. The suggested tenth- and eleventh-century dates at the Udal may be supported by Cille Pheadair (early eleventh) and Bornais (perhaps later tenth and fairly certainly eleventh). Bornais and Bostadh suggest a pre-platter phase of Viking pottery use, as Crawford originally suggested at the Udal. However, the evidence of continued platter use into the late twelfth-/early thirteenth-century at Cille Pheadair, and as late as the fourteenth century at Bornais, means that platter sherds cannot be used to identify specifically early Viking-Age sites. They indicate the continuation of a Viking-Age tradition of ceramic use over a longer period.

Both Cille Pheadair and Bornais support the identification of the Viking style of sagging-based bowls, cups and platters in use from *c.*1000 to the early thirteenth century. Bornais Mound 2 has not yet been studied in any detail. This site has the large stone longhouse of tenth-/eleventh-century date and an earlier, as yet undated, timber Viking phase (Sharples 2004). The pottery associated with this early timber phase has not yet been studied in detail, though it is thought that platter may be absent. Consequently, there is still some uncertainty about the nature of early Viking ceramic use. Crawford may be correct that pottery is introduced in his first Viking phase and the platters only appear in the tenth or eleventh century. Publication of Bostadh and Bornais Mound 2 may help to resolve this.

These Viking/late Norse ceramic forms have now been found on some fifty sites, varying from mere scatters of sherds to substantial eroding settlement and midden deposits. They are located throughout the Hebridean ceramic zone from Lewis to Tiree (Fig. 20.4). Detailed fieldwork on the other islands in this zone, following the South Uist work initiated by Parker Pearson, would undoubtedly locate further sites. However, uncertainty about dating means we cannot regard this as a Viking-period distribution, but rather a more loosely dated Viking to medieval indication of site occupation.

WIDER PARALLELS

Only two ceramic parallels have been traced for the Udal Viking style. Some of the Irish Souterrain Ware assemblages have pottery closely similar to the Udal Viking style. Much of the pottery is grassmarked, and forms include open bowls and cups with sagging bases. On the other hand, there are no platters, and the flat-bottomed cordoned pots are quite different in vessel proportions (Lane 1983, 352; Ryan 1973, fig. 2; Mallory and McNeill 1991, fig. 6.19). My review of Souterrain Ware museum collections in the late 1970s identified twenty-one Irish sites, out of ninety-one listed by Ryan, with pottery comparable to the Hebridean material; a few sites have closely similar material (Lane 1983, 350–8). Souterrain Ware is a common find on early medieval sites in north-eastern Ireland, principally occurring in Co. Antrim and Down, but with some finds in Armagh and Derry and, occasionally, elsewhere. It is normally said to date from perhaps as early as the eighth century until the twelfth century. Unfortunately, though a development from plain Souterrain Ware to decorated forms has been posited, there is insufficient detailed published evidence to allow us to differentiate the date of different assemblages. The sites with parallels to the Hebrides are overwhelmingly in Co. Antrim – eighteen out of twenty-one, and the best parallels are from three sites Larrybane, Ballintoy and Murlough Bay on the north Antrim coast. Unfortunately, none of these are closely dated (Lane 1983, 357). The nature of the relationship, if any, between the Hebridean assemblages and Souterrain Ware is still unclear.

One other area has comparable pottery. Excavations in the Faroe Islands have recovered pottery from a number of sites, though with some uncertainty about their dates. From Sandavagur comes a series of sagging-based bowls which look very similar to the Hebridean finds (Lane 1983, 348–9, fig. 30). I have not had an opportunity to study this material at first hand, and at present it is difficult to establish how similar it is, however Arge has noted similarities between pottery from Leirvik, of twelfth-/fourteenth-century date, and the bowls published by Parker Pearson from Cille Pheadair (Arge pers. comm.; Arge 1997, 32–4, fig. 6; cf. Parker Pearson et al. 2004b, fig. 7). It seems likely that this material is closely

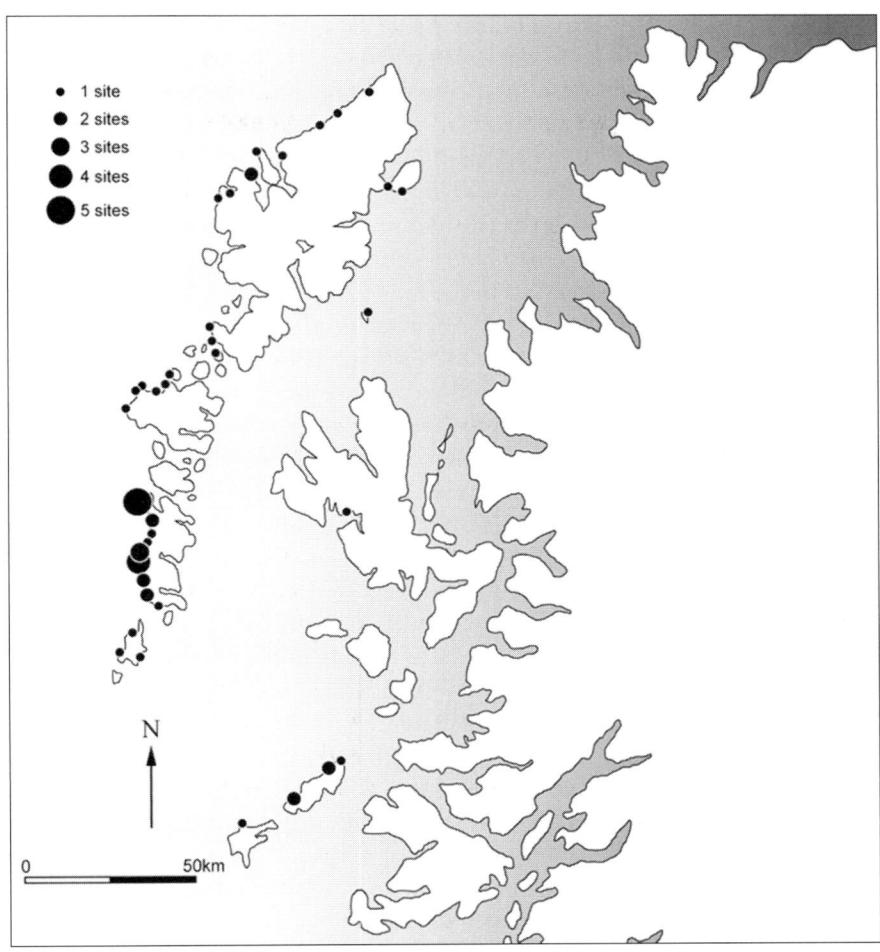

20.4 Distribution of Viking pottery in the Hebrides (© Alan Lane).

related to the Hebridean sequence, though it is perhaps significant that it is not thought to occur in early Viking levels where steatite is in use.

DISCUSSION

So, we can now demonstrate the nature of the Hebridean ceramic sequence from *c.*500 to 1400. The pre-Viking Plain Style is clearly a continuation of the Iron Age sequence and seems to be in full use up to the beginning of the Viking Age. But what date is the new Viking style and is it in use in the earliest phases of Viking settlement in the area?

As we have seen above, a significant percentage of the Udal level X material is in Late Iron Age Plain Style, but the new Viking style also appears. How is this to be interpreted? It may indicate the survival of part of the native population who continued to build pots in their native style and manner. Alternatively, these could be residual ceramics re-deposited in the Viking layer. It may be easier to agree on the importance of the new Viking-style pottery. These small cups and open bowls mark a significant change, and presumably indicate new eating and cooking habits. The new pottery construction technique could indicate new potters or perhaps an adaptation to the new forms which did not require the previous tongue and groove method. There are no obvious parallels for this new style on the Viking settlements of the Northern Isles or in the Scandinavian homelands where steatite, iron cauldrons and wooden vessels appear to be the dominant domestic utensils. The simple pottery and cup forms in the Hebrides may be skeuomorphs of Scandinavian stone and wood originals.

Steatite is common on the Viking settlements of the Northern Isles and pottery only reappears in this area in the late Norse period. This grass-tempered pottery is quite unlike the Hebridean forms (Graham-Campbell and Batey 1998, 223–5). It is striking that no steatite was recovered in the Udal excavations in contrast to its presence at Drimore, Bostadh, Cille Pheadair and Bornais. It is difficult not to regard the continuing use of pottery in the Viking-Age Hebrides as a sign of continuity, albeit heavily modified to make vessel forms which conform to new cultural norms. Crawford's view, that the Viking impact was 'sudden and totally obliterative in terms of local material culture' (Crawford 1981, 267), is not supported by the evidence of continuing pottery use but the new forms indicate something more complex than simple continuity.

CONCLUSION

It is now possible to trace the development of pottery in the Hebrides from *c*.AD500 to 1300 or 1400 with confidence. The arrival of the Vikings is recognizable in the sequence and impacts upon ceramic forms and technology. However, whether pottery is in use in the earliest Hebridean Viking settlements and the speed with which the new Viking style emerged remain to be demonstrated. Likewise, the relationship of the Viking style to Irish Souterrain Ware and the Faroese finds has hardly been touched on yet. Jennings and Kruse were keen to use the ceramic evidence to support their linguistic evidence against continuity in the Outer Hebrides and consequently to try to attribute the similarities in the Viking style to links with northern Ireland and a hypothesis of Irish potters being taken to the Viking settlements in the Hebrides and the Faroes. In my 1983 study, I discussed various possibilities for these similarities between pottery in northern Ireland and the Outer Hebrides, including the possibility of ceramic influence from, or to, Souterrain Ware. Given that pottery use seems to have been current in the Hebrides from the Neolithic to the nineteenth century, it seems more likely that pottery use is indicative of a stratum of local continuity.

How should the Hebridean settlement evidence be viewed? Crawford was of the view that the Udal evidence showed a sudden violent mid-ninth-century intrusion at the Udal (Crawford and Switsur 1977, 131). The evidence of rectangular structures directly on top of cellular buildings, without any intervening blown sand, implies direct chronological succession. He also claimed that the Udal shows immediate changes in pins, combs, ironwork, moulds and crucibles (Crawford 1975, 12; Crawford and Switsur 1977, 131; Crawford 1981, 267). If this is the case, the possible continuity of pottery use, but with the adoption of new vessel forms and techniques, is an interesting exception. None of the published evidence from Cille Pheadair or Bornais yet allows us to see the primary Viking phase in the Hebrides. Bostadh may have final pre-Viking and primary Viking evidence. Mound 2 at Bornais has a tenth-/eleventh-century hall house and an earlier timber phase, but this latter structure has not been fully excavated.

Ó Corráin has suggested that 'the most plausible and economic interpretation of the historical record' is that a substantial part of Scotland including the Western and Northern Isles and coastal mainland as far south as Argyll was conquered in the first quarter of the ninth century and that some settlements may have been established pre-825 (1998, 1). Unfortunately, none of the published evidence for the pre-Viking or the primary Viking settlements allows us to date them accurately, so we cannot yet establish an archaeological date for Viking takeover. Jennings and Kruse may well be right that the tendency of some archaeologists to underplay Viking impact is as much sociological as evidence-driven, but given appropriate publication and excavation we should in future be better placed to conduct the debate.

BIBLIOGRAPHY

Arge, S.V. 1997. 'Í Uppistovubeitinum: site and settlement', *Fróðskaparrit*, 45, 27–44.
Crawford, I. 1975. 'Scot (?), Norseman and Gael', *Scottish Archaeological Forum*, 6, 1–16.
Crawford, I. 1981. 'War or peace? Viking colonization in the Northern and Western Isles of Scotland reviewed' in H. Bekker-Nielsen, P. Foote & O. Olsen (eds), *Proceedings of the Eighth Viking Congress, Århus 24–31 August 1977* (Odense), pp 259–70.
Crawford, I. nd. *The West Highlands and islands: a view of 50 centuries* (Cambridge).
Crawford, I. & R. Switsur. 1977. 'Sandscaping and C14: the Udal, N. Uist', *Antiquity*, 51, 124–36.
Forster, A.K. 2004. 'Shetland and the trade of steatite goods in the North Atlantic region during the Viking and early medieval period' (PhD thesis, University of Bradford).

Graham-Campbell, J. & C.E. Batey. 1998. *Vikings in Scotland: an archaeological survey* (Edinburgh).

Harding, D.W. 2004. *The Iron Age in northern Scotland* (London).

Hines, J., A. Lane & M. Redknap (eds). 2004, *Land, sea and home: proceedings of a conference on Viking-period settlement, at Cardiff, July 2001* (Leeds).

Johnson, M. 2005. 'The pottery from Bostadh Beach, Isle of Lewis', unpublished draft report.

Lane, A. 1983. 'Dark-age and Viking-Age pottery in the Hebrides, with special reference to the Udal' (PhD thesis, University College, London).

Lane, A. 1990. 'Hebridean pottery: problems of definition, chronology, presence and absence' in I. Armit (ed.), *Beyond the brochs: changing perspectives on the Later Iron Age in Atlantic Scotland* (Edinburgh), pp 108–30.

Lane, A. 2005. 'The pottery' in N. Sharples (ed.), *A Norse farmstead in the Outer Hebrides: excavations at Mound 3, Bornais, South Uist* (Oxford), passim.

Lane, A. forthcoming. 'Ceramic and cultural change in the Hebrides, AD500–1300' in Jon-Viðar Sigurðsson (ed.), Celtic-Norse relationships in the Irish Sea, 800–1200 (Leiden).

Mallory, J.P. & T.E. McNeill. 1991. *The archaeology of Ulster from colonization to plantation* (Belfast).

Neighbour, T. & C. Burgess. 1997. 'Traigh Bostadh, (Uig Parish)', *Discovery and excavation in Scotland 1996*, 113–14.

Ó Corráin, D. 1998. 'The Vikings in Scotland and Ireland in the ninth century', *Peritia*, 12, 296–339.

Parker Pearson, M., N. Sharples & J. Symonds 2004a. *South Uist: archaeology and history of a Hebridean Island* (Stroud).

Parker Pearson, M., H. Smith, J. Mulville & M. Brennand 2004b. 'Cille Pheadair: the life and times of a Norse-period farmstead, c.1000–1300' in J. Hines et al. (eds), *Land, sea and home* (Leeds), pp 235–54.

Ryan, M. 1973. 'Native pottery in early historic Ulster', *Proceedings of the Royal Irish Academy*, 73, 619–45.

Selkirk, A. & W. Selkirk (eds). 1996. 'The Udal', *Current Archaeology*, 13:147, 84–94.

Sharples, N. 2004. 'A find of Ringerike art from Bornais in the Outer Hebrides' in J. Hines et al. (eds), *Land, sea and home* (Leeds), 255–72.

Sharples, N. (ed.). 2005. *A Norse farmstead in the Outer Hebrides: excavations at Mound 3, Bornais, South Uist* (Oxford).

Sharples, N. & M. Parker Pearson. 1999. '*Norse* settlement in the Outer Hebrides', *Norwegian Archaeological Review*, 32, 41–62.

Sharples, N. et al. 2004. 'The archaeological landscape of South Uist' in R.A. Housley & G. Coles (eds), *Atlantic connections and adaptations: economies, environments and subsistence in lands bordering the North Atlantic* (Oxford), pp 28–47.

Weber, B. 1999. 'Bakestones' in B.E. Crawford & B. Ballin Smith (eds), *The Biggings, Papa Stour, Shetland: the history and excavation of a royal Norwegian farm* (Edinburgh), 134–9.

Young, A. 1966. 'The sequence of Hebridean pottery' in A.L.F. Rivet (ed.), *The Iron Age in northern Britain* (Edinburgh), pp 45–58.

Viking-Age queens and the formation of identity

SHANNON LEWIS-SIMPSON

Of all the Viking kings who invaded, settled and/or briefly ruled in the York-Dublin axis, the historical record is practically silent about the women who shared their beds, married them and bore their children. In short, one is not told much of their queens. The few women who are prominently mentioned in the sources are notorious, their representations being the stuff of legend and folktale rather than portrayals of real people. One may ask, then, not why there is such a paucity of these women in the written record, but why any are mentioned at all, and for what purposes?

Digging through annals, chronicles and sagas, one does find references of King So-and-So's wife, or daughter given in marriage to another king, or mother of a king. Of these, there is Eadgyth, the royal pawn who embodies Christian virtue. There is Gormlaith/Kormlöð, the Irish princess-consort to three kings called the 'mother of the king of the foreigners'. And, finally, one should probably consider Auðr in djúpúðga who, after her marriage to the Norse king of Dublin, Óláfr inn hvíti, became one of the principal settlers of Iceland. The (dis)connections made between elite women and men represent dynastic connections between the Scandinavian, Irish and Anglo-Saxon elites and the desire or lack thereof to be politically affiliated with an Other. What is most interesting, however, is not what the contemporary chroniclers wrote about these inter/marriages, but how these alliances were spun by later writers in their attempts to rewrite the past.

EADGYTH, THE ROYAL VIRGIN

Although of the West-Saxon royal family, one might consider Eadgyth to have belonged to the Hiberno-Norse elite, at least for a brief period of time in 925. The Anglo-Saxon Chronicle MS 'D' is very matter-of-fact concerning her marriage:

> *Her Æþelstan cyning 7 Sihtric Norðhymbra cyng heo gesamnodon æt Tameweorðþige. iii. kalendas Februarius, 7 Æþelstan his sweostor him forgeaf* (ASC s.a. 925).
> 'Here King Athelstan and Sihtric, the king of the Northumbrians, came together at Tamworth on 30 January, and Athelstan gave him his sister'.

She is denied a name, she is *forgeaf* to Sigtryggr caech: clearly Eadgyth is not accorded any agency in her brother's dynastic transaction. Eadgyth is named by the thirteenth-century emendator of Roger of Wendover's *Chronica sive Flores Historiarum*, who expands this rather terse earlier chronicle entry. Althelstan gives away his sister *matrimonio honorifice* ('honourably in marriage') to *Sihtrico Danica natione progentio, Northanhumbrorum regi* ('Sigtyggr of the Danish nation, king of the Northumbrians') who subsequently *ob amorem virginis paganismum relinquens fidem Christi suscepit* ('for the love of the virgin, relinquishing paganism, accepted the Christian faith'). But, the new faith did not stick: he abandoned the wife along with Christ, went back to his gods, and then 'miserably ended his life' (*vitam miserabiliter terminavit*: Luard 1872, 446–7). Having preserved her virginity, Eadgyth died and went on to do many good works and miracles in death. Meanwhile, her brother made great use of Sigtryggr's untimely demise by subsequently annexing the Northumbrian kingdom, claiming his right to do so through his sister's marriage with the dead Hiberno-Norse king.

Eadgyth is sanctified in the amended chronicle as a royal and holy virgin, who attempts to bring the heathen Danish king to Christianity. She is not to blame for the failure of the marriage; rather the pagan king simultaneously rejects her and her religion, forfeiting his life in the process. The later account emphasizes both his ethnicity and religion, and Sigtryggr is portrayed here as the wicked pagan. Eadgyth, not her brother, is his Christian opposite. Somewhat resembling a plastic statue of a saint, she becomes a didactic image effectively used as propaganda to make manifest the miraculous victory of the Christian church against paganism. Furthermore, this later account makes much of the retention of Eadgyth's virginity: Eadgyth preserves the royal Wessex bloodline against invasion by the pagan Danes. The emphasis on the later account of Sigtryggr's having a different *genus*, or origin (implying both blood and also geographical origin or kinship), and *mores* (customs including religious belief) implies a wider ethnic boundary between Scandinavian and Anglo-Saxon than is perhaps suggested by the contemporary evidence (Hadley 2002; Lewis-Simpson 2005, 177–80). This theme of difference is certainly in keeping with the revisionist histories of the eleventh, twelfth and thirteenth centuries which increasingly cast the 'Danes' in an evil light as opponents of the righteous English (Reynolds 1983; Page 1987; Geary 1991; Cowen 2004).

GORMLAITH, *MATHAIR RÍGH GALL*

Sigtryggr did, however, sire sons, presumably by some other woman if Eadgyth indeed 'preserved her virginity' and her Wessex bloodline. One son's wife was not repudiated but outlived her husband, and her second husband as well. The obit of Gormlaith ingen Murchada in *Chronicum Scotorum s.a.* 1028 (recte 1030) states *Gormlaith ingen Murchadha mic Finn, mathair righ Gall .i. Sitricc, ocus righ Muman .i. Donnchadha mic Briain, moritur* (*Chronicum Scotorum*, 268–9: 'Gormlaith, daughter of Murchadh mac Finn, mother of the king of the foreigners, Sitriuc, and of the king of Munster, Donnchadh, son of Brian, *dies*'). The later *Corpus Genealogiarum Hiberniae* commemorates her alliances in the following telling quatrain (cited in Ní Mhaonaigh 2001, 18, n. 106):

> *Trí lémend ra ling Gormlaith,*
> *ní lingfea ben co bráth;*
> *léim i nÁth cliath, léim i Temraig,*
> *léim i Cassel, carnmaig ós chách.*

'Three leaps did Gormlaith perform,
Which no other woman will do till Doomsday:
A leap into Dublin, a leap into Tara,
A leap into Cashel, the plain with the mound which surpasses all'.

A king's consort thrice over, Gormlaith was first married to Amlaíb Cuarán (Óláfr Cuarán), king of Northumbria from 941 to 945 and of Dublin from 943 to 980 (Hudson 1994, 321; Ó Corráin 2001). As with Eadgyth, the match was more than likely controlled by her male relative, in this case her father, Murchad mac Finn, the king of Leinster and a political ally of Óláfr (Clarke 1998, 362). Gormlaith's son by Óláfr, Sigtryggr silkiskeggr Óláfsson, ruled Dublin from 989 to 1036. Óláfr died in 981 on pilgrimage to Iona after he had been defeated in battle by Máel sechnaill mac Domnaill, the king of Tara, whose wife or concubine Gormlaith is thought to have become in accordance with the quatrain above (Trindade 1986, 150; Ní Mhaonaigh 2001, 19–20). Gormlaith leapt to Cashel with Brian Bórama, king of Munster, who 'acquired [Gormlaith] in symbolic recognition of his supreme overlordship' (Trindade 1986, 150). Gormlaith's son by Brian was Donnchad, who became king after his father's death. Clearly it was thought important by these leaders to have this Leinster princess as consort, perhaps in the same way as Ælgifu/Emma was acquired by the conquering Knútr in England.

With Sigtryggr silkiskeggr of Dublin and Donnchad of Munster, she was a true mother of kings for both Norse and Irish. Although the quatrain in the later genealogies commemorates her alliances to three very important and prominent kings, her obit does not focus on Gormlaith as wife but places more importance on her as mother – and mother of a *rí Gall* at that. Due to her many unions, and the fact her sons and consorts are constantly at war with one another, one would think she would experience conflicting family allegiances. But in the early twelfth-century *Cogadh Gáedhel re Gallaibh* (*CGG*), as Máire Ní Mhaonaigh points out, Gormlaith is portrayed 'as a Leinster woman first and foremost'

(2001, 21). In an infamous encounter, Gormlaith is asked by her brother, Máel Mórda, king of Leinster, to sew a silver button on his tunic which was a gift from Brian.

> *Ro gab in rigan intinar, ocus tuc urcur isin tenid de, ocus ro bai ica cursacad, ocus ica gresacht a brathar, daig ba holc le moghsaine no dairse do chur do neoch ele fair, .i. an ní nar fhaom a athair no a shenathair riamh, ocus atbert fos co sirfeadh mac Briain ar a mhacsan ina diaigh, ocus gach duine déis aroile.*

'The queen took the tunic and cast it into the fire, and she began to reproach and incite her brother, because she thought it ill that he should yield service and vassalage, and suffer oppression from any one, or yield that which his father or grandfather never yielded; and she said also that Brian's son would hereafter require it from his son, and all other men afterwards' (*CGG*, 142, n. 15) and citation from the Brussels MS, p.143, note 15 (eclectic text).

The author is very quick to place distance between Gormlaith and Brian, and, more importantly, with *mac Briain* ('Brian's son') who is also her son, Donnchadh.In *CGG*, one sees Gormlaith as inciter, and she is cast as 'the prime instigator of the battle of Clontarf' (Ní Mhaonaigh 1995, 360). Trindade equates her to 'the Irish Helen, a woman who provoked an international incident and changed the course of history' (1986, 150). Gormlaith is also thoroughly cast in the role of evil instigator and machinator of Clontarf in *Brennu-Njáls saga*. Some scholars hypothesize that this rendition of the Battle of Clontarf has entered *Njáls saga* from a non-extant *Brjáns saga* composed by someone fluent in Irish (Lönnroth 1976, 226–36; Ó Corráin 1998, 447–52; Jonas Kristjánsson 1998, 270–1). Ó Corráin proposes that it was written as the Dubliners' answer to the *CGG*, which portrayed them in an unfavourable light, constituting a 'skilful reply and a diplomatic expression of loyalty [to the Ua Briain dynasty]' (1998, 450).

Gormlaith/Kormlöð and her son Sigtryggr silkiskeggr are introduced in *Njáls saga* as follows:

> *Þá kom ok þar konungr sá, er Sigtryggr hét, af Írlandi. Hann var sonr Óláfs kvárans; moðir hans hét Kormlöð. Hon var allra kvenna fegrst ok bezt orðin um allt þat, er henni var ósjálfrátt, en þat er mál manna, at henni hafi allt verit illa gefit, þat er henni var sjálfrátt. Brjánn hét konungr sjá, er hana hafði átta, ok váru þau þá skilið* (*Njáls saga*, 440).

'There was a king there, who was called Sigtryggr, from Ireland. He was the son of Óláfr kváran; his mother was called Kormlöð [Gormlaith]. She was the most beautiful of all women and best in all those things that were beyond her own control, but it is said that she was completely evil in everything for which she had self-control. There was a king called Brian, to whom she has been married, and now they were divorced.'

The source states that Gormlaith incites others to battle because she is a scorned woman: *En svá var hon orðin grimm Brjáni konungi eptir skilnað þeira, at hon vildi hann gjarna feigan* (441–2: 'She had such fierce thoughts towards King Brian after their divorce, that she eagerly wished him dead'). The saga author tells that she *eggjaði mjök* ('greatly urged') her son to seek the assistance of first Jarl Sigurðr of Orkney and then two Vikings, Bróðir and Óspakr, who are anchored off the Isle of Man (442). Jarl Sigurðr said he would help Sigtryggr under one condition: that he could marry Gormlaith and become king of Ireland should they defeat Brian: *Mælti hann þat til, at eiga móður hans ok vera siðan konungr í Írlandi, ef þeir felldi Brján* (444). Bróðir, who eventually kills Brian, makes the same demand (446). Sigtryggr agrees to the stipulations of both, with the blessing of his mother, who understands that her position and sexuality are being used to gain military support. Albeit portrayed as ultimately evil, Gormlaith is shown as having *sjálfráð* ('self-control' or 'sovereignty') over these assets of sex and bloodline, unlike Eadgyth who has no self-control over her circumstances. It is of interest to note that after the alliances have been made leading to the battle, Gormlaith exits the saga.

As with the contemporary and non-contemporary Irish sources, in the Old-Norse saga, marriage to or conquest of Gormlaith goes hand-in-hand with conquest of Ireland, and more specifically Dublin. But, there is a twist: she herself never appears to be conquered as such, but stays true to her Leinster kin or, in *Njáls saga*, her son – or anyone who opposes Brian. Her appearance in *Njáls saga* has perhaps less to do with a mythic remembrance of a Norse-Leinster alliance than with the saga narrative. There are many episodes of inciting women in *Njáls saga* (Hallgerðr the most memorable of these), and Lars Lönnroth remarks upon the similarities between her and Gormlaith (1976, 234). Gormlaith's inciting men to disastrous action is presaged by Hildigunnr's inciting of Flosi and his caustic response: '*Þú ert it mesta forað ok vildir, at vér tækim þat upp, er öllum oss gegnir verst, ok eru köld kvenna ráð*' (*Njáls saga*, 291–2: 'You are the greatest monster, and you would like us to take that up, which for us all will go worst, and cold are the counsels of women'). One can scarcely believe this dramatic episode would not be recalled by the audience with regards to Gormlaith's role in Clontarf. The inclusion of *Njáls saga* of the poem *Darraðarljóð* is also significant, as the supernatural women weaving with men's intestines and heads as loom weights are portrayed as controlling or weaving the battle's course, thus determining the lives and deaths of the warriors. They then discuss the outcome of the battle (Poole 1991, 134–40; Davidson 1998, 117–18). One may postulate that the author wished to make a comparison between the weaving women and

Gormlaith. Like the weaving women who control the course of the battle before it begins, Gormlaith also controls those that are to participate in the battle, enticing some warriors with her femininity and sexuality. The preamble to the battle and the poem are complementary in that both are controlled by feminine entities. Even if the saga author knew that the poem had nothing to do with Clontarf, as is argued by Russell Poole (1991, 124), it may be read as an extended metaphor of the power, and implied malevolence, exhibited by Gormlaith and other inciting female characters such as Hallgerðr and Hildigunnr earlier in the saga. One may suppose that a contemporary Icelandic audience would have understood and appreciated this conceit.

AUÐR LANDNÁMSKONA

In a hybrid society, intermarriage is bound to occur between cultural communities, especially among the elite. By marrying into powerful local families, medieval settlers 'could establish their position, since they would immediately acquire kin, property and patrons' (Bartlett 1993, 55). Certainly, that appears to be the case with Óláfr Cuarán's union with Gormlaith. That medieval Icelandic writers saw fit to remember such earlier intermarriages is perhaps in line with the Icelandic fascination with all things genealogical and ancestral. Indeed, one of Anthony Smith's criteria for the formation of an *ethnie* is the presence of a myth of common ancestry. These myths assist the individual to '"make sense" of their relocation' within a communal group (Smith 1999, 62). The first settlers to an area inevitably take on significance for the resulting community and Robert Bartlett argues that 'those who were present at [...societal] beginnings were rapidly mythologized and given special standing in the collective memory' (1993, 93). Although the *ethnie* is partially formed around 'origin myths', seemingly with an emphasis on blood origin, the very fact that an elite group would need to emphasize descent undermines the value of 'blood' in the creation of an ethnic group. In effect, origin myths are created purposefully 'in the head' by those who would manipulate others 'in the heart'. As well as bestowing special status on mythological forebears, genealogical texts also serve the purpose of validating current relationships between groups and peoples. 'Pre-literate peoples preserve versions of their history which explain current social groupings and institutions, and these versions may bear little relation to an historical sequence of events' (Dumville 1977, 85; see also Úlfar Bragason 2004). Although genealogy is usually looked upon as a fixed attribute, one which includes only specific members to a community on the basis of real or perceived blood ancestry or origin, it is apparent that myths of common ancestry form only one basis for inclusion to a specific community, and how writers present genealogical connections can bear little resemblance to the actual blood relationships of those discussed.

With this in mind, it is worth turning to Auðr in djúpúðga as the character most frequently cited as evidence of a strong matriarchal presence in the Viking-Age North Atlantic. The earliest record of her is found in *Íslendingabók*, where she is noted as the daughter of Ketill flatnef, called a *landnámskona*, and the mother of a long and distinguished lineage of Icelanders (26). *Landnámabók* notes that she married Óláfr inn hvíti, who *herjaði í vestrvíking ok vann Dyflinni á Írlandi ok Dyflinnarskíði ok gerðisk þar konungr yfir* ('harried in the Western Seas and won Dublin in Ireland, and the region of Dublin, and there he made himself king'). She is also named as the mother of Þorsteinn, who subsequently *gerðisk herkonungr; [hann vann] Katanes ok Suðrland, Ros ok Merrhœfi ok meir en hálft Skotland* ('became a warrior-king; [he won] Caithness and Sutherland, Ross and Moray, and more than half of Scotland' (*Landnámabók*, 136). *Eiríks saga* relates that Þorsteinn married Þuríðr and *þau áttu mörg börn* ('They had many children': 195).

Laxdæla saga recounts that Þorsteinn died in Caithness and that Auðr was there at the same time, presumably at his court, now controlled by Þorsteinn's killers. Left with no male to lead her large family, her subsequent actions in saga tradition are deemed remarkable. She escapes to Orkney, marries off several grandchildren and then relocates the whole family to Iceland. *Laxdæla saga* proclaims that *má af því marka, at hon var mikit afbragð annarra kvenna* ('one may observe from this that she greatly surpassed other women': 7). She arrives in Iceland, and *lét hon reisa krossa, því at hon var skírð ok vel trúuð* ('she had crosses raised, because she was baptized and very devout': *Eiríks saga*, 196). When she dies in a dignified manner of old age, her family ensures she is laid to rest properly (*Laxdæla saga*, 13). The author of *Laxdæla saga*, a source concerned with genealogical myth-making and conjecture of royal ancestors, makes little mention of the royal Óláfr preferring to concentrate on Auðr's connections across the North Atlantic in her role as *materfamilias*. This serves to connect Iceland with the greater North Atlantic world. Auðr very tangibly symbolizes the Scandinavian advance across the North Atlantic and the connections made along the way. She is a matriarch who is Christian and, like Eadgyth, she is a champion of the faith for later saga authors.

SUMMARY

Notwithstanding obvious differences in the tales of these 'queens', one could suggest that the portrayals of Eadgyth, Gormlaith and Auðr are used to represent connections and boundaries between the Scandinavian, Irish and Anglo-Saxon elites. The contemporary chronicles and early Icelandic histories might be thought of as having more veracity than later chronicles and sagas, but written sources do not give us the intimate details of contact between individuals of different cultures, nor do they give much indication as to contemporary attitudes towards this contact. This is not unique to the period. As Chris Gosden notes, 'many involved in face-to-face colonial encounters had little inclination or leisure to write down accounts of what happened' (2004, 6). Those who did write down accounts of cultural interaction generally did so because they were told to do so or were encouraged by an elite patron, as in the case of the writer of the *CGG*. With written accounts, not enough emphasis is placed on what the non-producers of myths – the audience – thought about these inter-ethnic connections and boundaries. One cannot presume that the whole community identified themselves with royal genealogical lists, for example. This prescriptive notion of identity, suggesting that the communal identity is created and prescribed by an elite, is not particularly in keeping with modern notions of ethnicity and identity as mutable and instrumental (for example, Jones 1997). Nevertheless, it must be said that the most visible manifestations of cultural identity contributing to ethnic identity are, in effect, those of the elite or created by or for an elite. The portrayals of Eadgyth, Gormlaith, Auðr and their international consorts should be read accordingly.

BIBLIOGRAPHY

ASC = Cubbin, G.P. (ed.). 1996. *The Anglo-Saxon Chronicle: a collaborative edition, 6: MS 'D'* (Cambridge).

Bartlett, R. 1993. *The making of Europe: conquest, colonization and cultural change, 950–1350* (Harmondsworth).

CGG = Todd, J.H. (ed. and trans.). 1867. *Cogadh Gaedhel re Gallaibh: the War of the Gaedhill with the Gaill, or, the Invasions of Ireland by the Danes and Other Norsemen* (London).

Chronica sive Flores Historiarum = Coxe, H.O. (ed.). 1841. *Rogeri de Wendover Chronica sive Flores Historiarum*, vol. 1 (London).

Chronicum Scotorum = Hennessy, W.M. (ed. and trans.). 1866. *Chronicum Scotorum: a chronicle of Irish affairs, from the earliest times to AD 1135*, Rolls Series, 46 (London).

Clarke, H.B., M. Ní Mhaonaigh & R. Ó Floinn (eds). 1998, *Ireland and Scandinavia in the Early Viking-Age* (Dublin).

Clarke, H.B. 1998. 'Proto-towns and towns in Ireland and Britain in the ninth and tenth centuries' in H.B. Clarke et al. (eds), *Ireland and Scandinavia*, pp 331–80.

Cowen, A. 2004. 'Writing fire and the sword: the perception and representation of violence in Viking-Age England' (PhD thesis, University of York).

Davidson, H.E. 1998. *Roles of the northern goddess* (London).

Dumville, D. 1977. 'Kingship, genealogies and regnal lists' in P.H. Sawyer & I.N. Wood (eds), *Early medieval kingship* (Leeds), pp 72–104.

Egils Saga = Sigurðr Nordal (ed.). 1933. *Egils Saga Skalla-Grímssonar*, Íslenzk fornrit, 2 (Reykjavík).

Eiríks saga = Einar Ol. Sveinsson and Matthías yórðarson (eds). 1935. *Eyrbyggja Saga, Brands yattr Orva, Eiríks saga rauða, Grænlendinga saga ok Grænlendinga yattr,* Íslenzk fornrit, 4 (Reykjavík), 195–237.

Geary, P.J. 1991. 'Ethnic identity as a situational construct in the early Middle Ages', *Medieval Perspectives*, 3:2 (1988), 1–17.

Gosden, C. 2004. *Archaeology and colonialism: cultural contact from 5000BC to the present* (Cambridge).

Hadley, D.M. 2002. 'Viking and native: rethinking identity in the Danelaw', *Early Medieval Europe*, 2:1, 45–70.

Holm, P. 1994. 'Between apathy and antipathy: the Vikings in Irish and Scandinavian history', *Peritia*, 8, 151–69.

Hudson, B. 1994. 'Knútr and Viking Dublin', *Scandinavian Studies*, 66, 319–35.

Íslendingabók = Jakob Benediktsson (ed.). 1968. *Íslendingabók. Landnámabók,* Íslenzk fornrit, 1 (Reykjavik).

Jesch, J. 1991. *Women in the Viking-Age* (Woodbridge).

Jochens, J. 1995. *Women in Old Norse society* (London).

Jonas Kristjánsson. 1998. 'Ireland and the Irish in Icelandic tradition' in H.B. Clarke et al. (eds), *Ireland and Scandinavia*, pp 259–76.

Jones, S. 1997. *The archaeology of ethnicity* (London).

Landnámbók = Jakob Benediktsson (ed.). 1968. *Íslendingabók. Landnámabók,* Íslenzk fornrit, 1 (Reykjavik).

Laxdæla saga = Einar Ól. Sveinsson (ed.). 1934. *Laxdæla saga,* Íslenzk fornrit, 5 (Reykjavík).

Lewis-Simpson, S.M. 2005. 'Strangers in strange lands: colonization and multi-culturalism in the age of Scandinavian expansion' (PhD thesis, University of York).

Lönnroth, L. 1976. Njáls saga: *a critical introduction* (London).

Luard, H.R. 1872. *Matthæi Parisiensis Chronica Majora: the Creation to 1066,* vol. 1 (London).

Ní Mhaonaigh, M. 1995. '*Cogad Gáedel re Gallaib*: some dating considerations', *Peritia*, 9, 354–77.

Ní Mhaonaigh, M. 1998. 'Friend and foe: Vikings in ninth- and tenth-century Irish literature', in H.B. Clarke et al. (eds), *Ireland and Scandinavia*, pp 381–402.

Ní Mhaonaigh, M. 2001. 'Tales of three Gormlaiths in medieval Irish literature', *Éiru*, 52, 1–124.

Njáls Saga = Einar Ól. Sveinsson (ed.). 1954. *Brennu-Njáls Saga,* Íslenzk fornrit, 12 (Reykjavík).

Ó Corráin, D. 1998. 'The Vikings in Scotland and Ireland in the ninth century', *Peritia*, 12, 296–339.

Ó Corráin, D. 2001. 'The Vikings in Ireland' in A.C. Larsen (ed.), *The Vikings in Ireland* (Roskilde), pp 17–27.

Ó Cróinín, D. 'Three weddings and a funeral: rewriting Irish political history in the tenth century' in A.P. Smyth (ed.), *Seanchas: studies in early and medieval Irish archaeology, history and literature* (Dublin), pp 212–24.

Page, R.I. 1987. '*A most vile people': early English historians on the Vikings* (London).

Poole, R.G. 1991. *Viking poems on war and peace: a study in skaldic narrative* (Toronto).

Reynolds, S. 1983. 'Medieval *origines gentum*: the community of the realm', *History*, 68, 375–90.

Smith, A.D. 1999. *Myths and memories of the nation* (Oxford).

Smyth, A.P. 1977. *Scandinavian kings in the British Isles* (Oxford).

Trindade, W.A. 1986. 'Irish Gormlaith as a sovereignty figure', *Études Celtiques*, 23, 143–56.

Úlfar Bragason. 2004. 'The politics of genealogies in *Sturlunga saga*' in J. Adams & K. Holman (eds), *Scandinavia and Europe, 800–1350* (Turnhout), pp 309–21.

The *ledung* and the continuity of warfare from the Viking Age to the Middle Ages: the example of Sweden

THOMAS LINDKVIST

The *ledung*, or *leding*, was the military naval organization in the three Scandinavian kingdoms that emerged during the Middle Ages, and question of continuity or discontinuity in the organizations that have to do with warfare in the Viking Age have been much discussed. The transition from the Viking Age to the Middle Ages has always been seen as a profound shift in the development of the Scandinavian societies. These changes are commonly understood as Christianization and the formation of kingdoms and states. One consequence is that the elites, secular and spiritual, became more socially distanced from the rest of the population.

Cavalry, archers and the castle were the essential components of medieval military, and consequently political, power. The coming of the knight and the introduction of the castle transformed Scandinavia during the twelfth and thirteenth centuries, later in Sweden than in Denmark. The great period of building castles in Sweden began in the middle of the thirteenth century. In the late thirteenth century the privileges of an aristocracy that served the king as knights on horseback were regulated, notably in the statutes of Alsnö 1280. The earliest evidence of cavalry in action in Sweden is the fight at Lena (or Kungslena) in Västergötland in 1208. The statutes of Alsnö, in effect, meant the establishment of a separate lay aristocracy that was a military elite (Rosén 1952). In his study of the making of Europe, Robert Bartlett distinguishes three roads of adaptation: conquest, defensive imitation and planned development. Sweden, as the other two Scandinavian kingdoms, experienced the third (Bartlett 1993, 72). The purpose of this military technological adaptation was not defensive, but a means of establishing and increasing power. However, the new military technology was in part introduced by migrating aristocrats mainly from northern Germany. Warfare on land became increasingly more important than warfare at sea. The Swedish *ledung* has mostly been discussed on the basis of the regulations in the provincial law codes. Sources on Swedish warfare are less rich than Danish and Norwegian ones.

The laws belong to a period when seaborne warfare became less important. That is why the *ledung* in the laws is more a fiscal imposition than a military duty. Its transformation into a fiscal imposition took place rather quickly in the reigns of Valdemar and Magnus (AD1250–1290; Lönnroth 1940, 57–136). Elements of continuity between older naval warfare and later medieval taxation and territorial systems have most recently been discussed by Kraft (2005).

The *ledung* is described in detail in four of the provincial law codes: *Upplandslagen* (the law code of Uppland), *Södermannalagen* (the law code of Södermanland), *Västmannalagen* (the law code of Västmanland) and *Hälsingelagen*. In Sweden, it is known only from certain provinces, those around Lake Mälaren, and northwards and southwards along the west coasts of the Gulf of Bothnia and the Baltic. In the province of Dalarna (Dalecarlia), it was simply a tax, one probably introduced during the late thirteenth or early fourteenth century. There is no evidence of a *ledung*, military or fiscal, in Västergötland in western Sweden.

In *Upplandslagen* from 1296, a mainly a fiscal *ledung* is pre-supposed: in effect, a military duty was turned into a tax. And there were many different kinds of taxes, replacements for various duties connected with the *ledung*. In *Södermannalagen* from 1327, it is assumed that the *ledung* could actually be rendered as a military venture. The *ledung* of the laws was probably a defensive organization, and this much is evident from the regulations of *Hälsingelagen*. If the *ledung* went overseas, beyond Aspasund in the Stockholm archipelago, there were no rights to demand *ledungslama*, or fines for not participating (*Hälsingelagen*, Konungabalken ch. 7). The laws set out the duty of the peasantry to provide the royal fleet with ships, men and victuals; and the further duty to guard the coasts. They also contained detailed regulations concerning the *ledung* as a tax, in cases where it was not demanded as a military duty (Lönnroth 1940, 62–6; Andræ 1960, 64–72). In certain periods, the *ledung* functioned as coast guard and defence organization. Attacks from the opposite shore of the Baltic are known, especially during the late twelfth century. In 1187, for example, the city of Sigtuna was burned and plundered by pirates, possibly from Estonia or Karelia. Other evidence for this kind of warfare is provided by several defensive constructions, citadels and forts in eastern Sweden, dated to the late twelfth century.

Reconstructions of an ancient military *ledung* based upon the regulations of the provincial law codes have been attempted. Gerhard Hafström estimated that the *ledung* of the provinces around Lake Mälaren consisted of 280 ships with roughly one hundred men each, thus a possible *ledung* of 28,000 men (Hafström 1949, 58–63). This has been questioned, not least by Adolf Schück. He stressed that the *ledung* prescriptions of the provincial law codes indicate a defensive organization (Schück 1950).

In an important study, Niels Lund has argued cogently that in Denmark the *ledung* of the king is more recent than assumed by previous research (1996). The Viking-Age *ledung* was based upon the retinues of the king and the magnates but, during the twelfth century, the king's prerogatives were so solidly based that he could impose on the peasantry – the free peasantry – the duty to participate.

Around 1170/1, the conditions governing the *ledung* were set out in law, but as a defensive organization (Lund 1996).

However, advanced organizations for maritime and warlike expeditions already existed in the ninth century. Areas on the Curonian coast were made tributary land of the Swedes, the Svear, by force (Blomkvist 2005, 203–14).

In *Upplandslagen*, there is a distinction between *liþ* and *leþung*, between the retinue and the mobilization of men/peasants. According to Erland Hjärne, these terms are not synonyms. It has been pointed out that *liþ* or *lið* are mentioned in runic inscriptions, while *leþung* or *leiðang* belong to the thirteenth century, perhaps with one possible runic exception. The inscription from Söderby in Gästrikland commemorates Egil, who died in Tavastia, *hann varð dauðr a Tafæistalandi*, while Brusi, his brother, led the *ledung* of the land (*Gästriklands runinskrifter*, nr. 13). However, the interpretation of the inscription is uncertain.

Sometimes runic inscriptions commemorate expeditions in the form of a *lið* (*Västergötlands runinskrifter*, no. 184; *Södermanlands runinskrifter*, nos 160, 217, 338; *Västmanlands runinskrifter*, no. 5; *Upplands runinskrifter*, nos 112, 348, 479, 611, 668; Larsson 1990a). There is no evidence of a king, chief or overlord controlling these seaborne forces, with the exception of the Ingvar expedition (Andræ 1960, 64–6). That expedition, of the middle of the eleventh century, probably in the 1040s, was definitely in the form of a cluster of retinues led by regional magnates. It is mentioned on about twenty-five runic inscriptions in the Lake Mälaren area (*Östergötlands runinskrifter*, nos 145, 155; *Södermanlands runinskrifter*, nos 9, 96, 105, 107, 108, 131, 173, 179, 254, 277, 281, 287, 320, 335; *Västmanlands runinskrifter*, no. 19; *Upplands runinskrifter*, nos 439, 644, 654, 661, 778, 1143). It had an organization like a *ledung* (Larsson 1990b). It was based upon the abilities of local lords, formal or charismatic, to muster men and resources. However, it was under the overall organizing control of Ingvar, and whether he be termed king or chieftain or *jarl* is of minor importance in this context (cf. Lund 1996, 111).

In *Östgötalagen*, there are remainders of a more aristocratic *ledung* than the conscript form of *Upplandslagen* and *Södermannalagen*. A special privileged group is mentioned, the men who held forty rowers or oarsmen at their own expenses, as well as *stallare* and *stekare*, that is, some form of serving office-holders. These men were entitled to a special fee as compensation for the killing of their men (*Östgötalagen*, Dråpsbalken, ch. 14:3). Aristocrats or magnates participate with their ships and men in the expeditions of the king or the *jarl*. This decree has been interpreted by Sven Tunberg as the first royal privileges of an emerging aristocracy in Sweden (1907). It was thus a new way of organizing warfare; ships with retinues could be mustered under the control of the king (Hjärne 1947, 18). Privileges were transferred from naval warfare to the knightly order – the privileges of Alsnö 1280 were the continuation of a service previously rendered by magnates with ships and retinue. There is, however, no systematic description of the fiscal system in *Östgötalagen* and thus there is no proper evidence of a *ledung* in Östergötland. The coastal areas could be burdened with higher taxes to the king and the *jarl*, which implies a tax that was a substitute for a military *ledung* (*Östgötalagen*, Byggningabalken ch. 28; Lönnroth 1940, 64).

The province of Östergötland and the diocese of Linköping were a political centre of the kingdom during the twelfth and early thirteenth centuries. Several known seaborne activities during that period originated in Östergötland. The kings of the Sverker dynasty were mainly residents of that province and they were sometimes involved in warfare and crusading activities on the other side of the Baltic, for example in 1142, 1164 and 1219, although it is uncertain whether or not some of these expeditions were on the initiative of the king (Lindkvist 1990, 63–7).

Areas became integrated within the province of Östergötland and/or the bishopric of Linköping. Gotland became a part of the Linköping bishopric and a tributary relationship to the Swedish king and jarl was established. The coastal area south of Östergötland, as well as the isle of Öland, became integrated in the political dominion of Östergötland and Linköping. Ecclesiastical integration of south-western Finland, including the Åland islands, was probably begun from Linköping (Sjöstrand 1994, 557–67). In 1197, Jarl Birger brosa was involved in a crusading expedition in what is now Estonia. Birger brosa, who was mostly resident in the province of Östergötland, was also much involved in establishing a stronghold on Öland. All of this required a developed offensive seaborne military organization.

In the thirteenth and early fourteenth centuries, it was possible to demand the *ledung*. It was not only a fiscal imposition: it could be transformed into a military obligation. And there were great seaborne campaigns, mainly under the name of crusades. There is an uncertain tradition of a crusade of Saint Erik the King in the 1150s and there were certainly crusading activities in the reign of his son, Knut Eriksson.

The term in Latin in the charters for *ledung* was *expeditio*, also used for a crusade. One of the first cases in Sweden was in 1266. Jarl Birger Magnusson donated a manor, Karleby, to the monastery of St John in Eskilstuna, including the royal rights with the exception of the *ius expeditionis*, which should be kept according to custom. The establishment of this spiritual institution in the late twelfth century indicates the arrival of crusade ideology (*DS* no. 518). The expeditions of Birger into present-day Finland and by the marshal Torgils Knutsson in Karelia and Ingria were considered crusades. Thus, the *ius expeditionis* could be understood as the duty to support or participate in warfare.

Birger Magnusson the *Jarl* undertook an expedition in the east, in 1238–40, against the Tavastians or Häme in Finland, and there was a subsequent expedition to the inner parts of the Finnish Gulf. The third Swedish crusade took place in 1293–5, led by the marshal of the realm, Torgils Knutsson, in the name of the minor king, Birger Magnusson. It resulted in the establishment of Viborg Castle in Karelia, and this remained for a long time the outpost of the kingdom of Sweden to the east.

A new campaign began in 1300, with Torgils Knutsson's assault on the area around the Neva estuary. According to the Erik chronicle the marshal had at his disposal, and on behalf of the king, the fairest navy ever seen, *then vänaste skiphär man hafuer seet*. The expedition started, according to the chronicle, at Whitsun, that is, the time prescribed in a manuscript of *Södermannalagen* as the time when the royal *ledung* fleet should be put to sea (*Erikskrönikan*, lines 1458–61; *Södermannalagen*, Konungabalken, Add. 2). It is mentioned in a manuscript of *Södermannalagen* from about 1335 or shortly after. It is thus possible that *Södermannalagen* follows the Erik chronicle (cf. Hafström 1965, 451).

In the late thirteenth century, control over the northern shore of the Finnish Gulf was established by the Swedish crown by war and conquest, probably accompanied by colonization of the coastal areas of the province of Nyland (Uusimaa) by a Swedish peasantry.

During this period, the late thirteenth century, the provincial law codes were written and here the rights and duties of the Christian and Europeanized monarchy were set out. From the middle of the thirteenth century, there was an increasing institutionalization of the political structure of Sweden, and this could be described as state-building. It also meant that the king gained firmer control over the provinces around Lake Mälaren. Opposition to, and revolt against, the Europeanized Christian monarchy were centralized in that area. Possible pagan incursions took place in the 1080s and 1120s. The *Folkungar*, a federation of magnates mainly based in the province of Uppland, standing in opposition to an increasingly centralizing kingdom, were defeated after several uprisings during the thirteenth century. In some respects, the Folkungar represented an ancient economic system, partly based on exchange of products, partly on overseas warfare. The Lake Mälaren area, and especially Uppland, was the centre of seaborne activities during the Late Viking Age. In 1247, after the battle at Sparrsätra, several burdens were imposed on the peasant communities of Uppland, notably fines and duties concerning the *ledung*. Duties to a local aristocracy were replaced by more or less permanent taxes paid to the king.

The late thirteenth century was also the period when the crusading tradition of St Erik the King and the martyr bishop Henry of Finland were invented, or re-invented. In these legends there is a memory of a 'first crusade' to Finland, possibly in the 1150s, but this is not known from contemporary sources.

The *ledung* could be used for offensive purposes during the late thirteenth and early fourteenth centuries. The *ledung*, at least the royal *ledung*, was perhaps invented or re-invented during the crusading wars and its organization was based on older traditions. The old *lið* organization was used for predatory expeditions, but it was never under royal control. The royal *ledung*, as it is known from the legal material, was probably recent – a military organization that could have had defensive purposes. The late twelfth century was a period when the kings in Sweden needed a defence organization.

From the late twelfth century to the beginning of the fourteenth, the Swedish kings or *jarls* were involved in several wars, crusades or pretended crusades, as well as in the consolidation a territorial overlordship in what is now Finland. The *ledung*, or the military organization used, was probably the kind implied in *Östgötalagen*, where the king or jarl relied on seaborne retinues of aristocrats and magnates. The *ledung* described in the provincial law codes of Svealand was mainly a fiscal duty; it belongs to a later stage. It was mainly an organization for taxation to finance, for example, the Swedish crusading wars in the east, but also perhaps to muster men for the campaign. The *ledung* was thus based upon traditions derived from the Viking Age. The emergence of a Christian kingdom transformed it into a military and fiscal instrument of a medieval state.

BIBLIOGRAPHY

Andræ, C.G. 1960. *Kyrka och frälse i Sverige under äldre medeltid* (Uppsala).
Bartlett, R. 1993. *The making of Europe: conquest, colonization and cultural change, 950–1350* (London).
Blomkvist, N. 2005. *The discovery of the Baltic: the reception of a Catholic world-system in the European North (AD1075–1225)* (Leiden).
DS = Liljegren, J.G. (ed.). 1829. *Diplomatarium Suecanum*, 1 (Stockholm).
Erikskrönikan = Pipping, R. (ed.). 1963. *Erikskrönikan* (Stockholm).
Gästriklands runinskrifter = Jansson, S.B.F. (ed.). 1981. *Gästriklands runinskrifter*, Sveriges runinskrifter, 15 (Stockholm).
Hafström, G. 1949. *Ledung och marklandsindelning* (Uppsala).
Hafström, G. 1965. 'Leidang. Sverige', *Kulturhistoriskt lexikon för nordisk medeltid*, 10, 450–6.
Hälsingelagen = Schlyter, C.J. (ed.). 1844. *Hälsingelagen*, Samling af Sweriges gamla lagar, 6 (Lund).
Hjärne, E. 1947. 'Roden: Upphovet och namnet. Området och jarlen', *Namn och bygd*, 35, 1–96.
Kraft, J. 2005. *Ledung och sockenbildning* (Västerås).
Larsson, M.G. 1990a. *Runstenar och utlandsfärder: aspekter på det senvikingatida samhället med utgångspunkt i de fasta fornlämningarna* (Lund).
Larsson, M.G. 1990b. *Ett ödesdigert vikingatåg: Ingvar den vittfarnes resa, 1036–1041* (Stockholm).
Lindkvist, T. 1990. *Plundring, skatter och den feodala statsmaktens framväxt: organisatoriska tendenser i Sverige under övergången från vikingatid till tidig medeltid* (Uppsala).
Lönnroth, E. 1940. *Statsmakt och statsfinans i det medeltida Sverige: studier över skatteväsen och länsförvaltning* (Göteborg).
Lund, N. 1996. *Lið, leding og landeværn: hær og samfund i Danmark i ældre medeltid* (Roskilde).

Rosén, J. 1952. 'Kring Alsnö stadga' in Y. Adolphson (ed.), *Festskrift till Gottfrid Carlsson* (Lund), pp 15–36

Schück, A. 1950. 'Review of G. Hafström, *Ledung och marklandsindelning* (Uppsala, 1949)', *Historisk tidskrift*, 70, 464–88.

Sjöstrand, P.O. 1994. 'Den svenska tidigmedeltida riksbildningsprocessen och den östra rikshalvan', *Historisk tidskrift för Finland*, 78, 530–73.

Södermanlands runinskrifter = Brate, E. and E. Wessén (eds). 1924–36. *Södermanlands runinskrifter*, Sveriges runinskrifter, 3 (Stockholm).

Södermannalagen = Schlyter, C.J. (ed.). 1838. *Södermannalagen*, Samling af Sweriges gamla lagar, 4 (Lund).

Tunberg, S. 1907. 'De äldsta världsliga privilegierna i Sverige', *Historisk tidskrift*, 27, 157–66.

Upplands runinskrifter = Jansson, S.B.F. and E. Wessén (eds). 1940–58. *Upplands runinskrifter*, Sveriges runinskrifter, 6–9 (Stockholm).

Upplandslagen = Schlyter, C.J. (ed.). 1934. *Upplandslagen*, Samling af Sweriges gamla lagar, 3 (Lund).

Västergötlands runinskrifter = Jungner, H. & E. Svärdström (eds). 1958–70. *Västergötlands runinskrifter*, Sveriges runinskrifter, 5 (Stockholm).

Västmanlands runinskrifter = Jansson, S.B.F. (ed.). 1964. *Västmanlands runinskrifter*, Sveriges runinskrifter, 13 (Stockholm).

Västmannalagen = Schlyter, C.J. (ed.). 1841. *Västmannalagen*, Samling af Sweriges gamla lagar, 5 (Lund).

Östergötlands runinskrifter = Brate, E. (ed.). 1911–18. *Östergötlands runinskrifter*, Sveriges runinskrifter, 2 (Stockholm).

Östgötalagen = Collin, H.S. and C.J. Schlyter (eds). 1830. *Östgötalagen*, Samling af Sweriges gamla lagar, 2 (Stockholm).

The baptism of Harald Bluetooth

NIELS LUND

Harald Bluetooth was baptized, immersed in a barrel, by Poppo, who had just convinced the king to convert by miraculously bearing in his hand a hot iron. So says the story, well known from the series of gilt copper plates from the church of Tamdrup, near Horsens in Jutland. So what is the problem, you might well ask. Well, there is more than one problem – which of course I do not promise to solve, only to draw attention to.

The plate depicting the baptism is one of a series of seven depicting the legend of Poppo. They originally belonged, probably, to a shrine of Poppo in the church of Tamdrup (Christiansen 1968), or to a golden altar or a retable (Nyborg 2002). Around 1600, they were fitted on the pulpit, mixed up with plates belonging to a golden altar of the type familiar from a number of other churches, and in 1873 they were brought to the National Museum in Copenhagen, where they are on display today.

There has been some discussion about the correct order of these plates. It is generally agreed that the first must be the one on which a bishop, or perhaps an archbishop (it cannot be determined because his mitre has been cut away), is talking to the king, presumably trying to persuade him that there is only one God. The king is lifting his right index finger towards the bishop (Fig. 23.1).

The next two plates depict the ordeal. One shows Poppo wearing an iron glove on his right hand, heating it in the fire (Fig. 23.3, Pl. 3). The other depicts him showing the glove to the king, lifting it in his left hand while carrying a book in his right (Fig. 23.2). The ordeal was considered positive if the hand remained unhurt, either immediately, or after it had been bandaged for eight days. This scene is often interpreted as the cleric showing his unscathed hand to the king after his ordeal. He is wearing a mitre and must therefore have earned his episcopate at this stage. According to another interpretation, because he is not yet wearing a halo, he is showing the glove to the king before the ordeal as if to say 'this is what I shall wear to give proof of my faith'. Since he is clearly heating the glove on his right hand, this order of things would involve a fraud, though a pious one, if afterwards he showed the king his left hand unscathed, while holding a book in his right. It is preferable, therefore, to place the scene showing the glove before that of the glove in the fire.

The fourth plate then shows the baptism (Fig. 23.4, Pl. 4). In those days, baptism involved full immersion, often in a river. In this case a barrel served, and the king is being baptized by a bishop with a halo. The remaining three plates depict various events that probably followed the baptism, the celebration of a mass, a prayer and the inauguration of a frontal.

This rendering in pictures of Poppo's ordeal and the baptism of Harald Bluetooth is generally understood as a pictorial representation of Widukind's written account:

> *Dani antiquitus erant Christiani, sed nichilominus idolis ritu gentili servientes. Contigit autem altercationem super cultura deorum fieri in quodam convivio rege presente, Danis affirmantibus Christum quidem esse deum, sed alios eo fore maiores deos, quippe qui potiora mortalibus signa et prodigia per se ostenderent. Contra haec clericus quidam, nunc vero religiosam vitam ducens episcopus nomine Poppa, unum verum deum patrem cum filio unigenito domino nostro Iesu Christo et spiritu sancto, simulacra vero daemonia esse et non deos testatus est. Haraldus autem rex, utpote qui velox traditur re ad audiendum, tardus ad loquendum, interrogat, si hanc fidem per semet ipsum declarare velit. Ille incunctanter velle respondit. Rex vero custodire clericum usque in crastinum iubet. Mane facto ingentis ponderis ferrum igne succendi iubet, clericumque ob fidem catholicam candens ferrum portare iussit. Confessor Christi indubitanter ferrum rapit tamdiuque deportat, quo ipse rex decernit. Manum incolumem cunctis ostendit, fidem catholicam omnibus probabilem reddit. Ad haec rex conversus Christum deum solum colendum decrevit, idola respuenda subiectis gentibus imperat, Dei sacerdotibus et ministris honorem debitum deinde prestitit. Sed et haec virtutibus merito patris tui adscribuntur, cuius industria in illis regionibus ecclesiae sacerdotumque ordines in tantum fulsere* (Widukind, Sachsengeschichte III:65).

'The Danes were Christians of old, but nevertheless worshipped the idols after the pagan manner. However, at a feast attended by the king a dispute arose about the worship, the Danes contending that although Christ was a god there were also other gods more powerful than he, since they showed the mortals more powerful signs and portents than Christ. Against this a clerk, who now leads a religious life, a bishop by the name of Poppo, gave testimony that there was one true God the Father with his only begotten Son and the Holy Spirit, the idols were only demons. King Harald, who is said to be eager to listen but slow to speak, now asked him if he was willing to prove this faith with his own body. He replied without hesitation that he would. The king then placed the cleric under custody till the following day. When morning had broken, he had a very heavy piece of iron heated in the fire and commanded the cleric to carry the red-hot iron for the catholic faith. The confessor of Christ picked up the iron without hesitation and carried it for as long as the king dictated. He showed his unscathed hand to everybody and thus rendered the catholic faith probable to them all.

23.1 *(left)* Tamdrup plate, depicting an archbishop/bishop and the king.
23.2 Tamdrup plate, depicting Poppo showing the iron glove to the king.

Converted to this, the king decreed that Christ should be adored as the only God and commanded his subjects to reject the idols. Afterwards he held the priests and God's servants in due honour. But this, too, must be ascribed to your father, through whose labour the church and the priests have come to such glory in those parts'.

Some discrepancies are, however, immediately obvious. Widukind has Poppo carry a lump of red-hot iron, not wear a heated glove. The glove first appears around 1100, in an account of the deeds of the bishops of Trier, and from here it found its way into other sources (Demidoff 1973). Saxo knew this version, although he attaches the whole story to Svein Forkbeard (X:11). This, however, is only a technical matter. There is a much more important discrepancy: Widukind, who wrote in 967–8, very close to the events, does not report the baptism of any king following on Poppo's ordeal.

One obvious explanation is that Widukind is not giving an account of Harald's conversion and baptism as such. In fact, he informs us that the Danes were Christians of old, but in spite of this still worshipped their ancient gods side by side with Christ, considering them more powerful in certain respects than Christ. Thus, they were syncretists, and that was a long-standing problem for the Church. It was not too difficult to persuade the pagans that Christ was a god, but harder to convince them that he was the only one. Bede, writing about King

23.3 *(left)* Tamdrup plate, depicting Poppo wearing the iron glove and heating it in the fire.
23.4 Tamdrup plate, depicting Poppo conducting the baptism.

Rædwald of East Anglia, who died no later than 627, tells that 'after the manner of the ancient Samaritans, he seemed to be serving both Christ and the gods whom he had previously served; in the same temple he had one altar for the Christian sacrifice and another small altar on which to offer victims to the devils' (*arulam ad uictimas daemoniorum*: *HE* II:15).

If we take Widukind at his word and accept that when Poppo paid his visit the Danes were already Christians, though in a half-hearted and imperfect way, then Poppo's task was neither to convert them to Christianity nor to baptize their king or his subjects. It was simply to persuade them that Christ was more powerful in all respects than their old gods. And that is precisely what Widukind records as the result of Poppo's efforts: the confessor of Christ picked up the hot iron without hesitation and carried it for as long as the king dictated. He showed his unscathed hand to everybody and 'thus rendered the Catholic faith probable to them all'. Thus converted, the king decreed that Christ should be adored as 'the only God' and commanded his subjects to 'reject the idols'.

It should cause us no surprise, then, that Widukind's account of what happened does not go on to describe the baptism of the king or the people. Although we know that the missionaries had difficulty persuading the Danes to accept baptism before they lay down on their deathbeds, we must assume that Widukind would not consider them Christians if, though believers, they remained unbaptized. Baptism was, after all, the admission ceremony to the church.

The most urgent questions to answer in this context, therefore, are not when and why Widukind's lump of iron became a glove, but when and why Poppo's ordeal came to be followed by Harald's baptism and, further, came to be seen as the turning-point in the conversion of the Danes from paganism to Christianity. Moreover, if at the time of Poppo's visit Harald was already a Christian and baptized, when was he baptized?

Later written sources offer scant help. Adam of Bremen claims that Harald was baptized by Otto the Great, who led a victorious expedition into Denmark and afterwards baptized the king and his family, including Svein Forkbeard, who is said to have been named after the emperor (II:3). Adam places these events in a chronological context that suggests that they took place around 947. However, it has long been clear that Otto's alleged expedition to Denmark never took place (Demidoff 1973, 45), and thus it could not have led to the baptism of Harald. Adam very probably invented it because it was important for him to exclude Cologne from any influence in the propagation of Christianity in Denmark. For the same reason he transferred the story of Poppo to another context, the baptism of the Swedish King Erik the Victorious (II:35).

The oldest history of Denmark, the *Roskilde Chronicle*, is extremely confused about the Jellinge dynasty. Basically, it takes over Adam's claim that Harald was fundamentally positive towards Christianity, while Gorm was negative, and it informs us that, having succeeded Gorm, Harald became a Christian. Nothing is said about how or by whom he was baptized. We know, or at least we believe, however, that it is probable that Harald did not succeed before AD958, the year of the burial in the northern mound at Jelling of what we think was Gorm's body.

Neither does Sven Aggesen know when Harald became a Christian. He tells us only that:

> *Haraldus Blatan filius superstes, qui et regni extitit heres, iuxta ritum gentilium in tumulis quasi gemellis et paribus secus regis curiam in Ialang quasi masoleis illustribus vtrumque parentem fecit humari* (Sven Aggesen, *En ny Text*, 79);
> 'Harald Bluetooth had both his parents buried according to heathen rites in almost identical mounds of equal size by the king's residence at Jelling, to serve as glorious mausoleums' (*Works of Sven Aggesen*, 61).

Sven also states that *Hic* [i.e. Harald] *primus idolatrie respuens spurcitias Christi crucem adorauit* ('he was the first king to reject the filth of idolatry and worship the cross of Christ'). This echoes Widukind's emphasis on the rejection of idolatry. We know, of course, that his parents did not get a mound each at Jelling: Thyre's grave has not been found, and the south mound was not completed until after 970.

Another source on which we have often relied for the date of Harald's baptism also seems to echo Widukind. In 968/969 Ruotger, a monk of St Pantaleon's in Cologne, wrote a biography of Bruno, the brother of King Otto, who was archbishop of Cologne from 953 to 965. During Bruno's episcopacy, Ruotger tells us, Harald, king of the Normans, *cum magna suę multitudine gentis regi regum Christo colla submittens vanitatem respuit idolorum* ('rejected the vanity of idolatry and submitted to the yoke of Christ, the king of kings, with a large number of his people': Ruotgeri *Vita Brunonis*, 40). Unlike Widukind, he does not say that the Danes were already Christians, but like Widukind he emphasizes the rejection of idolatry.

What Widukind meant by 'of old' is hard to tell. Poppo's ordeal, undertaken to correct them about the Faith, must have taken place no later than 965, when Bruno died. If the Danes had become Christians before that date, the available time does not seem to justify Widukind's words, because in 958 Harald gave his father a perfectly pagan burial. Would he have done so had he been Christian at that time, even to honour a pagan father? If so, his filial piety was set aside when probably only a few years later he transferred the remains of his father to the newly built church at Jelling.

We also know that, although there is little doubt that the Danes were familiar with Christianity long before the time of Harald Bluetooth, there are no traces of Christian practice before the middle of the tenth century. We have to consider the possibility that all Widukind knew about the state of Christianity in Denmark was that in 934 Henry the Fowler had forced Christianity upon the Danes, information that is found in the first book of Widukind's own *Sachsengeschichte* (I:40), and which he therefore probably believed to be true.

BIBLIOGRAPHY

Adam Bremensis. 1978. Gesta Hammaburgensis Ecclesiae Pontificum. *Quellen des 9. und 11. Jahrhunderts zur Geschichte der hamburgischen Kirche und des Reiches, ed. Werner Trillmich und Rudolf Buchner.* Ausgewählte Quellen zur deutschen Geschichte des Mittelalters, Freiherr vom Stein-Gedächtnisausgabe, 9 (Darmstadt).
Christiansen, T.E. 1968. 'De gyldne Altre I: Tamdrup-pladerne', *Aarbøger for nordisk Oldkyndighed og Historie*, 153–205.
Demidiff, L. 1973. 'The Poppo legend', *Medieval Scandinavia*, 6, 39–67.
HE = Bede. 1969. *Ecclesiastical history of the English people*, ed. B. Colgrave and R.A.B. Mynors (Oxford).
Nyborg, E. 2002. 'Inventar' in *Danmarks kirker* (Århus), 5111–46.
Ruotger. 1951. *Vita Brunonis*, ed. I. Ott, Monumenta Germaniae Historica, SRG NS, 10.
Saxo Grammaticus. 2005. *Gesta Danorum: Danmarkshistorien*, 2 vols, ed. K. Friis-Jensen, with P. Zeeberg (Copenhagen).
Sven Aggesen. 1915. *En ny Text af Sven Aggesøns værker*, ed. M.Cl. Gertz (Copenhagen).
Sven Aggesen. 1992. *The works of Sven Aggesen, twelfth-century Danish historian*, trans. E. Christiansen (London).
Widukind. 1977. *Sachsengeschichte*, ed. R. Buchner & F-J. Schmale, *Quellen zur Geschichte der sächsischen Kaiserzeit.* Ausgewählte Quellen zur deutschen Geschichte des Mittelalters. Freiherr vom Stein-Gedächtnisausgabe 8, hrsg (Darmstadt).

King Magnús Bareleg's adventures in the West: the making of a King's Saga

ELSE MUNDAL

The Norwegian king Magnús berfœttr ('bareleg') was the son of King Óláfr kyrri (d. 1093) and a certain Þóra Jóansdóttir, mistress of Óláfr kyrri. Magnús berfœttr succeeded his father as king of Norway, ruled for about ten years, and lost his life in a battle in Ireland in 1103, when he was nearly 30 years old.

In the relatively short period of Magnús berfœttr's rule, he led two warlike expeditions into Swedish territory and two to the West. In his first expedition to the West he spent the winter in the Suðreyjar (the Hebrides). In his second, he spent the winter in Ireland at the court of King Myrjartak (Muirchertach Ua Briain) in Kunnaktir (more correctly Kincora).

We do not know exactly when the oldest literature that mentions him was written. Sæmundr fróði's lost work about Norwegian kings most likely ended with Magnús góði (d. 1047). In stanza 40 of the poem, *Nóregs konunga tal* (*c.*1190), which was composed in honour of Jón Loptsson, Sæmundr's grandson, the anonymous skald states after the stanzas on Magnús góði that he now has told of the lives of ten Norwegian kings *sem Sæmundr sagði enn fróði* ('according to what Sæmundr fróði told'), before he continues with the later kings. It is of course not quite out of the question that Sæmundr could also have written about some of the later kings, or down even to his own time, but that is not what the text in *Nóregs konunga tal* indicates. Magnús berfœttr may have been mentioned in Ari fróði's lost *Konunga ævi*, if this work of Ari covered the period around 1100 (when Ari is mentioned as a source in later sagas of kings, it is always as a source for an earlier period).

The first who may have written in some length about the king is the anonymous author of *Historia Norwegie*. This Latin Norwegian chronicle was most likely written between 1160 and 1175 (Mortensen 2003, 24). However, only the first part is preserved and the text ends abruptly after St Óláfr's arrival in Norway in 1015. In the lost part, the author may have written of Magnús berfœttr.

The oldest text about King Magnús berfœttr is found in the Latin Norwegian chronicle, *Historia de antiquitate regum Norvagiensium*, written by Theodoricus *c.*1180. A few years later (*c.*1190) a chronicle or saga about this king is found in *Ágrip*, an anonymous Old Norse Norwegian work which tells of the Norwegian kings from Halfdan svarti to the beginning of the reign of King Sverrir (the last part is lost). Later, in the first decades of the thirteenth century, the saga of Magnús berfœttr, more or less based on *Historia de antiquitate* and *Ágrip*, but extended in several ways, is found in the Icelandic works *Morkinskinna*, in *Fagrskinna* (which certainly was written in Norway by an author whose nationality, Norwegian or Icelandic, is uncertain), and finally in Snorri's *Heimskringla*. His saga in *Morkinskinna* is not preserved in its original form, but in an extended recension deriving from the last decades of the thirteenth century. In addition *Orkneyinga saga* has many stories about King Magnús berfœttr's time in the Orkneys, and especially his treatment of the later saint, Jarl Magnús of the Orkneys, whom he tried to force to take part in his expeditions much against the will of the pious jarl. The original *Orkneyinga saga* was written late in the twelfth century, but the surviving manuscripts derive from a revised version which, according to most scholars, dates from the 1230s. Since it is impossible to know what belonged to the original *Orkneyinga saga*, what was added later, and what was changed, it is also difficult to establish where the anecdotes about King Magnús, preserved in the king-saga, should be placed in the chronological development of these stories. This problem will be referred to later.

The short saga about Magnús berfœttr – the longest version in *Morkinskinna* extends to forty printed pages – is a very interesting piece of literature if we wish to study the making of a king-saga as such, and here I include the development of the oral tradition and the later written tradition. This saga is relatively short: Magnús berfœttr was king for only ten years, and he died before he was 30. He lived an exciting life and this meant that there were stories to be told about him that could be characterized by the Old Norse adjective *söguligr* 'worth telling'. The oldest written text of some length about him is not contemporary, but neither was it written long after his death. Theodoricus's *Historia de antiquitate*, the oldest work in which Magnús berfœttr's history is preserved, was written eighty to ninety years after the events it recounts.

There probably was a history of Magnús berfœttr written even closer to his lifetime in *Historia Norwegie*, but Theodricus seems to be unaware of it. Therefore, Theodoricus must have based his chronicle on oral prose and skaldic tradition (which is not quoted), and of course he may have found something in Ari's *Konunga ævi*, if the period around 1100 was actually covered in Ari's work or in early works now lost.

The time-span of oral transmission – eighty to ninety years – is long enough to ensure that all possible witnesses to the events were dead, and memories from the time when some people could still remember events had begun to develop into oral tradition. Distance in time and space changes oral tradition, and narratives of events that took place far away tend to become less realistic and more fantastic than those of local events. Much of Magnús berfœttr's saga concentrates on his expeditions in the distant West. In the case of the king-sagas, their authors could, in many cases, build on tradition from two countries, Norway and Iceland. In the case of King Magnús berfœttr, the author of *Orkneyinga saga* could use Orcadian tradition as well. However, Ireland and Scotland, where the king's battles took place, were outside the Old Norse area where oral tradition about the king developed.

All the king-sagas and Theodoricus's Latin chronicle say is that in his first year Magnús shared the kingdom with his cousin Hákon, and that Hákon was very popular in Trøndelag because he reduced the taxes, but that then he suddenly died. All tell of a struggle, after Hákon's death, between King Magnús and Hákon's foster-father, Steigar-Þórir. Steigar-Þórir launched a new pretender to the throne, but King Magnús pursued Steigar-Þórir and his men who had run away to Hálogaland, captured him, and had him hanged together with one of his men. *Orkneyinga saga* does not tell the story: it merely states briefly that King Magnús had Steigar-Þórir killed (*Orkneyinga saga*, ch. 138).

Theodoricus, who wrote the oldest surviving text, does not say clearly that the two cousins were hostile to each other, nor does he mention how Hákon died, nor give any details about the hanging of Hákon's foster-father (*Historia de antiquitate*, ch. 31).

In the next text, *Ágrip*, written in Old Norse about ten years after, Theodoricus gives a fuller description (*Ágrip*, chs 46–7). We learn how Hákon died. He rode out hunting for a grouse, fell suddenly ill and died in the mountains. The narrative of the hanging of Steigar-Þórir has many new details, especially when compared with the older Latin chronicle. We learn that on the flight to Hálogaland Steigar-Þórir *had* to be carried by his men. The saga quotes two lines of a skaldic stanza, Steigar-Þórir's comment after he is taken prisoner, and some exchanges between the main characters of the saga, not lengthy dialogues of the kind we know from later Icelandic sagas – rather a few striking words that form a climax in dramatic scenes. In the sagas from the thirteenth century (*Morkinskinna*, ch. 40; *Fagrskinna*, ch. 80; *Heimskringla*, *Magnúss saga berfœtts*, chs 1–6), skaldic stanzas are now used to support the prose text. And a new macabre detail is added to the story about the hanging of Steigar-Þórir: he was so fat and heavy that his neck split open on the gallows. An account of how a king came to power and how he put down his enemies is a natural beginning to a saga. The authors could have found models for this both in European Latin chronicles and in oral tradition.

Apart from the king's fight against enemies or rivals in his own country, his warfare against neighbouring kingdoms is a standard component in Old Norse king-sagas. And so it is in the case of Magnús berfœttr. His fight against the Swedish king over land, which both claimed to have ended in King Magnús marrying the daughter of the Swedish king.

A third component found in most king-sagas are the king's expeditions to distant places – Viking expeditions, crusades to the Holy Land, journeys to Miklagarðr (Byzantium), and expeditions to the West that are seen more or less as a continuation of Viking expeditions. In the sagas of Magnús berfœttr, the stories about his two expeditions to the West make up the longest part of his saga, and offer many good examples of the development of a tradition that was favoured by distance. It is possible, I think, to point to some scenes that may have been at the core of the oral tradition, some probably old, and some that would need more time to develop.

In stories about warlike expeditions, the king's battles are often the backbone of the story, and we find very stereotypical scenes at the climax of battles. During his first expedition to the Western Isles, Magnús killed a certain Hugi according to Theodoricus *(Historia de antiquitate*, ch. 31). About ten years later, *Ágrip* relates that this Hugi was killed by a shot through the eye (*Ágrip*, ch. 49). The saga also says that he was shot by a man other than the king, but that this man attributed the shot to King Magnús. In the sagas from the thirteenth century – and in *Orkneyinga saga* as well – there are two men named Hugi (*Morkinskinna*, ch. 42; *Fagrskinna*, ch. 81; *Heimskringla, Magnúss saga berfœtts*, ch. 10; *Orkneyinga saga*, ch. 39). The one shot is protected by mail from head to foot, apart from his eyes. The shot is therefore a true master shot. And the man who attributed the master shot to the king is now said to be *háleyskr*, from northern Norway. We recognize here a scene known from many saga-battles: the unbelievably good shot. The bowman is, as in most cases, from northern Norway, and sometimes is clearly said to be Saami.

In the stories about Magnús's last battle in Ireland, in which he fell, the description of the battlefield is stereotypical, even in the oldest sources. The king and his men leave the ships and go ashore. The way inland is over swamps and fens. But when they returned to the shore, the Irish had come between them and their ships, and they were trapped. The king fell together with many of his men. This, in brief, is the story in Theodoricus's chronicle and in *Ágrip* (*Historia de antiquitate*, ch. 32; *Ágrip*, ch. 50). In the thirteenth-century sagas (*Morkinskinna*, ch. 44; *Fagrskinna*, chs 84–5; *Heimskringla, Magnúss saga berfœtts*, chs 24–5), we find more details about the battle and the king's death. Here we learn that the king was wounded by a spear that went through both his legs (thighs in *Heimskringla*). According to *Fagrskinna* and *Heimskringla*, he grasped the shaft between his legs and broke it, and said: 'Thus break we every leg-spar, men!' Brave and eloquent words from the wounded or dying hero are found in the climax in descriptions of battles in many sagas. A famous parallel are the last words of Þormóðr kolbrúnarskáld in the battle at Stiklestad. He pulled out the arrow which had gone through his heart, and said before he leaned back and died: 'Well has the king fed us. I am fat still about the roots of my heart'. *Orkneyinga saga* does not give any details here.

Not only eloquent words in prose, but also skaldic stanzas put in the mouth of the hero are sometimes found in the climax of battle scenes. *Morkinskinna* (ch. 44) quotes a stanza that King Magnús recited when his men took flight around him (the stanza is also found in the manuscripts. In *Fagrskinna* it is in the hand of Árni Magnússon, but it is uncertain whether it originally belonged to this saga).

The king says he is not homesick; the women in Trondheim (Kaupangr) will have to wait for him in vain this winter. His heart is in Dublin, where he knows a girl who does not deny him her love. He even uses an Irish word for 'girl' (*ingjan* from Irish *ingen*). Stanzas attributed to a hero in his last fight are normally not genuine. It is hard to imagine that dying heroes composed skaldic stanzas. King Magnús is not dying at this point of the story; he is still not wounded. But it is unlikely that the fleeing – or the fighting – men would stop to learn a skaldic stanza. It is, however, possible that this stanza is genuine after a fashion and was part of the oral tradition about the king's adventures in Ireland. It does not fit with the context of the written saga. When the king died, he was on his way to Norway. According to the stanza, he says that he is not going to Norway that winter but would stay in Dublin. The stanza may have been composed earlier in quite another setting, but placed in the story about the king's last battle to lead to the final climax in accordance with well known literary patterns where skaldic stanzas were used to create suspense before a climax.

The most fantastic story relating to King Magnús's expedition to the West is not mentioned at all in Theodoricus's chronicle and *Ágrip*. It occurs only in the king-sagas of the thirteenth century and in *Orkneyinga saga* (ch. 41). According to these, King Magnús and the Irish king Myrjartak became friends and partners. The king of Scotland, Malcolm, was the enemy, and King Magnús plundered and burned his country. To bring about peace, the Scottish king conceded to King Magnús all the islands west of Scotland so separated from the mainland by water that a ship with a fixed rudder could pass between the island and the mainland. When King Magnús approached the peninsula Sátírí (Kintyre) – which according to the Old Norse sources is a large land – he had a small ship dragged over the neck of land between the peninsula and the mainland. The king himself sat on the afterdeck holding the tiller, and took possession of the land. It is impossible to know with certainty whether this story was in the original *Orkneyinga saga*. Finnbogi Guðmundsson, who has compared the *Orkneyinga saga* text with the same story in *Heimskringla* (*Magnúss saga berfœtts*, ch. 10), draws the conclusion that the *Orkneyinga saga* text is the older, and he thinks the story was in the original *Orkneyinga saga* (Finnbogi Guðmundsson 1965, xiv). The story is also found in *Fagrskinna* (ch. 81) and *Morkinskinna* (ch. 42) and, even though there are some differences between the texts, the wording shows that all are related. This suggests that the story about how King Magnús berfœttr won Sátírí is directly or indirectly derived from the original *Orkneyinga saga*, if Finnbogi Guðmundsson is right.

In chapter 3 of *Orkneyinga saga*, there is a story about how the mythic King Heiti won part of Trøndelag by having his ship dragged over a neck of land – exactly in the same way as King Magnús won Sátírí. Finnbogi Guðmundsson, who argues that the three first chapters of *Orkneyinga saga* belong to the revised version (Finnbogi Guðmundsson 1965, xiv), held that the mythic story was modelled on the story of King Magnús winning Sátírí in *Orkneyinga saga* (ch. 41). It could also be the other way round. The story of the mythic king winning land could be modelled on the myth about the goddess Gefjon and how she took possession of Seeland, and the story about the mythic king could be the model for the fantastic story about King Magnús winning Sátírí.

It is difficult to say whether this story about King Magnús developed in oral or in written tradition. If the story in chapter 41 existed before the corresponding mythic story in chapter 3, it is likely that it developed in oral tradition. If the story about the mythic King Heiti existed in the original *Orkneyinga saga*, it is more likely that the author invented the entertaining story about King Magnús winning Sátírí with the mythic story as his model. In any case, the story would need some time to develop, and when it did it would become the core motif in the narrative of the warfare between King Magnús and the Scottish king.

On the basis of my comments above on the development of a few motifs, I will conclude with some more general remarks on the making of a king-saga, taking my examples from the sagas about King Magnús berfœttr.

The king's warfare against enemies in his own country, neighbouring kings, and his expeditions to remoter parts, constitute the major building blocks of the king-sagas. Stories about these must have made up a large part of the oral tradition about kings. The written tradition may have enhanced this. In relation to battles, and of course other topics, some more or less stereotypical scenes or motifs may have developed in the oral tradition – for example, stories about the good shot, striking words and the like. It is, of course, impossible to separate the oral from the written – striking and eloquent words did exist in oral tradition, and are to be found in early works like *Ágrip*.

A matter such as the king's marriage is, as we have seen, related to warfare too. A short notice concerning a marriage for political reasons is found in connection with King Magnús's expedition to Ireland and Scotland. On his way westward, the king left his young son Sigurðr, then about 9 years old, in the Orkneys, and made him king over the islands. According to *Heimskringla* and *Orkneyinga saga*, the king of Ireland sent his 5-year-old daughter to the Orkneys to be married to the young king as part of a pact of friendship (*Heimskringla, Magnúss saga berfœtts*, ch. 11; *Orkneyinga saga*, ch. 41). Ágrip (ch. 50) mentions that the two were married for a while. According to *Morkinskinna* and *Fagrskinna*, the young queen was the daughter of the Scottish king, and the marriage was obviously meant to end the war (*Morkinskinna*, ch. 43; *Fagrskinna*, ch. 81). Unfortunately, the story goes, the 9-year-old disliked his 5-year-old queen, and he left her behind when he returned to Norway.

Love and private life are not important matters in the sagas about King Magnús berfœttr, and that is the case in most king-sagas. Some of Magnús's illegitimate children are mentioned, but there are no stories about their mothers, though in some cases a name is mentioned. The king's private life and his love affairs may have been more important in the oral tradition than in the written sagas. As we saw, the stanza that King Magnús recited in his last battle has a love interest. Whether genuine or not, the poem is likely to have existed in oral tradition. If it was composed to fit the battle scene, we would expect it to be more in harmony with the surrounding prose. *Morkinskinna* (ch. 43) quotes three more stanzas attributed to King Magnús, and these must be characterized as love poetry (sts 155–7). They probably do not belong here originally, because the topos of love for an unknown woman indicate influence from later romances, but they may have existed in oral tradition before they were written down. They are incorporated in a very clumsy way, as if the author did not know quite what to do with this kind of tradition in a king-saga.

Skaldic verse is an important component in the making of a king-saga. As we have seen, the author of the Latin chronicle did not quote verse, but he may have used it as a source. The author of *Ágrip* quotes a *kviðlingr* (two lines) attributed to Steigar-Þórir. These lines are well-integrated in the story. In the saga about Magnús berfœttr in *Fagrskinna*, we have six stanzas or parts of stanzas in addition to Steigar-Þórir's lines; in *Heimskringla*, we have fourteen. Some of these stanzas are integrated in the story, and some are used as apparent witnesses to the truth of the prose text. We can observe here a development in the use of skaldic stanzas in the king-sagas. The earliest text quotes few, and mostly ones that are part of the story. In the next phase, the main function of skaldic stanzas is documentation, and their number is considerable. If genuine, or thought to be genuine, they must have existed in the oral tradition, even though they were not used by earlier authors. In *Morkinskinna* – and that means in the manuscript from the last part of the thirteenth century – there are no fewer than fifty stanzas in addition to Steigar-Þórir's *kviðlingr*. It is difficult to establish whether certain features or motifs in *Morkinskinna* cannot derive from the original early thirteenth-century saga. However, the number of stanzas in the saga of Magnús berfœttr is so great compared with the other king-sagas of the same period (*Fagrskinna* and *Heimskringla*) that it is reasonable to suggest that most stanzas were interpolated at a later time. The author, or rather a later scribe, seems to have known many skaldic stanzas and poems related to King Magnús, and in most cases he attributes them to well-known skalds. It is possible, however, that we can observe here a third phase in the development of the use of skaldic verse. Some stanzas seem to be inspired by the prose text itself, and lines from the prose text – for instance the brave words of some of the men present at Steigar-Þórir's hanging – now find their way into the skaldic stanzas.

BIBLIOGRAPHY

Ágrip = Bjarni Einarsson (ed.). 1984. *Ágrip af Nóregskonunga sögum*, Íslenzk fornrit, 29 (Reykjavik).

Fagrskinna = Bjarni Einarsson (ed.). 1984. *Ágrip af Nóregskonunga sögum*, Íslenzk fornrit, 29 (Reykjavik).

Finnbogi Guðmundsson. 1965. 'Formáli' in F. Guðmundsson (ed.). 1965. *Orkneyinga saga*, Íslenzk fornrit, 34 (Reykjavik).

Heimskringla = Finnur Jónsson (ed.). 1911. *Heimskringla: Nóregs konungasögur* (Copenhagen).

Historia de antiqutate = Theodoricus. 1880. '*Historia de antiqutate regum Norwagiensium*' in G. Storm (ed.), *Monumenta Historia Norvegiæ. Latinske Kildeskrifter til Norges Historie i middelalderen* (Oslo).

Morkinskinna = Finnur Jónsson (ed.). 1932. *Morkinskinna* (Copenhagen).

Mortensen, L.B. 2003. 'Introduction' in I. Ekrem & L.B. Mortensen (eds), *Historia Norvegie* (Copenhagen), 8–48.

Orkneyinga saga = Finnbogi Guðmundsson (ed.). 1965. *Orkneyinga saga*, Íslenzk fornrit, 34 (Reykjavik).

Urbanism and Christianity in Norway

SÆBJØRG WALAKER NORDEIDE

INTRODUCTION

The process of urbanization has been discussed in Norway for several centuries, often with the focus on which element was most important: the king, the Church or trade. However, the discussions have often been superficial, neglecting the basic premises of all three factors and the characteristics of the specific sites that became urban centres such as, for example, the make-up of the original inhabitants, when they were living there and what kind of activities they engaged in (Nordeide 1999). The perspective has often been ethnocentric, the town being mostly considered as an autonomous centre of trade and administration with a population that had a normal demographic profile. This is a well-known tendency in research into urbanization on the international level (for example, Pirenne 1925 [1956]). After some decades of large-scale urban excavations, we are now able to ask other questions of urban research and, to a certain degree, propose answers to them (see, for instance, Schia 1994; Nordeide 1990; Ulriksen 1996).

The prime objective of my postdoctoral project is to date the change from Norse paganism to Christianity in southern and central Norway (hereafter called 'south Norway'), to determine where the latest Norse and earliest Christian cults occur, and to trace any indication of influence on cult practices from Christianity to Norse (Nordeide, in preparation). A closer dating of the shift in religion will, one hopes, enhance our understanding of the chronological order in which the rise of monarchy, urbanization, and the establishment of the Church occurred in Norway, since these elements are obviously interlinked, one way or another. Rather unexpectedly, my preliminary results throw some new light on urbanization as well, as this paper briefly describes. To explain the background to my conclusions, I will briefly describe the archaeological material used in my analyses.

SELECTED MATERIAL

Archaeological material relevant to my investigations includes possible cult objects, excavated monuments, and cult sites in south Norway from about AD560 to 1100. Graves and cult houses (churches) offer the most frequent traces of cult from the late Iron Age and the early medieval period, and they dominate the material. My intention was to analyse all of south Norway, but this turned out to be too much for a three-year project. To maintain a large-scale perspective and

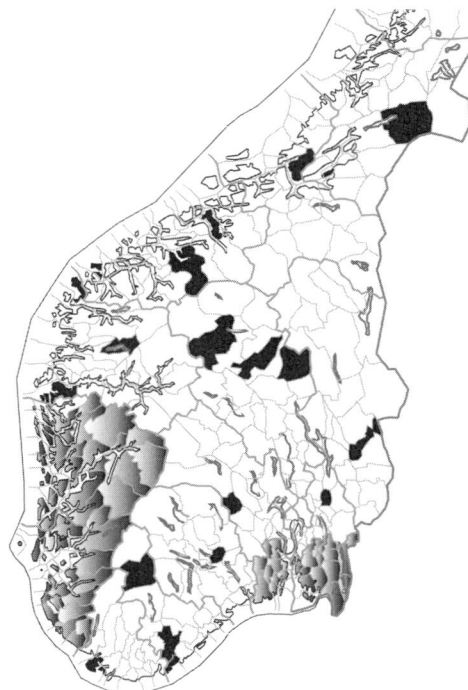

25.1 Southern and central Norway: selected research areas in black with areas of previously conducted relevant research in grey.

avoid yet another local study, I have selected twenty-two boroughs (Nor. *kommune*) as sources for the Norse material (Fig. 25.1). These units are carefully chosen to provide research data that might be representative of various locations, and to consider varying amounts, quality and types of information. In addition to these twenty-two boroughs, I have investigated the earliest towns in the area and all the excavations in south Norway that have revealed traces of an early Christian cult. The results of previous relevant local research are, of course, also taken into account.

For centuries, cultural heritage management, site recording, and artefact dating strategies have been used to authenticate the story told in the sagas, viz., that Norwegians were Christianized as a result of the battle of Stiklestad in 1030. Barrows and cairns with grave-goods have automatically been dated pre-1030, monuments with Christian graves are dated post-1030, and all evidence pointing in other directions has been met with serious scepticism or, probably, rejection. Towns, likewise, have been declared 'medieval', even if they are dated to the Viking period (Sognnes 1990; Christophersen 1990). The result is a sharp division between prehistory and the medieval period, and it is difficult to uncover true cultural differences or similarities across the division into periods. In my study of Christianization, it has been a challenge to match the real data with a reliable chronology and, in addition, to resist the dogmatic opinions of some curators concerning a chronology that is based on information in the sagas.

NORSE BURIALS

Burial customs in Norway were very heterogeneous in the late Iron Age (*c.*560–1050), and there are major regional differences. I have based the chronology of my material on information in museum archives, which in turn is mostly founded on typology. Occasionally, a coin gives a more reliable basis for the earliest possible date. Only three graves are dated by dendrochronology, but many churches are dated in this way, although none to as early as the eleventh century. The context of prehistoric burials is often poorly described, and many finds have reached a museum as a result of nineteenth-century farming. The number of graves known in each borough varies a great deal, depending on various circumstances. Some have very few, if any, known late Iron Age burials while, for instance, in Rauma, eighty-five burials are sufficiently well documented for my investigation. Urban archaeology usually offers a better chronology and fuller descriptions of context, but almost all finds date from after *c.*1000. In sum, this means that the basis for my statistics and chronology is uneven. Nevertheless, some patterns are evident and these cannot be explained other than by the existence of real differences in burial rituals in time and space.

I have analysed the Norse burials with respect to the treatment of the body (cremation or inhumation), the grave monument, the orientation of the burial, the number and types of grave-goods (if any), and the occurrence of symbols of belief. Space prevents me from going into details here, but a broad overview of the archaeological material clearly shows that burial traditions vary in many ways, and each small community may have peculiarities of its own. However, this does not necessarily mean that belief differed much from valley to valley, but the cult certainly did. I have also observed that in some areas an old burial tradition became revitalized and flourished towards the end of the Viking period, while elsewhere such activity ceased abruptly. This supports earlier findings on a more local scale, for instance, in the counties of Hordaland (Gellein 1997) and Vestfold (Kisuule 2000). The date at which Norse burials ceased varies from place to place, but the characteristics of hardly any Norse grave in any area can be identified as resulting from the influence of Christian burial customs.

Gender determination based on inventories of grave-goods shows that male graves dominate. Less than 20 per cent of all burials are female graves, but a considerable number are of double or of unknown gender. However, the ratio differs from place to place. Certainly, fewer females have been provided with a monumental burial and a wide range of grave-goods.

A decrease in barrow numbers in the late Iron Age is normally to be interpreted as the slow disappearance of the Norse cult. It is probably no coincidence that wherever Christianity appears, old burial traditions disappear at about the same time, for instance in Britain, even though the picture there is more complicated and cannot be explained in terms of religion alone (Dickinson 2002).

Early Christian legislation in Norway forbade the practice of the Norse cult. One theory is, however, that since barrows belonged to landowners, differences in the right to land may have caused differences in the occurrence of barrows (Solberg 2000, 268). The number of burial mounds may thus reflect how far the process of feudalism had gone. The relative number of female to male graves could, in that case, also reflect the relation of female to male landowners. Obviously, flat graves are not easily detected, and the true relation between the number of cairns and barrows and the number of flat graves is difficult to determine. However, if Solberg is right, conversion to Christianity does not fully explain the disappearance of barrows and cairns.

The latest dated Norse burials in various parts of south Norway show that Norse burial rituals ceased to be practised at different times in different places. The latest Norse barrow is at Nomeland in Valle, Aust-Agder, where the deceased, a woman, was given equipment for trading or barter, including weights and German, Anglo-Saxon, Danish and Norwegian coins, in addition to other rich grave-goods. One of the Norwegian coins provides a reliable date: it was struck as late as between 1065 and 1080, and the burial must have happened after that, perhaps as late as 1100. This indicates that the woman could scarcely have been isolated from external influences, although she did not necessarily have direct contact with these countries. This grave is typical for the county of Aust-Agder, in southernmost Norway, where several rather late Norse burials with many artefacts among the grave-goods (such as coins, weights and balances) may indicate trade and barter. In other areas, it is difficult to identify any graves later than AD950, and objects such as these are rare.

EARLY CHRISTIANITY IN NORWAY

Like the end of Norse burial practices, the appearance and date of the earliest traces of the Christian cult differ from place to place. Christian graves are not easily recognizable unless they are in a marked churchyard, preferably close to where a church still stands. The earliest churchyards found so far in Norway, two adjacent to one another on the island of Veøy in Romsdal, have been radiocarbon-dated to the first and second parts of the tenth century, perhaps even earlier (Solli 1996, 178). Since Veøy is close to Rauma, where Norse burials continued until at least *c.*1000, there must have been both Christian and non-Christian groups in the Romsdal area simultaneously (Nordeide in preparation).

Some time after the Veøy churchyards, a number of early remains of Christian cult practices have been found. An Anglo-Saxon coin from 1003–9 has been found in a Christian grave at Borgund, Sunnmøre (Herteig 1967; Skaare 1976, 160–1). The chronology of the cemetery at St Clement's Church in Oslo has recently been reconsidered, and new radiocarbon analyses show that the churchyard was most probably established during the first half of the eleventh century (Nordeide and Gulliksen 2007). An eleventh-century churchyard has also been found in Tønsberg. The origin of the city of Trondheim dates to the end of the tenth century, but so far no Norse burial site has been found in its vicinity unlike, for instance, the urban settlements of Birka and Kaupang. However, crosses and other possible Christian objects are found almost from the beginnings of urban Trondheim, and the first Trondheim inhabitants were probably Christians. The earliest graves there are radiocarbon-dated to around 1000 (*c.*980–1025: Ramstad 2002). Enkolpia were also produced in Trondheim from the second half of the eleventh century, no doubt in connection with the cult of St Olav, who died in 1030. Other churches or churchyards have not proved to be as early as those mentioned.

There is a striking correspondence between the oldest traces of Christian cults and the few early towns and centres in Norway, as at Trondheim, Veøy, Borgund, Tønsberg and Oslo (Fig. 25.2). The very earliest, Kaupang, existed from about AD800–960 and is surrounded by several cemeteries with hundreds of Norse graves (Skre and Stylegar 2004). No Christian cemetery has been uncovered here, although a few Christian symbols may have been found and a few graves may be influenced by Christianity. Four Thor's hammer symbols have been found at Kaupang, but none in the slightly later towns, even after more than thirty years of thorough excavations. The foundation of typical Christian towns seems to be slightly later than Kaupang. Veøy also seems to represent a variant in this picture, as the earliest Christian graves seem to be earlier than the population centre and contemporary with Norse graves in the surrounds.

DISCUSSION

The Agder area has a striking lack of medieval towns, and also differs from other areas in the frequency of Norse graves containing trading equipment, and also the occurrence of very late graves. Various Christian cults had been in existence for a long time in Trondheim before the woman in Aust-Agder was buried in a barrow. This might indicate that both trading and politics were decentralized and based on individuals or dynasties in Agder at a time when there were royal Christian centres in other parts of the country. The king appears in Agder through the royal manors, which are not distinguished by special or rich Iron-Age finds, but they are all connected to a (later) medieval church (Larsen 1978, 90, 160). This indicates that the king is associated with Christianity in this area as well, but at a later stage and not in connection with towns.

This tendency is also interesting in relation to information in written sources. They tell of passionate, missionary Christian kings who were baptized, often abroad, and brought missionaries back with them, for instance, King Hákon

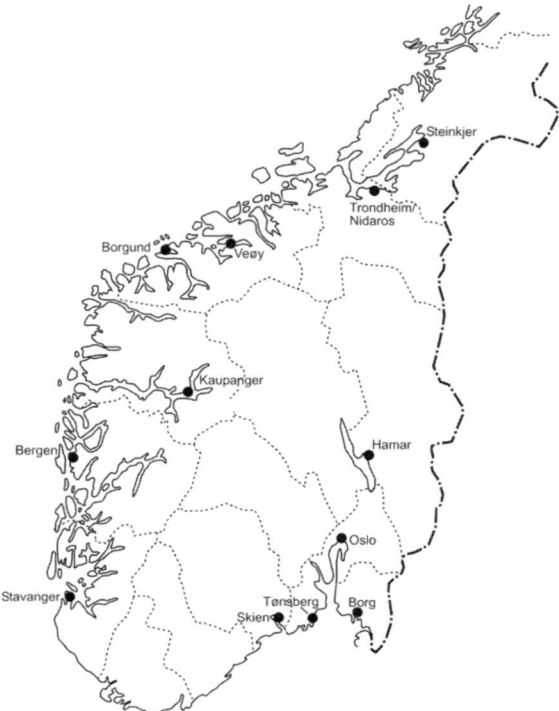

25.2 Medieval towns and central places within the present borders of southern and central Norway (drawing: Ellinor Moldeklev Hoff, Bergen Museum).

Haraldsson góði, who was raised in England. His ambitious goal was to convert the Norwegians. But how did he start, and how could he establish Christian communities?

According to the written sources, some kings founded the oldest towns in the late tenth and eleventh centuries, particularly King Óláfr Tryggvason, King Óláfr Haraldson (St Óláfr) and King Óláfr Kyrre. For instance, King Óláfr Tryggvason is reputed to have founded Trondheim in 997, and this information fits well with archaeological material. The correspondence between these Christian kings and the founding of towns may mark their attempt to establish Christian communities. The towns were centrally located in certain regions, and the new religion and Christian ideology could spread from them. The king would probably seek neutral or Christian ground for the town, which could be one explanation why Veøy became an incipient medieval town, while Kaupang did not.

Spreading Christianity was probably the most useful thing a 'wannabe-king' could do to become sole ruler of a large part of the country. Monotheistic Christianity had an ideology of hierarchical power with a unique Creator God at its acme, reflected on Earth by the clerical hierarchy and the king. The Church also offered know-how of great practical value, such as (improved) literacy, international language, organization and monumental buildings – of great symbolic value to the ruler.

Group One

King + Christianity + Loyal Landowners + Towns = State Formation

Group Two

Local Chiefs + Loyal Landowners + Norse Religions + Topography = Strong Local Society

25.3 Possible allies in the Christianization of Norway.

The king could not manage conversion alone. He needed a significant group of powerful allies who could share his interests, and they would have to see some obvious personal benefit in the undertaking.

On this assumption, it is natural to see at least two different groups (Fig. 25.3). Group One would support the king, who had a political programme with the ambitious goal of uniting people across various regions and relations. The towns were perhaps of greatest interest to the king as fora for creating and spreading the new ideology. The king would try to build Christian congregations, communities loyal to him. He naturally shared this goal with the Church. I claim that, more important than 'ports of trade' (Polanyi 1957), the towns and centres in Norway were established as 'ports of faith'. Even some landowners would find it beneficial to follow the king, at least those who could not aim for higher personal status on their own rather than in the service of the king. He or she would benefit from the king's co-operation, protection and loyalty. Some landowners had control over several kinds of high-quality craftsmen whose work had great symbolic value, as demonstrated in rich Viking-Age grave-goods. The manufacture and distribution of their products could benefit from improved organization and protection. Moreover, the construction of Christian churches was benefited by these craftsmen. People of a lower social standing probably had no influence or interest. The alliance was successful; the towns grew rapidly and soon became multi-purpose communities.

To point to the king and the Church as elements in urbanization is hardly a radically new idea. That the king was behind the foundation of towns, more or less, is the version told in the old sagas, and later historians (Gustav Storm (1899), for example) have also supported this view. Moreover, Edvard Bull (1918) argued that the Church was the most important element in the foundation of towns. However, early research of this type has been more inclined to look upon the town as a royal stronghold and an answer to administrative needs. It focused on the secular activity of the Church: income from penalties and tithes, paid in kind, brought crafts and trade in turn. The Church also generated a greater need for technology, materials and human resources, and led to permanent settlement, which again led to more crafts and more trade. The emergence of the town has primarily been discussed in terms of what kind of activity could lead to large numbers of people doing things other than those they would do in a rural district, things that, in sum, would make the settlement different from surrounding ones and give it the character of a 'town' (Helle and Nedkvitne 1977). These are, of course, necessary ingredients for a town to survive and grow. However, for the motivation behind the foundation of towns, I would point to the religious ideological by-products which the Church offered the king. More than anything else, the king needed an ideological change to legitimate his sole rulership. The towns became 'ports of faith' rather than 'ports of trade'.

However, some would not gain immediate benefit from this alliance. Group Two would consist of high-ranking landowners with local power, perhaps also living in the periphery of royal power, and they could attain higher status by trying to keep their established influence, probably based on close kindred. With some effort, they could even aspire to increased power for themselves by joining forces with their subjects to defend them against the king's efforts. If their power was based on the old system of belief, which it probably was, they would try to keep this up. These people, local chiefs and landowners in general, would probably benefit from conservative attitudes, in politics and religion, and try to keep things unchanged. This might explain the rich, late, Norse graves in Agder which, through their grave-goods, demonstrated that their occupants had wealth and a wide circle of trading contacts, but probably resisted urban trade and craftsmanship, Christianity, and the king. The topography of Norway probably helped this group; or, to put it another way, the topography of Norway was no benefit to anybody trying to unite its people.

The people forming Group Two would struggle against those who tried to conquer their region, and would focus on local values, cultural and human, and other resources. I suppose the relatively less mobile females would benefit more from this group than from the other. This was a successful alliance but only for a limited time.

CONCLUSION

Without going into detail, I have tried to highlight aspects that I think are important for understanding the king's need for urban centres as part of his striving to establish a monarchy. He needed the town as a 'start pack' to build up ideology as a Christian community. He brought Christian priests home with him, but had to give them a forum to act on. Late Norse graves in an area with no towns could indicate an area with less royal control. Although I think Christianity has been an important tool for the rise of a monarchy, it was not decisive. After all, we know of many non-Christian states.

The king needed Christianity as a support; it was far better than the Norse religion where several disunited gods were apparently contending for attention. It is probably not without reason that the ruler of the Roman Empire in a crisis in AD395 decided to make Christianity the official religion, the only legal one, at a time when only between 5 and 10 per cent of the population were Christian (Bagge 2004, 31). Christianity expected ethical behaviour and obedience to the emperor as God's representative on Earth. I end by illustrating my conclusion with King Magnus Lagabøter's law for the towns, enacted in 1276. He formulated the relation between God, the king and the people as follows (Robberstad 1923, 10):

1. This is the beginning of our chapter on the defence of the land, that Jesus Christ, the Crucified, true God and the son of God and Virgin Mary, king of all kings, and with whom all power, authority and honour rests, shall be the protector and defender of all the people of Norway.

2. In the same name of our Lord Jesus Christ, our lawful king of Norway, His servant, shall have authority to command and ban, and authority over our expeditions, and he shall rule by law and not by illegality, for God's honour, for his own benefit and for our need.

ACKNOWLEDGMENTS

Thanks to Richard Binns for improving my English. Sverre Bagge and Haki Antonsson also kindly helped me to translate the quotation from King Magnus Lagabøter's law for the towns.

BIBLIOGRAPHY

Bagge, S. 2004. *Europa tar form: år 300–1350*, 2nd ed. (Oslo).

Bull, E. 1918. 'Om oprindelsen til Oslo og de andre gamle norske byene', *St Hallvard*, 4, 65–80.

Christophersen, A. 1990. 'Trondheim: en middelalderby fra vikingtid', *Adresseavisen*, 11 September 1990.

Dickinson, T.M. 2002. 'What's new in early medieval burial archaeology?', *Early Medieval Europe* 2002 2:1, 71–87.

Gellein, K. 1997. 'Kristen innflytelse i hedensk tid? En analyse med utgangspunkt i graver fra yngre jernalder i Hordaland' (hovedfag thesis, University of Bergen).

Helle, K. & A. Nedkvitne. 1977. 'Norge: semtrumsdannelser og byutvikling i norsk middelalder' in G.A. Blom (ed.), *Det XVII nordiske historikermøte*, 1 (Trondheim), pp 37–126.

Herteig, A. 1967. *Innberetning for utgrævningene i Borgund i 1967* (unpublished report Bergen Museum, Middelaldersamlingene Topografisk arkiv).

Kisuule, A.E. 2000. 'De regionale forskjellene i gravmaterialet fra Østfold og Vestfold i vikingtiden: et uttrykk for tidlig kristen påvirkning samt maktpolitiske forhold i Viken' (Mag. art. thesis, University of Oslo).

Larsen, J.H. 1978. 'Utskyldriket. Arkeologisk drøfting av en historisk hypotese' (Mag. art. thesis, University of Oslo).

Nordeide, S.W. 1990. 'Activity in an urban community: functional aspects of artefact material in Trondheim from *c.*AD1000 to AD1600', *Acta Archaeologica*, 60 (1989), 130–50.

Nordeide, S.W. 1999. 'Urbaniseringsprosessen: på kvinners vilkår?' in G. Gundhus, E. Seip & E. Ulriksen (eds), *NIKU 1994–1999. Kulturminneforskningens mangfold*, NIKU Temahefte, 31 (Oslo), pp 44–8.

Nordeide, S.W. & S. Gulliksen. 2007. 'First generation Christians, second generation radiocarbon dates: the cemetery at St Clement's in Oslo', *Norwegian Archaeological Review*, 40:1, 1–25.

Nordeide, S.W. in preparation. *The Viking Age as a period of religious transformation: the Christianization of Norway from AD560–1150/1200.*

Pirenne, H. 1925 [1956]. *Medieval cities: their origins and the revival of trade* (Garden City).

Polanyi, K. 1957. 'Trade and market in the early empires: economies in history and theory' in K. Polanyi, C.M. Arensberg & H.W. Pearson (eds), *The economy as instituted process*, (New York, London), pp 243–70.

Ramstad, S. 2002. '"Gregoriuskirka": rekonstruksjon og funksjonell analyse' (hovedfag thesis, Norwegian University of Science and Technology).

Robberstad, K. 1923. *Magnus Lagabøters bylov* (Kristiania).

Schia, E. 1991. *Oslo innerst i Viken* (Oslo).

Skaare, K. 1976. *Coins and coinage in Viking-Age Norway: the establishment of a national coinage in Norway in the XI century, with a survey of the preceding currency history* (Oslo).

Skre, D. & F.A. Stylegar. 2004. *Kaupang vikingbyen: Kaupang-utstillingen ved UKM 2004–2005* (Oslo).

Sognnes, K. 1990. 'Trondheim: en vikingeby?', *Arbeideravisen*, 18 August 1990 (Trondheim).

Solberg, B. 2000. *Jernalderen i Norge* (Oslo).

Solli, B. 1996. *Narratives of Veøy: an investigation into the poetics and scientifics of archaeology*, Universitetets Oldsaksamlings Skrifter, n.s., 19 (Oslo).

Storm, G. 1899. 'De kongelige Byanlæg i Norge i Middelalderen', *Norsk Historisk Tidsskrift*, 3rd ser., 5, 433–6.

Ulriksen, E. 1996. *"Utkantens håndverkere og arbeidere": en aktivitetsanalyse av "Nordre Bydel" i middelalderens Tønsberg.* NIKU Temahefte 3.

Rebuilding the 'city of angels': Muirchertach Ua Briain and Glendalough, *c*.1096–1111

TOMÁS Ó CARRAGÁIN

In popular publications and some general surveys of European architecture, Glendalough is portrayed as a quintessentially Celtic monastery whose buildings are the result of a slow process of accretion beginning not long after its foundation in the sixth century (e.g. Conant 1959, 70–1; Altet 1997, 186–7). This view of the site used to be commonplace in studies of Irish architecture (e.g. Petrie 1845; Leask 1955), but in recent years it has been recognized that many of these churches are essentially Romanesque and they have been reassigned to the decade or two on either side of the year 1100 (e.g. Henry 1970, 150; O'Keeffe 1998, 121; 2003, 83–91; Harbison 1999, 322–3; Gem 2006). Nonetheless, while a number of them are commonly referred to in general discussions about early Irish architecture, the uniqueness of the group as a whole has not received due attention, and no one has offered a satisfactory explanation for this remarkable burst of, often experimental, building activity (Fig. 26.1). In this paper it will be argued that the key to understanding it lies in the relationship between Glendalough and the Hiberno-Norse port of Dublin.

THE BUILDINGS

The first phase of St Kevin's House (Plate 5), a barrel-vaulted church, is very similar to, but typologically earlier than, St Flannan's Killaloe, which Richard Gem (2006) has convincingly dated to *c*.1100. Its vaulted chancel with its northern side-chamber was probably added soon after it was built, possibly, in light of links discussed below, in response to the erection of St Flannan's which had a vaulted chancel from the outset. This addition, along with the three single-phase nave-and-chancel churches – Reefert, Trinity and St Kieran's – appear to be early instances of a new trend in Irish architecture of which St Flannan's represents the earliest securely dated example. The unusual south door of the chancel of St Kieran's finds a rare parallel in the chancel of Friar's Island, which I argue elsewhere is contemporary with St Flannan's (Ó Carragáin forthcoming). The western annex of Trinity, with its vault and belfry, are sufficiently close in form to the first phase of St Kevin's House to suggest that it was built within a few decades of it.

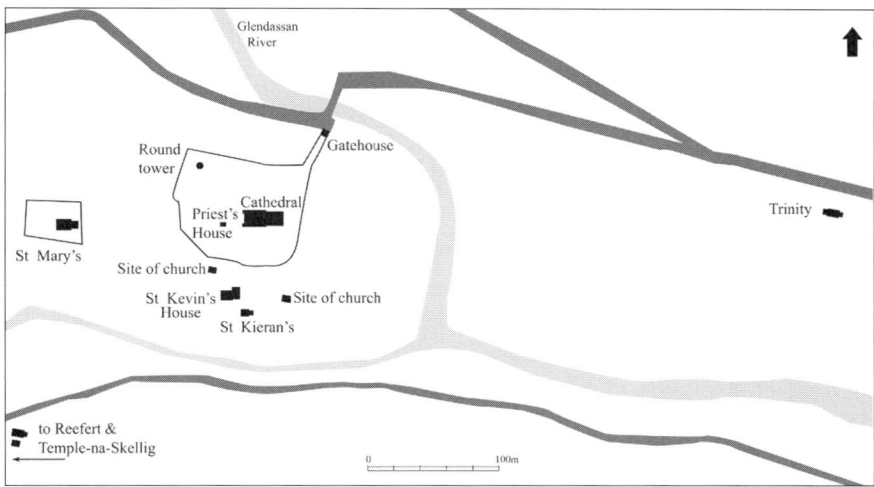

26.1 Map of Glendalough showing buildings and related features mentioned in the text.

There are also one or possibly two antae-less unicameral churches, a building type which does not become common until after *c.*1050: St Mary's and Temple-na-Skellig (Ó Carragáin 2005, 139–40). The plain west doorway of this latter church suggests that at least some of its fabric is pre-Romanesque. It also has an unusual twin-light east window which may be late twelfth-century, but because this church has been rebuilt virtually from ground level (Colles 1870, 198) we cannot determine whether or not it was an original feature. In addition to these churches, Glendalough also features a gatehouse with shallow antae and arches which are very similar to those of Reefert and Trinity. Its principal round tower has a round-headed doorway which could also conceivably date to this period.

We are on somewhat shakier chronological footing with the cathedral, which incorporates the fabric of a smaller church (Manning 2002). The deep antae of the enlarged church would normally suggest a tenth- or early eleventh-century date (Ó Carragáin 2005, 139), but here their dimensions are determined by the antae of the earlier building. The rubble tympanum and relieving arch above the doorway do not help us a great deal with dating; the earlier cathedral probably also had relieving arches over its D-shaped window tympana. Thus the architectural evidence does not allow us to date the enlarged church more closely than *c.*1000–1130. However, on the basis of historical probability, a date around 1100 seems most likely. It is important to emphasize that this is the only known instance of the wholesale rebuilding of a pre-Romanesque stone church. As far as we can judge, all other examples were the first stone churches at their particular locations and they were rarely altered at all until the later twelfth century (Ó Carragáin 2005, 142). This enlargement, which makes Glendalough Cathedral the second largest pre-Romanesque church in the country, would not have been undertaken lightly. At the risk of introducing circularity to the argument, it seems to me that the historical context suggested below for the rebuilding of the other churches is also the most likely context for it. It has been suggested that the granite abutments under the Transitional chancel arch of Dundry stone belong to an earlier chancel of the cathedral (O'Keeffe 2003, 84; also Long 1996, 251) but there are good reasons for doubting this, which I cannot go into here (Ó Carragáin forthcoming). Thus, whether or not it was enlarged in this period, the cathedral was probably the most traditional of all the Glendalough churches: a unicameral building with antae. This is what we should expect, for as late as *c.*1200 the principal churches at early Irish monasteries were generally more conservative in form than the subsidiary churches (Ó Carragáin 2007).

Even omitting the round tower and the enlargement of the cathedral, nine phases of building activity can confidently be dated to between *c.*1050 and 1150 and, as noted above, various scholars have dated most of them to the decade or two on either side of 1100. After Glendalough, the site with the most extant pre-1050 stone buildings is Clonmacnoise: it has a shrine chapel which may date from the ninth century, an early tenth-century cathedral, two or three churches which may date from the eleventh century (Temple Dowling and possibly two churches at the nunnery), and a round tower was which built in 1124 (*AFM*; Manning 2003, 86), that is six phases of construction spanning at least 220 years, as compared with nine phases in probably less than forty years. No other Irish site has more than three extant stone buildings which pre-date the full development of Hiberno-Romanesque. It must be remembered that what survives is a partial record, and only at a minority of sites can one be confident that a high proportion of the early stone churches are still extant. For example, we know that three more churches were standing at Clonmacnoise in the seventeenth century, but we have no information about the dates of their construction (Manning 1994). However, cartographic, annalistic and hagiographical evidence indicate that we are missing at least three churches at Glendalough also (O'Donovan 1838; *AFM* 1163; *VSH* I: 243–4). We are, I think, entitled to assume that this striking pattern bears some relation to the situation in the early medieval period (Hodder 1991, 132; Carver 2001).

Tellingly, in order to find a parallel for the level of building at Glendalough, we have to look to the Hiberno-Norse ports, and especially Dublin, though admittedly in this case our evidence is mainly documentary. Bradley (1992, 48–52; also Clarke 2004) shows that there were more than twenty urban and suburban churches in and around Dublin, and he argues that most of them were built in the eleventh century (Fig. 26.2). We only know the form of one of these, St Michael-le-Pole (Fig. 26.3; Gowan 2001), but the close similarity between its western belfry and those of St Kevin's House and Trinity, hints that the masons responsible for the Glendalough churches first encountered these new ideas in Dublin. The idea of engaged western belfries probably came from the Anglo-

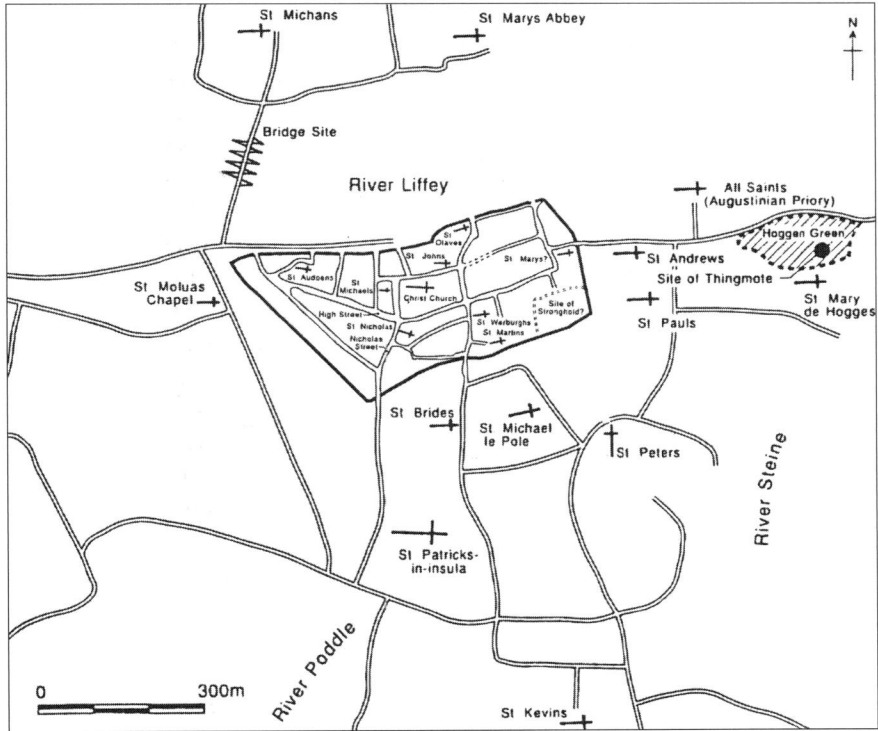

26.2 The urban and suburban churches of Dublin (after Bradley 1992, figs 2–3).

Scandinavian world (e.g. Heywood 1988; Blair 2005, 424–5), but the form of these examples derives from native free-standing round towers. This is generally true of the Glendalough churches: their thoroughly localized character suggests that they are a secondary response by masons primarily trained in the Irish architectural tradition to forms (barrel vaults, chancel arches etc.) which they encountered at some later stage in their careers, quite possibly in Dublin.

The question remains, why did these forms become so popular at Glendalough? By any reasonable chronological or formal criteria, most of these buildings are Romanesque and Romanesque buildings in Ireland have often been interpreted as expressions of the Church reform movement (e.g. Hughes 1966, 271–2; Gwynn 1992, 214; O'Keeffe 2000, 314–17). As discussed below, Glendalough was an enthusiastic participant in this movement, but so were other important Leinster churches such as Kildare (Gwynn and Hadcock 1970, 93) where there is no evidence for buildings of this date. In a study focused primarily on later Romanesque churches, O'Keeffe noted similar problems with the idea that Romanesque was a metaphor for reform. One of the most important conclusions he comes to is that 'the rationale [...] for building new churches with

The Old   Tower of Michael of Pole . Dublin .

26.3 View of St Michael-le-Pole, Dublin, by Gabriel Beranger, 1766 (after Gowan 2001, fig. 7).
Note the similarity between its western belfry and that of St Kevin's House (Plate 5).

Romanesque forms was not in the reform itself but in the politics surrounding it
and in the political environment which accommodated it' (O'Keeffe 2003, 284).
However, while he acknowledges that 'all buildings are political', he believes that
the Glendalough churches lack 'the level of political rhetoric' evident in their
successors at sites like Killaloe and Cashel (O'Keeffe 2003, 282). To my mind,
this is a doubtful conclusion which, intentionally or not, privileges decorative
sculpture over architectural form: it is almost as if buildings with sculpture
should be read as sophisticated political statements while undecorated buildings
grow out of the ground organically of their own accord. In fact, St Kevin's House
is arguably a more radical departure than the similar, but probably later, church
at Killaloe, and collectively the churches and other structures erected at
Glendalough around 1100 created a built environment without parallel at any
Irish monastery. Gem (2006, 83) comments that we lack a 'very specific historical
context' for St Kevin's House, but I will argue in the next section that it *is* possible
for us to identify a context for this unique church group.

THE POLITICAL CONTEXT

Glendalough's relationship with Dublin is the key to understanding these churches, not because it made new forms of architecture available, but because Glendalough had more to lose than any other site by the emergence of the port as a major ecclesiastical force in the late eleventh century. Dublin had a central role in Canterbury's plans to extend its authority over the Irish church. As early as 1074, in a decretum relating to the consecration of bishop Patrick, Canterbury referred to Dublin as *metropolis Hiberniae*, a phrase which can only be interpreted as 'metropolitan church of Ireland' (Holland 2000, 113–14; 2004, 160; Bethell 1971, 134). It was not until after 1096 that the full extent of Dublin's ambitions in this regard became clear. Glendalough, however, was in the front line when it came to Dublin expansionism and had to react to it at an earlier date; there is documentary evidence for tensions between the sites from the 1070s onwards (Doherty 2000). I have argued elsewhere that the competing interests of these major ecclesiastical powers is one of the reasons why more local sites in south Dublin and north Wicklow were provided with stone churches during this period than in any other area of the country (Ó Carragáin forthcoming).

Glendalough lost a lot of its interests in this area at the Synod of Kells in 1152. In order to understand how it was able to resist Dublin expansion before this we have to turn to secular politics. Glendalough's chief patrons, the Uí Lorcáin line of Uí Muiredaig, were the principal allies of the Uí Briain high kings in this part of Ireland and, as Toirdelbach Ua Briain extended his power eastwards, he promoted the Uí Lorcáin to the key kingship of north Leinster; the Uí Lorcáin in turn facilitated the Uí Briain dominance of Dublin (Mac Shamhráin 1996, 98–9, 152–3). Toirdelbach's son Muirchertach became high king in 1086. During the first decade of his reign, he apparently favoured Canterbury's involvement in the reform of the Irish Church. For example, along with various Irish bishops, he signed letters in 1096 asking Anselm of Canterbury to consecrate Samuel as bishop of Dublin and to establish a new see at Waterford with Mael Ísa as its bishop. Holland (2000, 127) argues that Muirchertach became aware of Dublin's ambitions in *c.*1096 or soon after, and that this was a key factor in his decision to reform the Irish church from within. Bishop Samuel seems to have been less politic and cautious than his predecessor, Patrick. Even Anselm of Canterbury reprimanded him for having a processional cross carried in front of him though he had not yet been elevated to the position of archbishop (Holland 2000, 134; 2004, 165). Samuel's behaviour may have been what alerted Muirchertach to Dublin's ambitions.

In the next fifteen years, Muirchertach pursued his new strategy energetically. He convened an initial reforming synod at Cashel in 1101, convinced Armagh to come on board soon afterwards (Holland 2000, 133–6) and, at Ráith Bressail in 1111, he oversaw the establishment of a new, papally approved, ecclesiastical hierarchy, independent of Canterbury. Most of the decisions regarding episcopal sees at Ráith Bressail were predictable enough, but in an extraordinary turn of events, Dublin was excluded from the hierarchy altogether and subsumed into an expanded diocese of Glendalough. As Mac Shamhráin observes, 'this unitary Glendalough-Dublin diocese was created to serve Ua Briain interests – combining, as it did, the Hiberno-Norse Scandinavian kingdom and the Uí Muiredaig relm' (Mac Shamhráin 2000, 53; 1996, 98–9). Glendalough, therefore, had a particularly important role to play in Muirchertach's vision of a reformed Church. However, this was to be a short-lived experiment. Muirchertach's power began to wane when he fell ill in 1114 and the new high king, Toirdelbach Ua Conchobair, had no interest in perpetuating his scheme. Dublin never accepted the Ráith Bressail arrangement and reasserted its independence in 1121 by sending a new bishop elect, Gréne, to Canterbury for consecration. Glendalough's worst fears about Dublin's ambitions would be realized in subsequent decades: it became a suffragan within a new archdiocese of Dublin in 1152 and was absorbed into the diocese of Dublin in 1212 (Mac Shamhráin 1996, 162).

But for a period of about fifteen years (*c.*1096–1111), it suited the high king of Ireland to promote Glendalough as the chief church of north Leinster, in order to circumscribe Dublin's unacceptable ambitions. This period was the high point of Muirchertach's authority in Ireland and abroad (Holland 2000, 131), and during it we know he 'exercised considerable influence over the affairs of Glendalough' (Mac Shamhráin 1996, 152–3). I believe that this provides us with a plausible context for the unprecedented building boom at the site, a boom which has already been dated to around this time on architectural grounds. Ideally, Muirchertach would probably have preferred to incorporate Dublin into his new diocesan structure. By giving Leth Moga (the south) one less bishop than Leth Cuinn (the north), the door was left ajar for a reconciliation with Dublin at some future date (Holland 2000, 145). But any reservations he may have had would not have been shared by the Uí Muiredaig, and the architectural evidence suggests that they whole-heartedly seized the opportunity which had been presented to them by Samuel's recalcitrance and Muirchertach's patronage.

A number of sources, some discussed below, point to the direct involvement of Muirchertach at the site during this period, and one in particular hints at the involvement of an important individual in Muirchertach's circle in the erection of at least one of its churches:

> Maeltrena, a noble priest and learned superior of Cro-Caeimhghin, the bosom fosterling of Ua Dunain, noble senior of Ireland, died, as became an ecclesiastic (*AFM* 1125).

Cró Coemgen is the barrel-vaulted church known as St Kevin's House (Plate 5) and Bishop Mael Muire Ua Dúnáin was Muirchertach's closest ecclesiastical ally:

the man who presided over the Synod of Ráth Breasail (Ó Corráin 1983). He gravitated to Muirchertach's circle soon after 1095: around the time that the king changed his policy towards Canterbury, Dublin and Glendalough. We do not know to what extent he influenced this change, but it seems unlikely to be mere coincidence that he is mentioned in one of only two annalistic references to St Kevin's House, especially in light of evidence, which I discuss elsewhere (Ó Carragáin forthcoming), that he was also involved in the building of similar barrel-vaulted churches at Kells and Killaloe. It is tempting to conclude that Mael Muire played some part in commissioning St Kevin's House and that he installed his 'bosom fosterling' as its superior. If so, then this may have taken place between 1096 and 1100, by which time the typologically later church of St Flannan's was probably built (Gem 2006). Whether the other buildings were built incrementally over the full period between c.1096 and 1111, or were mostly built in the immediate lead up to Ráith Bressail, is a matter of speculation.

'CIVITAS COEMGENI'

The aim of Muirchertach and his allies was to set Glendalough up as a legitimate alternative to Dublin, which by this time almost certainly had more stone churches than any other Irish site. Competitive emulation was therefore one of the motivations behind their building programme (on this concept see Renfrew 1986, 7–8). A number of the new churches probably replaced wooden ones including St Kieran's (Mac Shamhráin 1996, 139–41), Temple-na-Skellig, Reefert/Dísert Coemgen (*VSH* I: 242, 244) and St Kevin's House, which incorporates a door from an earlier church. It is possible, however, that some of the others were built on virgin sites. The dedication of the Trinity is unusual in the Irish context, and it may be significant that this is the official dedication of the cathedrals of both Dublin and Canterbury. The dedication of St Mary's is also quite unusual. It is probably the nunnery which appears to have been established at Glendalough in the period between the composition of Kevin's Latin and Irish lives (cf. *VSH* I: 239–40 with *BNÉ* I: 125–30). The architecture of St Mary's is consistent with the possibility that this happened in around 1100. Muirchertach's mother, Derborgaill, was married to the Ua Lorcáin king, Augaire (+1112 *AFM*), who must have been an important partner in the rebuilding of Glendalough, and she died there in 1098 (*AFM*). It is tempting to speculate that St Mary's was built to honour her, or else that she had a role in commissioning it before she died.

Apart from the number and character of its churches, it is possible that Glendalough emulated other aspects of the layout of Dublin. *Lebor na Cert* wishes 'fame to the king of Áth Cliath [Dublin] of the ramparts' (Dillon 1962, 110–11), while in a poem of c.1120 in the *Book of Leinster*, the *dún* of Dublin is listed as one of the seven wonders of Ireland (Wallace 1992, 45; Clarke 2000, 50). In this regard, it may be significant that the Glendalough gatehouse is the only stone example from any early Irish monastery (Plate 6). It is actually larger and more elaborate than the early twelfth-century example excavated at St Peter's Street, Waterford (Hurley 1997, 29). We cannot know without excavation, but it is possible that the enclosures around the site were remodelled at the time the gatehouse was erected. It cannot be mere coincidence that, in the political context outlined above, Glendalough was rebuilt in a way which probably made it appear more like one of the Hiberno-Norse ports than almost any other Irish ecclesiastical site. Those involved may well have been conscious that they were making it resemble an urban centre. The great Irish monasteries had always been conceived as *civitates*, and in the arrangement of their churches they may have emulated the layout of cities on the European mainland (e.g. Doherty 1985; Ó Carragáin 2003, 140). This term did not necessarily imply urbanism or even nucleation (Swift 1998), but a few sites, including Clonmacnoise and Armagh, had become nucleated (Bradley 1998). In the Glendalough hagiography there is a certain tension between idealized descriptions of the wild sylvan glen to which Kevin retreated and an awareness that this was not an ideal environment for a city to flourish in. In the Latin Life of Kevin, the saint negotiates with an angel about the size and character of his new *civitas*. He rejects the angels offer of fifty monks sustained by God with 'celestial bread' and eventually the angel promises that 'there will be for forever many thousands in it prosperous and without hardship, God giving to them already ample lands [...] a great city (*civitas magna*) will grow there' (*VSH* I: 246). The angel even offers to make the mountains into 'level plains most pleasant and fruitful', but Kevin stops short of this, not wishing to displace the wild animals of the glen. There is a similar duality between Glendalough as desert retreat and great city (*cathair*) in the Irish Lives: in one of them it is described it as 'a church with its hundreds ... a gracious Rome, city of angels' (*BNÉ* I: 144; II: 139–40).

In reality, it is doubtful if Glendalough was ever much more than a village, but around 1100 it was aiming to sideline a site which styled itself *metropolis Hiberniae*. Here, the term is used in the sense of metropolitan episcopal centre, but among the reformers of the period there was general agreement that metropolitans, and indeed all bishops, should be based in urban centres. This was enshrined in Canon 3 of the Council of London in 1075 and during Lanfranc's (1070–89) episcopacy, a number of diocesan centres were moved from old establishments in rural areas to walled cities (Whitelock et al. 1981, 608–9, 613; Cowdry 2003, 129), cities which, like Dublin, were experiencing an unprece-dented boom in stone church construction (Schofield 1994; Blair 2005, 416, 194). It can be argued that both Muirchertach and Mael Muire acknowledged this principal, for their last documented correspondence with Canterbury is a letter of 1096 requesting Anselm to establish a bishopric in Waterford because of its large population (Holland 2000, 124). Of course, the extent of urbanism or even nucleation of settlement in Ireland was miniscule compared to England, and most of the bishoprics established at Ráith Bressail in 1111 were, of necessity, at rural sites; but by around 1100 the only territorial bishoprics that had been established were in true *civitates*, and Glendalough's rival was the largest of these. In this context, it may have made sense for Glendalough to mimic aspects of the outward appearance of the new urban centres, even if it never achieved the critical mass to become one itself.

Having said that, the contrasts between the remodelled Glendalough and contemporary Dublin are also striking. While we know very little about the character of Christ Church in this period (Michael O'Neill in prep.), it seems likely that in Dublin, like cities throughout Europe (including the Hiberno-Norse ports in the twelfth century), episcopal and royal patronage and the architectural innovation that went with it, was focused, in the first instance, on the cathedral church. In contrast, if the enlargement of Glendalough Cathedral dates to this period, it only serves to emphasize the conservatism of this building in comparison to some of the smaller churches on the site, especially St Kevin's House. I have argued elsewhere that this church was occupied by ascetics and that it also had a reliquary function (Ó Carragáin forthcoming). While it is unlikely to mark the saint's original grave, a range of evidence suggests that it was a more important focus for his cult than the cathedral. Irish monasteries had long been characterized by a separation between the principal liturgical space and reliquary foci (Ó Carragáin 2003). Thus, at Glendalough, new architectural forms were used to perpetuate a tenet of the layout of Irish monasteries which had been established centuries earlier and which set them apart from their European counterparts. It should also be stressed that the new ideas evident at Glendalough may not all have come from Dublin. As O'Keeffe (2003, 83–4) points out, the antae projecting from the gatehouse suggest that its super-structure functioned as a chapel. In this regard its models may have been monastic gatehouses abroad (e.g. Morant 1995), rather than those of the Hiberno-Norse ports, though it should be noted that town gatehouses could also be used for religious purposes (e.g. Gilchrist 1995, 161, 173–4).

Clearly, then, those remodelling Glendalough were not aiming for slavish imitation of Dublin. The selective use of new ideas, sometimes in a way which reinforced peculiarly Irish traits, is perfectly in keeping with the new project which Muirchertach and his allies had just embarked upon: the creation of a reformed but independent Irish Church. Placed in this context, these individually modest buildings can collectively be recognized as a forceful political statement: a newly negotiated compromise between novelty and tradition. Henry commented that the illumination of Glendalough manuscripts of this period is characterized on the one hand by 'vivacity and inventiveness' and on the other by 'fidelity to old models' (Henry 1970, 53, 63–4). A similar ethos is evident in the rebuilding of the site itself.

ACKNOWLEDGMENTS

I am very grateful to the following for reading versions of this paper and/or discussing it
with me: Con Manning, Dr Richard Gem, Prof. Donnchadh Ó Corráin and Prof. Pádraig
Ó Riain. Any errors that remain are my own.

BIBLIOGRAPHY

AFM = O'Donovan, J. (ed.). 1851. *Annála ríoghachta Éireann: Annals of the kingdom of
Ireland by the Four Masters, from the earliest period to the year 1616*, 7 vols (Dublin).
Altet, X.B. 1997. *The early Middle Ages from late antiquity to AD1000* (Cologne).
Bethell, D. 1971. 'English monks and Irish reform in the eleventh and twelfth Centuries',
Historical Studies, 8, 111–35.
Blair, J. 2005. *The church in Anglo-Saxon society* (Oxford).
BNÉ = Plummer, C. (ed.). 1922. *Bethada Náem nÉrenn* (Oxford).
Bradley, J. 1992. 'The topographical development of Scandinavian Dublin' in F.H.A.
Aalen & K. Whelan (eds), *Dublin city and county: from prehistory to present* (Dublin),
pp 43–56.
Bradley, J. 1998. 'The monastic town of Clonmacnoise' in H.A. King (ed.), *Clonmacnoise
Studies 1* (Dublin), pp 42–56.
Carver, M. 2001. 'Why that? Why there? Why then? The politics of early medieval
monumentality' in A. MacGregor & H. Hamerow (eds), *Image and power in early
medieval Britain: essays in honour of Rosemary Cramp* (Oxford), pp 1–22.
Clarke, H.B. 2000. 'Conversion, church and cathedral: the diocese of Dublin to 1152' in
J. Kelly & D. Keogh (eds), *History of the catholic diocese of Dublin* (Dublin), pp 19–50.
Clarke, H.B. 2004. 'Christian cults and cult centres in Hiberno-Norse Dublin and its
hinterland' in A. MacShamhráin (ed.), *The island of Saint Patrick: church and ruling
dynasties in Fingal and Meath, 400–1148* (Dublin), pp 140–58.
Colles, J.A.P. 1870. 'Proposal to restore churches at Glendalough', *Journal of the Royal
Society of Antiquaries of Ireland*, 1, 194–201.
Conant, K.J. 1959. *Carolingian and Romanesque architecture, 800–1200* (London).
Cowdrey, H. 2003. *Lanfranc: scholar, monk and archbishop* (Oxford).
Dillon, M. 1962. *Lebor na Cert* (Dublin).
Doherty, C. 1985. 'The monastic town in early medieval Ireland' in H.B. Clarke & A.
Simms (eds), *The comparative history of urban origins in non-Roman Europe* (Oxford),
pp 45–75.
Doherty, C. 2000. 'Cluain Dolcáin: a brief note' in A.P. Smyth (ed.), *Seanchas: studies in
early and medieval Irish archaeology, history and literature in honour of Francis J. Byrne*
(Dublin), pp 182–8.
Gem, R. 2005. 'Saint Flannán's oratory at Killaloe: a Romanesque building of c.1100 and
the patronage of King Muirchertach Ua Briain' in D. Bracken & D. Ó Riain-Raedel
(eds), *Ireland and Europe in the twelfth century: reform and renewal* (Dublin), pp 74–
105.
Gilchrist, R. 1995. *Contemplation and action: the other monasticism* (London).

Gowan, M. 2001. 'Excavations at the site of the church and tower of St Michael le Pole, Dublin' in S. Duffy (ed.), *Medieval Dublin II* (Dublin), pp 13–52.

Gwynn, A. 1992. *The Irish church in the eleventh and twelfth centuries* (Dublin).

Gwynn, A. & Hadcock, R.N. 1970. *Medieval religious houses: Ireland* (London).

Harbison, P. 1999. *The golden age of Irish art* (London).

Henry, F. 1970. *Irish art in the romanesque period 1020–1170AD* (London).

Heywood, S. 1988. 'The round towers of East Anglia' in J. Blair (ed.) *Minsters and parish churches: the local church in transition* (Oxford), pp 169–78.

Hodder, I. 1991. *Reading the past: current approaches to interpretation in archaeology*, 2nd ed. (Cambridge).

Holland, M. 2000. 'Dublin and the reform of the Irish church in the eleventh and twelfth centuries', *Peritia*, 14, 111–60.

Holland, M. 2004. 'The twelfth-century reform and Inis Pátraic' in A. MacShamhráin (ed.), *The island of Saint Patrick: church and ruling dynasties in Fingal and Meath, 400–1148* (Dublin), pp 159–77.

Hughes, K. 1966. *The church in early Irish society* (London).

Hurley, M. 1997. 'The defences' in M.F. Hurley & O.B.M. Scully with S.J. McCutcheon (eds), *Late Viking Age and Medieval Waterford: excavations 1986–1992* (Dublin), pp 20–33.

Kelly, J. & D. Keogh (eds). 2000. *History of the catholic diocese of Dublin* (Dublin).

Leask, H. 1955. *Irish churches and monastic buildings*, vol. 1 (Dundalk).

Long, W.H. 1996. 'Medieval Glendalough: an inter-disciplinary study' (PhD thesis, Trinity College Dublin).

Mac Shamhráin, A. 1996. *Church and polity in pre-Norman Ireland: the case of Glendalough* (Maynooth).

Mac Shamhráin, A. 2000. 'The emergence of the metropolitan see: Dublin 1111–1216' in J. Kelly & D. Keogh (eds), *History of the catholic diocese of Dublin* (Dublin), pp 50–71.

Manning C. 1994. 'The earliest plans of Clonmacnoise', *Archaeology Ireland*, 8:1, 18–20.

Manning C. 2002. 'A puzzle in stone: the cathedral at Glendalough', *Archaeology Ireland*, 16:2, 18–21.

Manning, C. 2003. 'Some early masonry churches and the round tower at Clonmacnoise' in H. King (ed.), *Clonmacnoise studies, volume 2: Seminar Papers 1998* (Dublin), pp 63–95.

Morant, R.W. 1995. *The monastic gatehouse* (Lewes).

Ó Carragáin, T. 2003. 'The architectural setting of the cult of relics in early medieval Ireland', *Journal of the Royal Society of Antiquaries of Ireland*, 133, 130–76.

Ó Carragáin, T. 2005. 'Habitual masonry styles and the local organization of church building in early medieval Ireland', *Proceedings of the Royal Irish Academy*, 105C, 99–149.

Ó Carragáin, T. 2007. 'Skeuomorphs and spolia: the presence of the past in Irish pre-Romanesque architecture' in R. Moss (ed.), *Making and meaning: studies in Insular art* (Dublin), pp 95–109.

Ó Carragáin, T. forthcoming. *Churches in early medieval Ireland: architecture, ritual and memory* (New Haven and London).

Ó Corráin, D. 1983. 'Máel Muire Ua Dúnáin (1040–1117), reformer' in P. de Brún et al. (eds), *Folia Gadelica* (Cork), pp 47–53.

O'Donovan, J. 1838. *Letters containing information relative to the antiquities of the county of Wicklow: collected during the progress of the Ordnance Survey in 1838*. Reproduced in 1928 under the direction of Rev. Michael O'Flanagan (Bray).

O'Keeffe, T. 1998. 'Architectural traditions of the early medieval church in Munster' in M.A. Monk & J. Sheehan (eds), *Early medieval Munster: archaeology, history and society* (Cork), pp 112–24.

O'Keeffe, T. 2000. 'Romanesque as metaphor: architecture and reform in early twelfth-century Ireland' in A.P. Smyth (ed.), *Seanchas: studies in early and medieval Irish archaeology, history and literature in honour of Francis J. Byrne* (Dublin), pp 313–22.

O'Keeffe, T. 2003. *Romanesque Ireland: architecture and ideology in the twelfth century* (Dublin).

Renfrew, C. 1986. 'Introduction: peer polity interaction and socio-political change' in C. Renfrew & J.F. Cherry (eds), *Peer polity interaction and socio-political change* (Cambridge), 1–18.

Schofield, J. 1994. 'Saxon and medieval parish churches in the city of London', *Transactions of the London and Middlesex Archaeological Society*, 45, 23–145.

Swift, C. 1998. 'Forts and fields: a study of 'monastic towns' in seventh and eighth century Ireland', *Journal of Irish Archaeology*, 9, 105–25.

VSH = Plummer, C. (ed.). 1910. *Vitae Sanctorum Hiberniae* (Oxford).

Wallace, P. 1992. 'The archaeological identity of the Hiberno-Norse town', *Journal of the Royal Society of Antiquaries of Ireland*, 122, 35–66.

Whitelock, D., M. Brett & C. Brooke (eds). 1981. *Councils and synods with other documents relating to the English Church, Vol. I, AD871–1204* (Oxford).

Wilde, W. 1870. 'Memoir of Gabriel Beranger, and his labours in the cause of Irish art and antiquities, from 1760 to 1780, part 1', *Journal of the Royal Historical and Archaeological Society of Ireland*, 1, 33–64.

Culture clashes? The human remains from the Wood Quay excavations

BARRA O'DONNABHAIN

INTRODUCTION

The National Museum of Ireland undertook most of the archaeological excavations carried out in the Viking core of Dublin between 1962 and 1981. From 1974, this research was concentrated on a series of contiguous sites at Wood Quay, Fishamble Street II–III and John's Lane (Fig. 27.1). The excavations at these sites were directed by Dr P.F. Wallace and produced considerable information regarding the nature of the early settlement and the daily life of its inhabitants between the tenth and thirteenth centuries (Mitchell 1987; Lang 1988; Wallace 1992; Fanning 1994; Geraghty 1996; Heckett 2003; McCutcheon 2006). Human remains were a relatively common occurrence on all of the sites. Some complete skeletons and portions of skeletons were recovered, though much of the material recovered consisted of isolated bones. While some preliminary analysis of this material was carried out in the 1980s, the collection has recently been re-examined (O'Donnabhain forthcoming). As the human remains from the ninth-century cemeteries at Islandbridge and Kilmainham (O'Brien 1998) were not curated for the most part, and the tenth- to twelfth-century cemeteries have not been explored archaeologically, the skeletal material from Wood Quay and adjacent sites represents the largest extant collection of human remains from Viking-Age and Hiberno-Norse Dublin.

DATING AND CONTEXTS

The sites excavated between 1974 and 1981 covered an area of 1.8 hectares. Human remains were found in a number of different types of contexts. These included isolated human bones that were found in the general matrix at each of the sites; single skeletons; and multiple burials that may represent mass graves. The human remains have been dated on the basis of stratigraphic associations and can be divided into two temporal groups. The earlier of these consists of the skeletal remains recovered from tenth- and eleventh-century levels at the sites at John's Lane and Fishamble Street while the later group was recovered from twelfth-century levels at Wood Quay.

271

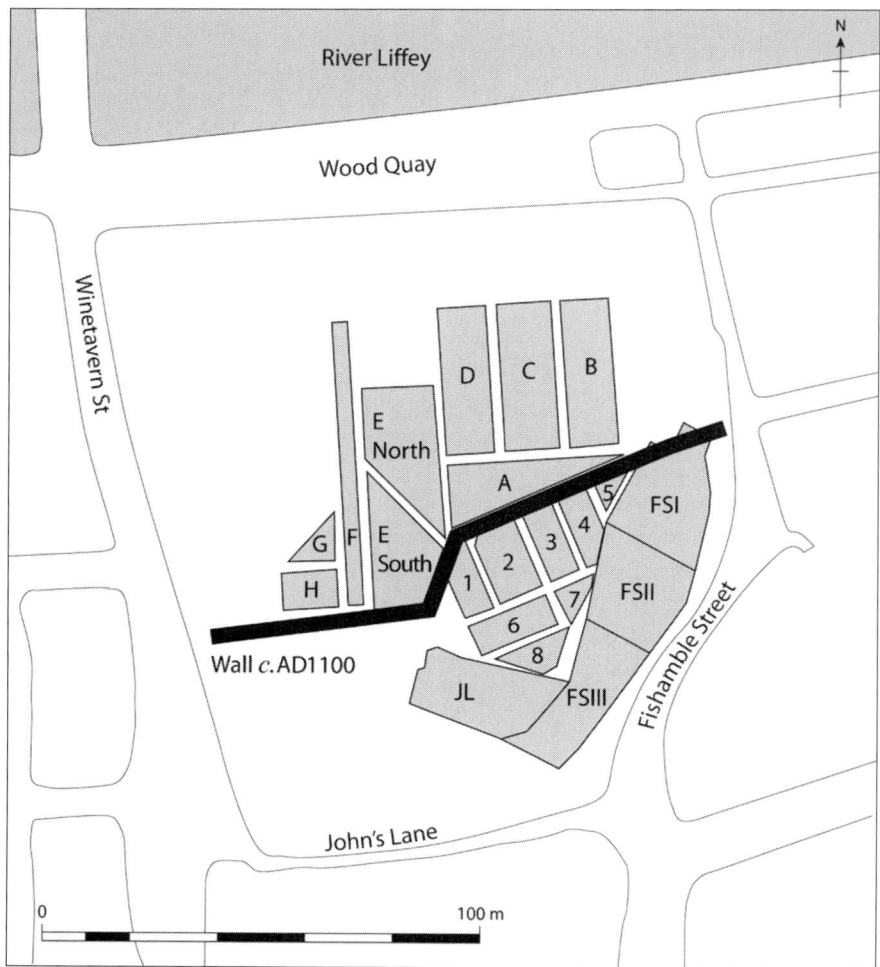

27.1 Dublin excavations, 1974–1981: A-H = Wood Quay; 1–8 = Fishamble Street (the Banks); FSI = Fishamble Street I; FSII = Fishamble Street II; FSIII = Fishamble Street III; JL = John's Lane.

Tenth- and eleventh-century remains

The earlier collection of human remains from John's Lane and Fishamble Street can be further subdivided into two sub-groups on the basis of the mode of their disposal. The first of these sub-groups consists of a small number of complete or nearly complete skeletons, while the second sub-group consists of isolated skulls, many of which have evidence of violent circumstances of death.

The skeletons were buried in shallow graves that were found at the lower levels of the sites at John's Lane and Fishamble Street III. Seven skeletons or portions thereof from these sites were available for study. Each of these appears to

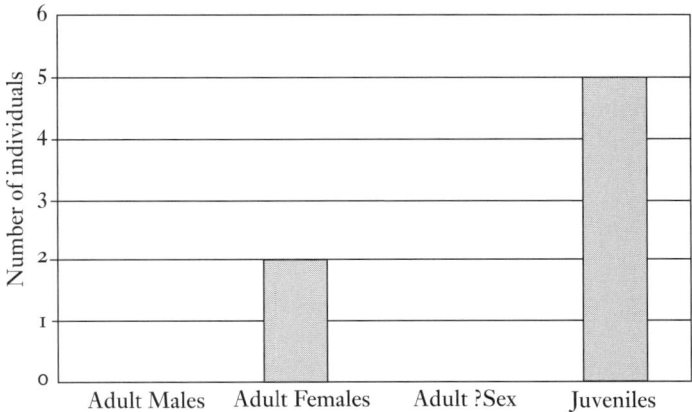

27.2 Age and sex distribution of tenth-/eleventh-century skeletons.

represent a discrete burial episode. Of the seven complete or partial skeletons, the position of the body could be determined in four of these: two of the burials from Fishamble Street III were flexed, while of those in John's Lane, one was semi-flexed and the other was an extended burial with the hands drawn up towards the face. At least five of the seven skeletons were associated with the first of the series of earth and gravel banks that were built along the foreshore at the northern margins of the settlement. The skeleton of a younger adult female was in a pit cut into the sterile boulder clay and may have pre-dated Bank 1 or been roughly contemporary with its construction. Portions of the skeletons of two children (5 to 10 years old and *c*.2 years old) were found in the fill of the ditch associated with Bank 1. The skeleton of another child (probably 8 to 10 years old) was associated with an early building at the lowest level of occupation. The skeleton of a fourth child (also probably 8 to 10 years old) was in the fill of a pit that cut the ditch associated with Bank 1. This latter was the earliest of the series of banks and is thought to have been primarily a flood defence in contrast to the more strategic features that were built later. Regardless of other functions, the banks marked the riverside boundaries of the settlement.

The age and sex data for this sub-group of skeletons are summarized in Figure 27.2 (in which the term juvenile implies individuals aged less than 18 years at time of death). While it has to be acknowledged that this is a very small sample, it is apparent that the articulated skeletons from the tenth-/eleventh-century levels represent the interment of children and some adult women along the northern perimeter of the early settlement. More recent excavations to the east of the Fishamble Street and John's Lane sites produced the grave of a 5 to 8 year old child in a similar riverside context (Simpson 1999). The radiocarbon date for this burial indicated that it may be contemporary with the early burials from the 1974–81 excavations (Simpson 2005). The extended and semi-flexed skeletons at John's Lane were interred with their heads to the west. The crouched burials do not conform to the standardized Christian burial practices. It seems likely that the early settlement had formal places of burial. If this were the case, these skeletons may represent individuals who did not merit inclusion in these cemeteries and were therefore people who for some reason occupied a socially marginal position. The liminal location of the burials along the riverfront may have been seen as an appropriate place of disposal for these particular individuals. The fact that these are the skeletons primarily of children and also of women might favour this view as, in many societies, these are cohorts of the population that can be treated more casually at the time of death. Whether or not these individuals were regarded as socially marginal, there was no evidence for any pathological conditions in this group of skeletons. That is not to suggest that they were healthy: six of the seven died prematurely. However, there was no skeletal evidence of the cause of death. In particular, there was no evidence of trauma or of violent injury to bone. This absence is in marked contrast to the second sub-group of remains from the tenth-/eleventh-century levels, which consists of a series of isolated skulls, seventeen in total, many of which have evidence suggesting that the individuals experienced a violent death. These skulls were found scattered across the early levels of three sites: John's Lane, Fishamble Street II and Fishamble Street III. The skulls were more or less evenly distributed across the three sites: six were found at John's Lane; another six were found at Fishamble Street II; while five were found at Fishamble Street III. At least three were found in pits (one of these a cesspit); two were found under or at the base of Bank 1, one was found on the boulder clay under Bank 3. The rest were found in the general matrices of the sites.

The age and sex data for the seventeen skulls are summarized in Figure 27.3. One of the skulls is probably that of a female, while a portion of one other is that of a 5 to 10 year old child. It is clear, though, that adult males dominate the collection of isolated skulls. Figure 27.3 presents a demographic profile dissimilar to the more complete skeletal remains of tenth- and eleventh-century date shown in Figure 27.2. This suggests that there is a different dynamic leading to the deposition of these heads, and it seems most likely that this was related to the evidence for trauma found in the skulls. Six of the total of seventeen (35.3 per cent) have evidence of wounds that can be attributed to acts of interpersonal violence rather than accidental injury. These lesions consist of both cutting wounds (four individuals) and blunt-force trauma (two individuals, including the child). None of these injuries had healed, indicating that the wounds were incurred at the time of death or thereafter. Furthermore, there is compelling evidence for decapitation in four cases. One has cut-marks to the skull while a second has cut-marks on the cervical vertebrae. Two more skulls were found with the first and second cervical vertebrae still attached, implying that the original deposit consisted of a head with the upper portion of the neck only. There is

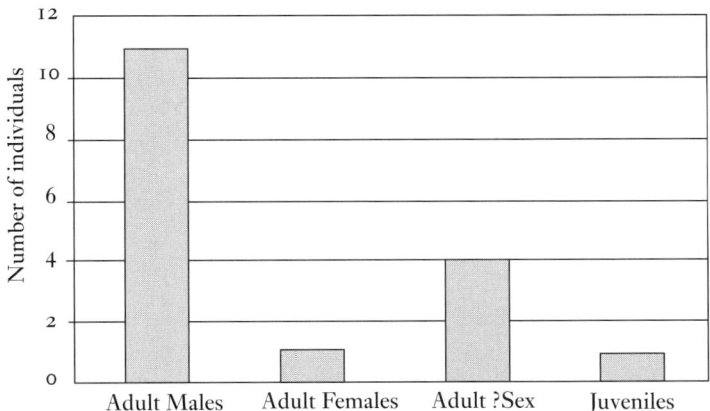

27.3 Age and sex distribution of tenth-/eleventh-century skulls.

damage to one individual that is consistent with an object being forced through the base of the skull and emerging at the top. This may indicate that the skull was put on display. The fact that the mandible was still attached indicates that the soft tissues of the head were still in place when this occurred and were also probably intact when the skull was eventually buried. This indicates that if the skull was displayed, this was for a relatively short time. Finally, at least two of the skulls had been buried with cattle crania. The first of these was buried with an intact cattle skull and a horn core, while the second appears to have been buried with a portion of cattle skull that included the horns and the attached portion of the skull vault.

The evidence, direct and indirect, of injuries in nearly 50 per cent of these mostly adult male individuals indicates that many of these people died in violent circumstances in which the head was removed from the body. While it is possible that this may represent some form of judicial execution, the presence of perimortem injuries in six individuals is suggestive of violent confrontations at the time of death. It is surely not coincidental that many of the heads were found adjacent to or associated with the banks marking the riverside boundary of the settlement. As was suggested with the casual disposal of the remains of children and some women, the concentration of skulls along the northern perimeter of the settlement may be indicative of the liminal status of this area that also rendered it appropriate for the disposal of miscreants. It is also possible that the concentration of skulls in this area is a reflection of the use of the perimeter of the settlement for the purpose of display.

It is tempting to relate these skulls to the descriptions of warfare and killings that are found in the contemporary literature. The Irish annals contain many references to decapitation and, more rarely, mention of the collection and perhaps display of the heads of defeated enemies. These references predate the arrival of the Vikings. A decapitation is mentioned in the Annals of Ulster in AD738, while a reference from 790 in the Annals of the Four Masters describes a decapitation where the head is taken away (*AU* 738.4; *AFM* 790.8). References to decapitation and the collection of heads increase in frequency in the ninth century and are specifically mentioned in descriptions of interactions between Irish and Viking groups. In 866, the Annals of Ulster relate how

> *Aedh m. Neill ro slat uile longportu Gall, .i. airir ind Fochla, eter Chenel n-Eugain & Dal n-Araide co tuc a cennlai & a n-eti & a crodha a l-longport er cath. Roiniudh foraib oc Loch Febail asa tuctha da .xx. dec cenn.*

> (Aed son of Niall plundered all the strongholds of the foreigners i.e. in the territory of the North, both in Cenél Eógain and Dál Araidi, and took away their heads, their flocks, and their herds from camp by battle. A victory was gained over them at Loch Febail and twelve score heads taken thereby (*AU* 866.4)).

The same battle is mentioned in the Annals of the Four Masters, though ascribed to the year 864.

> *Ro sraineadh for na Gallaibh, & ro cuireadh a n-ár. Ro tionóiled a c-cionna co h-aon-mhaighin a b-fiadhnuisi an righ, conadh dá fhichit décc cend ro comhairmheadh fiadha, do-rochair lais don chath-gleó-sin cenmota in ro créchtnaighthe díobh, & do bretha i n-othairlighibh écca lais, & ad-báithit cidh iar trioll dia n-gonaibh.*

> (The victory was gained over the foreigners, and a slaughter was made of them. Their heads were collected to one place, in presence of the king; and twelve score heads were reckoned before him, which was the number slain by him in that battle, besides the numbers of them who were wounded and carried off by him in the agonies of death, and who died of their wounds some time afterwards (*AFM* 864.3)).

This contemporary documentary evidence suggests that the taking of skulls as trophies or as a measure of the success of an expedition was an accepted practice in the warfare of this period. It may also suggest that at least some of the skulls found in the Dublin excavations may not represent the inhabitants of the Viking enclave but rather represent those who were perceived as enemies of the population of the settlement. Perhaps countering the suggestion that these skulls represent enemies is the fact that at least two of the severed heads had been buried with cattle crania. The inclusion of animal remains in the graves of people is a feature of Viking-Age burial practices in Scandinavia and in the Viking West, including Ireland (Sikora 2003/4). This association has also been reported more recently at other Irish sites. In Dublin, Simpson (1999) reported that a complete cattle skull was found in a pit adjacent to the grave mentioned above of a 5 to 8 year old child at Temple Bar West. The same site also produced a much larger pit that contained seven cattle skulls as well as portions of the vaults of two human skulls. Connolly and Coyne (2005) described the association of the remains of many animals, including cattle, with the Viking-Age burials at Cloghermore cave in Co. Kerry.

Twelfth-century remains

The twelfth-century remains from the 1974–81 excavations that were available for analysis were recovered from a series of eight graves located immediately north of (that is, outside) the defensive city wall that was built about AD 1100 (Fig. 27.1). The burials post-date the construction of the wall, which was one of the series of riverside defences that were built progressively towards the river, each time reclaiming another stretch of the foreshore. The river lapped against the north side of the wall and the graves consisted of shallow pits dug into the estuarine mud. This portion of the foreshore was subsequently covered by landfill associated with further reclamation that can be dated to about 1200 (Halpin 2000), so the twelfth-century date for the graves is secure. All of the skeletons were found concentrated along the base of the wall, primarily in the area of the excavation known as Strip E South, but also in Strip H (the remains from Strip H were not curated). It is possible that the skeletons recovered during the excavations represent only a fraction of what was originally deposited, as it seems likely that the burials were protected from the full force of the river current by a sigmoidal kink in the town wall that ensured that the areas in the lee of the wall in Strips H and particularly E South were relatively sheltered (see Fig. 27.1). Human remains were also found throughout the other strips excavated at Wood Quay, but these were disarticulated and perhaps reflect the action of the river current.

By the twelfth century, the population of Dublin had been Christian for at least a century. However, the burials outside the city wall do not conform to the norms of a formal Christian cemetery. The burials were haphazard and lacked the standardized body positions and orientations seen in Christian interments. The contents of the eight graves found in Cutting E South are summarized in Figure 27.4. Two of the burials were of individual skeletons that were deposited in shallow pits in the tidal mud of the estuary. The river probably covered the areas with the burials during high tides and it is possible that stones covering one semi-flexed skeleton were designed to weigh the corpse down. Two double graves were also present. One of these contained an adult and child, both of whom were in a flexed position, with the adult appearing to cradle the child. In contrast, the second double grave contained an adult and an adolescent who were interred head to toe, one on top of the other. The remaining four graves had minimum

Grave Number	MNI	Articulated remains Age and sex	Disarticulated remains Age and sex
1	1	YA♀	
2	1	M/OA♀	
3	2	YA♂ M/OA♀	
4	3	J, 10–13yrs	J, 6–7yrs OA♂
5	5	J, 6yrs OA♂	J, 6yrs J, 10–15yrs OA♀
6	2	J, 10–12yrs A ?♂	
7	3	OA♀	J, 3yrs J, 4–5yrs
8	6	M/OA	J, 1–1½yrs J, 6–7yrs OA♂ OA♂ OA♂

27.4 Table of remains found in graves at Wood Quay, Cutting E South (MNI = minimum number of individuals per grave; J = juvenile; A = adult; YA = younger adult; OA = older adult; M/OA = middle aged or older adult).

number of individuals (MNI) counts of between three and six, and may represent mass graves. These contained a mixture of articulated skeletons and portions thereof along with disarticulated remains. The mixed nature of the deposits was probably due to the effects of the river on these shallow graves. The MNI for the eight graves is twenty-three, and age and sex data for the collection are summarized in Figure 27.5. This demonstrates that men, women and children are represented in the deposit. There was no evidence of violent injury in the remains from the twelfth-century graves.

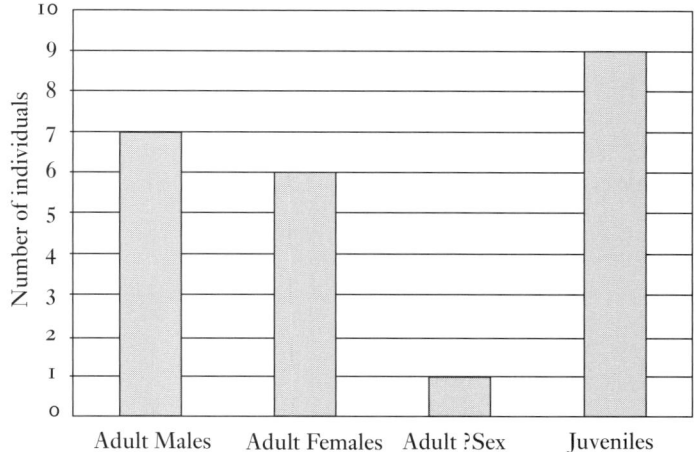

27.5 Age and sex distribution of twelfth-century remains.

The atypical nature of these burials raises questions as to the identity of the individuals. The presence of a relatively large number of people immediately outside the fortifications of a town might be suggestive of an invading force repelled at the walls. However, the preponderance of children and the presence of older adults would counter this scenario, and there was no skeletal evidence of violent injuries to any of these individuals. The demographic profile is more suggestive of people who lived within the settlement.

While there was no evidence to indicate causes of death, the atypical mode of burial suggests that Christian burial norms were abandoned for these people. This can occur at times of stress, when there is a peak in the death rate. The annals mention three occasions during the twelfth century (in 1162, 1170, 1171) when political strife resulted in the slaughter of some of the inhabitants of Dublin. The latter two of these dates also involved sieges (by the king of Leinster and the Anglo-Normans respectively) during which the population may have been starving or at least under increased nutritional stress. The annals also refer to epidemics during this period, in 1099 and 1116 – the latter described as a great pestilence (*AU* 1116.5). While these references to disease do not specifically mention Dublin, there could have been many situations during the twelfth century that presented the population of the settlement with elevated levels of mortality.

The age distribution among the adults in the twelfth century graves is summarized in Figure 27.6. When these data are combined with the number of children in the deposit, (those under 18 years at death represent just under 40 per cent of the total MNI), it is clear that the remains are dominated by the very young and the elderly. It seems likely that this group of burials represents a cross-section of the most vulnerable cohort of the population of twelfth-century Dublin. The burials present a mortality pattern that would be expected in

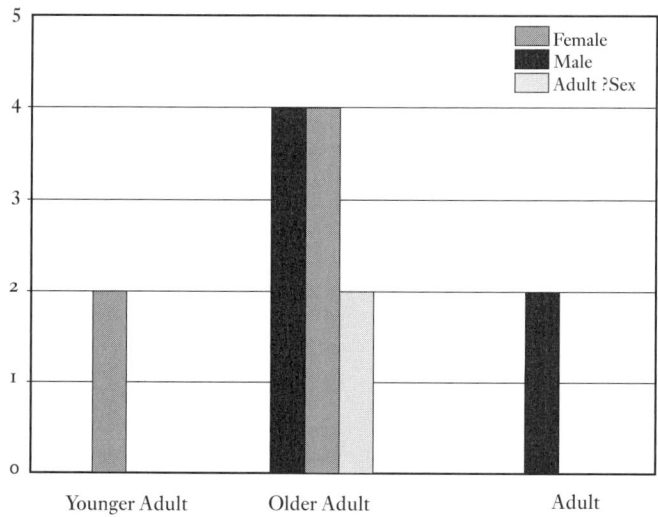

27.6 Adult age distribution, twelfth-century remains.

situations that result from a peak in morbidity, such as a protracted siege or an epidemic. The atypical location and mode of disposal of these bodies might indicate that the cemeteries normally used were not accessible or that the rate of mortality was so high that normal burial practices were suspended.

CONCLUSIONS

Although the cemeteries used by the population of Dublin between the tenth and twelfth centuries have not been explored archaeologically, the small collection of human remains found during the 1974–81 Dublin excavations provide us with some tantalizing evidence for a range of cultural behaviours centred on the disposal of human bodies and body parts. The collection represents at least three distinct burial processes, two from the tenth/eleventh centuries and one from the twelfth century. At least two of these may reflect violent clashes between the inhabitants of Dublin and their neighbours. The variability in behaviours may represent differences in attitudes to the body (over time and between the different cultural groups), which cannot be assumed to be universal or constant. The location of the remains, along the northern, riverside margins of the settlement, is probably significant and may also have implications in terms of how this particular space was viewed by the inhabitants of the town.

I suggest in this paper that the data indicate that the more complete skeletal remains represent the disposal of some of the more vulnerable of the town's inhabitants, though the nature of this vulnerability may vary. Along with the circumstances of burial, the age and sex profiles of the tenth-/eleventh-century remains suggest the casual disposal of individuals who were of low status within the settlement. The flexed nature of some of the early burials suggests that those who buried these dead were not following Christian burial practices.

The demographics of twelfth-century skeletons suggest that their deposition is primarily a reflection of a biological vulnerability rather than the social vulnerability of the earlier group. The two groups of skeletons also differ in another respect: the tenth-/eleventh-century remains seem to represent a number of discrete interments that may have taken place over a number of years, while it is possible that the twelfth-century graves represent a relatively short period of burial and may even represent a single calamitous event or set of such events that resulted in mass deaths among the town's inhabitants, leading to the suspension of normal social obligations governing the disposal of the dead.

Despite their haphazard nature, the graves in the estuarine mud reflect the determination of the living to remove the dead from the confines of the town. This may not have been the case with the skulls found in the tenth-/eleventh-century levels. It is likely that at least some of these were displayed, if only temporarily. The placing of body parts, especially skulls, of those who suffered violent deaths along the boundaries of settlements has parallels in many different cultural settings. The public display of body parts was one means by which social and political power was exercised and maintained. In the Dublin sites, the location of the skulls at the boundaries of the settlement must be significant. Placing the remains in liminal locations would have amplified the visual messages sent to those both inside and outside the town, while also reinforcing the symbolic exclusion of those whose heads were on display.

Perhaps the most tantalizing aspect of the human remains from the 1974–81 Dublin excavations is their potential to provide some insight into differing cultural perceptions of the body and attitudes to death. The tenth-/eleventh-century skulls were deposited at a time when there was a significant cultural gulf separating the inhabitants of the colonial enclave at Dublin from their indigenous neighbours. The annalistic references to decapitation suggest that for the native Irish, the severed head provided a means of gaining power over one's enemies. In the Scandinavian tradition, as expressed for example in the thirteenth century in the *Sigrdrífumál* in the *Codex Regius*, mantic abilities are ascribed to disembodied heads. This suggests a perspective in which the severed head was perceived as a potential source of power in itself. In this light, it is perhaps conceivable that the heads (whether on public display or buried) at the northern boundary of tenth-/eleventh-century Dublin had multiple meanings to the inhabitants of the settlement. Vanquished foes could concurrently have been perceived as respected adversaries, while graphic warnings to potential enemies or dissidents could also have been understood as apotropaic talismans.

BIBLIOGRAPHY

Connolly, M. & F. Coyne, with L.G. Lynch. 2005. *Underworld: death and burial in Cloghermore cave, Co. Kerry* (Bray).

Fanning, T. 1994. *Viking-Age ringed pins from Dublin* (Dublin).

Geraghty, S. 1996. *Viking Dublin: botanical evidence from Fishamble Street* (Dublin).

Halpin, A. 2000. *The port of medieval Dublin: archaeological excavation at the Civic Offices, Winetavern Street, Dublin, 1993* (Dublin).

Heckett, E.W. 2003. *Viking-Age headcoverings from Dublin* (Dublin).

Lang, J.T. 1988. *Viking-Age decorated wood: a study of its ornament and style* (Dublin).

McCutcheon, C. 2006. *Medieval pottery from Wood Quay, Dublin* (Dublin).

Mitchell, G.F. 1987. *Archaeology and the environment in early Dublin* (Dublin).

O'Brien, E. 1998. 'The location and context of Viking-Age burials at Kilmainham and Islandbridge, Dublin' in H.B. Clarke, M. Ní Mhaonaigh & R. Ó Floinn (eds), *Ireland and Scandinavia in the Early Viking Age* (Dublin), pp 203–21.

O'Donnabhain, B. forthcoming. The human remains from the Dublin excavations 1974–1981.

Sikora, M. 2003/4 'Diversity in Viking-Age horse burial: a comparative study of Norway, Iceland, Scotland and Ireland', *Journal of Irish Archaeology*, 12–13, 87–110.

Simpson, L. 1999. 'Director's findings: Temple Bar West. Dublin', *Temple Bar Archaeological Report*, 5.

Simpson, L. 2005. 'Viking warrior burials in Dublin: is this the longphort?' in S. Duffy (ed.), *Medieval Dublin VI* (Dublin), pp 11–62.

Wallace, P.F. 1992. *The Viking-Age buildings of Dublin* (Dublin).

Surtshellir: a fortified outlaw cave in West Iceland

GUÐMUNDUR ÓLAFSSON, KEVIN P. SMITH & THOMAS McGOVERN

INTRODUCTION

In recent years, $c.500$ Icelandic lava caves have been discovered, explored and mapped. More than 200 of these have produced some form of evidence for human occupation or activities, dating from the time of Iceland's initial settlement to the present day (Björn Hróarsson 2006). While many caves appear to have been used as animal sheds, archaeological remains in others suggest that these were used for human occupation over longer or shorter periods of time. Hidden entrances, fireplaces, sleeping alcoves and middens suggest that some may have been temporary hide-outs for outlaws. A smaller number have internal fortifications or other structures that suggest larger, more permanent or more contested occupations. Only two such caves had received some archaeological attention prior to the investigations discussed in this paper (Gísli Gestsson 1960; Guðmundur Ólafsson 2000; Sigurður Sveinn Jónsson and Björn Hróarsson 1992).

Gísli Gestsson's pioneering cave research at Hallmundarhellir, in the inner reaches of the western Icelandic Hallmundarhraun lava flow, demonstrated the potential for intact and unusual archaeological deposits to exist in the forbidding subterranean environments of Iceland's lava tubes. At Hallmundarhellir, Gestsson (1960) recorded dividing walls, partitions, hearths and a small assemblage of artefacts and bones hidden behind a massive wall that blocked the mouth of this sand-choked lava cave.

Further west in the Hallmundarhraun lava field, near its terminal end, investigations in the Víðgelmir cave in 1993 documented ephemeral features and a small assemblage of artefacts and faunal remains suggestive of a short visit by a small number of occupants intent on remaining hidden. These investigations, presented at the fourteenth Viking Congress in 2001, also provided strong evidence that charcoal from the settlement period, apparently gathered from very old standing trees or well-preserved logs and branches, could be up to 200 years older than the actual site they were taken from, providing an explanation for mysteriously 'old dates' from the Settlement period of Iceland (Guðmundur Ólafsson 2005, 204–6).

In 2001, an expedition by the National Museum of Iceland and Brown University explored the 3.5km long Surtshellir Cave, the longest lava cave in

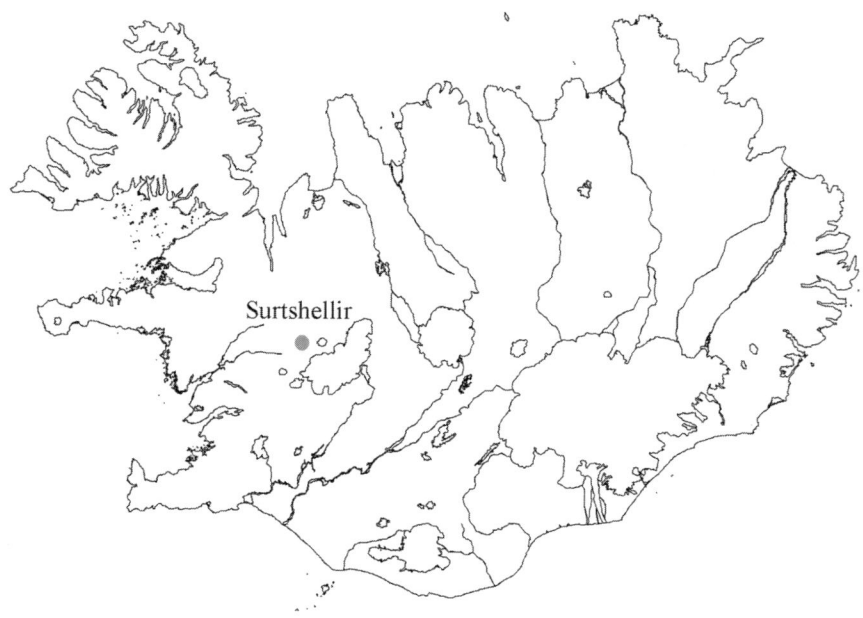

28.1 Location of Surtshellir in Iceland.

Iceland and one of seven caves known within the Hallmundarhraun lavaflow of West Iceland (Guðmundur Ólafsson et al. 2004; Fig. 28.1). This expedition sought to document traces of stone constructions within the cave, described periodically from the seventeenth century onward, but never scientifically explored, and to investigate reports that visitors were removing bones from deposits within the cave.

EARLY INHABITANTS OF SURTSHELLIR

The name Surtshellir means, variously, the 'Black Cave' or the 'Cave of Surtur', a powerful fire giant according to Norse mythology (Þórhallur Vilmundarson 1983, 124–5). Surtshellir is mentioned several times in Icelandic medieval literature and seems to have been well-known as a threatening place, inhabited by giants or outlaws.

According to the twelfth-century text *Landnámabók*, the first settler of Surtshellir was thought to be the giant Surtur. In the tenth century, however, two brothers named Þórarinn and Auðunn Smiðkelssynir became the leaders of an outlaw band, which was said to have occupied the cave. Eighteen outlaws from Surtshellir were reported to have been killed by local farmers in an ambush (*Landnámabók*, 75, 240).

In the fourteenth-century *Harðarsaga*, an outlaw is said to have fled from a fight with farmers near Hvalfjörður, to have taken refuge in Surtshellir with six other outlaws and then to have gathered more outlaws in the cave with him. They were finally driven away and later killed (*Harðarsaga*: 81–2). It is unclear whether the incidents described in *Landnámabók* and *Harðarsaga* represent separate episodes of outlaw activity or different accounts reflecting the same period of regional distress, as is suggested in the nineteenth-century *Hellismanna saga*, where Surtshellir is identified as the base of an outlaw band that fortified the cave in the late tenth century, preying on the surrounding countryside until routed by a coalition of local chieftains (*Hellismanna saga*: 399–466).

Surtshellir also plays an interesting role in *Sturlunga saga*. After taking his cousin and enemy Órækja, son of Snorri Sturluson, captive, Sturla Sighvatsson takes him in July 1236 on a 30km trip from Reykholt to Surtshellir to humiliate and punish him. He has him castrated and blinded *upp á virkið* ('on the top of the fortress': *Sturlunga saga*, 380–1). Which location this text means, whether a fortification wall or that part of Surtshellir that is today called Vígishellir ('fortified cave'), can be debated, but clearly the existence of a fortress in the cave was well known in the thirteenth century, and was considered to be the proper place for undertaking such a foul deed.

A closer look at outlaws in the Icelandic sagas shows that they were considered to be a serious problem, especially in the tenth century. Many raids on farmers' livestock by large groups of outlaws are described. The most notorious gang of outlaws is described in *Harðar saga*, where it is said that forty outlaws had stolen eighty wethers in one raid, and in another raid sixty outlaws tried to steal a herd of cows and bulls. In most sagas, this raiding goes on until the farmers finally get fed up and kill the outlaws. Outlaw stories usually follow the same pattern and even if it is often hard to separate legend from reality, they undoubtedly reflect some truth (*Harðar saga*, 74–5; Jón Árnason 1864, 300–4).

ARCHAEOLOGICAL EXCAVATION IN SURTSHELLIR

As previously mentioned, the presence of a fortification is implied in the written record and other remains, deeper in the cave, have been known for centuries. However, while the structural remains and midden deeper in the cavern were described as early as the 1600s, the fortification wall has never been described in detail and has, until recently, been covered through the summer by snow drifts that enter the cave through a collapsed portion of the ceiling. Even in the summer of 2000, it was entirely buried beneath snowdrifts, but warmer weather in the summer of 2001 exposed the wall completely.

In 2001 the first archaeological expedition into Surtshellir was undertaken to check on the condition of remains in the cave. Easy access to the cave has made it a popular tourist attraction, and rumours were circulating that the large pile of

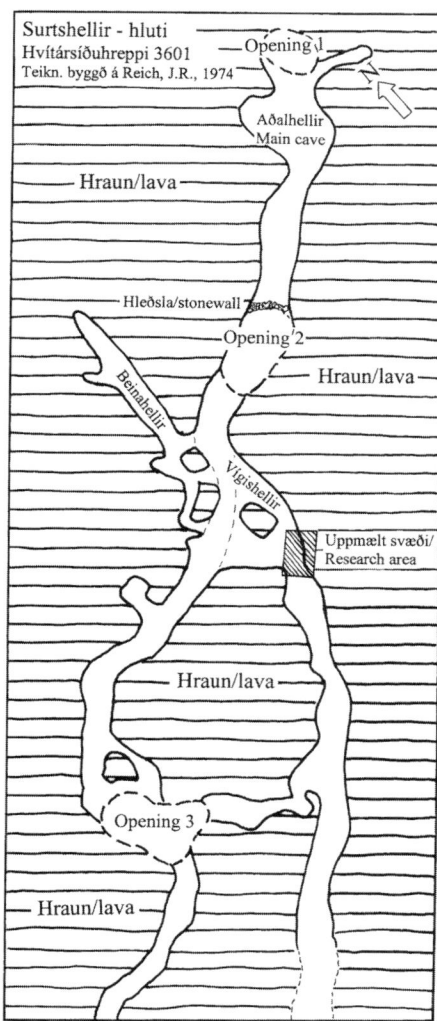

Surtshellir - hluti
Hvítársíðuhreppi 3601
Teikn. byggð á Reich, J.R., 1974

Opening 1

Aðalhellir
Main cave

Hraun/lava

Hleðsla/stonewall

Opening 2

Hraun/lava

Beinahellir

Vígishellir

Uppmælt svæði/
Research area

Hraun/lava

Opening 3

Hraun/lava

28.2 Plan of the Surtshellir cave and the research area (Guðmundur Ólafsson).

bones described by earlier explorers had disappeared into the pockets of souvenir hunters. As we entered the cave and transited its first roofed section, we were surprised to find our route blocked by a heavily built, dry-stone wall stretching across the width of the cave where we had earlier been required to climb a snowfield.

Bringing in a generator and good lights, the cave was properly lit for the first time in a thousand years. The dwelling area in a side cavern was mapped (Fig. 28.2) and part of its associated midden was excavated. Analyses of the finds have been conducted by the authors of this paper and radiocarbon dates have been analyzed by Árný Sveinbjörnsdóttir and Jan Heinemeier from the Aarhus-Reykjavik AMS-laboratory (Fig. 28.3).

While Víðgelmir was a short-term temporary hideout for one or two men, Surtshellir was a permanent dwelling for many men. The 3.5km long cave has three openings, each roughly 100m apart, formed by collapse of the ceiling.

A FORTIFICATION WALL

The stone wall stretches more than 13m across the width of the cave just before the second opening in its roof, c. 100m into the cave (Fig. 28.4). It still stands, in places, to a height of more than 2m and may originally have been higher, judging from the extent of the boulder field beside it. It is partly covered by blocks of rock fallen from the roof and from the collapse of the cave's ceiling behind it, indicating that the wall is older than the collapse and pre-dates the opening in the roof. At the top of the wall there are later additions, or a collapsed wall, said by

28.3 Graph showing radiocarbon dates, from charcoal and bones from a fireplace, in Surtshellir cave, in comparison to the age of the Lavaflow and the so-called Settlement layer (Árný Sveinbjarnardóttir, Jan Heinemeier, Guðmundur Ólafsson).

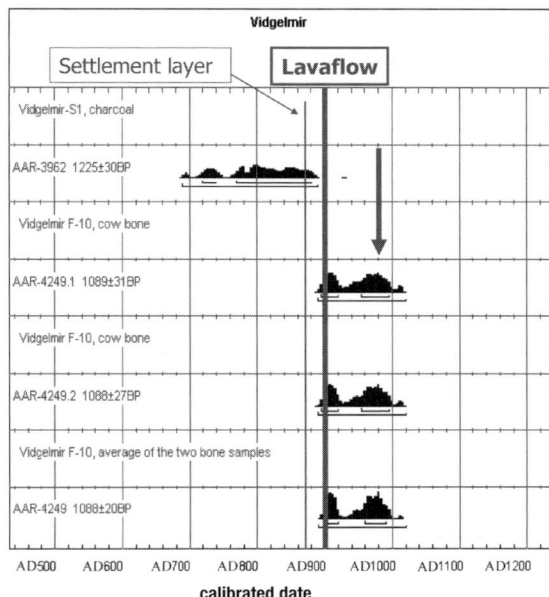

local informants to have been started in the mid-twentieth century above the earlier construction. Areas of concrete and iron rebar within smaller stones, loosely piled, make the identification of this later building episode quite simple. The original wall is well-built of large boulders laid so that their flat surfaces face forward to create a sheer, defensible wall. The amount of labour and effort that had to go into the construction of this wall suggests that it is the work of many men and that it probably served as a fortification to stop intruders. With the roof still standing and the wall stretching across its width in pitch darkness beyond the reach of light from the cave's natural entrance, the cave behind the wall would have been almost impenetrable.

Another indicator that the roof collapsed after the wall was built is that it would not have made sense to put up a fortification wall in this place if the opening was there, with the defenders having their rear open to attackers from above. This is also supported by the fact that collapse is still in progress, and many examples of recent collapse can be found throughout the cave.

SUBTERRANEAN HOUSE

Beyond the second opening in the roof, side galleries branch off the main cave, roughly 7.5m above the floor of the central passage. To the left is the so-called 'bone cave', which is said to have once had a huge pile of bones, now completely gone. To the right is the fortified cave, *Vigishellir*, which seems to have been the main dwelling area, with a stone building and a bone-rich midden (Fig. 28.5).

28.4 Part of the fortification wall, Surtshellir cave.

The presence of bone piles and a stone-walled structure in Surtshellir have been recorded since the seventeenth century (Eggert Ólafsson 1981, 137–46), and a single radiocarbon date was obtained from a cattle bone fragment in 1969 by the Icelandic author Halldór Laxness. These fragmentary records have been used in the past to suggest archaeological support for the historical narratives. However, the calibrated age of Laxness's date spans the entire Settlement and Commonwealth periods (AD870–1264) and could, therefore, reference activities undertaken at any point in the Early Middle Ages. Furthermore, in the absence of any detailed archaeological record of the cave's cultural features, no framework existed for protecting its archaeological resources, assessing the nature of the activities that once took place in Surtshellir, or comparing its deposits with those from other Icelandic sites associated with outlaw activity through historic references or archaeological inferences.

The stone-built structure in Vígishellir has some similarities in shape to the Viking-Age hall, with one side slightly curved (Fig. 28.6). It has, however, no central fireplace or long-hearth. This subterranean house is 7m long, 3.5m wide at the centre, and 2m wide at both gables. The walls, built of large boulders, stand up to 1m high. In some parts they are not very well built and may have been tampered with or restored in later times. Apparently, however, the walls have never been any higher and nothing indicates supports for a roof. While the house

28.5 Plan of the stone building with curved wall, a gable-end fireplace and the bone- midden in Vígishellir (Guðmundur Ólafsson).

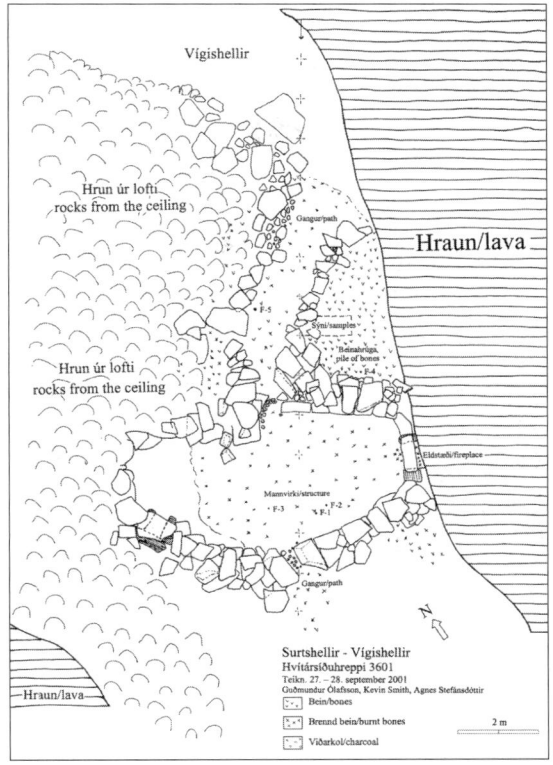

may have had a tent-like roof, it remains unclear why one would need a roof inside a cave, except, perhaps, to protect personnel and goods from dripping water. But why would one need a house in a cave anyway? Given that the Hallmundarhraun lava flowed just a few decades before the site was occupied, the lava would most likely have been comfortably warm. The house does not seem to be necessary as fortification. It is possible that it was a practical shelter inside the cave, but perhaps it functioned more as a symbolic gesture and was mainly built because of the inhabitant's psychological need to live in a house, even if it was not really needed inside the cave. The house is, after all, built across the width of the passage in which it is located, potentially closing off access to deeper parts of that passage. Interestingly, according to new speleological discoveries, this is not the only subterranean house that has been found in Icelandic caves. At least two other stone examples have been found, although they are from much later periods and are of different shape (Björn Hróarsson 2006).

The building has two entrances: one leading into the house from the main part of the cave system and the other leading into deeper parts of the cave behind the house, where no remains have yet been found. The fireplace seems to have been built into the gable and the floor is the lava rock covered, in part, by a very thin cultural layer comprised of ash, minuscule burnt bone fragments and few jasper

28.6 Overview of the building with curved walls and a gable-end fireplace (photo: Kevin P. Smith).

fire-starter splinters. The floor of the house seems to have been kept fairly clean and tidy. Instrumental Neutron Activation analyses of the jasper fire-starters show that they included fragments with trace-element geochemistries consistent with those recorded from local or regional West Icelandic jasper sources, as well as others whose chemical signatures suggest that they came from sources elsewhere in Iceland. In contrast, jasper fire-starters from the smaller outlaw shelter, Viðgelmir, and from the tenth-century iron production complex at Háls, 20km southeast of Surtshellir (Smith 2005), have each produced jasper assemblages with more homogeneous jasper geochemistries. The diversity of the jasper recovered from Surtshellir, despite the small size of the sample recovered in 2001, may imply that the cave's occupants came from a more disparate and diverse set of home districts, or that the cave was occupied several times by groups arriving from different regions, or a combination of these possibilities.

BONE-MIDDEN

To the northwest of the house is a bone-rich midden, 3.7m long and 2m wide (Fig. 28.7). A 1m long and 50cm wide trench was cut through the bone pile in 2001 and all recovered material was collected as bulk samples that were dry-screened through nested 4mm and 1mm screens, with the fine sediments retained for micro-artefact recovery.

28.7 The surface of the Vígishellir midden (photo: Kevin P. Smith).

The bone layer, when excavated, was only 7cm thick, but traces on the wall behind indicated that the pile of bones had originally been *c.*50cm thick. Bones at the surface are extremely well preserved, although they were all very fragmented as the occupants most likely obtained and utilized the marrow inside, even from the least marrow-producing bones. The bones showed severe butchery marks, but no gnawing marks by dogs.

Of the *c.*7500 bone fragments collected, 372 could be identified to species. Of these, ninety-four were cattle bones, twenty-seven were pig bones, fourteen were horse bones, with the remainder derived from goats and sheep. When compared to faunal collections from other Icelandic Viking-Age farmsites (Fig. 28.8), the mix of domestic animal bones present at Vígishellir shows a distribution pattern very similar to that of a fairly prosperous Settlement-Age farm. But when *all* of the major identified taxa are considered, the Vígishellir collection is exceptional – no other Icelandic collection from any period consists entirely of domestic mammals, and many Settlement-Age collections are instead dominated by wild species. This indicates a consumption pattern that is totally reliant on domestic animals for food. Those who accumulated this midden were not hunting or gathering food as other Viking-Age farmers were doing. Everything points to this being an outlaw settlement, not participating in any social activity, but stealing animals from the local farmers.

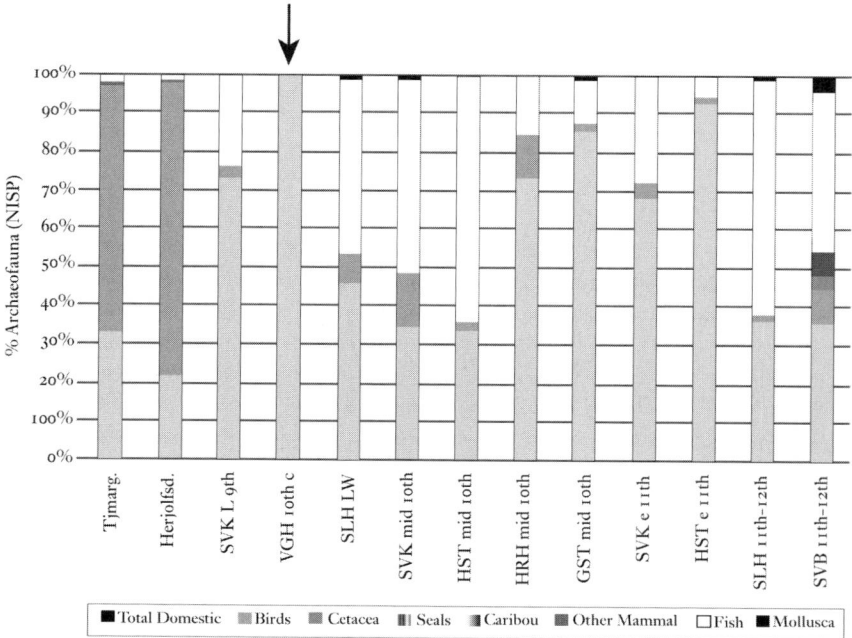

28.8 Proportions of domestic and wild taxa in quantifiable ninth- to twelfth-century
Icelandic archaeofaunas.

A comparison of the remains in the Viking-Age hideout caves in Víðgelmir
and Surtshellir shows that even though they are both arguably outlaw shelters
and were both occupied in the tenth century, they are very different sites. One
was used for only a few days; the other maybe several months or years. One
probably represents the activities of a single individual; the other indicates the
residue of many actions undertaken by group of people. Yet even if the occupants
of both caves preyed on neighbouring farms by stealing their livestock, it seems
that they tried to maintain a typical Viking farmer's lifestyle. These sites give us
a glimpse into the lives of outcasts in Viking-Age society.

DATING

The bone-rich deposit in Vígishellir can be dated both indirectly through
tephrochronology and directly through radiocarbon dating (Fig. 28.9). The lava
field in which Surtshellir and Vígishellir formed, Hallmundarhraun, rests above
the *landnám* tephra layer (Jóhannesson 1989), which has been independently
dated to AD871+/-2 (Grönvold et al. 1995). Two AMS radiocarbon dates (AAR-
7412 and AAR-7413) run on collagen from cattle bones collected in 2001 imply
a date for the deposit of AD690–960.

AAR–7412 (top layer)
1214±41 BP [AMS, *Bos taurus* bone fragment]
One sigma (68.2% probability)   calAD 770–890
Two sigma (95.4% probability)   calAD 680–950 [*680–900 (92.7%)*,
                                  920–950 (2.7%)]

AAR–7413 (basal layer)
1197±36 BP [AMS, *Bos taurus* bone fragment]
One sigma (68.2% probability)   calAD 770–890
Two sigma (95.4% probability)   calAD 710–960 [*710–750 (5.8%)*, *760–900*
                                  (82.6%), *920–960 (7.0%)*]

K–1435 (Laxness 1969)
1010±100 BP [Standard, *Bos taurus* bone fragment]
One sigma (68.2% probability)   calAD 900–1160 [*890–920 (5.4%)*,
                                  950–1160 (62.8%)]
Two sigma (95.4% probability)   calAD 780–1240 [*780–792 (0.9%)*,
                                  804–1223 (94.2%) 1233–1237 (0.3%)]

28.9 Radiocarbon dates from Vígishellir cave, Iceland.

With the *landnám* tephra providing a firm *terminus post quem* for the formation of the cave itself, the bone-bearing deposits tested in 2001 can be dated to the period AD880–960 with a high degree of certainty. Although these two AMS dates – on bones from the top and bottom layers of the thin deposit examined in 2001 – cannot be statistically separated, suggesting a rapid accumulation of the sampled portion of the midden, the standard radiocarbon date run on a cow bone by Halldór Laxness (1971) has a somewhat later calibrated age (Fig. 28.9: K–1435). While it is unknown whether Laxness's sample was recovered from the deposits sampled in 2001, from higher levels of the same midden, since removed, or even from deposits found in the now-empty *Beinahellir* gallery within Surtshellir, that date overlaps both of the new AMS age-ranges at two standard deviations. Together, the three dates support a late ninth- or tenth-century date that is generally consistent with the period of outlaw activity noted in medieval accounts.

QUERIES AND INTERPRETATIONS

Surtshellir is an unusual Viking-Age Icelandic site. Place-names within the cave, coupled with the documented archaeological features and deposits, suggest a relatively extensive and complex suite of archaeological remains including fortifications, a subterranean house, middens, and extremely thin and fragile occupation deposits. The main habitation zone is located *c.*200m from the cave's entrance, well beyond the penetration of any natural light. Separated from the entrance passages by a massive fortification wall and located in a hidden side passage, the house and its associated midden were obviously not meant to be accessible places. The thickness of the original midden layer, as indicated by remnants on the cave wall, shows that it must have accumulated over some time. AMS dates confirm a late ninth- or tenth-century date for the bone-bearing deposits, while the form of the adjacent structure bears some similarities to known Viking-Age halls. The massive wall spanning the main tunnel, the presence of fire-starter fragments from diverse and perhaps distant origins, and the unusual archaeofauna recovered from Vígishellir all match reasonably well with correlates one might reasonably derive from medieval accounts of the lairs of outlaw bands.

The 2001 archaeofauna from Vígishellir, while small and fragmented, shows both similarities with and differences from other known Icelandic Settlement-Age and Early Commonwealth samples. It would be anomalous (except in relative proportions of domestic mammals) even if it did not come from a cave with such a colourful legend. It lacks any of the fish, birds and shellfish common on Settlement-Age sites in Iceland, suggesting that the cave's occupants were not reduced to scavenging wild resources despite the site's marginal location – 10–15m underground in a lava field on the fringes of Iceland's uninhabitable interior highland.

Recent work indicates that farms 60km or more from the coast were regularly provisioned with preserved marine fish, sea birds and mammals, raw materials and other critical resources from the Settlement Period onwards (Smith 1995; 2004; 2005; Amundsen et al. 2005). If the cave's occupants were indeed outlaws, they may have been cut off from regular access to some resources because they no longer had access to the social networks that allowed such provisioning. Yet the mix of domestic mammals present suggests that the cave's occupants had the ability to acquire a wide range of domestic stock from surrounding farms, due perhaps to their success as raiders or to their support, willing or coerced, from nearby farms. Newborn calf bones, common in farm middens, are missing from this assemblage, and this may point to either seasonality in their raiding activity, problems in capturing young animals normally kept within farmyards, or a simple focus on adult animals that could provide more meat when slaughtered. Similarly, the site's apparent surplus of meat-rich long bones could reflect the butchery of some captured animals away from the cave, or raids on farm smoke-houses or meat stores. And yet the pattern of bone fragmentation also suggests that while the cave's occupants may have enjoyed considerable success in carrying off domestic stock, they had to process animal carcasses completely for meat, marrow, and bone grease. Perhaps they were attempting to get the most out of the animals they caught because they lacked other food sources (dairy produce, fish, birds, cereals), or possibly they attempted to limit their exposure to community retaliation by spacing their raids apart as widely as possible. Given the density of this midden, its composition and its reported larger size in previous times, it would appear that the occupants of the cave must have had a heavy impact on the economies of the farms around them.

CONCLUSION

The remains in the Surtshellir cave represent the work of a group of people who occupied the cave for some time during the tenth century. They put considerable efforts into building a massive fortification to ensure that no one could get to them and they built a subterranean house – possibly the oldest still-standing Viking-Age house in the world – which suggests that they planned to stay there for a long time. They lived only on domestic animals, most likely stolen from neighbouring farms, and must have put a lot of pressure on the surrounding region's economy. The material evidence from Surtshellir suggests that this unusual site was a Viking-Age shelter for a significantly large group of outlaws, matching quite well the Surtshellir legends recorded in the sagas and in *Landnámabók*.

Yet this is only part of the story. While Vígishellir's occupants built significant structures and dined on the meatiest portions of many animals, crushing their bones while burning few and carefully separating the burned from the unburned, these patterns differ significantly from those recorded at Víðgelmir, another probable outlaw shelter in the same lava field. At Víðgelmir, an untidy scatter of burned and unburned bones, tossed unsorted around a small unframed hearth on a hidden ledge, testifies to a short stay, perhaps lasting no more than a few days, by one or two people eating the least desirable portions of a cow (Eggert Ólafsson 2000). That these two nearly contemporaneous sites, located no more than 5–6km from one another, are so different suggests at the very least that the archaeological records of outlaws and cave sites in Iceland may be more complex than we currently realize.

BIBLIOGRAPHY

Amundsen, C.P., S. Perdikaris, T.H. McGovern, Y. Krivogorskaya, M. Brown, K. Smiarowski, S. Storm, S. Modugno, M. Frik & M. Koczela. 2005. 'Fishing booths and fishing strategies in medieval Iceland: an archaeofauna from the site of Akurvík, north-west Iceland', *Environmental Archaeology*, 10:2, 126–46.

Bigelow G.F. 1985. 'Sandwick, Unst, and the Late Norse Shetlandic economy' in B. Smith (ed.), *Shetland archaeology: new work in Shetland in the 1970s* (Lerwick), pp 95–127.

Björn Hróarsson. 1990. *Hraunhellar á Íslandi* (Reykjavík).

Björn Hróarsson. 2006. *Hellar á Íslandi I–II* (Reykjavík).

Eggert Ólafsson. 1981. *Ferðabók Eggerts Ólafssonar og Bjarna Pálssonar*, um ferðir þeirra á Íslandi árin 1752–1757, 1 (Reykjavík).

Enghoff, I.B. 2003. *Hunting, fishing and animal husbandry at the Farm Beneath the Sand, Western Greenland: an archaeozoological analysis of a Norse farm in the Western Settlement*, Meddelelser om Grønland: Man & Society, 28 (Copenhagen).

Gísli Gestsson. 1960. 'Hallmundarhellir', *Árbók hins Íslenzka Fornleifafélags*, 1960, 76–82.

Gísli Konráðsson. 1946. *Hellismanna saga* in Guðni Jónsson (ed.). *Íslendinga sögur II:* 399–466 (Reykjavík).

Grant, A. 1982. 'The use of tooth wear as a guide to the age of domestic ungulates' in B. Wilson, C. Grigson & S. Payne (eds), *Ageing and sexing animal bones from archaeological sites*, British Archaeological Reports, British Series, 109 (Oxford), pp 91–108.

Guðmundur Ólafsson, K.P Smith & A. Stefánsdóttir. 2004. *Rannsókn á minjum í Surtshelli*, Rannsóknaskýrslur Þjóðminjasafns, 2001, 8 (Reykjavík).

Guðmundur Ólafsson, T.H. McGovern & K.P. Smith. 2006. 'Outlaws of Surtshellir cave: the underground economy of Viking-Age Iceland' in J. Arneborg & B. Grönnov (eds), *Dynamics of northern societies: proceedings of the SILA/NABO conference on Arctic and North Atlantic archaeology, Copenhagen, May 10th–14th, 2004* (Copenhagen), pp 395–405.

Guðmundur Ólafsson. 2000. 'Fylgsnið í hellinum Víðgelmi', *Árbók hins Íslenzka Fornleifafélags*, 1998, 125–42.

Guðmundur Ólafsson. 2005. 'New evidence for the dating of Iceland's settlement: a Viking-Age discovery in the cave Víðgelmir' in A. Mortensen & S.V. Arge, *Vikings and Norse in the North Atlantic: select papers from the proceedings of the Fourteenth Viking Congress, Tórshavn, 19–30 July 2001* (Tórshavn), pp 200–7.

Halldór Kiljan Laxness. 1949. 'Lítil samantekt um útilegumenn', *Tímarit Máls og menningar* (May 1949), 86–130.

Halldór Laxness. 1971. *Yfirskyggðir staðir. Ýmsar athuganir. Aldur hellismanna* (Reykjavík), 96–105.

Haukur Jóhannesson. 1989. *Aldur Hallmundarhrauns í Borgarfirði*, Fjölrit Náttúruf-ræðistofnunar, 9 (Reykjavík).

Hermann Pálsson and P. Edwards (trans.). 1972. *The Book of Settlements (Landnámabók)*, University of Manitoba Icelandic Studies, 1 (Winnipeg).

Harðar saga = Þórhallur Vilmundarson and Bjarni Vilhjálmsson (eds). 1991. *Harðar saga*, Íslenzk fornrit, 13 (Reykjavík).

Hellismannasaga = Jón Árnason (ed.). 1864. *Þjóðsögur og ævintýri*, 2 (Leipzig), 300–4.

Karl Grönvold et al. 1995. 'Ash layer from Iceland in the Greenlandic GRIP ice core correlated with oceanic and land sediments', *Earth and Planetary Science Letters*, 135, 149–55.

Lyman, R.L. 1996. *Taphonomy* (Cambridge).

Matthías Þórðarson. 1910. 'Tveir hellar í Hallmundarhrauni', *Skírnir*, 84, 331–51.

McGovern, T.H. 1992. 'Bones, buildings, and boundaries: paleoeconomic approaches to Norse Greenland' in C.D. Morris & J. Rackham (eds), *Norse and later settlement and subsistence in the North Atlantic* (Glasgow), pp 157–86.

McGovern T.H., S. Perdikaris & C. Tinsley. 2001. 'Economy of landnám: the evidence of zooarchaeology' in A. Wawn & Þórunn Sigurðardóttir (eds), *Approaches to Vínland*, Sigurður Nordal Institute Studies, 4 (Reykjavík), pp 154–66.

McGovern, T.H. and S. Perdikaris. 2002. Preliminary report of animal bones from Hrísheimar, N. Iceland. Report on file with Fornleifastofnun Íslands and National Museum of Iceland (Reykjavík).

Outram, A.K. 1999. 'A comparison of Palaeoeskimo and medieval Norse bone fat exploitation in Western Greenland', *Arctic Anthropology*, 36:1, 103–17.

Perdikaris, S., C. Amundsen & T.H. McGovern. 2002. Report of animal bones from Tjarnargata 3C, Reykjavík, Iceland. Report on file with Fornleifastofnun Íslands (Reykjavík).

Sigurður Sveinn Jónsson & Björn Hróarsson. 1992. 'Fornminjar í íslenskum hraunhellum', *Surtur, ársrit Hellarannsóknafélags Íslands* (1992), 10–22.

Smith, K.P. 1995. '*Landnám*: the settlement of Iceland in archaeological and historical perspective', *World Archaeology*, 26:3, 319–47.

Smith, K.P. 2004. 'Independent people, householders and outlaws: reconciling economic autonomy, political centralization, and trade in medieval Iceland' paper presented at the 69th Annual Meeting of the Society for American Archaeology, Montréal.

Smith, K.P. 2005. 'Ore, fire, hammer, sickle: iron production in Viking-Age and early medieval Iceland', in R. Bork with S. Montgomery, C. Neuman de Vegvar, E. Shortell & S. Walton (eds), *De Re Metallica: studies in medieval metals*, AVISTA Studies in the History of Medieval Technology, Science and Art, 4 (Aldershot), pp 183–206.

Stefán Aðalsteinsson. 1991. 'The importance of sheep in early Icelandic agriculture', *Acta Archaeologica*, 61, 285–91.

Sturlunga saga = Örnólfur Thórsson (ed.). 1988. *Sturlunga saga*, 1 (Reykjavík), 181–458.

Þórhallur Vilmundarson. 1983. 'Surtshellir', *Grímnir: Rit um nafnfræði*, 2, 124–5.

Women in early towns

INGVILD ØYE

INTRODUCTION

The role of women in early towns has long been a rather neglected field of research. What do we know about women's role in these societies? What did women do and how numerous were they? And did they play the same role in Viking-Age proto-towns as in more developed medieval urban communities? In this paper, I will take a closer look at these questions, focusing on Scandinavian early towns in the Viking Age and Early Middle Ages and on some of the archaeological finds that may reflect female crafts – textile-production equipment and textile production – and thus, indirectly, the presence of women. Shedding light on women may also shed light on the urban structure, demographically, economically and socially.

THE ROLE OF WOMEN IN URBAN LIFE

A common feature of the populations in both medieval and later towns is an imbalance between the sexes, often with a surplus of men (Boserup 1970; Øye 2005). It has, however, been claimed that women formed a normal part of the population in Viking-Age urban communities, taking full part in manufacturing and commercial transactions, mainly as wives of merchants and craftsmen who ran small family businesses (Jesch 1991, 39). The gender issue has not been analyzed on a broader basis or as a special topic, either for proto-towns or early medieval towns. By focusing on some archaeological finds that may reflect female crafts and their practitioners in early urban contexts, I will draw attention to the role of women in textile production, a function that may have been far more important in the early urban communities than has hitherto been taken into account. Here, Birka, Hedeby, Bergen, Oslo and Trondheim will be used as examples (Fig. 29.1).

SEX RATIO AND SOCIAL POSITION

In general, we have little direct source material relating to the sex ratio in early medieval Scandinavian towns. For the Viking Age, however, the burial material from surrounding cemeteries has been used as an important source. At Hedeby,

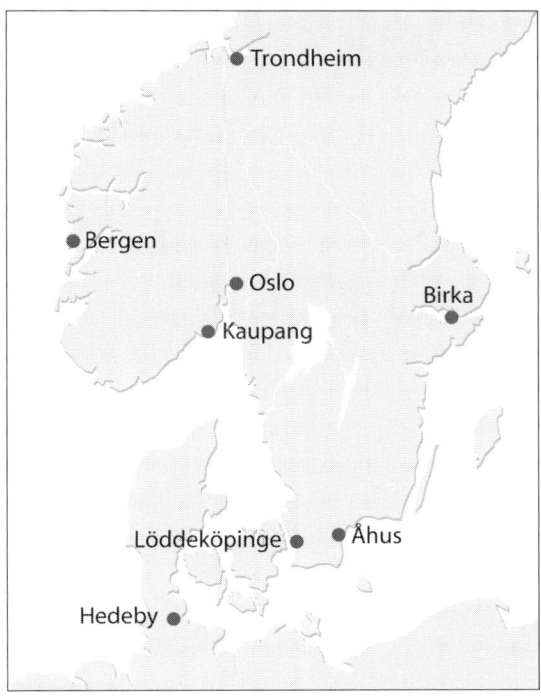

29.1 Locations referred to in the text.

for instance, a sample test yields an estimate of 38 per cent of the interred being women. According to Klavs Randsborg, women also had a lower average age of death than men (Randsborg 1980, 81). At Birka, the excavated graves that allowed an identification of gender indicated a distribution between the sexes actually in favour of women with a ratio of about 60:40. This high proportion may, however, be related to the fact that the graves of females are easier to recognize, as they contain more gender-specific finds, like jewellery. Even so, these results represent an extraordinary high proportion of buried women compared with burial customs in Viking-Age rural contexts. In Norway, the proportion is normally 1:5 in favour of men (Øye 2005, 82). Burials, then, can hardly be taken as a direct evidence for the actual sex ratio that prevailed. As not all members of society were granted monumental burials, they should, rather, be evaluated in a social context. The burials in the cemeteries around Birka and Hedeby, as well as at Kaupang in Norway (Blindheim and Heyerdahl-Larsen 1995; Stylegar 2007), do, however, reflect a mixed population, including children.

The social structure of the Birka population has been discussed by several scholars (see Gräslund 1980), to a greater extent than for the other Viking-Age towns. They have related the grave-finds to chieftains, rich merchants, ordinary people and thralls. A large number of the graves, considered to be more exclusive, are women's graves and it has been suggested that they may have been the wives of the merchants, many of them of Scandinavian origin (ibid., 80). But the

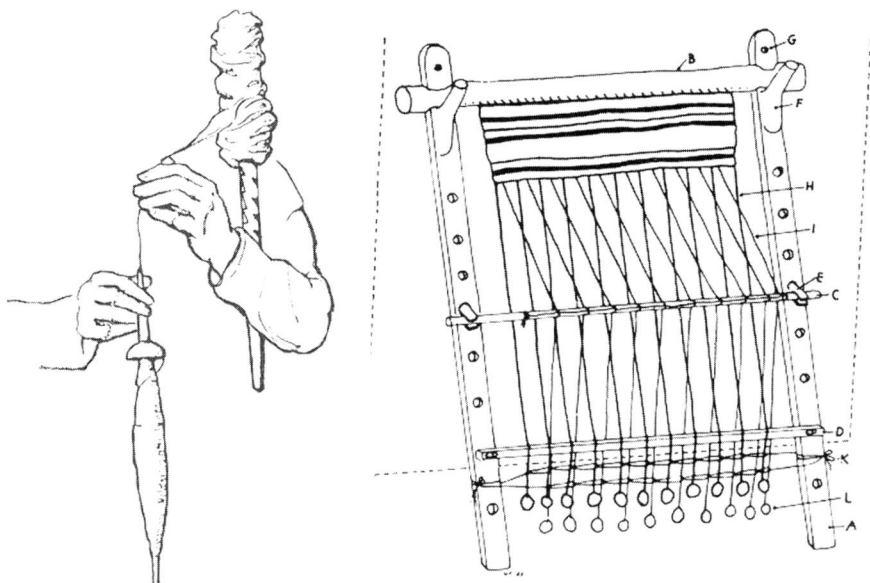

29.2 Spinning with a drop-spindle   29.3 The upright or warp-weighted loom
        (after Øye 1988).   (after M. Hoffmann 1964).

women may also have been active in commerce themselves; to a large extent, the graves that contained scales and weights were women's and even children's burials. Women's graves also contained textile-production equipment, but not always the same types as are found in the habitation areas (Andersson 2003), a finding that may also be of significance when looking at social status. My point of departure is that women's role in textile production may perhaps explain why many women apparently played such an important role in these early urban communities.

THE ROLE OF WOMEN IN TEXTILE PRODUCTION

The textile-production equipment from Birka and Hedeby, as well as that from Löddeköpinge and Åhus in Scania, have been analyzed by the Swedish archaeologist Eva Andersson (2000; 2003). Here, I shall draw on some of her results from a gender perspective, as the whole process of textile production – spinning and weaving on the warp-weighted upright loom, sewing, etc – seems to have been clearly defined as 'women's work' before it became an organized urban craft for male weavers (using the horizontal loom), tailors, fullers etc, in the High Middle Ages (cf. Øye 2005; 2006).

Andersson's analysis of the textile tools demonstrates that textile production in these early urban societies was both extensive and varied, and differed from

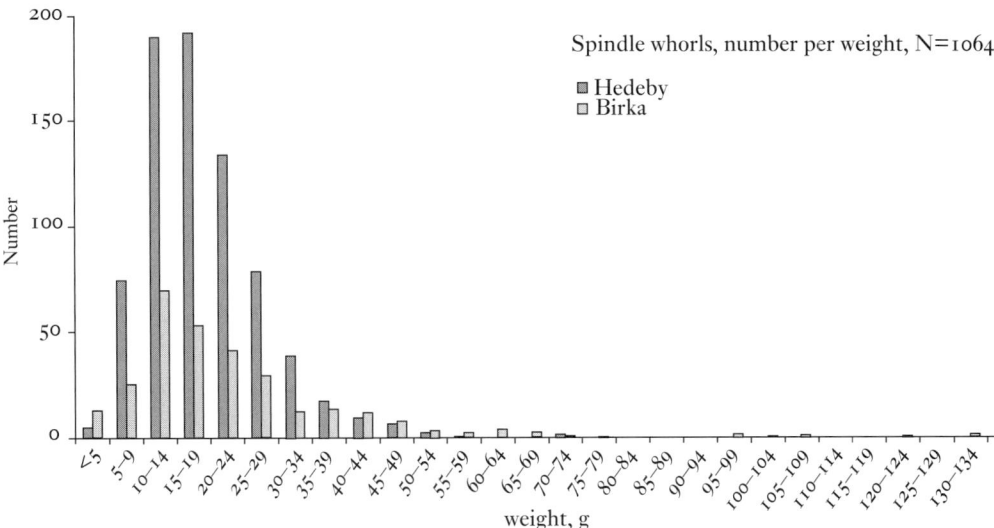

29.4 All registered spindle-whorls from Birka and Hedeby, according to weight (N=1064).

what is found in rural settlements. Although the equipment was rather simple – a couple of wool or linen combs, a few spindle-whorls of different sizes, sets of warp-weights for the upright loom and needles of different thicknesses were all that was needed to provide the textiles required for a household – the fine differences between the spindle-whorls and warp-weights and the variety in weight can be significant and reflect different types of quality and fabric (Figs 29.2–3). They are, therefore, also indicative of the degrees of specialization and standardization practised, and may therefore indirectly reflect women's roles either as producers for the household's own needs or, on a more specialized basis and on a larger scale, for wider groups of consumers.

Based on her analysis of textile tools found in Birka and Hedeby, Andersson claims that all types of textiles found in the burials – various qualities of woollen and linen cloth, from the most exclusive cloths to coarser fabrics – could have been produced at these sites. This is contrary to previous assumptions that local production in these places produced only coarse woollen cloth of poor quality (Andersson 2003, 53, 99).

Experiments have shown that the size and particularly the weight of spindle-whorls affect the type of thread produced. Even very small differences of 5g made a clear difference in the thickness of the yarn. The weight distribution of the spindle-whorls shows that all kinds of yarn were produced in several thicknesses, even the thinnest. With the lightest whorls (5–10g) it was possible to spin a very fine quality thread, but not the coarser ones (ibid., 25–6). When spinning with a whorl weighing 10–15g, the resulting thread is also very thin, provided that the raw material is fine-fibred. It is, therefore, interesting to note that the groups of whorls from which it was possible to spin very fine yarn are relatively well-represented in both Birka and Hedeby (Fig. 29.4). The weights of the spindle-whorls at both sites are concentrated around more or less the same weight groups. In Birka, the weights vary from less than 5g to 89g (with a few examples weighing more than 100g), while in Hedeby they vary from 4g to 75g. In Birka, whorls weighing between 5g and 29g are the most common, with a peak from 10g to 14g, while in Hedeby they are generally somewhat heavier, with whorls weighing between 10g and 25g forming the most common group, with a peak between 10g and 20g. At Hedeby, however, a clearer standardization of whorl morphology could be observed in terms of both size and weight, with many examples made on the same model with exactly the same shape, diameter and weight. Here, the large number of finds also indicates that production was on a large scale (ibid., 131).

The warp-weights also signify that different weights were used for different types of weave. Those that could be measured from Birka and Hedeby generally vary in weight between 200g and 1900g, with concentrations around 400–800g in Birka and between 300g and 600g in Hedeby.

Altogether, Andersson found that the textile-production equipment from urban contexts differs from that from rural sites, indicating a more standardized and specialized production, with a wider range of tools for producing a large range of qualities (2003, 135). Women, therefore, seem to have had a more specialized role in textile production in these communities than in ordinary rural households.

The majority of the dated textile-production equipment from Birka has been assigned to its latest settlement phases, 900–970, with most of it dating to the later phase, *c*.950–70 (Andersson 2003, 153). At Löddeköpinge, corresponding equipment is also concentrated in the late tenth century, going into the eleventh century. The production also seems to be more varied in the later phases. Textile production was most extensive when the settlement and activities were at their highest level (Andersson 2000). In Hedeby, however, the finds can only be dated to within a longer period of about 200 years. At Kaupang, a large amount of textile-production equipment has been found, of the same categories as those represented in Hedeby and Birka. This dates from its earliest phases to the middle of the tenth century, from the same period as the female burials in the surrounding cemeteries (Øye in press).

Generally, the finds of textile-production equipment derive from the whole habitation area in both Birka and Hedeby, and as yet there is no clear evidence that specific areas had workshops intended solely for textile production (Andersson 2003, 153). It appears that textile manufacturing, therefore, may have been connected with individual households. If that was the case, these were possibly extended kinds of households, probably with several single women. The find contexts at Löddeköpinge, however, show that many of the textile tools were directly related to sunken-floor huts, more than seventy in all, which were partly concentrated and partly scattered throughout the habitation area. As many as 80 per cent of the sunken huts contained textile-production equipment (Andersson 2000, 172–80), indicating that these were apparently workshops. Together, they represent a strong indication of specialized large scale production of textiles outside the household sphere. Sunken huts have also recently been found at Hedeby, but have not yet been investigated (von Carnap-Bornheim, pers. comm.). Proto-urban textile production, therefore, being on a larger scale and more specialized than that conducted in rural households, seems to have had a character of its own.

If we draw a parallel with the hierarchical and more organized textile production that prevailed further south in Europe in the same period (Herlihy 1990, 36), we will probably see a connection between textile production and women of lower rank. Since antiquity, the time-consuming and labour-intensive tasks of large-scale spinning and weaving had traditionally been performed by unmarried women of low rank, and many hands were needed to produce enough yarn and to weave the fabrics. Work was to a large extent carried out within gendered hierarchies and workplaces at that time, with women at both ends (ibid., 36, 60, 76; Øye 2006a).

Seen as primarily a female profession, textile production may also explain the relatively large representation of women in the urban burial assemblages noted above, since the women who organized and administered this work could have had a high status. The women who were given important burials probably represent this category. It may be indicative that warp-weights were not found in the Birka graves, while needle-boxes and more prestigious types of equipment were better represented in the burial deposits than in the Black Earth (Andersson 2003). Large-scale textile production needed a fair amount of administration and supervision, as well as a special competence for assessing the quality of the products. When cloth is used as a standard of value, it pre-supposes a certain degree of specialization and control in its manufacture, as expressed in the later Icelandic laws. Traditionally, husbandry and gardening that supplied the raw materials for textile production, also belonged to the female sphere (Øye 2005). It may well be the case, therefore, that both the administration and the whole economy of textile production were under female control. The heavy work of producing large sails, however, may have been a male activity during the Viking Age (Rabben 2002).

The demand for textiles of widely varying qualities, both prestigious and utilitarian products, including cloth, all kinds of clothes and garments, linen, tapestries, carpets, sails etc, must have been extensive in the new urban societies. The import of wool, flax and hemp from the surrounding countryside was therefore necessary. Experiments have shown that at least 6kg of wool was needed to produce two ordinary costumes of Viking-Age type for a couple. If a sheep yielded 1–2kg wool, then wool from between fifteen and thirty sheep was needed to spin enough yarn to produce ten new costumes. Still, it is possible that sheep yielded less wool, perhaps not more than half of this amount (Øye 2006b, 109 with references). For a sail of about 100m², about 75kg of the right quality wool was needed, requiring the shearing of about 225 sheep (Andersson 2003, 46–50), but perhaps as much as double that amount. Wool importation involved networks, economic transactions and an organization for distribution and storage. Women may have taken part in this industry, which apparently played an important role in Viking-Age towns.

WOMEN IN EARLY MEDIEVAL TOWNS

From the early part of the eleventh century, a marked increase in the market economy emerged in north-western Europe. The textile industry became increasingly professionalized and manufacturing was eventually taken over by men and organized through guilds (Goldberg 1992; Jacobsen 1995). How did these new conditions of large-scale manufacture and commerce affect domestic textile production and women's roles in the new urban communities of the Middle Ages?

Here I will briefly comment upon the development of textile production in three Norwegian early medieval towns, from their earliest stages to *c.*1250. I will make Bergen my starting-point as I have previously analyzed all of the medieval textile equipment from the largest excavated site there, Bryggen (Øye 1988). The Bryggen material contains more or less the same categories of equipment found at Hedeby and Birka and represents all processes, from the preparation of raw material to finished products. As at Birka and Hedeby there is a fairly high proportion of light spindle-whorls, with more than half of all the measurable spindle-whorls weighing between 5g and 20g indicating the spinning of light and fine yarn. Heavier examples also occurred, some even in excess of 150g, for the production of coarser thread (ibid., 40–1; Fig. 29.5a). There is also more variety in the material from Bergen than from rural contexts within the town's hinterland, and the same tendency is also revealed when the spindle-whorls from Viking-Age burials in Western Norway are considered (ibid., 52, 131). Turning to the warp-weights, the same weight groups are represented in Bergen as are evident at Birka and Hedeby, ranging from under 100g to more than 1300g, though 80 per cent of the weights weigh between 300g and 900g (ibid., 62–3).

The quantity of textile-production equipment from Oslo falls into more or less the same main categories as Bergen, with the spinning and weaving tools varying within more or less the same weight categories. Spindle-whorls range in weight from less than 5g to 64g, with the majority falling between 10g and 30g

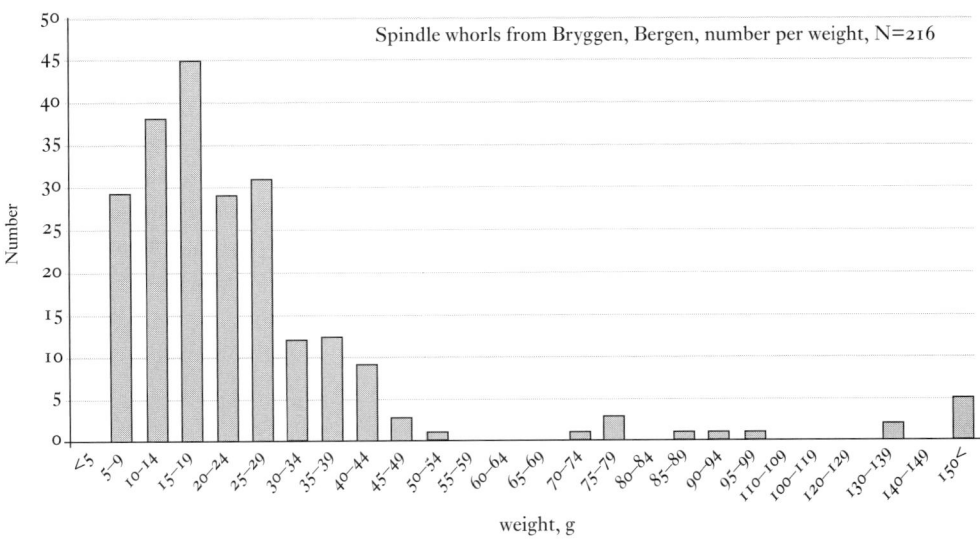

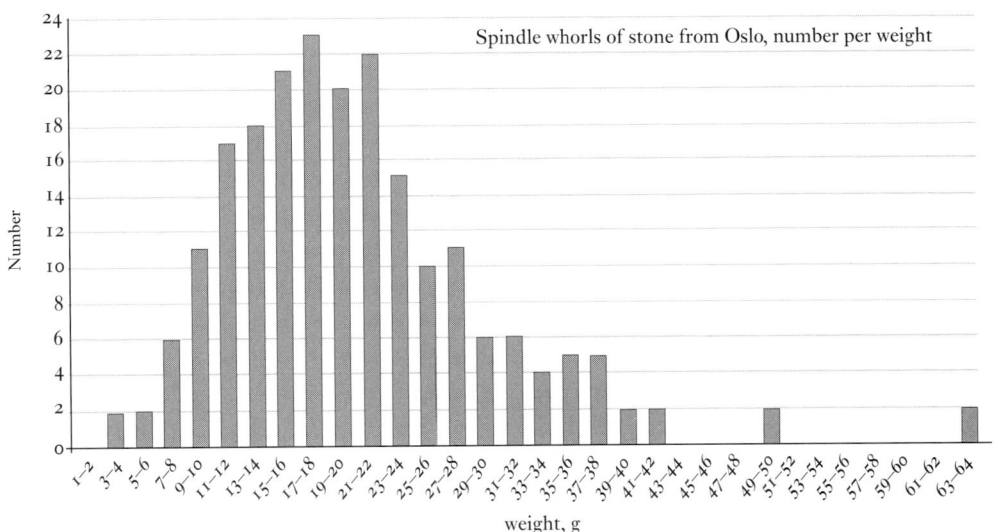

29.5 Weight distribution of measurable spindle-whorls from Bryggen (Bergen) (N=216; the whorls of wood are omitted) and Oslo (N=212; based on Molaug 1991, fig. 6a).

(Molaug 1991, 94; Fig. 29.5b). The warp-weights from Oslo normally weighed between 400g and 1300g, with most examples falling between 700g and 1100g (Rui 1991, 118–19), somewhat heavier than the Bergen material. In Trondheim, the textile-production equipment has been analyzed only on a quantitative basis (Nordeide 1994). The warp-weights have, however, been compared with the woven textiles to evaluate the quality of the production (Hagen 1994).

The temporal distribution of the finds indicates that textile production was of minor importance in the very earliest phases of all these Norwegian towns, and this may imply that women constituted a minor part of the population at that time. In Bergen and Oslo, textile production seems to have been of no importance before *c.*1130 at the earliest, but in Trondheim it emerges from *c.*1050 onwards. In all three towns, the busiest period for textile production using tools and techniques connected with female manufacture seems to have been the thirteenth century, slowing to decline in the next century. In Trondheim, this pattern also corresponds with other find-groups that reflect handicrafts.

Looking at the find contexts, many of the remains of textile tools were found *in situ* within buildings at both Bryggen and Oslo, reflecting a special working environment for female manufacture. At Bryggen, the spatial distribution over time shows an interesting pattern, with clusters of buildings tending to occur in the rear parts of the tenements in the northern part of the site, with a fairly stable location from the twelfth century until about 1300. After the middle of the fourteenth century, no such connections have been demonstrated (Øye 1988), which is not surprising considering that the Hanseatic League established its *Kontor* in the area around 1360. In Oslo, the weaving equipment is best represented around 1150. Here a similar pattern to Bergen can be recognized, where weaving took place in the inner parts of the tenements, but lasted for a shorter period, from *c.*1125 to 1225. In Oslo, many of the buildings with traces of upright looms also had hearths. After the opening decades of the thirteenth century the situation changed, and henceforward there were generally fewer buildings with warp-weights, and all without hearths (Rui 1991, 128–9).

These separate buildings within the urban tenements seem to have attracted special production of a kind that differed from the ordinary textile production known from rural contexts. Although they may have been focused within household settings, the households were probably extended with a female labour force with special competence, judging by the varied tools they have left. This pattern seems to break up at the same time as differentiated and specialized textile handicrafts were established, like weavers and tailors. The first definite find of the horizontal loom in Norway is from Trondheim, dated to around 1200, where weaving on upright looms seems to have lost its position by around 1300 (Nordeide 1994, 228, 230). A transitional period, where woollen textiles were woven both on the upright and horizontal loom by women and men respectively, seems to have lasted over a period of 150 years, judging by the textiles found (Hagen 1994).

Hand-spinning, however, was never taken over by men in the towns. The differentiation and specialization of textile production into several crafts clearly shows that the medieval towns broke up the old norms for the gender-based production, a process that can be recognized in most northern European towns. As a consequence, women lost their old position in textile production. Nevertheless, around 1300, the situation seems to have been somewhat fluid in many areas, where women and men also could work together, but where women now mostly assisted (Goldberg 1992, 332). This may also have been the situation in the three Norwegian medieval towns.

CONCLUSIONS

What do these studies tell us about women in early towns and what are their implications? The large amount of textile-production equipment in Viking-Age towns clearly shows that textile work, which was seemingly performed by women on a specialized basis, was a greater component in these towns than has hitherto been recognized, both economically and socially. The find contexts, burials, constructions and localization indicate that women belonging to different social strata were involved, both married (with children) and single. The female textile industry seems to have been most intensive in the later phases in the tenth century, and of less importance in the earlier stages. This may also have exerted influence on the demographic, economic and social patterns of these towns.

The medieval towns that emerged in the eleventh century show a similar development, with a relatively small-scale textile industry in the first phases and larger-scale production in the twelfth and thirteenth centuries. The evidence suggests a larger degree of specialization in Bergen and Oslo than has previously has been considered and may, therefore, imply that female textile workers played a more important role until about 1300. By the fourteenth century, however, the female textile industry seems to have been taken over by men and developed into more specialized crafts, relying on larger supplies of imported goods, including textiles from the fast-growing textile towns in England and on the Continent. For women, this may also have meant fewer work opportunities in the latter part of the Middle Ages, which may also have affected the demographic structure of the medieval towns.

BIBLIOGRAPHY

Andersson, E. 2000. 'Textilproduktion i Löddeköpinge: endast för husbehov?' in F. Svanberg & B. Söderberg (eds), *Porten til Skåne: Löddeköpinge under järnålder och medeltid*, Riksantikvareämbetet Skrifter, 3, Arkeologiska studier kring Borgeby och Löddeköpinge, 2 (Malmö), pp 158–87.

Andersson, E. 2003. *Tools for textile production from Birka and Hedeby*, Birka Studies, 8 (Stockholm).

Blindheim, C. & B. Heyerdah-Larsen. 1995. *Gravplassene i Bikjholbergene/Lamøya: undersøkelsene, 1950–1957*, Norske oldfunn bd. 2, Universitetets kulturhistoriske museer (Oslo).

Boserup, E. 1970 [1989]. *Woman's role in economic development* (London).

Goldberg, P.J.P. 1992. *Women, work and life cycle in a medieval economy: women in York and Yorkshire, c.1300–1520* (Oxford).

Gräslund, A.-S. 1980. *The burial customs: a study of the graves on Björkö, Birka: Untersuchungen und Studien* (Uppsala).

Hagen, K.G. 1994. *Profesjonalisme og urbanisering: profesjonalismeproblemet i håndverk belyst ved et tekstil- og vevloddsmateriale fra middelalderens Trondheim, fra 1000-tallet frem til slutten av 1300-tallet*, Universitets Oldsaksamlings Skrifter, n.s., 16 (Oslo).

Herlihy, D. 1990. *Opera muliebria: women and work in medieval Europe* (New York).

Hoffmann. M. 1964. *The warp-weighted loom* (Oslo).

Jacobsen, G. 1995. *Kvinder, køn og købstadlovgivning 1400–1600: lovfaste mænd og ærlige kvinder*, Danish Humanistic Texts and Studies, 1 (Copenhagen).

Jesch, J. 1991. *Women in the Viking Age* (Woodbridge).

Molaug, P. 1991. 'Sneller til håndtein' in E. Schia & P. Molaug (eds), *Dagliglivets gjenstander*, De arkeologiske utgravninger i Gamlebyen, 8 (Oslo), 81–112.

Nordeide, S.W. 1994. 'Håndverket' in A. Christophersen & S.W. Nordeide, *Kaupangen ved Nidelva*, Riksantikvarens Skrifter, 7 (Trondheim), 213–42.

Rabben, A. 2002. 'Med vevsverd og steikepanne: tekstilredskaper og kjøkkenredskaper i vestnorske mannsgraver fra yngre jernalder' (Master's thesis, University of Bergen).

Randsborg, K. 1980. *The Viking Age in Denmark: the formation of a state* (London).

Rui, L.M. 1991. 'Kljåsteiner: vevlodd' in E. Schia & P. Molaug (eds), *Dagliglivets gjenstander*, De arkeologiske utgravninger i Gamlebyen, 8 (Oslo), 113–30.

Rui, L.M. 1993. 'Kjønnsrollerelasjoner: et arkeologisk materiale fra middelalder-Oslo i feministisk perspektiv' (Masters thesis, University of Oslo).

Stylegar, F.-A. 2007. 'The Kaupang cemetries revisited' in D. Skre (ed.), *Kaupang in Skiringssal*, Kaupang Excavation Project Publication Series, 1 (Oslo), 65–126.

Øye, I. 1988. *Textile equipment and its working environment, Bryggen in Bergen ca1150–1500*, The Bryggen Papers, Main Series, 2 (Bergen).

Øye, I. 2005. 'Kvinner, kjønn og samfunn fra vikingtid til reformasjonen' in I. Blom & S. Sogner (eds), *Med kjønnsperspektiv på norsk historie* (Oslo), 21–101.

Øye, I. 2006a. 'Kvinner som tradisjonsformidlere: rom og redskaper' in R. Barndon, S.M. Innselset, K.K. Kristoffersen & T.K. Lødøen (eds), *Samfunn, symboler og identitet: festskrift til Gro Mandt på 70-årsdagen*. UBAS, Nordisk, 3, Universitetet i Bergen Arkeologiske Skrifter (Bergen), pp 439–53.

Øye, I. 2006b. 'Landbruket i historisk lys' in K. Helle (ed.), *Vestlandets historie bd.1* (Bergen), pp 76–129.

Øye, I. in press. Textile-production equipment, Kaupang Excavation Project Publication Series, 8 (Oslo).

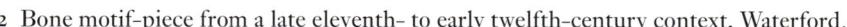

1 Ragnarök, as depicted in the graffito on the tower at Skipwith, East Yorkshire.

2 Bone motif-piece from a late eleventh- to early twelfth-century context, Waterford.

3 Tamdrup plate, depicting Poppo wearing the iron glove and heating it in the fire.

4 Tamdrup plate, depicting Poppo conducting the baptism of Harald Bluetooth.

5 St Kevin's House, Glendalough, Co. Wicklow from the north.

6 The Gatehouse, Glendalough, Co. Wicklow from the south.

14 Liknatr's memorial stone, Ardre church, Gotland (photo: Sören Hallgren, ATA).

15 The Tjängvide picture stone, parish of Alskog, Gotland.

16 The first sunken featured building at Sveigakot, looking northeast.

17 The late tenth-century hall at Sveigakot, looking east.

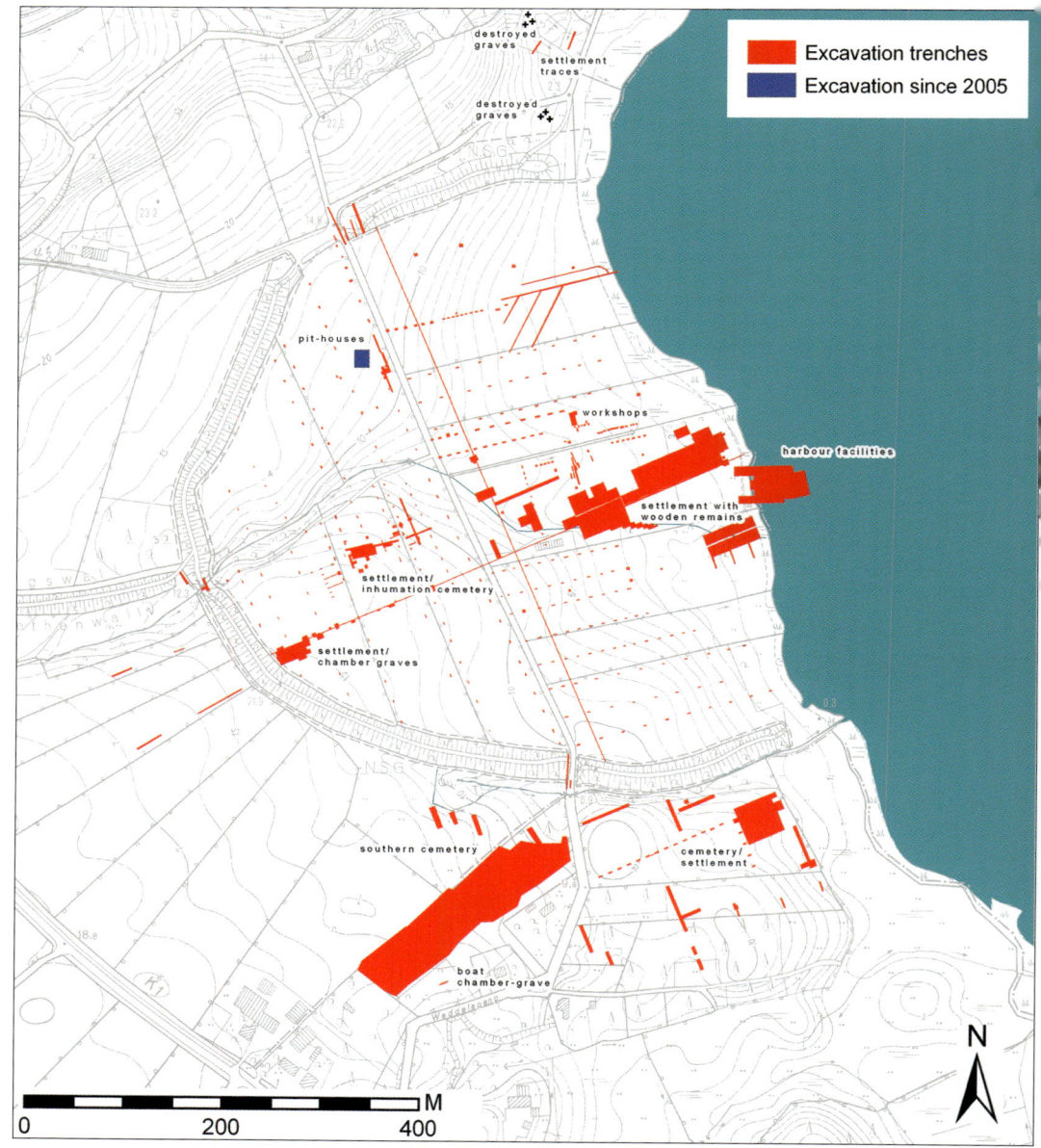

18 Plan of Hedeby, showing the areas excavated since 1900.

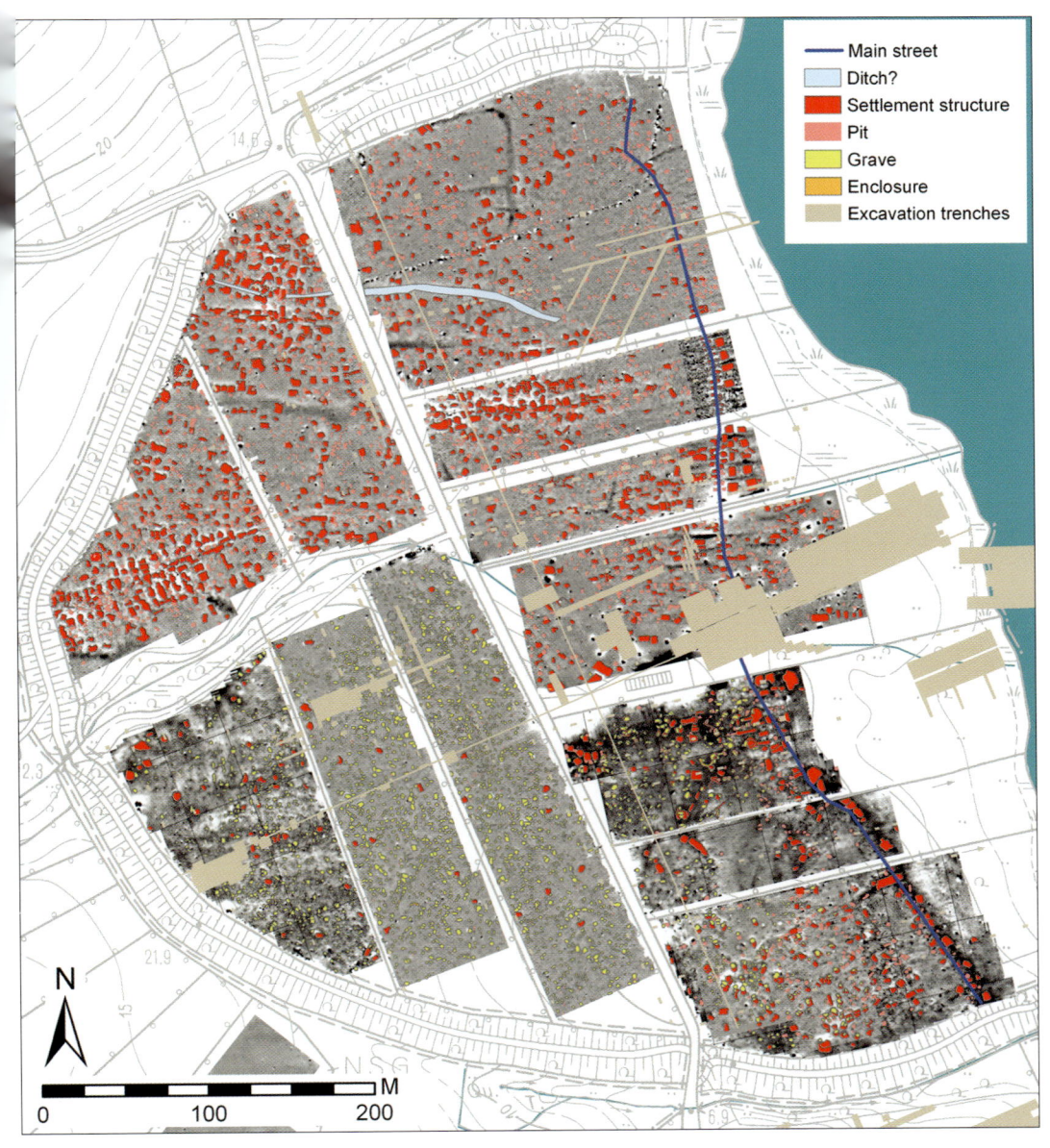

19 Plan of Hedeby, showing the interpretation of data derived from geophysical prospection methods.

20 Portrait of Colonel Sempronius Stretton (courtesy of National Portrait Gallery, London).

21 Excavations at Fishamble Street, Dublin.

22 Excavations at Fishamble Street, Dublin.

Bridging the distribution gap: inscribed swords from Denmark

ANNE PEDERSEN

INTRODUCTION

Swords were doubtless the most prestigious and valuable weapons of the Viking Age. Famous swords were remembered by name, and the blades and handles of many surviving weapons attest to the skill and care shown in their manufacture. Among the most notable weapons are those with an inscription or inlaid symbols on the blade, the most common being the name VLFBERHT combined with an hourglass or lattice motif on the reverse of the blade (see Stalsberg, this volume). Such swords were noted by weapon enthusiasts and antiquarians even in the early nineteenth century and are today known across most of northern Europe with one apparent exception, southern Scandinavia including present-day Denmark, which has long featured as a 'white spot' at the centre of many distribution maps (Cf. Müller-Wille 1971; Geibig 1991). Nevertheless, inscribed blades have come to light in recent years, and the aim of this paper is to focus on a small number of swords with inscriptions and other distinctive marks that attest to the far-reaching international contacts of Viking-Age Denmark.

When Herbert Jankuhn published his survey of VLFBERHT swords in 1951, the only weapon mentioned from Denmark was an unprovenanced example in the collections of the National Museum in Copenhagen, a sword of Petersen's Type E with a double Omega-like symbol on one side of the blade and an unidentified mark on the other (Appendix no. 1; Jankuhn 1951, 215). In a survey published twenty years later, Michael Müller-Wille included a total of 99 swords, but again with no examples from Denmark (Müller-Wille 1971, 71, 83), a situation repeated in the distribution map published by Alfred Geibig in 1991, where no originals or copies are marked for Denmark and Scania, in spite of the increased number of finds from the surrounding Continental and especially Norwegian and Baltic regions (Geibig 1991, 121, 192). The gap was, however, narrowed by the inclusion of an almost complete sword of Petersen's Type V, recovered from the flat grave cemetery of Hedeby in 1906. The blade is covered by remains of organic material from the scabbard, but X-ray photography has revealed traces of letters that suggest the name VLFBERHT (Geibig 1990, 254, no. 28). A second sword from Hedeby, excavated in 1905 and possibly also a grave find, has an incomplete and illegible inscription (Geibig 1990, 254, no. 31).

By all accounts, the lack of inscriptions from Denmark was not caused by any lack of awareness on the part of Danish scholars. On the contrary, they had every opportunity of seeing an exceptionally well-preserved VLFBERHT blade of Norwegian origin in the collections of the Oldnordisk Museum in Copenhagen, the sword moreover featuring as a type example in the widely read *Nordiske Oldsager i Det Kongelige Museum i Kjöbenhavn* (Worsaae 1859). It was part of a collection of prehistoric antiquities acquired by the museum in 1812 and assembled by Captain, later Major, C.H. Sommer during his stay in Norway. The museum inventory number 780 records 'ten iron swords of the usual length and width, some single, others double edged … all recovered from burial mounds' (Undset 1878, 33). The blade of number 4, a Petersen Type S sword, shows a typical lattice-and-line ornament on one side and, on the other, a common version of the name VLFBERHT in which the letters V and L are joined together and the cross at the end is placed between the letters H and T. The position of the inscription, unusually close to the cross-guard, indicates that the blade may have been re-hilted and possibly shortened in the process (Peirce 2002, 100). A second sword from Sommer's collection (inv. no. 780, no. 3) bears simple hourglass and circle/line markings, but no name (Undset 1878).

Despite such finds and the evident interest of antiquarians and archaeologists in the weaponry and weapon burials of the Viking Age, no inscriptions appear to have been identified during the nineteenth and early twentieth centuries. A possible explanation may be sought in the corroded state of many Danish swords and the difficulties involved in removing versus preserving the remains of wooden scabbards surviving on the blades. Considering that only about 160 more or less complete Viking-Age swords are preserved from Denmark, in contrast to more than 2,500 from Norway, the reluctance to attempt any analysis which might damage the weapons is understandable. It was not until the 1950s that X-ray photography became widely recognized as a useful tool in identifying inscriptions and other inlays on corroded swords (Cf. Jankuhn 1951, n. 90), but another four decades were to pass before the first inscribed weapons were recorded in Denmark.

INSCRIBED SWORDS

In the early 1990s, Bjarne Lønborg, conservator in Fyns Stiftsmuseum, identified inscriptions on three swords, one of them a burial find from Fyn, the other two found in wetland contexts in Sjælland and in Jylland. The sword from Fyn (Appendix no. 7) was recovered in 1978 when a small cemetery was examined at Rosenlund in connection with the construction of a motorway from Nyborg to Langeskov east of Odense (Jacobsen and Thrane 1994). The accidental find of a lump of corroded iron led to the discovery of the remains of a wooden chamber in which the deceased had been buried with a full range of weapons and two full sets of riding equipment, one apparently placed in an annex to the burial chamber proper. Judging by the nature of the burial and its contents, the deceased was a prominent individual and one who might well have been known to or even associated with the man who, in the early tenth century, was accorded an impressive ship burial at Ladby, only 10km to the north of Rosenlund (Sørensen 2001).

Like the VLFBERHT sword from Norway, the sword from Rosenlund belongs to Petersen's Type S, and although less elaborate than other related swords, the guards and pommel are decorated with silver wire. The blade is much corroded. However, later X-ray examination revealed remains of pattern-welded letters that could be interpreted as the initial letters +VLF, leaving no doubt that this was indeed an VLFBERHT blade fitted with a Scandinavian-type hilt and one with a definite Danish provenance (Plate 7) (Lønborg 1994, 10).

Apart from the inscribed sword, the weapons from Rosenlund include a spearhead of Petersen's Type K with elaborate silver inlay in a herring-bone pattern on the socket, and a shield boss of Scandinavian type. The axehead, on the other hand, is as yet unique in a Danish context. It is characterized by an elongated blade and unusually long spurs or projections at the shaft hole and belongs to a small group of exclusive, decorated axes deposited in burials of the tenth century (Plate 8). Although not identical, the closest parallels from Denmark are two inlaid axes from Trelleborg in Sjælland and Over Hornbæk in Jylland (Nørlund 1948, 136, XXXVI; Nielsen 1991). The origin of these weapons is assumed to lie in the area south and southeast of the Baltic, and axes with features similar to the axe from Rosenlund are known from Lunow, near the Oder, and the river Havel in Brandenburg (Cat. Speyer 1992, 96; Cat. Magdeburg 2001, 78). Like the swords, these axes are prestige weapons, and were also presumably of considerable economic value, which may have been acquired in exchange – peaceful or otherwise – or as gifts from foreign partners and allies.

The second inscribed sword identified by Lønborg, a Petersen Type V, was found during drainage work near Jørlunde, in northern Sjælland, some time before 1924 (Appendix no. 2). Although only partially preserved, the inscription is clearly readable as the name VLFBERHT (Lønborg 1994, 10). The usual cross at the end of the name is lacking and it is uncertain whether it was left out in the smithing process or has vanished due to corrosion. The reverse of the sword shows an hourglass figure set between transverse lines.

The third sword was recovered from spoil unearthed during construction of a waste-water pipeline in Randers in 1992 (Appendix no. 11). The exact find spot is not known but was probably the 'Hospital Meadow' immediately north of the river Gudenå (Stidsing 1999, 93). The sword is broken and incomplete, the presence of a now missing pommel being indicated by two rivet holes in the upper guard (Fig. 30.1, left). Judging by the shape of the guards, the sword may have

30.1 Two swords from Randers parish, Jylland (photo: Kulturhistorisk Museum Randers, Hans Grundsøe).

belonged to Petersen's Type H. The blade carries an inscription but appears also to be pattern-welded, a most unusual combination judging by the known VLFBERHT swords (Cf. Jankuhn 1951, 224; Geibig 1991, 116). The inscription is distorted and difficult to decipher, as the two sides of the blade overlap in the X-ray. The model was very likely the name VLFBERHT (Cf. Lønborg 1994, 10), but the distortion suggests an imitation rather than an original, and it is uncertain whether an inscription or rather the typical hour-glass pattern was intended on the reverse.

Another four swords can be added to the ones identified by Lønborg. Two were noted in 1994 when fourteen corroded swords from Danish weapon burials were examined by X-ray. The purpose of the study was primarily to identify the hilt-type and thus determine the probable date of the weapon (Pedersen 1995). Nevertheless, two of the photographed swords proved to have definite traces of an inscription, and the possibility remains open for three others. The first sword comes from Frølunde Fed, in southwest Sjælland (Appendix no. 4), and was submitted to the National Museum in 1887 along with an iron spearhead. The two weapons were found together at a depth of about 50cm in an old beach on a promontory separating a small inlet (now dried-up) from Storebælt. According to the finder, 'there was only the usual sandy earth at the place where the sword was found'. No stones or bones were observed, but two such weapons found together in a beach ridge suggest the possibility of a disturbed weapon burial rather than an accidental loss or a weapon deposit. The inscription on the blade of the sword is incomplete but faint traces of the first letters in the name VLFBERHT are preserved, along with a figure resembling a double H. The sword is but one of three silver-inlaid swords of Petersen's Type S from the same small area in southwest Sjælland. In 1860 two others were recovered from the site of a destroyed burial mound on the former island of Magleø in Korsør Nor (the location in Holbæk county cited by Brøndsted (1936, 188) for the Magleø swords is mistaken). They were included in the personal collection of King Frederik VII, the king having discovered and cleaned the inlay on one of the swords himself (Worsaae 1861, 291).

An incomplete sword of Petersen's Type V (Appendix no. 6) comes from an equestrian burial disturbed in 1885 during gravel-digging, possibly on the high ground of Hobyskov, on a promontory west of the former Rødby Fjord on the island of Lolland. The artefacts from the grave, apart from the sword, included an axe, an iron stirrup elaborately decorated with silver and copper, and a horse bit, and were acquired by the National Museum in 1893 from a private collection (the records of which state that the artefacts had been found in a gravel pit together with a second stirrup and a spur). The riding equipment is typical of the middle of the tenth century, and X-ray analysis supports the classification of the sword as a Type V rather than X, as suggested by Brøndsted (1936, 182). Faint traces of inlay are found on both sides of the blade, most likely representing part of an inscription on one side and the remains of a rhombic pattern, similar to that known from other VLFBERHT blades, on the reverse.

Whereas all the five swords mentioned above appear to be more or less obvious variations or distortions modelled on the name VLFBERHT, a Petersen Type X sword represents a different group (Appendix no. 9). This came to light in 1951 when an equestrian burial was exposed during roadworks between Ranum and Næsby in northern Jylland (Vesterhimmerlands Museum Aars; Cf. Brøndsted 1960, 439). Poor weather threatened to destroy the burial and hindered detailed documentation of the find. However, the precise location of the grave was identified in 1992. The grave consisted of an oval pit sunk deep into the subsoil. At its base, iron artefacts were located in a compact concentration beneath and behind large stones, the sword lying with the hilt to the west. The inscription is difficult to decipher, but it clearly differs from the others with a predominance of N-like figures. It is possible that it should be ascribed to the INGEL-group or that the inscription represents letters similar to, for instance, +INNOMINED (Cf. Geibig 1991, 123). Parallels for the riding equipment in the grave from Norway and Sweden suggest a date in the very late tenth century for the burial, when the practice of equestrian burial was coming to an end in Denmark. A poorly preserved sword (Appendix no. 5), recovered in the autumn of 1981 on

Kildegårds Mark in southern Sjælland, should possibly be added to the list of swords with inscribed names. The sword had been caught in the teeth of a harrow, and only the blade and lower guard of the hilt have survived, the latter showing traces of silver, copper and brass inlay. The shape of the guard indicates a sword of Type H. The remains of a leather scabbard were visible within the layer of corrosion covering the blade, and although X-ray examination revealed positive evidence of an inscription, it could not be deciphered.

GEOMETRIC SIGNS AND SYMBOLS

Apart from the swords with more or less readable inscriptions, Danish weapon finds include a few swords with geometric symbols and other markings on the blades. No detailed study of these has yet been carried out, and it is likely that future research will lead to additional examples to the ones listed here.

In 1998 a second sword of Petersen's Type H (Appendix no. 12) was found in Randers at a depth of 2m in the River Gudenå, close to the railway bridge. It measures 95cm in length and is extremely well preserved due to the lack of oxygen at the river bottom (Fig. 30.1, right). The guards and pommel are inlaid with silver and copper in a braided pattern and the flat surfaces towards the blade and grip are covered with brass sheet. Remains of the scabbard, which was made of wood lined with fur, are still preserved along most of the blade but have been removed over a short section in order to determine the condition of the iron. The blade shows no trace of an inscription. However, there is little doubt of the quality of the weapon, and X-ray has revealed traces of inlay on both sides about 7cm below the lower guard. On one side the inlay forms a possible knot-like motif, and on the other a symbol consisting of two circles (each about 2.1cm in diameter), separated by a faint line across the blade. Similar symbols are known from Continental blades of the eighth and ninth centuries (Westphal 2002, 273).

West of Randers, the Gudenå is joined by the River Nørreå flowing from west to east, the broad river valley thus creating a formidable hindrance to north-south going traffic. A crossing is located at Fladbro (bro = 'bridge') to the west of the confluence of the rivers. Several Viking-Age swords have been dredged from the river in the vicinity, an indication of the significance of the site. As yet, no inscribed blades have been recorded, but one incomplete sword, presumably of Petersen's Type H, is fitted with a pattern-welded blade with a symbol shaped like a figure-of-eight (Appendix no. 10; Fig. 30.2). A similar symbol is seen on the pattern-welded blade of a definite Type H sword from Sjørring Lake, in northwest Jylland (Appendix no. 8). This sword was recovered in the late nineteenth century, along with other Viking-Age weapons and artefacts, when a canal was cut across a narrow ridge of land that separates Sjørring Lake to the west from Sperring Lake to the east. Up to modern times, the route between the

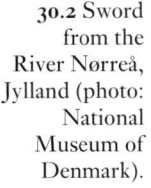

30.2 Sword from the River Nørreå, Jylland (photo: National Museum of Denmark).

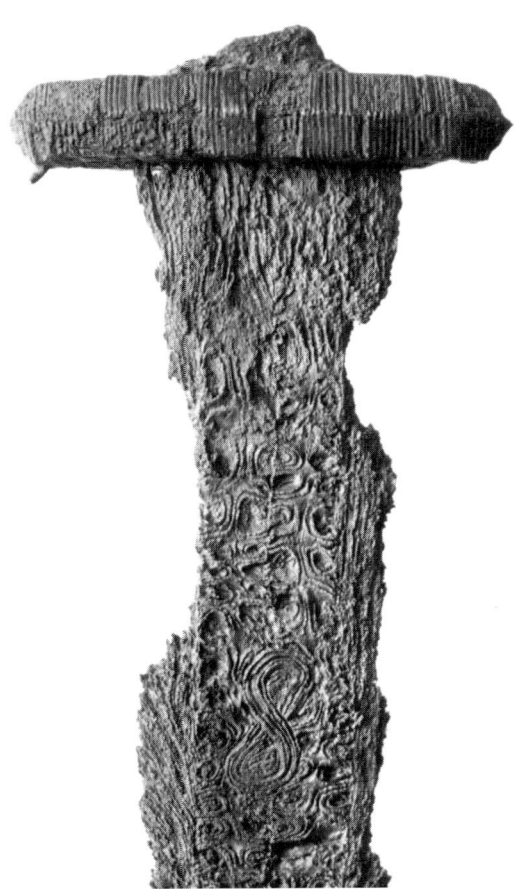

two lakes formed a strategically important link between northern and southern Thy. The site, thus, was similar in this respect to the crossing points over the rivers Nørreå and Gudenå.

Yet another sword, a Petersen Type X from Lake Tissø in Sjælland (Appendix no. 3), was recently examined in an attempt to identify the inscription or symbols faintly visible on its surface. X-ray analysis provided no definite evidence of a name, despite the traces on the better preserved side of the blade (Peter Pentz, Curator, the National Museum, pers. comm.). However, the reverse showed a clearly defined pattern reminiscent of the lattice motif of many VLFBERHT and INGELRII swords (Fig. 30.3; Geibig 1990, 117). Finally, a related sword, an earlier variant of Petersen's Type X, from Bösarp in the southwest corner of Scania, depicts symbols in the form of a Greek cross on one side and a circle on the other (Appendix no. 13, Strömberg 1961, II: 57).

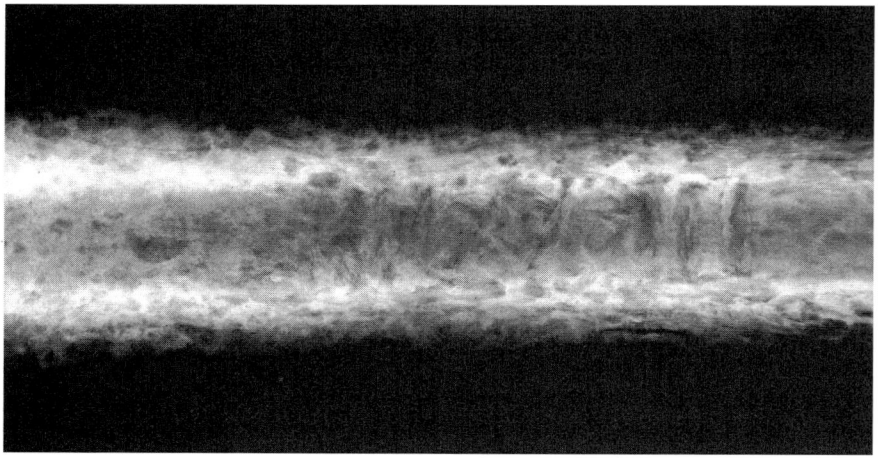

30.3 X-ray of the pattern on the reverse of the sword from Tissø, Sjælland
(photo: National Museum of Denmark).

CONCLUSIONS

It is now possible to close the distribution gap between western Europe and northern Scandinavia that was so glaring in Geibig's map of 1991 (see Fig. 30.4). Modern X-ray examination has revealed at least six Danish swords with traces of inscriptions. Of these, the three from Jørlunde, Frølunde Fed and Rosenlund appear to be true if not complete representations of the name VLFBERHT, whereas the others may be copies or derivatives, in which only a distorted imitation of the original lettering was achieved. In the case of the late tenth-century sword from Næsby, it is conceivable that a different name or type of inscription was intended.

A further six swords, including the one from Bösarp in Scania, depict symbols or geometric markings on the blade. The pattern identified on the sword from Tissø resembles the common motif on the reverse of many VLFBERHT swords, but there is no conclusive evidence for a corresponding reading of the faint obverse inscription. Likewise, it is not possible to decipher the inscription of the sword from Kildegårds Mark. The markings on the other swords are either single symbols, a figure-of-eight or a cross versus a circle on the Bösarp sword, or composite symbols consisting of several elements. The use of such symbols emerged in the centuries prior to the Viking Age, but presumably they served similar purposes as marks of quality or origin.

Compared to the total number of swords surviving from the Viking Age, the recorded blades with inscriptions or symbols together form only a minor, widely distributed group. Judging by the hilts, the blades were in use over a long period of time from the ninth to the eleventh or even twelfth century, and as indicated

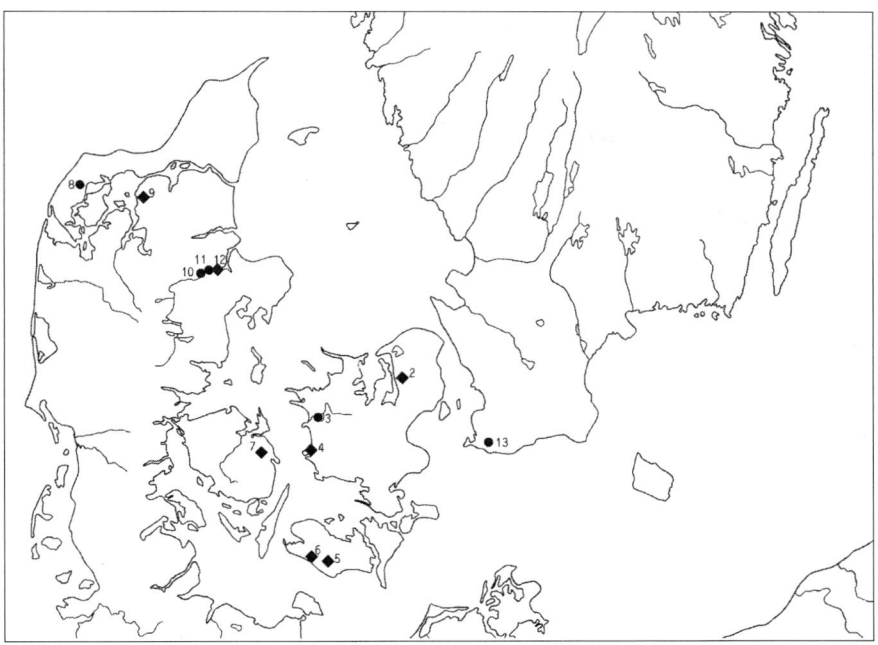

30.4 Distribution of swords with inscriptions (diamond) or markings (dot) from Denmark and Scania.

by the Norwegian sword mentioned above, the blades may have been re-hilted either as a repair or to meet changing requirements. Nevertheless, most appear to be fitted with hilts typical of the ninth and tenth centuries and this is also the case in Denmark (Müller-Wille 1971, 75). Apart from the unprovenanced sword of Petersen's Type E, the main types H, S, V and X are represented.

The three swords from Hoby, Rosenlund and Næsby all derive from equestrian burials, indicating that their owners belonged to a prominent or élite milieu. Likewise, the find circumstances for the sword from Frølunde suggest a disturbed weapon burial and, if so, one that contained an association of decorated sword and spear, thus also indicating a certain wealth and status. By contrast, the sword from Tissø was recovered from a lake and has been interpreted as evidence of a weapon deposit, possibly of a religious nature, rather than an accidental loss (Jørgensen and Petersen 1996, 25). A similar interpretation may apply to the swords from Jørlunde, the Nørreå/Gudenå river system and Sjørring Lake.

A basic survey of swords (other than burial finds) with a known provenance within Denmark, Schleswig and Scania has revealed about seventy more or less intact blades with preserved parts of the grip, guards and pommel. Surprisingly, many are from wetland contexts – rivers, bogs and lakes. In addition, eleven swords of Frankish, Scandinavian, Anglo-Saxon and East European origin have come to light in the harbour region at Hedeby (Geibig 1999). The wetland finds include sword-types not represented in Danish burials, among them three examples of Petersen's Type D from the early Viking Age. At least twenty-two of these swords, including the examples from Hedeby harbour and the above-mentioned sword recovered from the River Gudenå in 1998, feature traces of scabbards which support a ritual interpretation rather than loss related to conflict or intense traffic, as might be envisaged for Hedeby or the river crossings. Many wetland finds may therefore represent the ritual deposition of valuable weapons still protected by their scabbards, just as swords from graves were frequently deposited inside their scabbards.

The origin of the VLFBERHT blades has been sought in the Rhine area, although it remains uncertain whether the name refers to a single workshop or, judging by the variation of marks and inscriptions, a number of workshops working within the same tradition (Geibig 1991, 121). Misrepresented inscriptions have been interpreted as evidence of imitation. Geibig has distinguished three categories of copies: blades made by other, less prominent masters; copies with more or less accurate inscriptions manufactured outside of the Frankish empire; and finally blades with inscriptions added later (ibid., 122). The find from Hedeby is viewed as an original VLFBERHT blade. A few of the Danish examples may likewise be imports or at least very accurate copies, whereas others may have been manufactured locally, either in an attempt to fake high quality blades for commercial reasons or to create a copy of an otherwise unattainable prestige weapon. In either case, the imitations attest to the desirability and value of the imported blades. Thus, although still few in number, the Danish finds fit well within the general pattern. Quality weapons were no less sought after in Denmark than in the neighbouring countries.

APPENDIX: INSCRIBED SWORDS/SWORDS WITH MARKINGS FROM
DENMARK AND SCANE

1. Unknown provenance, Denmark
The National Museum UI/1364. J. Petersen Type E, length *c*.74cm. Double omega separated by a line.
Unknown circumstances.
Jankuhn 1951, 215.

2. Jørlunde, Jørlunde parish, Sjælland
Fyns Stiftsmuseum A1775, transferred to Museet Færgegården. J. Petersen Type V, length 91.5cm. Partially preserved +VLFBERHT inscription with complete name but lacking a cross at the end; hourglass between transverse lines on reverse.
Lake or river, recovered during drainage work before 1924.
Lønborg 1994.

3. Tissø, Store-Fuglede parish, Sjælland
The National Museum D111/1957. J. Petersen Type X, length 94cm. Lattice motif and lines across one side of the blade.
Lake deposit, exposed when the water table in Lake Tissø was lowered.
Jørgensen and Petersen 1996, passim.

4. Frølunde Fed, Tårnborg parish, Sjælland
The National Museum C5821. J. Petersen Type S, preserved length 44cm. Initial letters VLF followed by uncertain letters.
Presumably a disturbed weapon burial, non-expert recovery around 1887.
Brøndsted 1936, 189.

5. Kildegårds Mark, Sædinge parish, Lolland
The National Museum D111/1982. J. Petersen Type H (?), length 82cm. Illegible inscription.
Single find, recovered 1981.
Unpublished.

6. Hoby, Gloslunde parish, Lolland
The National Museum C7331. J. Petersen Type V, preserved length 75.5cm. Faint traces of lettering and lattice motif.
Equestrian burial, non-expert recovery 1885. Tenth century.
Brøndsted 1936, 182, fig. 92.

7. Rosenlund (Røjerup), Rønninge parish, Fyn
Odense Bys Museer 4100x174. J. Petersen Type S, length 91cm. Initial letters +VLF.
Equestrian burial, excavated 1978. Tenth century.
Jacobsen and Thrane 1994; Lønborg 1994.

8. Sjørring Lake, Jylland
The National Museum C1272. J. Petersen Type H, length 84.6cm. Figure-of-eight on pattern-welded blade.
Single find from the lake, acquired 1878.
Unpublished.

9. Næsby, Ranum parish, Jylland
Vesthimmerlands Historiske Museum 867/C226. J. Petersen Type X (?), length 84.5cm. Inscription, uncertain reading.
Equestrian burial, excavated 1951. Late tenth century.
Unpublished.

10. River Nørreå, Grensten parish, Jylland
The National Museum C6374. J. Petersen Type H (?), length 87cm. Figure-of-eight on pattern-welded blade.
Single find from the river, recovered around 1890.
Unpublished.

11. Hospitalsengen 1, Randers parish, Jylland
National Museum C32332/Kulturhistorisk Museum Randers 0234x1. J. Petersen Type
H (?), length 89.2cm. Distorted name on one side of the blade, illegible letters or signs
on the reverse.
Near or in the River Gudenå, recovered 1992.
Lønborg 1994; Stidsing 1999.

12. Hospitalsengen 2, Randers parish, Jylland
National Museum C34297. J. Petersen Type H, length 94.5cm. Possible interlace or knot-
like motif on one side of the blade, two circles separated by a line across the blade on the
other.
River Gudenå, recovered 1998.
Stidsing 1999.

13. Bösarp, Bösarp parish, Scania
Lunds Universitets Historiska Museum 24925. J. Petersen Type X, length 81.7cm. Greek
cross on one side of the blade, circle on the reverse.
Single weapon burial, uncovered 1926.
Strömberg 1961, II: 57, Taf. 40:4.

BIBLIOGRAPHY

Brøndsted, J. 1936. 'Danish inhumation graves of the Viking Age', *Acta Archaeologica*, 7,
    1936, 81–228.
Brøndsted, J. 1960. *Danmarks Oldtid* III. Jernalderen, 2nd ed. (Copenhagen).
Cat. Magdeburg 2001 = M. Puhle (ed.), *Otto der Grosse: Magdeburg und Europa*, vol. 2,
    Katalog [Kulturhistorisches Museum Magdeburg 27 August–2 December 2001]
    (Mainz).
Cat. Speyer 1992 = *Das Reich der Salier 1024–1125: Katalog* [Speyer, Historisches
    Museum der Pfalz 23 March–21 June 1992] (Sigmaringen).
Geibig, A. 1990. 'Zur formenvielfalt der schwerter und schwertfragmente von Haithabu',
    Offa, 46, 1989 (1990), 223–60, Taf. 1–7.
Geibig, A. 1991. Beiträge zur morphologischen entwicklung des schwertes im mittelalter:
    eine analyse des fundmaterials vom ausgehenden 8. bis zum 12. jahrhundert aus
    sammlungen der Bundesrepublik Deutschland, Offa-Bücher, 71 (Neumünster).
Geibig, A. 1999. 'Die schwerter aus dem hafen von Haithabu', *Berichte über die ausgrabungen
    in Haithabu 33: das archäologische Fundmaterial VI* (Neumünster), 9–91.
Jacobsen, J.A. & H. Thrane. 1994. 'Vikinger under motorvejen ved Langeskov', in J. Hertz
    & S. Nielsen (eds.), *5000 år under motorvejen* (Copenhagen), pp 72–5.
Jankuhn, H. 1951. 'Ein Ulfberht-schwert aus der Elbe bei Hamburg' in K. Kersten (ed.),
    *Festschrift für Gustav Schwantes zum 65: Geburtstag dargebracht von seinen Schülern
    und Freunden* (Neumünster), pp 212–29.
Jørgensen, L. & L. Petersen 1996. 'Vikinger ved Tissø: gamle og nye fund fra et handels-
    og håndværkscenter', *Nationalmuseets Arbejdsmark*, 1996, 22–36.
Lønborg, B. 1994. 'Mærkevare', *Skalk*, 1994/3, 8–10.

Müller-Wille, M. 1971. 'Ein neues ULFBERHT-schwert aus Hamburg: verbreitung, formenkunde und herkunft', *Offa*, 27, 1970 (1971), 65–91.

Nielsen, B.H. 1991. 'Langbladsøksen', *Skalk*, 1991/2, 9–13.

Nørlund, P. 1948. Trelleborg, *Nordiske Fortidsminder*, 4:1 (Copenhagen).

Pedersen, A. 1995. 'Vikingetidens grave med våben og hesteudstyr i det gammeldanske område: inventar og datering, idé og hensigt' (PhD thesis, Aarhus University).

Pierce, I.G. 2002. *Swords of the Viking age* (Woodbridge).

Petersen, J. 1919. *De norske vikingesverd: en typologisk-kronologisk studie over vikingetidens våben*, Videnskapsselskapets Skrifter II, Hist.-Filos. Klasse 1919, 1 (Oslo).

Stidsing, E. 1999. 'To pragtsværd fra vikingetiden', *Kulturhistorisk Museum Randers Årbog* 1999, 93–7.

Strömberg, M. 1961. *Untersuchungen zur jüngeren eisenzeit in Schonen*: I Textband, II Katalog und Tafeln, Acta Archaeologica Lundensia, Series in 4°, 4 (Bonn).

Sørensen, A.C. 2001. *Ladby: a Danish ship-grave from the Viking age*, Ships and Boats of the North, 3 (Roskilde).

Undset, I. 1878. *Norske Oldsager i Fremmede Museer* (Kristiania).

Westphal, H. 2002. *Franken oder Sachsen? Untersuchungen an frühmittelalterlichen Waffen.* Studien zur Sachsenforschung, 14 (Oldenburg).

Worsaae, J.J.A. 1859. *Nordiske Oldsager i Det Kongelige Museum i Kjöbenhavn* (Copenhagen).

Worsaae, J.J.A. 1861. 'Danske Vikingesværd tilhørende Hs. Majestæt Kongen', *Illustreret Tidende*, 2:89, 291–2.

Ninth-century Viking entries in the Irish annals: 'no 'forty years' rest'

EMER PURCELL

The Irish annals preserve one of the best records of Viking activities in north-western Europe. Though they contain very little detail about the nature and form of Viking settlement in Ireland, they give some indication of where and when they were most active. Most scholars acknowledge a decrease in activity during the ninth century, but they disagree about when it began; the decline is usually assigned to sometime between the late 840s and the 880s. Discussion of this subject, in the past, has been influenced by the idea presented in *Cogad Gáedel re Gallaib* that Ireland experienced 'forty years' rest' from the Vikings (Todd 1867, 27–9). However, Donnchadh Ó Corráin (1996, 224) has shown this to be a biblical topos used by the compiler(s) of the saga. In the course of my research, I compiled a database of all extant ninth-century entries concerning Vikings, and subsequently carried out a quantitative and qualitative analysis of them. The quantitative analysis shows that the most significant decline in Viking-related entries occurs in the late 850s. A summary of the methodology, problems and findings of this research is presented here.

The study began with the extraction of all ninth-century Viking-related entries from the Irish annals. The primary sources consulted were the *Annals of Ulster* (*AU*), the *Annals of Inisfallen* (*AI*), *Chronicum Scottorum* (*CS*), the *Annals of Clonmacnoise* (*AClon*), the *Annals of Boyle* (*AB*), the *Annals of Roscrea* (*AR*), the annals in the *Book of Leinster* (*LL*), the *Annals of the Four Masters* (*AFM*), the annals contained within the text known as the *Fragmentary Annals* (*FA*), and the early twelfth-century saga *Cogad Gáedel re Gallaib* (*CGG*). Unfortunately, one cannot use the *Annals of Tigernach* (*ATig*) for this period, as there is a lacuna in the text from 766 to 973.

The textual history of the Irish annals is a subject of much debate with regard to their origins, chronological structure and inter-textual relations. Scholars, generally, agree that a common source originating in the Columban foundation at Iona forms the ancestor text which lies behind the extant annals (Mac Niocaill 1975, Charles-Edwards 2006). This chronicle left Iona *c*.740 and was continued at a monastery in the Irish midlands until *c*.911 (Hughes 1972, 107, Grabowski & Dumville 1984, 55). At this point, a version of the chronicle seems to have been continued at Armagh (*AU*) and another (or others) at Clonmacnoise (*CS*, *ATig*, *AClon*); hence close textual similarities are evident between *AU* and *CS* in the ninth century.

METHODOLOGY

All Viking entries from the period 795 to 900 were extracted and imported into a database, in the hope that this would shed some light on how the annals relate to one another and how this may or may not influence our understanding of the references. Material was excerpted from printed textual editions and/or from editions available on the Corpus of Electronic Texts website (www.ucc.ie/celt). As some structure was necessary, *AU* was chosen as the anchor text because it has the fullest geographical range and also preserves the oldest linguistic forms of Irish (Ó Máille 1910). Each entry was entered in Latin and/or Irish and in English translation, thus providing the basis for a comparative study of the texts and their transmission. This had the additional benefit of drawing attention to issues about editorial translation. Each text was colour-coded and thus unique entries were easily identified. The period AD825 to AD875 was chosen for intensive quantitative analysis. Analysis is based on references excerpted from the annals, and one must acknowledge the inherent dangers involved in isolating information in this way. Frequent recourse to the annals themselves was necessary in order to view each entry in context and, to some extent, a qualitative analysis of entries from 795 to 900 helped resolve this problem (Chapter 3, PhD Dissertation).

QUANTITATIVE ANALYSIS

Quantitative analysis of references to the Vikings in the Irish annals for the period 825–75 was based only on entries in four sets of annals; *AU, CS, AI* and *AFM*. Though *AFM* is a seventeenth-century compilation, it contains some unique entries evidently contemporary with the events they describe, and some additional material not recorded in other annalistic compilations. *AClon, FA, CGG, AR, AB* and *LL* were excluded. The problem with excluding the heavily interpolated annals (*FA*) or the saga literature (*CGG*) is that they do contain unique information and therefore these texts were included in the qualitative analysis.

As David Dumville (1985, 76) has pointed out, A. Martin Freeman's edition of the *Annals of Connacht* (1944) was the first modern edition in which annal entries for each year were demarcated and numbered. Seán Mac Airt's edition of *AI*, and Mac Airt and Gearóid Mac Niocaill's edition of *AU* followed that practice, and it is adopted and extended in CELT's online editions of the annals. The practice has also been implemented by T.M. Charles-Edwards in his reconstruction of *The Chronicle of Ireland* (2006). Numbering of entries allows one to see the importance of the Viking activities in a given year; for example, five out of nine entries in *AU* 837 concern them (*c*.55 per cent). However, conclusions based simply on the number of entries are a crude and flawed indication of activity. Firstly, one entry may record two events that should really be counted as two separate entries. Secondly, some entries have become conflated in the transmission of the text. Thirdly, numbering of entries is often a matter of modern editorial judgment. Conversely, two events are sometimes separated when, clearly, they formed part of the same episode. Even if the entries are straightforward, that is, one entry per event, they may not accurately reflect varying levels of Viking activity. For example, only one reference out of three may refer to them, but that one reference may be twice as long as the two non-Viking entries combined. A more effective (though not entirely flawless) method in conducting this kind of analysis is to count the number of words devoted to them per entry per year. For example, in *AU* 837, 94 out of a total of 139 words (*c*.67 per cent) are devoted to them. The results of these calculations are shown in Appendix 1, a year-by-year calculation of the number of entries and the number of words per annal. *AFM*'s chronology is sometimes seriously dislocated. For example in the years 831–2, 843–4 and 856–7, events recorded are anywhere from two to three years behind the dates supplied, for these events, by other annals. In the database, an attempt was made to synchronize the *AFM* entries with the other annals, but for present purposes the solution was to average the number of entries and words for these years and, when spread over a five year period, the overall numbers were not affected. Thus Appendix 2 contains totals for 825–75, divided into five-year periods.

There are inherent difficulties in the selection and the objective treatment of source material in this way. The criteria adopted for inclusion of entries were quite broad. All references to acts perpetrated by, or on, the Vikings, or on their settlements were included. All records which detail their involvement, whether or not they were the principal agents, were counted. For example, I include the entry for *AU* 850, where Cináed mac Conaing, king of Northern Brega, rebelled against Máel Sechnaill mac Máele Rúanaid, king of Southern Uí Néill, with the aid of the Vikings. Entries regarding expeditions or exploits conducted overseas by Vikings who were (or who had once been) based in Ireland, were also included in calculations. For example, I include the entry in *AU* 866 where Amlaíb and his brother Auisle, along with the Foreigners from Ireland and Scotland went to Foirtriu, plundered Pictland, and exacted hostages as guarantee of tribute. Likewise, *AU*, *CS* and *FA* §254, all record the death in 856 of Horm, *toísech na nDubgennti*, in Wales. This death notice is included in the word count because Horm had been active in Ireland for some years previously. Some of the annal entries are augmented by quatrains of verse and where these poems make reference to the Vikings they have been included; for example, AFM 868 contains additional verses on the battle of Cell Ua nDaigri, Killineer, near Drogheda, Co. Louth (*OG* 1910, 214).

In some cases, problems occur because an event may be recorded in a number of annals, but only one source may attribute the event to the Vikings; for example, *AU* 840 records the burning of Armagh but *AClon* and *AFM* specify that Armagh was burned by the Foreigners. Unless the source clearly states Viking involvement, then the reference is not included in the calculations, even when other annals assign the event to them. At times, the annals disagree as to who was responsible for an event; for example, *AU* 842 records that Commán, abbot of Linn Dúachaill, was killed by the heathens and the Irish, while *CS* and *AFM* (perhaps deliberately) do not mention Irish involvement. Surprisingly, despite the many statements of modern historians to the effect that the annalists are biased observers, they are, on the contrary, remarkably frank and matter-of-fact in their descriptions of Viking raids (Byrne 2005, 609). In addition, scribes had the opportunity during the transmission and/or transcription of a chronicle to attribute attacks to them, particularly in laconic entries where no perpetrator is mentioned.

Numbering entries causes many problems, not least in regard to the unbalanced impression they may convey of Viking activity. Obituary notices seem to pose particular problems for modern editors when dividing entries. Sometimes all the ecclesiastical or secular obits are grouped together as one entry (as they may or may not have been in the original chronicle), but sometimes they are demarcated separately; and thus an unrepresentative picture is created. For example, there may be twelve entries for a year, but five of these may be obits. Dumville (1985, 76–7) has argued that 'the criteria for division, though never explicitly stated, have been that a combination of new subject and new sentence defines a new entry ... This method has made for a revolution in precision of reference to entries in Irish chronicles, and has therefore made text-historical exegesis significantly easier'. Unfortunately, these criteria have not been consistently applied, and for precise referencing to annals there must be an agreed standard for demarcating entries.

Editorial judgment determines the division of entries; for example, in Charles-Edwards's reconstruction of the *Chronicle of Ireland*, he chooses to separately demarcate the Kalend entries (854.1), but sometimes Kalends are included with the first entry (855.1). Though not explicitly stated, this demarcation seems to be based on a decision to include Kalends with the first entry when it is derived from *AU* but have a separate Kalend entry when the first entry comes from another set of annals. Dumville (1985, 76, 78–80) draws attention to another problem: the inappropriate grouping of unrelated *mirabile*-statements into single entries in Mac Airt and Mac Niocaill's edition of *AU*. Furthermore, in their edition of *AU*, they make the following two notices into one entry as *AU* 836.10: *Uastatio crudelissima a gentilibus omnium finium Connachtorum. Ar catha forsin Dess Tuaisceirt o genntib.* The common factor in these accounts is the Vikings, and perhaps the feeling that these acts were carried out by the same band, and this seems to determine how the events are presented in the edition. Similarly, in the online edition of *AFM* available on www.ucc.ie/celt, *s.a.* 835.10 (*recte* 836) three separate events are recorded as one entry: (1) *Cluain Mhór M' Aedhocc do losccadh oidhche Nodlacc la Gallaibh, & sochaidhe mór do mharbhadh leo, amaille lé braighdibh iomdhaibh do bhreith leo.* (2) *Derthech Glinne Da Locha do losccadh leó dna.* (3) *Crioch Connacht uile do diothláithriughadh leó mar an c-cédna.* The common factor once more is the Vikings. Is there an inherent assumption that it was the same band that conducted these raids on Clonmore, Co. Wexford, Glendalough, Co. Wicklow, and in Connacht? The demarcation of this entry is based on the fact they are the principal agents in these three events. *Charles-Edwards' Chronicle* links the raid on Glendalough with the raid on Kildare by Vikings from Inber nDeae. According to the original numbering, only two entries out of fifteen relate to the Vikings in this year, when in fact there are five entries out of fifteen (55 words out of 94). Editorial judgment again comes into play in *AU* 841, when the establishment of the *longphoirt* at Dublinn and Linn Dúachaill are grouped as one entry, while in *CS* (online edition www.ucc.ie/celt) and in *Charles-Edwards' Chronicle*, the events are divided into two separate entries.

Entries are also influenced by the transmission of the extant text. An example of this occurs in 837. The annals relate that the heathens inflicted a defeat on Uí Néill at Inber na mBarc. *AClon* alone states that Uí Néill defeated the Vikings. John O'Donovan (1851, i, 455) in his edition of *AFM* suggested that Conell Mageoghagan turned defeat into victory to glorify Uí Néill. In 847, *AU* and *CS* state that Loch Ramor, Co. Cavan, was attacked by Máel Sechnaill, king of Southern Uí Néill, in the course of a war against Luigne and Gailenga who had been plundering Mide 'in the manner of the heathens'. *AFM* records that they had been plundering 'at the instigation' of the Foreigners. The difference between 'manner' and 'instigation' is a significant one:

> *AU* 847: *Toghal Innsi Locha Muinnremair la Mael Sechnaill for fianlach mar di maccaibh bais Luigne 7 Galeng ro batar oc indriudh na tuath more gentilium* 'Mael Sechnaill destroyed the Island of Loch Muinremor, overcoming there a large band of wicked men of Luigni and Gailenga, who had been plundering the territories in the manner of the heathens'.

> *AFM*: *Toghail insi Locha Muinreamhair lá Maol Sechlainn, mac Mael Ruanaidh, for fiallach mór do mhacaibh báis Luicchne 7 Gaileng ro bhádar occ innredh na t-tuath a h-ucht Gall, go ro mallartnaighit lais* 'The demolition of the island of Loch Muinreamhar by Maelseachlainn, son of Maelruanaidh, against a great crowd of sons of death, i.e. malefactors of the Luighni and Gaileanga, who were plundering the districts at the instigation of the foreigners; and they were destroyed by him'.

More (in the *AU* entry), derived from the noun *mōs* or *mōris*, may mean: 'custom, habit, mood, manner, fashion, character', though it may also mean 'move, stir, agitate, affect, provoke, disturb' when derived from the verb *moueō* (*OLD* 1982, 1136–9). In the seventeenth century, the Four Masters chose to render *more* as *a h-ucht*, again a word with a similar range of possible meanings (*DIL* 1983, 624–5), but which O'Donovan correctly translates as 'instigation'. There is a nuance of meaning, translation and interpretation here; the entry, as presented in *AFM*, implies collusion with, rather than mere imitation of, the Vikings. Ó Corráin (1979, 304–5) suggests that the description of the Gailenga and the Luigne as *maicc báis* (sons of death) may reflect a partisan account by annalists based at Clonard, given that community's connection with Clann Cholmáin. The only previous Irish-Norse alliance recorded was the 'martyrdom' of Commán of Linn Dúachaill by the heathens and the Irish in 842. Three years after events at Loch Ramor, in 850, Cináed was to rebel against Máel Sechnaill with the aid of the Foreigners. In 854, *AU* relates that Máel Sechnaill marched against the men of Mumu, as far as Inneoin na nDéise, Mullaghnoney, Newchapel, near Clonmel, Co. Tipperary (*OG* 1910: 460). *AU* and *CS* do not mention the Vikings, but *AFM*, rather tendentiously, states that he did so because the men of Munster had opposed him at 'the instigation of the foreigners': *Maoil Sechlainn, rí Ereann do dhul a Mumhain, co ráinicc Indeoin na n-Déisi, 7 do-bert a n-gialla 7 a oighréir uatha, ar ro thriallsat frithbhert fris a h-ucht echtaircheinel*. Máel Sechnaill, himself, was not averse to their assistance; *AU* relates in 856 that he opposed the heathens with the support of the Gallgoídil (Foreign-Irish).

Calculating the total number of words devoted to the Vikings in the Irish annals is probably the most effective means of identifying the many peaks and troughs of recorded ninth-century activity. The texts were downloaded from the CELT website, and words were counted electronically. Therefore, these calculations include all interpolated entries and all words as expanded or supplied by editors. Appendix 1 shows the total number of words recorded per annal and the number of words devoted to them in each source. Appendix Two shows the total number of words recorded as calculated over five-year intervals, 825–75. Appendix 1 allows the material to be viewed in context; for example, we can see clearly whether there were few Viking entries in a particular set of annals, or whether the year was a quiet one, at least for record-keeping in general. The figures may either confirm or undermine our expectations of activity for a given year. There are certain years when one would expect a high proportion of words to be devoted to the Vikings; for example, 837 marks the arrival of large fleets on the River Boyne and on the River Liffey, 120 ships in total. The expected rise in activity is confirmed; in *AU* a total of 94 of 139 words are concerned with the Vikings. In contrast, we know they over-wintered in 840 and 841, and one would expect a significant increase in words concerning them, but these years appear relatively quiet. In 840, *AU* devotes 40 of 113 words to the Vikings, and *CS* 14 of 57. In *AU* 841, 31 of 102 words detail their activity, though, in *CS* all 45 words relate to them. In this year, the annals record the Viking base on Lough Neagh;

the establishment of the *longphoirt* at Dublinn and Linn Dúachaill (from which they raided into Tethbha, Laigin and Uí Néill); as well as raids on Clonenagh, Clonard and Killeigh (all in one expedition?). It is tempting to interpret the relative lack of raiding as an indication that the Vikings were occupied with establishing their base camps. In 842, *AU* devotes 82 words out of a total of 127 to them. This rise in activity is accompanied by a greater geographical spread in raiding. Vikings from Narrow Water, Co. Down, raided Castledermot, Co. Kildare; Vikings from Linn Dúachaill (Co. Louth), raided Clonmacnoise (Co. Offaly), and *AU* states that Vikings from Dublin raided Birr and Saighir Ciaráin (Co. Offaly) – *CS* is silent about their origins while *AClon* and *AFM* record that the raiders were from the River Boyne, or from Linn Dúachaill, respectively. Despite some confusion, the annalists seem keen to identify each raiding party and the base from which it came. Obviously, there was some degree of communication and interaction during raiding, but one wonders what difference the base camp of the heathens made. Was there a contemporary relevance for these distinctions? No doubt the location of the raiding party's base would dictate how likely (and/or how often) the victims could expect to be subjected to other attacks. In addition, the noting of these bases is in itself a tacit recognition of the settlement of the Vikings in Ireland in the 840s.

There are no Viking entries for 843, but there is a general decline in the number of words in the record of this year, *AU* is down from a total of 127 words in 842 to just 85. Is this decline in recorded Viking activity a reflection of reality? It is important to be aware that this discussion is based wholly on the annalistic record; many raids both on ecclesiastical and secular sites went unrecorded, particularly in areas that were not well served by the extant annals. Etchingham (1996, 21) notes that the 'two regions [the central east and the Shannon-Brosna basin] in which Viking raids on churches are concentrated happen to be those in which ecclesiastical affairs in general can be shown to be disproportionately well documented'.

The most striking calculation is the overall percentage of words devoted to the Vikings in each of the annals. The figures are unexpectedly low when one considers that the second quarter of the ninth century is generally regarded as the peak of Viking activity in Ireland. For the period 825–75, the annals devote the following percentages of their total word count to the Vikings: *AU* 32 per cent, *CS* 40 per cent, *AI* 18 per cent and *AFM* 30 per cent. I have been broad in my criteria for inclusion of references. In fact, if the criteria limited the record to purely Viking activity then the numbers would be even lower. According to these figures, the peak period of activity is 841–5; there is a slight decline in 846–50; a more marked decrease is evident in 851–5; and the lowest figures occur in 856–60. There is a slight decline in the overall number of words written in the 850s, but there is a corresponding decline in the number of words devoted to the Vikings. For example, in *AU* 856–60 only 77 out of a total of 473 words are concerned with the Vikings. In the period 866–70, the number of words devoted to them rises significantly, but this is due to the relatively long description of the destruction of the *longphoirt* in the north, by Áed Finnliath, king of Northern Uí Néill, and his subsequent defeat of the Vikings at Loch Foyle. Viking word-counts are also augmented by the long accounts of the battle of Killineer in 868.

Generally, the data presented in Appendix 2 confirms that there is a discernible drop in Viking activity, as recorded in the annals, in the mid-ninth century. Etchingham (1996, 10, 14) argues that the paucity of Viking entries in the late ninth century reflects a change in the nature of annalistic writing rather than a decline in activity. It is important to emphasize that the figures presented here include both raids on churches and secular encounters. The annalists were writing quite a lot at the peak of Viking activity. There is no agreement amongst the annals themselves as to the highest number of words: the peak years vary slightly from one source to the other. It must be restated, however, that there is a complex inter-textual relationship between the annals in this period and it is a simplification to treat them as independent sources.

'FORTY YEARS' REST'

Numerous and varied arguments have been advanced in regard to the impact of the Vikings on the monastic *scriptoria*. There is no evidence for D.A. Binchy's (1975, 119) much-quoted 'profound – one might say shattering effect upon native Irish institutions'. These figures indicate that, in the ninth century, the Vikings had minimal impact on annalistic writing in terms of productivity, i.e. the number of words written by the annalists in this period, when one compares it to others. In the future I hope to carry out a comparative study of tenth-, eleventh- and twelfth- century entries. The number of words recorded does fluctuate but, in general, there is no radical change in the quantity of material. Dumville (1982, 327–8) argues for an impact on annalistic writing itself in the ninth century, and this may (or may not) be true about content or style, or in the increasing use of the vernacular, but it has no bearing on the quantity of the record.

Etchingham (1996, 2) presents a review of previous scholarly opinion on the decline of raids in the ninth century. Hughes (1972, 157) had suggested that 830–80 was the 'period of intense Viking pressure', and that this was followed by a calm period, 880–920. Peter Sawyer, (1971, 206–7) in his original review of the material, proposes that 873–913 was the period of 'forty years' rest', but in a subsequent analysis he (1982, 84–5) argues that there was a concentration of activity in 820–50 and a reduction thereafter. Ó Corráin (1972, 94, 109) argues that the period of the great raids was over by the early 850s or 860s. Mac Cana (1975) argued that decline began about 875 and, taking *CGG* at its word,

suggested that the lull 'stretched back into the reign of Máel Sechnaill son of
Máel Rúanaid, who died in 862'. Obsession with the notion of a period of forty
years' rest, as noted in CGG, has quite muddied the argument and has led to ill-
starred attempts to link: (1) the ninth-century decline in Viking raids; (2) the
expulsion of Vikings in 902; and (3) their subsequent return to Waterford in 914
and Dublin in 917. This is impossible. As we have seen, the decline begins in the
late 840s, and the lowest figures occur in the late 850s. In addition, the model
does not work, as there is a slight increase in Viking entries in the late ninth
century. Either way, one cannot find a period of forty years' respite from attack
or incursion, despite the statement in *CGG* (Todd 1867, 27–9):

> *Bai, imorro, arali cumsana deraib Erend fri re .xl. bliadan can inred Gall .i. o
> remis Maelsechlainn mic Mailruanaid cusin mbliadain re nec Flaind mic
> Mailseclaind, ocus co gabail rigi do Niall Glundub. Is and sin ro hathlínad Eriu
> do longsib Gall. Is and dna tanic longes la Hacond ocus la Cossa Nara
> corgabsat ar Loch Da Caech.*

> 'Now, however, there were some rest to the men of Eirinn for a period of
> forty years without ravage of the foreigners; viz., from the reign of
> Maelseachlainn, son of Maelruanaidh, to the year before the death of
> Flann, son of Maelseachlainn, and the accession to the throne of Niall
> Glundubh. It was then came a fleet under Haconn and under Cossa-Nara,
> and seized on Loch da Caech'.

As previously stated, Ó Corráin (1996, 224) argues that this reference is in
fact a biblical topos which *CGG* borrowed: 'He [the author of *CGG*] sees the lull
in Viking attacks in the late ninth century in biblical terms'. Etchingham quite
correctly has drawn attention to the way in which the notion of the 'forty years'
rest' influenced Charles Doherty's and Francis John Byrne's maps of Viking
activity in the *New History of Ireland*, ix (Moody, Martin & Byrne 1984, 19–21).
In a recent synthesis, Doherty (1998, 295) presents a review of the progress in
our understanding of the Viking period. However, he continues to view the
period from 837 to 876 as one of intense raiding and semi-permanent
settlements and, though he cites Ó Corráin's work, he maintains the view that
'the period 876 to 916 saw a relative respite from raids, hence the term 'forty
years' rest' as the writer of *Cogadh Gáedhel* called it'.

Etchingham (1996, 5) argues that Sawyer's tabulations were the most
scientific but were based only on *AU* and did not include *AFM*, which, quoting
Kelleher, he regards as the fullest of the extant compilations, especially for the
later ninth century. While *AFM* does contain some unique references, and some
additional material not found in the other annals, the figures clearly show that
the total number of words used to relate Viking activity of all kinds, including
church raids, amounts to approximately 30 per cent of *AFM*'s word count for

the period 825–75 and only 19.5 per cent of entries (as they are currently presented in the CELT edition). More importantly, figures calculated over five-year intervals demonstrate that *AFM* witnesses a decline in Viking entries in line with *AU*, the lowest figures for both annals occurring in 856–60. Decline impacts slightly later in *CS*, the lowest figures being in 861–5. My survey includes *AU*, *CS*, *AI* and *AFM*, and all annals, within a period of five years or so, display a marked reduction in the number of words devoted to the Vikings. My analysis shows decline in the late 850s, approximately ten to fifteen years before the traditional date of the 870s as proposed by some previous studies.

Etchingham attributes the decline to a change in the nature of annalistic recording. He argues (1996, 12) that the annalists ceased to record events in relation to ecclesiastical affairs, with the exception of obituary notices:

> On the face of it, there is a loose coincidence between this contraction in the record of ecclesiastical events generally after 840 and the observed drop in recorded Viking raids on churches after 850. Indeed, the reduced frequency of Viking raids on churches is manifest in the annals already by the second half of the 840s, which makes the coincidence rather closer.

On closer examination of Etchingham's analysis of ecclesiastical events (excluding obits of churchmen) in the annals 731–900, there is a noticeable decline from 841 (1996, 12, fig. 4). This is followed by a modest recovery at 851, precisely the point where there is a decline in church raids as shown by Etchingham's figures or a decline in all Viking activity as shown by my figures. Etchingham (1996, 14–15) does acknowledge that the change in church raids is perceptibly greater than other ecclesiastical events:

> Granted this important caveat about change in the character of the annals, a real pattern in the chronology of Viking raids on churches in the ninth century can, in fact, be detected. … inspection of Figure 3 reveals that the mid-century down-turn is perceptibly greater in the case of Viking raiding activity than in the case of other ecclesiastical events.

Decline in the annals is reflective of a change in the nature of Viking activity itself.

MID-NINTH CENTURY DECLINE

Etchingham (1996, 4, 22) argues that 'the period designated a 'forty years' rest' in *CGG* was not characterized by any appreciable change in the pattern of church-raiding, but by a reduced involvement in Irish dynastic politics on the part of the Vikings'. In the mid-ninth century, as Clarke (1990–2, 97) and

Ó Corráin (1998a, 425) have shown, the Irish were quite successful in resisting the Vikings, which may partly account for this change. According to *AU*, the year 848 was a devastating one for the Vikings, for they suffered considerable losses at the hands of Irish kings: at Forach they lost 700 men, at Sciath Nechtain 1200, at Daire Dísert Do Chonna 1200, and at Dún Maíle Tuile 500.

In the past, scholars have also attributed decline to the loss of the effective leadership of Amlaíb and Ímar in the 870s (Etchingham 1996, 53), and in the later ninth century to a concentration of Viking interest overseas, particularly in north-west England and Iceland (Ó Corráin 1997, 92). The figures discussed earlier show a marked reduction from the late 840s through to the 860s, approximately six years before the capture of York (*c.*866), almost ten years (if not more) before the loss of Amlaíb and Ímar, and perhaps a few decades before the settlement of Iceland in the late ninth century.

In Ireland, the period from the late 840s to the 850s is distinguished by the establishment of more temporary and permanent bases, and the arrival of the sons of the king of Laithlinn: Amlaíb, Ímar and Auisle (for discussion of identification of Laithlinn see Ó Corráin 1998b; 2007; Etchingham, this volume). Leaving aside *AFM*'s record that Munster opposed Máel Sechnaill at the instigation of the Foreigners, in 854 and 855 there are no Viking-entries; F.J. Byrne (2005, 617), based on an account in *FA* §239, suggests that Amlaíb organized the colony in Dublin and then left for Man or the Hebrides. The lack of activity in these two years may testify to Amlaíb's success in taking control of the situation in Ireland; in 853, *AU* records *Amhlaim m. righ Laithlinde do tuidhecht a n-Erinn coro giallsat Gaill Erenn dó, & cis o Goidhelaib* viz. that he extracted tribute from the Irish, and perhaps more importantly, he gained the submission of his countrymen already operating in Ireland. Political alliances cemented through intermarriage between the Norse and the Irish occur during this period; for example, Amlaíb was married to the daughter of Áed Finnliath, king of the Northern Uí Néill. Archaeological evidence for the ninth century has until recently relied upon stray finds, hoards and the grave-goods discovered in a small number of isolated burials as well as the cemeteries unearthed during the construction of the railway line at Kilmainham-Islandbridge in Dublin (for most recent summary see Ó Floinn 1998). In historical discussions, the ninth century is characterized as the pure Viking period, but Stephen Harrison (2001, 70–1) has recently shown that many ninth-century spears and shield-bosses show distinct Insular influence, and the same may be said of some types of Viking silver brooches (Sheehan 1998, 81–2). An increase in Irish and Viking interaction may partly explain a decline in references in the source material. Had a significant element of the Viking population become settled? In 866, *AU* records:

> *Aedh m. Neill ro slat uile longportu Gall, .i. airir ind Fochla, eter Chenel n-Eugain*
> *& Dal n-Araide co tuc a cennlai & a n-eti & a crodha a l-longport er cath.*

'Aed son of Niall plundered all the strongholds of the foreigners i.e. in the territory of the North, both in Cenél Eógain and Dál Araidi, and took away their heads, their flocks, and their herds from camp by battle (?)'.

The reference implies that there were *longphoirt* along the coastline, and Ó Corráin (1997, 90) proposes that Áed Finnliath, king of Northern Uí Néill, was taking back the littoral from the Vikings. It also shows just how successful the Vikings had been in establishing bases in the mid-ninth century. There were others at Linn Dúachaill and Dublin 841; Cork 848; Carlingford Lough 852; Youghal 866; and Clondalkin 867.

In 2003, during test-trenching for the construction of the N25 Waterford Bypass, archaeologists discovered evidence of ninth-century Viking settlement, at Woodstown, on the banks of the River Suir, just three miles upriver from Waterford city (Russell et al. 2005). The site has yet to be decisively identified in the source material (Downham 2004; Ó Cíobháin 2005). Archaeological evidence, to date, suggests that the site was occupied from the mid-ninth to mid-eleventh century and the initial establishment of Woodstown clearly belongs to a key period in the mid-ninth century when the Vikings were keen to establish bases in Ireland. John Sheehan suggests that some of these bases may have been established with trading in mind, as the archaeological evidence for trade – weights, silver, balance scales etc – that has come to light in Woodstown and Dublin, as well as various potential longphort sites, is very impressive (2008, 290–3). Trading may also account for a reduction in raiding in the late 850s.

My analysis of the ninth-century Viking entries in the Irish annals shows that there is a reduction in references in the late 850s. Furthermore, these figures show that there is no radical decrease in the number of words written by the annalists, and even where there is a slight decrease, a more marked decrease in Viking references can be determined. Decline in entries is reflective of a change in the nature of Viking activity in Ireland due to (1) the successful resistance of Irish kings, (2) the arrival and subsequent reign of Amlaíb and Ímar, and (3) the establishment of strategic bases and settlements.

ACKNOWLEDGMENTS

I wish to thank my supervisor Donnchadh Ó Corráin, as well as Kevin Murray, Máirín Mac Carron, Anne Connon and John Sheehan, who read drafts of this article.

Total number of entries and words devoted to the Vikings in the Irish annals, AD825–75 (first column = Viking entries/words; second column = total number of entries/words)

YEAR	AU Entries	AU Words	CS Entries	CS Words	AI Entries	AI Words	AFM Entries	AFM Words
825	6 17	44 159	6 9	45 68	0 1	0 12	6 19	50 143
826	0 11	0 87	0 6	0 35	0 0	0 0	0 11	0 76
827	2 10	37 131	0 2	0 247	0 0	0 0	2 13	26 432
828	4 7	59 86	1 3	15 27	1 2	30[a] 36	3 13	24 82
829	0 4	0 78	0 3	0 24	0 2	0 12	0 7	0 41
830	0 9	0 72	0 4	0 27	0 1	0 15	0 12	0 76
831	2 11	35 130	1 4	19 37	0 1	0 6	1 7	22 89
832	6 9	62 98	5 10	52 79	0 1	0 6	4 13[b]	63 157
833	5 14	42 141	2 4	16 47	1 4	11 31	3 12[c]	62 157
834	1 11	27 121	2 5	21 43	0 3	0 17	2 14	24 103
835	3 12	23 140	1 2	16 25	0 1	0 5	1 15	21 247
836	3 10	56 194	3 5	34 71	0 1	0 5	2 15	55 194
837	5 9	94 139	9 12	111 128	0 0	0 0	11 20	178 231
838	1 10	15 112	1 3	14 33	0 1	0 33	1 15	18 150
839	3 10	45 145	2 3	19 35	0 1	0 6	2 14	26 134
840	3 8	40 113	1 7	14 57	0 1	0 33	2 12	41 157
841	2 5	31 102	4 4	45 45	0 1	0 7	3 7	47 118
842	8 13	82 127	5[d] 7	50 63	0 1	0 8	6 15	63 127
843	0 9	0 85	0 4	0 31	0 1	0 5	0 0	0 0[e]
844	2 4	17 27	1 3	17 35	0 1	0 14[f]	2 14	25 130
845	6 12	122 175	5 6	110 125	1 1	20 20	6 17	145 259
846	2 12	26 124	1 7	20 95	0 1	0 16	3 16	53 279
847	1 9	38 101	1 5	37 77	0 1	0 7	3 13	60 222
848	4 9	73 112	5 7	86 104	1 3	13 29	6 14	102 170
849	2 12	38 122	2 8	35 108	0 1	0 7	3 21	59 218
850	1 4	48 101	1 5	47 87	0 3	0 17	2 12	75 186
851	2 8	40 165	1 4	32 97	0 1	0 10	3 14	47 254
852	3 8	68 136	2 6	52 81	0 1	0 7	3 18	61 152
853	2 6	26 91	2 3	27 61	0 3	0 22	3 16	39 172
854	0 4	0 58	0 3	0 36	0 1	0 13	1 7	29[g] 83
855	0 6	0 66	0 3	0 30	0 1	0 12	0 7	0 58
856	4 8	45[h] 105	5 8	47 95	0 2	0 13	4 14	52 158
857	1 5	14 67	1 5	13 47	1 2	13 34	0 7	0 49
858	0 5	0 94	1 3	25 88	0 3	0 16	1 9	30 168
859	2 5	18 108	1 4	8 71	0 2	0 34	3 9	112[i] 148
860	0 4	0 99	0 1	0 54	0 1	0 9	1 6	11 147

a Both MacAirt (1951, 127) and Grabowski (1984, 53) identify this entry as an early Viking incursion in Cork. I include it in figures here though I am not convinced.   b *AFM* some events are recorded *s.a.* 830 and 831. So added recte years 832 and 833 and divided by two.   c *AFM* some events are recorded *s.a.* 831 and 832. So added recte years 832 and 833 and divided by two.   d These figures do not include the raid on Kinnity, Co. Offaly.   e Entries in *AFM* for this year are dislocated.   f *AI* has only one entry for this year, the plundering of Dún Masc, though the Vikings are not specifically mentioned. The other annals date the attack to 845.   g Like *AU* and *CS*, *AFM* records Máel Sechnaill's attack on Mumu, but adds he did so at the 'instigation of the Foreigners'.   h Includes reference to death of Horm in Wales. i *AFM* (and *FA*) record Viking presence at Rathugh; *AU* and *CS* do not.   j *AU* and *CS* record the invasion of Mide by Áed Finnliath and the Vikings; *AFM* omits the Vikings, so is not included in word-

YEAR	AU Entries		AU Words		CS Entries		CS Words		AI Entries		AI Words		AFM Entries		AFM Words	
861	1	2	8	17	1	3	22	31	0	2	0	14	2	6	43[j]	93
862	1	6	16	103	0	6	0	62[k]	0	1	0	6	2	11	47	185
863	2	4	61	88	1	4	12	38	0	1	0	12	4	11	84	144
864	1	5	16	75	2	5	25	69	0	1	0	7[l]	2	12	30	156
865	0	6	0	80	0	5	0	52	0	2	0	52	0	10	0	95
866	2	5	64	104	1	2	24	40	1	1	17	17	3	8	162	213
867	3	9	60	143	0	4	0	22	1	1	11	11	3	16	50	157
868	1	8	68	174	1	8	92	141	0	3	0	25[m]	3	12	281	592
869	1	10	18	123	1	6	19	65	0	1	0	6	2	20	45	206
870	3	8	87	178[n]	2	5	24	51	0	1	0	6	2	16	78	248[o]
871	3	9	52	116	2	4	38	55	0	1	0	10	1	13	9	110
872	0	9	0	79	0	6	0	98	0	2	0	14	1	10	20	140
873	1	8	9	94	2	4	12	31	1	3	19	31	2	15	14	140
874	1	5	8	69	0	3	0	33	0	1	0	11	1	11	7	82
875	2	6	21	66	0	2	0	15	0	1	0	17	0	1	9	66
Total	108	410	1753	5520	85	245	1295	3216	8	73	134	756	121	620	2469	8194
%	26		32		35		40		11		18		19.5		30	

APPENDIX 2

Number of words and entries devoted to the Vikings (first column = Viking entries/words; second column = total number of entries/words)

Year	AU Entries		AU Words		CS Entries		CS Words		AI Entries		AI Words		AFM Entries		AFM Words	
830[p]	12	58	140	613	7	27	60	428	1	6	30	75	11	75	100	850
835	17	57	189	630	11	25	124	231	1	10	11	65	11	61	192	753
840	15	47	250	703	16	30	192	324	0	4	0	77	18	76	318	866
845	18	43	252	516	15	24	222	299	1	5	20	54	17	53	280	634
850	10	46	223	560	10	32	225	471	1	9	13	76	17	76	349	1075
855	7	32	134	516	5	19	111	305	0	7	0	64	10	62	176	729
860	7	27	77[q]	473	8	21	93	355	1	10	13	106	9	45	175[r]	670
865	5	23	165	363	4	23	59[s]	252	0	7	0	91	10	50	204	673
870	10	40	297	722	5	25	159	319	2	7	28	65	13	72	616	1416
875	7	37	90	424	4	19	50	232	1	8	19	83	5	50	59	538

count.   k *CS* does not mention that the Vikings accompanied Áed Finnliath and Flann son of Conaing when they plundered Mide.   l All the annals, except *AI*, record that Dermait, king of Corcu Bascinn, was drowned by Amlaíb.   m *AI* has quite a short entry regarding the battle of Killineer, it does not record the involvement of the Vikings.   n Word-count includes raid on Laigin/Áth Cliath by Áed Finnliath and the raid on Dumbarton by Amlaíb and Ímar.   o Word-count includes raid from Áth Cliath to Gowran by Áed Finnliath.   p Word-count includes 6 years from 825 to 830.   q *AU* lowest number of words devoted to the Vikings.   r *AFM* lowest number of words devoted to the Vikings since the late 820s.   s *CS* lowest number of words devoted to the Vikings since the late 820s.

BIBLIOGRAPHY

AClon = Murphy, D. (ed.) 1896. *The Annals of Clonmacnoise*, Dublin.

AI = Mac Airt, S. (ed. & trans.) 1951. *The Annals of Inisfallen*, Dublin.

AFM = O'Donovan, J. (ed. & trans.) 1856. *Annála ríoghachta éireann: annals of the kingdom of Ireland by the Four Masters, from the earliest period to the year 1616*, 7 vols, Dublin, i–ii.

AR = Gleeson, D.F. & S. Mac Airt, (eds). 1958. The Annals of Roscrea, *Proceedings of the Royal Irish Academy*, 59C, 137–80.

ATig = Stokes, W. (ed. & trans.). 'The Annals of Tigernach', *Revue Celtique*, 16 (1895), 374–419; 17 (1896) 6–33, 116–263, 337–420; 18 (1897) 9–59, 150–303, 374–91 (repr. 2 vols, Felinfach 1993).

AU = Mac Airt, S. & G. Mac Niocaill, (ed. & trans.) 1983. *The Annals of Ulster (to AD 1131)*, Dublin.

Binchy, D.A., 1975. 'The passing of the old order' in B. Ó Cuív, (ed.), *Proceedings of the International Congress of Celtic Studies Dublin 1959*, Dublin, 1962, 119–32; reprinted as *The Impact of the Scandinavian Invasions on the Celtic-Speaking Peoples, c.800–1100AD*, Dublin.

Byrne, F.J., 2005. 'The Viking age' in D. Ó Cróinín, (ed.), *A new history of Ireland: prehistoric and early Ireland*, Oxford, 1, pp 609–34.

CGG = Todd, J.H. (ed. & trans.) 1867. *Cogadh Gaedhil re Gallaibh*, RS 48, London.

Charles-Edwards, T.M. (ed.). 2006. *The chronicle of Ireland: translated with notes and introduction*, Liverpool.

Clarke, H.B. 1990–2. 'The bloodied eagle: the Vikings and the development of Dublin, 841–1014', *Irish Sword*, 18, 91–119.

Clarke, H.B., M. Ní Mhaonaigh, and R. Ó Floinn, (eds). 1998. *Ireland and Scandinavia in the Early Viking Age*, Dublin.

CS = Hennessy, W.M. (ed. & trans.) 1866. *Chronicum Scottorum*, RS 46, London.

DIL = 1983. *Dictionary of the Irish Language; based mainly on Old and Middle Irish Materials* (compact edition), Dublin.

Doherty, C. 1998. 'The Vikings in Ireland: a review' in H.B. Clarke et al. (eds), *Ireland and Scandinavia*, pp 288–330.

Downham, C. 2004. 'The historical importance of Viking-Age Waterford', *Journal of Celtic Studies*, 4, 71–96.

Dumville, D.N. 1982. 'Latin and Irish in the *Annals of Ulster*, AD431–1050' in D. Whitelock, R. McKitterick, and D.N. Dumville, (eds), *Ireland in early medieval Europe: studies in memory of Kathleen Hughes*, Cambridge, pp 320–41.

Dumville, D.N. 1985. 'On editing and translating medieval Irish chronicles: *The Annals of Ulster*', *Cambridge Medieval Celtic Studies*, 10, 67–86.

Dumville, D.N. 1997. *The churches of North Britain in the first Viking-Age*, Whithorn.

Etchingham, C. 1996. *Viking raids on Irish church settlements in the ninth century*, Maynooth Monographs, Series Minor 1, Maynooth.

Etchingham, C. 2007. 'The location of historical *Laithlinn/Lochlainn*: Scotland or Scandinavia?' in M. Ó Flaithearta, (ed.), *Studia Celtica Upsaliensia: Proceedings of a Symposium of the Societas Celtologica Nordica, Uppsala, 2004*, Uppsala, pp 11–31.

FA = J.N. Radner, (ed. & trans.) 1978. *Fragmentary Annals of Ireland*, Dublin.

Freeman, M.A. (ed. & trans.) 1944. *The Annals of Connacht (AD1224–1544)*, Dublin.

Freeman, M.A. (ed.) 1924–7. 'The annals in Cotton MS Titus A. XXV', *Revue Celtique*, 41, 301–30; 42, 283–305; 43, 358–84; 44, 336–6, (i.e, 336–61.)

Grabowski, K. and D.N. Dumville, 1984. *Chronicles and annals of medieval Ireland and Wales: the Clonmacnoise group of texts*, Woodbridge.

Greene, D. 1975. 'The influence of Scandinavian on Irish' in B. Almqvist, & Greene D. (eds), *Proceedings of the Seventh Viking Congress, Dublin 1973*, Dublin, pp 75–82.

Harrison, S.H. 2001. 'Viking graves and grave-goods in Ireland' in A.C. Larsen, (ed.), *The Vikings in Ireland*, Roskilde, pp 51–75.

OG = Hogan, E. 1910. *Onomasticon Goedelicum*, Dublin.

Hughes, K. 1966. *The Church in early Irish society*, London.

Hughes, K. 1972. *Early Christian Ireland: introduction to the sources*, London.

LL = Best, R.I., O.J. Bergin, M.A. O'Brien & A. O'Sullivan, (eds) 1954–83. *The Book of Leinster*, 6 vols, Dublin.

Mac Niocaill, G. 1975. *The Medieval Irish Annals*. Medieval Irish History Series 3, Dublin.

Moody, T.W., F.X. Martin, & F.J. Byrne, (eds) 1984. *A New History of Ireland 9: maps, genealogies, lists*, Oxford.

Ó Cíobháin, B. 2005. 'Cammas hUa Fathaid Tíre and the Vikings: significance and location', www.vikingwaterford.com.

Ó Corráin, D. 1972. *Ireland before the Normans*, Dublin.

Ó Corráin, D. 1979. 'High-kings, Vikings and other kings', *Irish Historical Studies*, 21, 283–323.

Ó Corráin, D. 1996. 'Vikings I: "Forty years" rest', *Peritia*, 10, 224.

Ó Corráin, D. 1997. 'Ireland, Wales, Man and the Hebrides' in P. Sawyer, (ed.), *The Oxford Illustrated History of the Vikings*, Oxford, 83–109.

Ó Corráin, D. 1998a. 'Viking Ireland – afterthoughts' in H.B. Clark et al. (eds), *Ireland and Scandinavia*, 421–52.

Ó Corráin, D. 1998b. 'The Vikings in Scotland and Ireland in the ninth century', *Peritia*, 12, 296–339.

Ó Floinn, R. 1998. 'The archaeology of early Viking-Age Ireland' in H.B. Clarke et al. (eds), *Ireland and Scandinavia*, pp 131–65.

Ó Máille, T. 1910. *The language of the Annals of Ulster*, Manchester.

O'Brien, R., P. Quinney & I. Russell, 2005. 'Preliminary report on the archaeological excavation and finds retrieval strategy of the Hiberno-Scandinavian site of Woodstown 6, Co. Waterford', *Decies*, 61, 13–122.

OLD = *Oxford Latin Dictionary*. Oxford 1982

Purcell, E. Ninth-century Viking settlement in Ireland: a study (PhD, University College Cork, in progress).

Sawyer, P.H. 1971. *The Age of the Vikings*, London.

Sawyer, P.H. 1982. *Kings and Vikings*, London.

Sheehan, J. 1998. 'Early Viking-Age silver hoards from Ireland and their Scandinavian elements' in H.B Clarke et al. (eds), 1998. *Ireland and Scandinavia*, pp 166–202.

Sheehan, J. 2008. 'The *longphort* in Viking Age Ireland', *Acta Archaeologica*, 79, 282–95.

The metal detector and the Viking Age in England

JULIAN D. RICHARDS & JOHN NAYLOR

INTRODUCTION

Metal detector users know more about the location of many categories of archaeological sites than do most archaeologists. This is particularly true for Anglo-Saxon and Viking-Age England. The boom in survey by remote sensing and aerial photography since the 1970s may have multiplied the known density of late prehistoric and Roman sites, and many late medieval settlements can be recognized from the earthwork remains of tofts and crofts or inferred from modern settlement patterns, but the more ephemeral enclosures and post-built timber structures of the period AD400–1000 remain elusive to traditional fieldwork methods (Richards 2000; 2001). Their scarcity has fuelled debates about numbers of settlers, and left the field open for place-name scholars. It has also meant that the main period of settlement nucleation in lowland England has long remained contested, with room for Anglo-Saxon, Viking, or Norman influence.

The advent of the metal detector has changed all that. Metal detecting probably reached the peak of its popularity in England around 1980, although the equipment is now more refined and the users more proficient. By the time of the first comprehensive survey of metal detecting in England in 1995 it was estimated that there were still perhaps 30,000 detectorists, of whom about 12,000 belonged to clubs affiliated to the National Council for Metal Detecting, and a further 3,000 were members of the Federation of Independent Detectorists (Dobinson and Denison 1995). At the time of writing, it is estimated that there are still some 8,000 or so metal detectorists active in England and Wales (Paynton 2006). The effects of detecting are difficult to quantify, but it is clear that tens of thousands of artefacts are recovered annually. The Portable Antiquities Scheme (PAS) database has records of over 200,000 archaeological objects, but this largely reflects only recently reported finds, and it is probably the tip of the iceberg (Paynton 2006). At the British Museum, for instance, about two-thirds of all Anglo-Saxon, medieval and post-medieval metal artefacts inspected between 1988 and 1995 were found by detectorists, together with nearly nine out of ten hoards and about half of all coins (Dobinson and Denision 1995). These finds have the potential to transform our knowledge of past material culture and, if find spot information is recorded, to revolutionize our knowledge of settlement and trading patterns as well (see, for example, Naylor 2004; Ulmschneider 1999; 2000).

Initial archaeological reactions to the growth of the hobby were largely negative and many archaeologists accused so-called 'treasure hunters' of looting archaeological sites, destroying the nation's past without proper record. Nowadays, there is wider acceptance that apart from a small number of illegal nighthawks (despised as much by other detectorists as by archaeologists), the majority of detectorists in England are responsible users with a genuine interest in the past and detailed knowledge of artefacts and archaeology (Paynton 2006). It is recognized that the real culprit is modern agricultural practice and that most finds are recovered from the ploughsoil, in which they are being abraded with each new ploughing and would eventually be destroyed without record, if it were not for the activities of detectorists. Nonetheless, the subject still gives rise to strong opinions, as a scan of *britarch*, the online discussion forum for British Archaeology quickly reveals (see also papers in Thomas and Stone forthcoming). From an early stage, however, some archaeologists recognized that it was important to try to work with metal detectorists. The late Tony Gregory in Norfolk, as well as Kevin Leahy in Lincolnshire, encouraged responsible metal detectorists to report their finds and to record their provenance. In East Anglia, where many Anglo-Saxon and Anglo-Scandinavian sites are known solely from detected finds, the tradition of cooperation has been maintained by John Newman in Suffolk, Andrew Rogerson in Norfolk, and by the late Sue Margeson and her successor, Tim Pestell, at Norwich Castle Museum. However, in the 1990s, during discussions leading up to the passing of the 1996 Treasure Act, it was recognized that there was a pressing need to establish a national scheme to record artefacts recovered by members of the public.

THE PORTABLE ANTIQUITIES SCHEME

The medieval law of Treasure Trove was replaced in England and Wales by a new Treasure Act in 1996. The new act gave legal protection to certain categories of artefacts and coins. To count as Treasure, in broad terms, finds must be at least 300 years old and contain more than 10 per cent gold or silver, although any associated finds, groups of ten or more coins, or two or more prehistoric finds of any material, are also classed as Treasure. Other artefacts, however, including single copper-alloy coins or artefacts are not covered by the Act. Consequently, apart from occasional finds of hack-silver and silver ingots, Anglo-Scandinavian stray finds rarely fall within the legal definition of Treasure. Nonetheless, it was recognized that many of the finds made by members of the public, whilst not being treasure, were important for our knowledge of the past, but were not being recorded because of the absence of appropriate resources and systems.

In March 1996, what was then the Department of National Heritage (DNH: now the Department for Culture, Media & Sport (DCMS)) published *Portable Antiquities: A Discussion Document*. The aim of this document was to complement the impending Treasure Act, address the issue of non-treasure archaeological finds and to propose solutions for dealing with these. After consultation, it was agreed that a scheme for the voluntary recording of all finds was required. As a result, in December 1996, the DNH announced that funding would be provided for two years for a programme of six pilot schemes, starting in September 1997. The project was ultimately overseen by the DCMS and administered by the Museums & Galleries Commission (now Museums, Libraries & Archives Council (MLA)). The pilot schemes were based in museums and archaeology services in Kent, Norfolk, the West Midlands, North Lincolnshire, the northwest and Yorkshire. In each place a Finds Liaison Officer (FLO) was appointed to act as a point of contact for finders. Their role was to record finds, to provide further information if possible and, providing finds did not qualify as Treasure, to return them to the finder. The six posts and schemes were co-ordinated by a further post which was based at, and funded by, the British Museum. Some areas, such as Norfolk, had already developed good relationships with detectorists; other areas, such as the northwest, did not have systems in place for recording such finds.

Initially, finds were recorded using either the host organizations' existing systems or systems unique to that organization, but it was recognized that a standardized, computerized system for recording finds was needed. An online national database was launched in 1999 to enable wider access to the information collated by the scheme. During the first year of the pilot scheme, over 13,500 objects were recorded. The scheme was very successful, but further funding was needed to extend it nationally. Bids were successfully put forward to the Heritage Lottery Fund (HLF) to fund five more FLO posts, commencing in January 1999. The five new FLO posts were based in museums and archaeology services in Dorset and Somerset (one post covering two counties), Hampshire, Northamptonshire, Suffolk and Wales. Shortly after this, a further application was made to the HLF to provide comprehensive coverage of the whole of England and Wales, and this was eventually put in place from April 2003, bringing about the scheme as it exists today. The full scheme comprises a network of thirty-six FLOs, between them covering each county in England and the whole of Wales, plus five specialist finds advisers and management and systems support. Finally, from April 2006 the scheme secured full funding from the DCMS, until March 2008. Administration of the scheme changed hands from MLA to the British Museum. Also in April 2006, the Portable Antiquities Scheme central unit became an official department within the British Museum, the *Department of Portable Antiquities & Treasure*.

METAL DETECTING AND VIKING-AGE ENGLAND

The study of the period AD700–1050 has much to gain from harnessing these new data. Pedersen (2005) has discussed the information gained from Viking-

Age finds reported in Denmark, and collaboration with German metal detectorists has illuminated the distribution of activity within the ramparts at Hedeby. In lowland England early medieval settlements have been particularly unresponsive to traditional survey methods, but the large quantities of copper-alloy objects in circulation have meant that Anglo-Saxon and Anglo-Scandinavian objects are well represented, and that many hitherto unknown sites have been discovered. Indeed, the only known Viking inhumation cemetery from England, at Cumwhitton in Cumbria, was discovered by a metal detectorist (Brennand 2006). The use of the metal detector has even given rise to a new category of site, referred to as the 'productive site' (see Pestell and Ulmschneider 2003). It is, however, argued that these are simply a product of the means of recovery, and that many excavated sites are similarly 'productive', if the number of non-ferrous metal objects is quantified (Richards 1999a).

Nonetheless, Cottam, East Yorkshire (Richards 1999b), remains one of the few excavated and published productive sites where occupation extends into the Anglo-Scandinavian period, and more sites are known only from concentrations of objects and coins. Leahy (2004) has described the large number of pieces of copper-alloy costume jewellery decorated in an Anglo-Scandinavian style which have been recovered from Lincolnshire, and the possible Anglo-Saxon trading site and Viking winter camp at Torskey has yielded Viking silver and Arabic dirhams (Blackburn 2002). The North Yorkshire site known by the fictional name of Ainsbrook (after its finders Mark Ainsley and Geoffrey Bambrook) may represent a similar category of site to Torksey.

THE VIKING AND ANGLO–SAXON LANDSCAPE AND ECONOMY PROJECT

The Viking and Anglo-Saxon Landscape and Economy (VASLE) Project was established in October 2004 with a three-year research grant from the Arts and Humanities Research Council (AHRC). By utilizing coin and artefact data for the period AD700–1050, primarily recovered by metal-detecting, the aims of the project are: (1) to plot national distributions of artefact types in order to chart social and economic development and change; (2) to study settlement hierarchies by defining characteristic assemblage 'fingerprints'; and (3) to study the development and settlement morphology of specific sites through limited fieldwork. It is hoped that these will feed into the broader aim of improving our understanding of the development of settlement landscape and economy in the early medieval period.

For reasons of space, this paper will focus on the first of these aims and will illustrate the results for the Viking Age with a small number of selected examples. The full results and an interactive database are to be published in the online journal *Internet Archaeology* at the end of the project.

One of the most important objectives has been the determination of the nature of constraints and bias in the data. A number of techniques have been developed to assess this, built around GIS-based analysis exploring the VASLE data against a range of control data (Figs 32.1–2) and a number of base maps including a 'constraints' base map (Figs 32.3–5). This was specifically designed to illustrate where finds recovery may be problematic, limited or unduly affected by modern features, using layers for urban areas, forests, lakes and the limits of ploughzone farming. We have also used basic topographic mapping, comparing data to the height of land and river systems, and have produced plots of kernel density to determine areas of relatively higher concentrations of finds across the country.

In assessing the potential constraints on recovery, it was decided that the best approach would utilize as many records as possible from all periods, rather than a period-specific dataset such as VASLE's. The data for this was compiled from all material with grid references held by the PAS dating from early prehistory to the modern period, a total of 122,379 records. This gives a broad overview of metal-detected data across England and Wales into which period-specific datasets can be compared and conclusions drawn relating to settlement patterns for particular periods. The density of all PAS records in Figure 32.1 shows a greater concentration of finds in the south and east, especially East Anglia, Kent, North Lincolnshire and parts of Yorkshire, with large numbers also visible in the central Midlands, especially Northamptonshire. In northwest England, Wales and the southwest (Devon and Cornwall) noticeably fewer finds are known.

It is clear that urbanism and the limits of ploughzone farming are the major constraints on data collection, but any area where access is restricted, including woodland and military 'danger' zones also have a negative effect on recovery. Urbanism has a two-fold effect – there are virtually no finds made in built-up areas, with little detecting and few stray finds, but conversely, clusters of finds are often made in the immediate vicinity of many larger towns and cities, as a result of detectorists working on land relatively local to them. Across the country, most finds have been made below 100m OD, and the vast majority below 300m OD, although some can be seen at this height in the southern Pennines. Historical landscape elements have also affected recovery patterns produced, with the majority of finds made dating to the period pre-AD1500. It is most obvious in areas such as the Weald, and the finds around the Wash, where archaeological work has illustrated a low density of occupation for much of pre-modern times.

A critical question in attempting to utilize such distributions for research, however, must be the extent to which distribution patterns are a product of constraints on modern recovery of artefacts and how much they can be considered a real indicator of ancient settlement patterns. Obviously, it is clear that this is a difficult question to answer, and it must be recognized that there is much regional variation, producing the complex patterns summarized above.

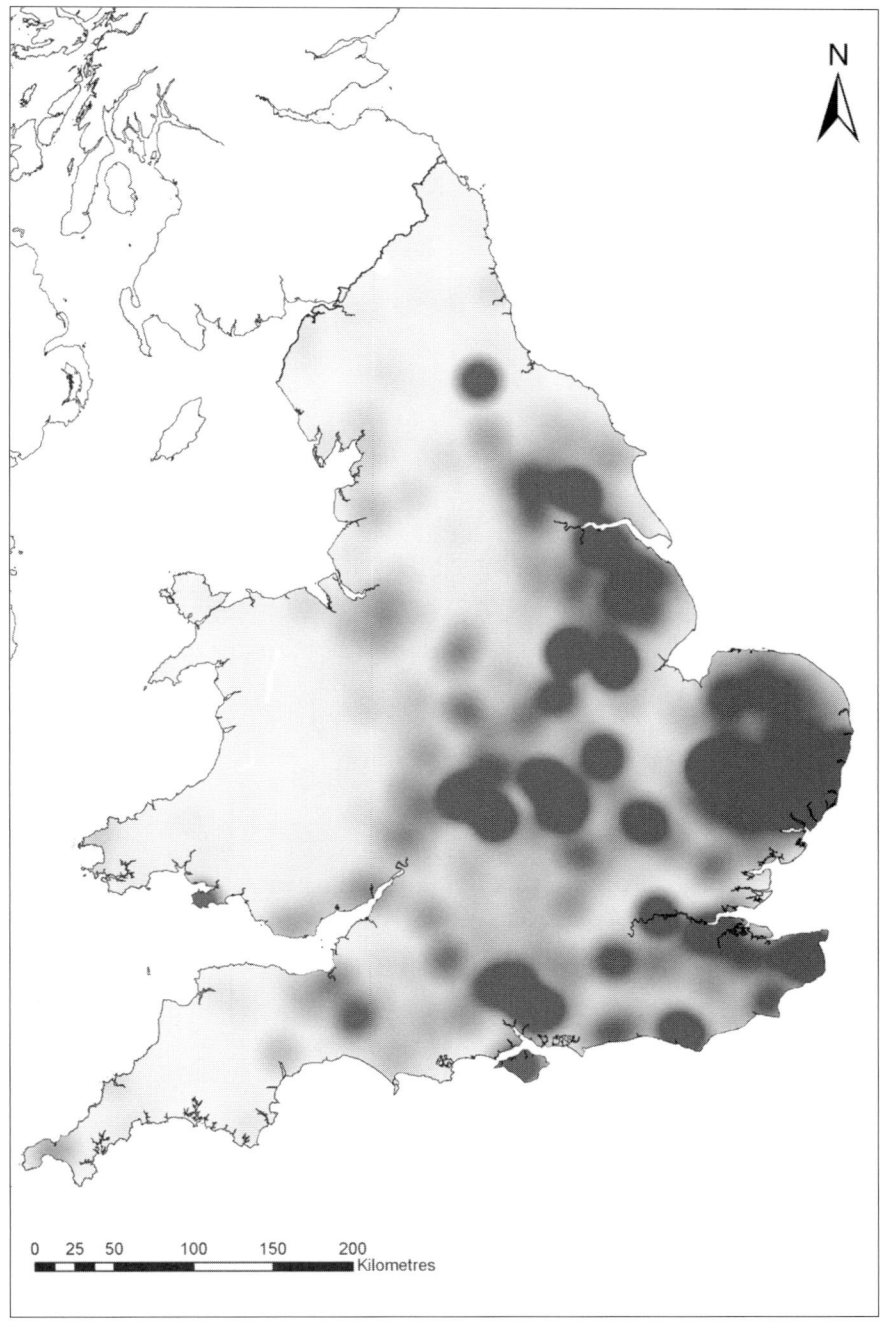

32.1 Density plot for all Portable Antiquities Scheme data, as at July 2006.

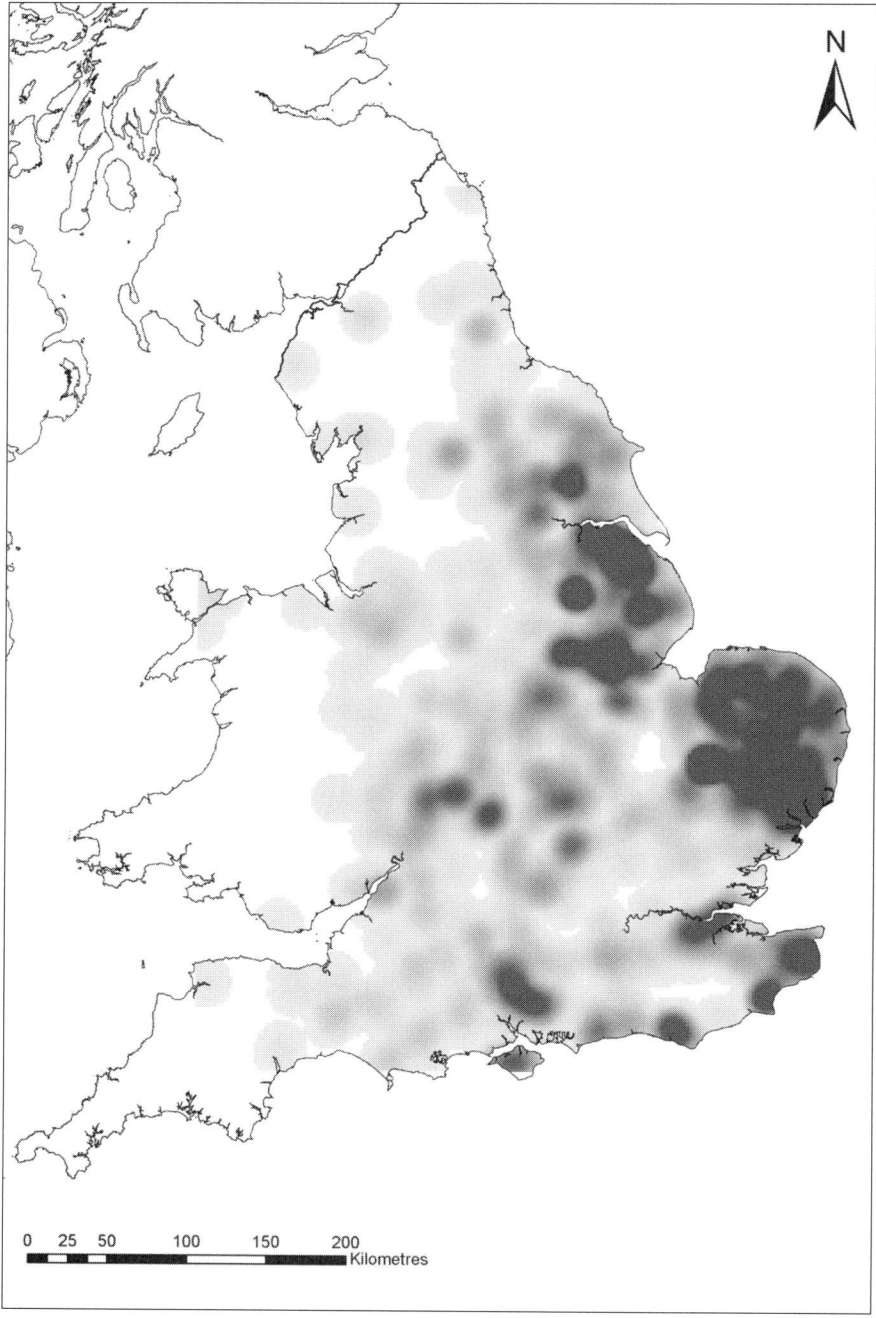

32.2 Density plot for Viking and Anglo-Saxon Landscape and Economy/Portable Antiquities Scheme records, as at end of October 2005.

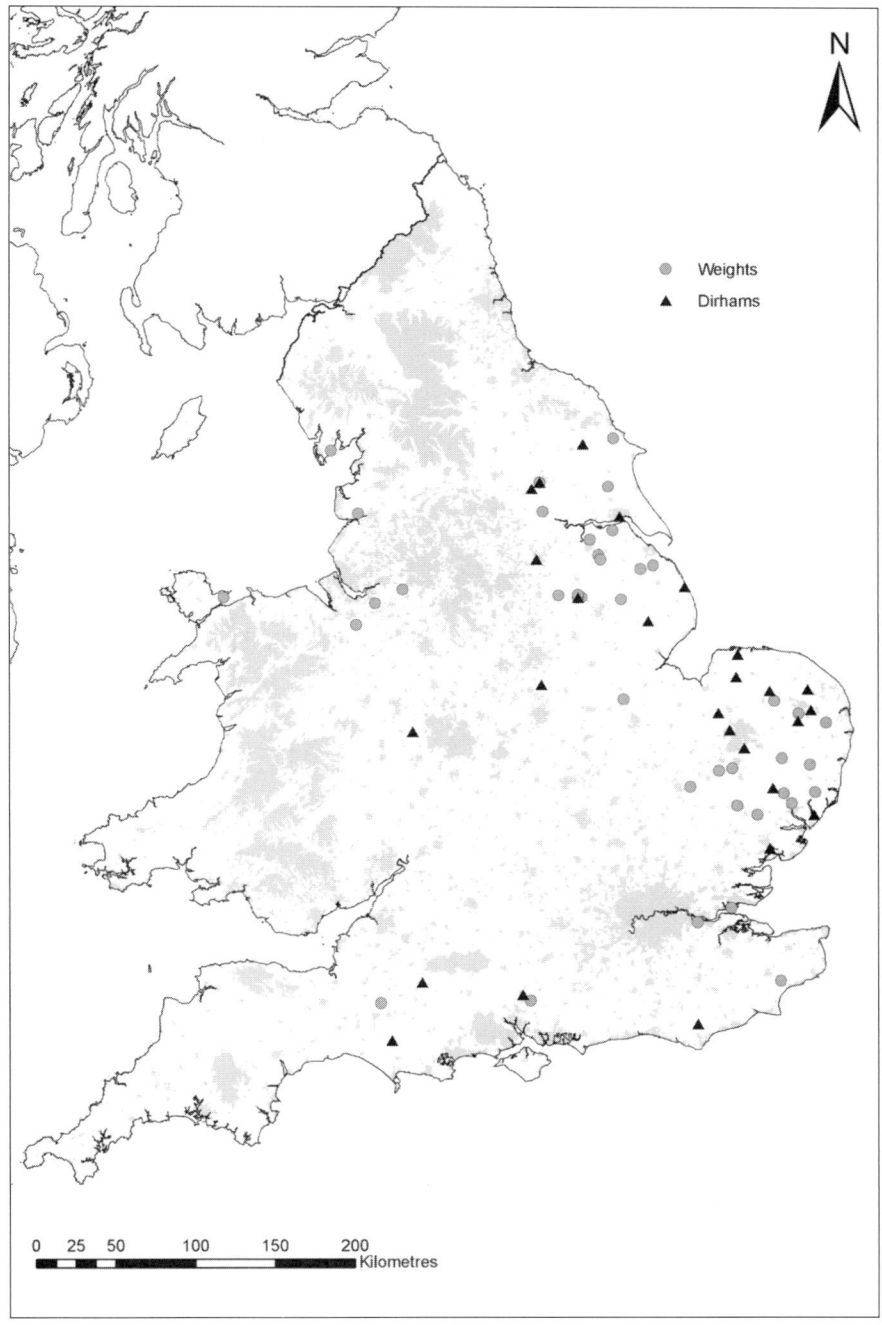

32.3 Distribution of weights and dirhams, against possible constraints on data recovery.

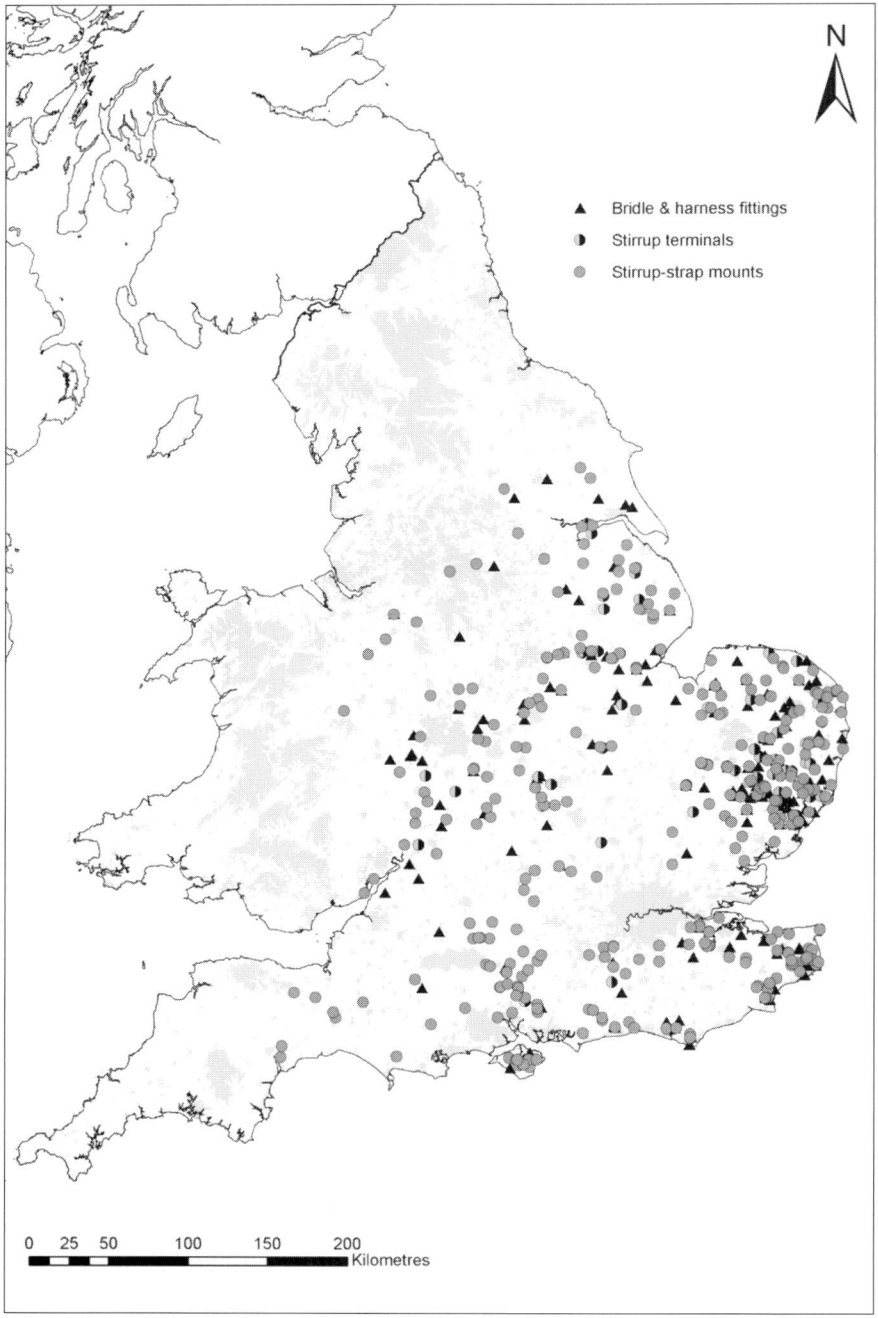

32.4 Distribution of horse-fittings and related objects, against possible constraints on data recovery.

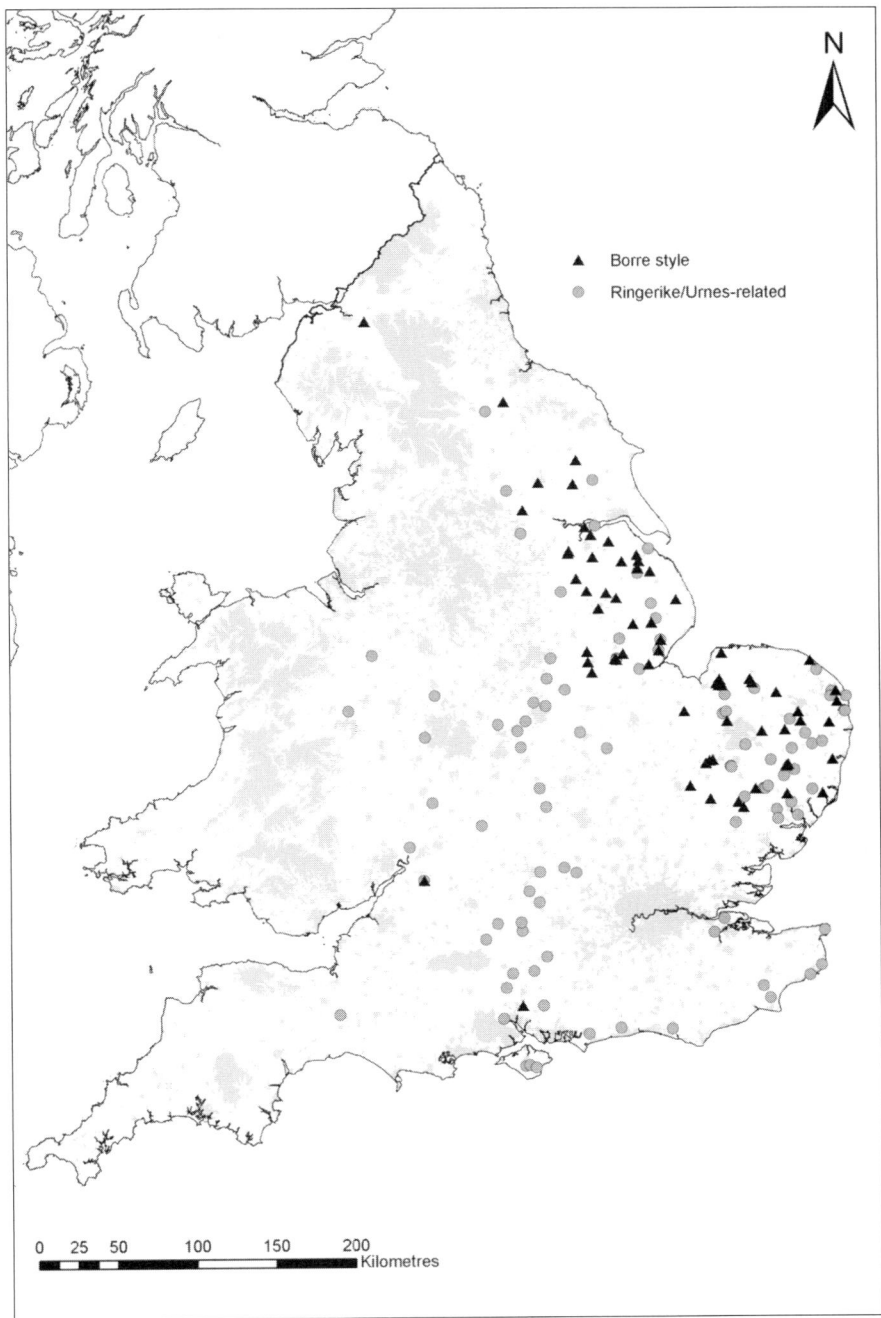

32.5 Distribution of Borre-style and Ringerike/Urnes-related style objects, against possible constraints on data recovery.

Some of the higher densities relate to those areas where finds reporting is well established (even though Norfolk and Suffolk finds have been recorded in local systems and are under-represented in the national database). However, in general, we can be quite confident that the dearth of finds on higher ground is an indication of ancient settlement patterns and not just the limits of arable agriculture, especially given that even on higher ground *within* the ploughzone the number of finds made is generally lower. In eastern England (excluding the northeast and southeast), constraints on data recovery are generally low, and so here it is likely that the distributions have a basis in ancient patterns of settlement. In the northeast, there are known problems of access to land and so the sparse distribution there is governed by constraints on modern recovery. Southeast England faces very similar problems to the northwest and much of the Midlands. Those associated with urban areas are most pertinent, and the density of finds immediately outside these areas would be expected across the country. Therefore, in the Midlands, northwest and southeast, outside of the highland areas, it should be expected that a more general spread of finds should be seen but urban areas distort this picture to produce a biased pattern.

The data derived from the PAS forms the basis for the mapping of artefact distributions for the period 700–1050, and has been cleaned and amended where necessary (for further discussion of this process, see Naylor and Richards 2005). It should be noted that additional information about single coin finds has been derived from the Corpus of Early Medieval Coin Finds (EMC) maintained at the Fitzwilliam Museum, Cambridge, but is not used here.

The PAS-derived VASLE database contains 3,379 records, over 96 per cent of which have at least a four-figure national grid reference. As for the overall PAS data, the density of this data in Figure 32.2 shows a greater concentration of finds in the south and east, especially East Anglia, northern and eastern Kent, the Sussex coastline, North Lincolnshire, and the Vale of York and Yorkshire Wolds. However, the differences between the density distributions for 700–1050 and the total density are most important, as these cannot result from differential recovery. Any differences must, therefore, relate to specific factors determining the loss of portable artefacts in the Anglo-Saxon and Viking period.

The major variations relate to areas in the west. There are fewer VASLE finds and correspondingly lower densities in the northwest, south Wales or the Midlands, and virtually no early medieval finds have been made in southwest England. As for most pre-Conquest periods, the Weald has produced few finds, and this corresponds well with most early medieval archaeology. Variations are also present in East Anglia, especially in northeast Suffolk, where the relative finds density is very low. These variations must be a reflection of settlement patterns in the period.

Turning to distributions of specific finds categories associated with Viking activity, the correspondence between these distributions and documented areas of activity gives further support to the reliability of the distributions, although one should be wary of circular arguments.

The presence of weights is an indication of transactions involving the weighing of silver or gold, rather than those reliant on a monetary economy. Balances are frequent finds from Scandinavian burials, and weights often turn up on sites associated with Scandinavian activity, such as Torksey. Arabic dirhams must have been brought to England by those who had passed through or had contact with Scandinavian-dominated areas. The main concentration of weights and dirhams recorded by the PAS is to be found in Eastern Yorkshire, Lincolnshire and East Anglia, as seen in Figure 32.3, although there are some coastal outliers in Dorset, Cheshire and the northwest. Dirhams are concentrated particularly in Norfolk, whereas weights are common in Suffolk and North Lincolnshire. Where they have been reported, dirhams are likely to have been correctly identified, although the identification of Viking weights may depend more on the experience of the local FLO. Although the total number of finds is small, it is unlikely that further discoveries will radically alter the distributions.

These are all areas where the Viking Great Army was active, and where land was subsequently partitioned with Viking settlers, although the relative absence of such finds from the central Midlands and the area that had been controlled by Mercia and later Wessex must be significant. Referring to the general density of finds from the period 700–1050 (Fig. 32.2), the south Midlands, Hampshire and the southeast each produce high densities of coins and other artefacts. The absence of weights and dirhams is a real one, and must relate to fewer transactions with those from Scandinavia or carried out in a Scandinavian fashion, apart from near to the coast or major rivers. Again, the fact that these are to the west of Winchester, and around Chester and Preston, must relate to a small Scandinavian presence in these regions.

The distributions of bridle and harness fittings, stirrup terminals and stirrup-strap mounts are all roughly co-terminus, justifying the strategy of treating them together as relating to equestrian activity. These are stray finds, rather than from graves, although one should remember their association with late tenth-century aristocratic male burial in Denmark (Roesdahl 2006). Stirrups found in 1884 near Magdalen Bridge in Oxford were originally thought to have been casual losses but have been re-interpreted as coming from an equestrian burial (Blair and Crawford 1997). Stirrups are thought to have been introduced by the Vikings and finds of stirrups in the Danelaw have been regarded as indicating the presence of Danish cavalry in eleventh-century armies (Graham-Campbell 1992; Seaby and Woodfield 1980). Williams (1997) has catalogued over 500 stirrup-strap mounts with elements of Ringerike or Urnes style ornament, which were attached to iron stirrups. These were probably in use for a relatively short period of time, between 1025 and 1100. These may represent a short-lived fashion, possibly of an elite cavalry group, initiated during Knútr's reign and certainly with Scandinavian affiliations.

There is a fairly wide distribution of these equestrian artefacts throughout lowland England, much less constrained than the distribution of weights or dirhams, although there are notable differences from the overall distribution of objects of 700–1050. The main concentration of finds from Norfolk and Suffolk follows the general pattern, as do the smaller groupings in the southeast, and in Hampshire and the Isle of Wight. However, as well as these foci, the distribution also extends across southern England, and into the West Midlands and Warwickshire, where there are otherwise few finds of the period. On the other hand, there are no recorded finds in the northwest, and few north of the Humber. The finds are clearly indicative of an eleventh-century southern-based equestrian class, although the number of finds suggest that this was quite substantial and probably included more than the traditional societal elites.

Finally, it is instructive to compare the distributions of artefacts decorated in the Borre style, with those decorated in a Ringerike or Urnes style (Fig. 32.5). To a great extent, the distribution of Ringerike or Urnes-related objects corresponds to the distribution of equestrian equipment seen in Figure 32.4, and includes many of the same objects, although the southeast is sparse. Nonetheless, this wide distribution can be seen as the area of eleventh-century Scandinavian influence, under Knútr. By contrast, the Borre-style objects represent a much more northern and eastern Scandinavian focus in the second half of the ninth and early tenth century. Borre-style objects are almost entirely constrained to Norfolk, Suffolk, Lincolnshire and Yorkshire, with very few outliers. Clearly, the fashion for brooches decorated in this style was limited to areas with significant numbers of Scandinavian settlers in the partitions of land following the campaigns of the Great Army. Although the areas lie within the areas of Scandinavian-influenced place-names, the foci are very different, with a lower density of finds than place-names north of the Humber and in the northwest, and a higher density in East Anglia. There is a smaller number of Jellinge-style objects whose distribution is coterminous with that of the Borre-style artefacts, but an almost complete absence of Mammen-style artefacts, which corresponds with the absence of documented Scandinavian activity between 900 and 980.

CONCLUSION

To conclude, mapping of the entire PAS dataset provides us with some important conclusions regarding the potential constraints on recovery of artefacts by metal-detection. The data is a complex interplay of factors, with geography (topography, river valleys, wetlands), modern constraints (urbanism, limits of ploughzone farming, forests, military zones), and underlying historical landscape elements all affecting the patterns of finds produced. The two most important factors immediately visible as having major effects on data-recovery are the nature of modern urbanism and natural topography/limits of plough-zone. Comparing VASLE-period data to this allows for the distribution pattern to be adequately assessed with respect to both modern constraints and, with care, to patterns of early medieval settlement.

The plotting of artefacts of specific classes has the potential to illustrate economic transactions as well as cultural zones, and the use of decorative style to demonstrate ethnicity, as the few examples presented here have shown. The core distribution of Viking weights and dirhams is similar to that of Borre-style ornament, although the outliers show that Scandinavian economic activity was not entirely constrained to those areas where people wore Scandinavian-style dress. In the ninth century this was very regionalized, focused on Norfolk, Suffolk, Lincolnshire and parts of Yorkshire. Outside of this eastern zone, people followed Anglo-Saxon costume styles and jewellery. Maybe these constraints reflect the extent to which Scandinavian influence was limited to specific areas, following the partitions of land recorded in the *Anglo-Saxon Chronicle*. There is then a gap of about a hundred years before we see the widespread dispersal of Urnes- and Ringerike-style objects across lowland England, under the reign of Knútr, and the presence of a mobile equestrian class who carried the new style throughout southern England, but failed to have much influence in the north. Artefact distributions must be treated with care, and the statements made here should be regarded as preliminary, but by harnessing the results of metal detecting we hope to have demonstrated their potential to refine our understanding of the development of a multi-cultural society in England during the Viking Age.

ACKNOWLEDGMENTS

We are grateful to Mark Blackburn of the Fitzwilliam Museum, and to Roger Bland, Helen Geake, Simon Holmes and other colleagues from the Portable Antiquities Scheme for their help and encouragement in using their data-sets. We are also grateful to the countless metal detectorists who have made this research possible by logging their finds with the EMC and PAS databases. The background map detail used in the figures in this paper is based on copyright digital map data owned and supplied by HarperCollins Cartographic, and is used with permission. Contours are derived from LANDMAP datasets and are used with permission. The project's website can be found at <http://www.york.ac.uk/depts/arch/vasle/>. The project was funded by the AHRC under Research Grant APN18370.

BIBLIOGRAPHY

Blackburn, M. 2002. 'Finds from the Anglo-Scandinavian site of Torksey, Lincolnshire' in B. Paszkiewicz (ed.), *Moneta Mediævalis: Studia numozmatycze i historyczne ofiarowane Profesorowi Suchodolskiemu w 65, rocznicęurodzin* (Warsaw), pp 89–101.

Blair, J. & B.E. Crawford. 1997. 'A Late-Viking burial at Magdalen Bridge, Oxford?', *Oxoniensia*, 62, 135–43.

Brennand, M. 2006. 'Finding the Viking dead', *Current Archaeology*, 204, 623–9.

Dobinson, C. & S. Denison 1995. *Metal detecting and archaeology in England* (York).

Graham-Campbell, J. 1992. 'Anglo-Scandinavian equestrian equipment in eleventh-century England', *Anglo-Norman Studies*, 14, 77–89.

Leahy, K. 2004. 'Detecting the Vikings in Lincolnshire', *Current Archaeology*, 190, 462–8.

Naylor, J. 2004. *An archaeology of trade in Middle Saxon England*, British Archaeological Reports, British Series, 376 (Oxford).

Naylor, J. & J.D. Richards 2005. 'Third-party data for first class research', *Archeolgia e Calcolatori*, 16, 83–91.

Paynton, C. 2006. 'Is the war finally over?', *Current Archaeology*, 206, 38–9.

Pedersen, A. 2005. 'The metal detector and the Viking Age in Denmark' in A. Mortensen & S.V. Arge (eds), *Vikings and Norse in the North Atlantic: select papers from the proceedings of the Fourteenth Viking Congress, Tórshavn, 19–30 July 2001* (Tórshavn), pp 402–11.

Pestell, T. & K. Ulmschneider (eds). 2003. *Markets in early medieval Europe* (Macclesfield).

Richards, J.D. 1999a. 'What's so special about 'productive sites'?' in T. Dickinson & D. Griffiths (eds), *The making of kingdoms: Anglo-Saxon studies in archaeology and history*, 10 (Oxford), 71–80.

Richards, J.D. 1999b. 'Cottam: an Anglian and Anglo-Scandinavian settlement on the Yorkshire Wolds', *Archaeological Journal*, 156, 1–110.

Richards, J.D. 2000. 'Anglo-Saxon settlements and archaeological visibility in the Yorkshire Wolds' in H. Geake & J. Kenny (eds), *Early Deira: archaeological studies of the East Riding in the fourth to ninth Centuries AD* (Oxford), pp 27–39.

Richards, J.D. 2001. 'Finding the Vikings: the hunt for Anglo-Scandinavian rural settlement in the Northern Danelaw' in J. Graham-Campbell et al. (eds), *Vikings and the Danelaw: proceedings of the Thirteenth Viking Congress* (Oxford), pp 269–77.

Roesdahl, E. 2006. 'Aristocratic burial in Late Viking-Age Denmark: custom, regionality, conversion' in C. von Carnap-Bornheim (ed.), *Universitätsforschungen zur Prähistorischen Archäologie*, 139, pp 169–83.

Seaby, W.A. & P. Woodfield, 1980. 'Viking stirrups from England and their background', *Medieval Archaeology*, 24, 87–122.

Thomas, S. & P. Stone. forthcoming. Metal detecting and archaeology, (Newcastle).

Ulmschneider, K. 1999. 'Archaeology, history, and the Isle of Wight in the Middle Saxon Period', *Medieval Archaeology*, 43, 19–44.

Ulmschneider, K. 2000. 'Settlement, economy and the "productive" site: Middle Anglo-Saxon Lincolnshire AD650–780', *Medieval Archaeology*, 44, 53–79.

Williams, D. 1977. *Late Saxon stirrup-strap mounts*, Council for British Archaeology Research Report, 111 (York).

From Scandinavia to Spain: a Viking-Age reliquary in León and its meaning

ELSE ROESDAHL

Viking artefacts are known from many European countries – objects produced within Scandinavia, produced abroad in Scandinavian taste, or produced in local versions of that taste – sometimes designated, for example, as Hiberno-Norse or Anglo-Scandinavian. Such artefacts are normally considered to be products of raids or trade, or of settlement or mercenary activity in the region. In some countries many such objects are found. Only a single Viking object, however, is known from Spain. This is a small box which probably came thence from Scandinavia as an aristocratic gift in the late tenth century. It is now in the treasury of the collegiate church of San Isodoro in León, in northern Spain, on the pilgrims' road to Santiago de Compostela (Fig. 33.1), in an area that had been Christian since late Roman times (as opposed to most of Spain, which came under Muslim rule in the early eighth century).

DESCRIPTION AND RESEARCH HISTORY

The box (Figs 33.2–4), which is now empty, is cylindrical with a protruding 'ear' at the top; it is 4.5cm high and 3.3cm in diameter. The material is antler, the 'ear' being carved from a tine. The lid and base are of gilt copper-alloy. The body is carved in open-work between a narrow rim at top and bottom. The rims have a recess to accommodate the lid and base respectively, and the upper rim is extended towards the centre so as to give added strength. It is not known whether there was a similar treatment of the base. The ornament, in the Scandinavian Mammen style, is tight, intricate and well-organized, and the surface is carefully polished. The main motif is a bird. Its head, with huge eyes and marked beak, is formed from the 'ear'. The wings are folded below and the legs spread out to both sides. The wings and legs are interlaced with knots and four 'snakes' with small heads. Two further, smaller snakes interlace with the ornament on top of the bird's head. Two fairly large holes below the bird's beak interfere with its wings and are probably secondary, while a wide opening right beneath the beak seems to be an original feature (Figs 33.2–3). The lid and base are also in openwork and in late Mammen style. Four copper-alloy nails attach the base to the cylinder. The simple lid-hinge must be secondary. Indeed, small vertical holes in the top rim, which seem to correspond with holes and remains of a nail in the lid, indicate that the lid was originally also nailed to the body.

353

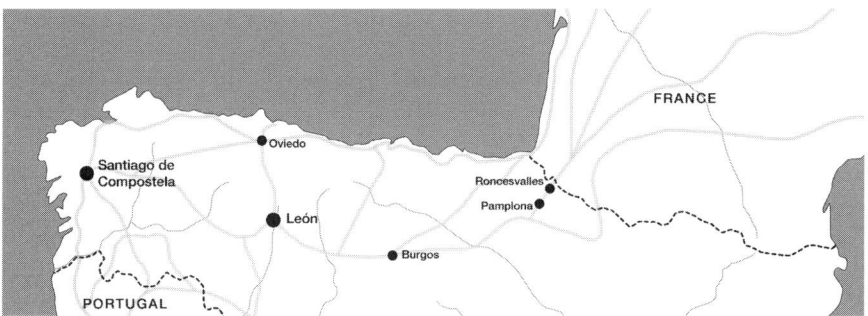

33.1 Northern Spain, showing location of León (drawing: Louise Hilmar).

The above description is based on visual inspection of the box in its exhibition case on a visit to León in July 1999, and on a series of good photographs taken in 1990 of the object while it was out of the case, by Jan Skamby Madsen. These photos are also the basis of the drawings in Figures 33.5–6.

On the basis of photographs, the material has been identified as red-deer antler by a zoologist (Jørgensen 1990), and not ivory, bone or walrus-ivory as has been stated in previous publications (see below), although it is notoriously difficult to distinguish between red-deer and reindeer antler. A recent popular book on San Isidoro and its treasury describes the box as being of reindeer antler (Vinayo 1998, 46); but the author (pers. comm., 8.11.2000) has stated that this identification was not based on zoological determination. The identification is presumably based on the recognition of the object as Scandinavian, with a consequent conception of reindeer as a Scandinavian animal. Red-deer antler seems a more acceptable alternative.

The known history of the object and its publication must be briefly outlined. As already mentioned, it is part of the treasury of the collegiate church of San Isidoro in León. Nothing is known about its early history. It was first published, with six text lines and two photographs, in a catalogue of this treasury in 1925–6, where it was described as a possible reliquary of ivory of Anglo-Saxon origin (Gómez-Moreno 1925, 195; 1926, figs 195–6). Adolph Goldschmidt picked up on it quickly and included it in his catalogue of Romanesque ivories; he argued that it was a reliquary and stated it was of bone and held a relic (Goldschmidt 1926 [1975], no. 298). He was well aware of its date and Scandinavian origin, but the relevant volume of his ivory corpus, which listed the Cammin (Kamień) and Bamberg caskets and other related material, had been published eight years earlier (Goldschmidt 1918 [1969], nos 189, 191–2). The León box, therefore, appeared in the 'wrong' Goldschmidt volume (IV instead of II) and remained largely unknown to students of the Viking Age. Danielle Gaborit-Chopin was aware of the box and included it in her 1978 book on medieval ivories, identifying it as a Scandinavian pyx of walrus ivory (Gaborit-Chopin 1978, cat. no. 84). But it was not until 1990, when Eduardo Morales of the Spanish

33.2 View of the León box
(photo: Jan Skamby Madsen).

33.3 View of the León box
(photo: Jan Skamby Madsen).

Embassy in Copenhagen, and Jan Skamby Madsen, then at the Viking Ship Museum in Roskilde, travelled in Spain in search of Vikings, that the box was 'rediscovered', so-to-speak and the material identified. Subsequently, it was widely published in newspapers and popular articles and became well-known in Viking circles (e.g. Jørgensen 1990; Skamby Madsen 1992, 18; Morales 1991; 2004).

PARALLELS, FUNCTION AND MEANING

As already noted, the box is the only Viking object known from Spain. It is clearly of Scandinavian workmanship, finely carved in the Mammen style and therefore datable to the mid- to second half of the tenth century (on the Mammen style, see Wilson & Klindt-Jensen 1966, 95–133; Fuglesang 1991; Wilson 1995, 115–41).

It has no exact parallel, but small cylinder-shaped objects are not unknown in Viking-Age contexts. Some, as those from Årnes and Å in Norway and another from Wolin, are also finely carved and in the Mammen style, while others, from London and Bornish in Uist, have rather coarse Ringerike-style ornamentation. The function of such cylinders is unknown. It has been suggested that they served as knife-handles or containers for sewing-gear (Wilson & Klindt-Jensen

33.4 View of the León box (photo: Jan Skamby Madsen).

1966, pl. XLV, fig. 57; Graham-Campbell 1980, nos 495, 500; Fuglesang 1991, figs 17–18; Sharples 2000, 14; (information on the Wolin cylinder kindly supplied by Blazej M. Stanislowski (2002); cf. Backhouse, Turner & Webster 1984, cat. no. 116)). The ornament of the metal lid and base-plate is quite well paralleled in Scandinavian and Anglo-Scandinavian brooches of the tenth century, as well as on some mounts on the late tenth-century Cammin and Bamberg caskets (e.g. Jansson 1984, 60, fig. 8:2; Muhl 1990, taf. 22; Wilson 1995, 117). No other small boxes or cylinders, however, have metal lids, and none are in openwork or have a protruding 'ear' like that on the León box. Nor do they have its bird motif.

This motif is, however, well known in contemporary Scandinavian art. Some of the fine mounts in King Gorm's grave at Jelling (c.958), for example, take the form of birds, and the same is true of the Cammin and Bamberg caskets (e.g. Müller-Wille 1982, abb. 11; Muhl 1990, taf. 26). This bird motif has no specific religious significance; it was, for example, used on Thor's hammers as well as cross pendants and bird pendants (e.g. Roesdahl 1981; Roesdahl & Wilson 1992, nos 104, 181, 265). With its big eyes, pronounced beak and folded wings, the León bird must be a bird of prey, probably a falcon or other hunting bird. In my opinion, it is clear that the bird motif was an aristocratic symbol (Roesdahl 2002, 105). There is, then, good comparative material from Scandinavia. But the León box is unique in both quality and motif, as well as in the fact that it is in openwork. It is also distinctive because it is preserved in the treasury of an

33.5 The ornament from the León box, height 4.5cm
(drawing: Louise Hilmar, based on a series of photos).

33.6 The lid and base of the
León box. Not to scale
(drawing: Louise Hilmar,
based on photos).

important church. It must have been the container of something precious, and
the openwork indicates that the contents should be seen, not hidden, and could
be touched. The box was also permanently closed; both lid and base were once
nailed to the body. The real treasure, therefore, was the now lost contents, as was
probably the case with many other splendid boxes, some of which came to places
far from where they were produced, such as the Franks casket, the Cammin and
Bamberg caskets and medieval Limoges caskets (Webster 1999; Goldschmidt 1918
[1969], nos 191–2; O'Neill & Egan 1996). In the light of its late tenth-century date –
Denmark's official conversion was in *c*.965 – the León box was probably a reliquary
as originally postulated by Goldschmidt, not a pyx (cf. *Lexikon des Mittelalters* 1994,
VII: 'Pyxis'), and it may well have been made in Denmark. If this interpretation is
correct, it is perhaps the earliest known Scandinavian reliquary (for a possible
contemporary example see Roesdahl 1977).

It has been variously suggested that the box reached León from the Isle of
Man, where so many fine stone crosses decorated in the Mammen style survive,
or that its appearance might be due to Viking incursions in northern Spain, or
that it was presented to San Isodoro together with other gifts by King Fernando
I (reigned AD1037–65) and his queen (Morales 1991, 46; on Manx crosses see

Kermode 1907 [1994]). This latter proposition seems not unlikely. León is situated on a cultural crossroads, in an area of great interest to Christians. The town was the capital or royal residence of the kingdom of León, and is not far from Santiago de Compostela, where the cult of St James had been celebrated since the early ninth century. León is actually on the pilgrims' road to Santiago, where pilgrims from lands to the north of the Pyrenees are first recorded at the shrine of St James in the early tenth century, although pilgrimages to Santiago do not seem to have developed into a mass phenomenon before the eleventh or twelfth century (*Lexikon des Mittelalters* 1991, V: 'León'; 1994, VII: 'Santiago de Compostela'; Vinayo 1972). Furthermore, although Santiago and León were situated in the Christian part of the Iberian Peninsula, they were located close to the border of what was, in the late tenth century, Muslim territory. León was indeed stormed by Almanzur in 987, and Santiago was destroyed by him in 997. Vikings had plundered Santiago some thirty years earlier, occupying the region in the years between 968 and 971 (Fabricius 1897, 130; Vinayo 1972). It is of interest, incidentally, that the Spanish Arab At-Tartuschi visited Hedeby in about 970.

The church of San Isodoro itself was founded in 1063 – long after the box was made – by King Fernando I after victories over the Moors, and the relics of San Isodoro himself were translated there from Seville. Fernando had united the realms of León and Castile in 1037, and San Isodoro became the burial church of his dynasty. It was, then, a church of great distinction, closely associated with royalty, and succeeded earlier churches on the site (Vinayo 1972; 1998). The box could well have been in royal possession for some time before it came to San Isodoro, and may initially have been in another royal chapel or church in the region, perhaps even in León itself.

I have argued elsewhere (Roesdahl 1998) that the León box should be seen in the context of the Cammin and Bamberg caskets (in present northern Poland and southern Germany respectively) and the so-called Saint Stephen's sword, now in Prague. All are decorated in the Mammen style and, like the León box, are preserved in European churches of high status (see also Goldschmidt 1918 [1969], nos 189, 191–2). I have also suggested that these extremely high quality objects were aristocratic gifts from Scandinavian royalty – probably Harald Bluetooth or perhaps Svein Forkbeard – to European princes, kings and emperors, their Christian contemporaries. Aristocratic gift-exchange is a well-known phenomenon, and gift-exchanges between Scandinavian and European princes in the Viking Age are well recorded in written sources. León is a long way from Denmark, but lies in a very interesting area, and the box is in a very interesting church. Its size and compactness also make it easy to transport.

In conclusion, I would suggest that this box with its once precious contents, undoubtedly a relic, was presented by royalty or high aristocracy from newly converted Denmark to royalty in Christian Spain, represented by a king fighting the pagan Moors and who lived on the road to Santiago. If this interpretation of the box is correct, it implies that a vision of Christian northern Spain, of battles against the Moors and of the cult of St James in Santiago de Compostela was present in aristocratic circles in Scandinavia in the earliest period of Viking Christianity in the late tenth century.

ACKNOWLEDGMENTS

I am very grateful to Jan Skamby Madsen for kindly providing his photos of the box; to Magdalena Valor for help with contacting Antonio Vianyo about the material of the box; and to Christopher Grøndahl Pedersen for the translation into Danish of Antonio Vinayo's letter, as well as of the text in Gómez-Moreno 1925–6. I also wish to thank David M. Wilson for discussions on the box and for transforming my 'English' into English.

BIBLIOGRAPHY

Backhouse, J. et al. (eds). 1984. *The golden age of Anglo-Saxon art* (London).
Fabricius, A. 1897. 'Normannertogene til den spanske Halvø', *Aarbøger for Nordisk Oldkyndighed og Historie* (1897), 75–160.
Fuglesang, S.H. 1991. 'The axehead from Mammen and the Mammen style' in M. Iversen (ed.), *Mammen: Grav, kunst og samfund i vikingetid* (Højbjerg), pp 83–107.
Gaborit-Chopin, D. 1978. *Elfenbeinkunst im Mittelalter* (Berlin) [trans. from *Ivoires du Moyen Age* (Fribourg, 1978)].
Goldschmidt, A. 1918 [1969]. *Die elfenbeinskulpturen* II *aus der zeit der karolingischen und sächsischen Kaiser VIII–XI jahrhundert* (Berlin).
Goldschmidt, A. 1926 [1975]. *Die elfenbeinskulpturen* IV *aus der romanischen zeit XI–XIII jahrhundert* (Berlin).
Gómez-Moreno, M. 1925–6. *Catalogo monumental de Espana: provincia de León. Texto, Láminas* (Madrid).
Graham-Campbell, J. 1980. *Viking artefacts: a select catalogue* (London).
Jansson, I. 1984. 'Kleine rundspangen' in G. Arwidsson (ed.), *Birka II:1. Systematische analysen der gräberfunde* (Stockholm), pp 58–74.
Jørgensen, J.H. 1990. 'Vikinger i Spanien: sensationelt historisk fund', *Politiken* (Copenhagen) 13 December 1990, 2. sektion, 3.
Kermode, P.M.C. 1907 [1994]. *Manx crosses: with an introduction by D.M. Wilson* (Angus).
Lexikon des mittelalters. 1977– (München and Zürich).
Morales, R.E. 1991. 'Arte vikingo in Espana', *Revista de arqueología*, 7:121, 41–7.
Morales, R.E. 2004. '"San Isodoro-æsken" i León' in *Vikingerne på den Iberiske Halvø* (Madrid), 118–25 [trans. *Los Vikingos en la Península Ibérica* (Madrid, 2004)].
Muhl, A. 1990. 'Der bamberger und der camminer schrein: zwei im Mammenstil verzierte prunkkästchen der Wikingerzeit', *Offa*, 47, 241–420.

Müller-Wille, M. 1982. 'Königsgrab und Königskirche', *Bericht der Römisch-Germanischen Kommission*, 63, 349–412.

O'Neill, J.P. & T. Egan (eds). 1996. *Enamels of Limoges* (New York).

Roesdahl, E. 1977. 'Danmarks ældste relikvieskrin', *MIV. Museerne i Viborg amt* 7, 26–33.

Roesdahl, E. 1981. 'En tusindårig guldfugl', *hikuin* 7, 205–8.

Roesdahl, E. 1998. 'Cammin – Bamberg – Prague – Léon: four Scandinavian *objects d'arts* in Europe' in A. Wesse (ed.), *Studien zur archäologie des Ostseeraumes: festschrift für Michael Müller-Wille* (Neumünster), pp 547–54.

Roesdahl, E. 2002. 'Harald Blauzahn: ein dänischer Wikingerkönig aus archäologischer sicht' in J. Henning (ed.), *Europa im 10. jahrhundert: archäologie einer aufbruchzeit* (Mainz am Rhein), pp 95–108.

Roesdahl, E. & D.M. Wilson (eds). 1992. *From Viking to Crusader: Scandinavia and Europe, 800–1200* (Copenhagen & New York).

Sharples, N. 2000. *The Iron Age and Norse settlement at Bornish, South Uist: an interim report on the 2000 Excavations*, Cardiff Studies in Archaeology, 18 (Cardiff).

Skamby Madsen, J. 1992. *Les Vikings Danois* (Copenhagen).

Vinayo, A.G. 1972. *L'ancien royaume de León Roman* (Zodiaque).

Vinayo, A. 1998. *Colegiata de San Isodoro* (León).

Webster, L. 1999. 'The iconographic programme of the Franks Casket' in J. Hawkes & S. Mills (eds), *Northumbria's golden age* (Stroud), 227–46.

Wilson, D.M. 1995. *Vikingatidens konst*. Signums svenska konsthistoria (Lund).

Wilson, D.M. & O. Klindt-Jensen. 1966. *Viking art* (London).

The sagas and courtly love

DANIEL SÄVBORG

In his history of literature, Finnur Jónsson (1920–4) devotes 1,629 pages to Old Norse literature before 1300. Only a hundred of these are devoted to literature with a direct connection to foreign literature. He discusses *riddarasögur* in eighteen of these pages, and religious and learned literatures are also discussed very briefly. Since Jónsson's time, there has been a tendency among scholars to emphasize the importance of continental culture for Old Norse civilization. In the 1960s, these tendencies reached their peak. *Norrøn fortællekunst* (1965) concentrated on translations such as saints' lives and *riddarasögur*. In *Skáldasögur* (1961), Bjarni Einarsson claimed that the skald sagas were dependent on continental literature. In several works, Lars Lönnroth emphasized the great importance of continental culture and literature in thirteenth-century Iceland. He claimed that the continental and the indigenous literature did not flourish separately in Iceland, but were cultivated in the same circles. In an article (1964) on what he called *tesen om de två kulturerna* 'the theory about the two cultures', he contested the opinion *att den inhemska sagalitteraturen producerats och konsumerats i en annan sorts miljö än den samtida översättningslitteraturens* 'that the indigenous saga literature was produced and consumed in a type of environment other than that of the contemporary translated literature' (1967, 181). His conclusion is that the indigenous saga literature in every respect was dependent on the translated works. He claims that 'the style and subject matter of "family sagas" are often derived from foreign literature' (1965, 20). His rejection of the notion of 'the two cultures' leads him to reject the idea of the Icelandic family saga as a unique genre, one *sui generis*; rather, on the literary grounds it is impossible to posit a difference between translated works and indigenous sagas.

Nowadays, all scholars agree that the Old Norse culture was part of a common European culture. But what was the nature of foreign influence? How deep was it? How strong was the indigenous tradition compared to the foreign? That is what I discuss here. My point of departure is the theme of love.

In continental courtly poetry, love is frequently a main subject. This type of poetry became known in Old Norse as *riddarasögur*. According to the standard view among scholars, the translations are not faithful. The typically courtly character of the depiction of love is said to be more or less ruined (e.g. Mitchell 1959, 465; Jónas Kristjánsson 1997, 323; Einar Ól. Sveinsson 1953, 41; Bonath 1985, 13). Many scholars talk about a lack of interest in love, they claim that love descriptions are omitted or abbreviated, that the emotions are moderated compared to the originals, etc. – all under the influence of the indigenous saga style.

This opinion may seem to reject the idea of a strong continental influence on the family sagas. However, many scholars appear to believe in a fusion of the two. Thus, the *riddarasögur* as well as the family sagas could then be seen as hybrids of Old Norse and continental tradition. This accords with Lönnroth's idea that it is impossible to make a distinction between indigenous and translated literature.

The standard view about *riddarasögur* is that there was an Old Norse dislike of typical courtly love and its love depiction. Is that correct?

In medieval Scandinavia there are a lot of runic inscriptions with text in Latin, for example quotations from love poems known from *Carmina Burana* about fire of love and so on, there are also objects with the text *amor, flos amoris, omnia vincit amor* etc (Liestøl & Sanness Johnsen 1980–90, 11–15). There are also several works of art from the fourteenth century depicting loving couples in a typically continental courtly way. These are evidence of an appreciation of continental literature and its depiction of love.

What of the *riddarasögur*? First, it seems necessary to establish what is typical in the depiction of love in courtly poetry. Firstly, love frequently begins with love-sickness, where the power of passion causes the lover terrible pain. Secondly, *frauendienst* is a common phenomenon – a man is the humble servant of a lady to make himself worthy of her love. And thirdly, love is described in a florid language with many metaphors, where love frequently is described as a fire, with many adjectives etc. The love descriptions are full of long analyses of the emotions. Persons openly confess their love to the beloved and they comment on it in monologues and dialogues. Repetition and fullness of detail are typical features. The descriptions of all emotions are full of extreme effects.

The oldest of all *riddarasaga* manuscripts is a Norwegian one from *c.*1250–70, just a short time after the translation was made. This manuscript contains two courtly works with a lot of love depiction, *Pamphilus* and *Strengleikar*. *Pamphilus* is entirely about love. Here we find love-sickness with a detailed description of the trembling body, open confessions of love (98, 103, 104, 105), long monologues about love (102–3, 96, 118), dialogues between the loving couple, love complaints, florid constructions like *fagrliga faðmaz* ('embrace beautifully', 107) and *brennandi ást* ('burning love', 118), metaphorical and allegorical descriptions of the emotions etc (98, 116, 119). This Old Norse text is full of typically courtly love description. *Strengleikar* contains many stories where love is always an important element. Here we find love-sickness (22–6, 68, 70), *Frauendienst* (72), monologues about love (68–70), confessions of love (26, 232), amorous addresses to the beloved (26, 28, 38, 74, 198, 240), fire metaphors (24) and florid contructions about love of different kinds (30, 34, 66, 198). And works like *Pamphilus* and many of the *strengleikar* are hardly abbreviated at all compared to the originals. The works in the oldest *riddarasaga* manuscript show that Old Norse translators in the thirteenth century reproduced the courtly love depictions of their continental originals without real distortions.

There certainly exist abbreviated *riddarasögur*, for instance *Tristrams saga* and *Parcevals saga*, and sometimes the abbreviations and omissions are important, for instance in *Ívens saga* and *Erex saga*. But it should be noted that the features which are most important in the love depictions of the continental poetry still remain. The monologues about emotions and the psychological analyses are shorter in these *riddarasögur* than in the originals, but they are still typical features. The same is true of many of the other typical features of courtly love, for instance the open love confessions, the amorous addresses, the love sickness, the fire metaphors, the florid constructions, *Frauendienst*, and the extreme reactions of grief on the death of the beloved (e.g *Tristrams saga*, 8–11, 13, 15, 51, 57, 63, 66, 82, 99, 101, 110, 111, 112; *Ívens saga*, 37, 57, 59–60, 63–4, 104; *Erex saga*, 11, 36–7, 54–5, 56). My conclusion is that *riddarasögur* are much closer to the continental courtly tradition than is normally claimed. They reproduce most of the love depiction and love concept of the continental originals. The archaeological evidence from Scandinavia supports that view. There was an appreciation of the courtly love tradition in Old Norse culture. The picture given by scholars in the 1960s is confirmed – though continental literature seems to have been even more appreciated in Iceland than they claimed.

Were indigenous and foreign literary works appreciated in the same circles or in different ones on Iceland? In medieval Norway we find vernacular skaldic poems and quotations from Virgil on the same objects, the quotations of *Carmina Burana* are written with indigenous runes etc. This indicates that the continental poetry was appreciated in the same circles as the indigenous tradition. Lars Lönnroth has shown that the same scribes wrote *riddarasögur* and indigenous sagas (1964, 74). Thus, it seems clear that indigenous works like the family sagas and courtly works like *riddarasögur* were appreciated in the same circles. Here Lönnroth seems correct. But what about his further conclusions? Are the family sagas fundamentally influenced by the continental literature? Is there only one literary tradition in thirteenth-century Iceland, a fusion between the continental and the indigenous?

At first we have to establish what is typical of love depiction in the family sagas. Love and erotic matters are primarily depicted through a limited group of motifs. A man and a woman talk to each other, a man and a woman sit together, usually the formula *sitja/setjask hjá* is used, a man visits a woman, or a saga character gives a gift of clothes to his beloved (cf. Sävborg 2002, 47, 52–4, 63, 66). These motifs make up most of the love depictions in the family sagas. The style of love depictions in the family sagas also has some characteristics. Firstly, the saga authors depict the emotions by describing the external behaviour of their characters, but do not describe or explain their psychology. Secondly, there is generally a moderating tendency: strong emotions are mentioned through meiosis, discreet words and constructions like *leggja hug á* instead of 'love' (cf. Sävborg 2002, 64); strong emotions are expressed through moderate behaviour. Finally, there is the indirect tendency: the saga characters almost never confess their emotions to the beloved; and they usually do not mention their own emotions at all, except in stanzas claimed to be authentic, but drawn from works that already exist. In the prose, emotions are instead sometimes mentioned by other saga characters or in references to public opinion (cf. Sävborg 2002, 46, 63). These features are in contrast to the love depiction of the courtly literature. This is certainly a genuinely indigenous tradition.

What of the family sagas that are claimed to be deeply influenced by courtly literature and especially by courtly love depiction? How is the love depiction in these sagas related to the courtly and the indigenous traditions respectively?

Let us start with *Laxdœla saga*. Jónas Kristjánsson explicitly ascribed to 'Courtly influence' the love depiction in this saga (1997, 274). Ole Widding sees influence from *riddarasögur* on the saga regarding 'hele udformningen' of the motif of Kjartan's and Guðrún's love (1965, 86). This is probably the standard view among scholars today.

There are, in fact, some clear instances of continental influence in the saga: descriptions of magnificent clothes, decorated shields, and so on. But what of the love story that dominates the main plot? Strangely, love between Kjartan and Guðrún is never explicitly mentioned in the saga – no love-sickness, no fire metaphors, no florid constructions about their emotions, no love monologues, no love confessions, no *Frauendienst*. On the contrary, Kjartan humiliates his Guðrún. The story begins with the Sælingsdalslaug episode. Here we find the motifs of talk and visit, and their love is referred to as 'friendship'. Óláfr pái later refers to the public opinion about their friendship – a meiosis for love, mentioned indirectly by another person. Kjartan's love for Guðrún is later indicated by his choosing to return to Iceland to marry Guðrún instead of staying in Norway as King Óláfr's man and as husband of the king's sister. Kjartan shows no reaction when he gets the message about Guðrún's marriage to Bolli, but in the continuation his sorrow is indicated several times, primarily through his behaviour – long silence and a reluctance to play games, and through explicitly mentioned *eptirsjá*, but it is mentioned only indirectly in his sister's reference to public opinion about this. *Eptirsjá* is also experienced by Guðrún, again expressed by a reference to public opinion. In an extensive passage in the saga the head cloth, with its emotional charge, is used to emphasize Kjartan's and Guðrún's affection for each other. There are many other saga-like indications of emotions in this part of the saga: blush, silence etc. Only in the concluding scene does Guðrún herself mention her love, but her wording is ambiguous and thus there is no real confession. In the entire love story there is no courtly technique of love depiction and there are no traces of the courtly love concept. The entire love story is told within traditional saga technique.

What about *Kormáks saga?* Bjarni Einarsson called Kormákr 'Tristan Íslands' (1961, 163), and he ascribed to it a fundamental influence from *1100-tallets høviske litteratur* 'the courtly literature of the twelfth century' (1976, 115). Love is never mentioned in the prose of *Kormáks saga* either, but is indicated through traditional saga motifs. We recognize the motifs of talk and visit, the formula *sitja hjá*, the gift of clothes (this time rejected), and kisses. Love is mentioned in the prose only in a meiosis-wording (*þokki*), and only indirectly by another person. In fact, it is explicitly mentioned only in quoted stanzas. The lover's conduct towards his beloved is rude and quite without 'courtly' *Frauendienst*. There is no love-sickness, no florid constructions etc.

Björn Magnússon Ólsen described *Gunnlaugs saga ormstungu* as *en ridderlig Elskovsroman paa nordisk Baggrund, en islandsk strengleikr i Sagastil* 'a chivalric love romance on Nordic ground, an Icelandic *strengleikr* in saga style' (1911, 10). He talks about the continental influence on it and about the 'sentimental end' of the saga (10). This is probably the standard view among scholars today.

This saga also lacks courtly characteristics such as love-sickness and fire metaphors. Emotions are mentioned more frequently than in other sagas, and this has been used as an argument for continental influence by, for example, Alison Finlay (2001, 237) and Vésteinn Ólason (1998, 215). But if we examine these instances more closely we find that all the explicit mentions of emotions are indirect and in true saga style: the emotions are mentioned by others in references to public opinion or in proverbs (*Gunnlaugs saga*, 54, 55, 87, 89). We are far away from continental poetry and *riddarsögur* with its explicit and repeated references to love in monologues and confessions.

Many scholars have described the end of the saga as sentimental and have claimed that it is influenced by continental poetry. On the contrary, the account of the grieving Helga gazing on Gunnlaugr's coat is typical of a saga scene: it depicts only external behaviour and avoids all explicit references to emotions, and it uses the motif of a gift of clothes. The mistake of the scholars is easily explained by an old prejudice that saga style is unable to create a strong emotional effect. Scholars have noticed that the episode is emotionally powerful and have therefore confused powerful emotion with sentimentality. The next step has been to connect sentimentality with courtly influence, and so they have not noticed that the episode uses only traditional saga technique to achieve the emotional effect. The saga character of the episode becomes clear if we compare it with descriptions of similar situations in courtly literature. In continental poems, and in Old Norse translations like *Tristrams saga* and *Ívens saga*, the comparable grief scenes are dominated by faints, attempts to commit suicide, self-hurt, wild crying, tearing of clothes and hair, unrestrained lamentation etc. There is no hint of anything of the sort in the description of Helga's grief in *Gunnlaugs saga*.

These three family sagas tell of strong and lifelong love. It is clear, at the same time, that all use the tools of saga tradition in their love depictions. There are no courtly characteristics, neither in depiction nor concept. They seem to show, in contradistinction to the standard view, that there was a highly developed indigenous Old Norse tradition of love depiction with a character of its own. No continental influence can be detected in these sagas. But we still have not fully answered the question whether there is a fusion between the two traditions. We must return to the *riddarsögur*. Is there any influence from the indigenous tradition of love depiction in that genre? In fact, several scholars have claimed that *riddarasögur* are fundamentally influenced by the saga literature (e.g. Kretschmer 1982, 192; Reynard 2004, 250; Jónas Kristjánsson 1997, 322).

I have listed the most typical elements of love depiction in the family sagas. If they have influenced the *riddarasögur* we should, in consequence, be able to find these elements in *riddarasögur*. However, I have found no instances where the Norse translators adapt their original to the indigenous technique. The motifs and formulas of saga, as well as its style, are totally lacking in even the most abbreviated *riddarasögur*.

The only similarity between *riddarasögur* and family sagas in respect of the love is a negative one: they usually have a less explicit depiction of emotions than the courtly romances of the continent and they lack some of their characteristics. However, this similarity is too superficial to use as an evidence for literary influence. Saga technique is, after all, not characterized by the absence of a certain type of love depiction, but of the presence of another type. The love depiction in, for example, *Erex saga* certainly seems poor compared to the French original. But the love depiction in family sagas like *Laxdæla saga* is not characterized by poverty – on the contrary, it is a phenomenon as sophisticated as that in the courtly romances. *Erex saga* certainly lacks much of the courtly love depiction of its original, but it lacks even more of the typical love depiction of the family sagas. My conclusion is that the *riddarasögur* of the thirteenth century are not at all influenced by the contemporary family sagas, at least in respect of their love depiction.

We now return to the assertions of Lars Lönnroth. My investigation has confirmed his views on some points, but not on others. Lönnroth is right about two important matters. Continental culture did indeed play an important role in Iceland just when the indigenous saga literature flourished. I mean that the Icelanders adopted continental trends to a much greater degree than scholars usually claim. Continental and indigenous literature were appreciated in the same circles on Iceland; the two met in the same persons. But that does not mean that there was a literary fusion in medieval Iceland. In the genre of family sagas there is a highly developed and peculiar tradition of love depiction, not influenced by the continental tradition. It is fundamentally different from the description of love in the *riddarasögur*, a genre that closely follows the tradition of the continent and is not influenced by the family saga tradition. In his discussion of 'the two cultures', Lönnroth does not distinguish between cultural environment and literary individuality. If we talk about the former, we have to reject the idea of 'two cultures'; if we talk about the latter it is, on the contrary, legitimate to talk about two different cultures in medieval Iceland.

In conclusion, in medieval Iceland there are two traditions of love depiction – courtly and saga-like. On most points they are in bold contrast with each other. Courtly love in its pure continental form was a popular phenomenon in literature at the same time and in the same circles in which indigenous saga literature flourished. Yet my researches show that these two traditions hardly influenced each other at all. They lived, side by side, without meeting.

BIBLIOGRAPHY

Bjarni Einarsson. 1961. *Skáldasögur: um uppruna og eðli ástaskáldasagnanna fornu* (Reykjavík).

Bjarni Einarsson. 1976. *To skjaldesagaer: en analyse af Kormáks saga og Hallfreðar saga* (Bergen).

Björn Magnússon Ólsen. 1911. *Om Gunnlaugs saga ormstungu: en kritisk undersøgelse* (Copenhagen).

Bonath, G. 1985. 'Introduction to Thomas', *Tristan* (Munich).

Einar Ólafur Sveinsson. 1953. *The Age of the Sturlungs: Icelandic civilization in the thirteenth century* (Ithaca).

Erex saga = Blaisdell, F.W. (ed.). 1965. *Erex saga Artuskappa*, Editiones Arnamagnæanæ, Ser. B, 19 (Copenhagen).

Finlay, A. 2001. 'Skald sagas in their literary context 2: possible European contexts' in R. Poole (ed.), *Skaldsagas: text, vocation and desire in the Icelandic sagas of poets* (Berlin), pp 232–71.

Finnur Jónsson. 1920–4. *Den oldnorske og oldislandske litteraturs historie*, 2nd ed., 3 vols (Copenhagen).

Gunnlaugs saga = Sigurður Nordal & Guðni Jónsson (eds). 1938. *Gunnlaugs saga ormstungu*, in *Borgfirðinga sögur*, Íslenzk fornrit, 3 (Reykjavík), 49–107.

Ívens saga = Blaisdell, F.W. (ed.). 1979. *Ívens saga*, Editiones Arnamagnæanæ, Ser. B, 18 (Copenhagen).

Jónas Kristjánsson. 1997. *Eddas and sagas: Iceland's medieval literature*, 3rd ed. (Reykjavík).

Kormáks saga = Einar Ól. Sveinsson (ed.). 1939. *Kormáks saga*, in *Vatnsdæla saga*, Íslenzk fornrit, 8 (Reykjavík), 201–302.

Kretschmer, B. 1982. *Höfische und altwestnordische erzähltradition in den Riddarasögur* (Hattingen).

Laxdæla saga = Einar Ól. Sveinsson (ed.). 1934. *Laxdæla saga*, Íslenzk fornrit, 5 (Reykjavík).

Liestøl, A. & Sanness Johnsen, I. 1980–90. *Norges innskrifter med de yngre runer*, 6 (Oslo).

Lönnroth, L. 1964. 'Tesen om de två kulturerna', *Scripta Islandica*, 15, 3–97.

Lönnroth, L. 1965. *European sources of Icelandic saga-writing: an essay based on previous studies* (Stockholm).

Lönnroth, L. 1967. 'Svar till min fakultetsopponent', *Samlaren: tidskrift för svensk litteraturhistorisk forskning*, 88, 178–90.

Mitchell, P.M. 1959. 'Scandinavian literature' in R.S. Loomis (ed.), *Arthurian literature in the Middle Ages: a collaborative history* (Oxford), pp 462–71.

Norrøn fortællekunst = Bekker-Nielsen, H. (ed.). 1965. *Norrøn fortællekunst: kapitler af den norsk-islandske middelalderlitteraturs historie* (Copenhagen).

Pamphilus = Holm Olsen, L. (ed.). 1940. *Den gammelnorske oversettelsen av Pamphilus: med en undersøkelse av paleografi og lydverk* (Oslo).

Reynard, L. 2004. 'Når en roman av Chrétien de Troyes blir til en norrøn saga: fra Yvain ou Le Chevalier au Lion til Ívens saga', *Historisk tidsskrift*, 83, 245–59.

Strengleikar = Cook, R. & M. Tveitane (eds). 1979. *Strengleikar: an Old Norse translation of twenty-one Old French lais. Edited from the Manuscript Uppsala De la Gardie 4–7 – AM 666 b, 4°* (Oslo).

Sävborg, D. 2002. 'Kjartan och Guðrún – en kärlekssaga?', *Tidskrift för litteraturvetenskap*, 31, 41–68.

Tristrams saga = Kölbing, E. (ed.). 1878. *Tristrams saga ok Ísöndar*, in *Die nordische version der Tristan Sage* (Heilbronn), 5–112.

Vésteinn Ólason. 1998. *Dialogues with the Viking Age: narration and representation in the sagas of the Icelanders* (Reykjavík).

Widding, O. 1965. 'Islændingesagaer' in H. Bekker-Nielsen (ed.), *Norrøn fortællekunst: kapitler af den norsk-islandske middelalderlitteraturs historie* (Copenhagen), pp 72–91.

Life and death among the Picts and Vikings at Westness

BERIT J. SELLEVOLD

Between 1968 and 1984, the little cemetery at Westness on Rousay, in the Orkney Islands, was archaeologically investigated by Sigrid Kaland of the University of Bergen. Radiocarbon dates show that the cemetery was in use between the seventh and eleventh centuries (Sellevold 1999), and many generations of the local population of the Westness farm were buried there during these five centuries. However, towards the end of the cemetery's functioning period it also became the final resting place for the Viking settlers, as evidenced by grave constructions and grave-goods (Kaland 1987).

The first Viking grave at Westness was accidentally discovered in 1963 by Ronald Stevenson of the Westness farm. The grave contained rich grave-goods, including two oval brooches and a beautiful silver gilt ornamental ring pin with gold filigree and amber inlays, which had probably been made in Scotland in the eighth century. There were also beads, a weaving batten, bronze straps, fragments of a bronze bowl, and two wool combs in the grave (Kaland 1987, 23). The grave contained the skeletal remains of three individuals, two young adult females and a full-term foetus or newborn child. There are no archaeological records of the recovery of these remains and nothing is known about the grave itself.

The excavated part of the cemetery (Fig. 35.1) contained between thirty and forty graves, both Pictish and Viking. In the Pictish graves, there were no grave-goods and the dead were deposited supine (extended on the back) in narrow, full-length, shallow graves. The graves of the Vikings showed greater variety. Some were rectangular without grave-goods, others were oval-shaped, and yet others were boat-shaped. The oval-shaped graves were lined with stone slabs standing on edge, with a higher slab behind the head. Some of these graves were also covered by slabs. Among the objects in the Viking graves were weapons – such as swords, axes, spears, arrows and shield bosses, tools – such as sickles, adzes and weaving implements, and jewellery (Kaland 1987, 26).

THE SKELETAL INVESTIGATIONS

There were between thirty and forty graves in the cemetery, but some of the graves did not contain any skeletal parts. In all, the remains of twenty-nine individuals were disinterred. These skeletal remains not only derive from different generations but also from two different population groups, Orkney Picts and Norse Vikings, and thus represent a cross-section of the Westness population over five centuries. Among the questions of interest in the skeletal investigations was whether or not there were discernible differences between the skeletons from the two population groups. This issue will be discussed below. Other questions dealt with the sex- and age-distribution of the material, statures, pathological conditions and congenital and other anomalies.

SEX AND AGE

The graves of men, women and children were intermingled in the cemetery. There were no areas reserved for either sex or for specific age-groups. Among the skeletons that could be sex determined there were eleven males and twelve females. The remains of five children and one adult could not be sex determined. The sex- and age-distribution in the material is outlined in Figure 35.2.

The youngest individual in the cemetery was an unborn child in the fifth or sixth month of foetal development. The remains of this foetus were found in the pelvic region of the skeleton of a young adult female. There were also remains of three infants/small children of less than one year old, and of one seven- to eight-year-old child. The remains of the infants could not be sex determined, but the small size of the teeth of the child suggests that it may have been a girl. One skeleton was age-determined to *c.*16–17 years and was sex-determined male.

The remaining twenty-three individuals were all adults. Among the ten grown males, nine could be allocated to age groups – one young and eight middle-aged adults. There were no old males. Among the twelve females there were five young adults, two middle-aged and five old individuals. On average, the women at Westness lived longer than the men. The mean age at death for those who survived childhood was 41 years for males and 45 years for females.

STATURES

The twelfth-century source *Historia Norvegiae* describes the Picts as 'a diminutive race, little more than pygmy in stature' (Thomsen 1987, 1). It was therefore with considerable interest that the stature calculations for the skeletal remains were carried out: would the results corroborate the ancient myth?

It was possible to calculate the statures of seven males and eight females based on the maximum length of the thigh bone (Trotter & Gleser 1952, 1958). The average stature for males was 174cm (5 feet 8 inches), while the average for females was 160cm (5 feet 3 inches). Amongst the seven males, five from Pictish graves had exactly the same stature, all being 171cm tall. The other two were

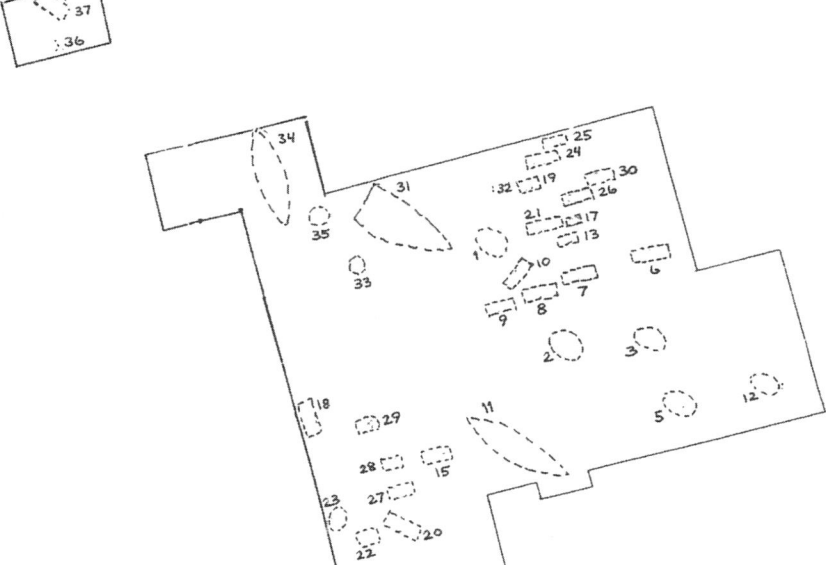

35.1 The archaeologically investigated part of the Westness cemetery
(based on S. Kaland's working sketch).

buried in Viking boat graves. They stood out as being much taller than the five Picts, being 180cm in height. However, even though the five Pictish males were shorter than the Vikings, the Picts are far from being 'pygmies', as suggested in *Historia Norvegiae*. The statures of the Pictish males lie well within the range of contemporary male statures in north-western Europe.

Among the eight females for whom statures could be calculated, six were between 160 and 165cm in height, while two were considerably shorter, at 152cm and 154cm. The shortest was buried in a Norse grave and the slightly taller one in a Pictish grave.

PATHOLOGICAL AND ANOMALOUS CONDITIONS

There are some very interesting pathological and anomalous conditions in the Westness skeletons. Some pathologies, such as degenerative joint disease (osteoarthritis) and dental caries, are frequently seen in ancient skeletal remains, but other conditions found in the Westness assemblage are more rarely observed. Some of these are described below.

Age group	Males		Females		Indeterminate		Total	
	n	%	n	%	n	%	n	%
Foetus	–	–	–	–	1	16.7	1	3.4
Small child	–	–	–	–	3	50.0	3	10.3
Big child	–	–	–	–	1	16.7	1	3.4
Adolescent	1	9.1	–	–	–	–	1	3.4
Young adult	1	9.1	5	41.7	–	–	6	20.7
Middle-aged	8	72.7	2	16.7	1	16.7	11	37.9
Middle-aged/old	–	–	3	25.0	–	–	3	10.3
Old	–	–	2	16.7	–	–	2	6.9
Grown	1	9.1	–	–	–	–	1	3.4
Sum	**11**	**100**	**12**	**100.1**	**6**	**100.1**	**29**	**99.7**

35.2 Table showing sex- and age-distribution in the Westness skeletal assemblage.

Osteoarthritis: degenerative joint disease

Changes caused by degenerative joint disease are among the most commonly observed pathologies in ancient skeletal remains. Osteoarthritis is probably the result of normal wear and tear, but systemic and genetic predispositions are important factors in the development of this disease (Rogers & Waldron 1995, 32–3). In some cases, however, the pathological changes are sequelae of an injury or other trauma. In the Westness assemblage, several individuals were affected by degenerative joint disease, both in small and large joints. Most changes were found in the small joints of the spine.

Trauma

Fractured bones and fractured teeth are often found in archaeological skeletal remains and there were numerous fractured bones in the Westness skeletons. One of the more noticeable bone fractures was observed in a skeleton of undetermined sex – possibly a male – from one of the Norse graves. There was a badly healed fracture of the left collar bone and pathological changes in the surrounding bones (Fig. 35.3). Øivind Larsen, who studied the bone, suggested that the injury may have been the result of torture (Larsen 1972). The changes to the bone are consistent with the arms having been tied behind the back at the wrists, after which the individual was strung up by the wrist ties. The individual clearly lived for some time after the traumatic event, as the fracture healed and there were pathological changes in the joints of the other bones of the shoulder girdle, where secondary osteoarthritis had developed as a consequence of the injury.

There were also healed fractures in many of the other skeletons, in some instances in several bones. The skeleton of an elderly female had ten fractured ribs, a fractured wrist, and a fractured vertebra in the lower spine, all of which had healed. In a male skeleton there was a fractured right collar bone, six fractured ribs and a fractured vertebra in the lower spine, all of which had also healed.

Almost all of the fractures were found in the Pictish skeletons. All afflicted individuals had survived for many years after the fractures were incurred: the fractures had healed and the bones had been remodelled. The numerous fractures and the many skeletal changes due to trauma indicate that life at Westness was harsh and physically challenging.

Tuberculosis
Among the very interesting pathological findings in the Westness skeletal assemblage are signs of tuberculosis in two skeletons, an elderly and a young female, both Pictish. In both skeletons there were several pathologies in the chest region. The elderly female had numerous osteoarthritic changes in the joints of the chest and shoulder girdle, but most notable were the changes in the tenth thoracic vertebra and the associated tenth rib. There is a 19mm deep cyst or abscess into the left side of the vertebral body and the cyst continues onto the tenth left rib and goes deep into its enlarged head (Fig. 35.4). The supporting structures (trabeculae) surrounding the cyst have become dense (sclerotic). This is a characteristic sign of skeletal tuberculosis (Ortner & Putschar 1985, 141–76). During the excavation of this skeleton, fragments of thin bony plates were recovered and labelled as 'bony matter from within the rib cage'. These fragments are probably what Don Brothwell calls 'plaques of pleural calcification' (1981, 132).

The other skeleton with signs of tuberculosis was that of a young female with foetal bones in the pelvic region. As in the skeleton of the older female, there were several pathological changes in the chest (thoracic) region, and there were also thin, bony plate fragments – calcified pleura – in the rib cage. An irregularly shaped bony lump was found among the left ribs, while another was found in the pelvic region among the foetal bones. The presence of pleural calcifications in association with other pathological changes provides important evidence of possible tuberculosis (Steinbock 1976). A diagnosis of tuberculosis in these two individuals might be verified by analyzing extracted aDNA (ancient DNA: Aufderheide & Rodríguez-Martin 1998, 127, 133) but such a test, unfortunately, was outside the scope of this study.

Based on osteological evidence, it has been established that tuberculosis was present in Europe by the Neolithic period (Aufderheide & Rodríguez-Martin 1998; Ortner & Putschar 1985), but finds of bones affected by the disease are not numerous. For example, only one case was found in a large assemblage of several thousand skeletons from early medieval Lund, southern Sweden (Arcini 1999, 121).

The skeleton of the young pregnant female has been radiocarbon-dated to AD650–85 and that of the older female to AD432–642 (both dates are calibrated and corrected for the marine component). If these two, in fact, did suffer from

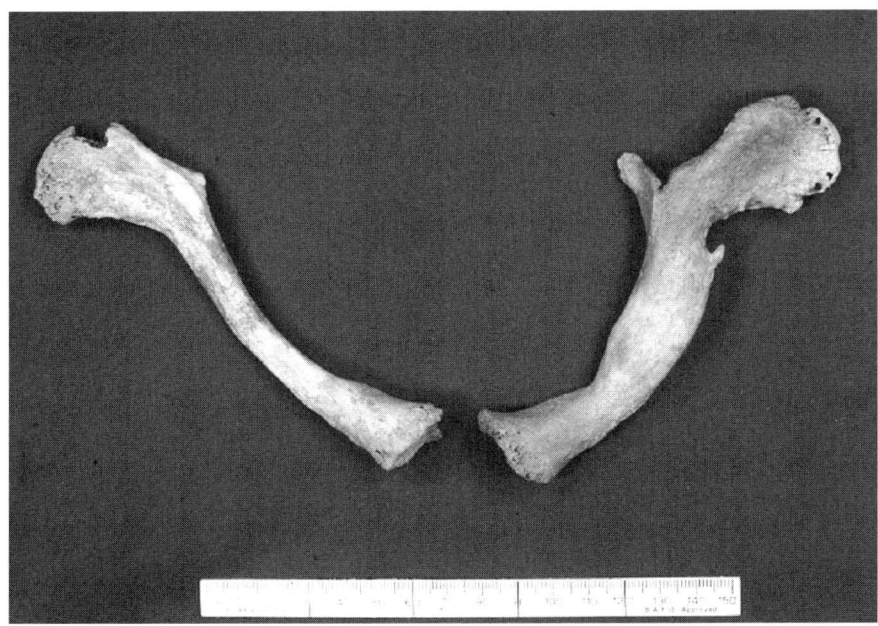

35.3 Fractured and badly healed left collar bone of a middle-aged individual, possibly a male (Grave 1) (photo: Berit J. Sellevold).

35.4 Traces of a cyst in the tenth thoracic vertebra and rib in the skeleton of a middle-aged/old Pictish female (Grave 7) (photo: Berit J. Sellevold).

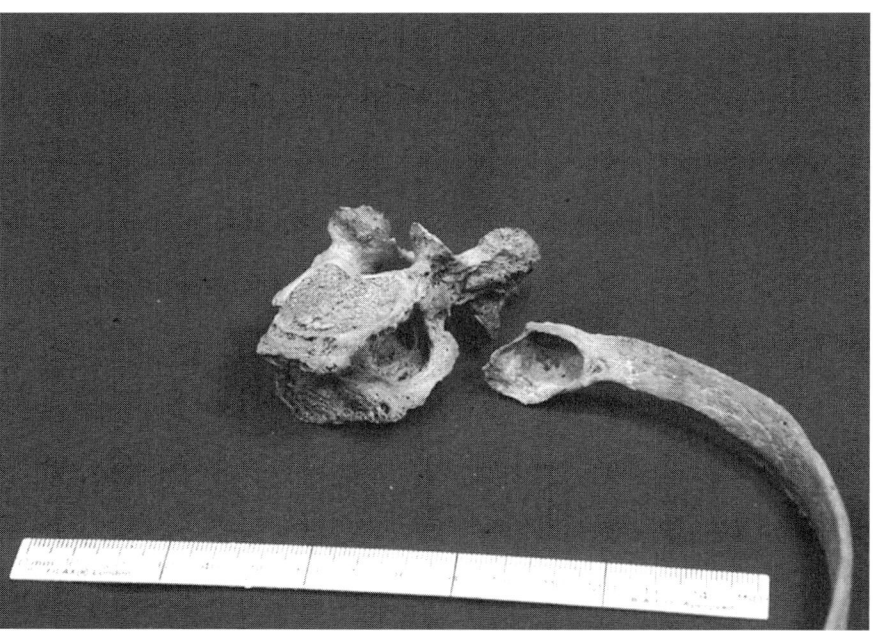

tuberculosis, the cases would be among the earliest found in Britain. So far, the earliest find of tuberculosis in England was reported by Mays and Taylor (2003) in a skeleton from Tarrant Hinton in Dorset, dated to between 400 and 230BC. As for Britain as a whole, Mays and Taylor cite a total of thirteen published finds, the earliest of which dates to the first century AD. Stirland and Waldron claim that 'few unmistakable cases have been diagnosed in contexts earlier than the medieval period [in Britain]' (1990, 221). It would seem that more research is needed with regard to the presence of tuberculosis in prehistoric British skeletal remains.

The earliest case of tuberculosis in Norway is found in a skeleton dating to between AD600 and 800, that is, the Merovingian period, and is thus roughly contemporaneous with the two finds at Westness. The Norwegian skeleton was of a middle-aged male from the island of Gisløy in Øksnes parish, Nordland (Larsen 1973; 1986).

A pregnant woman

As mentioned above, the skeleton of the young female with signs of tuberculosis was found with foetal bones in the pelvic region. In other words, she was pregnant when she died. The foetus was in the fifth or sixth foetal month. The pelvis was rather high and relatively narrow, and there were a number of anomalous changes in the pelvic bones. Giving birth to a fully developed foetus would have been most difficult and possibly very dangerous, both for the mother and the child. However, the woman died prior to parturition, perhaps of tuberculosis or other causes which were unrelated to the pregnancy.

Trepanation scars?

Trepanation is a surgical operation in which a part of the skull bone is removed. Trepanation scars have been registered in archaeological finds from the Stone Age to the present in many parts of the world (Jennbert 1991; Bennike & Brade 1999). Some of the patients died during the procedure but, surprisingly, others often survived and the hole in the skull healed. In Danish prehistoric skeletons, for example, a remarkable 79 per cent of the individuals with trepanation scars survived the procedure, as evidenced by signs of healing around the wound (Bennike 1985, 97). Sometimes the operation seems to have been performed as a therapeutic measure related to cranial fractures (Jørgensen 1988), but the reason may equally well be sought in ritual magic and religious practices (Jennbert 1991).

Two of the Westness skulls had depressions in the cranial vault bones. The skull of a middle-aged Norse female had a non-penetrating, roughly circular depression on the frontal bone, measuring approximately 10mm in diameter and approximately 1.5mm in depth. The internal surface of the bone was smooth and slightly thickened, while externally the depression was roughened in the middle with a groove around its perimeter. The depression resembles a completely healed trepanation.

The skull of a middle-aged Pictish male had three small, circular depressions on the left parietal bone, located close to each other; each was approximately 3mm in diameter. There was no change on the internal surface of the bone. A similar case has been reported in the skull of a pre-Inca Peruvian adult male which had three unhealed trepanation holes close together, interpreted as representing an attempt to treat a cranial fracture in the area (Jørgensen 1988, 3). The depressions on the Pictish skull may represent such healed trepanation holes.

Congenital anomalies
In addition to changes caused by trauma and pathologies, there may be traces of congenital and/or heritable anomalies in ancient skeletal remains. In the Westness skeletal assemblage, there are a number of remarkable congenital anomalies, but those found in the skeletons of a young adult female, an adolescent male and a small child are especially interesting. Each of these individuals was born with only eleven pairs of ribs and all had spinal anomalies. Both the young male and the female had pronounced overbites (the dental occlusion of the child could not be determined). In addition, in spite of their relatively young ages, the male and female had ossified hyoid bones (the bone to which the tongue is attached), which is a developmental anomaly; usually, ossification of this bone takes place much later in life.

In addition to the congenital anomalies noted above, there were also pathological changes in these three skeletons. The child had several fused vertebrae, and had noticeable enamel hypoplasias in several teeth. Enamel hypoplasia is a manifestation of disrupted dental enamel formation, and may be linked to periods of ill health, starvation or nutritional deficiency. The location of the enamel formation disturbance testifies to the age at which the disruption occurred, because dental enamel forms at a constant rate during foetal life and childhood (Hillson 1996). In this child, all four deciduous upper and lower central incisors had signs of disrupted enamel formation in the form of dark brown to black stains located centrally on the incisive edges of the teeth. The location of the enamel formation disruption shows that it had occurred in the fifth foetal month.

These three individuals, with their similar congenital anomalies, were probably closely related. The radiocarbon dates of the female and the child are very close in time: the female skeleton is dated to AD665–790 while that of the child dates to AD670–770. The young male lived at a slightly later time than the female and the child, AD770–1020. All three were buried fairly close together in the northern part of the cemetery.

Dental occlusion
One of the congenital anomalies mentioned above is dental occlusion. This anomaly was, in fact, one of the more remarkable aspects of the Westness population. Among the seventeen skeletons which had surviving jaw bones or

jaw bone fragments, the dental occlusion could be examined in eleven cases, namely four males and seven females. Six of these eleven individuals had noticeable horizontal overbites, four had edge-to-edge bites, while one had an underbite (Sellevold & Kaland 2003).

The six individuals with marked overbites were all buried very close to each other in Pictish graves in the northern part of the cemetery. Three of the four individuals with edge-to-edge bite were buried in the southern part of the cemetery, while one was buried among the individuals with overbites in its northern part. The individual with an underbite was the male buried in the northernmost of the Viking boat-shaped graves.

Five of the six individuals with marked overbites were female and one was male. In each of these six dentitions the upper incisors stuck far out over the lower incisors, the overjet being between 6 and 10mm. In all six dentitions the molars were in approximately normal occlusion, which means that it was the incisor occlusion which created the characteristic overbite. Figure 35.5 shows a skull with such an overbite, with an overjet of 10 mm.

CONCLUSION

The Norse settlement of the Orkney Islands in the Viking Age has been described in written sources and in the sagas. It would seem that the Vikings took over the local farms and that there was continuity in the occupation of the land. *Orkneyinga Saga* mentions Sigurðr of Westness on Rousay. Grave constructions and burial customs in the Westness cemetery show the presence of two different population groups. The results of the investigations of the skeletal remains also point to the existence of two population groups. Several skeletal traits and observations of conditions seem to serve to distinguish the indigenous Pictish population from the Norse settlers. While far from being 'pygmies', the Pictish males were quite a bit shorter than the Norse males. Other distinguishing features are the many congenital, heritable traits in the Pictish skeletons which are not found in the Norse ones. One such trait is the congenital absence of the twelfth pair of ribs in three individuals, another is the marked overbite found in many of the Pictish skulls. The congenital traits point to a close biological relationship between the Picts.

The graves of both population groups were intermingled in the cemetery. The Viking graves did not disturb any of the existing Pictish graves, indicating that the latter must have been marked above ground in some way. There is no sharp break in continuity evident in the radiocarbon-dating of the skeletons of the two population groups. All of this might be indicative of a period of peaceful coexistence. There is also a general absence of signs of violence in the skeletal remains, though the Viking male in the northernmost boat-shaped grave may

35.5 The skull of a young adult female with pronounced overbite (Grave 24)
(photo: Berit J. Sellevold).

have met with a violent end. Four arrow points were found among the bones of his skeleton and one or more of these may have killed him, even though the arrows had not left any marks on the bones.

The cause of death could not be unequivocally determined for any of the individuals in the Westness cemetery. The skeletal remains bear signs of hard physical labour, ill health and disease. Bone fractures were not at all unusual. At least two individuals possibly suffered from tuberculosis. Life at Westness must have been arduous.

BIBLIOGRAPHY

Arcini, C. 1999. *Health and disease in early Lund: osteo-pathological studies of 3,305 individuals buried in the first cemetery area of Lund, 990–1536* (Lund).
Aufderheide, A.C. & C. Rodríguez-Martin. 1998. *The Cambridge encyclopaedia of human paleopathology* (Cambridge).
Bennike, P. 1985. *Paleopathology of Danish skeletons* (Copenhagen).
Bennike, P. & A.-E. Brade. 1999. *Middelalderens sygdomme og behandlingsformer i Danmark* (Copenhagen).
Brothwell, D.R. 1981. *Digging up bones: the excavation, treatment and study of human skeletal remains* (London).
Hillson, S. 1996. *Dental anthropology* (Cambridge).

Jennbert, K. 1991. 'Trepanation from Stone Age to Medieval Period from a Scandinavian perspective' in K. Jennbert, L.O.G. Larsson, R. Petré, & B. Wyszomirska-Werbart (eds), *Regions and reflections: in honour of Märta Strömberg*, Acta Archaeologica Lundensia, 8:20 (Lund), pp 357–78.

Jørgensen, J.B. 1988. 'Trepanation as a therapeutic measure in ancient (Pre-Inka) Peru', *Acta Neurochirurgica (Wien)*, 93, 3–5.

Kaland, S. 1987. *The Norse connection: Orkney-Norway, 800–1500* (Bergen).

Larsen, Ø. 1972. 'Eine schlüsselbeinbeschädigung aus der Wikingerzeit: folge einer folterung', *Medizinhistorisches Journal*, 7, 197–200.

Larsen, Ø. 1973. 'Ein fall von tuberkulose aus Nordnorwegen in der Merowingerzeit', *Medizinhistorisches Journal*, 8:1, 77–88.

Larsen, Ø. 1986. 'Tuberkulose i Skandinavia: første kjente tilfelle', *Tidsskrift for Den norske lægeforening*, 7, 106.

Mays, S. & G.M. Taylor. 2003. 'A first prehistoric case of tuberculosis from Britain', *International Journal of Osteoarchaeology*, 13, 189–96.

Ortner, D.J. & W.G.J. Putschar. 1985. *Identification of pathological conditions in human skeletal remains* (Washington, DC).

Rogers, J. & T. Waldron. 1995. *A field guide to joint disease in archaeology* (Chichester).

Sellevold, B.J. 1999. *Picts and Vikings at Westness: anthropological investigations of the skeletal material from the cemetery at Westness, Rousay, Orkney Islands*. NIKU Scientific Report, 10 (Oslo).

Sellevold, B.J. & S. Kaland. 2003. 'Dental conditions among Picts and Vikings in Orkney' in E. Iregren & L. Larsson (eds), *A tooth for a tooth* (Lund), 65–70.

Steinbock, R.T. 1976. *Paleopathological diagnosis and interpretation: bone disease in ancient human populations* (Springfield).

Stirland, A. & T. Waldron. 1990. 'The earliest cases of tuberculosis in Britain', *Journal of Archaeological Science*, 17, 221–30.

Thomsen, W.P.L. 1987. *History of Orkney* (Edinburgh).

Trotter, M. & G. Gleser. 1952. 'Estimation of stature from long bones of American whites and negroes', *American Journal of Physical Anthropology*, 10, 463–515.

Trotter, M. & G. Gleser. 1958. 'A re-evaluation of estimation of stature based on measurements of stature taken during life and long bones after death', *American Journal of Physical Anthropology*, 16:1, 79–124.

Colonel Sempronius Stretton and the reprovenancing of a Viking-Age hoard

JOHN SHEEHAN

INTRODUCTION

There are various difficulties in the study of Ireland's Viking-Age hoards, particularly those discovered during the eighteenth and nineteenth centuries. The antiquarian records of their discovery and composition vary a great deal in detail and quality and often the hoards themselves do not survive, having gone to the melting pot. Frequently, in addition, depending on the antiquarian involved, the coins that occasionally occur in these hoards attract more interest than do their non-numismatic elements. In some instances, therefore, a judgment about the provenance and nature of a particular hoard must be arrived at not only on the basis of the available antiquarian evidence but also on the object-types known to have been in the hoard, their date-ranges, and other related factors. This paper presents a study of one early nineteenth-century discovery, heretofore referred to as 'the west of the Co. Kilkenny' hoard.

The main evidence for this find, a silver mixed hoard of coins and 'ingots in the form of rings', is contained in the writings of John Lindsay, the eminent nineteenth-century Cork numismatist, who noted it briefly in his seminal work *A View of the Coinage of the Heptarchy, etc* (1842, 125). Therein he stated:

> A few years since a large parcel of Anglo-Saxon coins, together with several silver ingots in the form of rings, each of the weight of three ounces, were found in the west of the County Kilkenny; about sixty of the coins, all of Edgar, and with one exception without heads, came into the possession of Colonel Stretton, C.B. Athlone.

The implication seems to be that this individual, Colonel Stretton, did not obtain the entire find, though it is clear that he secured 'about sixty' of the coins. It is not stated what happened to the non-numismatic element of the hoard which, it is proposed below, comprised standard ingots.

Over the past fifty years, this hoard has been noted in academic papers on various occasions. In each case, it has been referred to as having a provenance in the west of Co. Kilkenny, on the basis of the information published by Lindsay (Thompson 1956, no. 207; Dolley and Martin 1959, 175–82; Dolley 1966, 51, no. 116; Hall 1974, 78; Graham-Campbell 1976, 63, 67; Blackburn & Pagan

1986, 297, no. 170; Sheehan 1998a, 200). On the basis of its numismatic content, Dolley dated the deposition of the hoard to *c*.975 (1966, 51) while Blackburn and Pagan have proposed a date of *c*.970 (1986, 297, no. 170); see also Bornholdt Collins, this volume). The purpose of the present paper is to argue that this Kilkenny provenance is erroneous, being based on a misunderstanding of Lindsay's, and to demonstrate that it is far more likely that the hoard derives from the barony of Kilkenny West, in the Lough Ree area of Co. Westmeath, some 125km north of Co. Kilkenny.

COLONEL SEMPRONIUS STRETTON

The key to the puzzle lies in the name, background and relationships of the person whom Lindsay recorded as the owner of the coins from the hoard, 'Colonel Stretton, C.B., Athlone'. He may be identified, with a great degree of certainty, as Sempronius Stretton (1781–1842), a colonel in the British Army who was awarded the C.B. (Companionship of the Order of the Bath) in recognition of his military services during the Napoleonic Wars (Plate 20). Originally from Lenton, Nottinghamshire, he is perhaps best known for his series of drawings and watercolours, now in Canada's National Archive, of the Mohawk people and their settlements, made in 1803–6 while he was serving as a young lieutenant with the 49th Regiment at Quebec. Having been promoted to a company in the 40th Regiment of Foot (2nd Somersetshire) (Wickes 1974, 59–60), he served under Wellington in Portugal and France during the Napoleonic Wars. He spent two months in Ireland during this period – in Cóbh, Co. Cork, and Athlone, Co. Westmeath, following the sinking of his military transport at the mouth of Bantry Bay in October 1814. He returned to the Continent in time to serve with distinction at the Battle of Waterloo the following year. In the years after the war, his regiment was in Scotland and then Ireland, being stationed in Athlone from 1822 to 1824 in response to a rise in agrarian disturbances in this district. During this period, the regiment was described as being 'most conspicuous in suppressing outrage and aiding the civil power ... they well supported the character they obtained on the numerous scenes of active service in which they were engaged' (*Connaught Journal*, 20 March 1823). In 1821, Stretton married the Honorable Catherine Jane Massey, from Co. Limerick, who died some months later. He retired from the army in 1823, with the rank of colonel.

So far, we have demonstrated that Sempronius Stretton was familiar, to some extent at least, with Athlone, a midland barracks town of note, where Lindsay places his Colonel Stretton. It is also the case that both Lindsay's colonel and the one stationed in Athlone during 1822–4 were Companions of the Order of the Bath, an uncommon distinction. Clearly, they were one and the same person.

Two further points of relevance emerge about Stretton. Firstly, his connections with Athlone did not end in 1824, for six years later he took as his second
wife the Honorable Anne Handcock, youngest daughter of Richard Handcock,
on whom the barony of Castlemaine was entailed. The seat of this family was
Moydrum Castle, just outside Athlone (Lodge 1833, 90). Secondly, it transpires
that the Nottingham family he derived from was locally renowned for its interest
in antiquarian matters. His father was William Stretton (1755–1828), the well-
known Nottingham architect, builder and antiquarian (Marcombe 1999). *The
Stretton Manuscripts*, a privately printed account of the family published in 1910,
note that William 'had a taste in articles of *vertu*, of which, at the time of his
death, he possessed an extensive museum' which included 'specimens of his
coins, Nuremburg tokens, seventeenth-century Nottinghamshire tokens, seals,
monastic paving tiles, and other objects' (Robertson 1910). With such a
background, it is not surprising that Colonel Stretton took an interest in the
Viking-Age coins from Ireland and, indeed, acquired them.

Following his army career, Stretton spent several years travelling on the
Continent, returning occasionally to the family home in Nottinghamshire.
During this period, the mid-1820s, it is recorded that he 'made many valuable
contributions to his father's extensive museum' (Robertson 1910). It was
presumably during this time, probably specifically in 1822–4, that the coins from
the hoard from Ireland were brought to Nottingham, for his father died in 1828.
Sempronius inherited the property, though he appears to have generally lived
elsewhere until his death in 1842 (Marcombe 1999). Being childless from both
his marriages, he willed Lenton Priory, the family home, to his brother Severus
(1793–1884). He never resided there, however, and it was rented out. There are
indications that prior to eventually selling the house in 1880, Severus disposed
of some, at least, of the collection of antiquities that had been built up by his
father and contributed to by his brother. In 1848, for instance, he gave to Sir
Henry Dryden 'a large earthenware jug, fourteen encaustic tiles, and a small
piece of carved masonry, found on the site of Lenton Priory', and these were
subsequently acquired by what is now Nottingham Castle Museum (Robertson
1910). Moreover, in 1855 he put up for auction at Sotheby's 'the cabinet of the
late William Stretton, Esq., Lenton Priory, Nottinghamshire' (*Sotheby's sale
catalogue* March 17–20, 1855).

Dolley and Martin researched the history of the coins from the so-called west
of Co. Kilkenny find, of which, according to Lindsay, 'about sixty ... all of
Edgar' were acquired by Sempronius Stretton, and identified them with the
fifty-seven Anglo-Saxon coins of Eadgar that were sold at the 1855 Sotheby's
sale of William Stretton's cabinet (1959, 175–82; *Sotheby's sale catalogue*, lots
410, 412–18). Given that no mention was made of the ingots from this hoard at
the sale, it may be assumed that they had been disposed of at an earlier date or,
indeed, that they had never been acquired by Sempronius Stretton. It should be

noted that Lindsay's account of the find only states that he came into possession of the coins from the hoard (1842, 125). The ingots were not among a separate collection of William Stretton's antiquities that was acquired by Nottingham City Museum through a later collector, John Toplis, and it may safely be assumed that they are lost.

THE HANDCOCKS

As has been noted above, in 1830 Stretton married the Honorable Anne Handcock, the youngest daughter of the future 2nd Lord Castlemaine of Moydrum Castle, just outside Athlone. The Handcock family, originally from England, was granted its Irish lands during the Cromwellian plantations and remained one of the most prominent landowning dynasties in the midlands until the 1920s (Sheehan 1978, 43–7). Moydrum Castle, a Gothic Revival edifice, was built by the 1st Baron Castlemaine, following his elevation to the peerage in 1812.

Stretton may have become acquainted with the Handcocks during his period as a high-ranking officer in Athlone some years earlier when, presumably, there was regular social interaction between this Anglo-Irish family and the officers from the nearby garrison. Certainly this was the case in later decades, as in 1846, for instance, when Lord Castlemaine presided at the nearby Lough Ree boating regatta where 'the attendance was large and fashionable – the lake crowded with small crafts, decked in their gayest colours – while the splendid band of the 75th Regiment, stationed in a boat at a short distance form the shore, playing at intervals select pieces, rendered the scene at once animated and delightful' (*Westmeath Independent*, 8 August 1846).

What is of particular interest about Stretton's new inlaws in the present context, however, is that they had substantial estate interests in a place called Kilkenny West. This is a barony and a civil parish located some 7km north-east of Athlone and it is bounded on its west side by Lough Ree, a large lake on the River Shannon. Given that much of the barony was part of the Handcock estate, it now seems virtually certain that the find-location of the hoard acquired by Stretton was actually from this part of Co. Westmeath and not from the west of Co. Kilkenny, as reported by Lindsay. Lindsay may be excused for his error of changing Kilkenny West into 'the west of the county Kilkenny', as it is perhaps unlikely that a Cork city gentleman would be familiar with the local geography of Westmeath, a county that lay some 220km to the north.

It seems certain, therefore, that Stretton's hoard was found in the barony of Kilkenny West, Co. Westmeath. Its date of discovery is unknown, though it may have been during the years 1814 or 1822–4, or indeed beforehand, as these were the periods during which he was stationed in Athlone. It is also possible that it was unearthed somewhat later, closer to the 1830 date of his marriage to Anne

Handcock, as he presumably also spent some time in the area then. However, given that the coins formed part of his father's collections in Nottingham, and that he had died by this time, this latter possibility seems the less likely one. Lindsay's 1842 account of the find, unfortunately, is of little use in arriving at a conclusion concerning the date of its discovery, for he only states, rather vaguely, that it had been found 'a few years since'. On the basis of the available evidence, therefore, it seems most likely that its discovery was made sometime between 1814 and 1824, though it remains possible that it had been unearthed sometime prior to this.

A HARE ISLAND CONNECTION?

The re-provenancing of the Stretton hoard to Kilkenny West, Co. Westmeath, raises an intriguing possibility that deserves consideration; namely, that the find may represent portion of one of the two lost Viking-Age hoards – one of gold and the other of silver – that were discovered on Hare Island in 1802, for this island is also located in the barony of Kilkenny West. In fact, there is a further and more intriguing potential connection between the finds in that the Handcocks had a grand shooting-lodge, complete with planned gardens, on this island. It is not known when exactly they got ownership of the island, or whether they were the proprietors in 1802, the year of discovery of the gold and silver hoards. The earliest definite record of their ownership is in 1826 (Brewer 1826, 246), while local tradition holds that the lodge was built in 1812.

The evidence for the Hare Island finds, which were first recognized as Viking-Age hoards by Graham-Campbell (1974, 269–72), is mainly contained in Vallancey's *Collectanea de Rebus Hibernicis* (1804, 255–7, figs 1–4). Unfortunately, both hoards were consigned to the melting pot some time after their discovery. Vallancey recorded that they were discovered 'a few yards distant' from one another, and that the gold hoard comprised ten gold arm-rings, of varying types, a number of which he illustrated. This find is by far the largest gold hoard known from the Viking Age, amounting to slightly in excess of 5kg in weight. The most diagnostic of its arm-rings finds parallel in terms of form and ornamentation to Hiberno-Scandinavian 'ribbon-bracelets', a type which occurs, either as hack-silver fragments or whole, in two early tenth-century coin-dated hoards from northern England, those from Cuerdale, deposited *c.*905–10, and Bossall/Flaxton, deposited *c.*927. On this basis, it seems likely that the Hare Island gold hoard was deposited during the period encompassing the later ninth and early tenth centuries. The second hoard, according to Vallancey, comprised 'a number of silver anklets, with some ingots'. From his illustration of one of these 'anklets' it is obvious that they were, in fact, penannular arm-rings of the well-known Hiberno-Scandinavian broad-band type (Sheehan 1998a, 178–80). These were in circulation during the later ninth and early tenth centuries and, on the basis of their occurrence in coin-dated hoards, appear to mainly date to the period between *c*.880 and *c*.930.

Although the finder of the Hare Island hoards, a 'peasant', declined to name their find-spot, an Athlone silversmith reported to Vallancey that they were found locally. Another informant, however, identified by Vallancey as 'Colonel Handcock of Willbrook', informed him that it was believed that the location of the find-spot was on Hare Island. It is uncertain who this individual was, but Willbrook was an alternative name for Moydrum, the seat of the main line of the family. Perhaps he is to be identified as William Handcock, 1st Baron and Viscount Castlemaine (1761–1839), who was created Baron Castlemaine only in 1812 and may thus have been simply referred to as 'Colonel Handcock' prior to this. If so, he was the future uncle-in-law of Sempronius Stretton.

Graham-Campbell has proposed that the deposition of the two Hare Island hoards might date to the period of the Hiberno-Scandinavian occupation of the lake between 921/22 and 936, first by the Limerick Vikings and then by the Vikings of Lough Erne (1974, 272). Hare Island is a large island on which are the remains of an important early medieval ecclesiastical site, known in the annalistic sources as *Inis Ainghin*. A large enclosure at nearby Ballaghkeeran, on the Westmeath shore of the lake, has been interpreted as the location of the historically attested Scandinavian *longphort* on Lough Ree (Fanning 1983, 221; Sheehan 2008, 284–5), though it has also been suggested that the *longphort* may have been situated within the monastic enclosure on Hare Island itself (Graham-Campbell and Sheehan, forthcoming).

Could there be any connection between the Kilkenny West find and either of the Hare Island hoards? On first consideration it seems possible, given the facts that all three were found within the same small barony, are associated with Lough Ree, and appear to have been connected, directly or indirectly, with the same family. Furthermore, it is not inconceivable that they were found at the same time as, although the Kilkenny West hoard was probably discovered sometime between 1814 and 1824, it could have been unearthed sometime prior to this and the Hare Island hoards were discovered in 1804. Given the margins of error that are often evident in the details supplied by nineteenth-century antiquarians, it seems possible that a connection existed between these finds and that the 'Kilkenny West' find may represent a portion of one of the two lost Hare Island hoards.

On archaeological grounds, however, this possibility appears unlikely. Gold and silver appear to have functioned somewhat differently in the Scandinavian economy during the Viking Age, at least until reduced to bullion, and consequently it is rather unusual for these metals to occur together in the same find. It is not surprising that the two Hare Island hoards, as reported by Vallancey, divide into one consisting exclusively of gold ornaments and the other

36.1 Unlocalized Viking-Age hoard from Co. Cork (British Museum 1851, 3–31, 3).

36.2 Ingot from a hack-silver hoard from Ladestown (Rushy Island),
Lough Ennell, Co. Westmeath (NMI 1988.135a).

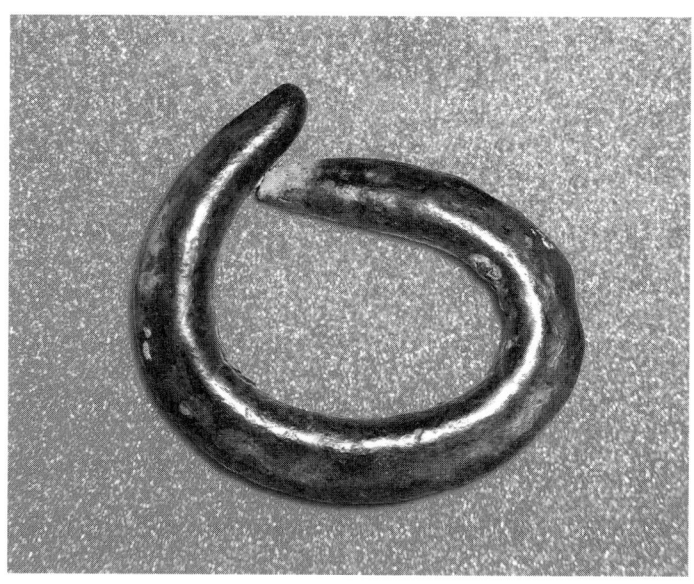

only of silver (Graham-Campbell and Sheehan, forthcoming). On this basis, it seems unlikely that the silver coins and ingots of the Kilkenny West hoard could have formed part of the same deposit as the Hare Island gold arm-rings. Moreover, while there are strong grounds for dating each of the Hare Island hoards to the later ninth and early tenth centuries, the numismatic content of the Kilkenny West find indicates that it was buried some decades later, *c*.970.

It seems, therefore, that it is only geographical and circumstantial evidence – to do with the Handcock family – which appears to link the Hare Island finds with the Kilkenny West hoard. The logical conclusion is that there was no connection and that they represent separate hoards.

THE HOARD IN CONTEXT

On the basis of its numismatic content, Dolley dated the deposition of the hoard to *c*.975 (1966, 51, no. 116), while Blackburn and Pagan have amended this to *c*.970 (1986, 297, no. 170). The only recorded information about the non-numismatic element of the hoard is what Lindsay noted, that it contained 'several silver ingots in the form of rings, each of the weight of three ounces' (1842, 125). The use of the words 'ingots in the form of rings' is unusual and suggests that Lindsay was either describing unornamented arm-rings, which he may have considered as serving the same function as ingots, or standard ingots that had been bent into something approaching hoop form. It seems unlikely that the former is the case, if only because arm-rings are rarely known to occur in coin-dated hoards from Ireland dating from the 930s onwards. Furthermore, when ingots do occur in association with arm-rings in Ireland's ninth- and tenth-century hoards, the rings are most often of Hiberno-Scandinavian broad-band type, and there is no evidence that this form continued in circulation anywhere near as late as 970, the deposition date of the Kilkenny West hoard. Rather, it is ingots which tend to dominate the coin-dated finds of the second half of the tenth century.

It seems, therefore, that the non-numismatic element of the Kilkenny West hoard consisted solely of ingots and that these had been bent into hoops 'in the form of rings'. Ingots given this treatment do actually occur in Ireland's hoards. An unlocalized hoard from Co. Cork, for instance, now in the British Museum, comprises an oblong ingot bent into an ovoid loop through which two hack-silver fragments of arm-rings have been looped (Sheehan 1998b, 153; Fig. 36.1). Another example, bent into a hoop so that one terminal touches against the underside of the other, forms part of an unpublished hack-silver hoard from a probable crannóg at Ladestown (Rushy Island), Lough Ennell, Co. Westmeath (Fig. 36.2). This hoard, which also contains a coin of Aethelraed II, indicating a *terminus post quem* of 979 for its deposition, is of particular interest in the present context in that it provides another instance of the circulation of ingots of this type in the midlands during the later tenth century.

Silver ingots form a significant element of Viking-Age hoards throughout the Viking world, and functioned primarily as a simple means of storing bullion. They occur, in either complete or hack-silver form, in at least half of the eighty recorded ninth- and tenth-century hoards from Ireland that contain non-numismatic material. Seventeen of this total also contain coins, and thus their deposition dates may be determined. All of these are of tenth-century date, though the large number of ingots and ingot-derived hack-silver in the Cuerdale, Lancashire, hoard, deposited *c*.905–10 and originating in large part in Hiberno-Scandinavian Dublin (Graham-Campbell 1987, 332–6), serves to illustrate that ingots must also have been in circulation in Ireland during the closing decades of the ninth century. Lindsay noted that each ingot in the Kilkenny West hoard weighed 'three ounces', i.e. 93.6g. If it is assumed that at least four ingots comprised the find, on the basis that this number is unlikely to exceed Lindsay's 'several', this results in a minimum estimate of *c*.374g for the weight of the non-numismatic element of the hoard.

ACKNOWLEDGMENTS

The author is grateful to Michael Kenny, National Museum of Ireland, for information on the date of the coin from the Ladestown hoard; Ann Inscker, Nottingham City Museums and Galleries, for information on its Stretton collections; the National Portrait Gallery, London, for permission to reproduce the portrait of Sempronius Stretton; Nick Hogan, Department of Archaeology, University College Cork, for assistance with the illustrations.

BIBLIOGRAPHY

Blackburn, M. & H. Pagan. 1986. 'A revised check-list of coin-hoards from the British Isles, *c*.500–1100' in Blackburn, M.A.S. (ed.), *Anglo-Saxon monetary history: essays in memory of Michael Dolley*, Leicester, pp 291–313.

Brewer, J.N. 1826. *The beauties of Ireland: being original delineations, topographical, historical, and biographical, of each county*, vol. 2.

Dolley, R.H.M. 1966a. *Hiberno-Norse coins in the British Museum*, London.

Dolley, R.H.M. & J.S. Martin. 1959. 'New light on a tenth-century find from the west of the county Kilkenny', *Numismatic Chronicle*, 1959, 178–82.

Fanning, T. 1983. 'Ballaghkeeran Little, Athlone, Co. Westmeath', *Medieval Archaeology*, 27, 221.

Graham-Campbell, J.A. 1974. 'A Viking-Age gold hoard from Ireland', *Antiquaries Journal*, 54, 269–72.

Graham-Campbell, J.A. 1976. 'The Viking-Age silver hoards of Ireland' in B. Almqvist & D. Greene (eds), *Proceedings of the Seventh Viking Congress, Dublin 1973*. Dublin, pp 31–74.

Graham-Campbell, J.A. 1987. 'Some archaeological reflections on the Cuerdale hoard' in D.M. Metcalf (ed.), *Coinage in ninth-century Northumbria: the tenth Oxford symposium on coinage and monetary history*. British Archaeological Reports, British Series, 180. Oxford, pp 320–44.

Graham-Campbell, J.A. & J. Sheehan, forthcoming. 'Viking-Age gold and silver from Irish crannógs and other watery places', *Journal of Irish Archaeology* (2009).

Hall, R. 1974. 'A check-list of Viking-Age coin finds from Ireland', *Ulster Journal of Archaeology*, 36–7 (1973–4), 71–86.

Lindsay, J. 1842. *A View of the coinage of the heptarchy, etc.* Cork.

Lodge, E. 1833. *The peerage of the British Empire*, London.

Marcombe, D. 1999. 'The last days of Lenton Priory', *Studies in Church History: Subsidia 12: Life and Thought in the Northern Church, c.1100–c.1700*.

Robertson. G.C. (ed.). 1910. *The Stretton manuscripts: being notes on the history of Nottinghamshire by William Stretton (of Lenton Priory)*, Nottingham.

Sheehan, J. 1978. *South Westmeath: farm and folk*, Dublin.

Sheehan, J. 1998a. 'Early Viking-Age silver hoards from Ireland and their Scandinavian elements' in H.B. Clarke, M. Ní Mhaonaigh & R. Ó Floinn (eds), *Scandinavia and Ireland in the Early Viking Age*, Dublin, pp 166–202.

Sheehan, J. 1998b. 'Viking-Age hoards from Munster: a regional tradition?' in M.A. Monk & J. Sheehan (eds), *Early Medieval Munster: archaeology, history and society*. Cork, pp 147–63.

Sheehan, J. 2008. 'The *longphort* in Viking-Age Ireland', *Acta Archaeologica*, 79, 282–95.

Thompson, J.D.A. 1956. *Inventory of British coin hoards, AD600–1500*, London.

Vallancey, C. 1804. 'Of golden implements and ornaments of gold and silver found in Ireland', *Collectanea de Rebus Hibernicis*, vol. 4, pt. 2, 237–89.

Wickes, H.L. 1974. *Regiments of foot: a historical record of all the foot regiments of the British army*, Reading.

Weapons and warfare in Icelandic place-names

SVAVAR SIGMUNDSSON

In one of the Icelandic sagas, *Reykdœla saga ok Víga-Skútu*, we are told that one summer a ship arrived from across the ocean at Húsavík in Iceland. It belonged to three brothers:

> Vagn hét einn ok var kallaðr spjót, annarr Nafarr ok var kallaðr sax, Skefill inn þriði ok var kallaðr sverð. [...] Svá er sagt, at hverr þeira bræðra átti þat vápn, sem við var kenndr. Þeim þótti þau í bezta lagi sinnar eigu, ok létu sér aldri hendi firr ganga.
>
> ('One was named Vagn and called Spear, the second was Nafar and nicknamed Short-sword, and the third was Skefill who was nicknamed Sword. [...] It is said that each of the brothers owned the weapon for which he was nicknamed. It seemed to them that these were their best possessions and they never let them get far from their hands': *Reykdœla saga*, 205).

In 1940, Björn Sigfússon, the editor of this saga in the series *Íslenzk fornrit*, wrote in his commentary that it was very unusual to name men after such common weapons. The main parallels are: Narfi spjót (Narfi the Spear) who was killed in 1205 (*Bǫglunga sǫgur*, ch. 5, 445); Þóroddr hjálmr (the Helmet) appears in *Landnámabók* (229) and *Ljósvetninga saga* (78); and Þorleikr geir (the Spear) figures in the Melabók version of *Landnámabók* (118). Björn Sigfússon says that there is no indication that such by-names were more common in Norway than in Iceland (*Reykdœla saga*, 205).

It is not the purpose of this paper to further discuss the topic of men named after weapons; instead I will discuss places in Iceland named after arms, armour and combat. The weaponry of Icelanders appears in excavated graves, for instance in Baldursheimur in Mývatnssveit, northern Iceland, which was discovered 1860 and 1861 as the result of erosion. Kristján Eldjárn says of the man buried there that 'he was buried fully armed, with an axe, shield and girt with a good sword. These were obvious necessities for any real free man in the Age of Settlement, an age traditionally named after the Vikings in neighbouring countries' (1963, 1). Similar equipment can be seen from a pagan grave near Kaldárhöfði in southern Iceland.

Jón Ólafsson (b. 1705) from Grunnavík was a scholar and became the secretary of Árni Magnússon, the collector of manuscripts in Copenhagen. He wrote that the subject matter of the Icelandic sagas can be described in three words: *Bændur flugust á* ('Farmers went a-fighting' (KB Add. 3, fo. 7v; see

Sverrir Tómasson 2003, 326). Manuscript drawings, for example those from the legal code *Jónsbók*, depict various types of weaponry, including a hood reminiscent of guerilla warfare past and present.

I shall now turn to those place-names in Iceland which evidently involve terms for weapons or armed combat.

VOPN ('WEAPONRY')

Vopn is the general term for all kinds of weaponry, defensive and offensive. *Vopnafjörður* is mentioned in *Landnámabók* and gets its name from Eyvindr vápni Þorsteinsson, who came from Strind in Trondheim, Norway (*Landnámabók*, 289). Þórhallur Vilmundarson thought that the fjord got its name from a long, thin spit of land (now named Kolbeinstangi) that extends into it, which could resemble the shape of a sharp weapon and thus have acquired the name **Vápn* and the fjord **Vápni* (*Grímnir* I: 137–8). *Vopnahóll* in Vopnafjörður was perhaps thought to be the burial mound of Eyvindr vápni (*Frásögur*, 12). It is difficult to decide at present whether the spit of land was a sufficiently distinctive feature to give a name to the fjord, and no comparable place-name is known today. It is, however, easy to find an explanation of the place-name in a personal male name. Vápni Herjólfsson is also mentioned in *Landnámabók*, and so this personal name was not unknown.

Vopnalág (*lág* = 'hollow'). This name is found in two places in Iceland, and one of them is the subject of a battle legend. This is a horseshoe-shaped hollow, about 300m long and 1–2m deep, situated in the land of Kalmanstunga in Borgarfjörður, in western Iceland. Legend has it that a band of outlaws was attacked there while they were sleeping, some being slain in the hollow and others being chased from there and killed (*Árbók* 2004, 186, 279).

Vopnahús (*hús* = 'house'). There is no explanation of the place-name Vopnahús in Neðra-Apavatn, southern Iceland. In the hayfield south of Orustadalur is a long hollow, called Vopnahús (*Örnefnaskrá*), divided by a small hill. The word was current in Icelandic for Latin *armamentarium* and Danish *tøjhus* ('arsenal'), but it seems unlikely that such a house stood in this place.

SPJÓT ('SPEAR')

The word *spjót* appears as a place-name element in locations that may possibly resemble a spear in appearance. *Spjótaflaga*: in Galtareyjar, Djúpeyjar in Skarðsþing in Breiðafjörður, western Iceland (*Sókn*. 2003, 111; map in *Árbók* 1989, 118). *Spjóthólmar* is the name of three islets near Fremri-Langey in Breiðafjörður. The spear of Einar skálaglam is thought to have drifted ashore there (*Sókn*. 2003, 120; *Grímnir* III: 132; map in *Árbók* 1989, 112). It is unlikely that a spear drifted ashore in these islets and the legend most likely arose to explain a pre-existing name.

There are examples of spears actually having been discovered in places named after spears. *Spjótsmýrr* is a meadow just north of the hayfield at Þóroddsstaðir in Hrútafjörður, northwestern Iceland. *Grettis saga* relates that when Sturla Þórðarson the lawman was an old man the spear of Grettir, with which Grettir slew Þorbjörn øxnamegin, was discovered in a place 'now called Spjótsmýrr', though the saga adds that some sources say that he was slain at Miðfitjar (*Grettis saga*, 157). The place-name Miðfitjar is now lost, but Spjótsmýri is still known (Þorsteinn Jósepsson & Steindór Steindórsson 1984, V: 228). This example demonstrates how place-names for particular locations could have emerged long after events allegedly associated with them, when some material remains apparently related to these events were found. Likewise, *Spjótsmýri* in Marðareyri in Grunnavík, in the West Fjords, is said to derive its name from the discovery of a spear there (*Frásögur*, 429).

SVERÐ ('SWORD')

The place-name *Sverðskelda*, north of Fáskrúður in western Iceland, is comparable to Spjótsmýri, as it is a place where a weapon was said to have been discovered. Þórólfr Ósvífursson concealed the sword that Kjartan had received as a gift from the king of Norway in a bog, but Án inn hvíti found the sword and returned it to Kjartan (*Laxdœla saga*, 142). As previously mentioned, the word *sverð* could be a by-name and the place-name *Sverðsstaðir* in Norway, which occurs in the appendix to *Skarðsárbók* (1958, 191), could be an example of just that.

SKJÓMI ('SWORD')

The word *skjómi* ('brightness, light, radiance') occurs as a sword-name and as such probably means 'the polished, shining one'. *Skjómaborg* is a high, rocky hill southeast of an old boundary-wall in Hróarsdalur in Skagafjörður, northern Iceland. The name has in recent times changed to Skjónaborg, and people accordingly believe it to be named after a horse called *Skjóni* as this is a well-known horse-name in Iceland (*Örnefnaskrá*).

VIGR ('SPEAR')

The word *vigr*, which occurs as the name of several islands, is thought to describe the shape of these islands. *Vigur* is an island in the West Fjords (*Sókn.* 1952, II: 135). There is a skerry of the same name in Álftafjörður, eastern Iceland (*Sókn.* 2000, 545, 568), and a third instance applies to a large rocky skerry in the middle of Lónsvík, in southeastern Iceland, which is girt by cliffs but grassy on top (*Sókn.* 1997, 29). The latter is said to resemble the shape of a sword when seen from a certain place in Stafafjöll (*Örnefnaskrá*). Vigur is also an island-name in Orkney, as is Vigra in Norway (*Grímnir* III: 131).

Vigra-. A few place-names with the first element *Vigra-* (gen. pl.) are known in Iceland:

Vigrafjörður is now known as Sauravogur, in western Iceland. This place-name appears in *Landnámabók* (118–19), the ancient list of Icelandic fjords (*Fjarðatal*, 127), and *Eyrbyggja saga* (9).

Vigralækur. In Staðarsveit, in western Iceland, *c*.1380 (*DI* III: 344).

Vigravík. On Akranes, in western Iceland, 1397 (*DI* IV: 196).

It is not certain that these names contain *vigr* in the sense of 'island resembling a spear'. *Vigri* means 'gray seal, female seal', thus the word *vigraselur* may refer to (female) seals with a litter in the outer skerries (*Grímnir* III: 131–2).

BRANDR ('SWORD')

Brandr was formerly such a common personal name that it is impossible to distinguish it from the sword-term *brandr* or some other weapon. Moreover, *Brandur* or *surtarbrandur* could be a geological term meaning 'jet'.

Brandurinn. This is the name of an island near the Westman Islands (Þorkell Jóhannesson 1938, 35). It is, however, shaped like a horseshoe and is therefore unlike the weapon *brandr* in shape.

FLEINN ('SPEAR')

The word means 'spike' but also signifies a 'shaft, light spear' or a 'sharp-edged weapon' in Old Icelandic. *Fleinn* is the name of a basalt layer that is more bulky above than below and has a pointed top (*Árbók* 2002, 251). This *Fleinn* gives its name to the dale *Fleinsdalur* between Leirufell and Sandfell in the parish of Kolfreyjustaðir, in eastern Iceland (*Sókn.* 2000, 399). The name, therefore, does not have to refer to the weapon as such.

GEIRR ('SPEAR')

This word meant 'spear', but could also denote some other type of thrusting weapon in Old Icelandic. Five men bear the name Geirr in *Landnámabók*, thus in the case of place-names containing *Geirs-* it is impossible to determine whether the personal name is involved or if the locations were so-named because they bore some similarity to the weapon-type. Place-names with the element *Geir-* are more likely to involve a comparison with the weapon: *Geirland* in Síða, southern Iceland, *Geirhólmur* in Hvalfjörður, western Iceland (which is also often named *Geirshólmur*), *Geirhólmi* in Flatey, western Iceland, and *Geirhnúkur* (two instances). A name like *Geirinn* and names with the first element *Geira-* could well involve the masculine noun *geiri*, meaning 'triangular strip' as in clothing.

SAX ('SHORT SWORD'/'LARGE KNIFE')

The meaning of the place-name *Saxa*, a cleft or ravine in eastern Iceland (*Sókn.* 2000, 453), is quite uncertain. This is also the case in the compound *Saxagjá* in Látrabjarg (*Sókn.* 1952, I: 214), where it seems rather unlikely that the weapon-term appears in the first element.

Saxahváll (now Saxahóll) is near Snæfellsjökull in western Iceland. The farmstead of this name is named after Saxi Álfarinsson, according to *Landnámabók* (110), and he is the only man by that name in this source.

ÖR ('ARROW')

Only the place-name *Örvasandur* in Ytri-Álftavík in Borgarfjörður, northeastern Iceland, could contain this weapon-term as its initial element, but no feature in the local landscape seems likely to give rise to the name (*Örnefnaskrá*).

ÖXI ('AXE')

This word means 'axe', used as weapon and tool. Jón Ólafsson describes the axe of Skarphéðinn, the so-called Rimmugýgur (1994, 14–15), which he claimed to have seen. The word appears in place-names, uncompounded like *Öxi*. A cliff named Öxi, most of which extends into the sea (*Örnefnaskrá*, Steinanes) is located in a chain of cliffs in western Iceland. This is also the name of a partition- or plinth-shaped cliff off the shore in Ófeigsfjörður, western Iceland (*Árbók* 2000, 101). Thirdly, this appears as the name of a heath and road in eastern Iceland (*Sókn.* 2000, 273). The word also appears compounded in place-names such as:

Axarsker. The shape of this skerry, located in Þverhamar, Breiðdalur, eastern Iceland, resembles a 'snag-horned' axe (a type of halberd-like axe).

Öxará. This place-name occurs near Þingvellir, the site of the annual legal assembly in southern Iceland. It is also the name of a river and farm in Ljósavatnsskarð in northern Iceland. There is a legend about the origin of the instance near Þingvellir. When the settler Ketilbjörn of Mosfell and his men travelled early in the spring from Skálabrekka to explore the land, they came upon a frozen river, made a hole in it and dropped an axe into the hole (*Haukdæla þáttr* in *Sturlunga saga* I: 57). This legend looks like a later explanation of the place-name. It is interesting, however, that Myrkavatn, the lake which forms the source of Öxará, is remarkably similar in shape to an axe-blade. A comparable legend is not known in connection with Öxará in northern Iceland.

Øxarfjörður. In northeastern Iceland. *Landnámabók* relates that Einar Þorgeirsson and his companions placed an axe on the mountain Reistargnúpr (= Axarnúpur, *Sókn*. 1994, 200) and named the fjord Øxarfjörður (*Landnámabók*, 285). The legend reflects a ritual land-taking. It has also been suggested that it is an explanatory tale arising after the settlement era and associated with a Christian cross.

SKJÖLDR ('SHIELD')

This word denotes a protection or defensive armour in battle, a 'shield', but it is also used as a name for a convex feature in the landscape. It occurs commonly, as the following examples show. The (male) personal name Skjöldr was the name of Óðinn's son and of a Swede who appears in *Njáls saga*, but it does not occur in *Landnámabók*, and is not known as a personal name in Iceland. It seems likely, therefore, that landscape features resembling the shape of a shield give rise to some of the place-names involving *skjöldr*.

According to legend, Skjaldarey in Breiðafjörður got its name because the shield of Þórður Ingunnarson is said to have drifted ashore there (*Laxdæla saga*, 100). Similarly, Skjaldey, also in Breiðafjörður, is said to be the place where the shield of Einar skálaglam drifted ashore according to *Landnámabók* (123; also Skjaldarey: *Sókn*. 2003, 120).

Skjaldarhæð. Two low elevations in the landscape of Tvídægra in western Iceland; close to Kjarardalur are the Dofinsfjöll mountains. The meaning of Dofinsfjöll is unclear. According to *Heiðarvíga saga* (*Frásögur*, 137), the name was Dofansfjöll, but the place is now named Skjaldarhæð, which is flat on top and shield-like in shape (*Árbók* 2004, 300).

Skjalda(r)staðir is a farm in Öxnadalur, northern Iceland (*Sókn*. 1972, 151–2, 159–60), possibly from the personal name *Skjöldur*.

Skjaldbreið(ur). A high (1066m) shield volcano close to Þingvellir in southern Iceland, which gets its name from its shape (Þorsteinn Jósepsson & Steindór Steindórsson 1984, IV: 114). A lake northwest of Mallandsvík on Skagi, in northern Iceland, also bears this name. Another example is the volcano at Brunasandur in southern Iceland.

BARDAGI ('COMBAT, BATTLE')

Bardagi is the name of a hill in western Iceland (across from the farm Dvergasteinn). An ancient sword is supposed to have been discovered there around 1880 (*Árbók* 1949, 70). The name recalls the Battle of Hastings in England, which is the name of a monastery erected to commemorate the battle of 1066.

Bardagagrund. The place-name Bardagagrund, 'battlefield', occurs in two places. One is the hayfield of Hringsdalur in Arnarfjörður, western Iceland, where the farmer Hringur is thought to have been slain (*Frásögur*, 408, 410). Close to this is Víghella, where some spear-fragments and other remains have been found (*Sókn.* 1952, 233). Another is a plain by the hayfield in Otradalur, in the aforementioned Arnarfjörður, but it is not known to what battle the place-name is supposed to refer.

ORRUSTA ('BATTLE')

In western Sweden there is the island Orust, but explanations of its name among Swedish scholars are not entirely clear; perhaps the main explanation is 'the island by the shore where fishing is good'.

Orustubalar. Located in the land of Hánefsstaðir in eastern Iceland. A sword was discovered there in the nineteenth century, so it is possible that a battle occurred in the place (*Árbók* 2005, 201).

Orustudalur. Located in Flói in southern Iceland. It is the only *Orustu-* place-name in *Landnámabók* (353, 375). It is also mentioned in *Flóamanna saga* (244) as the location where the battle of Önundr bíldr and Gunnar Baugsson took place (*Árbók Hins íslenzka fornleifafélags* 1882, 55). It is also attested in Neðra-Apavatn, Laugardalur, southern Iceland (*Örnefnaskrá*).

Orustuhóll. There are several occurrences of this place-name in Iceland with, in some cases, stories of battles having taken place at these locations. For instance, a conical gravel-hill close to Eilífsdalur, in southwestern Iceland, bears the name and *Kjalnesinga saga* tells of a battle beside this hill: 'The cairns by Orustuhóll near Eilífsdalur in Kjósarsýsla, where the brothers Helgi and Vakr fought Búi, as the same saga [*Kjalnesinga saga*] relates' (*Frásögur*, 344, 346). Another example, once called Melrakkahóll (*Finnboga saga*), occurs south of Dælir in Fnjóskadalur, in northern Iceland. A battle took place here according to *Ljósvetninga saga*, and it was then called Kakalahóll. A third example names a hill in Loftsstaðir in Flói, southern Iceland, where it is said that the slaves of some settlers fought (Bjarni Harðarson 2001, 103).

Orustuhólmur. This name occurs close to Tjaldanes in Saurbær, western Iceland, and is named in *Kormáks saga* (254) = Orustuhólmi (*Árbók Hins íslenzka fornleifafélags* 1881, 66). 'There are many cairns there, which show that men where slain there' (*Sókn.* 2003, 181).

Orustuhváll. This hill is named in *Egils saga* (291) as the place where Steinar Sjónason and Þorsteinn Egilsson fought.

Orustustaðir. Two examples of this name are on record: in Jökuldalur, eastern Iceland, and a farm on Brunasandur, southern Iceland (*Sókn.* 1997, 188). It is uncertain whether *orusta* could be a topographical name element, but Orustuhóll suggests this possibility and the word may in fact be traced back to **urriston* 'uprising' (Ásgeir Bl. Magnússon 1989, 694). Names like Orustudalur, where the second element of the compound means something opposite to an elevation, may thus refer to combat.

ÓFRIÐUR ('HOSTILITY, WARFARE'; LIT. 'UN-PEACE')

The word ófriður occurs as an element in at least three place-names:
Ófriðarstaðir. This name occurs at Hafnarfjörður in southwestern Iceland (now Jófríðarstaðir) and at ruins in the land of Ábær in northern Iceland. The latter site has never been the location of a farm and there are legends of a battle there long ago (Bjarni Einarsson 1989, 14–15).

Ófriðarvík. In Ófeigsfjörður in western Iceland (*Árbók* 2000, 101). Two shepherds are believed to have fought there, but the sea is rough in this area and that could be the true origin of the name.

ØRLYGI ('BATTLE')

This word is thought to originally mean 'peace-breaking'. It is, perhaps, a loanword in Norse from Middle Low German, like Swedish *örlig*, *örlog*, and Danish *orlog*. The word may not be a loan, however, as place-names demonstrate that the personal name Ørlygur occurs in Iceland during the settlement era (Guðrún Kvaran & Sigurður Jónsson 1991, 607). It is also known as a poetic noun or as a name for a shield in poetic noun- or name-lists, the so-called *þulur*.

Örlygshöfn. In the West Fjords. Three men with this name occur in *Landnámabók* and this harbour is named after Ørlygr Hrappsson (*Landnámabók*, 53–4) = Örlogshöfn (*Sókn.* 1952, I: 211).

Örlygsstaðir. This is a field in the land of Víðivellir in Skagafjörður, northern Iceland, which may have given its name to the battle of Örlygsstaðabardagi in 1238. Bjarni Einarsson suggested (1989, 13–15) that the name arises from this battle, which is described in *Sturlunga saga*. A battle is known to have taken place at Örlygsstaðir in Helgafellssveit, western Iceland, but the first element of this farm-name could elsewhere be the personal name Ørlygr, which occurs in *Landnámabók* and some sagas.

There are other forms of this element in Icelandic place-names:

Örlaugsvík. In Æðey in northwestern Iceland. This was a place for embarking when the harbour was frozen over. Possibly from *ørlygi*, but the personal name Örlaugur occurs in the twentieth century (Guðrún Kvaran & Sigurður Jónsson 1991, 606–7).

Örlogsgrunn. A fishing-ground from Bjarnareyjar in Breiðafjörður, western Iceland.

Örlögsey (now *Örlygsey*). A small island near Grísanes in the parish of Helgafell, western Iceland (*Sókn*. 1970, 186).

VIRKI ('FORTIFICATION')

This word means, among other things, 'fortification', but it also appears to have the less specific sense 'building, structure' or 'something resembling a fortification'. There are many examples of this word in Icelandic place-names. Virki, or compounds involving the word, is used for a hill, crag, cairn or suchlike. There are, however, some places with a real fortification, for example in Mýrar in Dýrafjörður, western Iceland: 'This fortification was built by Þórður kakali when he lived there, as a defence against his enemies. It was destroyed a few years ago to make a lawn or grassy plain. The wall of the fortification could be seen until that time. This is close to the church' (*Örnefnaskrá*).

Borgarvirki is a rocky hill near the farm Stóraborg in northwestern Iceland (= Þórðarvirki). It is 'obviously built in the manner of the ancients and like a round fortification [...] in which Vígabarði sought refuge according to legends, as *Heiðarvíga saga* relates' (*Frásögur*, 462). It is considered unlikely that men actually defended themselves there.

Hrolleifsvirki in Sléttuhlíð, northern Iceland. 'Perhaps named after the Hrolleifur who appears in *Vatnsdæla saga* or *Landnámabók*' (*Frásögur*, 500). Considered to be a deserted farm (*Sókn*. 1954, 155).

In a way similar to *Virki* serving as the name of crags or hills, the name *Kastali* or 'Castle' is widely used in western Iceland for similar features in the landscape, especially in the hayfields of farms.

VÍG ('KILLINGS (IN BATTLE)')

Vígaflötur. The kinsmen Þorkell Geitisson and Bjarni Brodd-Helgason fought in this place according to *Vápnfirðinga saga*, but the place-name is now lost (*Örnefnaskrá*, Eyvindarstaðir).

Víghella is an raised flat stone in Marðareyri in Grunnavík, in or near Spjótsmýri (*Frásögur*, 429).

Víghóll is supposed to be a name for a place where executions or slayings are said to have occurred. Þórhallur Vilmundarson (1994) is of the opinion that, in most cases, the original name was Veghóll or 'Road-hill', on the basis that most of these hills are located close to roads. It might also be considered that killings were more likley to occur on well-travelled roads.

VÍGI ('DEFENSIVE FORTIFICATION')

This occurs both as the first and second element of place-names:

Vígishellir = Beinahellir. A part of the Surtshellir cave in western Iceland (*Árbók* 2004, 188).

Kóreksstaðavígi. An isolated crag surrounded by columnar basalt close to the farm Kóreksstaðir in Útmannasveit, northeastern Iceland (*Grímnir* II: 106–8).

VÍKINGR ('VIKING')

Finally, I will mention Vikings, who also make an appearance in Icelandic place-names. However, it should be noted that Víkingr was also a (male) personal name in ancient times according to *Landnámabók*. The word *víkingr* does not only mean 'a seafarer'. It also carries the sense of 'drive, energy', 'a very hard worker' or 'work-horse'; in this sense, the word *víkingr* is indeed used as the name for a horse, at least in later times: the *Víkingssteinar* get their name from a horse named Víkingur who was found lying there and unable to stand up (*Örnefnaskrá*, Stóri- og Minninúpur in southern Iceland).

Víkingur. A fishing landmark in Holtssókn in Önundarfjörður, western Iceland (*Sókn.* 1952, II: 104).

Víkingavogur is in Papey in eastern Iceland.

Víkingavatn. A lake and a farm in Kelduhverfi in northern Iceland (*Sókn.* 1994, 212, 214).

Víkingshóll is a hill just beside the lake, and old legends say that the man who gave his name to the lake, hill and farm was the original settler.

Víkingsá marks the boundary to the bottom of Víkingsdalur in northern Iceland.

Víkingsfjall. A mountain north of Öxnadalsheiði, in northern Iceland.

Víkingsgil (now Skarfsstaðagil). At Skarfsstaðir in Hvammssveit in western Iceland (*Sturlunga saga* I: 312).

Víkingslækur. There are two instances of this name. The first applies to a farm at Rangárvellir, in southern Iceland, as noted in *Landnámabók* (356, 362–3). The second is the name of a brook in Heiði, Skaftafellssýsla, southern Iceland.

Víkingsstaðir. This name is applied to a deserted farm in Þingeyjarsýsla, northern Iceland (*Sókn.* 1994, 151) and to a farm in Vallahreppur, eastern Iceland (*Sókn.* 2000, 302).

The conclusion of this survey of Icelandic place-names that contain or possibly contain words for weapons or armed combat is that some of them surely bear witness to the hostilities and weaponry of the Viking Age. In some cases, place-names testify to hostilities while in others they simply exist because of a landscape feature's resemblance to a weapon type. Legends of battles could, of course, also have given rise to place-names in later times. Icelandic place-names do not, perhaps, add much to our knowledge of the Viking Age or the behaviour of the Vikings. They have, however, supported memories of these times and provided material for the sagas. I am not of the opinion that the sagas are, to any great extent, built on place-names that actually describe natural features. Rather, I believe that place-names preserve reflections of events that took place long ago and that they bear witness to the life and death of people in various periods. But the place-names could also, of course, have changed with the passing of time in accordance with changes in people's perceptions of the past.

BIBLIOGRAPHY

Árbók = *Ferðafélag Íslands. Árbók.* 1928– (Reykjavík).
Árbók Hins íslenzka fornleifafélags. 1881– (Reykjavík).
Ásgeir Bl. Magnússon. 1989. *Íslensk orðsifjabók* (Reykjavík).
Bjarni Einarsson. 1989. 'Örlygsstaðir?', *Véfréttir sagðar Vésteini Ólasyni fimmtugum 14. febrúar 1989* (Reykjavík), 13–15.
Bjarni Harðarson. 2001. *Landið, fólkið og þjóðtrúin: kortlagðir álagablettir og byggðir trölla, álfa, drauga, skrímsla og útilegumanna í Árnesþingi* (Selfoss).
Bǫglunga sǫgur = Finnur Jónsson (ed.). 1913. *Bǫglunga sǫgur: eirspennill – AM 47 fol – Nóregs konunga sögur: Magnús góði – Hákon gamli* (Oslo).
DI = *Diplomatarium islandicum* I–XVI. 1857–76 [1952–72] (Reykjavík).
Egils saga = *Sigurður Nordal* (ed.). 1933. *Egils saga Skalla-Grímssonar*, Íslenzk fornrit, 2 (Reykjavík).
Eyrbyggja saga = Einar Ól. Sveinsson & Matthías Þórðarson (eds). 1935. *Eyrbyggja saga*, Íslenzk fornrit, 4 (Reykjavík).
Fjarðatal = Haraldur Matthíasson (trans.). 1986. *Íslenzkir sögustaðir* (Reykjavík), IV: 127–8.
Flóamanna saga = Þórhallur Vilmundarson & Bjarni Vilhjálmsson (eds). 1991. *Harðar saga*, Íslenzk fornrit, 13 (Reykjavík).
Frásögur = Sveinbjörn Rafnsson (ed.). 1983. *Frásögur um fornaldarleifar 1817–1823* (Reykjavík).
Grettis saga = Guðni Jónsson (ed.). 1936. *Grettis saga Ásmundarsonar*, Íslenzk fornrit, 7 (Reykjavík).
Grímnir. Rit um nafnfræði, 3 vols. 1980–96 (Reykjavík).
Guðrún Kvaran & Sigurður Jónsson. 1991. *Nöfn Íslendinga* (Reykjavík).
Jón Ólafsson. 1994. 'On the weapons of the ancients', *Árbók Hins íslenzka fornleifafélags* (1994), 14–15.

Kristján Eldjárn. 1963. 'Fornaldarkuml í Baldursheimi', *Hundrað ár í Þjóðminjasafni* (Reykjavík), 1.

Landnámabók = Jakob Benediktsson (ed.). 1968. *Íslendingabók. Landnámabók*, Íslenzk fornrit, 1 (Reykjavík).

Laxdæla saga = Einar Ól. Sveinsson (ed.). 1934. *Laxdæla saga*, Íslenzk fornrit, 5 (Reykjavík).

Ljósvetninga saga = Björn Sigfússon (ed.). 1940. *Ljósvetninga saga með þáttum: Reykdæla saga ok Víga-Skútu. Hreiðars þáttr*, Íslenzk fornrit, 10 (Reykjavík), 1–106.

Njáls saga = Einar Ól. Sveinsson (ed.). 1954. *Brennu-Njáls saga*, Íslenzk fornrit, 12 (Reykjavík).

Reykdæla saga = Björn Sigfússon (ed.). 1940. *Ljósvetninga saga með þáttum: Reykdæla saga ok Víga-Skútu. Hreiðars þáttr*, Íslenzk fornrit, 10 (Reykjavík), 149–243.

Skarðsárbók = Jakob Benediktsson (ed.). 1958. *Skarðsárbók: Landnámabók Björns Jónssonar á Skarðsá* (Reykjavík).

Sókn. = *Sýslu- og sóknalýsingar Hins íslenzka bókmenntafélags*. 1839- (Reykjavík).

Sturlunga saga = Jón Jóhannesson, Magnús Finnbogason & Kristján Eldjárn (eds). 1946. *Sturlunga saga*, 3 vols (Reykjavík).

Sverrir Tómasson. 2003. '"Bændur flugust á." Þrjár athugasemdir Jóns Ólafssonar í Grunnavík um fornbókmenntir', *Gripla*, 14, 325–6.

Þorkell Jóhannesson. 1938. *Örnefni í Vestmannaeyjum* (Reykjavík).

Þorsteinn Jósepsson & Steindór Steindórsson (eds). 1984. *Landið þitt Ísland* (Reykjavík), 1–5.

Þórhallur Vilmundarson. 1994. 'Víghóll', *Lesbók Morgunblaðsins*, 26 March, 7–11.

Örnefnaskrá = Place-name records in Stofnun Árna Magnússonar í íslenskum fræðum – Örnefnasafn.

The Finglas burial: archaeology and ethnicity in Viking-Age Dublin

MAEVE SIKORA

INTRODUCTION

In 2004 a grave containing two oval brooches, a comb and a casket was found at Church Street, Finglas, northwest of Dublin city (Fig. 38.1). The burial was an unexpected discovery during the final stages of excavation of a number of medieval ditches (Kavanagh, pers. comm.). The brooches, comb and casket mounts were deposited in the National Museum of Ireland almost immediately after discovery and were conserved in the Museum's conservation laboratory. Burials with oval brooches are a relatively rare feature of Viking-Age archaeology in Ireland. Prior to the Finglas discovery the last find was made in 1900/1901 near Arklow, Co. Wicklow, in a grave that has been dated to the first half of the tenth century (Ó Floinn 1998b, 31–4). The particular form of the Finglas brooches represents the first of its type to be found in Ireland.

LOCATION

Although it is now part of the greater Dublin area, cartographic sources indicate that Finglas was originally a small village (Ball 1920, 83–4; Tutty 1973, 68). The earliest historical record of the monastery of Finglas is an entry in the *Annals of the Four Masters* for the year 758, recording the death of Faelchu of Finnghlais. Its principal association was with St Canice, who is also linked to Kilkenny (Walsh 1888, 11; Ball 1920, 114; Gwynn & Hadcock 1970, 384; Tutty 1973, 66; O'Dwyer 1977, 55). Although relatively little is recorded about the monastery, references to a scriptorium there in the ninth century suggest that it was considered a significant foundation (Ó Corráin 1998, 432). The annals refer to a number of scribes at Finglas in the later eighth and ninth centuries (*Annals of Ulster* 796, 812, 838, 867). Finglas, along with Tallaght, is also noted as one of the 'eyes' of Ireland during the eighth and ninth centuries, and it was linked with Tallaght in the Céli Dé movement (Ball 1920, 84; Harbison 1992, 330; O'Dwyer 1977, 31).

In the later Viking Age, Finglas found itself within the hinterland of Hiberno-Norse Dublin (*Dyflinarskiri*) and its inclusion in a list of churches in the 1179 letter of Alexander III provides interesting evidence of continuity with pre-

38.1 Location of Finglas, Co. Dublin.

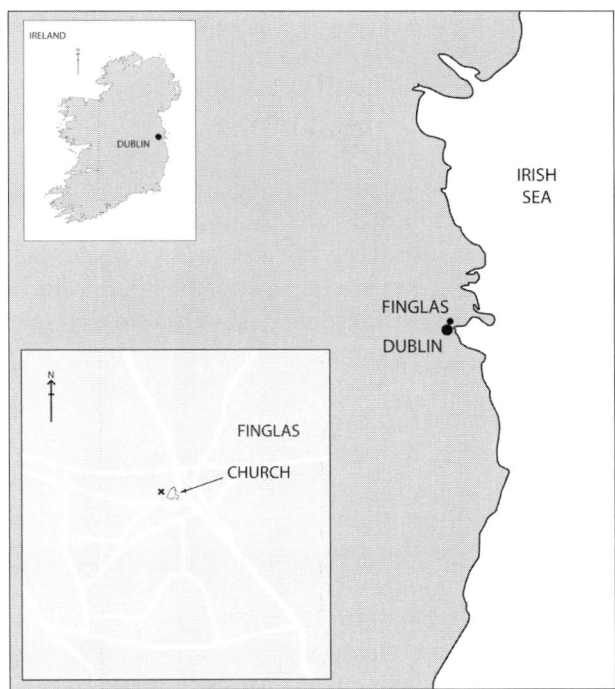

Viking times (Bradley 1988, 55–9). A ditch excavated by John Kavanagh on the site containing twelfth-century material supports this evidence (Kavanagh, pers. comm.). The present church at Finglas dates to the twelfth century and later (Ball 1920, 114–15). A granite high cross which is now located to the south of the church is classified as one of Harbison's South Leinster group, all of which, apart from Finglas, lie south of the River Liffey (Ball 1920, 114; Harbison 1992, 376). Although the burial was outside the current church wall, it is situated very close to the monastic site (Kavanagh, pers. comm.). Kavanagh's excavation at the site revealed evidence for a substantial ditch, measuring 4.2m wide, which is believed to date to the early medieval period. Lines of enclosure around Finglas may also be inferred by an examination of the first edition of the Ordnance Survey map. Test excavations carried out in 1993 in advance of road construction also revealed evidence for a ditch which may be connected to the monastic enclosure (Halpin 1996, 12).

THE BURIAL

The skeleton, identified as a female aged between 25 and 35 years at death (Kavanagh, pers. comm.), was buried with two oval brooches, a comb and a wooden box or casket decorated with bone plates. The body was placed southwest/northwest, with the head to the southwest. The brooches were in the customary position for female Scandinavian burials, fastening the dress-straps just below the shoulders (Jansson 1985, 221), while the comb and box were on the right pelvis. The finger bones of the left hand were found underneath the brooch, indicating that the hand had probably been underneath the dress-strap. The remains had suffered considerable damage. The skull was at a higher level than the rest of the body, and had been disturbed, while the comb and box had also been badly damaged. The legs had been truncated above the knees, and the left shoulder and upper arm were missing. A number of animal bones were also found on the upper torso, but due to the level of disturbance it is doubtful that these are contemporary deposits.

CASKET

The casket was probably made of wood, but only the mounts remained. It was not possible to determine whether the comb was contained within the casket or whether the artefacts were placed side by side.

Two complete and eight fragmentary strips survive, all of which appear to be of bone, as the cancellous structure on the reverse or undecorated side of the strips resembles bone rather than antler (see MacGregor 1985, 8–29). All of these were decorated with sawn oblique lines executed in two different ways: four parallel narrow lines alternating with a plain surface, or continuous thicker sawn incisions. Looking at the first type, a slight difference in width between the incisions suggests that they were made with a single-bladed saw; however, the decoration is finely executed. Within this style, three different motifs were used: two strips have opposed chevron decoration (Fig. 38.2), two are decorated with z-form oblique lines, and three with s-form lines. At least two of these strips appear to have decorated the lid of the casket. Apart from those with opposed chevron decoration, which appear to be longer, the strips appear to have been of regular dimensions, measuring approximately 120mm long by 20mm wide. Three strips decorated with wider incisions of continuous z-form oblique lines decorated either the side or base of the casket. All of the strips were originally attached to the box by means of iron nails.

Unfortunately, the exact form of the casket cannot be reconstructed due to the incomplete nature of the find, but the fact that no hinges or handles were found may be an indication that the box was of relatively simple construction with a sliding lid, in contrast to more complex caskets such as those from some of the graves at Birka (Arbman 1940, 259–73). Caskets with simple sliding lids occur in Norwegian burials from as early as the Migration period (Shetelig 1912, 116).

As yet, no parallels are known for the occurrence of a casket in a Scandinavian grave in Ireland, but a number of mounts, related to the Finglas examples, have

38.2 Sample of bone mounts, decorated with opposed chevron decoration, from the Finglas casket.

38.3 Fragment of the single-sided composite comb from the Finglas burial.

been found during excavations in Hiberno-Norse Dublin and also in Waterford and Cork: at Christchurch Place, Dublin, the lid of a box was recovered with a number of bone mounts still attached (NMI reg. no. E122:16343; Ó Ríordáin 1981, 44), while the side of a wooden casket excavated in tenth-century levels at Fishamble Street has a border of bone strips decorated with oblique lines similar to the Finglas casket (NMI reg. no. E190:7108). A number of casket mounts were found during excavations in Waterford: one which has similar decoration to Finglas dates to the mid-twelfth century (see Hurley et al. 1998, 64, fig. 22; see also Cleary et al. 1997, 258, figs 6 and 228, fig. 114, no. 7, for examples from Cork). A portion of a wooden box lid with bone mounts, which was found at Coppergate in York, probably dates to the eleventh century (McGregor 1999, 1954–7), but some bone and antler strips were also found from approximately ninth-century contexts (McGregor 1999, 1954).

COMB

The surviving piece, measuring 49mm long, consists of one end of the comb and includes its two connecting plates and a section of its tooth plate. It is a single-sided composite comb, made of antler, with side-plates that are plano-convex in both outline and cross-section (Fig. 38.3). The surviving ends of the connecting plates are decorated with incised parallel lines, and an incised motif is visible near the broken edges. None of the teeth remain in place, but thirty-two loose examples were found scattered in the vicinity; beading is evident on many of them, indicating that the comb was used prior to deposition. Based on the number of these teeth alone, the comb would have measured 90mm long, but it is more likely that it was at least 150mm in length.

The comb appears to be similar to Dunlevy's type F1 (Dunlevy 1988, 363–4) or Ambrosiani's 'Group A' combs, specifically type A3, but without the animal-head terminals (see Ambrosiani 1981, 63). Group A combs are distinguished by their plano-convex shape, both in the length of the comb and in cross-section, and there appears to be a correlation between this type of comb and decoration with lines parallel to the edge of the plate. The type dates from the ninth century and is frequently found in Norway, where it continued to be used in the tenth century. Group A combs are generally considered to be of Scandinavian origin and Dunlevy argues that the small number of this type known from Ireland, combined with the fact that some of the motifs used on them are paralleled on combs from Scandinavia, suggests that some were imported into Ireland rather than being manufactured there (1988, 364). Combs are known from a number of other Scandinavian graves in Ireland (see Bøe 1940, 66, 76; Dunlevy 1988, 395; Simpson 2003, 131–3) but are not of frequent occurrence (Harrison 2001; Ó Floinn 1998a).

OVAL BROOCHES

Although only one of the oval brooches is complete (Fig. 38.4, Plates 9–11), the surviving fragments of the other (Fig. 38.5) indicate that they formed a matching pair. The complete brooch lay on the right shoulder, while the remains of the second were found in the area of the left. X-ray fluorescence analysis has shown that the brooches are cast gilt brass with inlaid silver and glass. The decoration consists of applied animal figures and fields of cast gripping-beast motifs. The complete brooch measures 82.24mm long by 61mm wide. The following discussion focuses on the latter brooch.

Framework
The framework for the decoration on the surface of the brooch is formed of two principal elements: a cast moulding, *c*.2mm wide, oval in plan, which divides the upper surface from the side, and a pair of parallel flat strips which run the length of the brooch on either side of the central mount. In brooches of similar type found in Scandinavia, the ridge is formed instead of twisted silver wire (see Jansson 1985, 31; Capelle 1968, 103). The flat strips are decorated with inlaid silver, which would also have been ornamented with coils of silver wire which do not survive: eight on one side and ten on the other (Fig. 38.6). Each coil of wire probably surrounded a central silver granule. The silver strips, which measure 36mm in maximum length by 7.8mm in maximum width, terminate in round boss mounts at each end. Each of these mounts is in turn connected to the edge of the brooch by a series of parallel ribs, which are nicked transversely, and taper towards the rim. Although their fastening pegs are visible on the underside of the brooch, none of these four bosses survive, but they were probably analogous to those in a corresponding position on the pair of brooches of the same type from grave 550 at Birka (Jansson 1985, 31). Between the bosses at each end is a smaller, 13mm long, biconcave strip of inlaid silver decorated in the same manner as the two longer strips.

Surface decoration
The decoration on the surface of the brooch consists of fields of cast gripping-beast motifs, all of which are gilt (Fig. 38.7). Four fields are placed symmetrically on the top of the brooch, within the area enclosed by the oval moulding: two in the centre, at either end of the central mount, and one at each side. Outside of the central area, the decoration is also arranged symmetrically, with two large motifs on either side flanked at each end by a smaller design. Two small panels of decoration are also visible at each end of the brooch, outside the applied animal figures. Although some differences in form are notable between the

38.4 The complete oval brooch from the Finglas burial.

38.5 Surviving fragments of the second oval brooch from the Finglas burial.

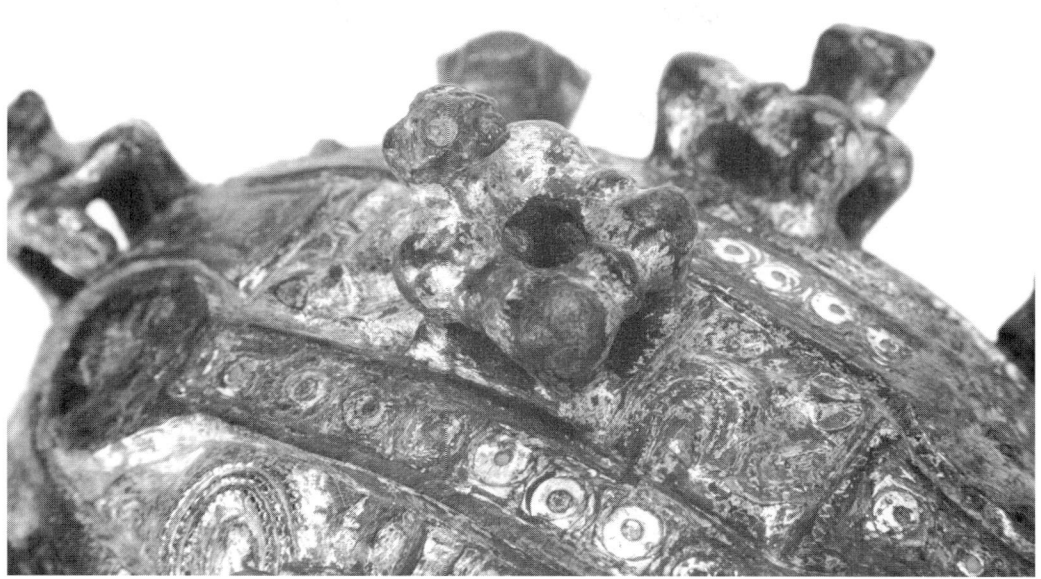

38.6 Detail of the complete brooch, showing inlaid silver.

38.7 Detail of complete brooch, showing cast gilt gripping-beast motif.

matching pairs of fields, the beasts on all panels are of similar type. Apart from the fields on either side of the central mount, which are of abstract form, the beasts have a triangular head and a clearly defined neck, somewhat similar in form to the heads represented on the Berdal type P15 brooch from grave 557 at Birka (Jansson 1985, 27), and those on the sides of the pair from grave 42 at Hedeby (Capelle 1968, 103, Taf. 7, 2c). The bodies are formed of a rather abstract series of concentric arcs, some of which are nicked transversely similar to the patterns on the pair of brooches from grave 550 at Birka (Jansson 1985, 31).

Protruding decoration
Perhaps the most striking feature of the brooch is the protruding animal ornament. Two different types are represented, whole animals/figurines and larger animal heads. In both cases, the animals clearly resemble bears, with short snouts, rounded ears and round inset glass eyes (Plates 9–11).

The figurines consist of bear heads placed on four-legged mounts. Five such animals are present on the brooch and these are arranged in a cruciform fashion with one in the centre and one at each end and on either side of the brooch. The heads are placed on the 'hind legs', giving the impression that the animals are seated. The bears are made of gilt brass and have round bulging glass eyes. The mounts vary in size, particularly in terms of their heads. Four-legged mounts occur on a number of other oval brooches, including the pairs from graves 550 and 552 at Birka (Arbman 1940, Taf. 59; Jansson 1985, 28–31). A single animal mount from a grave at Kaupang is also comparable, although the animal head is placed on one of the legs, rather than on a pair (grave C27997C in N. Bikjholberget gravefield: Blindheim et al. 1981, 219).

Four bear heads are positioned in between the bear figurines on the edges of the brooch, outside the dividing moulding. They appear to be larger versions of the heads on the whole animals. These are also of brass and have glass eyes, but they appear to have traces of silver or zinc coating rather than gilding (most of which has worn off). The fastening pegs for these heads are clearly visible on the underside of the brooch.

The edge of the brooch has a plain everted flange above which is a single row of cast beading. Both the catch plate and the base of the pin survive on the underside, though the latter is obscured by a clump of fossilized textile. Although detailed examination has yet to be carried out, there appears to be at least two different types of textile represented here (E. Wincott Heckett, pers. comm.).

DISCUSSION

The oval brooch is one of the most characteristic types of Viking-Age antiquities, occurring both in female burials in the homelands as well as in areas of

Scandinavian colonization. It is an indigenous Scandinavian personal ornament type, which developed from a small plain dress-fastener into a larger ornate piece decorated with zoomorphic motifs (Wilson & Klindt-Jensen 1966, 40). Some types were mass-produced, and mould fragments have been recovered from excavations at major Viking-Age centres such as Ribe, Birka and Hedeby. These brooches are seen as having a practical function in fastening dress-straps, and are generally found in pairs (Jansson 1985, 221). However, they must also have had social and religious significance and their decoration may be interpreted as carrying symbolic meaning (Capelle 1968, 89; Hayeur Smith 2005, 83).

Classifications used for studying oval brooches are mainly based on that published by Petersen (1928), though subsequent studies by Paulsen (1933), and more recent work by Capelle (1968) and Jansson (1985), on the Hedeby and Birka material respectively, are also taken into account. The pair from Finglas may be classified as belonging to Petersen Type 23/24 (hereafter P23/24), which are distinguished by the presence of applied protruding decoration combined with a double band of decoration along the spine (Petersen 1928, 12; see also Paulsen 1933, 30). Although technically these are two different types, Paulsen (1933, 29), Capelle (1968, 43) and Jansson consider them as a single group. Rygh also illustrates a brooch of this type from a grave at Horne, Romedal, Hedmark, which is classified as R646 (Rygh 1885). The types date to early in the series of Viking-Age oval brooches and late in the sub-grouping of so-called Berdal brooches, with a date centring on the second half of the ninth century (Petersen 1928, 19; Paulsen 1933, 31; Capelle 1968, 42–4; Jansson 1985, 222). While Berdal brooches are generally more popular in southern Scandinavia than in Norway (Jansson 1981, 1), this particular sub-type is most commonly known from Norway (Capelle 1968, 113; Jansson 1985, 32). It is a rare type which is highly decorated and very skilfully produced. Apart from Finglas, eleven finds – either of single brooches or pairs – of Type P23/24 are known; the majority are from Norway, with further examples on record from Denmark, Sweden and Iceland (Petersen 1928, 19; Paulsen 1933, 29; Capelle 1968, Taf. 7, Karte 13; Jansson 1985, 32). Few of these have well-documented find circumstances, and some are unpublished (Jansson 1985, 32; for lists of examples see Rygh 1885, 33 (R646); Petersen 1928, 19; Paulsen 1933, 30; Jansson 1985, 32).

Among those with recorded contexts is the unique pair from grave 550 at Birka (Arbman 1943; Jansson 1985) and the pair from grave 42 at Hedeby (Capelle 1968). Similarities between the Finglas brooch and the Birka and Hedeby pairs include the form of the brooches and the presence of protruding animal ornament, as well as the use of gilding and silver inlay (Capelle 1968, 103; Jansson 1985, 31). The pair of brooches from Horne, though they exhibit some differences from the Finglas brooch, also has traces of silver inlay (Rygh 1885, 33). The Finglas brooch is at least 1cm shorter than those mentioned above. In the cases of both the Birka and Hedeby examples, the framework of decoration differs from Finglas in that the strips of silver are both concave, giving the top field of the brooch a biconcave shape; the strips on the Finglas brooch are straight, and thus the fields of decoration are also straight. The Finglas example also differs from these two pairs in having extra applied decoration in the form of the larger bear heads and in its lack of a band of twisted silver wire framing the decoration on the top and middle fields.

The surface decoration on the Birka and Hedeby pairs appears to be more sophisticated than that on the Finglas brooch, particularly on the side fields. In the case of the latter example, the body of the animal is reduced to a series of concentric lines in contrast to the well-defined limbs of the beasts on the Birka brooches (Jansson 1985, 31). Despite this, the Finglas brooch is an exceptionally beautiful artefact and extensive effort has clearly been invested in the production of its ornate applied animals. The use of glass eyes on these brooches appears to be of rare occurrence, and it is not replicated on either the Birka or Hedeby examples, although it is seen on the equal-armed brooch from the high-status ninth-century grave at Gausel, Rogaland (Petersen 1928, 51; Børsheim and Soltvedt 2002, 28). Interestingly, Petersen compared his Type P23, from Bjorke, Hedrum, Vestfold, to the Gausel brooch.

The gilding, silver inlay, glass, and quantity of applied decoration on the brooch set it apart as a piece of outstanding craftsmanship. At Birka, women buried with oval brooches decorated with silver, albeit of the P51C type, tended to represent a higher social class (Jansson 1985, 226). It seems likely that the Finglas pair would also have marked the wearer out as a person of high rank, particularly in an Irish context, where this type of artefact seems to have been quite rare. The high status of this woman might also be inferred by the presence of a casket in her grave, a rare find in the context of Viking-Age Ireland.

Some previous studies have discussed the meaning of the art on oval brooches (Capelle 1968, 87). In the context of the applied decoration on the Finglas brooches, it is interesting to note the significance of the bear in Scandinavian mythology, in which the animal is specifically associated with the cult of Óðinn (Ström 1980). At Kaupang, bear bones were found in association with a rich boat-grave (S. Bikjholberget, grave K/VIII) which also contained a sword, spearhead, two axes and a shield among other items (Blindheim & Heyerdahl-Larsen 1995, 117, 128). Blindheim and Heyerdahl-Larsen suggested that the interred was a bear-hunter who lost his life while hunting, and noted that bear bones are not unusual in the context of Iron-Age graves and have been interpreted as being associated with magic and ritual. The associations between this animal and magic have recently been considered by Price in his discussion of the finds from Storsjö lake on Frösö island, where the remains of what appears to be a Viking-Age sacrificial grove were excavated. The remains of a large number of animals, including five bears, were discovered around the stump of a birch tree (Price 2002, 61). Bearskins, identified by the presence of claws and paw-bones, are also known from Scandinavian Iron-Age graves (Shetelig 1912, 146–7; Price 2002, 374, also 367–78 for discussion of bears in relation to sorcery and aggression in Late Iron-Age Scandinavia). Is it possible that the owner or the person who commissioned the Finglas brooches was affiliated to a bear cult or to the cult of Óðinn?

CONCLUSIONS

The majority of Scandinavian graves known in Ireland appear to date to the period between AD840 and 950, with an emphasis on the latter half of the ninth century (Ó Floinn 1998a, 138; Harrison 2001, 74–5). Around 80 per cent of these are found within five kilometres of Dublin (Harrison 2001, 65–6), a trend supported by the Finglas find. The contents of these burials, along with other categories of evidence, reflect a Norwegian-dominated presence in Ireland during this period (Ó Corráin 1997, 84; Ó Floinn 1998a, 140; Wamers 1998, 60). Both the brooch and comb from Finglas are early Viking-Age types and can be paralleled in Norwegian contexts (Petersen 1928; Petersen 1951). On present evidence, therefore, there is nothing to contradict the idea that this burial dates to the period of the first phase of Scandinavian activity in Ireland.

The location of the burial close to a monastic site poses interesting questions concerning the cultural affiliations of the interred and those who interred her. This phenomenon, however, is not unprecedented in the Viking world: Bersu's excavation at Balladoole (Bersu & Wilson 1966, 13) and burials at Peel on the Isle of Man (Freke 2002, 73) are both examples, as is Donnybrook in south Dublin (O'Brien 1998, 220), while the Scandinavian burials at Islandbridge may also have been on the site of a pre-existing Christian cemetery, and those at Kilmainham may have been within the precincts of the monastic site of Cell Maignenn (O'Brien 1998, 203; Ó Floinn 1998a, 132). The exact find-place of the burials in the Phoenix Park is not known, but Ó Floinn suggests that it may have been at or near the early ecclesiastical site at Cell Moshamóc (Ó Floinn 1998a, 134).

Burial is a valuable category of evidence as it represents an act of deliberate deposition, and the location of the Finglas burial, as well as its contents, should be considered a conscious act. The presence of brooches suggests that the woman was buried in traditional Norse dress, a detail often interpreted as a marker of Scandinavian ethnicity (Graham-Campbell 2002, 97; Hayeur Smith 2004). Gräslund has argued that the presence of brooches, combs and other personal accessories connected with the clothing of the deceased, should not be considered as grave-goods per se, and are thus not necessarily indicative of a pagan rite (1987, 85). She does, however, categorize artefacts such as boxes, buckets and other vessels, as specifically grave-goods, and therefore probably suggestive of a pagan rite. Using this method, we might consider the brooches and comb at Finglas as personal accessories, but the casket as a grave-good.

Pagan burial in a Christian milieu could be interpreted as an attempt to accentuate that which is different about a set of beliefs of a culture that feels isolated or under threat (Carver 1995; Hayeur Smith 2004, 79). But, given its location in a Christian context, it might also be argued that the Finglas burial represents an attempt at the cohesion of two different cultural perspectives in a time of transition. As previously noted (Ó Floinn 1998a, 163), the role of Scandinavian women, and perhaps of the woman buried at Finglas, may have been crucial in forming political alliances in the early Viking period in Ireland.

Note added in press
Since this paper was submitted, the author had the opportunity of examining oval brooches in the collection of the Archaeological Museum in Stavanger. Of particular interest is S.2095, an oval brooch from Fristad, Rogaland, which is a very similar to the Finglas brooch (see Petersen 1928, 21). Both brooches are comparable in size, are gilded all over and feature analogous cast gripping-beast decoration, applied animal ornament and silver inlay. The Fristad brooch has four animal heads, possibly representing bears, and five four-legged mounts. The animal heads probably had glass eyes similar to the Finglas brooch, but none survive. That the Finglas brooch should be so similar to one from this part of Norway is not unexpected, since the involvement of people of this region in Ireland in the early Viking-Age has been demonstrated very clearly (Wamers 1998, 57).

ACKNOWLEDGMENTS

I am very grateful to the excavator, John Kavanagh, for allowing me to study the artefacts from the grave. I am also grateful to Ian Riddler and Nicola Nartowska for their assistance with the identification of the casket mounts and the comb; to Elizabeth Wincott-Heckett for her comments on the textile; to Valerie Dowling, Senior Photographer and to John Murray of Graphic Design Department in the National Museum of Ireland for the photography and illustrations respectively; to Dr Paul Mullarkey of the Conservation Department in the Museum for carrying out preliminary x-ray fluorescence analysis on the brooches, for drawing my attention to the Fishamble Street casket, and for comments on the text. Thanks are due to Mary Cahill for reading and commenting on the text, and to Raghnall Ó Floinn for reading the text, for advice on historical sources and suggestions for parallels for the casket mounts. I would also like to thank Åsa Dahlin Hauken and Nathalie Hanna for their assistance while in the Archaeological Museum in Stavanger.

BIBLIOGRAPHY

Annals of Ulster (to AD1131), ed. and trans. S. Mac Airt & G. Mac Niocaill, Dublin 1983.
Ambrosiani, K. 1981. *Viking age combs, comb making and comb makers in the light of finds from Birka and Ribe*, Stockholm Studies in Archaeology, 2 (Stockholm).

Arbman, H. 1940–3. *Birka I: die gräber*, 2 vols (Stockholm).

Arwidsson, G. (ed.). 1989. *Birka II 3: systematischer analysen der gräberfunde* (Stockholm).

Ball, F.E. 1920. *Southern Fingal being the sixth part of a history of county Dublin* (Dublin).

Bersu, G. & D.M. Wilson, 1966. *Three Viking graves in the Isle of Man*, Society for Medieval Archaeology Monograph Series, 1 (London).

Blindheim, C., Heyerdahl-Larsen, B. & R.L. Tollnes. 1981. *Kaupang-funnene, Bind I*. Norske Oldfunn, 11 (Oslo).

Blindheim, C. & B. Heyerdahl-Larsen. 1995. *Kaupang-funnene, Bind II*, Norske Oldfunn, 16 (Oslo).

Bradley, J. 1988. 'The interpretation of Scandinavian settlement in Ireland' in J. Bradley (ed.), *Settlement and society in Medieval Ireland: studies presented to F.X. Martin, o.s.a.* (Kilkenny), pp 49–78.

Bøe, J. 1940. 'Norse antiquities in Ireland', pt. III in H. Shetelig (ed.), *Viking antiquities in Great Britain and Ireland* (Oslo).

Børsheim, R.L. & E. Soltvedt. 2002. *Gausel: utgravingene 1997–2000* (Stavanger).

Capelle, T. 1968. *Der metallschmuck von Haithabu: studien zur wikingischen metallkunst* (Neumünster).

Carver, M.O.H. 1995. 'Ancient boat burial in Britain: ancient custom or political signal?' in O. Crumlin-Pedersen & B. Munche (eds), *The ship as a symbol in prehistoric and medieval Scandinavia* (Copenhagen), pp 111–24.

Clarke, H.B., M. Ní Mhaonaigh & R. Ó Floinn (eds). 1998. *Ireland and Scandinavia in the Early Viking Age* (Dublin).

Dunlevy, M. 1988. 'A classification of early Irish Combs', *Proceedings of the Royal Irish Academy*, 88C, 341–422.

Edwards, N. 1990. *The archaeology of early medieval Ireland* (London).

Freke, D. (ed.). 2002. *Excavation on St Patrick's Isle Peel, Isle of Man, 1982–88: prehistoric, Viking, medieval and later*, Centre for Manx Studies Monographs, 2 (Liverpool).

Graham-Campbell, J. 2002. 'Tenth-century graves: the Viking-Age artefacts and their significance' in D. Freke (ed.), *Excavation on St Patrick's Isle Peel, Isle of Man, 1982–88: prehistoric, Viking, medieval and later*, Centre for Manx Studies Monographs, 2 (Liverpool), pp 83–98.

Gräslund, A. 1987. 'Pagan and Christian in the Age of Conversion' in J.E. Knirk (ed.), *Proceedings of the Tenth Viking Congress: Larkollen, Norway, 1985*, Universitets Oldsaksamlings Skrifter Nyrekke, 9 (Oslo), pp 81–94.

Gwynn, A. & R.N. Hadcock. 1970. *Medieval religious houses, Ireland* (London).

Harbison, P. 1992. *The high crosses of Ireland: an iconographical and photographic survey*, vol. 1 (Bonn).

Halpin, E. (ed.). 1996. 'Excavations on the route of the Finglas by-pass, Finglas, Co. Dublin', unpublished excavation report submitted to the Department of Environment, Heritage and Local Government.

Harrison, S.H. 2001. 'Viking graves and grave-goods in Ireland', in A.C. Larsen (ed), *The Vikings in Ireland* (Roskilde), pp 61–75.

Hayeur Smith, M. 2004. *Draupnir's sweat and Mardöll's tears: an archaeology of jewellery, gender and identity in Viking-Age Iceland*, British Archaeological Reports, International Series, 1276 (Oxford).

Hayeur Smith, M. 2005. 'Breaking the mould: a re-evaluation of Viking-Age mould-making techniques for oval brooches', in R. Ordell Bork, S. Montgomery, C. Neuman de Vegvar, E. Shortell & S. Walton (eds.) *De Re Metallica: the uses of metal in the Middle Ages* (London), pp 81–100.

Hurley, M.F. & O.M.B. Scully, with S.W.J. McCutcheon. 1998. *Late Viking-Age and medieval Waterford: excavations 1986–1992* (Waterford).

Jansson, I. 1981. *Economic aspects of fine metalworking in Viking-Age Scandinavia: economic aspects of the Viking Age*, British Museum, Occasional Paper, 30 (London).

Jansson, I. 1985. *Oval brooches: a study of Viking period standard jewellery based on the finds from Björkö (Birka)*, Sweden (Uppsala).

Kavanagh, J. 2005. 'Excavation at Church Street, Finglas, Dublin', unpublished excavation report submitted to Department of Environment, Heritage and Local Government.

MacGregor, A. 1985. *Bone, antler, ivory and horn: the technology of skeletal materials since the Roman period* (London).

MacGregor, A. et al. 1999. 'Craft, industry and everyday life: bone, antler, ivory and horn from Anglo-Scandinavian and Medieval York', in P.V. Addyman (ed.), *The archaeology of York: the small finds*, 17:12 (York).

Ní Mhaonaigh, M. 1998. 'Friend and foe: Vikings in ninth- and tenth-century Irish literature', in H.B. Clarke et al. (eds), *Ireland and Scandinavia* (Dublin), pp 381–402.

O'Brien, E. 1998. 'The location and context of Viking burials at Kilmainham and Islandbridge, Dublin', in H.B. Clarke et al. (eds), *Ireland and Scandinavia*, pp 203–21.

Ó Corráin, D. 1997. 'Ireland, Wales, Man and the Hebrides', in P. Sawyer (ed.), *The Oxford Illustrated History of the Vikings* (Oxford), pp 83–109.

Ó Corráin, D. 1998. 'Viking Ireland – afterthoughts', in H.B. Clarke et al. (eds), *Ireland and Scandinavia*, pp 421–52.

Ó Cúiv, B. 1988. 'Personal names as an indicator of relations between native Irish and settlers in the Viking Period', in J. Bradley (ed.), *Settlement and society in medieval Ireland: studies presented to F.X. Martin, o.s.a.* (Kilkenny), pp 79–88.

O'Dwyer, P. 1977. *The spirituality of the Célí Dé reform movement in Ireland, 750–900* (Dublin).

Ó Floinn, R. 1998a. 'The archaeology of the early Viking age in Ireland', in H.B. Clarke et al. (eds), *Ireland and Scandinavia*, pp 131–5.

Ó Floinn, R. 1998b. 'Two Viking burials from Co. Wicklow', *Wicklow Archaeology and Society*, I, 29–35.

Ó Ríordáin, B. 1981. 'Aspects of Viking Dublin', *Medieval Scandinavia*, 2 (Odense).

Paulsen, P. 1933. *Studien zur Wikinger-Kultur*, Forschungen zur Vor- und Frühgeschichte aus dem Museum vorgeschichtlicher Altertürmer in Kiel, I (Neumünster).

Petersen, J. 1928. *Vikingetidens smykker* (Stavanger).

Petersen, J. 1951. *Vikingetidens redskaper* (Oslo).

Price, N. 2002. *The Viking way: religion and war in Late Iron Age Scandinavia* (Uppsala).

Rygh, O. 1885. *Norske Oldsager* (Christiania).

Shetelig, J. 1912. *Vestlandske graver fra Jernalderen* (Bergen).

Simpson. L. 2003. 'Excavation at South Great George's Street' in I. Bennett (ed.), *Excavations 2001* (Bray) no. 382 (i.e. Excavations 2001).

Ström, Å. 1980. 'Björnfällar och Oden-religion', *Fornvännen*, 4, 266–70.

Thomas, C. 1971. *The Early Christian archaeology of north Britain* (Glasgow).

Tutty, M.J. 1973. 'Old Dublin Society', *Dublin Historical Review*, 26:2, 66–73.

Twohig. D.C., R.M. Cleary, M.F. Hurley, & E. Shee Twohig, *Skiddy's Castle and Christ Church, Cork: Excavations 1974–77 by D.C. Twohig* (Cork).

Walsh, R. 1888. *Fingal and its churches: a historical sketch of the foundation and struggles of the Church of Ireland* (Dublin).

Wamers, E. 1998. 'Insular finds from Viking-Age Scandinavia', in H.B. Clarke et al. (eds), *Ireland and Scandinavia*, pp 37–72.

Wilson, D.M. & O. Klindt-Jensen. 1966. *Viking art* (London).

The first phase of Viking activity in Ireland: archaeological evidence from Dublin

LINZI SIMPSON

THE *LONGPHORT* OF *DUIB-LINN*

This paper summarizes recent emerging archaeological evidence that is starting to fill in the gaps in our knowledge in regard to the evolution of Viking Dublin, especially in the less well-known initial period of contact, from the early to mid-ninth century. The Irish annals, contemporary monastic records, document these earliest violent contacts, recording the first raids along the northern coast of Ireland in the late eighth century, with gradual penetration of the internal waterways system by the early ninth century (MacShamhráin 2002, 43–5). Their initial contacts with the Liffey estuary culminated in AD841 in the first over-wintering at a place known as *Duib-linn* where they set up a *longphort*, an Old Irish word translating as 'ship place'. That this was not an isolated event is indicated by that fact that a second *longphort* was established further up along the coast at a place known as *Linn Dúachaill* (near Annagassan in modern Co. Louth).

The site that the Vikings chose was not a virgin site, as the annalistic sources record the presence of a monastic settlement at *Duib-linn* (Old Irish, 'Black Pool'). It is thought that the monastery may have been sited close to a large pool on the Poddle waterway, just south of Dublin Castle, in the Poddle Valley (Clarke 2000, 3; Fig. 39.1). Little is known about this ecclesiastical site apart from the fact that, following its occupation by the Vikings, it disappears from the records. The Viking base is also described by the annalists as being at *Áth Cliath* (Old Irish, 'Ford of the Hurdles'), suggesting that there were two distinct settlements at the mouth of the Liffey, known by two different names, one (*Duib-linn*) certainly ecclesiastical, the other (*Áth Cliath*), possibly a pre-Viking secular settlement.

The *longphort* provided a secure stronghold where warriors could gather to form raiding parties and perhaps, more importantly, where the booty from these raids, such as precious goods and slaves, could be stored, traded and distributed without having to make a risky seaward journey. The economic operation at Dublin was very impressive: a recent calculation, based on the annals, has estimated that in one year alone at least 1000 Viking warriors from Dublin were killed in various battles around the country and it was still not enough to collapse the settlement (Duffy 1996, 1–2). It was a bold move in a foreign land and one which was not welcomed by the indigenous population, as demonstrated in AD849 when the *longphort* was attacked by the Irish and comprehensively destroyed. The eight years it had been in operation, however, could not be wiped out so easily, and it was evidently rebuilt and reoccupied, as in AD902 the *longphort* was attacked again by the combined forces of two powerful Irish kings and the foreigners were driven out, as recorded in the annals (Duffy 1996, 1–2).

THE TENTH-CENTURY SETTLEMENT AT DUBLIN

The Viking warriors came back in AD917 after their earlier expulsion and re-established a settlement on a prominent high ridge overlooking the Liffey, the site of the famous Wood Quay/Fishamble Street excavations (Wallace 1985, 103–45). This settlement was enclosed by a series of clay embankments from the early to mid-tenth century onwards and various sections of the interior have now been excavated, revealing details of post-and-wattle houses, within defined plots, accessed by a myriad of timber pathways and roads. These deposits can be dated, for the most part, from the early tenth to the early twelfth centuries, the evidence from later centuries having been removed by the destructive impact of the cellars of the great houses built in the Georgian era, which were constructed over so much of the historic core of Dublin. The settlement was walled in *c.*1100, but was successfully captured by the English just seventy years later.

The extensive excavations in the historic core (Fishamble Street, Christ-church Place, Winetavern Street, John's Lane) within the walled town, however, did not locate any deposits which the excavators could confidently ascribe to the ninth century, although the obstacles to so doing at the time, in the absence of definite dating mechanisms, have to be taken into account. The lack of early material presented something of a problem in Viking studies, creating a physical divide between, on the one hand, the well-documented *longphort* (and the 'foreigners' of Dublin), of which no trace could be found, and, on the other, the thriving international port established after their return to Dublin in AD917, a settlement which excavations have so graphically illustrated.

Prior to the evidence of archaeological excavations, speculation regarding the development of Dublin was confined mainly to cartographic studies. Simms postulated what she thought was the evolution of the town in a simple graphic (Fig. 39.2): (A) represented the site of the *longphort* nestling in the crook of the Poddle and Liffey rivers, which later formed the core of the tenth-century town; (B) represented the westward expansion along High Street, which occurred in the late tenth/eleventh century (Simms 1979, 25–41; 2005, 15–65); and (C) represented the northern expansion and reclamation along the river banks carried out by the Anglo-Normans in the thirteenth century. This basic conjectural urban developmental sequence has stood the test of time, being

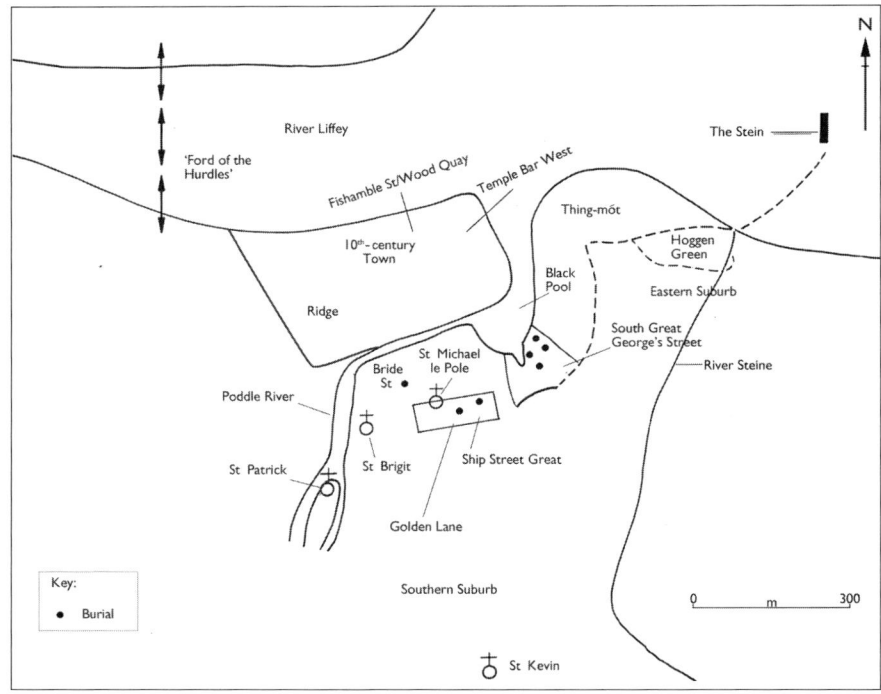

39.1 Viking settlement at *Duib-linn*, Dublin.

supported by the substantial archaeological evidence now coming from Dublin. The excavations at Fishamble Street/Wood Quay established that the eastern side of the settlement was the oldest, the levels dating to the early tenth century, while excavations along High Street indicated the westward expansion postulated by Simms. Excavations on the northern side of the city, along the riverfront, confirmed what the documentary sources suggested – that this area was reclaimed in the thirteenth century.

TEMPLE BAR WEST

However, levels earlier than the tenth century remained elusive until the Temple Bar West campaign, a research excavation which was located to the west of Fishamble Street in the north-east corner of the embanked settlement (Simpson 1999; 2001; 2005; Fig. 39.3). These excavations finally identified ninth-century settlement patterns in the form of small sunken structures, followed by two phases of domestic post-and-wattle houses and animal pens, which were within roughly defined plot enclosures. These houses were probably built sometime in the late ninth century, but the excavations also established that there was no

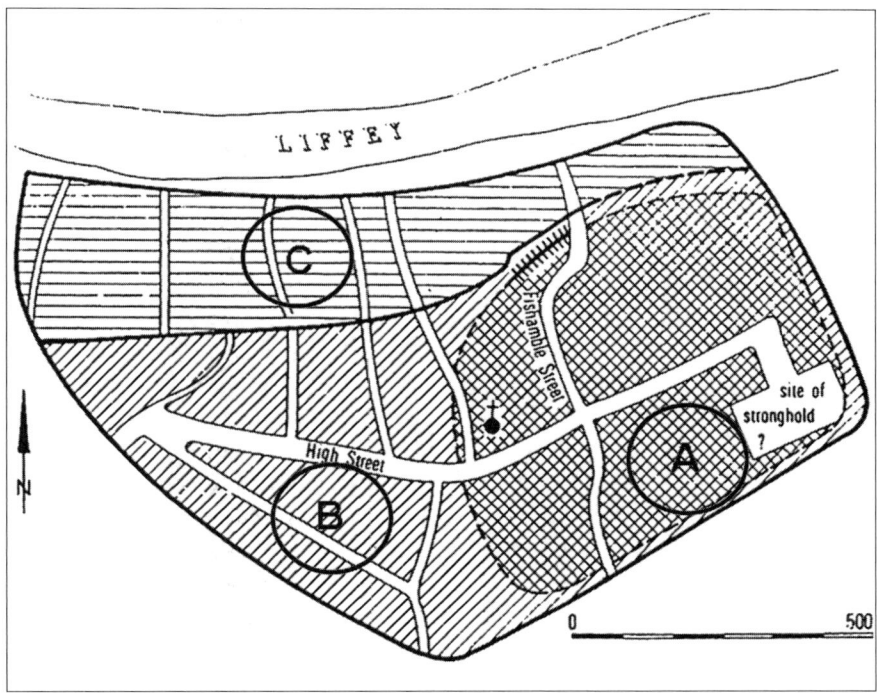

39.2 The development of Viking-Age Dublin (after Simms 1979; 2005).

break in occupancy on the site, despite the period of 'expulsion' between AD902 and 917, recorded in the annals. Thus, although the Viking warriors were expelled in 902, we must presume that this was confined to the ruling elite and that life at Dublin went on as usual, albeit with a reduced population.

Certain facts about the early levels could be ascertained. The sunken structures were an early habitation feature at Temple Bar West, but these could probably be dated, by radiocarbon determinations, to the late ninth century. A cluster of three was identified, very small (measuring on average 3m by 4m), apparently indicative of small-scale or even temporary settlement on the banks of the Liffey. These might have been more widespread originally, as examples were also found during earlier excavations at Winetavern Street/Wood Quay and Christchurch Place, to the south and west (Simpson 2000, 19). The post-and-wattle buildings that followed were also significant, and dated similarly but, more importantly, they respected the line of the River Poddle, which bordered the settlement on the east. Thus it was the Poddle rather than the Liffey that was the defining topographical feature at this time.

There were several problems, however, with identifying Temple Bar West as the nucleus of ninth-century settlement, or even as the elusive *longphort*. The sequence of radiocarbon determinations appeared to suggest a date in the late

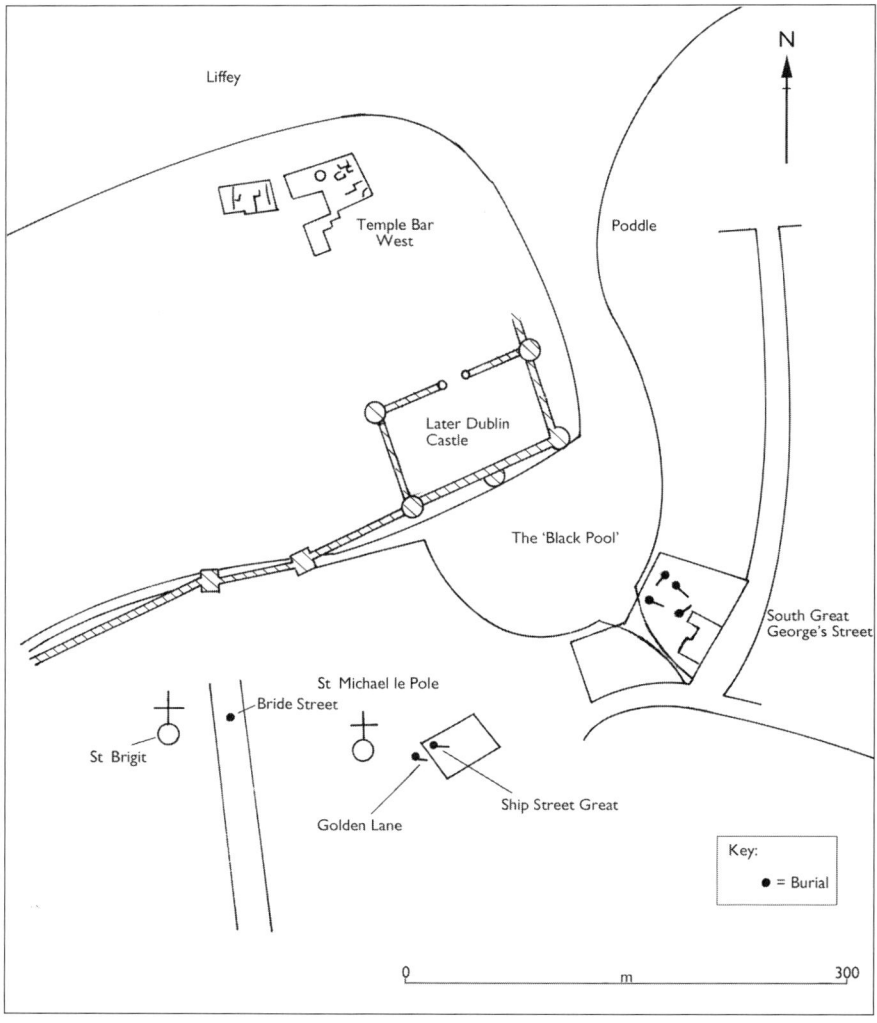

39.3 The locations of recent excavations in Viking-Age Dublin.

ninth rather than the mid-ninth century, and there was a distinct lack of defences on the eastern (Poddle) side. In addition to this, the early levels appeared to be confined to a very small area, in the crook of the Poddle and the Liffey. The conclusion that was eventually reached was that this settlement probably constituted undefended domestic activity, which represented overspill from the *longphort*, concentrated along the Poddle, and that the *longphort* lay further south along this channel. In such a scenario, the most likely contender for the location of the *longphort* itself was the naturally-defended site of Dublin Castle to the south of Temple Bar West.

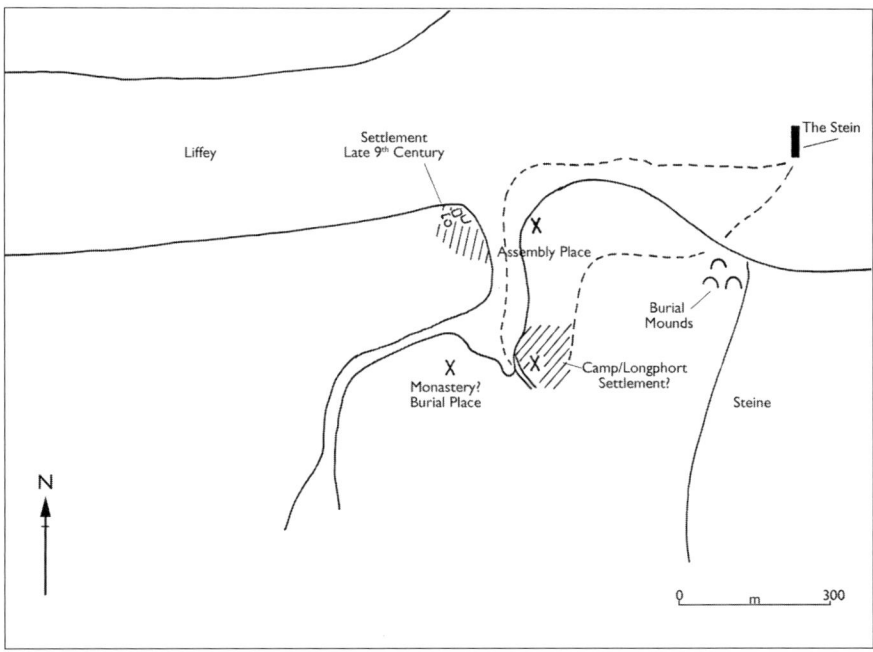

39.4 The eastern suburb.

39.5 A re-assessment of the development of Viking-Age Dublin.

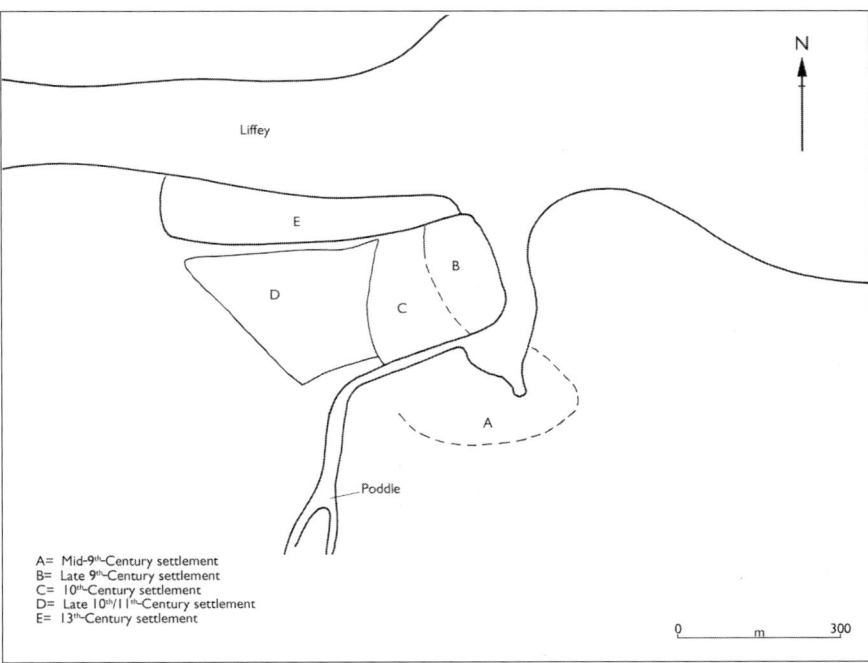

A= Mid-9th-Century settlement
B= Late 9th-Century settlement
C= 10th-Century settlement
D= Late 10th/11th-Century settlement
E= 13th-Century settlement

THE PODDLE VALLEY

But the more recent archaeological findings from a large site at South Great George's Street have started to unravel this neat topographical package that would have everything happening north of the Poddle, on the high ridge where the walled town was later located (Simpson 2004; 2005). This new evidence is now suggesting that the first Viking settlement-activity dating to the ninth century was well outside the later walled town in the low-lying Poddle Valley on the southern approach to Dublin and that the naturally-defended ridge or prominence surrounded on almost three sides by water and fronting directly onto the Liffey, represents only part of a developmental sequence, which started in a quite different topographical location. The decision to establish the tenth-century defended settlement at Fishamble Street/Wood Quay, west of the undefended domestic activity at Temple Bar West, was, then, a specific and calculated action which resulted in a deliberate shift in the settlement, presumably to a more favourable location.

SHIP STREET GREAT BURIAL

South Great George's Street was a large site (*c.*100 m by 65m), which encompassed the southern bank of the supposed 'Black Pool' (Simpson 2005). Preservation in general was not good but the presence of an inlet from the pool ensured that a swathe of deposits survived, in a central band across the site. Interest had been considerably heightened by the unexpected discovery of a partial Viking skeleton at Ship Street Great, to the southwest of the site. The remains consisted of the upper torso of a young male, between 17 and 20 years old, with a finger ring, a silver ring, a decorated bead and a fragment of corroded iron, all originally around his neck. A fragment of a pattern-welded sword suggested that it was likely that this represented a Viking warrior burial. The dating confirmed this but produced a surprisingly early date: he had a 95 per cent probability of dating to between AD665 and AD865, the intercept date of which, at AD790, potentially placed him extremely early in the Viking sequence (the first documented raid on Ireland being in 795AD).

   The new burial was presumed to form part of a series of 'individual warrior burials', which have been found dotted around Dublin in the nineteenth century, one of which was recovered in 1860 close by at Bride Street with a sword, spearhead and shield boss as grave-goods. Other burials have been found at Kildare Street, Cork Street, Donnybrook, and to the north of the Liffey at Dollymount and the Phoenix Park (Ó Floinn 1998, 44). But, unlike the graves found earlier, the Ship Street Great burial could be scientifically dated, his age and sword a fair indicator that he was a Viking raider, perhaps one of the well-documented 'foreigners' attached to the *longphort*. This burial was also important for a second reason, its close proximity to the potentially important ecclesiastical site known as the church of St Michael le Pole. The stone church (and attached small round tower) has been suspected of being an early foundation and excavations clarified that it was constructed in *c.*1100. However, it was built on top of earlier burials and habitation deposits, which could be dated by radiocarbon determinations to the eighth century (Gowen 2001, 13–52).

This and other early evidence raised the possibility that St Michael le Pole represented the lost site of the monastery of *Duib-linn*, which is mentioned in the annals before and contemporaneously with the establishment of the *longphort* in AD841, and then curiously disappears, although there is no firm evidence that the Vikings were actually responsible for its extinction. In this context, the location of the two burials, at Ship Street Great and Bride Street, could not be written off as random, their position at least alerting us to the possibility that both burials may have represented re-use by the Vikings of a known Christian burial site.

SOUTH GREAT GEORGE'S STREET

The Ship Street Great burial was influential in determining the archaeological strategy for the South Great George's Street excavation, and the result was a research-focused planning requirement for the total excavation of the footprint of the new building development. This quickly proved justified when the work uncovered a total of four Viking warrior burials spread out across the eastern side of the site. All were young strong males (under 25 years) and three had been buried with grave-goods: the first came complete with a shield boss and dagger, while the second also had the fragmentary remains of a second shield boss. The third had a fine decorated bone comb and a decorated zoomorphic (hare) headed pin, as well as an unidentified copper-alloy object and a blade, while the fourth, which consisted only of a pair of legs, was surrounded by 21 fragments of animal bone. Also of note were burnt wooden objects with two of the burials (Daly 2005, 64).

It was clear that these burials were similar in type to the Ship Street Great burial and this was confirmed by their dates. Two of the burials have a 95 per cent probability of dating to between AD670 and 880 (with an intercept date of AD770), which was identical to the Ship Street Great dating, while the third had a 95 per cent probability of dating to between AD689 and 882 (with an intercept date of AD782). The fourth, while generally consistent within the date-range, had a later intercept date of AD885 and he had a 95 per cent probability of dating to between AD786 and 955. In general, the dating sequence suggests that the burial of these young warriors, around the rim of the natural pool assumed to be the eponymous *Duib-linn*, can be related to the first phase of Viking contact with

Dublin, sometime from *c.*800 onwards. Isotope analysis indicates that two of the men were from Scandinavia, while the other two were from somewhere in the British Isles, possibly the western coast of Scotland (Simpson 2005, 50–3).

Since the South Great George's Street excavations, a second large-scale excavation at the site of St Michael le Pole at Golden Lane finally uncovered what is thought to be an Early Christian cemetery, with evidence of burial ongoing throughout the Viking period (AD700–AD1200: O'Donovan 2007). Included among the burials were several outlying interments, one of which was a Viking warrior, located 15m west of the Ship Street Great example. This skeleton, of which only the lower half survived, was also buried with grave-goods, which included a spear head, buckle and strap-tag end, a knife and two lead weights (O'Donovan 2006, 17).

Habitation at South Great George's Street
Perhaps the most exciting element of the South Great George's Street excavations was the fact that the site also produced evidence of related habitation and settlement: the warriors were interred in an area that was already settled and continued to be settled into the eleventh century at least. Thus, the South Great George's Street site produced the first evidence in Dublin of Viking habitation outside what was later the walled town. The earliest levels revealed that there was a natural valley running through the site towards the *Dubh-linn* or pool on the north, with higher settled ground to the east. This valley was periodically under water in the very early stages, possibly as a result of flooding from the pool, which was tidal. At this time, the higher ground on the eastern side was defended by two successive linear slot-trenches, both of which originally held some sort of a palisade fence, as associated post-holes and nails were found. A large ditch was then cut into the break in slope, measuring 4m by at least 2m high, and this was subsequently filled in and converted into a clay bank.

The enclosed area was evidently occupied, as demonstrated by the remains of hearths, surfaces, post-holes and domestic pits. An analysis of one of the hearths (into which one of the burials was interred) suggests that it was a domestic fire where foodstuffs were being prepared (cereal and grains). In addition to this, the early clay levels produced a large volume of animal bone and shells, indicative of considerable numbers of people living in the vicinity.

The valley was subsequently completely flooded, creating a pool at the western side of the site, and this produced diagnostic Viking artefacts including a well-preserved iron axe-head, two lead weights (75.7g and 25.68g), an iron shears and iron tweezers. More importantly, the gravels also produced a number of distinctive clench bolts or rivets, probably from clinker-built vessels, suggesting that there were boats in the water in this location, presumably accessing the pool from the Poddle. Some of the structures they occupied also survived in the form of large distinctive post-holes, one of which appeared to be very long, measuring at least 12m in length. Despite the large size, the essential elements of the Viking-type Dublin house were recognizable. The roof was supported by large internal load-bearing supports, flanking the main central aisle, which was floored at least twice in stone and it had a hearth at one end. A radiocarbon determination from one of the post-holes produced a 95 per cent probability of dating to between AD793 and 971, with an intercept date of AD889.

A further three levels of occupation were identified on the site, which comprised houses, hearths, pits, gullies etc, although the stratigraphy was, by comparison to the average depth of Viking deposits (3m) within the city walls, relatively shallow, measuring less than 0.3m in depth. Occupation continued on the site for some time, however, as a second large structure was dated by radiocarbon determinations to between AD894 and 1011, with an intercept date of AD979.

The results of the excavation

The excavation, then, has identified a defended area that was occupied in the early to mid-ninth century, where buildings were constructed and food was prepared. Unfortunately, we have no way of knowing whether the site was continuously occupied or just occupied in the 'raiding' season, although the large amount of butchered bone does attest to a settlement of some longevity. The dates for the warriors suggest a timeframe which is tantalizingly early, although there are increasing concerns about the reliability of such finely-tuned results. For example, a high fish diet is thought to affect such radiocarbon determinations. Despite this, it can be stated with some certainty that there was some sort of Viking settlement at the South Great George's Street site, where warriors were interred, the dates of which, at the very least, coincide with the historically documented dates of the *longphort*. This settlement was outside what was later to become the main trading port (Fig. 39.4), suggesting a deliberate shift in occupation, possibly as part of a planned re-foundation by the ruling elite following their documented return to Dublin in AD917.

The site of the primary settlement also sheds light on other aspects of Dublin's history. It was located in the Poddle Valley, rather than the high ridge towards the Liffey, which refocuses attention on an area that cannot now be described, implying a subsidiary role, as the 'southern suburb', but must be viewed as the primary hub of early settlement at Dublin. The Golden Lane excavations have established the presence of what is likely to be a large Early Christian cemetery at the church site of St Michael le Pole, which can possibly now be identified as the monastery of *Duib-linn*. The Viking presence on the banks of the pool so close to the monastic site, and the fact that the spread of warrior burials included at least one that lay almost within the cemetery, makes it likely that they were responsible for the demise of the monastery, as they appear to have been occupying land close to if not at the site and they buried their dead in the surrounding area.

The continuation of the usage of the cemetery from the ninth to the twelfth century is also illuminating as it confirms that there was a significant ecclesiastical profile in this area throughout the Viking period, demonstrated by the concentration of churches with native dedications, St Patrick's, St Bridget's, and St Kevin's (Clarke 2002, 7). This location, on the southern side of the Poddle waterway, may also help explain the importance of the eastern suburb to Viking Dublin, which is well-attested, albeit in a later period, by both the place-name and the archaeological evidence. This includes the location of the *þingmót* or assembly place, a cemetery in the form of burial mounds and a large upright stone in the River Liffey, known as the *Stein* or latterly the 'Long Stone', which is said to have marked the position of the first Viking landing (Duffy 2005, 351–60; Clarke, 2002, 6). The distinctive alignment of South Great George's Street, as it curves around the rim of the pool, indicates that it was a very early route linking the southern and eastern suburb, with little or no reference to the ridge where the tenth-century settlement was later established.

So, in conclusion, the accepted evolution of the Viking settlement at Dublin has to be amended to include the most recent archaeological evidence (see Fig. 39.5). The primary activity, dated to the early to mid-ninth century, was located on the rim of the pool, close to the church of St Michael le Pole (A), straddling what were later to become the eastern and southern suburbs of the walled city. The focus at this date was on the pool and the Poddle waterway. The next phase is represented by small-scale associated settlement further north on the channel by the late ninth century, at the confluence of the Poddle (B), and this probably originally extended further westwards, scattered along the banks of the Liffey. By the early tenth century, (B) has been engulfed by the establishment of the embanked settlement, demonstrated by a westward shift towards Fishamble Street/Christchurch Place (C), which formed the core of new settlement. A continuing emphasis on the westward expansion can be documented by the excavations along High Street (D), dated from the late tenth century onwards, eventually culminating in the construction of the city wall between 1100 and 1120.

BIBLIOGRAPHY

Clarke, H.B. 2002. *Dublin Part 1 to 1610*, Irish Historic Towns Atlas (Dublin).
Clarke, H.B., M. Ní Mhaonaigh & R. Ó Floinn (eds) 1998. *Ireland and Scandinavia in the Early Viking Age* (Dublin).
Daly, C. 2005. 'From Valhalla: conservation of a group of Viking grave-goods' in S. Duffy (ed.), *Medieval Dublin VI* (Dublin), pp 62–77.
Duffy, S. 1996. 'The historical background' in G. Scally, 'Excavations at 5–7 Exchange Street Upper/33–34 Parliament Street, Dublin' (unpublished stratigraphic report submitted to the former *Dúchas*: the Heritage Service, now Department of the Environment, Heritage and Local Government, National Monuments Section), 1–14.

Duffy, S. 2005. 'A reconsideration of the site of Dublin's Viking thing-mót' in T. Condit & C. Corlett (eds), *Above and beyond: essays in memory of Leo Swan* (Bray), pp 351–60.

MacShamhráin, A. 2002. *The Vikings: an illustrated history* (Dublin).

O'Donovan, E. 2006. 'There is an antiquarian in us all', *Archaeology Ireland*, 19:3, 16–17.

O'Donovan, E. 2007. 'The Irish, the Vikings and the English: new archaeological evidence from excavations at Golden Lane, Dublin' in S. Duffy (ed.), *Medieval Dublin* VIII, pp 36–130.

Ó Floinn, R. 1998. 'The archaeology of the Early Viking Age in Ireland' in H.B. Clarke et al. (eds), *Ireland and Scandinavia*, pp 132–65.

Simms, A. 1979. 'Medieval Dublin: a topographical analysis', *Irish Geography*, 23, 25–41.

Simms, A. 2001. 'Origins and early growth' in J. Brady & A. Simms (eds), *Dublin: through space and time* (Dublin), pp 15–65.

Simpson, L. 1999. *Director's findings*, Temple Bar Archaeological Series, 5 (Dublin).

Simpson, L. 2000 'Forty years a-digging: a preliminary synthesis of archaeological investigations in Medieval Dublin' in S. Duffy (ed.), *Medieval Dublin I* (Dublin), pp 11–68.

Simpson, L. 2004. 'Viking Dublin: the ninth-century evidence begins to unfold – Temple Bar West, Ship Street Great and South Great George's Street' in E. Rosedahl & J.-P. Schjødt (eds), *Treogtyvende tværfaglige vikingesymposium* (Aarhus), pp 47–63.

Simpson, L. 2005. 'Viking warrior burials: is this the *longphort?*' in S. Duffy (ed.), *Medieval Dublin VI* (Dublin), pp 11–62.

Wallace, P.F. 1985. 'The archaeology of Viking Dublin' in H. Clarke & A. Simms (eds), *The comparative history of urban origins in non-Roman Europe: Ireland, Wales, Denmark, Germany, Poland and Russia from the ninth Century to the thirteenth Century*, British Archaeological Reports, International Series, 255/1 (Oxford), pp 103–45.

Wallace, P.F. 1988. 'Archaeology and the emergence of Dublin as the principal town of Ireland' in J. Bradley (ed.), *Settlement and society in medieval Ireland: studies presented to F.X. Martin, O.S.A.* (Kilkenny), pp 123–60.

Close ties and long-range relations: the emporia network in early Viking-Age exchange

SØREN M. SINDBÆK

A lasting fascination of the Viking Age is its wide-scale connectivity. During the period, long-range communication attained a reach and intensity previously unknown in Europe beyond the frontier of the former Roman Empire. Yet in recent times, exchange has been somewhat neglected in Viking studies in favour of internal social hierarchies and cultural codes. This paper will seek to explain why long-distance exchange was indeed a vital aspect of Viking culture. It points to a new approach to this theme by analyzing exchange as a network. In this perspective, a critical difference is evident between the many local trading-places and the few international emporia. The latter stand out as sites with a special significance for the historical development of exchange-network, and for the social forms of exchange.

EXCHANGE IN VIKING CULTURE

In recent years a culturist turn has brought new inspiration to Viking studies. Relieving the former predominance of political and economic perspectives, it has brought symbolic and ritual aspects to the foreground of even formerly prosaic fields like settlement archaeology or cultural geography.

Within this new frame of study, a particular group of sites occupies an unusually marginalized position. Traditionally, the great emporia of the early Viking Age, for example Ribe, Hedeby or Birka, are considered key places in Europe of the eighth to ninth centuries AD. Their extraordinarily detailed archaeological records have contributed to making this period a favourite focus of studies in the early history of exchange (e.g. McCormick 2001; Verhulst 2002; Gustin 2004). Yet these places are now often presented as sites of limited cultural significance. The communication and exchange they signify are regarded as secondary aspects of a social order revolving around power and rituals. Thus, emporia are portrayed as little more than extensions of royal power (Näsman 2000). Allegedly lacking collective institutions, monuments, history and identity, they are dismissed as 'non-places' – sites of economic importance indeed, but not invested with cultural meaning (Hodges 2000, 70). Even when their populations are acknowl-edged as communities in their own right, their social importance is assessed as modest compared with the world of the great chieftain's halls.

Significantly, this is argued not only for the Scandinavian cultural area, but equally for Christian western Europe. The major emporia of the Carolingian world are observed to be separate from the main Christian cult-centres with important relics, unlike those of both the Merovingian and Ottonian periods. They are described as belonging to a period of experimentation, occupying 'a specific and probably non-representative place in the exchange-system as a whole' (Theuws 2004, 137).

The notion of 'non-places' is certainly a controversial assessment of what are indeed the only Scandinavian sites of the early Viking Age named in contemporary sources. And if they were an experiment, it appears to be one that ran successfully for a century or more. The recent disparagement of these sites rather points to a failure in our recognition. Trading-places have been perceived in a frame of economy, rather than one of culture. This calls to mind the criticism famously made by Bronislaw Malinowski, of identifying culture with the exotic symbols of myths and cosmologies without reference to the cultural practice in which the same symbols become intelligible (Malinowski 1954).

The emporia-network is a case in point of the way in which economy is cultural. Long-distance exchange and the sites associated with it were essential aspects of culture. As a counterpart to the hierarchical, ritualized structures given attention to in recent studies, they left a loophole for social dynamics and sustained an awareness of other possible worlds. Moreover, they gave a very specific character to communications of the period.

TRANSIT ROUTES, CENTRAL PLACES AND NETWORKS

Over the years, the study of Viking-Age exchange and communication has been influenced by models and perceptions, which appeared historically in succession, but continue to be present in contemporary discourse. These models have developed in response to a growing empirical basis, as well as to changing theoretical approaches; but they also reflect a general progress in the understanding of communication, which can be traced in subjects ranging from geography to statistics. New developments in both aspects have been introduced in the last few years and these, I shall argue, open a new and promising perspective.

Early synthesis pictured a very limited number of trading-towns positioned along a single great trunk-route, connecting western Europe with Russia and the east. A well-known example is the map published by Herbert Jankuhn (1956; cf. also Jankuhn 1953; Fig. 40.1). The empirical basis for this map was a relatively small number of focused research excavations. Its theoretical framework was a traditional historical archaeology, working in the margins of written sources, i.e. focusing on the sites mentioned therein. The map reflected a culture-historical synthesis most coherently articulated in Sture Bolin's adaptation of the Pirenne

Thesis: towns came to Scandinavia as Viking expeditions made a by-pass for the Mediterranean trade supposedly blocked by the Arab conquests (Bolin 1953; Swedish version published 1939). The outlook was evidently diffuse: trade passed Scandinavia in transit, and the impetus for urbanism came from the old cultural centres.

As for the underlying perception of communication and exchange, Jankuhn acknowledged his debt to the discipline of transport-geography, which had matured in the early twentieth century, effectively as an academic complement to railroad-planning. As the latter implied systems that were established or altered only at a high initial cost, early transport-geography was concerned mostly with rather simple and stable systems of routes. Its abstract view of communication can be equated in this respect with the mathematical paradigm known as classical graph theory.

More recent reconstructions of Viking exchange have envisaged a dense pattern of sites, suggesting that each would have acted as 'central place' to a region. This approach can be illustrated by the map presented by Johan Callmer at the twelfth Viking Congress in Stockholm in 1993 (Callmer 1994; Fig. 40.2). The new image reflects, of course, a vastly expanded empirical basis, increasingly supplied by a growing antiquarian system. But it also reveals a theoretical outlook associated with processual archaeology – a propensity to trust less in particular historical sources than in general models, even when supported sometimes by little empirical evidence. Unlike Jankuhn's map, many of the sites indicated by Callmer were never named in written documents and had been subject only to limited archaeological fieldwork.

The framework underlying the map was the geographical central-place model, which predicts evenly dispersed sites acting as centres for regional redistribution (Christaller 1966). The implied view – that the development of urban milieus was rooted in local processes – denotes an evolutionistic outlook, also contained in the idea of 'urbanization', which the map was intended to illustrate. Being concerned with cumulative dynamics in a large system, it is hardly a coincidence that the central-place model was cultivated in geography in the same period when random graph theory emerged in statistical science. Both are conceptually related to typical forms of communication in twentieth-century mass society.

Today, several developments point towards a new departure. Many excavations and new sites have been added since the last map was published. More importantly, a considerable number of old and new excavations have recently been worked through and published, both in major emporia like Ribe and Kaupang (Bencard et al. 1981–2004; Feveile 2006; Skre & Pilø 2007), and in smaller trading sites like Sebbersund or Ralswiek (Birkedahl 2000; Herrmann 2005). In addition, an overview has begun to form of the hundreds of inconspicuous rural sites encountered in rescue-excavations in recent decades –

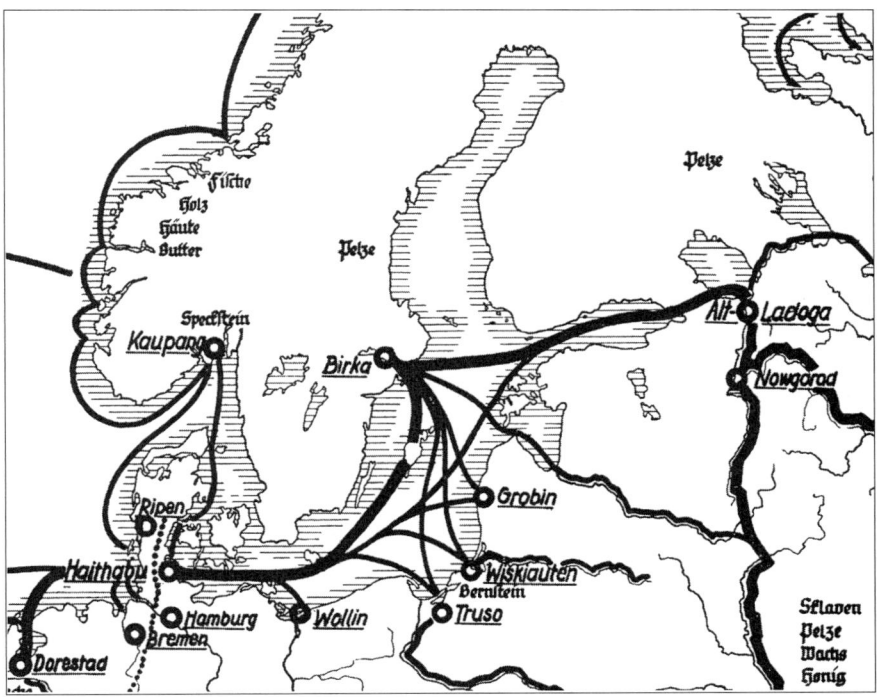

40.1 A single great trunk-route of long-distance trade marked the external impetus to urbanism in Scandinavia in Herbert Jankuhn's 1950's culture-historical synthesis (after Jankuhn 1956).

the very sites to which the trading-sites were central (Jacobsson 2000; Sindbæk 2005; Tegnér 2005). Whereas former generalizations had to issue from rather impressionistic comparison, we now have an opportunity to make a specific, contextual assessment of a large number of sites.

In the meantime, a rapid development in the understanding of communication has been triggered by the growth of electronic communication, of which the growth of the Internet is the most prominent expression. This has led to a series of pioneering studies that seek to analyze complex, interconnecting systems in terms of specific morphology, rather than mere cumulative trends. The striking homologies observed in structures as different as neural networks, electric power systems, social groups, and the Internet leads the researcher to suggest a basic similarity in the architecture of networks, and to propose a series of new models to account for their properties (see, for example, the popular presentation in Watts 2003).

Complex network theory opens a new approach to the study of exchange and communication in early history, suggesting that details in the development and arrangement of connections were decisive for the robustness of systems, for the possibility of control, and thus for the historical development of exchange and

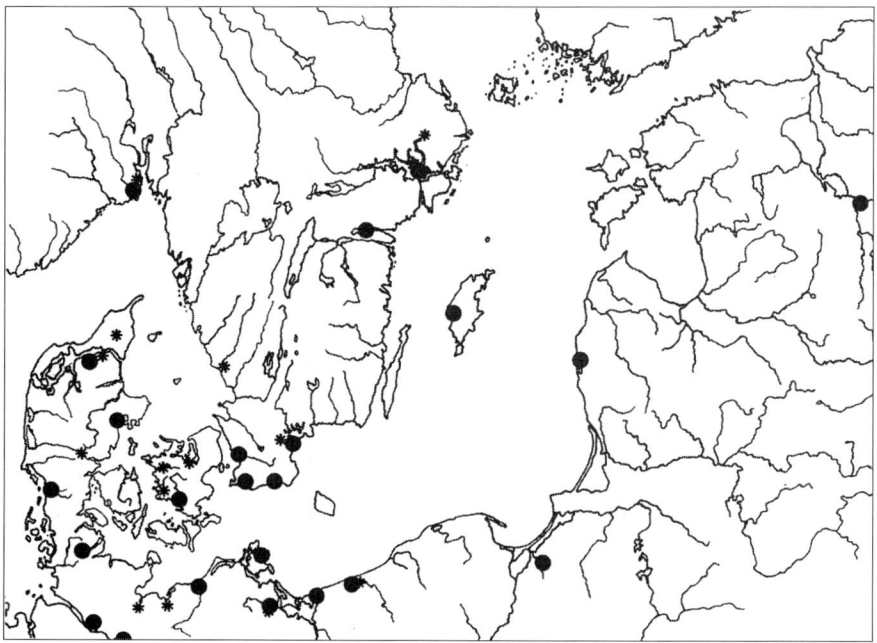

40.2 A large number of sites are proposed as 'central places' in Johan Callmer's map, where urbanism is seen to evolve from local process (after Callmer 1994).

communications. As I will show, these insights can suggest a critical difference in our understanding of early Viking-Age emporia, and the way in which they linked Scandinavia to the world beyond.

THE EMPORIA NETWORK

How did early Viking-Age trade operate as a network? An essential feature to notice is the particular role of the emporia. Urban life was once considered alien to Scandinavia in the Viking Age. But in recent years, the list of sites associated with trade and urbanism has grown lengthy. Embryonic towns are now claimed in some regions to have outnumbered the municipal towns of the late medieval period. Some have even been proclaimed as new Hedebys or Birkas. Yet, as more detailed information is published, a fine distinction becomes apparent between the few nodal points and the many regional markets. Archaeology defines a small group of sites as centres on quite another scale than other possible trading-places. This appears most clearly from a range of imported items.

One example of this is the group of soft, yellow earthenware known collectively as Badorf-type ware. This typical Rhineland product occurs regularly

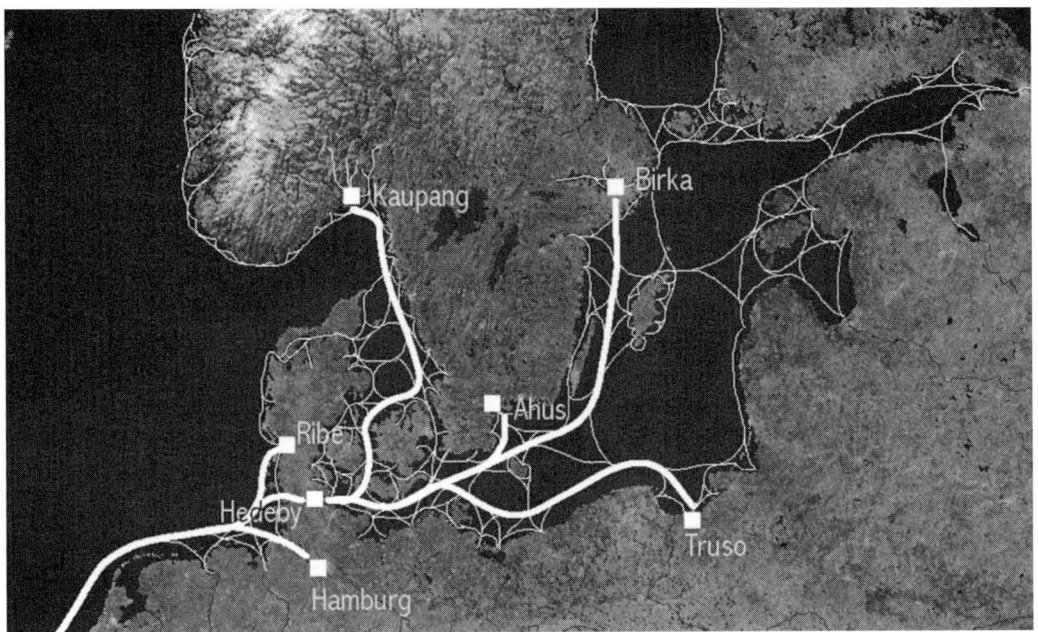

40.3 The dynamics of long-distance traffic constitutes a few sites as hubs of an entirely different scale than the many local markets. In the network perspective, these hubs create short-cuts, which make the large world 'small' – a process which transcends the division between local and external (drawing: Søren M. Sindbæk).

in a particular group of sites: Ribe in Denmark, Kaupang in south Norway, Birka and Åhus in Sweden, Truso in Poland, and Groß Strömkendorf and Hedeby in Germany; but unlike many other west European products, its distribution beyond these locations is non-existent except for a few coastal sites in southwestern Denmark and northern Germany (Sindbæk 2007). This strictly limited distribution is repeated in contemporary sites in England (Brown 2003, 23), and is a pattern which suggests that the imported vessels arrived in both regions as traders' items rather than traded items (cf. Hodges 1982, 58). Their occurrence may therefore be taken mostly to reflect the presence of travellers from the Rhineland.

Similar distributions are shown by several other groups of finds (see Callmer 1998) which indicate large-scale production in two particular crafts – bronze-casting and bead-making. The significant feature of these crafts was not the particular specialization of the craftsmen, but the fact that they consumed raw materials imported from a distance. They were thus directly dependent on the same steady supplies through long-distance exchange that are reflected in the imports.

Long-distance exchange, then, evidently took place in bulk along routes between a very small number of localities (Fig. 40.3). It is not trade as such that distinguishes these hubs from many lesser markets. The latter were obviously important for local trade and communicated with the nodal points – but not with the long-distance traffic between them. The essential observation is that the number of important centres of long-distance trade in early Viking-Age Scandinavia should not be counted in dozens. There were many local markets, but few nodal points of an incipient urban character.

THE SMALL WORLD OF THE VIKINGS

The presence of the emporia as hubs had an important implication for the system of early Viking-Age communication as such. This is brought out by the observations of recent network studies. One property which has caught particular attention in these studies, is the so-called 'small world phenomenon'.

Most geographically organized networks are highly clustered: neighbours link to neighbours, who in turn link mostly to the same neighbours etc. In this situation, one will expect the path between two random nodes in a large network to be a very long one on average. Yet, many networks are shown to possess subtle topological features that create much shorter paths than expected. This is the essence of the often-repeated phrase that all people on earth are connected through less than 'six degrees of separation' (cf. Watts 2003).

A small world does not warrant that a network can be easily navigated, as no individual knows more than a fraction of the whole system, but it implies that news, innovations, viruses or even material objects may spread more directly than any single person can account for. The abundant material that did travel across remarkable distances in the Viking Age strongly indicates that a small world formation was in play.

A small world network can develop in a number of ways. One model invokes occasional random links, or 'weak ties', that cross between otherwise distant nodes. But it appears that many small-world networks build on a different principle: they combine a small fraction of 'rich' nodes having very many links with large number of 'poor' ones having very few. This has been called a scale-free architecture, as it combines nodes of entirely different scale.

As we have seen, a small group of sites can be identified in Viking-Age Scandinavia in which the number of non-local objects is significantly more than in average sites. The few written sources of the period also suggest that a limited number of sites enjoyed a special status. In so far as a scale-free distribution is defined broadly as one composed of sites of vastly different scale, this most likely applies to Viking-Age exchange. If this is true, it will have been vulnerable to an occupational disease of this type of network.

The structure of scale-free networks makes them robust against random failure, but vulnerable to attack directed at the hubs. While mature, robust networks typically connect across hierarchical levels, a scale-free network approaching a state of hierarchy becomes vulnerable to systematic breakdown. The removal of even a single central node may cause large sections of the network to fall out. This seems to be exactly what happened repeatedly in Viking-Age exchange. Several episodes in accounts like Anskar's *vita* describe how connections deteriorated dramatically if a key actor died. But even on the institutional level of ports and routes, it is evident how apparently successful emporia could be deserted within a few years if connections failed or reconfigured (Palmer 2003, 50; Feveile 2006, 52).

The oft-celebrated global connections of Carolingian and Viking-Age Europe were held together by a tiny core of travellers, passing between an even smaller number of locations. While this network was sometimes remarkably effective, it was also extremely vulnerable. The path from structure to collapse was never more than a few steps long.

SOCIAL TIES

The structure of the early Viking-Age communication network sketched here has an important implication for the understanding of the social institutions of exchange. It is often claimed that the regular exchange between strangers in a market necessitates a third party to maintain a monopoly of violence and act as sanction against fraud or violation (e.g. North 1990, 57). For this reason, a royal or seigniorial supervision is sometimes assumed in every beach-market in the Viking world. The observations made above should cause one to question this assumption.

Even though things were exchanged regularly over long distances in early Viking-Age Scandinavia, their long-distance movement took place almost exclusively between the few emporia. In other trading-places, one will also have encountered imported things, but most probably they were brought by people who had travelled to emporia and returned to their home region. In the local markets, exchange will have been conducted within a social environment where most people knew most others, and few knew none. In this situation, the necessary sanction was provided by the informal constraints of existing social ties (North 1990, 120). Any fraud will have led to repercussions from relatives bound by personal and family honour.

Only in the emporia did exchange regularly extend beyond the ties of regional communities. Certainly these are also the sites in which we find the most unambiguous evidence of royal supervision and military protection. But the structure of the emporia-network points to an important social dimension even in these international gateways. The population of an emporium was not incomparably larger than that of a large village. It was bound by regular traffic to distant neighbours in the trading-network, and we have every reason to assume that close personal contacts were maintained along the same routes as bulk-traffic in this network. Even the local travellers, who conducted exchange between the emporia and the local markets, are likely to have been a restricted group of people, most of whom travelled repeatedly and were known personally by people in the emporia as well as in their home regions.

In this way, long-distance exchange could take place between people who were no more socially distant than people in an individual region. A quern stone might travel in a few steps from a quarry in the Rhineland to a farm in Jutland without ever changing hands between actual strangers. If this was indeed how early Viking-Age exchange operated, the need for third-party sanction will have been very modest compared to that required in the mature network of the later Middle Ages, which linked large numbers of towns with crowds of strangers.

CONCLUSION

The links which sustained long-distance connections in early Viking-Age Scandinavia moved on a narrow gauge. The number of large hubs was extremely limited: we find the same few sites emphasized in written sources and in the analysis of archaeological assemblages. Perhaps no more than a few dozen hubs like Birka, Hedeby, Dorestad or Rome linked all of Europe in the ninth century. Moreover, it was mostly the same few groups of people who travelled recurrently between these sites. Whether mercenaries, merchants or missionaries, they were specialized travellers, somehow separate from the mass of society. Within this group, the road from Rome to Birka was swift. But beyond them, there were few if any links reaching outside local clusters.

The critical difference between early medieval exchange and the modern world of globalization is not the scale of connections, but their pervasiveness, and hence robustness. Viking-Age communication was able to generate remarkably far-reaching contacts and sometimes to conduct extensive exchange through these circuits. But it was rarely able to sustain them over long periods of time or in the face of crisis.

In all plainness, the emporia network had a very special ability: it was able to achieve regular, long-distance exchange through a net of essentially social ties. It was so, however, only so long as these ties were considered of a mutually beneficial nature.

BIBLIOGRAPHY

Bencard, M. et al. (eds). 1981–2004. *Ribe Excavations 1970–76*, 5 vols (Aarhus).
Birkedahl, P. 2000. 'Sebbersund – en handelsplads med trækirke ved Limfjorden – orbindelser til Norge' in Karmøy Kommune (ed.), *Havn og handel i 1000 år. Karmøyseminaret 1997* (Stavanger), pp 31–40.

Bolin, S. 1953. 'Mohammed, Charlemagne and Ruric', *Scandinavian Economic History Review*, 1, 5–39.

Brown, D.H. 2003. 'Bound by tradition: a study of pottery in Anglo-Saxon England' in D. Griffiths et al. (eds), *Boundaries in early medieval Britain*, Anglo-Saxon Studies in Archaeology and History, 12 (Oxford), 21–7.

Callmer, J. 1994. 'Urbanization in Scandinavia and the Baltic region *c*.AD700–1100' in B. Ambrosiani & H. Clarke (eds), *Developments around the Baltic and the North Sea in the Viking Age: proceedings the Twelfth Viking Congress, Hässelby slott, 1993*, Birka Studies 3 (Stockholm), pp 50–90.

Callmer, J. 1998. 'Archaeological sources for the presence of Frisian agents of trade in Northern Europe *c*.AD700–900' in A. Wesse (ed.), *Studien zur archaeologie des Ostseeraumes, von der eisenzeit zum mittelalter: festschrift für Michael Müller-Wille* (Neumünster), pp 469–81.

Christaller, W. 1966. *Central places in southern Germany* (Englewood Cliffs).

Feveile, C. (ed.). 2006. *Det ældste Ribe: udgravninger på nordsiden af Ribe å 1984–2000* (Aarhus).

Gustin, I. 2004. *Mellan Gåva och Marknad: handel, tillit och materiell kultur under vikingatid* (Lund).

Herrmann, J. 2005. *Ralswiek auf Rügen: die slawisch-wikingischen Siedlungen und deren hinterland. Teil III – die funde aus der hauptsiedlung.* Beiträge zur Ur- und Frühgeschichte Mecklenburg-Vorpommerns, 37 (Schwerin).

Hodges, R. 1982. *Dark Age economics: the origins of towns and trade AD600–1000* (London).

Hodges, R. 2000. *Towns and trade in the age of Charlemagne* (London).

Hodges, R. 2006. *Goodbye to the Vikings? Re-reading early medieval archaeology* (London).

Jacobsson, B. 2000. *Järnålderundersökningar i Sydsverige: katalog för Skåne, Halland, Blekinge och Småland* (Lund).

Jankuhn, H. 1953. 'Der fränkisch-friesische handel zur Ostsee im frühen mittelalter', *Vierteljahresschrift für Sozial- und Wirtschaftsgeschichte*, 40, 193–243.

Jankuhn, H. 1956. *Haithabu: ein handelsplatz der Wikingerzeit*. 3., ergänzte Auflage. (Neumünster).

Malinowski, B. 1954. *Magic, science and religion, and other essays* (Garden City, NY).

McCormick, M. 2001. *Origins of the European economy: communications and commerce, AD300–900* (New York).

North, D.C. 1990. *Institutions, institutional change and economic performance* (Cambridge).

Näsman, U. 2000. 'Exchange and politics: the eighth-early ninth century in Denmark' in C. Wickham & I. Lyse Hansen (eds), *The long eighth century: production, distribution and demand*, The transformation of the Roman World, 11 (Leiden), pp 35–68.

Palmer, B. 2003. 'The hinterlands of three southern English emporia: some common themes', in T. Pestell & K. Ulmschneider (eds), *Markets in early medieval Europe: trading and 'productive' sites, 650–850* (Macclesfield), pp 48–60.

Sindbæk, S.M. 2005. *Ruter og rutinisering: strukturationen af fjernudveksling i Nordeuropa ca. 700–1000* (Copenhagen).

Sindbæk, S.M. 2007. 'Networks and nodal points: the emergence of towns in early Viking-Age Scandinavia', *Antiquity*, forthcoming.

Skre, D. & L. Pilø (eds). 2007: *Kaupang in Skiringssal: excavation and surveys at Kaupang and Huseby, 1998–2003 – background and results*, Kaupang Excavation Project, 1 (Aarhus).

Tegnér, M. 2005. *Järnålderundersökningar i Skåne: katalog över arkeologiska undersökningar 1960–2000* (Lund).

Theuws, F. 2004. 'Exchange, religion, identity and central places in the Early Middle Ages', *Archaeological Dialogues*, 10:2, 121–38.

Verhulst, A. 2002. *The Carolingian economy* (Cambridge).

Watts, D.J. 2003. *Six degrees: the new science of networks* (London).

Ailikn's wagon and Óðinn's warriors: the pictures on the Gotlandic Ardre monuments

ÞÓRGUNNUR SNÆDAL

The conversion of Gotland was no walk-over victory for the Christians. As a matter of fact, it took approximately two centuries from *c.*1030 when the new religion first began to influence the society after the visit of St Olaf (*Guta saga*, ch. 14, 8–9) until the heathen faith was finally denounced somewhere around 1220 in the first sentence of the Guta Law, which states: 'This is the first of our laws, that we shall refuse heathendom and accept Christianity and all believe in one God Almighty' (*Lex Gotlandiæ*, 36). During this long period, heathens and Christians lived side by side, and throughout the twelfth century the pagans continued to bury their dead in grave-fields with the customary grave-gifts, while the Christian buried theirs in graveyards (Thunmark-Nylén 1989, 213–15).

THE ARDRE MONUMENTS

Given this mixed society, it ought not to surprise us to find the two religions intermixed on memorials from this century. And indeed this is the case on two monuments found in Ardre church in southeast Gotland during restoration in the summer of 1900. Beneath the church floor were revealed the remains of an older church, probably built around 1170 (Snædal 2002, 94). In the floor of this older church lay a magnificent picture stone and several smaller stones adorned with runes, characters and ornamentation (G 111–14, *Gotlands runinskrifter* I: 199–220). There were four runic monuments associated with two different families. I deal here only with the monuments of one of these families, the memorials of Liknatr and his wife Ailikn. The inscription on Liknatr's stone (Fig. 41.1; Plate 14) reads:

⚕ utar + ak + kaiRuatr + ak + aiuatr + þaR + setu + stain + ebtir + liknat + faþur ⚕ sen + ⚕ raþialbr + ak + kaiRaiaut- + þaiR kiarþu + merki + kuþ + ubtir + man + saaran ⚕ likraibr + risti + runaR

Óttarr auk GaiRvatr auk Aivatr, þaiR settu stain eptiR Líknat faður senn. RáðþialfR auk GaiRniautr, þaiR giarðu merki góð yptiR mann snaran. Lík(n)raifR rísti rúnaR.

Ottarr and Gairvatr and Aivatr they raised this stone in honour of their father Liknatr. Raðþialfr and Gairniautr made good monuments for a quick man. Liknraifr carved the runes.

Some years or decades later, the sons erected a four-sided monument with exquisite ornamentation, now unfortunately badly damaged, to honour their mother (Fig. 41.2, Plate 12). The runic inscription along the edges tells us:

syniR : liknata[r]... ...arua : merki : kut : ebtir : ailikni : kunu : koþa : moþur : ... s : auk : kiaruataR : auk : liknuiaR : : kuþ a-... ...n : heni : auk : kieruantum : merki : m-... ...ua : aR : men : sin : ...R : i : karþum : aR : uaR : uiue meR : : h...

SyniR LíknataR ... giarva merki gutt eptiR Ailikni kunu góða, móður ... auk GaiRvataR auk LíknvíaR. Guð auk (?) ...nádin(?) henni auk giervandum. Merki ... aR menn siá ... í Garðum aR vaR Vívé(?) meR...

Liknatr's son's had a good monument made in honour of Ailikn, a good woman, Ottar's and Gairvatr's and Liknvi's mother. God and the mother of God save her and those who made it, the biggest memorial that one can see, in Garda [...]

The rest cannot be fully interpreted as parts of the inscription are missing and the prayer is a reconstruction (Snædal 2002, 73–4).

The stones must have stood somewhere near the church. They are not much weathered and traces of red paint can still be seen in the deep lines of Ailikn's monument, they cannot have been out in the open for more than some fifty or sixty years before they were laid down in the church floor around 1170, which sets the time-frame for the Ardre monuments to the first or maybe the second quarter of the twelfth century (Snædal 2002, 93–102).

The small crosses at the beginning and end of the text on Liknatr's stone and the prayer in Ailikn's inscription prove that the family had accepted Christianity. Despite this, the pagan world is very much present on the monuments. Between the beautiful dragons on one face of Liknatr's stone a male figure is sitting on a stool with a chest or a low table in front of him (Fig. 41.1). This must be Óðinn, as he is usually portrayed on the picture stones sitting on a stool inside a house. Possibly he is here shown as the wise man sitting on the chair of the sage, giving out good advice to people, as told in the Eddaic poem *Hávamál*. In his right hand he is presumably holding Draupnir, the ring which propagates itself into eight new rings every ninth night (Snorra Edda, 82).

41.1 Front face of Liknatr's memorial stone (G113), Ardre church, Gotland
(Photo: Sören Hallgren, ATA).

41.2 Ailikn's monument (G114), Ardre church, Gotland. The runic inscription begins on the front (complete) side while a warrior's entry to Valhalla is depicted on the fourth (broken) side (photo: Sören Hallgren, ATA).

THE *EINHERJAR*

Trapped between the dragons on the front side of Ailikn's monument is a small running figure with a sword on his left side and a mead horn in his right hand (Fig. 41.2, right). This equipment proves that this is an *einherji*, one of Óðinn's heroes in Valhalla, appearing to hurry to the daily war games. Snorri Sturluson describes in his *Edda* how these warriors get dressed every day, take their weapons and go out on the yard to fight and cut each other down. When it is time for breakfast, they ride home to Valhalla to sit down to eat the everlasting pork from Sæhrímnir and drink the mead that runs endlessly from the teats of the goat Heiðrún (Snorra Edda, 57–8).

But to qualify as an *einherji* you had to die in a battle and, indeed, on the second side of the monument we see a battle going on: a man with a broadaxe is chasing some hapless fellow and two helmeted warriors seem to be chasing someone else (Fig. 41.3).

41.3 The second side of Ailikn's monument, depicting a battle (photo: Sören Hallgren, ATA).

41.4 The third side of Ailikn's monument, depicting a fallen warrior among snakes and dragons (photo: Sören Hallgren, ATA).

On the third side of the monument, a fallen warrior is depicted among interlaced dragons (Fig. 41.4) and on the fourth side a warrior is arriving to Valhalla on Sleipnir, equipped with his sword and seemingly carrying a rucksack (Fig. 41.2, left). It has been suggested that the Gotlanders believed that Óðinn sent his own horse to carry the most honoured guests to Valhalla (Nylén and Lamm 1988, 68–70). Above the rider stands a fully armed man, taking a swig of beer from his mead horn and around them the war games seem to be in full swing.

THE WAGON

The shape of Ailikn's monument and other monuments of the same form, the oldest are from the seventh century, has always baffled me. I understood their form only when I happened to take a closer look at a picture stone from Grötlingbo parish, probably of early eleventh-century date (Nylén and Lamm 1988, 102–3). It shows a woman riding in a wagon, with curved sides of almost exactly the same form as the Ardre monument (Fig. 41.5). It is my belief that the form of these stones is copying the wagons used on Gotland during this period and that the form is obviously inspired by the heathen belief that women rode in wagons to the realm of death. The Eddaic poem 'Brynhildr's Hel Ride' (*Helreið Brynhildar*) tells that the Valkyrie Brynhildr was burnt in a wagon covered with precious fabrics and that she rode in this wagon down the Hel-way (Taylor and Auden 1969, 113). According to grave finds in many places in Scandinavia, Viking-Age women (and even some men) were sometimes buried in wagons, though not, as far as I am aware, in Gotland (Stæcker 2002, 15–20).

TOWARDS GLAD-HOME?

But where did Gotlandic women ride in their wagons after death? The *Edda* and other written sources tell us next to nothing about the fate of women in general after death, but the Gotlanders certainly must have had a definite belief as to where their women were heading in their wagons, and it seems clear that some of them went straight to Valhalla, or at least to Óðinn's realms. In front of the woman in the wagon on the Grötlingbo stone stands another woman, or is it a Valkyrie, ready with a mead horn just as in the scenes when a warrior arrives to Valhalla. This proves that even women came to a place where they were received with a swig of mead. That they are in Óðinn's domain is also made clear by the presence of the *valknútr*, the symbol of the power of Óðinn, seen on several picture stones (Ellis Davidson 1982, 147).

But what did these women do in Valhalla? Maybe they joined the ranks of Valkyries, whose duty it was 'to lay and decorate the tables and to look after the

41.5 Fragment of picture stone from Grötlingbo parish, Gotland
(photo: Harald Faith-Ell, ATA).

beer vessels and, as their name indicates, to ride out and decide which men were
to fall on the battlefield, thus gaining the right to be Óðinn's warriors forever'
(Snorra Edda, 53). Óðinn was clearly the most celebrated god on Gotland and
his presence is very much felt on the picture stones.

It is also possible that this wagon-ride had something to do with Freyja as the
goddess of noble women. She travels in a wagon and is strongly linked with
Óðinn, as told by Snorri: 'wheresoever she rides to the strife, she has one-half of
the kill, and Óðinn half. Her dwelling is Fólkvangr ('Battlefield') and her hall is
Sessrúmnir ('the hall with many seats')' (Snorra Edda, 41–2). Both names can
equally well describe Valhalla. And the fact that Freyja owns one-half of the kill
makes her out as some kind of a head Valkyrie.

When Egill Skallagrímsson had decided to starve himself to death he was
joined by his daughter Þorgerðr, who declares that she is not going to eat
anything until she can 'sup with Freyja' (*Egils saga*, 244; Ellis Davidson 1982,
114–16). This seems to indicate that heathen people, at least to a certain degree,
were able to decide where they wanted to spend their afterlife.

Perhaps it was believed on Gotland that noble women, and men to of course,
could choose to join Óðinn/Freyja and their warriors in Valhalla or at least go to
Glaðsheimar ('Glad-Home'), where according to the Eddaic poem The Lay of
Grímnir (*Grímnismál*) Valhalla is situated:

Glaðsheimr heitir inn fimmti	*The fifth is Glad-Home*
Þars in gullbjarta	*where, golden-bright,*
Valhöll víð of þrumir;	*The Hall of Valhalla stands*
En þar Hroftr kýss	*There Hropt, the Doomer*
Hverjan dag	*daily chooses*
Vápndauða vera	*warriors slain by weapons*
(*Eddukvæði* I: 86)	(Taylor and Auden 1969, 65)

It seems that Valhalla is indeed depicted on two picture stones, one is that found in the church at Ardre, while the other one is from Tjängvide, in the nearby parish of Alskog (Plate 15); both are of tenth-century date. On these stones we see men and women mingling outside a building with big doors which must be Valhalla, famous for its many big doors, and the place must therefore be Glad-home. On the Tjängvide stone, the warrior on Sleipnir has already got his mead horn. Two women are present, one is receiving the warrior and the other is engaged in some kind of game or battle with a man, it seems likely that they are Valkyries. Given the name *Glaðsheimar*, one cannot avoid the thought that the bent over figures on both the Ardre and the Tjängvide stone are meant to show a *leikari* ('jester') turning somersaults, thereby illustrating the entertainment offered in those merry dwellings. On a picture stone from Väskinde church, dated to the period 400–600, one can see figures doing somersaults over horses (Nylén and Lamm 1988, 27). In *Færeyinga saga* the hero Sigmundr Brestisson is said to have amused Sveinn, the son of the Norwegian earl Hákon with all kinds of *fimleikar* ('agility'): *Sigmundr kom ser j tal vid Suein jalls son ok lek firir honum marga fimlæika ok hendi jalls son mikit gaman at honum* (Flateyjarbók 1860 I: 136; *Kulturhistoriskt lexikon* X: 462).

Although Liknatr's and Ailikn's memorials are at least 150 years younger than the Ardre and Tjängvide picture stones, the motifs are much the same. It is my belief that there must be a connection between those stones and the Ardre stones and I also believe that there must be a connection between the figure of Óðinn on Liknatr's stone and the motifs on Ailikn's memorial, and that those motifs must have something to do with the their life and faith (after I presented my paper at the Viking Congress in Cork, Signe Horn Fuglesang suggested that the picture stones of Tjängvide and Ardre were erected by ancestors of Liknatr and Ailikn, and this is of course possible).

Liknatr and Ailikn must have been born around the middle of the eleventh century and were almost certainly raised in heathen beliefs; they may have remained faithful to the old gods even though their children had become Christians. Ailikn can very well have had some religious function, which explains the motifs and splendour of her memorial. Her Christian sons were certainly aware of the fact that only the grace of God could grant their mother access to Paradise. Maybe they hoped that their prayer would save her soul and that she, being a good woman, would be accepted in heaven, though at the same time they honoured her with a monument shaped and ornamented in old Gotlandic tradition, thereby allowing her to ride to Valhalla in her stony wagon if that were *her* choice.

BIBLIOGRAPHY

Almgren, B. (ed.). 1967. *Vikingen* (Göteborg).
Andrén, A. 1989. 'Dörrar till förgångna myter: en tolkning av de gotländska bildstenarna' in A. Andrén (ed.), *Medeltidens födelse: symposier på Krapperups borg* (Lund), pp 287–319.
Böttger-Niedenzu, B. 1982. Darstellungen auf gotländischen bildsteinen, vor allem des typs C und D, und die frage ihres zusammenhangs mit stoffen der altnordischen Literatur (unpublished manuscript, Vitterhetsakademiens bibliotek, Stockholm).
Eddukvæði I = Guðni Jónsson (ed.). 1949. *Eddukvæði*, 2 vols (Reykjavík).
Egils saga = Sigurður Nordal (ed.). 1933. *Egils saga Skallagrímssonar*, Íslenzk fornrit, 2 (Reykjavík).
Ejder, B. 1969. *Dagens tider och måltider* (Lund).
Ellis Davidson, H.R. 1982. *Gods and myths of northern Europe* (Oxford).
Flateyjarbók = Guðbrandr Vigfusson & C.R. Unger (eds). 1860. *Flateyjarbók*, 3 vols (Christiania).
Gotlands runinskrifter = Jansson, S.B.F. & E. Wessén. 1962. *Gotlands runinskrifter*, (Stockholm).
Guta saga = Peel, C. (ed.). 1999. *Guta saga: the history of the Gotlanders* (London).
Jansson, I. (ed.) 1983. *Gutar och vikingar: historia i fickformat* (Stockholm).
Kulturhistoriskt lexikon = I. Andersson et al. (eds). 1956–78. *Kulturhistorisk leksikon for nordisk medeltid fra vikingetid til reformationstid* (Malmö).
Lex Gotlandiæ = Wessén, E. 1945. *Lex Gotlandiæ. Svetice et Germanice*, Corpus Codicum Suecicorum Medii Aevi, 5 (Copenhagen).
Lindqvist, S. 1941–2. *Gotlands bildsteine*, 2 vols (Stockholm).
Ljungberg, H. 1938. *Den nordiska religionen och kristendomen* (Stockholm).
Nylén, E. & P. Lamm. 1988. *Stones, ships and symbols* (Visby).
Snædal, Þ. 2002. *Medan världen vakar: studier i de gotländska runinskrifternas språk och kronologi*, Runrön, 16 (Uppsala).
Snædal, Þ. 2005. 'Ailikn's wagon and Odin's warriors: about the pictures on the Ardre monuments', *Viking Heritage* 2:05, 9–13.
Snorra Edda = Guðni Jónsson (ed.). 1949. *Edda Snorra Sturlusonar* (Reykjavík).
Stæcker, J. 2002. The woman on the wagon: pagan Scandinavian burials in a Christian perspective', *Viking Heritage* 1:02, 15–18.
Taylor, P.B. & W.H. Auden (trans.). 1969 [1973]. *The Elder Edda* (London).
Thunmark-Nylén, L. 1989. 'Samfund och tro på religions-skiftets Gotland', *Medeltidens födelse Symposier på Krapperups slott*, 1 (Lund), 213–32.
Thunmark-Nylén, L. 1990–1. 'Vikingatid eller medeltid?', *Tor*, 141–201.
Wilson, D.M. 1995. *Vikingatidens konst*, Signums svenska konsthistoria, 2 (Lund).

Ulfberht revisited: a classification

ANNE STALSBERG

INTRODUCTION

For over a century, Viking-Age sword blades signed Ulfberht have attracted the interest of archaeologists. Ulfberht is a Frankish man's name, but it is unknown who or what he was. Anders Lorange, in his pioneering study of Norwegian Viking-Age swords, discusses the various spellings of the name (Lorange 1889, 18–20).

On the reverse sides of one-third of these blades, geometrical patterns, or marks, have been documented. The signatures and reverse marks consist of steel rods, often pattern-welded, welded onto the steel blade, which was polished and probably etched so that the inlays were clearly visible (Fig. 42.1). The blades themselves are not pattern-welded. So far it has been possible to collect fairly reliable information about 166 Ulfberht blades from twenty-three countries in Europe, mainly Northern Europe, and especially Norway. They were used over a period of two centuries or more, from around AD800. The blades are generally thought to have been forged in the lower Rhine area in the Frankish realm (until AD911 under the Carolingians, later under the Saxon Ottonians), but it has been postulated that the blades with 'incorrectly' written Ulfberht signatures might be imitations or fakes forged in the countries where they have been discovered (e.g. Stalsberg 1989, 20–2; Geibig 1991, 121–3). It is hard to believe that the variants of the signatures and the reverse marks, or their combinations, were shaped at random; they may have indicated various things, such as the user, owner, lord, smith, smithy, quality or forging method, or they may have chronological significance. To discuss the significance of the variants of signatures and reverse marks, a classification of them is needed and this is the aim of this article. Other signatures are also known, but only the Ulfberhts are numerous enough for the type of classification proposed in this paper.

ULFBERHT

The name Ulfberht is not known from written contemporary sources (Jankuhn 1951, 117–18; Müller-Wille 1970, 91). It is, however, clear that the signing of sword blades with Latin letters originated in a culture where Latin letters were used around AD800, that is, in the Carolingian Empire. Lorange identified the name as Frankish (1889, 18) and linguists have narrowed its homeland to the

42.1 Signature and reverse mark on a sword blade in Bergen University Museum (B882), provenanced to Vestfold, Norway (after Lorange 1889, table II, fig. 2).

lower Rhine area/North Germany (Jankuhn 1951, 217; Müller-Wille 1970, 91; Harald Bjorvand, pers. comm.). This localization is supported by the fact that the earliest Ulfberht blades are found in the Rhine (D-8 Mannheim; D-9 Speyer). A name may have wandered, but it is unlikely that the weapon-smith Ulfberht would have been allowed to wander freely: he must have been abducted as a valuable armament craftsman. Until proved otherwise, the genuine Ulfberht blades must be regarded as having been forged in the Frankish realm, initially under the Carolingians, probably on the lower Rhine.

GENUINE OR FALSE ULFBERHT BLADES?

Imitations may have been made outside Ulfberht's home area. Alfred Geibig (1991, 122) distinguishes between originals forged within the Frankish realm and imitations forged either within or outside this area, perhaps near the place where they were used or deposited. He also notes blades onto which signatures were welded later, probably also near the places where they were used or deposited. If the incorrect writing of the signature is a criterion of imitation, two blades from Frankish Germany are especially interesting because their signatures are not 'correct' (D-1 Frankfurt a.M.; D-8 Mannheim). There is no reason *not* to regard them as Frankish, that is, as Frankish imitations or inexperienced work. It is not (yet) possible to establish which blades were made outside the Frankish realm, but there are blades which clearly show that smiths outside this area did inscribe blades: two Late Viking-Age blades found in the Ukraine, for instance, are signed with Cyrillic letters (cf. Stalsberg 2003, with references). Strictly speaking, however, this does not conclusively prove that the actual blades were forged in the Ukraine (or that other incorrectly inscribed blades were forged in other places outside the Frankish area), as steel bars for signatures and marks can be added to an old blade (Andresen 1993; Kasper Andresen, pers. comm.).

The Ulfberht signature is often referred to as a sign of high quality. However, on some blades the bars of the signatures and reverse marks have partly or completely fallen out, leaving only their impression on the blade. This is a sign of insufficiently careful heating (Kasper Andresen, pers. comm.). Such poor quality work is, to my knowledge, found on two blades from Germany, one from Spain, two from Norway, two from Poland and one from the Ukraine (Geibig 1991, Abb. 86; Taf. 108; Oakeshott 2000, fig. 30; Peirce 2002, 101; von zur Mühlen 1975, Taf. 10; Sarnowska 1955, Rys. 1; Kirpiničkov 1966, Tab. V-5; Kirpiničkov and Stalsberg, forthcoming). It is notable that signatures and reverse bars have also fallen out of 'correct' Ulfberht blades. There are many elements which must be taken into account in the distributional and chronological studies of the Ulfberht blades, but a systematization of the different signatures and reverse marks is basic for such studies.

VARIANTS OF SIGNATURES AND REVERSES (Fig. 42.2)

This classification of signatures and reverse marks is based both on publications (Geibig 1991, 192–4) and on Kirpičnikov's unpublished examinations of blades in Norwegian museums (Kirpičnikov and Stalsberg, forthcoming); the relevant documentation varies from a couple of words to fully published swords. It is possible to place 105 signatures and 100 reverse marks into one of the groups, and 139 blades are datable on the basis of their hilts (the blade chronology not being sufficiently developed). Both signatures and reverses marks are each classified into six groups, with one further miscellaneous group in each case resulting from the problem of indefinable inlays (as the blades are often poorly preserved). The grouping is based solely on the outline and orthography of the signatures and the outlines of the reverse marks, based on drawings and photographs, the quality of which is often poor. It has not been possible to take quality, the order of the forging of the rods or other details into considerations. The author has seen many of the Norwegian swords, but also relies on Kirpičnikov's unpublished drawings and descriptions. Signatures and marks are often difficult to see, both on the swords themselves and on X-ray photos. The interpretations of both, to a large extent, depend on the scholar's experience. It

1. + VLFBERH+T   (46 - 51 ex.)

2. +VLFBERHT +   (18 - 23 ex.)

3. VLFBERH+T   (4 - 6 ex.)

4. +VLFBERH+T+   (1 - 2 ex.)

5. + VL FBERH+T   (10 ex.)

6. +VL EBERHIT   (17 ex.)
    +VL FBEHT +
    +VL FBERH +
    +VL FBERH+T
    +VL FBERTH

7. non definable   (31 - 32 ex.)

I ||| ⋈ ||| (29 ex.)

II || ⊗ |+ ||| ⋈ ||| (8 ex.)

III |||⋈|||⋈||| (9 ex.)

IV || ⋈⋈ || (19 ex.)

V ||⋈| |||⋈|| (23 ex.)
     |||⋈|||

VI   + INGEFLRII +   (5 ex.)
    + VLFBERH+T
    III C +✝ ꙅ II
    IINIOMINEDMN

VII   non definable   (6 ex.)

42.2 Variants of signatures (left) and reverse marks (right) on Ulfberht blades, with the number of examples in each group indicated (© Anne Stalsberg).

goes without saying that assignation to groups has not been a simple matter, because of issues of preservation and documentation, and for this reason the numbers are not fixed.

Signatures 1–4 have all the letters in 'Ulfberht' correctly written and in correct sequence. *Signatures 1* are the most numerous of these. *Signatures 5* have all letters of the name present, but it seems that the last letters are more simply welded since the horizontal bars in the letters H+T are not made separately, but by one single horizontal bar uniting the elements. *Signatures 6* are incorrectly written signatures and have been regarded as imitations or falsifications. *Signatures 7* are clearly enough Ulfberhts, but they are so badly preserved that they cannot be assigned to any of the defined groups.

Reverse marks I–V are geometrical figures. The *reverse marks I* group comprises twenty-nine blades, while there are eight blades in the *reverse marks II* group; the latter marks appear to the author as unsuccessful attempts to make *reverse marks I*, especially the middle figure of the mark to the right. *Reverse marks III* are repetitions of the main figure. *Reverse marks IV* are characterized by a longer braid. *Reverse marks V* are simpler than the preceding types, with the bars often being irregularly placed in the central figure. They give an impression of being less well shaped and, surprisingly, three of them are found in the Frankish realm (2 in Germany, 1 in the Netherlands). *Reverse marks VI* are all unique forms. The Belgian blade has a cross potent on the reverse, while the Russian example has vertical bars and omega figures. The most remarkable sword in this group, from the Leipzig area, features a reverse mark which is an abbreviation for *in nomine Domini* (IhNIOMINEDMN), and is dated to the eleventh-twelfth centuries (Herrman and Donat 1985, 376). This must be one of the latest Ulfberht blades, and is the only known Ulfberht signature that is combined with a Christian inscription. *Reverse marks VII* are not well enough preserved to be assigned to one of the defined groups. No reverse marks are published for sixty-seven blades and it is consequently unknown whether all Ulfberht blades had reverse marks.

Geometrical figures like the Ulfberht reverses cannot be taken on their own as indications of a blade being an Ulfberht example, since such marks are also found on blades without signatures. Kirpičnikov has found such figures on more than thirty of the 105 blades he examined in Norway. Other kinds of geometrical marks, without signatures, were found on around twenty blades, which indicates that marks were often welded onto blades.

DATING

Petersen's typological dating of the sword hilts is followed here, but with some modification in the light of recent research. The dating scheme allows only wide assignations, to the early Viking Age (EVA: ninth century), middle Viking Age (MVA: late ninth/tenth century) and late Viking Age (LVA: mid-tenth century and into the Middle Ages). It is not a straightforward matter to place all of the hilts into even these broad periods, since their date-ranges overlap. For example, handle-type H is placed into EVA since, according to Petersen (1919, 99), it occurs most commonly during the first half of the ninth century, with fewer occurrences in the second half, but the type also exists into the middle of the tenth century (with this last dating appearing to be contextual). It is, indeed, a problem that Petersen does not clearly separate type- from contextual-dating. In some cases, his suggested dating is based on an overly-narrow dating of the Ulfberht blades to the first half of the tenth century (Petersen 1919, 101, 131–2, 152). In one case, the author has deviated from his dating sequence, and has moved the type-O hilts back from the late ninth/tenth centuries to the ninth century. Petersen himself noted that it is difficult to separate types K and O-III, but he separated them chronologically because of the Ulfberht blades (Petersen 1919, 31). The hilt of a sword from Gjersvik (N-10) is decorated with a Carolingian vine, which suggests an earlier date, of the ninth century. Two hilts from Croatia are, in the author's opinion, not type-K, as proposed by Vinski, but rather O-III, based on the inadequate drawings in Vinski (1983, Abb. 10–1, 15–3). It should be noted that there is no compelling reason to date the latest types, X, Y, Z, to the eleventh century, since they originated during the tenth century (Petersen 1919, 165, 171, 177). The one sword that seems to be late is the already noted D-13, from Sachsen, with the reverse IINIOMINEDMN inscription. As a result of these considerations, the hilt-types are dated thus in the Appendix: EVA: Mannheim (Mh), E, H, K, M, N, O; MVA: I, Q, R, S, T, V, W; LVA: X, Y, Z.

DISCUSSION

Reference to the information in the Appendix demonstrates that Norway, with forty-four examples, has the largest number of Ulfberht blades, followed by Sweden and Finland, Russia, Estonia and Eastern Prussia (the Kaliningrad area in Russia). In the Frankish realm itself (Germany, the Netherlands and Belgium), there are a total of twelve examples (+3 from unknown finds location in Germany). In the EVA and MVA, most swords are found in Norway, while by contrast there are only two MVA and one LVA examples in Frankish Germany. Only in the LVA are there fewer blades from Norway than from Germany and Belgium. If this map were simply read as showing mute archaeological objects, Ulfberht's homeland would have been identified as Norway, which has the earliest finds and the most varied material. However, the objects are not mute, as they bear a lower Frankish, north German name. It goes without saying that many swords may be found only where there were many swords originally, but one can hardly believe that the Franks had so few swords compared to the Norwegians. The main explanation is that in the pagan countries to the north and east of the Frankish realm, grave-goods were given to the dead, which was normally not the case in Christian countries. The overwhelming number of finds in Norway, therefore, is the result of a generous burial practice which gave the dead equipment for the afterlife. The swords found on the Christian continent have been found in rivers, where they were lost or perhaps sacrificed (Steuer 1999a, 316).

The varied intensity of research strongly influences the numbers of recorded finds. Most Ulfberht blades in Sweden, Russia and the Ukraine were identified by Kirpičnikov. In Norway, he identified eighteen unknown Ulfberhts in addition to the twenty-six that were already on record (Kirpičnikov and Stalsberg, forthcoming). In Finland, Leppäaho's research revealed a number of Ulfberht swords (1964). I know of no such systematic searches from other countries (but see Pedersen, this volume).

The variants of the adverse signatures and reverses do not seem random, since the signatures could be grouped into only four correctly written groups, and the reverse marks into only five variants. *Signatures 5* and *6*, and the *Reverse marks VI*, comprise only a few unique deviations and do not influence the overall impression that the variants must have been made intentionally and have a meaning.

Geographically *Signatures 1* and *2* are most numerous in Norway, and also occur to some extent in Sweden and Finland, with only few in Carolingian/ Frankish Germany. *Signatures 3* and *4* are few in number, but most are from Norway and they are not found in Germany. *Signatures 5* are most numerous in Norway, with only one each in Sweden, Finland, Latvia and Russia, which supports the idea that they are imitations, not forged in the Frankish realm. The incorrectly written *Signature 6* shows the same main distribution, but three are found in the Frankish realm (2 Germany, 1 Belgium). It is remarkable that on one very fine sword (D-8), an early Mannheim-type found in Mannheim and datable to *c.*800, the smith has forgotten to 'write' the letter R and the reverse is slightly aberrant from *Reverse mark IV*. The blade-smith obviously was uncertain or untrained.

Reverse marks I and *II* have the same distribution pattern as *Signatures 1 and 2*. *Reverse marks III* have been found in Norway, Sweden, Estonia and Latvia; *Reverse mark IV* in Norway, Sweden, Finland, Russia, Latvia and Ireland. The simple *Reverse mark V* is found in Frankish Germany, which is unexpected, since the author would *a priori* expect more careful work from Ulfberht's homeland. As seen on the find table, there are many combinations of signatures and reverse marks. *Signature 1 / Reverse mark I* is the most numerous of these, with seventeen blades, but there is no obvious pattern in their distribution. *Signature-1 / Reverse mark III* are known only from Norway (three blades), Estonia (one blade) and Latvia (one blade). *Signature-1 / Reverse mark IV* is also known only from Norway (three blades). There are no obvious patterns in the distribution of the remaining combinations.

On the other hand, if one looks at the analogies of one sword, the combinations may be informative. For example, a sword from Norway (N-30 Gravråk) has a type-K hilt, with the name *Hiltipreht* on the lower hilt, and a blade with *Signature 1* or *2* and *Reverse mark IV*. The closest analogy is a sword from Ireland (IRL-1 Ballinderry), which has a hilt which must have been made in the same workshop in the Carolingian Empire. Kirpičnikov reads the Norwegian example as *Signature 1*, while the Irish specimen clearly has *Signature 2*; both blades have *Reverse mark IV*. The signature on the Norwegian blade is only partly legible; Müller-Wille (1970, Abb. 2) published it as 'LFB', while Kirpičnikov completed it and read it as *Signature 2*. The two last letters are hardly visible; Leena Airola, a metal conservator in the Museum of Natural History and Archaeology, NTNU, Trondheim, has made several X-ray photographs of it, but neither she nor I have been able to decipher these letters. If the two swords are so similar, except for the signatures, might it be that the blades were provided by two smithies or blacksmiths? Or were they of different qualities? If, on the other hand, the Norwegian blade has the *Signature 1 / Reverse mark IV* combination, I know of only two analogous blades, both from Middle Norway: H-hilt from Levanger, 75km north of Gravråk, and possibly X-handle from Vikna, 180km north of Gravråk. On this basis, one may speculate further concerning who forged what, when and where, and how the blades ended up here, with two EVA handles and one LVA handle. It might, for example, mean that the blades are contemporary, while the hilt had been modernized in Vikna.

Swords with *Signature 2/Reverse mark IV* combinations are more numerous, with seven blades: from Ireland (Ballinderry); Norway; Sweden; Finland; and Russia. None are known from the Frankish realm. They are only known in areas which had relations with Scandinavia – such as Ireland, Timerevo on the Upper Volga, and Häme in Egentliga Finland. I do not dare speculate on what this might mean.

It is notable that incorrectly written signatures and 'simple' reverse marks have been found in the Frankish realm, the supposed land of origin of these blades. Presumably this simply indicates that the smiths were not literate (or were less able).

The chronological analysis of the different signatures, reverse marks and their combinations reveals similar non-concentrated distributions, but some have a clearer chronological distribution. Generally, there are more EVA hilts with Ulfberht blades than from the two other periods. The code EVA-MVA-LVA with the numbers of occurrences is helpful in providing a quick survey of the data. The distribution of *Signatures 1* is 11–20–13, and of *Reverse marks I* 5–11–5, and they are most numerous during MVA. The combination *Signature 1/Reverse mark I* is also most frequent in MVA: 2–9–2. The EVA *Signature 1* is found in Norway, Sweden, Finland, Estonia, the Ukraine and the Netherlands, but not in Frankish Germany, where only later examples are found, namely one MVA and four LVA. The combinations *Signature 1/Reverse mark I* follow the same distribution. Surprisingly, these are not known in Ulfberht's homeland in Germany, but again, the many finds in Norway and Sweden serve to distort the distribution maps.

Signature 2 blades are chronologically distributed, 15–4–3, and the *Reverse marks IV* follow the same pattern: 10–4–4. These must be regarded as generally early, even if they are also known from MVA and LVA. The *Signatures 2* are known from Frankish Germany and the Netherlands, while *Reverse mark IV* is not represented there. The scattered and unsystematic chronological patterns may, for example, indicate that blade and hilt did not leave the workshop as a complete sword, but that the blades were fitted with hilts later, or vice versa.

Neither the geographical nor the chronological distributions give any clear information about where and when the blades were spread. Nor do the distributions help much in separating 'genuine' from 'imitated' Ulfberht blades. Meticulous examination and documentation are very important for further discussion of these blades.

CONCLUSION

As noted above, the distribution patterns of the variants of signatures and reverse marks are difficult to interpret. They pose more questions than they provide answers. In reality, the data provides only one answer: there was not *a* blacksmith Ulfberht, since Ulfberht blades seem to have been forged for a period of two centuries, unless the Ulfberht who lived under Charlemagne left behind a large arsenal of blades which was taken into use successively. The usual explanations are that the signature was used by several smithies or smiths, perhaps of the same dynasty, or that the signatures had become a widely imitated sign of quality used by various smiths in various countries. However, it may simply be that Ulfberht was not a smith himself, but a literate man who was the producer of swords, with smiths doing the actual forging. It would be natural that the armament and weapons were controlled by a high-positioned man, such as the constable or marshall. Weapons were also produced in monasteries, and some bishops and abbots were also warlords. In this connection, it struck me that the Ulfberht signature starts with a cross. I know only one professional group of men having an initial cross in their signatures: Catholic bishops. The numismatist Jon Anders Risvaag was struck by the similarity between the position the author suggested regarding the Ulfberht blades and that of medieval moneyers known from England, France and, perhaps later, Norway. The moneyers had a licence from the king to strike coins, or they were the king's servants, and were responsible for the coins being made according to standard forms and quality, even if the enterprise was private (J.A. Risvaag, pers. comm.; Metcalf 2001). The workers were probably illiterate, which may explain why one of the two oldest known Ulfberht signatures (D-8) is written +ULFBEHT+. Coining was kept under strict control, but so too must have been armament production, especially towards well-known, fierce and ruthless foes like the Vikings. Trade in weapons was strictly controlled in the trading towns, but smuggling could not be prevented (Steuer 1999b, 408). Some of Charlemagne's *capitularia* ban the sale or export of weapons, including horses, to foreigners (Horn Fuglesang 2000, 179). Inside the empire, craftsmen were dependants on the king, bishops or other chieftains. The workshops were located in royal courts, aristocratic estates and, not least, in monasteries. Around AD820, a plan for the redevelopment of St Gallen Abbey in Switzerland was prepared by monks from Reichenau Abbey. The proposed developments were never carried out, but it is important to note that a building with workshops, among them for shield-makers and sword-makers, was planned. Furthermore, these workshops were designed to be accessible only through a central control chamber (Steuer 1999a, 321; Steuer 1999b, 413; Capelle 1999, 424).

The archaeological evidence shows that Carolingian/Frankish weapons were spread outside the realm. Weapons could be contraband or gifts on special occasions; arsenals could be robbed and weapons taken from fallen enemies. Ransom was another method practiced by the Vikings. The *Annales Bertiniani* state that in AD869 a Saracen prince demanded at least 150 swords as part of the ransom for the archbishop of Arles (Steuer 1999a, 318). It may also be that the Vikings abducted sword-smiths, for learning was a person-to-person process, even more so than today.

The chronology of the swords is confusing, since signatures and reverse marks are found with hilts dating to different periods of the Viking Age. It may simply be that the owners changed the hilts on old blades, but the answer may also be more sophisticated than that. If the Ulfberht blades were reserved for the royal or ecclesiastical retinues, for officers, or for special military detachment, it may be that favoured officers/soldiers were given an Ulfberht blade from the arsenal, where blades had been kept for a long time. If a blade manufactured, let us say, in the first half of the ninth century was given to an officer or warrior in 925, the hilt attached then would be of a later type. This may explain the seemingly inexplicable dating of signatures and reverse marks. Such a problem cannot be solved until there are methods to date the steel blade directly. The systematization of the blade signatures and reverse marks offered in this paper does not solve the problem of dating, but having a systematic overview of the variants of the Ulfberht blades does allow for more advanced discussion in the future.

APPENDIX

Variants of signatures and reverse marks on Ulfberht blades with their hilt-types and dating (in accordance with hilt-types). The find spots are localized only by country (borders as in 2007), indicated by a letter – the international identification letter of motor vehicles. The letters pRU indicate Eastern Prussia, now the Kaliningrad area in Russia.

	ADVERSE							REVERSE							HILT-TYPE		
	1	2	3	4	5	6	7	I	II	III	IV	V	VI	VII	EVA	MVA	LVA
B-1	x																X
-2	x			x													X lt
CH-1	x									x							X
CZ-1			x														Y
-2						x		x								T	
D-1				x				x									X
-2 *						x										W	
-3	x								x								X
-4	x							x								R	
-5	x												x				X
-6	x													x			Y
-7 *	x												x				X
-8					x			x							Mh		

	ADVERSE							REVERSE							HILT-TYPE		
	1	2	3	4	5	6	7	I	II	III	IV	V	VI	VII	EVA	MVA	LVA
-9		x										x			Mh		
-10	x											x					X
-11	x						x										X
-12	x							x									X?
-13 *							x				x						X lt
DK-1							x									S	
-2	?	?														V	
-3							x									S	
E-1		x										x					X
EST-1															T		
-2	x																
-3					x												
-4	?	?						x							H		
-5					x									x	E		
-6																	
-7	x									x						T	
-8	?				x	x										T	
-9																	Z
F-1																	X lt
FIN-1	x							x									
-2						x		x									
-3						x				x					I		
-4	x											x					X
-5	x							x									
-6									x								
-7	x							x									
-8	x							x									Y
-9			x										x				
-10				x									x			T	
-11		x															
-12			x					x									
-13	x														M		
-14		x									x				H		
GB-1			x														Z
-2							x				x						X
-3							x					x			N		
-4							x									S	
HR-1		x													O-III		
-2							x								O-III		
I-1							?										
IRL-1		x									x				K		
-2					x										H		
IS-1																V	
-2							x							x		V	
LT-1		S															
-2																	
LV-1		x										x			Y		
-2	x								x								Z
-3	x							x								T	
-4							x				x						X
-5				x						x					H		
-6																	
-7																	Z
N-1	x							x									

	ADVERSE							REVERSE							HILT-TYPE		
	1	2	3	4	5	6	7	I	II	III	IV	V	VI	VII	EVA	MVA	LVA
-2							x										
-3	x							x									R
-4		x									x				H		
-5	x									x							R
-6	x							x							H		
-7	x																
-8	x							x							H		
-9					x						x				H		
-10		x									x				O-III		
-11	x															V	
-12					x								x			R	
-13																S	
-14							x									T	
-15															N		
-16		x										x			H		
-17				x								x				S	
-18			x											x			Z
-19	x																Z
-20	x															Q	
-21		x												x		Q	
-22				x				x							O-II		
-23			x								x						late
-24	x															R	
-25	x							x								Q	
-26						x									H		
-27						x					x					S	
-28	x							x								I	
-29					x			x									Y
-30	x										x				K		
-31	?	?					x				x						X
-32				x							x					I	
-33				x									x		H		
-34						x							x		H		
-35	?	?											x		H		
-36				x											H		
-37	x										x				H		
-38		x														V	
-39		x											x		H		
-40	x												x		Mh		
-41																R	
-42	x								x							I	
-43				x												V	
-44	x							x							H		
NL-1															H		
-2	x	?											x		H		
-3							x	x								T	
PL-1					x												
-2																	Z
-3																	
-4																S	
-5					x												Y
-6																S	
-7																	Y
RUS-1				x				x									X

	ADVERSE							REVERSE							HILT-TYPE		
	1	2	3	4	5	6	7	I	II	III	IV	V	VI	VII	EVA	MVA	LVA
-2							x	x								V	
-3																V	
-4		x									x				E		
-5			x										x		E		
-6	x							x								V	
-7																V	
-8							x				x				E		
-9																I	
-10																S	
-11					x			x							H		
pRU12																V	
-13							x	x							H		
-14																	X
-15																W	
-16						x										T	
-17							x					x					X
-18																V	
-19															H		
-20																	
-21																	
-22																	
-23																	
S-1	x														H		
-2		x									x						X
-3	x							x							H		
-4		x									x				H		
-5		?								x					H		
-6		x									x				H		
-7		?								x					H		
-8							x			x							
-9						x						x					
-10						x						x			O		
-11							x				x					V	
-12					x											V	
-13		x								x						I	
-14							x								H		
-15							x								H		
-16	x									x							
-17				?						x							
UA-1	x															T	
-2	x										x				H		
-3	x							x								V	
-4	x								x							S	
-5	x							x								S	
-6							x							x		T	

ACKNOWLEDGMENT

A warm thank-you is extended to my colleagues for their invaluable comments and discussion during two seminars on the topic of this paper.

BIBLIOGRAPHY

Andresen, K. 1993. 'Dekor og innskrift på vikingsverd: hvordan ble de utført?', *SPOR*, 1, 38–9.

Capelle, T. 1991. 'Handwerk in der Karolingerzeit' in C. Stiegemann & M. Wemhoff (eds), *Kunst und kultur der Karoligzeitnerzeit: beiträge zum katalog der ausstellung. Paderborn 1999* (Mainz), 424–9.

Geibig, A. 1991. *Beiträge zur morphologischen entwicklung des schwertes im mittelalter: eine analyse des fundmaterials vom ausgehenden 8. bis zum 12. jahrhundert aus Sammlungen der Bundesrepublik Deutschland*, Offa-Bücher, 71 (Neumünster).

Herrmann, J. & P. Donat. 1985. *Corpus archäologischer quellen zur frühgeschichte auf dem gebiet der Deutschen Demokratischen Republik (7–12 Jahrhundert)* (Berlin).

Horn Fuglesang, S. 2000. 'Skriftlige kilder for karolingisk våpeneksport til Skandinavia?', *Collegium medievale*, 13, 177–82.

Jankuhn, H. 1951. 'Ein Ulfberht-schwert aus der Elbe bei Hamburg' in K. Kersten (ed.), *Festschrift für Gustav Schwantes zum 65: geburtstag dargebracht von seinen Schülern und Freunden* (Neumünster), pp 212–29.

Kirpičnikov, A.N. 1966. *Drevnerusskoe oružie*, vol. 1 (Moskva-Leningrad).

Kirpičnikov, A.N. & A. Stalsberg. forthcoming. The Norwegian-Russian sword project (Trondheim; St Petersburg).

Leppäaho, J., 1964. *Späteisenzeitliche Waffen aus Finnland*, Finska forminnesföreningens tidskrift, 61 (Helsinki).

Lorange, A. 1889. *Den yngre jernalders sværd* (Bergen).

Metcalf, D.M. 2001. 'The premises of early medieval mints: the case of eleventh-century Winchester' in R. La Guardia (ed.), *I Luigi della Moneta: atti del Convegno Internazionale 1999, Milano* (Milano), pp 59–66.

Mühlen, B. von zur. 1975. *Die kultur der Wikiknger in Ostpreussen*, Bonner Heft zur Vorgeschichte, 9 (Berlin).

Müller-Wille, M. 1971. 'Ein neues Ulfberht-schwert aus Hamburg: verbreitung, formenkunde und herkunft', *Offa*, 27, 1970 [1971], 65–91.

Oakeshott, E. 2000. *Sword in hand* (Minneapolis).

Petersen, J. 1919. *De norske vikingesverd* (Kristiania).

Peirce, I. 2002. *Swords of the Viking Age* (Woodbridge).

Sarnowska, W. 1955. 'Miecze wczesnośredniowieczne w Polsce', *Światovit*, 21, 276–323.

Stalsberg. A. 1989. 'Mønstersmidde sverd og varjagerkontroversen', *Norks våpenhistorisk selskap. Årbok 1988* (Oslo), 7–31.

Stalsberg, A. 2003. 'Til spørsmålet om lokal eller fremmed produksjon av sverdblades fra vikingetiden i Skandinavia' in P.P. Toločko (ed.), *Družinni starožitnosti central'no-shidni Evropy VIII–XI st.: materialy mižnarodnogo pol'ovogo arheoligičnogo seminaru* (Černihiv), 148–59.

Steuer, H. 1999a. 'Bewaffnung und Kriegesführung der Sachsen und Franken' in C. Stiegemann & M. Wemhoff (eds), *Kunst und kultur der Karoligzeitnerzeit: beiträge zum katalog der Ausstellung. Paderborn 1999* (Mainz), 310–22.

Steuer, H. 1999b. 'Handel und wirtschaft in der Karolingerzeit' in C. Stiegemann & M. Wemhoff (eds), *Kunst und kultur der Karoligzeitnerzeit: beiträge zum katalog der Ausstellung. Paderborn 1999* (Mainz), 406–16.

Thålin-Bergman, L. & A.N. Kirpičnikov. 1998. 'Neue untersuchungen von schwertern der Wikingerzeit aus der sammlung des Staatlichen Historischen Museums in Stockholm' in A. Wesse (ed.), *Studien zur archäologie des Ostseeraumes* (Neumünster), pp 497–506.

Vinski, Z. 1983. 'Zu karolingischen schwertfunden aus Jugoslawien', *Jahrbücher des römisch-germanischen Zentralmuseum*, 456–501.

Toftanes and the early Christianity of the Faroe Islands

STEFFEN STUMMANN HANSEN

INTRODUCTION

During 1982–7 the National Museum of the Faroe Islands (Føroya Fornminnis-savn) conducted a large-scale excavation of a Viking-Age farmstead at Toftanes in the settlement of Leirvík, on Eysturoy (Stummann Hansen 1988; 1989; 1991; 1993). This produced a rich assemblage of artefacts, including a number of unique wooden objects. Some of these could easily be identified as, for instance, bowls, spoons, barrel staves, tallies, rivets, gaming boards, and so on. The archaeological evidence indicates that the farmstead was established in the late ninth century or no later than the first half of the tenth century. This dating has been substantiated by nine radiocarbon dates, which indicate that the farmstead was established no later than AD860–970 (Vickers et al. 2005).

In 2002, a research grant from SILA, the Greenland Research Centre at the National Museum of Denmark, provided the opportunity to conduct a more detailed study of a major part of the artefact assemblage, including the extensive wooden material, aiming at a full publication of the site. This study has resulted in important observations that form part of the basis for this paper. In particular, it led to the identification of two wooden crosses among the Toftanes assemblage, providing a challenge to the traditional view of the date and nature of early Christianity in the Faroe Islands.

THE CROSSES

One of the cross-shafts is preserved to a length of 38.5cm, while the horizontal transept has a width of 19cm. The two parts of the cross were joined by a centrally placed wooden rivet. The cross-shaft, presumably, was furnished with a pointed base (Fig. 43.1). The edges of the upper part of the shaft and of the arms were serrated, while its lower part had straight edges.

The second cross is represented by a fragment of the shaft, 35cm in length. It is clearly broken at the lower end, which probably was pointed. This cross also had a central perforation through which a wooden rivet joined its two parts. The cross is characterized by having hollowed angles (Fig. 43.2), in the Irish style. Both crosses were made of larch (*Larix*) which presumably was driftwood ultimately deriving from the rivers of northern Russia.

43.1 Wooden cross from Toftanes
(photo: Føroya Fornminnissavn,
Haldane Joensen).

43.2 Fragment of wooden cross of 'Irish type'
from Toftanes (photo: Føroya Fornminnissavn,
Haldane Joensen).

The two separate pieces of the first cross were found within a short distance of each other in a layer representing the establishment phase of the farmstead (Fig. 43.3). This contained, among other things, a lot of waste wooden material and a high number of wooden artefacts. The second cross was found in even earlier deposits, superimposed by the above-mentioned layer. One of the first things that happened in the establishment phase of the site was an impressive engineering work which involved drainage ditches being dug in the natural peaty surface. These were approximately 20cm deep and were soon filled up with peaty soil containing waste materials and artefacts, including the cross-fragment. The ditches and their contents were covered by the establishment layer noted above. Thus, the second cross is probably older than the first, though the difference in terms of age may be very small. Both layers were covered by the extension to the long-house (XI) and the firehouse (XII), both of which can be dated to the tenth century.

43.3 The Toftanes site with an indication of where the crosses were found
(photo: Føroya Fornminnissavn, S. Stummann Hansen).

CULTURAL CONTEXT

There are good parallels for the wooden crosses from Toftanes, especially among those from the churchyard in Herjolfsnes (Inuit: Ikigaat) in the Eastern Settlement of medieval Greenland. During excavations in the early twentieth century, a number of burials were found here which the excavator, Poul Nørlund, dated to *c.*1150–1450. These burials initially became famous for the well-preserved garments they contained. However, approximately sixty wooden crosses were also found in this churchyard, most of them placed either on top of the wooden coffins or on the chests of the corpses. They varied in length between *c.*11cm and 69cm (Nørlund 1924, 197–219). The wooden crosses from Toftanes have many similarities in form as well as scale with these crosses from medieval Greenland.

Nørlund grouped the wooden crosses from Herjolfsnes into a number of types. The later piece from Toftanes may be assigned to Nørlund's Type D, which he defined as 'crosses having semicircular and segmental hollows at the intersections' (ibid., 205–10). To this group he ascribed a total of fourteen crosses, of which the tallest measured some 49cm by 27.4cm. It is characterized by the limbs being joined by means of notches and a single tree-nail with a large round head. The closest parallels for the Toftanes example among the Herjolfsnes wooden crosses are nos 139, 142 and 143, as well as a rune-inscribed wooden cross, no. 136 (ibid., 207–8, fig. 145; 277–80, fig. 5).

There is hardly any doubt that the form of this type of cross was influenced by the form of Irish crosses of the early medieval period, including the famous high crosses. This specific type is well represented at the Herjolfsnes site. Thus Nørlund stated:

> [W]e are so fortunate to have, among the crosses from Herjolfsnes, at least one group of such pronounced shape that its origin can be established with the greatest certainty. It is that extensively found type on which the angles are hollowed with circular cuttings, sometimes broad and open semicircles, sometimes small and narrow almost quite closed circles [...]. It is the simplified 'Celtic Cross' which was so long in extensive use on stone monuments – both on standing crosses and recumbent slabs – in the British Isles, especially in Scotland and Ireland (Nørlund 1924, 216–17).

However, while the wooden crosses from Herjolfsnes were found in funerary contexts, those from Toftanes derive from a simple rural farmstead.

When Nørlund published the wooden crosses from Herjolfsnes, he interpreted them as burial crosses. This interpretation was justified by the fact that they were all found in the churchyard, and typically on top of the wooden coffins or placed on the chests of the corpses. Thus the crosses were regarded as having been produced specifically for use in burial contexts. Although other wooden crosses were subsequently found at the excavation of the farmstead of Sandnes (Inuit: Kilaarsarfik) and its attached church-site in the Western Settlement of medieval Greenland (Roussell 1936, 17–18), as opposed to churchyards, Nørlund's original interpretation was accepted by other scholars. More recently, wooden crosses have also been found at another Western Settlement farmstead, the 'Farm Beneath the Sand' (Danish: Gården Under Sandet, abbreviated GUS), which has no adjacent church-site (Berglund 1998, 50–1).

However, on the basis of a re-interpretation of the crosses from Norse Greenland and of other wooden crosses found in medieval contexts, for instance, at Bryggen in Bergen (Herteig 1969, fig. 66; Liestøl 1980–90, 49–50, 87–90) and in Trondheim (Hagland 1986, 12–13), Nørlund's original interpretation has now been seriously challenged. Thus it has been suggested that the crosses from medieval Greenland should be interpreted as devotional rather than burial crosses (Liestøl 1980–90, 90; Stoklund 1984; Berglund 1998, 49). Such crosses were probably placed within the dwelling houses of the farmsteads for the purpose of protecting the inhabitants from 'evil'. The fact that these crosses typically seem to have had a pointed base indicates that they were placed in some kind of staff. In some cases, as evidenced in the Herjolfsnes churchyard, the crosses subsequently accompanied the deceased to the grave and thereby ended up functioning as burial crosses.

THE EARLY CHRISTIANITY OF THE FAROE ISLANDS

It remains to explain how wooden crosses appear on a Viking farmstead at Toftanes at a period when, according to saga tradition, the inhabitants of the Faroe Islands were pagan. There are various indications of strong Irish cultural influences in the Faroe Islands during the Viking Age. Thus, the Faroese linguists Jakob Jakobsen and Christian Matras drew attention to a number of Irish loan-words in the Faroese language (Jakobsen 1902; Lockwood 1977; 1978; Matras 1939; 1954; 1955; 1956; 1957; 1965; 1981). In this connection it is interesting to note that some shielings of the Viking-Age and early medieval periods, identified at several locations in the mountainous Faroese landscape, have place-names attached to them that contain not the Old Norse word *sætr*, but the Old Irish word for shieling, *áirge*. The latter appears, for instance, as *ergi* and *argi* in a number of Faroese place-names, for example Ergisdalur and Argisbrekka (Dahl 1970; Fellows-Jensen 1980; 2002; Mahler 1989; 1991a; 1991b; 1993; 1996; Matras 1957; Matras et al. 2004).

In Iceland, several Viking-Age burials have been found containing typical pagan grave-goods, for instance horse gear, boats, weapons and impressive brooches (Eldjárn 2000). Curiously, these types of burials have not been found in the Faroe Islands, where the only two graveyards dating to the Viking Age so far identified are Yviri í Trøð, in Tjørnuvík (Dahl and Rasmussen 1956), and Við Kirkjugarð, in the present-day churchyard in Sandur (Arge and Hartman 1992). At Tjørnuvík, the burials contained only a small selection of mundane objects, of which the most characteristic is a ringed bronze pin of Hiberno-Scandinavian type. Two pins of the same type were found at Toftanes (Stummann Hansen 1988, 69–70, fig. 9; 1989, 139, fig. 11; 1991, 49, fig. 9). The burials were dated to the tenth century by the excavator, based on the archaeological assemblage (Dahl 1971, 65). Later this date was substantiated by radiocarbon dates on bones from two burials, providing the dates AD991 and AD999 respectively (Arge 2001, 11).

The burials in Sandur all had an east-west orientation and only contained a few small personal objects. This may indicate that they are Christian. One of the few objects found was a fine bronze fragment with ornamentation that is clearly of Irish design and origin (Arge 2001, 9–11). The burials have been dated to the tenth and/or early eleventh century (Arge 2001; Arge and Hartman 1992, 17–20).

If it is accepted that people at Toftanes – and generally in the Faroe Islands – were Christian throughout the tenth century, it may help to explain why classic pagan Viking graves, of the types found in contemporary Scandinavia, Ireland, Scotland, Orkney, Shetland and Iceland, have not turned up in the Faroe Islands. But where, then, were the Viking-Age Faroese buried? Dahl stated, in dealing with the lack of Viking-Age graves in the Faroe Islands:

Grave-goods are, however, rare. Let us consider why so few have been found. Professor A.W. Brøgger came to the conclusion that the settlers who went to the Faroe Islands came mainly from Agder and Rogaland in Norway and brought the burial traditions of their home region with them. Another possibility is that a number of settlers, as already mentioned, came from a Christian milieu in the Atlantic islands and brought Christian burial customs to the Faroe Islands early in the Viking era – burying their dead in churchyards unaccompanied by grave-goods (Dahl 1971, 65).

He furthermore stated:

> Written records about the churches in the Middle Ages – their number, appearance, inventory, and ornamentation – are completely lacking. It appears certain, however, that during the Middle Ages, or at least shortly after the arrival of Christianity circa 1000, there were a few more churches than the 39 which are mentioned after the Reformation in circa 1540. A number of smaller churches or chapels – *bønhús* – are known to have fallen into disuse at this time, no doubt particularly due to the disappearance of the income from the bishopric's large land holdings which were expropriated by the monarchy as 'crown land'. In many villages one can still see the overgrown plots of such deserted, medieval prayer houses, which clearly have had stone walls (Dahl 1976, 24).

Thus, the answer to the questions about the final resting places for the Faroese of the Viking Age may lie in the so-called *bønhúse* ('prayer houses'), of which the ruins may still be seen at a number of locations around the islands (Joensen 1951, 86).

These small church buildings were placed centrally within churchyards enclosed by circular or sub-circular dikes. The best preserved example of this type of site is at Leirvík (Plate 13), while another fine example is known from Velbastaður (Stummann Hansen and Sheehan 2006). Surviving place-names are testimony that such structures were once present all over the islands. Regrettably, none of these sites have so far been the subject of archaeological excavation.

The interesting thing about these church sites in the present context is their surrounding circular or sub-circular dykes. This feature is not known from contemporary Scandinavia, and can reasonably be regarded as a feature which culturally had its roots in the early Christian environment in Ireland. It can be found in a line from Ireland to the Western Isles, the Northern Isles of Scotland, the Faroe Islands, Iceland and all the way up to the Eastern Settlement of Norse Greenland. These small churchyards, with their circular or sub-circular dykes, represent another material indication that the Viking-Age emigrant communities in the North Atlantic were strongly influenced by the Irish Christian world (Stummann Hansen and Sheehan 2006).

The implication of the above-mentioned evidence is that the Faroe Islands, from the beginnings of their history, were subject to a strong Irish or Hiberno-Scandinavian, and thereby Christian, influence – or, to go one step further, that a major part of the people who settled in the Faroe Islands in the Viking Age originated from an Irish and Christian world. Ethnically, they had a mixed Hiberno-Scandinavian background. Many probably derived from Scandinavians, who had already settled in the Irish Sea region by early in the ninth century, especially in the Western Isles, where they soon integrated with the Christian Irish communities (Smyth 1984, 169–74).

Such a hypothesis seems to be substantiated by recent genetic work on the Faroese population, which indicates that a majority of the male settlers had a Scandinavian ancestry (Jorgensen et al. 2004) while the major part of the female settlers had a British/Irish ancestry (Als et al. 2006). The explanation for this may be that the Western Isles, Skye and Iceland represented a 'frontier' to the Vikings in the North Atlantic region which attracted lone Viking males, who later established families with females from Britain and Ireland. Closer and more secure areas like Orkney, Shetland and the north-western coast of Scotland, on the contrary, facilitated primarily family-based settlement. The population of the Faroe Islands thus fit well into the pattern of male and female admixture proportions of the North Atlantic region (Goodacre et al. 2005).

That the Faroe Islands came under the Norwegian Crown and Church and, thereby, into a pure Scandinavian world in the medieval period is indisputable. Much evidence, however, indicates that the Faroe Islands housed a Christian community from the earliest phases of the Viking-Age *landnám* period and it owed this to the Irish world rather than to Scandinavia.

BIBLIOGRAPHY

Als, T.D., T.H. Jorgensen, A.D. Børglum, P.A. Petersen, O. Mors & A.G. Wang. 2006. 'Highly discrepant proportions of female and male Scandinavian and British Isles ancestry within the isolated population of the Faroe Islands', *European Journal of Human Genetics*, 14, 497–504.

Arge, S.V. 2001. 'Forn búseting heima á Sandi', *Frøði*, 2001/2, 4–13.

Arge, S.V. & N. Hartmann 1992. 'The burial site of við Kirkjugarð', *Fróðskaparrit*, 38–9, 5–21.

Berglund, J. 1998. 'Christian symbols' in J. Arneborg & H.C. Gulløv (eds), *Man, culture and environment in ancient Greenland: report on a research programme*, Danish Polar Centre Publication, 4 (Copenhagen), pp 48–54.

Dahl, S. 1970. 'Um ærgistaðir og ærgitoftir', *Fróðskaparrit*, 18, 361–8.

Dahl, S. 1971. 'The Norse settlement of the Faroe Islands', *Medieval Archaeology*, 14 (1970), 60–73.

Dahl, S. 1976. 'Timber churches of the Faroes', *Faroe Isles Review*, 1:2 (1976), 24–8.

Dahl, S. & J. Rasmussen 1956. 'Víkingaaldargrøv í Tjørnuvík', *Fróðskaparrit*, 5, 153–67.

Eldjárn, K. 2000. *Kuml og haugfé úr heiðnum sið á Íslandi*, 2nd rev. ed, ed. A. Friðriksson (Reykjavík).

Fellows-Jensen, G. 1980. 'Common Gaelic *áirge*, Old Scandinavian *Ærgi* or *Erg?*', *Nomina*, 4, 67–73.

Fellows-Jensen, G. 2002. 'Old Faroese *Ærgi* yet again' in A. Johansen (ed.), *Eivindarmál: heiðursrit til Eivind Weyhe á seksti ára hansara 25. apríl 2002*, Annales Societatis Scientiarum Færoensis Supplementum, 32 (Tórshavn), pp 89–96.

Goodacre, S., A. Helgason, J. Nicholson, L. Southam, L. Ferguson, E. Hickey, E. Vega, K. Stefánsson, R. Ward & B. Sykes. 2005. 'Genetic evidence for a family-based Scandinavian settlement of Shetland and Orkney during the Viking period', *Heredity*, 95, 129–35.

Hagland, J.R. 1986. *Runefunna: ei kjelde til handelen si historie. Fortiden i Trondheim bygrunn, Folkebibliotekstomta*, Meddelelser, 8 (Trondheim).

Herteig, A.E. 1969. *Kongers havn og handels sete: fra de arkeologiske undersøkelser på Bryggen i Bergen, 1955–68* (Oslo).

Jakobsen, J. 1902. 'Keltisk indflydelse paa Færøerne', *Tingakrossir* (January 1902), repr. in J. Davidsen (ed.). 1957, *Jakob Jakobsen, Greiner og ritgerðir* (Tórshavn).

Joensen, H.D. 1951. 'Træk af Færøernes Begravelsesforhold', *Dansk Ligbrændingsforenings beretning for 1951*, 85–110.

Jorgensen, T.H., H.N. Buttenschön, A.G. Wang, T.D. Als, A.D. Børglum & H. Ewald. 2004. 'The origin of the isolated population of the Faroe Islands investigated using Y-chromosomal markers', *Human Genetics*, 115, 19–28.

Liestøl, A. 1980–90. 'Bryggen i Bergen: dei latinske innskriftene' in J.E. Knirk (ed.), *Norges innskrifter med de yngre runer*, 6:2 (Oslo), pp 1–96.

Lockwood, W.B. 1977. 'Some traces of Gaelic in Faroese', *Fróðskaparrit*, 25, 9–25.

Lockwood, W.B. 1978. 'Chr. Matras' studies on the Gaelic element in Faroese: conclusions and results', *Scottish Gaelic Studies*, 13, 112–26.

Mahler, D.L.D. 1989. 'Argisbrekka: nye spor efter sæterdrift på Færøerne', *Hikuin*, 15, 147–70.

Mahler, D.L.D. 1991a. 'Argisbrekka: new evidence of shielings in the Faroe Islands', *Acta Archaeologica*, 61, 60–72.

Mahler, D.L.D. 1991b. 'Sæterdrift på Færøerne i Vikingetid og tidlig Middelalder? En model' in J.P. Joensen et al. (eds), *Nordatlantiske foredrag*, Annales Societatis Scientiarum Færoensis, Supplementum, 15 (Tórshavn), 29–41.

Mahler, D.L.D. 1993. 'Shielings and their role in the Viking-Age economy: new evidence from the Faroe Islands' in Batey, C.E., J. Jesch & C.D. Morris (eds), *The Viking Age in Caithness, Orkney and the North Atlantic: select papers from the proceedings of the Eleventh Viking Congress, Thurso and Kirkwall, 1989* (Edinburgh), pp 487–505.

Mahler, D.L.D. 1996. 'Landskab og landbrug på Færøerne i vikingetid og tidlig middelalder', *Bol og By*, 1, 8–24.

Matras, A.K. et al. 2004. 'A Viking-Age shieling at Skarðsvík, Fugloy', *Fróðskaparrit*, 51, 200–11.

Matras, C. 1939. 'Færøerne: ortnamn', *Nordisk Kultur*, 5 (Stockholm), 53–9.

Matras, C. 1954. 'Làmh chearr í føroyskum máli', *Fróðskaparrit*, 3, 60–77.

Matras, C. 1955. 'Soppur í føroyskum og sopp í írskum', *Fróðskaparrit*, 4, 15–31.

Matras, C. 1956. 'Caigeann og køkja', *Fróðskaparrit*, 5, 98–107.

Matras, C. 1957. 'Gammelfærösk ærgi, n., og dermed beslægtede ord', *Namn og Bygd*, 44:14, 51–67.

Matras, C. 1965. 'Írsk orð í føroyskum', *Almanakkin fyri tað ár eftir Kristi føðing 1966* (Copenhagen), 22–32.

Matras, C. 1981. 'Korkadalur', *Fróðskaparrit*, 28–9, 78–80.

Nørlund, P. 1924. *Buried Norsemen at Herjolfsnes*, Meddelelser om Grønland, 67:3 (Copenhagen).

Roussell, Aa. 1936. *Sandnes and the neighbouring farms*, Meddelelser om Grønland, 88:2 (Copenhagen).

Smyth, A.P. 1984. *Warlords and holy men: Scotland, AD80–1000* (Edinburgh).

Stoklund, M. 1984. 'Nordbokorsene fra Grønland', *Nationalmuseets Arbejdsmark*, 1984, 101–13.

Stummann Hansen, S. 1988. 'The Norse landnam in the Faroe Islands in the light of recent excavations at Toftanes, Leirvík', *Northern Studies*, 25, 58–84.

Stummann Hansen, S. 1989. 'Toftanes: en færøsk landnamsgård fra 9–10 århundrede', *hikuin*, 15, 129–46.

Stummann Hansen, S. 1991. 'Toftanes: a Faroese Viking-Age farmstead from the 9th–10th centuries AD', *Acta Archaeologica*, 61, 44–53.

Stummann Hansen, S. 1993. 'Viking-Age Faroe Islands and their southern links in the light of recent finds at Toftanes, Leirvík' in Batey, C.E., J. Jesch & C.D. Morris (eds), *The Viking Age in Caithness, Orkney and the North Atlantic: select papers from the proceedings of the Eleventh Viking Congress, Thurso and Kirkwall, 1989* (Edinburgh), pp 473–86.

Stummann Hansen, S. & J. Sheehan. 2006. 'The Leirvík "bønhústoftin" and the early Christianity of the Faroe Islands, and beyond', *Archaeologia Islandica*, 5, 27–54.

Vickers, K., J. Bending, P.C. Buckland, K.J. Edwards, S. Stummann Hansen & G. Cook. 2005. 'Toftanes: the palaeoecology of a Faroese *landnám* farm', *Human Ecology*, 685–710.

Cosmic aspects of sanctuaries in Viking-Age Scandinavia with comparisons to the West-Slavic area

OLOF SUNDQVIST

Adam of Bremen's description of Uppsala from 1075 is probably one of the most important pieces of evidence for the existence of sanctuaries in pre-Christian Scandinavia. However, this description has been much debated. Some decades ago, historians of religion argued that it was reliable since it was contemporary with the events it described. Indeed, Adam built his narrative on hearsay, but his informants were eyewitnesses. In recent research, scholars are more sceptical (Hultgård 1997), arguing that Adam's text is permeated with rhetorical embellishments and missionary strategies. Some scholars have also found mythical elements in it. The temple, the tree and the well, for instance, are actually descriptions of a mythical landscape. These authorities argue that Adam misunderstood the mythical traditions surrounding Valhalla, Yggdrasill and the well of Urðr, and confused it with reality. Therefore, they believe that Adam's text cannot be accepted as a trustworthy source on Viking-Age sanctuaries (Bruun and Jónsson 1909; Alkarp 1997).

In my opinion, these connections may lead to another conclusion. In what follows, I argue that the mythical references in Adam's description render a cultic reality. The temple, the tree and the well may deliberately have been arranged as a reflection of the mythical landscape. This is not unique to Uppsala, as this can be seen at cultic places in other parts of Scandinavia and the continent as well. In my opinion, these cosmic references to Uppsala had significance for the rulers. Uppsala was not only a place for the famous temple, it was also a political and economic centre. The rulers of Uppsala used mythical traditions about the cosmos and the divine world in order to gain legitimacy and power. For instance, the members of the famous Ynglinga family viewed themselves as the god Freyr's offspring and during sacrifices they performed ritual roles (Sundqvist 2002).

There are some problems attached to this assertion, mainly with the sources. Extensive accounts about cosmology are not preserved in Eastern Scandinavian traditions. They appear only in Old Norse materials written down in thirteenth-century Iceland. We are uncertain of their prevalence outside of Iceland, or whether they ever existed in Viking-Age Uppsala. In my opinion, however, there never was a centralized institution or organized priesthood which could formulate normative world-views and ritual practices over all of Scandinavia. On the other hand, there might have existed mythical and ritual themes which were spread over wide geographic areas and were stable over time. Some notions may have been transmitted by aristocratic groups who made contacts with each other via marriages, gift-giving systems and trade.

SANCTUARIES AS REFLECTIONS OF COSMOS

The idea that the sanctuary of Uppsala reflected cosmic aspects is related to a general theory in the history of religion, elaborated mainly by Mircea Eliade (1957 [1987]). He has argued that temples, cult places and towns in several societies mirror a mythical symbolism. Sanctuaries, such as the temple of Jerusalem, were imitations of a transcendent model. This symbolism is also evident in the early Christian basilicas and medieval cathedrals. In modern theoretical debate, Eliade's ideas have sometimes been regarded as problematic (McCutcheon 1997, 42, 74–100). He has, for instance, been criticized for his universal perspectives and lack of consideration for specific cultural contexts. A number of scholars also disagree with Eliade's apolitical interpretation of cosmic myths. Therefore, it feels somewhat risky to apply his ideas without stating some reservations.

During the last number of years, Eliade's ideas have been applied to the Scandinavian context. Lotte Hedeager, for instance, has argued that the central place at Gudme, in Fyn, was arranged according to a mythical model (2001). The hall, the workshops and the lake were organized in a way that resembled Ásgarðr. This interpretation can be supported by the place-name; the name *Gudme*, i.e. *Guðheim*, actually means 'the home of the gods'. Hedeager points to important aspects which were overlooked by Eliade, namely that the sanctuary at Gudme also had political and economic functions. Gudme, in essence, was a site for the elite. The cosmic symbolism at this site can therefore be related to political motifs and can be seen as part of the mechanism which creates authority. I shall now turn to Adam's description of Uppsala and see if there are any connections between myth and the real cultic topography.

THE TEMPLE

Adam of Bremen's work on the history of the archdiocese Hamburg-Bremen was written in 1075/76. In Book 4, chapter 26, he describes the temple in Uppsala (*Ubsola*):

> In this temple [*Ubsola*], totally adorned with gold, the people worship statues of three gods, the most mighty of them, Thor, has his throne in the middle of the banquet room, Óðinn and Freyr have their places on either side (Schmeidler 1917).

In the marginal note 139, the temple is described in more detail:

> It is said that a golden chain surrounds the temple, hanging over the gables of the building, glowing brilliantly towards those who approach (Schmeidler 1917).

This description resembles mythical conditions. In *Gylfaginning*, Snorri describes a *hóf* ('temple, hall') at a place called Gladsheim, which was decorated with nothing but gold: 'It was their [the gods] first act to build the temple that their thrones stand in, twelve in addition to the throne that belongs to All-father [Óðinn]. This house is the best that is built on earth and the biggest. Outside and inside it seems like nothing but gold' (ch. 14). According to *Grímnismál* (st. 8), this building seems to be identical with Valhalla. Similar to the Uppsala temple, this house has seats for the deities. Óðinn has the high-seat there (*Gylfaginning*, ch. 14), and the Einherjar can drink their fill there every day (*Gylfaginning*, ch. 39; *Grímnismál*, sts 23–5). The parallels between the Uppsala temple and Valhalla are striking. In both places the gods are enthroned in a gold-adorned building. There are also other similarities. When Adam described the temple in Uppsala, he probably did not aim at describing a building exclusively intended for idols and ritual objects. Behind the term *templum*, a great multifunctional hall could be concealed, i.e. a room for banquets, which reminds one of Valhalla. It has been noticed that Adam applied the term *triclinium* when describing the room where the idols stood (Dillmann 1997). In both classical and medieval Latin, this term denotes 'dining-room' and 'room for ceremonial banquets'.

Archaeologists have found remains of structures in Gamla Uppsala that may be related to a cultic building. In 1926, Sune Lindqvist discovered post-holes beneath the stone church, which he interpreted as the remains of a rectangular temple. New investigations have shown, however, that this interpretation must be rejected (Nordahl 1996). Remains of a hall to the north of the church were, however, discovered in the late 1980s. This hall burned down around 800. It was probably replaced by another hall, which might have stood on the spot of the present church. There is a huge terrace at this location, indicating a building about 70m in length (Andrén 2002, 326), and some of Lindqvist's post-holes may be related to it. Knowledge of this late Viking-Age hall may have reached Adam through his informants and inspired his description of the temple.

In recent research, it has been emphasized that Iron-Age halls had cultic functions in Scandinavia (Herschend 1999). Sometimes they appear at places with sacred place-names, such as Helgö and Gudme. Archaeological finds support the assertion that these buildings occasionally were adorned with gold, like Valhalla. Melted gold was discovered in connection with one of the post-holes of the hall at Gudme. According to Frands Herschend, the posts at Gudme might have been decorated with gold, but resulting from a fire the gold may have melted and trickled into to the post-hole (Gräslund 1997, 108).

THE TREE AND THE WELL

Adam also commented on the surroundings of the Uppsala temple in note 138:

> Beside this temple stands an enormous tree, spreading its branches far and
> wide; it is green, in winter as in summer. [...] There is also a well there,
> where heathen sacrifices are commonly performed (Schmeidler 1917).

This description also resembles information from mythical traditions about
Yggdrasill and its wells. According to Snorri, Yggdrasill was, of all trees, the
biggest and the best. Its branches spread out over the whole world and extended
across the sky. One of its roots reached down towards Mimir's well, where Óðinn
deposited his eye in order to drink of the knowledge that the well contained.
Another root was located among the gods at Urðr's well and the third root
extended down to the well called Hvergelmir (*Gylfaginning*, ch. 15). Even if
Snorri described three different wells, they are usually interpreted as different
names of one and the same mental image, that is, the cosmic well (Simek 1995,
205). The tree and the well(s) are also mentioned in Eddic lays as being related
to each other. In, for instance *Grímnismál* (st. 44), it is narrated that the ash
Yggdrasill 'is of all trees best'. The detail that the tree was always green and
stood beside a well is mentioned in *Vǫluspá* (st. 19):

An ash I know there stands,	*Ask veit ek standa,*
Yggdrasill is its name	*heitir Yggdrasill,*
a tall tree, showered	*hár baðmr, ausinn*
with shining loam.	*hvítaauri.*
From there come the dews	*Þaðan koma döggvar,*
that drop in the valleys.	*þærs í dala falla.*
It stands forever green over	*Stendr æ yfir, grænn*
Urðr's well.	*Urðar brunni* (Dronke 1997)

Eddic lays also mention that the tree extended its branches wide (*Fjölsvinnsmál*,
sts 13–14). As the tree in Uppsala, the cosmic tree in the myths seems to stand
beside an important building. According to *Grímnismál* (sts 25–6), there was a
tree called Læraðr situated beside Valhalla (*á höllo Heriafǫðrs*: cf. *Gylfaginning*,
ch. 39).

These similarities between Uppsala and the mythical traditions have, as I
mentioned above, been taken by some scholars in the past as indications that
Adam based his account on myth and confused it with reality. Thus, they argue,
Adam's account cannot be taken seriously. In opposition to this view, I think that
Adam's description is reliable. The existence of trees and wells is very common
in texts referring to Germanic sacred seats. In the ecclesiastical polemics against

pagan customs, the expression *arbor et fons* seems to announce a pagan cultic place. It appears in texts from the *concilium* at Tours in AD567 to the *capitularia* in the age of Charlemagne (e.g. *Concilium Turonense*: Maasen 1893, 133; *Capitulatio de partibus Saxoniae*: Boretius 1883, 69). Sometimes the tree is represented by a cosmic pillar in these texts. Rudolf of Fulda, for instance, mentions that the Saxons worshipped wells and green groves. They also worshipped a great tree-trunk, called Irminsul, which supported the world (*Translatio S. Alexandri*: Pertz 1829, 676).

Cultic trees and cosmic pillars are also attested in Scandinavian contexts. According to the U-version of *Hervarar saga*, a sacrificial tree, called *blóttré*, stood at the assembly-place of the Swedes. During cultic feasts, this tree was reddened with blood from the animals (*Hervarar saga*: Jón Helgason 1924, 160). Many scholars have associated the cosmic tree with the ritual tree, in Swedish called *vårdträd*, which appears in more recent sources. Such a tree was often situated in the farm, close to the house (Ström 1961). Sacrifices were performed at these trees in connection with weddings and child-births. These customs remind us about the great oak, ON *barnstokkr* ('the child trunk'), which was placed in the middle of the hall of the Völsungs, according to *Völsunga saga* (Guðni Jónsson and Bjarni Vilhjálmsson 1943, 6). There is archaeological support for cultic trees in Sweden. During excavations underneath the church of Fröson, numerous animal bones were discovered in association with a mouldered birch stump; 60 per cent of the bones belonged to wild animals, mostly bears, and 40 per cent were domestic animals. The bones and the stump were dated to the tenth century (Iregren 1989). It should be noted that the church was called *Hoffs kirkio* in a document from 1408. Still today, a place south-east of the church is called *Hov*. It has been argued that the Hov-names in Jämtland refer to buildings where cult practices were carried out (Vikstrand 1993). Thus, we cannot rule out the possibility that we have a structure at Fröson similar to that in Uppsala; a cultic house situated close to a cultic tree.

Cultic trees may not always have been a real tree, as in Fröson. According to Anders Andrén, the triangular stone-settings called *treuddar*, which have been found at several places in Sweden, should be interpreted as symbolic expressions of the world-tree Yggdrasill, with its three roots (Andrén 2004, 406). One such Viking-Age setting is situated just outside the cultic hall at Helgö (Zachrisson 2004). It contained ritual depositions, such as crucibles, bread, arrowheads and pottery. Under the stone setting, in the middle, a single post-hole was found, dating to the Vendel Period. Perhaps a cosmic pillar of the Irminsul-type stood there before the stone setting was made.

Scholars have tried to identify Adam's sacred well in Uppsala. David Damell has suggested that it is the little lake at Myrby träsk, close to Old Uppsala, where a high content of phosphorus was detected (Damell 1980). There is much evidence to support the existence of sacrificial lakes and bogs in Scandinavia from different times and places, at for instance Thorsbjerg, Vimose, Nydam, Kragehul, Illerup and Skedemosse (Ilkjær 1990; Fabech 1994; Carlie 2000; Hagberg 1967–77). The most interesting of these is the little lake at Tissø, Zealand (Jørgensen 2002). The place-name Tissø has been interpreted as 'the lake dedicated to the god Tyr' (Brink 2001). In this lake, several finds have been made which have been interpreted as sacrificial objects. At the settlement beside the lake, a local elite raised a huge ceremonial hall. Palisade enclosures were situated in connection with the south-western part of the hall and enclosed a small structure that was interpreted as a cultic house. A similar pattern is also in evidence at Järrestad, Scania, with a hall, an enclosed area with a small cultic building, and beside this hall, sacrificial wells and springs (Söderberg 2005, 211). At Gudme, too, the great hall is situated beside a lake, though there are as yet no recorded finds from this lake. It is not impossible, however, to imagine that the topography of these sites, like Uppsala, was structured according to a certain mental figure or mythical model.

UPPSALA AS A REDUPLICATION OF ÁSGARÐR

One thing that not is mentioned in Adam's text, but has been revealed by recent excavations, is that a palisade also enclosed the ritual area in Uppsala. It was located at Norra Gärdet and has been dated to the early Viking Age. Its dimensions indicate that it could not be used for defensive purposes and it seems better to interpret it as a symbolic demarcation (Gräslund 1997, 111). In the mythic world, there were fences (ON sing. *garðr*) which enclosed different places (Heggstad et al. 1993, 139). According to Snorri, one of these fences was called *Miðgarðr* and it was built as a fortification round the world against the hostility of giants (*Gylfaginning*, ch. 8). The concept indicates that it was located in the middle of the world. In this place lived people, the gods and other divine beings. The specific place where the gods resided was called *Ásgarðr* (*Gylfaginning*, ch. 9) and Valhalla was situated here as well as Yggdrasill and the well of Urðr. Snorri mentions that the Master Builder built a fortified castle (*borg*) for the gods (*Gylfaginning*, ch. 42). That some of these notions also existed in eastern Scandinavia may be attested by an earthfast rune-inscribed rock at Fyrby, Södermanland (Sö 56), where the inscription notes that Håsten and Holmsten were the most rune-skilled men in Midgard (*mænnr rynasta a Miðgarði*: Jansson 1963 [1987], 138).

It is thus not impossible to imagine that the religious topography and cult at Uppsala, were reflections of the cosmic Ásgarðr. Perhaps real symbols in Uppsala represented the world-tree Yggdrasill and the mythical well(s). The cultic building in Uppsala and the activities that took place at this location might very well have reflected life in Valhalla. As was the case at Ásgarðr, Uppsala was enclosed by a fence. All these ritual attributes in Uppsala were probably markers indicating an *axis mundi*, the centre of the universe.

TEMPLES IN THE NORTH-WESTERN SLAVIC AREA

The mythical-ritual configuration of temple, tree and well found in Uppsala is also visible at cult sites in continental Europe, especially among north-western Slavic people. In comparison to the materials available to the historian of Scandinavian religion, the picture of Slavic temples is impressive (Słupecki 1993). There is good evidence in the written sources for temples at, for instance, Radogosc, Szczecin, Wolin, Wolgast, Garz and Gutzkow. In addition, possible cultic buildings have been found by archaeologists at Feldber, Wolin, Groß Raden, Ralsiek, Parchim and Wroklaw. From the perspective of the present paper, a description of the temple at Szczecin (Stettin), Pommern, is very interesting (Słupecki 1993, 250, 265). This description was made by Herbord in his twelfth-century biography of Bishop Otto of Bamberg, and it is based on eyewitness information. According to Herbord, there were four temples (*continae*) in Stettin when Otto arrived. The principal one, called the temple of Triglav, was built with amazing reverence and skill. Herbord called the cultic buildings *contina*, which is equivalent to old slave *kančina* ('temple'). After describing the principal temple and a three-headed-idol, he states:

> There was also a huge oak-tree with lots of leaves there, and a most pleasant spring near it. The simple people regarded it as seat of a deity and held it in great esteem (*Herbordi Vita Ottonis Ep. Babenb*: Pertz 1856, 794).

The ritual structure including temple, tree and well reminds us of Uppsala. It should be noted that Stettin, like Uppsala, was a site associated with rulers.

CONCLUSIONS

In this paper, I have argued that Adam's description of Uppsala is based, if not in detail at least in essence, on reliable information regarding the cultic building, the tree and the well. Since cultic halls, in combination with specific trees and/or wells, lakes or bogs, recur at other places, I suggest that this structure reflects a wide spread cosmological tradition. The mythical symbolism seen at Uppsala had several functions. On a religious level, it indicated that this site was a threshold to the divine world. At this place, man could meet the divine powers by means of performing rituals such as sacrifices. It had also ideological and power implications for the rulers of Uppsala. When the ruler appeared, the scene needed to be set with specific properties. Religious symbols, such as representations of the cosmic hall, tree and well, created the appearance that the ruler's authority came from a realm beyond politics, society and the natural world. Aspects of such symbolism and ideology are also observable at other rulers' sites in Scandinavia and, perhaps also, on the continent.

BIBLIOGRAPHY

Alkarp, M. 1997. 'Källan, lunden och templet: Adam av Bremens Uppsalaskildring i ny belysning', *Fornvännen*, 92, 155–61.

Andrén, A. 2002. 'Platsernas betydelse: norrön ritual och kultplatskontinuitet' in J. Jennbert et al. (eds), *Plats och praxis: studier av nordisk förkristen ritual*, Vägar till Midgård, 2 (Lund), pp 299–342.

Andrén, A. 2004. 'I skuggan av Yggdrasil: trädet mellan idé realitet i nordisk tradition' in A. Andrén et al. (eds), *Ordning mot kaos: studier av nordisk förkristen kosmologi*, Vägar till Midgård, 4 (Lund), pp 389–430.

Boretius, A. (ed.). 1883. *Capitulatio de partibus Saxoniae*, Monumenta Germaniae Historica, Legum Sectio II, Capitularia Regum Francorum, 1 (Hanover).

Brink, S. 2001. 'Mythologizing landscape: place and space of cult and myth' in M. Stausberg et al. (eds), *Kontinuitäten und brüche in der religionsgeschichte: festschrift für Anders Hultgård zu seinem 65, Geburtstag am 23.12.2001* (Berlin & New York), pp 76–112.

Bruun, D. & Finnur Jónsson. 1909. 'Om hove og hovudgravninger på Island', *Aarbøger for nordisk Oldkyndighed og Historie*, 2:24, 245–316.

Carlie, A. 2000. 'Käringsjön: en offerplats för bondebefolkning eller ledarskikt? Studier kring en romartida kultplats och dess omland i södra Halland', *Tor*, 30, 123–64.

Damell, D. 1980. 'Om en fosfatkarta över fornminnesområdet vid Gamla Uppsala' in Å. Hyenstrand (ed.), *Inventori in honorem: en vänbok till Folke Hallberg* (Stockholm), pp 64–7.

Dillmann, F.-X. 1997. 'Kring de rituella gästabuden i fornskandinavisk religion' in A. Hultgård (ed.), *Uppsalakulten och Adam av Bremen* (Nora), pp 51–73.

Dronke, U. (ed.). 1997. *The Poetic Edda, II: mythological poems* (Oxford).

Eliade, M. 1957 [1987]. *The sacred and the profane: the nature of religion* [trans. W.R. Trask, *Das Heilige und das Profane*] (San Diego, New York & London).

Fabech Ch. 1994. 'Reading society from the cultural landscape: south Scandinavia between sacral and political power' in P.O. Nielsen et al. (eds), *The archaeology of Gudme and Lundeborg* (Copenhagen), pp 169–83.

Faulkes, A. (ed.) 1988. *Edda: prologue and Gylfaginning* (London).

Gräslund, A.-S. 1997. 'Adams Uppsala: och arkeologins' in A. Hultgård (ed.), *Uppsalakulten och Adam av Bremen* (Nora), pp 101–15.

Guðni Jónsson & B. Vilhjálmsson (eds). 1943. *Völsunga saga*, Fornaldar sögur Norðurlanda, 1 (Reykjavík).

Hagberg, U. 1967–77. *The archaeology of Skedemosse I–IV* (Stockholm).

Hedeager, L. 2001. '*Asgard* Reconstructed? Gudme: A "Central Place" in the North' in M. de Jong et al. (eds), *Topographies of power in the early Middle Ages* (Leiden), pp 467–507.

Heggstad, L. et al. 1930 [1993]. *Norrøn ordbok* (Oslo).

Herschend, F. 1999. 'Halle' in H. Beck et al. (eds), *Reallexikon der Germanischen Altertumskunde*, 13, 414–25.

Hultgård, A. 1997. 'Från ögonvittnesskildring till retorik. Adam av Bremens notiser om Uppsalakulten i religionshistorisk belysning' in A. Hultgård (ed.), *Uppsalakulten och Adam av Bremen* (Nora), pp 9–50.

Ilkjær, J. 1990. *Illerup Ådal. 1: die lanzen und speere. Textband*, Jutland Archaeological Society Publications, 25:1 (Aarhus).

Iregren, E. 1989. 'Under Frösö kyrka: ben från en vikingatida offerlund?' in L. Larsson & B. Wyszomirska (eds), *Arkeologi och religion: rapport från arkeologidagarna, 16–18 januari 1989*, University of Lund Institute of Archaeology Report Series, 34 (Lund), pp 119–33.

Jansson, S.B.F. 1963 [1987]. *Runes in Sweden* (Stockholm).

Jón Helgason (ed.). 1924. *Hervarar saga. Heiðreks saga. Hervarar saga ok Heiðreks konungs* (Copenhagen).

Jørgensen, L. 2002. 'Kongsgård – kusted – marked: overvejelser omkring Tissøkompleksets struktur og funktion' in K. Jennbert et al. (eds), *Plats och praxis: studier av nordisk förkristen ritual*, Vägar till Midgård, 2 (Lund), pp 215–47.

Maasen, F. (ed.). 1893. *Concilium Turonense*, Monumenta Germaniae Historica, Legum Sectio, 3, Concilia, 1, Concilia Aevi Merovingici (Hanover).

McCutcheon, R.T. 1997. *Manufacturing religion: the discourse on* sui generis *religion and the politics of nostalgia* (Oxford).

Neckel, G. & H. Kuhn (eds). 1914 [1983]. *Edda: Die Lieder des Codex Regius. Nebst verwandten Denkmälern*, 1 (Heidelberg).

Nordahl, E. 1996. *... templum quod Ubsola dicitur ... i arkeologisk belysning*, Aun, 22 (Uppsala).

Pertz, H. (ed.). 1829. *Translatio S. Alexandri*, Monumenta Germaniae Historica, Scriptorum, 2 (Hanover).

Pertz, H. (ed.). 1856. *Herbordi Vita Ottonis Ep. Babenb*, Monumenta Germaniae Historica, Scriptorum, 12 (Hanover).

Schmeidler, B. (ed.). 1917. *Magistri Adam Bremensis Gesta Hammaburgensis Ecclesiae Pontificium*, Scriptores Rerum Germanicarum in Usum Scholarum, Ex Monumentis Germaniae Historicis, 3rd ed. (Hanover).

Simek, R. 1984 [1995]. *Lexikon der germanischen Mythologie* (Stuttgart).

Słupecki, L.P. 1993. 'Die Slawischen tempel und die frage des sakralen raumes bei den Westslawen in vorchristlichen Zeiten', *Tor*, 25, 247–98.

Ström, F. 1961. 'Heliga träd', *Kulturhistoriskt lexikon för nordisk medeltid*, 6, 373–4.

Sundqvist, O. 2002. *Freyr's offspring: rulers and religion in Ancient Svea Society*, Acta Universitatis Upsaliensis, Historia Religionum, 21 (Uppsala).

Söderberg, B. 2005. *Aristokratiskt rum och gränsöverskridande: Järrestad och sydöstra Skåne mellan region och rike 600–1100*, Riksantikvarieämbetet Arkeologiska undersökningar Skrifter, 62 (Lund).

Vikstrand, P. 'Förkristna sakrala ortnamn i Jämtland', *Namn och bygd*, 81, 49–84.

Zachrisson, T. 2004. 'The holiness of Helgö' in H. Clarke & K. Lamm (eds), *Excavations at Helgö XVI: exotic and sacral finds from Helgö*, Kungl. Vitterhets Historie och Antikvitets Akademien (Stockholm), pp 143–75.

The making of a centre: the case of Reykholt, Iceland

GUÐRÚN SVEINBJARNARDÓTTIR

INTRODUCTION

Unlike in Scandinavia, permanent urban centres do not seem to have developed in Iceland in the medieval period. But centres where people met seasonally, both to trade and hold assemblies, are known from early on and, by the late thirteenth century, when fishing became more common as an industry, camps were created where fishermen stayed during the winter fishing season. A historical explanation for the non-development of permanent urban centres in Iceland in the medieval period is, on the one hand, poverty and the small size of the population and, on the other, a political decision made by parliament which was initiated by chieftains fearing competition with foreign traders for the workforce. Foreigners were banned from overwintering in fishing camps and the Icelandic people were not permitted to live permanently in them (Helgi Þorláksson 1979, 159–60). So far, archaeology has not contributed much to the debate. This is due to change, however, with the completion of the investigations currently taking place at two of the known medieval trading centres, Gásir in Eyjafjörður and Kolkuós in Skagafjörðun, both in the north of Iceland.

The rest of the North Atlantic area settled by the Norse, namely the Scottish Isles, the Faroe Islands and Greenland, was also sparsely populated, thus lacking the basis for a permanent urban society. Although some evidence of medieval urban development is emerging from the Scottish Isles (Owen 2005), no such evidence is available from either the Faroes or Greenland. Trading centres may yet be discovered in these areas, but trade may also have been carried out largely at or through major religious and political centres. There is evidence of this, for example, at the bishop's seat at Garðar in Greenland, where a quantity of the bone around the walrus tusk root (walrus *maxilla*) was found during archaeological investigations, walrus ivory being the main trade item in Greenland in medieval times (McGovern 1985). This seems to indicate that this product was prepared for export at the site.

The political, religious and cultural centres of Iceland's Commonwealth period (AD930–1262) possessed the means to produce and exchange goods and are therefore likely to have served an important function in that area. The basis of wealth lay in agriculture during this period, so these centres were located in areas of good farming land. As a result, many of them were located far from the

seashore. One of these centres is Reykholt in Borgarfjörður (Fig. 45.1), which
was one of the earliest church centres in the country and the estate of the writer
and chieftain Snorri Sturluson during the first half of the thirteenth century.
This site forms the core of the Reykholt project, which involves archaeological,
historical, environmental and literary research (Guðrún Sveinbjarnardóttir
2000). One of the aims of the project is to investigate what role land-use played
in the process of centralization of power in the Commonwealth period. Much of
the environmental work in the Reykholt area has been carried out by members
of the 'Landscapes circum *landnám*' project (Edwards et al. 2004), funded by the
Leverhulme Trust. In this paper, some of the historical, archaeological and
environmental evidence, which throws light on the rise of Reykholt as a centre,
is discussed.

THE HISTORICAL BACKGROUND

The whole of Borgarfjörður, where the farm Reykholt is located, is thought to
have been acquired by the chieftain Skallagrímr, one of the earliest settlers
(*Landnámabók*, 70–1; *Egils saga*, 72–5). He built his farm at Borg, from where
the name of the area is derived. According to the sources, he gave or sold sections
of his land to other settlers, including the one who took the tongue of land
between the rivers Hvítá and Reykjadalsá, and lived at Breiðabólstaður
(*Landnámabók*, 74). Reykholt was established on this land. The medieval written
sources indicate that the whole area was rapidly divided up into individual
holdings.

Although Reykholt is only mentioned in *Landnámabók* as the location of a
warm pool used by the inhabitants of Breiðabólstaður, which lies *c.*1km further
east and up the hill, there are indications in the same source of early occupation
at the site. This is now supported by radiocarbon dates from charred barley from
the earliest occupation levels, with the date-range falling between the late tenth
and mid twelfth centuries (SUERC-8208: 950±35BP, cal. AD1010–1170.
SUERC-8207: 975±35BP, cal. AD990–1160).

One of the earliest settlers, Úlfr Grímsson, took the land between the Hvítá
river and the glaciers to the south and lived in Geitland, an inland area *c.*25km
due east of Reykholt. According to *Landnámabók*, a relative of his lived at
Reykholt four generations later (*Landnámabók*, 77–8), an estimated eighty to a
hundred years after the date of the initial phase of settlement. The connection
between Reykholt and Geitland is reflected in the earliest preserved church
charter from the late twelfth century (*DI* I: 279–80), where Geitland is listed as
one of the resource areas belonging to Reykholt. It is generally accepted that
Landnámabók, preserved in a thirteenth-century version and based on a lost
twelfth-century one, should be regarded as reflecting the needs of the time in

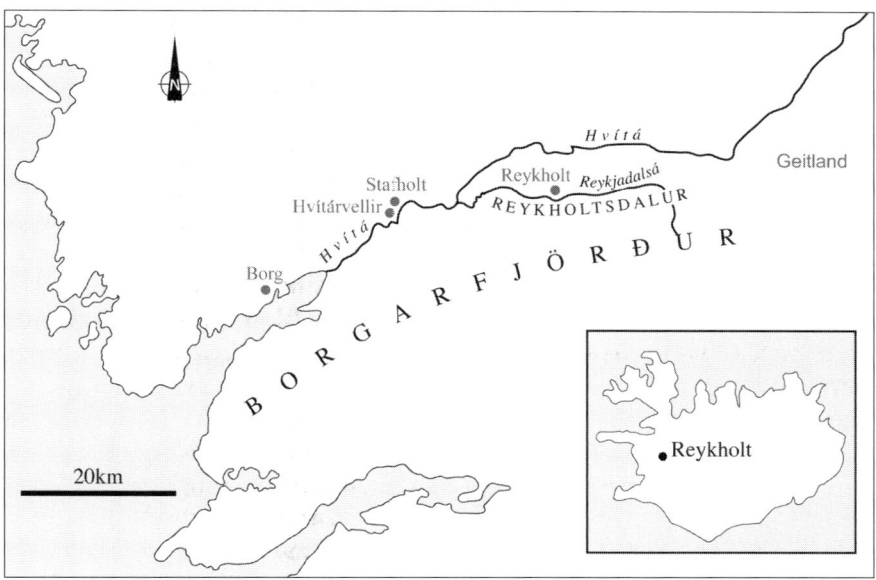

45.1 Location map showing Reykholt and some of the sites mentioned in the text.

which it was written rather than as an accurate account of the settlement process. One suggestion is that the main reason for its compilation was to register land ownership (Sveinbjörn Rafnsson 1974), which might serve to explain the connection displayed in it between Reykholt and Geitland as an attempt to secure Reykholt's ownership of a valuable resource.

An alternative hypothesis is that Geitland was indeed an early settlement site. With its good grazing land, but thin soil-cover that was subject to erosion by wind-blown sand and glacial rivers, it is a typical candidate for an early inland settlement where, typically, occupation did not last for long (Guðrún Sveinbjarnardóttir 1992). Other farm-sites are known in the area (Guðmundur Ólafsson 1996, 74–81), although they have not been investigated and their dates of occupation are therefore not known. It seems a legitimate hypothesis that Geitland's connection in the written sources with Reykholt indicates that its occupants may have moved away to settle at Reykholt, having secured the land from Breiðabólstaður, keeping Geitland as an area providing extra resources. Archaeological investigations might just establish which of the above hypotheses is more likely to be true.

The earliest archaeological evidence from Reykholt indicates that the site may have been settled as early as *c.*AD1000, at about the time Christianity was introduced into Iceland. Although the date of the earliest church, still under investigation, has yet to be established, these new dates seem to put to rest the suggestion that the reason for the establishment of the farm so close to the site of Breiðabólstaður was that a church was first erected at the site, the location being attractive on account of the warm pool (Orri Vésteinsson 1996, 79–92; Helgi Þorláksson 1998, 52–3). The proximity to the hot spring may have been a deciding factor when the decision was taken to establish a farm in this location. There is ample archaeological evidence – especially in the form of stone-built conduits – for the use of the geothermal resource from early on. These and other impressive constructions discovered at the site are also a sign of its high status (Guðrún Sveinbjarnardóttir 2005; 2006).

There are several indications that Reykholt had become the central farm in the area, as well as a church centre, by the early twelfth century (Helgi Þorláksson 2000, 13; Benedikt Eyþórsson 2003, 21–2). The first noteworthy chieftain in residence was Páll Sölvason, who lived there in the mid twelfth century (*DI* I: 186), and it was from his son that Snorri Sturluson acquired Reykholt for himself and moved there in *c*.1206 (*Sturlunga saga* I: 241–2). Between then and the High Middle Ages, the estate became considerably richer through Snorri's marriages, both his own and those he arranged for other members of his family.

THE CHURCH

The key to Reykholt becoming a major estate seems to have been the establish- ment and good management of the church, which became a major church with a resident priest in the twelfth century (Benedikt Eyþórsson 2005, 55–6). The earliest churches in Iceland were private, established by individual farmers who endowed property to them. Gradually these churches accumulated more wealth through gifts and as a result of good management by those who ran them. If we assume that a farm was established at Reykholt around AD1000, together with a church, the initial farmer must have been a person of reasonable means. He may have been a descendant of one of the initial settlers who were, on the whole, prosperous farmers and chieftains, providing further support for his connection to the initial settlement site in Geitland.

The earliest church charters state that the church owns the homeland plus three neighbouring holdings: Breiðabólstaður and Reykir with the cottage Háfur on the north side of the river, and Hægindi on the south side (*DI* I: 466–80). Estimates of farm boundaries in the valley in the medieval period, based on various strands of evidence (Fig. 45.2), show that the Reykholt estate is the largest in area, but topographical analysis has revealed that it does not contain most of the best type of farming land – the marshland which lies, lower down, at the mouth of the valley (Guðrún Sveinbjarnardóttir et al. in prep.). The land rises inland, and soils get thinner and less fertile. Reykholt lies in the middle of the valley, at the inland edge of which this change in the land begins to have

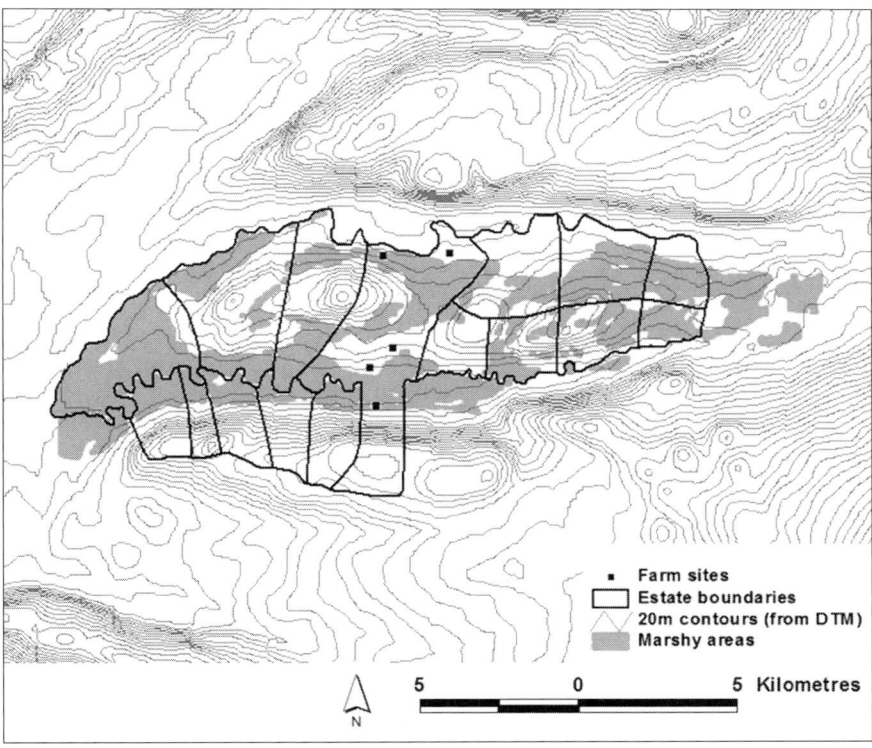

45.2 Map showing estimated boundaries in the medieval period and the location of farm-sites within the Reykholt estate (adapted from Orri Vésteinsson et al. 2002).

effect. The farm lies at the junction of major medieval communication routes (Tryggvi Már Ingvarsson 2001, 32), which may have been a deciding factor in its success. Since the land was neither of top quality nor particularly extensive, the prosperity of the estate will have depended heavily on the extra resources it owned as well as on good management. The Reykholtsdalur valley does not provide any mountain pasture areas, so these had to be sought further afield. According to the twelfth-century charter, Reykholt owned a shieling area and fishing rights in Kjarardalur, woodland in Sanddalur and Þverárhlíð, and grazing in Hrútafjarðarheiði, all to the north of the large glacial river Hvítá, grazing in Faxadalur to the south, as well as in Geitland in the interior, where there was also woodland (*DI* I: 279–80) (Fig. 45.3). Woodland was important as a source of fuel and for iron-working, and grazing areas and shielings were an important part of the economy which was based on animal farming. The main products that could be exchanged for imported wares were cloth and butter, before fish became the main export.

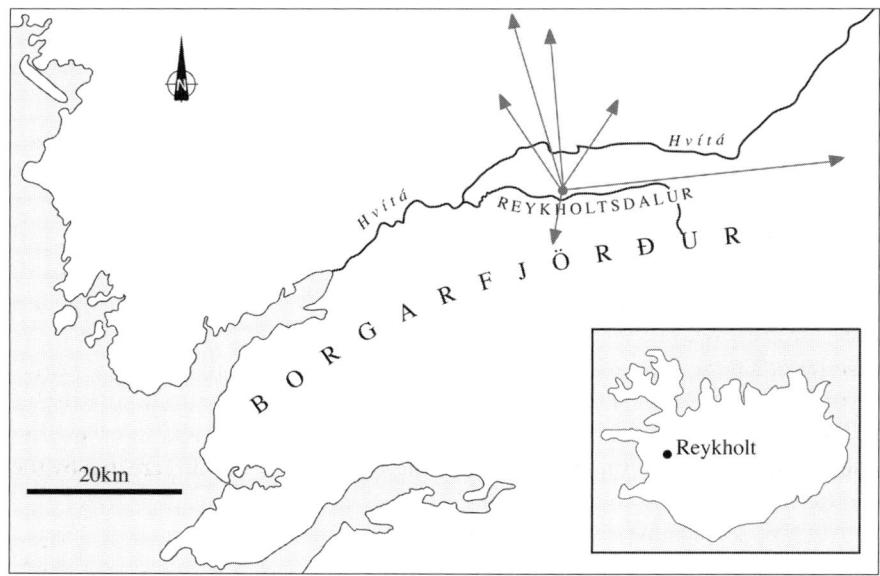

45.3 Map showing locations of resource areas belonging to Reykholt in the late twelfth century.

THE ENVIRONMENTAL AND ARCHAEOLOGICAL INVESTIGATIONS

One of the aims of the Reykholt project is to try to explain the success of an estate like Reykholt on the basis of its management and use of resources. For this purpose, soil samples have been taken, both within and outside the site, and subjected to palaeo-ecological analysis in order to throw light on the economy of the farm. Some of the results (Guðrún Sveinbjarnardóttir et al., 2007) are reported below.

There is evidence to support the account in the twelfth-century charter of cereal-growing at the site. The charred barley grains, which fall between the late tenth and mid-twelfth centuries, may have been grown locally on account of their small size, indicating poor growing conditions. Weeds associated with the grains also support their possible local origin (Hillman 1991). Cereal production in medieval Iceland was limited and confined to climatically suitable areas. This type of agriculture was a sign of high status, and will have enhanced the economic status of the farm considerably. Cereal-growing is mentioned in the 1224 church charter (*DI* I: 466), but not in 1358 (*DI* III: 122–3), indicating that by that time it had been abandoned. This form of agriculture is thought to have been abandoned everywhere in Iceland by the fifteenth century, when cheap cereal became available from abroad (Björn Þorsteinsson 1980).

A midden at the site, radiocarbon-dated to between the late tenth and mid-thirteenth centuries on the basis of samples from sheep and cattle bones, charred seeds and barley (SUERC-267: 875±45BP, cal. AD1030–1260; SUERC-164: 915±40BP, cal. AD1020–1210; SUERC-163: 930±65BP, cal. AD980–1250), produced large quantities of a beetle remains. The dominant species, *Aglenus brunneus*, is characteristic of foul grain residues and other warm man-made accumulations, such as rotting vegetation and manure. It was probably introduced to the site in imported grain, and its survival may be connected to the warmth provided by the hot springs. Barley grains were found in the deposit. Barley was used for brewing, but there is not enough evidence to suggest that this was the case here. There is an account in *Sturlunga saga* (I: 315) of Christmas drinks being served at Reykholt by Snorri Sturluson in 1226 following a Norwegian fashion, indicating that this was regarded as unusual in Iceland and was therefore a sign of high status. If the drinks were home-brewed, the warmth created by the geothermal resources would certainly have facilitated the brewing process.

A seal bone, retrieved from the same midden, as well as one found at the neighbouring cottage farm site Háls, which was occupied between the mid-tenth and late thirteenth centuries (Smith 1995, 334), demonstrates that this inland area had access to maritime resources. Fish bones from the midden indicate a trade in fish. At this time the nearest trading centre lay *c.*25km to the west of the site.

TRADE AND TRADING GOODS

The site of the trading centre is frequently referred to in medieval sources. It lay on the Hvítá river, close to the farm Hvítárvellir. It was one of the main harbours and trading centres in Iceland, operated from the late twelfth century or earlier until *c.*1340, when it was replaced by a harbour in Hvalfjörður. The latter location was a more suitable site for trade in dried fish, which was by then a major trade item (Helgi Þorláksson 1979).

The other main trading centres, contemporary with Hvítá, were Eyrar on the south coast, now the location of the village Eyrarbakki, where no remains of the medieval centre are recorded, and Gásir in the north, where building remains are being investigated. At Kolkuós in Skagafjörður, also under investigation, remains of a medieval trading place are being eroded away by the sea. It is possible that the site at Hvítá suffered a similar fate, caused by the river, which has changed its course through the centuries. Alternatively, it may have been obscured by deposits brought in by the river. A recent geophysical survey in the area did not identify a definite location for the site (Horsley 2006).

There was a local assembly close by, probably also used for seasonal trading. All this activity shows the importance of this area in the medieval period. During the first half of the thirteenth century, it was presided over by Snorri Sturluson who, according to *Sturlunga saga* (I: 271, 304, 335), used the harbour frequently. Wares would have been brought to the country from far away places in exchange for locally produced items. There is, for example, a reference to cereal being landed at Hvítá in 1202 (*Sturlunga saga* I: 240).

Before fish became the main export item, homespun cloth (*vaðmál*) served this role. This and dairy products, also an important trade item, were products of sheep-rearing, the main type of animal husbandry practiced, some of which took place at shieling sites within the mountain pastures. Several such sites are associated with Reykholt from early on. In the late twelfth-century charter, a shieling in Kjararardalur, north of the Hvítá river, is mentioned (*DI* I: 279–80). The sources indicate that it was moved down the valley in the sixteenth century, perhaps as a result of erosion which is evident in the area, and this has been supported by radiocarbon dates obtained on charcoal thought to belong to the last occupation phase (SUERC-512: 395±35BP, cal. AD1430–1530; SUERC-5122: 290±35BP, cal. AD1480–1670). There may also have been a shieling in Geitland, although such activity at the site is not mentioned in the earliest sources. In Faxadalur, the grazing area to the south of Reykholt, there are building remains, but the site is first referred to as a shieling in *c*.1600 only. Three other places may have had shielings belonging to Reykholt, but these are less certain.

Although there is limited information in the written sources about the imports brought to Hvítárvellir, they are likely to have included iron for making tools. Evidence of iron-working, in the form of slag, was found at the Reykholt site. Wood for house-building is another likely import. There are several accounts of building activities at Reykholt in *Sturlunga saga*, one of which tells of wood being fetched from Skagafjörður in the north in 1233 for building a living room (*stofa*) (I: 362). It seems likely, in this instance, that the wood was imported and that it was being transported from Kolkuós, the trading centre in Skagafjörður. It seems unlikely that it was driftwood, since Reykholt did not own rights to driftwood in the north at this time, but rather in the Western Fjords (*DI* III: 122–3). Wood samples from the site have been analyzed and identified as both imported wood and driftwood (Ólafur Eggertsson 2006). The right to collect driftwood was an important economic asset, the largest holders of which were the church farms. These were also the households with the economic means to import wood.

The artefacts found at the site give some idea of the types of imports brought into the site in the medieval period, when the trading centre on Hvítá was in operation. In addition to cereal, they include pottery from England and Germany, window glass, a glass beaker from France and various metal objects (Guðrún Sveinbjarnardóttir and Aldred 2006). All of these finds indicate the high status of the site.

CONCLUSION

Various strands of evidence suggest that Reykholt was established as a farm, at about the same time that Christianity was introduced into Iceland, by a prosperous farmer who erected a church at the site. It was located close to the initial farm in the Reykholtsdalur valley, and took over its role as the central place. The choice of location may have been influenced by the proximity of the site to hot springs. The heat generated is likely to have benefited cereal cultivation, mentioned in the written sources, and archaeological evidence shows that hot water and steam were channelled into the farm site. The homeland was neither extensive nor particularly good quality, but through the church the farm acquired additional resource areas in far away places. It was, therefore, already well established as a centre when Snorri Sturluson took it over in the first half of the thirteenth century.

The wealth of the site doubtless served as a major appeal to Snorri, but its other advantages seem to have played a part too. Before he acquired Reykholt, he owned Stafholt, another equally wealthy church centre that was located close to a local assembly site and a trading centre. Despite this, Snorri chose to make Reykholt the centre of his domain. A major factor in this choice may have been its location in the centre of the area over which he presided, and the fact that it stood at the junction of the main communication routes to the west, northwest and south. The importance of this is emphasized in an account in *Sturlunga saga* (I: 303–4), when Snorri holds his daughter's wedding at Reykholt, despite the fact that he is at the time residing at Stafholt, in order to make it easier for the Bishop of Skálholt to attend. The attraction of the easily accessible hot water is also clearly evident from the many references in *Sturlunga saga* (I: 319, 388, 456) to the warm pool at the site and to Snorri spending time in it.

BIBLIOGRAPHY

DI I = Sigurðsson, J. (ed.). 1857–76. *Diplomatarium Islandicum, 834–1264*, Íslenzkt fornbréfasafn, 1 (Copenhagen).
DI III = Þorkelsson, J. (ed.). 1896. *Diplomatarium Islandicum, 1296–1415*, Íslenzkt fornbréfasafn, 3 (Copenhagen).
Edwards, K.J., P.C., Buckland, A.J. Dugmore, T.H. McGovern, I.A. Simpson & G. Sveinbjarnardóttir. 2004. 'Landscapes *circum landnám*: Viking settlement in the North Atlantic and its human and ecological consequences – a major new research programme' in R.A. Housley & G. Coles (eds), *Atlantic connections and adaptations: economies, environments and subsistence in lands bordering on the North Atlantic*, Symposia of the Association for Environmental Archaeology, 21 (Oxford), pp 260–71.
Egils saga = Nordal, S. (ed.). 1933. *Egils saga Skalla-Grímssonar*, Íslenzk fornrit, 2 (Reykjavík).
Eyþórsson, B. 2003. 'Í þjónustu Snorra', *Sagnir*, 23, 20–6.

Eyþórsson, B. 2005. 'History of the Icelandic Church, 1000–1300: status of research' in Þorláksson H. (ed.), *Church centres: church centres in Iceland from the 11th to the 13th century and their parallels in other countries* (Akranes), pp 19–69.

Guðmundur Ólafsson. 1996. *Friðlýstar fornleifar í Borgarfjarðarsýslu*. Rit Hins íslenska fornleifafélags og Þjóðminjasafns Íslands, 2 (Reykjavík).

Guðrún Sveinbjarnardóttir. 1992. *Farm abandonment in medieval and post-medieval Iceland: an interdisciplinary study*, Oxbow Monograph, 17 (Oxford).

Guðrún Sveinbjarnardóttir (ed.). 2000. *Reykholt in Borgarfjörður: an interdisciplinary research project*, Workshop held 20–21 August 1999 (Reykjavík).

Guðrún Sveinbjarnardóttir. 2005. 'The use of geothermal resources at Reykholt in Borgarfjörður in the medieval period: some preliminary results' in A. Mortensen & S.V. Arge (eds), *Viking and Norse North Atlantic: select papers from the proceedings of the Fourteenth Viking Congress, Tórshavn, 19–30 July 2001* (Tórshavn), pp 208–16.

Guðrún Sveinbjarnardóttir. 2006. 'Reykholt, a centre of power: the archaeological evidence' in E. Mundal (ed.), *Reykholt som makt- og lærdomssenter* (Reykholt), pp 25–42.

Guðrún Sveinbjarnardóttir & O. Aldred. 2006. *Reykholtskirkja. Fornleifárannsókn 2006* (Interim Report), National Museum of Iceland (Reykjavík).

Guðrún Sveinbjarnardóttir, E. Erlendsson, K. Vickers, T.H. McGovern, K.B. Milek, K.J. Edwards, I.A. Simpson, I.A. & G. Cook. 2007. 'The palaeoecology of a high status Icelandic farm'. *Environmental Archaeology*, 12.2, 187–206.

Guðrún Sveinbjarnardóttir, I.A. Simpson & A.M. Thomson, in prep. 'Landscapes circum *Landnám*: integrated historical and topographical analysis of settlements in Reykholtsdalur, Iceland'.

Helgi Þorláksson. 1979. 'Miðstöðvar stærstu byggða', *Saga*, 1979, 125–64.

Helgi Þorláksson. 1998. 'Hruni: um mikilvægi staðarins fyrir samgöngur, völd og kirkjulegt starf á þjóðveldisöld'. *Árnesingur*, 5, 9–72.

Helgi Þorláksson. 2000. 'Icelandic society and Reykholt in the twelfth and thirteenth centuries with special reference to Snorri Sturluson' in Guðrún Sveinbjarnardóttir (ed.), *Reykholt in Borgarfjörður: an interdisciplinary research project*, Workshop held 20–21 August 1999 (Reykjavík), 11–20.

Hillman, G. 1991. 'Charred remains of grains and seeds from the site Reykholt in Iceland'. Unpublished report.

Horsley, T.J. 2006. *Hvítárvellir, Borgarfjörður, Iceland*. Report on Geophysical Surveys, April – May 2005, for Snorrastofa.

Landnámabók = Jakob Benediktsson (ed.). 1968. *Íslendingabók. Landnámabók*, Íslenzk fornrit, 1 (Reykjavík).

McGovern, T.H. 1985. 'The arctic frontier of Norse Greenland' in S. Green & S. Perlman (eds), *The archaeology of frontiers and boundaries* (New York), pp 275–323.

Ólafur Eggertsson. 2006. 'Viðargreiningar', appendix 2 in Guðrún Sveinbjarnardóttir & O. Aldred, *Reykholtskirkja: Fornleifárannsókn 2006*. National Museum of Iceland (Reykjavík), 24.

Orri Vésteinsson. 1996. 'The Christianization of Iceland' (unpublished PhD thesis, University College London).

Orri Vésteinsson, T.H. McGovern & C. Keller. 2002. 'Enduring impacts: social and environmental aspects of Viking-Age settlement in Iceland and Greenland', *Archaeologia Islandica*, 2, 98–136.

Owen, O. 2005. 'Scotland's Viking 'towns': a contradiction in terms?' in A. Mortensen & S.V. Arge (eds), *Viking and Norse North Atlantic: select papers from the proceedings of the Fourteenth Viking Congress, Tórshavn, 19–30 July 2001* (Tórshavn), pp 297–306.

Smith, K.P. 1995. '*Landnám*: the settlement of Iceland in archaeological and historical perspective', *World Archaeology*, 26:3, 319–47.

Sturlunga saga = Jón Jóhannesson et al. (eds). 1946. *Sturlunga saga* (Reykjavík).

Sveinbjörn Rafnsson. 1974. *Studier i Landnámabók* (Lund).

Sveinbjörnsdóttir, Á., J. Heinemeier, & G. Guðmundsson. 2004. '14C dating of the settlement of Iceland', *Radiocarbon*, 46:1, 387–94.

Þorsteinsson, B. 1980. *Íslensk miðaldasaga* (Reykjavík).

Tryggvi Már Ingvarsson. 2001. 'Leiðir tveggja alda í nágrenni Reykholts í Borgarfirði' (BA thesis, University of Iceland, Reykjavík).

Ethnicity and class in settlement-period Iceland

ORRI VÉSTEINSSON

INTRODUCTION

In AD880 – give or take a decade or so – one or two men built a hut on the shore of a small lake that forms part of a chain of lakes and ponds in an extensive marshland south of the great inland lake Mývatn, in Iceland's northeastern highlands. Mývatn is some 50km from the coast at 277m above sea level; a considerably higher altitude than most inhabitable parts of the country. While rich in fish and birdlife, Mývatn represented an extreme environment for the settlers who had begun to arrive there a few years previously. Barley cultivation had proved difficult and the yields of the milch-cows were far below what they were used to. There was, however, plenty of hay to be had on the lakeshores and in the marshlands south, west and north of the lake, and summer grazing was plentiful and easier to manage than in the more densely wooded lowlands. Winter grazing had proved surprisingly good too, because even if the winters were cold, the snowfall was light so the livestock could nearly always find snow-free patches or shrubs sticking up from the snow to graze. These conditions were proving to be consistent, and some of the settlers had begun to think of ways to make the most of the opportunities they presented. Some dreamed of sheep stations, others thought that large herds of cattle could be raised for beef production, while yet others believed that a cattle-dairy economy of the sort they were accustomed to in their homelands in Northern Europe could be established by increasing the number of milch-cows to offset the low milk yields.

Our hut-builders were the agents of one such cattle-dairy enthusiast who had chosen this site to establish a small dairy farm. The site was on a narrow strip of dry land covered in shrubs and the occasional willow and birch tree between the lakeshore and a vast lavafield stretching eastwards to the base of a high mountain range. The hut was so small, only 2.8m by 2m, that there was no room for a hearth in it (Fig. 46.3) and instead they built two pit-hearths outside the hut.

Once they had completed building the hut, a post-built structure with either wood planks or wattle filling the gaps between the posts, they started working on a byre (Fig. 46.2). This was to hold up to twenty head of cattle and so they stripped the turf off an area measuring 11m by 4.4m, creating a sunken feature at most 30cm deep. Along the central axis of this building they dug a channel and in this they placed stone slabs to make an even pavement for the greater ease of scooping out the manure. Later, possibly in the following year, they started work on a permanent dwelling. For this they dug a sub-rectangular pit, some

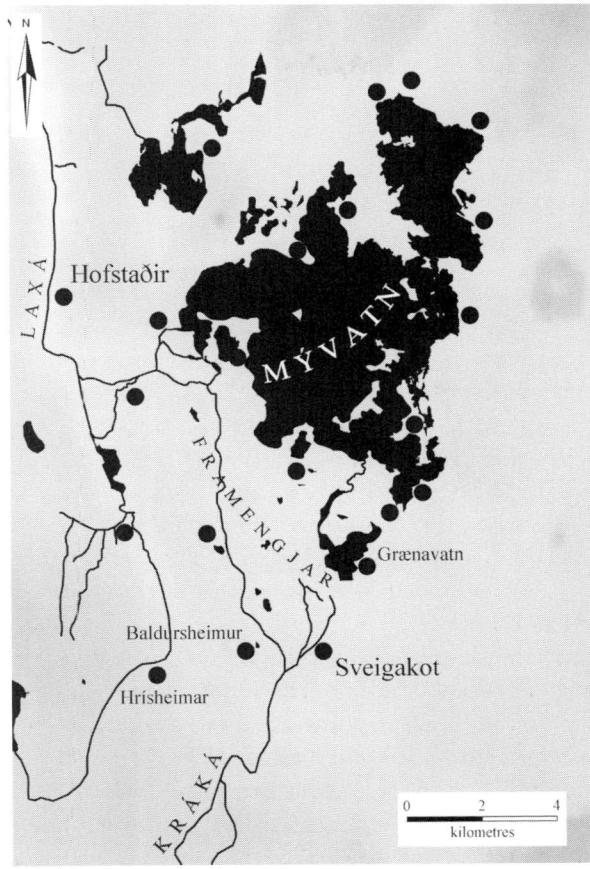

46.1 Map of Mývatnssveit showing places mentioned in the text. The dots indicate some of the farm sites likely to have been contemporary with Sveigakot.

60cm deep and 5m by 4m in area, down-slope of their hut (Fig. 46.4). Initially, this had a large entranceway facing onto the lakeshore only a few metres away. For the coming decades, this was the small farm's dwelling, housing at most a nuclear family, possibly only one or two individuals at a time. The interior was rearranged several times, the simple floor-level hearths shifted around repeatedly; possibly signifying frequent changes in occupancy.

This building had been abandoned by the middle of the tenth century – as had the byre – and other sunken-featured dwellings were built instead, one of them also showing signs of repeated remodelling (Figs 46.2 & 46.5). It was only in the second half of the tenth century, possibly in its final years, that a hall was built at the site (Plate 16). While very small, this is a typical Norse Viking-Age hall, with concave long walls, a three-aisled construction and a centrally placed hearth. By this time, the economy of the farm had changed. Attempts at large-scale dairy farming had long been abandoned, replaced by a greater emphasis on sheep rearing. The farm was already set on a downward spiral although it was to remain functioning – if intermittently – until the end of the twelfth century.

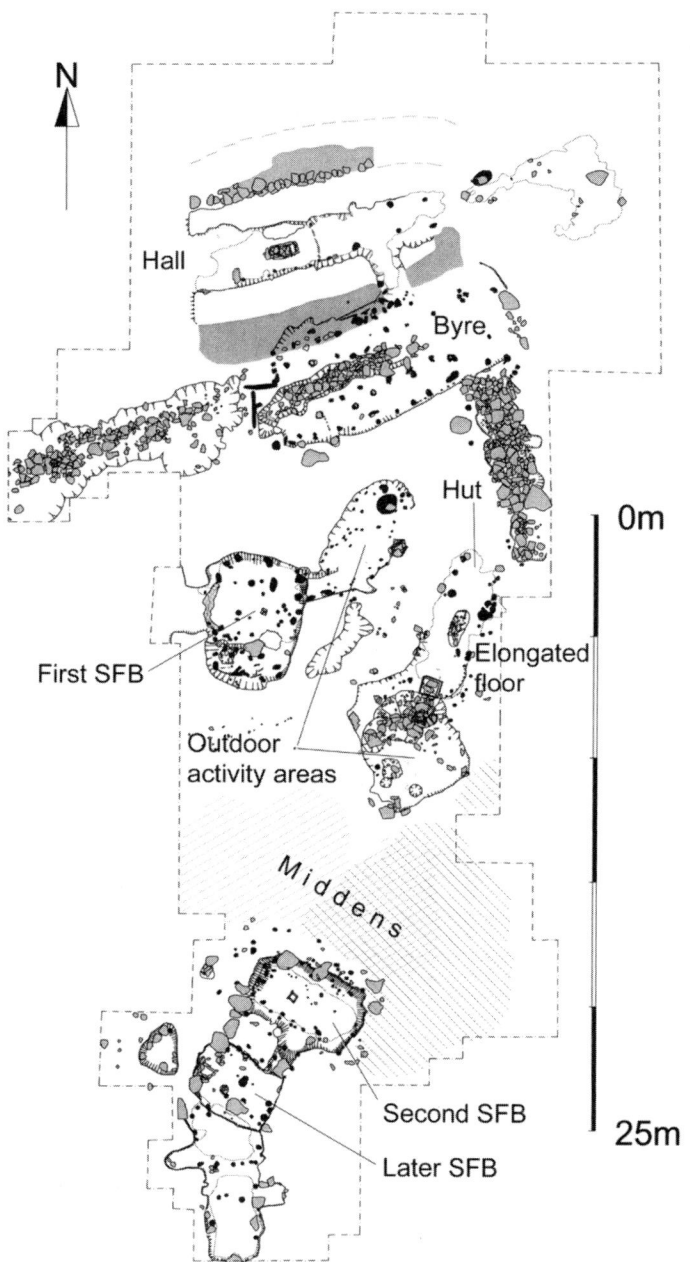

46.2 Plan of Sveigakot showing the main excavated features datable to the ninth and tenth centuries.

ARCHAEOLOGICAL RESULTS FROM SVEIGAKOT

The above description of events is based partly on the results of excavations in 1999–2006 at the site, which now goes by the name of Sveigakot, partly on educated guesses, and partly on pure speculation. As this paper is being written, the last season of fieldwork is barely over and much work remains unfinished in dating and analyzing individual features at the site. A fuller account of the archaeology of Sveigakot must therefore await another opportunity, but a number of important observations may be made, providing the basis for a discussion about ethnicity and class in settlement period Iceland.

Firstly, people had arrived in Sveigakot extremely early. In fact it is, along with Hrísheimar, located 4km due west (an apparently higher status site – Fig. 46.1), the earliest dated human settlement in northern Iceland. The occupation post-dates the *landnám* tephra of AD871±2 (Grönvold et al. 1995) but predates a mid-tenth-century tephra labelled V~940 (Sigurgeirsson et al. 2002; 2008). Occupation deposits lie directly on top of the *landnám* tephra, suggesting that people were there very soon after it had been deposited, and at least two buildings, the byre and the sunken-featured dwelling described above, had gone through several phases of remodelling and became abandoned before the deposition of the mid-tenth-century tephra. While a wide margin of error must be allowed, a guess of AD880 as a commencement date for the occupation is not unreasonable.

Secondly, Sveigakot was a very small farm. While the byre compares well in size with other recorded Viking-Age byres in Iceland – of which at least five examples are known, in addition to twelve byres in Þjórsárdalur dating to the eleventh to thirteenth centuries (Bruno Berson 2002) – indicating that the Sveigakot cattle were close to average in numbers, the domestic architecture of the site is of very small dimensions. The sunken-featured dwelling (Fig. 46.4) is less than half the size of the smallest halls so far known in Iceland – the later hall at Sveigakot and a late tenth-century hall at Eiríksstaðir in western Iceland (Guðmundur Ólafsson 2001), both little more than 40m². It is possible that the second sunken-featured dwelling (Fig. 46.5), measuring only 4.4m by 2.3m, was to begin with contemporary with the first one, thus adding a few square metres to the total living space, but even so there is hardly room for more than a single nuclear family – or a few farmhands, if Sveigakot was an outpost rather than a farm. Attempts at reconstructing the area and quality of land belonging to Sveigakot also suggest that this was a very modest holding, smaller in area and poorer in resources than the surrounding farms. Vegetated land belonging to Sveigakot cannot have covered much more than 3.5km², of which as much as 1.2km² may have been a lake. That makes it up to five times smaller than Hofstaðir, with 15km² (Simpson et al. 2004, 474–8). While the material culture of the post-V~940 deposits at Sveigakot compares well – in terms of absolute numbers and diversity – with the contemporary but apparently higher status

46.3 The initial hut under excavation, looking south.
46.4 The second sunken-featured building under excavation, looking south. The photograph shows the structure in its final stages when the pit had become largely infilled with floors and occupation debris and when a central hearth had been built, possibly suggesting influence from Norse hall architecture.

46.5 Aerial photo of Sveigakot showing its landscape setting, looking southeast. The site itself is left of centre and the area between it and the River Kráká would have been marshland or a lake in the Viking Age. Modern hay fields from the Baldursheimur farm can be seen in the top right corner.

sites at Hrísheimar and Hofstaðir, the artefact assemblage from the earliest phase of occupation at Sveigakot is both very small and nondescript. Against this, the animal bone assemblage from the early period at Sveigakot does not suggest a radically different herding strategy from other contemporary sites in the region – if there was a difference it was in the absolute numbers of livestock – and possible stress indicators are no more apparent at Sveigakot than the other sites (Thomas H. McGovern, pers. comm.). Taken together, the evidence seems to suggest a small holding originally aimed at maximum production with a minimal crew, which later became more balanced, with a larger household but a less intensive production strategy better suited to the local environment.

Thirdly, the domestic architecture excavated at Sveigakot is unique among the substantial corpus of Viking-Age farm sites in the North Atlantic. Sunken-featured buildings (SFBs) seem to have been ubiquitous on Icelandic Viking-Age farmsteads, where they are most commonly associated with halls and seem to have been used either as temporary shelters – often re-used when more permanent housing had been established – or as special-purpose buildings. Functions such as bath houses, weaving sheds and slaves' quarters have been suggested (Þór Magnússon 1973; Nanna Ólafsdóttir 1974; Guðmundur Ólafsson 1980; Einarsson

1992; Milek 2006, 210–47). These ancillary SFBs exhibit a number of similarities: they have oven-like fireplaces in or near one corner; they tend to produce few artefacts, with a high proportion of objects related to textile production; most of them show no signs of an entrance and their occupation layers tend to be very thin, suggesting short periods of use. Isolated SFBs have also been excavated (at sites like Gjáskógar and Hólmur – Milek 2006, 215), but these share the same general characteristics as those associated with halls. By contrast, the two main SFBs at Sveigakot have substantial and multiple floor layers, many types of hearths in various positions on the floor, very distinct entranceways and a very limited artefact assemblage with no particular indications of textile-working. Furthermore, they are not associated with a hall. It is possible, of course, that a hall belonged to the early phase of occupation and was situated some distance away from the preserved cluster of ruins, in an area now completely denuded. A scatter of lava stones imported to the site was recorded some 10m east of the excavation area, possibly indicating the former presence of a structure, but whether this was a hall and to which phase it belonged is impossible to say. It is also possible that a building which had been erected on top of the original hut, and which is believed to have been in use when the V~940 tephra was deposited, was a tiny hall (Fig. 46.2). Here a substantial floor-layer, measuring 6m by 2m with a centrally placed hearth, was excavated. This looks very much like the central aisle of a miniature hall, but as no indications whatsoever were found of the walls that would have belonged to such a structure, it seems unsafe to postulate that it was. Instead, it seems that this is a new type of structure, paralleled only by the final phase of the second sunken-featured dwelling at Sveigakot, when the original cut had become full of floor layers and occupation debris, and a larger building with a floor area of 7.3m by 3.2m and a central hearth was built on top (Fig. 46.5). These considerations aside, it is clear that the two main SFBs at Sveigakot were dwellings; they were in use for a long time and they are significantly different from SFBs found elsewhere in Iceland ancillary to halls. It is therefore unnecessary to postulate the existence of a contemporary hall at Sveigakot. Rather, it seems that these SFBs were the only dwellings at Sveigakot for the first two to three generations of its occupation and that the post-V~940 hall is the earliest one at the site, replacing the later sunken-featured dwelling and/or the curiously formed surface buildings already mentioned.

So, to sum up: Sveigakot is early, marginal and poor, and architecturally divergent from the norm. All these points raise a number of important questions relating to the origins, intentions and social relations of the people who colonized Iceland in the ninth and tenth centuries. First among these is perhaps: 'Why would anyone have wanted to cross the North Atlantic to live in a place like Sveigakot?' (Plate 17). The obvious answer, that nobody would have wanted to do so, has implications for our understanding of how the *landnám* was organized.

MODELS OF *LANDNÁM*

In traditional historiography, there are two principal models of how the *landnám* was organized, both of which were originally devised by thirteenth-century scholars. One is the 'farmer model' according to which the *landnám* was characterized by independent farmers, necessarily of some means, who left their patrimonies in Norway or the Norse colonies in Britain, sailed to Iceland on their own ships and claimed land for themselves and their descendants. It is clear that the compilers of *Landnámabók* ('The Book of Settlements') envisaged that such colonists would normally claim much more land than was needed for a single holding, but it is also clear that they envisaged that each such claim would, as a rule, only have one farmstead to begin with and that the claim would only start to be divided up as new generations came of age and established new farmsteads. According to this model, the infilling of the landscape would be a gradual business, with each original claim becoming divided into ten holdings on average as time went by. Ólafur Lárusson (1944, 24–32) presents a case-study of how this would work out. If this model were true, however, one would expect marginal places like Sveigakot and W48 in Greenland (Orri Vésteinsson et al. 2002, 106) to be established towards the end of the settlement process, not at its beginning as the archaeological evidence suggests.

The other model is sometimes called the 'slave model', but also the 'Skallagrímr model', the latter in reference to *Egils saga*'s famous description of Skallagrímr Kveldúlfsson's colonization of Borgarfjörður (72–8). According to this model, the settlement was characterized by large groups of people, led by a chieftain who claimed large tracts of land which were divided between followers and freedmen and the chieftain's own estates. The latter, in turn, could be split into a core farm and out-stations manned by slaves. Following this model, the colonization process could be a relatively speedy one and superficially, at least, it looks as if Sveigakot would fit this sort of scenario much better.

It is obvious that these two models have very different implications for the social structure that was to emerge: the farmer model resulting in a society made up of numerous small, culturally homogenous units, more or less similar in political and economic strength, whereas the slave model would imply fewer and larger such units, with a greater degree of ethnic diversity and social differentiation. The models are in no way mutually exclusive – both types of colonization can have taken place side by side – and few scholars have felt that they needed to select one above the other. It is also clear, however, that the farmer model has long been considered as the prevalent and most influential type of colonization that would have shaped the social order that emerged in Iceland during the course of the tenth century (see, for example, Byock 2001, 9–11; Gunnar Karlsson 2000, 14–15, 25–7).

Both models are simplistic and have not proven particularly useful when trying to make sense of the growing body of archaeological data relating to the colonization of Iceland. Nor have they proven useful in the analysis of settlement patterns. It is based on the analysis of settlement patterns that new hypotheses have been proposed (Orri Vésteinsson 1998; Orri Vésteinsson et al. 2002; 2006, 32–44) which regard the colonization as a complex process, where each stage has certain characteristics which should be identifiable archaeologically. A basic tenet of this new model is the distinction between large, complex settlements, often nucleated, which tend to occupy the best land and have access to the greatest range of resources, and smaller settlements which often occur in rows or groups and tend to be similar in size, with a more limited access to resources. These latter settlements were planned, representing more than two-thirds of all holdings in the country. The fact of the planning implies both a level of intent and organization that is not adequately explained by the farmer or slave models. These only seek to characterize the behaviour of individual colonists, as if each operated in complete isolation from anyone else. It makes more sense to theorize that the colonists' behaviour was dictated by the influence of other colonists, requiring a more dynamic model of explanation.

At some point in the ninth century successful farming settlements became established in Iceland. Somebody had to be first, but once it had been shown that people could survive in this new country, the settlements will have begun to multiply. We do not know whether this was a slow or fast process, but it must have reached a point at some stage where competition arose between the settlements. In the initial phase of colonization, when settlements were still few, survival will have been the colonists' main concern. Interaction between settlements is likely to have been limited, and characterized either by cooperation or attempts at annihilation, rather than competitive strategies. However, once a number of successful settlements had been established, it would have become easier for new colonists to establish new settlements, and the settlements will have begun to become concerned about their possibilities for expansion and the threat of encroachment from others. The only way to substantiate a claim and to prevent others from settling there is to settle it yourself, and for this people were needed. It is at this point that the colonization will have begun to progress very rapidly, with each settlement striving to fill the landscape it wanted to claim for itself with subject or dependent settlements. It is uncertain how difficult this was. Maybe the Icelandic colonists had great trouble convincing enough people to come and settle in their claims and had to resort to cunning schemes to get them to come – memories of such ploys may be preserved in the story of Eiríkr rauði's advertising methods for his new colony in Greenland (*Íslendingabók*, 13; *Landnámabók*, 132). Maybe there were hundreds of families in Norway and the Northern Isles of Scotland who were just waiting for the opportunity to have their own small farm in Iceland, and even made their way there themselves on the off-chance that they would make their dreams come true. Even if that was the case and eager colonists were arriving in droves, some early settlers will have had more trouble than others in getting people to settle on their land. The availability of new colonists may not have solved all the problems of those already established who wanted to man their claims. They will have wanted people who were dependent on them, who could be controlled and kept on the land, not people of independent means who might become uppity and troublesome, and maybe leave their land next year when a better opportunity arose elsewhere. All sorts of scenarios can be imagined, but it seems likely that there was at some point a rush to colonize all easily inhabitable space in Iceland. The archaeological evidence suggests that this will have been in the decades immediately following the deposition of the *landnám* tephra in AD871±2, and during this rush all sorts of methods must have been used to obtain settlers. It can be imagined, and the Sveigakot evidence may suggest this, that ethnicity was not a major concern of the organizers of settlements. Anybody with basic farming skills would do, and perhaps the more dependent or even unfree the newcomers were the better it was for the organizers. In this light, it is worthwhile examining the likelihood that some of the planted settlers were unfree and whether the group may have been multi-ethnic, drawn from all over Northern Europe rather than specifically Scandinavia and Britain. First let us consider the matter of slavery.

SLAVERY IN SETTLEMENT-PERIOD ICELAND

There is good evidence that slavery existed in Iceland during the Viking Age, although its duration and economic significance is debated. Barring one debt-slave in the 1170s, noted in *Sturlu saga* (*Sturlunga saga*, 83), there is no evidence for slavery in the contemporary sagas describing events in Iceland from the second half of the twelfth century onwards, and from this it has been deduced that slavery had become obsolete in Iceland before 1200 (Gunnar Karlsson 2000, 52). The evidence consists, on the one hand, of considerable, if not comprehensive, legislation about slavery in *Grágás*, the Commonwealth period legislation preserved in two late thirteenth-century versions and, on the other, of descriptions of slaves in the Book of Settlements and Sagas of Icelanders, from which it is clear that the authors of these largely thirteenth-century texts thought that slaves had been very much a normal part of the Viking-Age economy (Foote 1977; Karras 1988). The image of slavery presented in the sagas is of household slaves. They are described as menial workers, sometimes valued and loyal, sometimes objects of ridicule, often foreign and always single, without family or blood-relations. Scholars have tended to follow this lead and imagine that Icelandic slavery during the Viking Age was akin to plantation slavery in the early modern Americas, with large groups of slaves running estates for a largely idle class of landowners (Agnarsdóttir and Árnason 1983; Jakobsson 2005). This is possible, but other scenarios are also imaginable and the legislation does seem to point in a different direction – to the fact that Viking-Age slavery was more akin to serfdom.

Landnámabók does mention slaves in charge of farms. Geirmundur heljarskinn settled in Breiðafjörður but also claimed extensive lands in Hornstrandir, on the northern coast of Vestfirðir, where he installed slaves in charge of three farms (*Landnámabók*, 154–5). Friðmundr, the slave of Ingimundr gamli, is also said to have settled Forsæludalur – no doubt to be understood as a subject *landnám* within the larger claim of Ingimundr (*Landnámabók*, 218–19). It is possible that the reader was supposed to infer that Friðmundr had been freed, as settlements by freedmen are not uncommon. At least seventeen of these are recorded in the Book of Settlements, mostly within larger claims of the Skallagrímr-type of settlers, but there is also at least one example of an independent settlement by a freedman, that of Þórir dúfunef in Flugumýri, the freedman of the Norwegian nobleman Yxna-Þórir (*Landnámabók*, 235). All this tells us is that thirteenth-century scholars thought it was conceivable that slaves could be in charge of farms, but whether this had any more basis in reality than the household slaves is uncertain.

There is not room here to discuss the legal evidence for slavery in *Grágás* in detail, but an examination of the evidence reveals that while the Icelandic laws on slavery share a number of elements with Scandinavian laws, particularly Gulaþingslög, they are also different in significant ways (Dennis, Foote and Perkins 1980, I: 172–4, 181–2; 2000, II: 45, 70–1, 180; see also Karras 1988, 96–121). It transpires that the legislators thought that Icelandic slaves could have families and relatives, and they could own property. They were partly responsible for their own misdeeds – the owner was not necessarily liable if the slave broke the law – and slaves could receive compensation if they were injured. Finally, Icelandic slaves could be manumitted much more easily than Scandinavian slaves. In particular, the responsibility of the Icelandic slave-owner diminished much more rapidly once the slave had been freed.

Judging by the laws, it seems that Icelandic slave-owners – no doubt the very group most likely to be able to influence the legislation and make it work in their favour – were not at all keen to bind their slaves closely to them. On the contrary, they seem to have been happy to let their slaves take responsibility for themselves in their dealings with third parties, and obstacles on the way to freedom were as minimal as could be. This does not smack of a plantation-type of slavery, where slaves needed to be kept on a tight rein. Rather, the legal evidence seems to suggest a society where slavery was possibly widespread but not considered economically or socially vital. This might become explicable if we imagine that unfree people were brought to the country to become farmers, to man the lands claimed by early settlers. In the rush we have already postulated, one of the simplest ways to obtain people would have been to buy them on the slave-markets in northern Europe (about which frighteningly little is known, although

it is universally assumed that slaves would have been one of the principal commodities in the North European emporia that began to emerge in the seventh
and eighth centuries). It is not necessary to persuade unfree people to move to
an alien country in the middle of the outer sea and their dependent status will
have been automatically secured from the outset. Once established on a piece of
land, it may not have been crucial to maintain the unfree status of such people
for many generations. If their dependent status could be secured by other means
(by controlling their access to resources, for instance, renting of livestock, and/or
by creating personal bonds through decent treatment), their lack of freedom
could be as much a hindrance as a boon to the owner.

It is quite possible that unfree people continued to be brought in long after
the rush had abated, but the character of the legislation does seem to suggest that
the social necessity for slavery in Viking-Age Iceland had more to do with the
need to bring people in against their will than to keep them unfree once settled
in the country. It is possible that the taunt, referred to in one of the versions of the
Book of Settlements, that the Icelanders were descended from slaves and villains
(*Landnámabók*, 336) had more truth to it than the compilers wanted to admit.

MULTI-ETHNIC ORIGINS OF THE ICELANDERS

Icelandic scholars have long been pre-occupied with the origins of Icelanders,
and enormous efforts have been expended in attempts to wring information
from all sorts of evidence, ranging from the medieval literature to modern DNA.
The literary, linguistic and material cultural evidence all suggests that the culture
that became established in Iceland was very Norse, but that does not mean that
all – or even the majority – of the settlers were born in Scandinavia or espoused
some sort of Norse identity. Apart from a few fantastic hypotheses, the debate
has mainly been concerned with the proportions of Norse versus Celtic or
British elements in the founding population, with a subsidiary concern about the
role of Norse settlers from colonies in the British Isles, who may or may not have
become more British/Irish than Norse by the time they left for Iceland. Most
recently, analyses of DNA in modern Icelanders have been used to suggest that
while the men seem to have come primarily from Scandinavia, the majority of
the women originated in the British Isles (Agnar Helgason et al. 2000; 2001).
These studies might be seen to imply a rather rootless, non-family based,
pioneering society where men of one ethnicity obtained partners from another
through unconventional means. But they could also simply suggest that women
were proportionately few in the pioneering phase, and that while those
individuals did not perhaps reflect well the cultural make-up of the group as a
whole, they had a proportionately large influence on the gene-pool of subsequent
generations. Be that as it may, these studies aimed only to compare the relative

weight of British versus Scandinavian DNA in the gene-pool of modern Icelanders. They did not aim to pick up on the possible contribution of DNA from other parts of northern Europe and must therefore be considered inconclusive on that front.

The possibility of some of the settlers coming from outside the usual suspect regions of Britain and Scandinavia is raised by the sunken featured dwellings at Sveigakot. While SFBs are ubiquitous in all parts of Northern Europe before and during the Viking Age, they only seem to have been used as primary dwellings in urban contexts (e.g. in Aarhus and Hedeby: Clarke and Ambrosiani 1991, 63; von Carnap-Bornheim et al., this volume) and in rural areas east of the Elbe (Donat 1980). In eastern Europe, from the Baltic to the Ukraine, SFBs were the prevalent dwelling-type from the early up to the High Middle Ages, and people hailing from those regions – the same people who are likely to have been in considerable supply on the slave-markets – would have regarded a sunken-featured dwelling as a normal kind of abode. It is also possible that the Sveigakot sunken dwellings were built by townspeople – in many ways towns like Hedeby would have been the easiest recruitment grounds simply because of population density – but it is perhaps more questionable that town-dwellers would have transferred architectural styles specifically adapted to urban environments to a decidedly rural setting like that of Sveigakot.

The exact origins or ethnicity of the settlers of Sveigakot will remain a mystery. What matters is that they chose (or were made) to build in a fashion that eschews any obvious Norse cultural symbolism. The same holds true for their material culture. Pre-V~940 artefacts are exceedingly rare at Sveigakot, numbering twenty pieces at the most, representing less than 2 per cent of the whole assemblage, and none of them are culturally diagnostic. This is in contrast to the post-V~940 assemblage – associated with the small hall with bow-shaped walls – which contains a number of artefacts loaded with Norse cultural symbolism, such as a knob from an oval brooch and a dragon-shaped head of a bone pin.

CONCLUSIONS

So far, Sveigakot is an anomaly – there is no other known site with the characteristics described above. It may be just that, an exception to the rule, which would then not allow us to draw any general conclusions about the nature of colonizing society in Iceland. The nature of the archaeological remains, however, gives reason to believe that Sveigakot is not so anomalous, and that earlier excavation methods would not have revealed the type of deposits and structures that make Sveigakot a novelty in the corpus of Icelandic archaeological sites. Until the 1990s, excavation of Icelandic farm-sites tended to be limited to structures visible on the surface, and normally only the insides of the buildings were examined (Orri Vésteinsson 2004). Middens were not excavated, except as parts of farm mounds, and negative features outside buildings would not be identified unless they were indicated by depressions. At a site like Sveigakot, these methods would only have resulted in the identification of the small hall, the only structure visible on the surface at the start of the excavation, thus missing the first, and crucial, chapter of the story. It was extensive open-area excavation, initially designed to define and excavate the sheet middens, which allowed the detection of the unusual buildings from the earliest phase of occupation at Sveigakot. It is possible, therefore, that the reason no comparable remains have yet been found in Iceland is not that they are rare, but simply that they have not been recognized. Whether this is the case or not, only time and further research will tell, but here, at least, the possibility will be entertained that Sveigakot is in no way an extraordinary place.

The inferences suggested here about the ethnicity and unfree status of the inhabitants of Sveigakot are not the only ones that can reasonably be drawn from the archaeological evidence. This evidence does not prove mixed or non-Norse/British ethnicity or the existence of serfdom in Viking-Age Iceland. It does, however, raise the possibility of such interpretations, and these have the virtue of fitting into models of how the colonization proceeded.

For Mývatnssveit, we can postulate the following (see also Adolf Friðriksson et al. 2004, 197–200). Once settlement had been established on the coast, it would only have been a matter of time before exploration upriver from the bay of Skjálfandi would have revealed information about the large inland lake Mývatn and its rich resources. The rich fish- and bird-life on the lake and in the River Laxá which drains it (see McGovern et al. 2006) will no doubt have attracted hunters, if not settlers, at a very early stage in the settlement process. The earliest camps are likely to have been around the confluence of the Rivers Laxá and Kráká (see Fig. 46.1), by the outlet from the lake where nature's bounty is greatest, and it may be that farming was very much secondary to hunting to begin with. Once people started to colonize Mývatnssveit for farming purposes, the most attractive area will have been Framengjar, the great swathe of meadow-land stretching some 6km southwards from the lake and covering an area of approximately 30km². Apart from proximity to the lake and its resources, Framengjar will have produced enough fodder to support a small number of farms, and it is the only area around the lake where a number of farms could have been established in close proximity to each other. On other sides of the lake, settlement is limited to a single row of farms on the shore. It is possible that the early settlers of Framengjar worked as a team – there are at least no indications that one settlement was more original or able to claim a lion's share of the resources. The principal settlements, judging from late medieval patterns, are fairly evenly spaced and the resources are divided fairly evenly between them. However amicable and heterarchical this small community of, perhaps, five original settlements was, there will still have been competition between them for land and resources, perhaps increasingly so after the initial phase of colonization was over, when bare survival had been achieved and people did not have to rely on each other's good will to the same life-saving degree as before. Let us consider two of these possibly early farms, Baldursheimur and Grænavatn, deemed so from their prime locations, primary farm-names, and the association of the former with a rich pagan burial (Kristján Eldjárn 2000, 200–3) and the latter's high taxation value in later times. These two farms would have been on the edge of the initial wave of settlement, and they would both have had extensive hinterlands with possibilities for further settlement. In this case, the hinterlands of the two farms overlap in the area east of Kráká (where Baldursheimur is on the western bank) and south of Grænavatn. It would have mattered to the people of these farms what happened in these hinterlands, and they are likely to have wanted to control them, if only to make sure that nobody else could claim them and/or occupy them. It is in these conditions that the need for dependent settlers would have arisen. It makes excellent sense for either Grænavatn or Baldursheimur to establish a dependent farm exactly where Sveigakot is, on the Grænavatn side of the river, but directly across from Baldursheimur, in order to substantiate a claim and to hinder the other from doing the same.

If this need for dependent settlers arose on this scale, the procurement of the settlers is unlikely to have been handled by the farmers, who were themselves basically subsistence farmers competing for limited resources. Only in sagas do Icelandic farmers routinely sail abroad to seek fame and fortune. A more prosaic explanation would see them relying on others, either agents who were in the business of shipping people to Iceland or, perhaps more likely, chieftains who had the connections and clout to help their followers in this way. Either way, the settlers of places like Sveigakot would have been pawns in a struggle for resources, power and prestige.

BIBLIOGRAPHY

Adolf Friðriksson, Orri Vésteinsson & T.H. McGovern. 2004. 'Recent investigations at Hofstaðir, Northern Iceland' in R.A. Housley & G. Coles (eds), *Atlantic connections and adaptations: economies, environments and subsistence in lands bordering the North Atlantic* (Oxford), pp 191–202.

Agnar Helgason, Sigurðardóttir, J. Nicholson, B. Sykes, E.W. Hill, D.G. Bradley, V. Bosnes, J.R. Gulcher, R. Ward & K. Stefánsson. 2000. 'Estimating Scandinavian and Gaelic ancestry in the male settlers of Iceland', *American Journal of Human Genetics*, 67, 697–717.

Agnar Helgason, E. Hickey, S. Goodacre, V. Bosnes, K. Stefánsson, R. Ward & B. Sykes. 2001. 'mtDNA and the islands of the North Atlantic: estimating the proportions of Norse and Gaelic ancestry', *American Journal of Human Genetics*, 68, 723–37.

Anna Agnarsdóttir & Ragnor Árnason. 1983. 'Þrælahald á þjóðveldisöld', *Saga*, 21, 5–26.

Bjarni F. Einarsson. 1992. 'Granastadir-grophuset och andra isländska grophus i ett nordiskt sammanhang: deras funktion och betydelse i kolonisationsförloppet i Island', *Viking*, 1992, 95–119.

Berson, B. 2002. 'A contribution to the study of the medieval Icelandic farm: the byres', *Archaeologia Islandica*, 2, 34–60.

Byock, J. 2001. *Viking-Age Iceland* (Harmondsworth).

Clarke, H. & B. Ambrosiani. 1991. *Towns in the Viking Age* (Leicester).

Dennis, A., P. Foote, & R. Perkins (ed. and trans.). 1980, 2000. *Laws of early Iceland: Grágás*, 2 vols, University of Manitoba Icelandic Studies, 3, 5 (Winnipeg).

Donat, P. 1980. *Haus, hof und dorf im mitteleuropa vom 7. bis 12. Jahrhundert* (Berlin).

Egils saga = S. Nordal (ed.). 1933. *Egils saga Skalla-Grímssonar*, Íslenzk fornrit, 2 (Reykjavík).

Foote, P.G. 1977. 'Þrælahald á Íslandi: Heimildakönnun og athugasemdir', *Saga*, 15, 41–74.

Grönvold, K., N. Óskarsson, S.J. Johnsen, H.B. Clausen, C.U. Hammer, G. Bond & E. Bard. 1995. 'Ash layers from Iceland in the Greenland GRIP Ice Core correlated with oceanic and ash sediments', *Earth and Planetary Science Letters*, 135, 149–55.

Guðmundur Ólafsson. 1980. 'Grelutóttir: landnámsbær á Eyri við Arnarfjörð', *Árbók hins íslenzka fornleifafélags*, 1979, 25–73.

Guðmundur Ólafsson. 2001. 'Eiríksstaðir: the farm of Eiríkr the Red' in A. Wawn & Þ. Sigurðardóttir (eds), *Approaches to Vínland*, Sigurður Nordal Institute Studies, 4 (Reykjavík), 147–53.

Gunnar Karlsson. 2000. *Iceland's 1100 years: the history of a marginal society* (Reykjavík).

Íslendingabók = Jakob Benediktsson (ed.). 1968. *Íslendingabók. Landnámabók*, Íslenzk fornrit, 1 (Reykjavík).

Karras, R.M. 1988. *Slavery and society in medieval Scandinavia* (New Haven & London).

Kristján Eldjárn. 2000. *Kuml og haugfé í heiðnum sið á Íslandi*, 2nd ed. ed. Adolf Friðriksson (Reykjavík).

Landnámabók = Jakob Benediktsson (ed.). 1968. *Íslendingabók. Landnámabók,* Íslenzk fornrit, 1 (Reykjavík).

Magnús Á. Sigurgeirsson, Orri Vésteinsson & Hafliði Hafliðason. 2002. 'Gjóskulagarannsóknir við Mývatn – aldursgreining elstu byggðar' in Orri Vésteinsson (ed.), *Archaeological investigations at Sveigakot 2001, with reports on preliminary investigations at Hrísheimar, Selhagi and Ytri Tunga*, (Reykjavík), 108–10.

Magnús Á. Sigurgeirsson, Ulf Hauptfleisch & Árni Einarsson. 2008. 'Gjóskulög frá tímabilinu 700–1250 e.Kr. í botnseti Mývatns' in Guðrún Alda Gísladóttir & Orri Vésteinsson (eds), *Archaeological investigations at Sveigakot 2006* (Reykjavík), 61–6.

McGovern, T.H., S. Perdikaris, A. Einarsson & J. Sidell. 2006. 'Coastal connections, local fishing and sustainable egg harvesting: patterns of Viking-Age inland wild resource use in Mývatn District, Northern Iceland', *Environmental Archaeology*, 11, 187–205.

Milek, K. 2006. 'Houses and households in early Icelandic society: geoarchaeology and the interpretation of social space' (PhD thesis, University of Cambridge).

Nanna Ólafsdóttir. 1974. 'Baðstofan og böð að fornu', *Árbók hins íslenzka fornleifafélags*, 1973, 62–86.

Ólafur Lárusson. 1944. 'Úr byggðasögu Íslands', *Byggð og saga* (Reykjavík), 9–58.

Orri Vésteinsson. 1998. 'Patterns of settlement in Iceland: a study in prehistory', *Saga-Book of the Viking Society*, 25, 1–29.

Orri Vésteinsson. 2004. 'Icelandic farmhouse excavations: field methods and site choices', *Archaeologia islandica*, 3, 71–100.

Orri Vésteinsson, Helgi Þorláksson & Árni Einarsson. 2006. *Reykjavík 871±2. Landnámssýningin: the settlement exhibition*, trans. Anna Yates (Reykjavík).

Orri Vésteinsson, T.H. McGovern, & C. Keller. 2002. 'Enduring impacts: social and environmental aspects of Viking-Age settlement in Iceland and Greenland', *Archaeologia Islandica*, 2, 98–136.

Simpson, I.A., G. Guðmundsson, A.M. Thomson & J. Cluett. 2004. 'Assessing the role of winter grazing in historic land degradation, Mývatnssveit, Northeast Iceland', *Geoarchaeology*, 19, 471–502.

Sturlunga saga = Örnólfur Thorsson (ed.). 1988. *Sturlunga saga* (Reykjavík).

Sverrir Jakobsson. 2005. 'Frá þrælahaldi til landeigendavalds: Íslenskt miðaldasamfélag, 1100–1400', *Saga*, 43:2, 99–129.

Þór Magnússon. 1973. 'Sögualdarbyggð í Hvítárholti', *Árbók hins íslenzka fornleifafélags*, 1972, 5–80.

Hedeby, the settlement and the harbour: old data and recent research

CLAUS VON CARNAP-BORNHEIM, VOLKER HILBERG,
SVEN KALMRING & JOACHIM SCHULTZE

INTRODUCTION

The famous site at Hebeby is very important for the early medieval history of not only the North Sea and the Baltic regions but also of Scandinavia and the continent. In recent years, especially since 2002, a new stage in its research has been arrived at through the development of various initiatives in and around the site. The new approaches have been concentrated on the reappraisal of older excavation features from the settlement and the harbour (Plate 18), the application of geophysical prospection methods (Plate 19) and selective small-scale excavations. The employment of metal detectors has succeeded in opening a new window onto our understanding of the later Hedeby, complementing the information gleaned from conventional field-walking conducted in the 1960s and 1970s. As a result, a body of new finds has been secured which constitutes a substantial expansion on the Hedeby artefact record, particularly of the tenth and eleventh centuries.

The combination of two-dimensional surface data with those allowing a three-dimensional view into the structure of the site is of fundamental importance for the further exploration of Hedeby. Among the first group are those data gained from the geophysical prospection of entire areas. The surveying revealed a logical and homogenous grid of pathways and roads which, in some zones, even allowed the identification of the layout of individual plots and their buildings (Plate 19). Luckily, the site was apparently completely abandoned in the second half of the eleventh century, so that later developments rarely disturbed the early medieval structures. No exact dates have yet been ascertained for these structures though, undoubtedly, they belong to the relatively early phases of the settlement, most likely the tenth century.

In recent years, prospecting using metal detectors has enjoyed great success, especially in the southern Scandinavian sites of Tissø and Uppåkra. A corresponding strategy suggested itself for Hedeby, and not only for reasons of comparability. The extraordinarily interesting material recovered from this exercise shows that large areas of the latest settlement layers, those of the eleventh century, have been destroyed by ploughing. The initial mapping of the

511

results allows the identification of areas of find concentrations and of specific function, verifying the high value of the evidence from find material derived from already known contexts. This prospecting, obviously geared to locating metal finds, is complemented by the field-walking that was conducted by K. Schietzel in the years 1967–72 and in 1995. They resulted in the recovery of a wealth of ceramic finds and iron slag, as well as other non-metal finds. From the combination of these approaches, geophysical prospection and metal-detecting, it will prove possible in the future to deduce a highly differentiated picture of the later settlement.

All of this new information is supplemented by a re-evaluation of the old excavations alongside the evidence from new excavations, which provides a three-dimensional picture (albeit limited in parts). In the recording, classification and interpretation of documentation from excavations extending over a century, the key has proven to be the high-performance GIS programmes which have been successfully employed for the older settlement excavations and for the harbour excavation. Now, for the first time, it is possible to deal with the huge amount of data, as exemplified by the 25,000 structural timbers recorded from the 5000m² settlement excavation, though the stratigraphic information is extremely complicated and not always easy to interpret. Nevertheless, it is clear from the results that we shall shortly have to bid farewell to some fondly held pictures of the site's settlement topography and of the harbour's structure and use.

The technology now exists to enable the combination of the 2-D coarse-resolution aerial data with the 3-D high-resolution detail data of Hedeby. Inevitably, as a result, new research questions and models of interpretation will emerge. We can describe in some detail the important position of this place within the network of early medieval central places and can, in quite good detail, make out its special function in the political and military events of the ninth, tenth and eleventh centuries. Furthermore, there is now no doubt whatsoever that Hedeby was of great significance for the Christianization of the north. Questions pertaining to Hedeby's relationship with her surrounding countryside are, however, more difficult to answer and only an outline of the reciprocal network of relations is identifiable. In the coming years, however, it will be possible to introduce quite another question into the discussion – a question referring wholly to relations within the settlement itself. For the first time, we can attempt to define functional units within the large settlement. For instance, the significance of the pit-houses in the western, relatively higher area of the settlement will be shown to be quite distinct from that of the hall-houses in the eastern harbour area near the Noor. In the future, a question of utmost importance will be whether we can differentiate and interpret private space (e.g. within the fenced plots) from the public space (e.g. the paths and open spaces/ market squares). In this regard, the harbour jetties, whose character as private or public structures cannot yet be determined with certainty, will be central to the discussion. The town as a space for social and political interaction is becoming recognizable and this is happening in individual segments of time which, in optimum cases, are high-resolution. This means that new perspectives on the Hedeby research, which count on the combination of successful excavation activity with the results of modern prospecting methods, are now being defined. By way of example, three areas of study have been singled out here to be considered in more detail. These result from the geophysical prospection pertaining to the internal organization of the settlement area within the semi-circular rampart, as well as recent investigations of the settlement and the harbour of Hedeby.

ARCHAEOLOGICAL AND GEOPHYSICAL PROSPECTION

The Viking-Age *emporium* of Hedeby is situated at the narrowest part of the Cimbrian peninsula, near the Danevirke, the southern Danish border in the Middle Ages. Accessible both from the west and the east, Hedeby possessed a key position in connecting the trading systems of the North Sea with the Baltic basin. The place is known from written records since the year 804 and developed in the ninth century into the leading *emporium* or proto-town of the Danish kingdom, until its final destruction in 1066. Its functions and political role were then transferred to Schleswig/Slesvig on the other side of the Schlei/Slie fjord. Hedeby itself is well-known for the extensive archaeological research done on it by German archaeologists since 1900 (Plate 18). In 1897, Sophus Müller from the National Museum of Denmark identified the huge semi-circular rampart at the western side of the Haddebyer Noor with the place mentioned on Viking-Age runic inscriptions, found nearby, as Hedeby (Müller 1897, 636–42, figs 395–6).

An important contribution to the Hedeby research programme is provided by systematic archaeological prospection. During the 1960s and 1970s, K. Schietzel conducted a systematic field survey within the semi-circular rampart. The materials collected consist mainly of pottery and soapstone sherds, iron slag, and production waste in metal and glass, and these finds contributed much to our understanding of the whole settlement complex (Schietzel 1981, 21–2, map 23). Since 2003, systematic metal-detector surveys have been carried out with the assistance of the Bornholmske Amatørarkæologer and a German amateur group of metal-detector users from Schleswig-Holstein. During six campaigns, about 11,000 metal finds were collected and their locations measured precisely with a D-GPS system (Hilberg 2007; 2009). A pre-Viking-Age phase to the site became apparent for the first time with the discovery of some significant objects from the late Germanic Iron Age, concentrated in the southern area inside the rampart. With these metal-detected finds, knowledge of the settlement complex has increased considerably. For many different object types, like ornaments, coins or weights, we now have larger assemblages at our disposal. In addition, the continental influence on Hedeby is clearly visible from the ninth century onwards in the artefact assemblages. Most of the material dates to Hedeby's later phases, coming from its disturbed or destroyed upper layers. For the eleventh century, the large number of German and Scandinavian coins, riding equipment and ornaments decorated in late Viking-Age art-styles point to the *emporium*'s lively role in the Danish North Sea empire up to the 1060s and 1070s (Hilberg, 2007).

Since 1952, different geophysical methods, on both sea and land, have been used for archaeological purposes at Hedeby (Stümpel and Borth-Hoffmann 1983; Utecht and Stümpel 1983; Kramer 1998–9). A new project of large-scale geophysical research started in 2002 when, during a field-work season spanning three weeks, approximately 29ha inside and outside the semi-circular rampart were analyzed using Fluxgate- and Caesium-magnetometers and ground-penetrating radar (Plate 19). The different prospection methods applied in recent years have provided new data for the development of the whole settlement complex (Hilberg 2007; 2009).

Inside the semi-circular rampart, the density of anomalies is very high. The northern area is characterized in the magnetogram by parallel courses and many rectangular structures with high magnetism. According to the investigations done with ground-penetrating radar, some of these latter features are up to 1.7–1.8m in depth and could, therefore, be sunken-featured buildings. Comparable pit-houses were excavated in the surrounding areas. Schietzel, in his surface-survey, collected a high amount of iron-slag in this north-western part of the site, concluding that iron was processed there (Schietzel 1981, maps 28–9; Westphalen 1989, 28–36, figs 5–7). The magnetic structures in this area of the settlement could be interpreted as workshops (Jankuhn 1986, 92). While precise dating is impossible at the moment, these structures seem to belong to Hedeby's later phase of the tenth to eleventh centuries. Within the north-eastern area of the rampart, the survey detected a lot of rectangular structures with high magnetism, sometimes aligned. These could also be interpreted as sunken-featured buildings or workshops. Workshops for metal-casting and glass-production, which were lying immediately next to each other, are on record from previous excavations and dated to the ninth and tenth centuries. It was this area which Jankuhn designated as the 'quarter of craft activities' in the 1940s and later (Jankuhn 1944; 1977; Hilberg 2009, fig. 8). A linear structure runs parallel to the shore and possesses small magnetic structures lying in pairs opposing each other (Plate 19). This seems to be a street extending along the whole shoreline for a length of *c.*530m, accompanied by houses on both sides. The feature crosses the main area excavated by Jankuhn and Schietzel and was visible there in all layers, and was frequently designated a main street of the settlement (Jankuhn 1943, 38–40, 49–50, fig. 4; 1986, 98–9, figs 39–40; Schietzel 1969, 19–21; Randsborg 1980, fig. 23). The street also crosses a small stream by means of a narrow bridge, the construction of which is dendro-dated to the year 819 (Eckstein 1976; Schietzel 1969, 21–6, figs 10–14). Consequently, the street must have existed from as early as the early ninth century, but without more precise data, such as that provided by new excavations, its actual extent at that time is still unknown. Streets stretching along the shore seem to be a characteristic of early medieval trading centres, such as Sigtuna and Dublin (Clarke and Ambrosiani 1991, 138–41, figs. 5.5 (Dublin), 4.23 (Sigtuna)). In Hedeby, this main street was apparently crossed by several other streets running from the harbour zone to the core areas of the settlement, as shown by Jankuhn's and Schietzel's excavations and also detected in the magnetometer survey.

To the southwest of the settlement, outside the rampart, lay a huge cemetery area with a boat-grave of mid-ninth-century date as a focal point (Plate 18). Within the rampart, in the southwestern zone stretching from the rampart to the *c.*6 m-contour, thousands of small anomalies with a lesser degree of magnetism were investigated in 2002 (Plate 19). They could be interpreted as burials, with ring-ditches being detected in some cases (Steuer 1984, 203–9; Eisenschmidt 1994, 38; 2004, 302). A superimposition of the cemetery with house structures is known from Knorr's and Jankuhn's excavations, and this points to the usage of this area for housing and production activities since the tenth century (Jankuhn 1986, 107, 110). The existence of settlement structures in the entire south-western area is demonstrated by the 2002 magnetometer survey. The density of detected houses seems to be lower than in the northern parts of Hedeby, but the whole area inside the rampart seems to have been settled. Furthermore, the data from both the surface-survey and systematic metal-detection point to settlement activities. But further research is needed to decide if the cemetery area within and without the late tenth-century rampart originally formed one burial ground.

In 2005, new small-scale excavations started to verify the results and interpretations of the geophysical research. The existence of pit-houses in the higher, sandy areas was attested and hundreds of soil samples were collected for further geophysical analyses. Careful excavation and sieving of the spoil revealed two pit-houses, each consisting of two phases. One of these houses was destroyed by fire, though its remains survived in an excellent state of preservation, and thousands of small finds dating from the second half of the tenth century to the middle of the eleventh century were recovered from it. Discoveries like this have contributed to the enlargement of our knowledge of Hedeby's position and role in the international trading system, especially for the late tenth and the eleventh centuries. The supposed decline of the emporium around 1000 can now be doubted (Jankuhn 1986, 222; Hill 2001, 107).

THE EVALUATION OF THE SETTLEMENT EXCAVATION

The evaluation of the structural timbers with regards to house construction and settlement structure from Jankuhn's and Schietzel's excavations offers numerous and far-reaching possibilities for interpretation. At the same time, the large number of preserved timbers poses a great challenge in proceeding with the analyses. In just one 1300m² area on the Haddebyer Noor, some 12,000 structural timbers were recovered from cultural layers up to 2m in depth (Fig. 47.1). In order to handle the data of the individual timbers better and to be able to sort out single timbers with the help of clear criteria, the data is at present being transferred to the computer. For this, a process was developed which combines the possibilities of Geographical Information Systems (= GIS; ArcGIS from ESRI) and data banks (Access). First of all, the plans are scanned, geo-referenced and digitized. Then the data (altitude, slope, shape, working, measurements, burn traces, dendrochronological dating, etc) of each individual timber are entered in coded form into the tables of GIS or the data bank. In the same way, stones or discolouration (plans and sections) can be processed. At a later point in time, the finds will also be entered into GIS and combined with the structural features. Once all the data has been entered, GIS offers the possibility of the visual presentation of selections of timbers with certain characteristics so that the problems associated with the sorting out of single structures of correspondingly clear criteria will be alleviated. A simplified 3-D presentation (extrusion of the cross-sections of the structural timbers as far as their upper and lower edges) facilitates their initial relative chronological classification, whereby the absolute chronological dating can be achieved in many cases by dendrochronology. The evaluation shows that dendrochronological dates must be assessed with caution and they should always be tested against other criteria, especially the stratigraphy. In many cases, the re-use of structural timbers could be ascertained and in some cases the number of re-used timbers outweighed those of the actual building phase. In all, some 4,300 structural timbers from the 1966–9 excavations were sampled for dendrochronology and about 3,200 of these could be dated. The distribution of the dating of the individual samples shows a clear concentration in the ninth century, whereas the tenth and eleventh centuries are barely represented (Fig. 47.2). This latter finding does not, necessarily indicate a drop in settlement activity however, and it may be accounted for by the less favourable conditions of preservation in the upper layers. This is also verified by the many finds of the tenth century, and even of the eleventh century, which were found in the course of metal detecting (see above). What is surprising, on the basis of this dating evidence, is that at the time of the earliest historical accounts of Hedeby in the years 804 and 808, the excavated areas were apparently not yet intensively settled. This did not happen until around the 830s. One may assume that the damp areas close to the Haddebyer Noor were at first not settled, not only because they were so low down but also because they were repeatedly threatened by flooding (Schultze 2005). Against the background of the total number of dendrochronological datings, the early dating of the north-south street stands out.

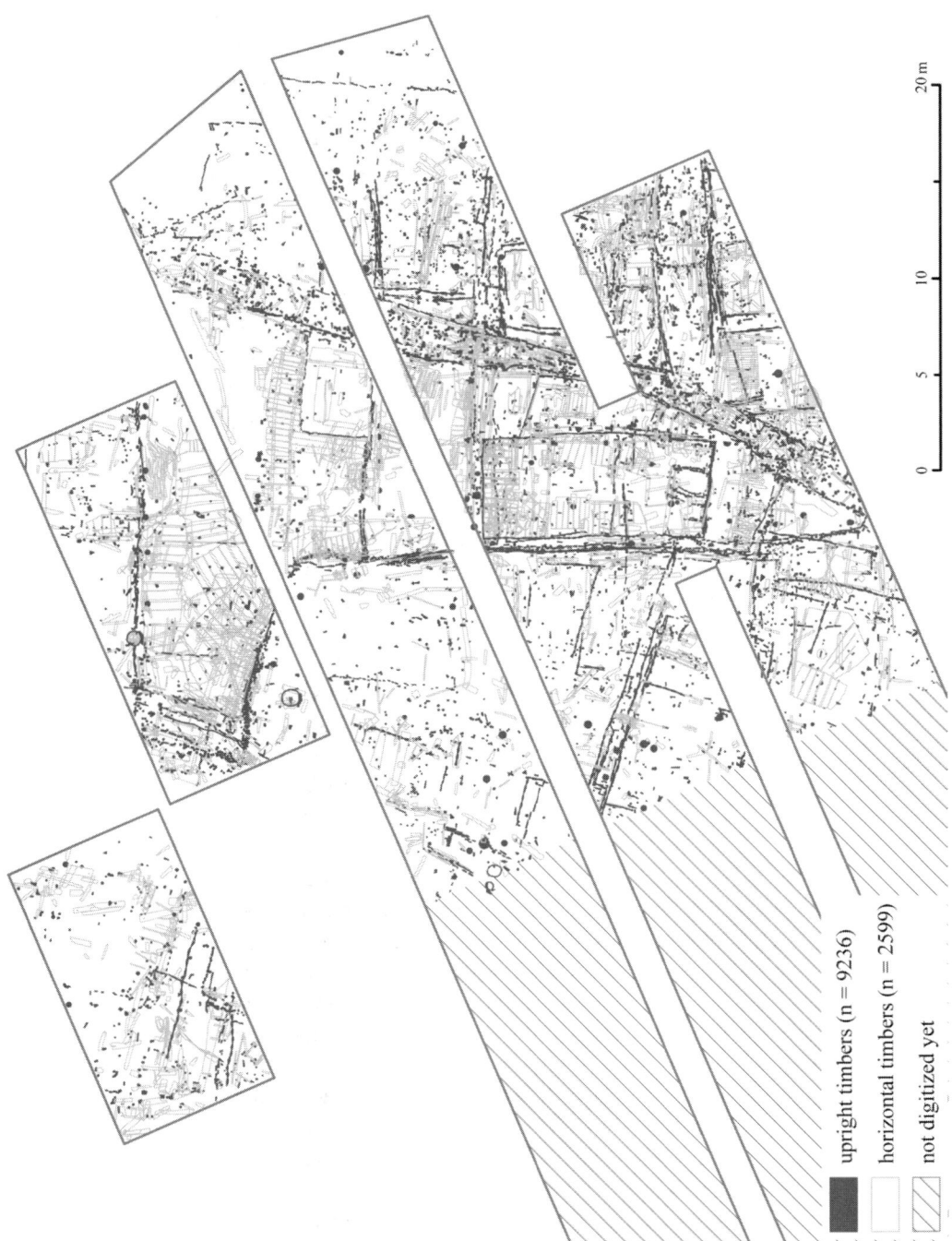

47.1 Plan of the recovered timbers from the 1966–9 excavation in the examined area close to the Haddebyer Noor.

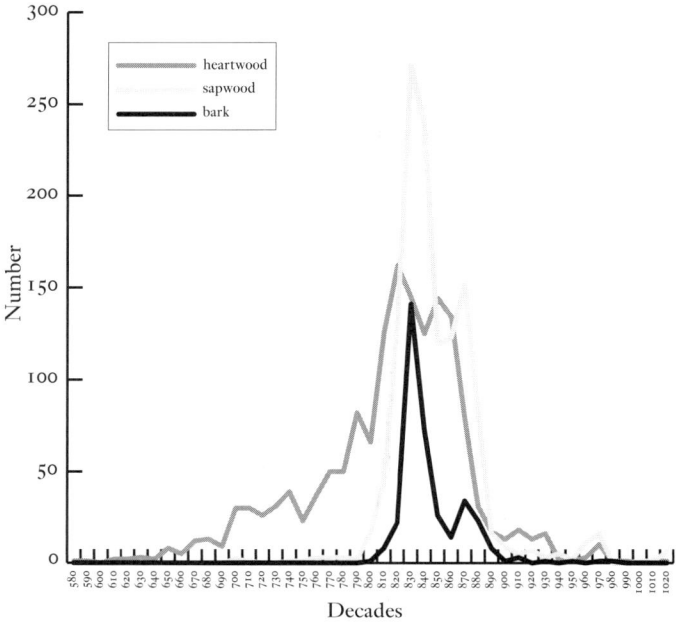

47.2 Distribution of the dendrochronological dating of all samples taken from the settlement excavation, 1966–9.

Following earlier attempts at sorting out the settlement structure (especially Jankuhn 1943, 28–51; Eckstein and Schietzel 1977, 154–7; 1984, 175–80; Schietzel 1981, 65–9), the present evaluation succeeded in enabling an almost complete sequence of settlement to be presented in a small area of the site. It spans the ninth century completely and, in this case, even reaches into the middle of the tenth century; the hearths found in the uppermost layers without preserved timbers indicate an even later construction date. In this section of the settlement, a very quick building sequence could be ascertained, this feature also being confirmed in other zones. One extreme example is a house which was built anew four times in seven years, each time after burning down. Of special interest, too, was the observation made on the small settlement section that the very cramped construction pattern could change over the course of time. There are examples of paths being deliberately built over, though presumably these were byways and not main paths. In evaluating larger areas, the frequency and location of such building-over episodes will now have to be clarified so that conclusions may be drawn about larger property units.

As already observed by Rudolph (1936a; 1936b), Jankuhn (1986, 95–6) and Schietzel (1981, 37–44; 1984c), there was a multitude of differently constructed wooden buildings in Hedeby. The main type of building is one of framework construction (*Gerüstbauten*). In contrast to its rural surroundings, where internal framework constructions are usually found, the wall framework building (*Wandgerüstbauten*) dominates in Hedeby. The inclined outer supports recorded from one building, which appear to point to the early use of the rafter roof in this region, is a peculiarity (see Eckstein and Schietzel 1977, 151–4; 1984, 171–4; Schietzel 1981, 43–4, 61–4; Schmidt 1999, 64, 102–3; Schultze 2008). The latest form of the wall framework buildings (*Wandgerüstbauten*) are frame constructions with interrupted sills being tenoned between the posts (*Pfosten-Schwellriegelbauten*), which are typical of high medieval Schleswig (Vogel 1992). Alongside Hedeby's framework buildings there were also smaller houses such as palisade constructions, where all the timbers of the walls took on the weight of the roof equally, and log buildings (see Schietzel 1981, 42).

The detailed observation of the structural features allows one to make various statements about the fashioning of the Hedeby terrain by its people. In the very flat, damp areas close to the Haddebyer Noor, one of the main concerns of the people was how to stay dry. It has been observed that the floor level within houses here was higher than the ground outside. Rainwater ran from the plot to the pathways lower down, which were apparently used as sewage channels when rain fell; this necessitated the wooden substructures of the pathways. Small sewage drains were built to channel the water in the direction of the stream or the Haddebyer Noor (Schultze 2006; 2008).

RESULTS OF RECENT RESEARCH IN THE HARBOUR OF HEDEBY

Considering the significance of Hedeby as one of the major commercial centres of the Viking Age, it is important to take a look at its topographical situation. Hedeby, as noted above, is situated at a most favourable position for trade and communication at the narrowest point of the Cimbrian peninsula on the Schleswig isthmus. This point is even more restricted by the natural barrier landscapes of marshes and lowlands in the west and the fjord-like Schlei in the east, narrowing it down to a strip only 15km wide. The site itself is located far inland at the Haddebyer Noor, a small inlet at the inner end of the Schlei. Two vital traffic routes ran through the Schleswig isthmus and could be controlled by the fortifications of the Danevirke/Danewerk and by the settlement of Hedeby itself. A north-south axis was formed by the Hærvej/Ochsenweg, which ran overland from Viborg in the north down to the river Elbe in the south and which can be traced back to the Bronze Age. Even more important from a trading perspective was the east-west axis between the Baltic and the North Sea, from the Schlei in the east, over the land bridge and down the rivers Eider and Treene to the Wadden Sea. The counterpart to the harbour of Hedeby on the Baltic side was presumably Hollingstedt, which formed the North Sea harbour for traffic crossing the isthmus (Jankuhn 1986, 117–19; Brandt 2002, 83–6; 102–3).

Beyond this, the topographical situation was geo-strategically characterized by its position within the borderland between the Danes, Frisians, Saxons and Slavs (Obodrites), which constituted another important factor for trade and cultural exchange.

Since Hedeby, as a major commercial centre, had to have a special harbour area to handle its trade activities, the question of the construction of the harbour and its facilities had already a risen by the 1930s (Jankuhn 1936, 98). Interest in the harbour persisted and led to the harbour excavation in 1979–80 (Plate 18), under the direction of K. Schietzel (Schietzel 1984b). So far, apart from a few short preliminary reports, only a small section published in connection with the Hedeby ships (Crumlin-Pedersen 1997, 63) has dealt with the harbour features revealed in this campaign.

In connection with the excavation of Wreck 1, a long, slender personnel carrier of prime workmanship from the end of the tenth century, the substructures of some harbour facilities were encountered. They appeared as regularly spaced rows of posts and continued from the Haddebyer Noor right to the shore, being interpreted as the supports of landing-stages or jetties. Including expansion to the north and south in the second season of the excavation, an area of around 2200m² was excavated; this represents approximately 1.5 per cent of the former harbour area within the Noor. In addition, two small adjacent parts of the shore were uncovered in the extensions of 1980.

The general plan of the excavated area in 1979–80 shows all the registered posts and post-holes, and through these the outlines of different harbour facilities appear in the straight lines which are formed by the rows of posts (Fig. 47.3). Apart from the harbour facilities themselves, a shore defence and parts of the former landward development were detected next to the coast within the excavated area of the harbour (Kalmring *in preparation*). Although wood preservation in Hedeby is extremely good because of the deposition of sediments and the rise of the water level, only the substructures of the harbour facilities have survived in the form of regularly placed rows of posts, though the picture derived from these can be complemented by the inclusion of the post-holes. From this evidence, it is possible to reconstruct the facilities as open pile works, through which water could flow. Individual structures vary in from 9m to in excess of 54m in length (inclusive of later extensions) and from 4m to 13m in breadth. Even though it is not possible to say to which structure every post or post-hole belonged, we can comprehend the interior structure as well as the outlines of the facilities. Even though the structures were repaired every spring because of the damages caused by ice-drift, there are regularities in the positioning of the posts of the interior bays, and the position of the bays in relation to each other are clearly discernable.

During the excavation, samples of structural timbers made from oak which possessed a sufficient number of growth-rings were taken from the more than

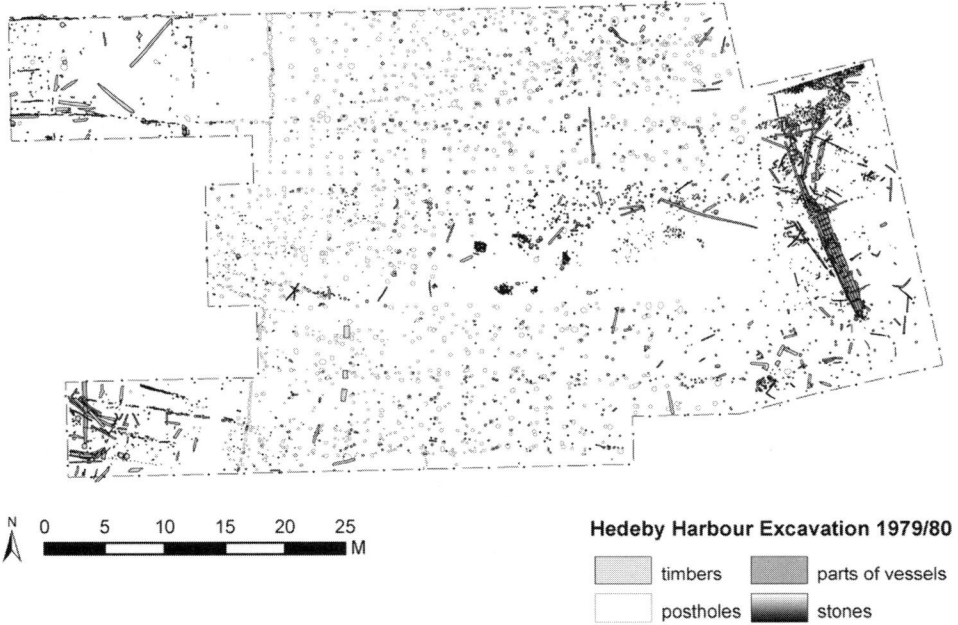

N
0   5   10   15   20   25
M

Hedeby Harbour Excavation 1979/80

timbers   parts of vessels

postholes   stones

47.3 Plan of the 1979–80 excavated area of Hedeby harbour.

47.4 Schematized plan of harbour facilities at Hedeby, showing phasing of the development.

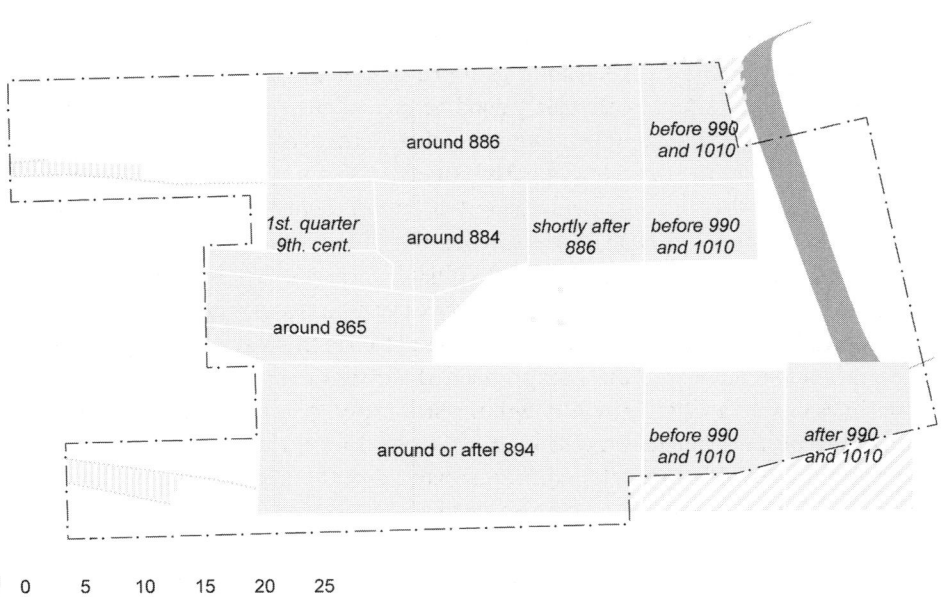

around 886

before 990
and 1010

1st. quarter
9th. cent.

around 884

shortly after
886

before 990
and 1010

around 865

around or after 894

before 990
and 1010

after 990
and 1010

N
0   5   10   15   20   25
M

2000 timbers recovered. Using these samples, the dating of the structures was achievable by the dendrochronological determination of age (Eckstein & Schietzel 1984). From about 50 per cent of the total number of tested timbers only 15 per cent could be dated. The overall distribution of felling dates showed a strong peak around AD880/890 and a weaker one around AD840. But, rather than indicating that the development of the harbour took place in two main phases, this picture simply reflects the usage of different wood-qualities in different areas of the harbour (Kalmring 2003). An earlier suggestion of an extremely early dating for one harbour facility to around 725–750 (Crumlin-Pedersen 1997, 68), which would be even older than the oldest artefacts from the central settlement area of Hedeby, could not be sustained. Following a phase where the shore has been used as a beach market with a simple landing place, the first wooden access to a landing place was constructed at the end of the last third of the ninth century. By the end of the century, a large extension with jetties was constructed in order to give high-sea cargo carriers a swimming berth (Fig. 47.4). Due to the disposal of waste materials from the settlement in the harbour basin, combined with the increasing size of the cargo carriers before 990 and 1010 – the assumed date of the sinking of the royal personnel carrier Wreck 1 – the jetties had to be extended further. The wrecking of this ship and its superstructure in the south of the excavation area provide evidence for activity here in the first half of the eleventh century (Kalmring 2008).

One of the main results of the analysis of the harbour excavation is the recognition that the harbour facilities were not simply formed by several individual jetties extending at right angles from the shore onto the open water. Instead, these single structures often adjoin one another on their shoulders and were even connected by smaller breakers. In this way, the facilities quickly developed into a large, u-shaped platform with an area of nearly 1500m², and they served not only for mooring purposes, but also as the market place of the early town (Kalmring in preparation). Therefore, the harbour of Hedeby seems to be of key interest for the understanding the urbanization process in northern Europe.

BIBLIOGRAPHY

Brandt, K. 2002. 'Wikingerzeitliche und mittelalterliche besiedlung am ufer der Treene bei Hollingstedt: ein flusshafen im Küstengebiet der Nordsee' in K. Brandt et al. (eds), *Haithabu und die frühe stadtentwicklung im nördlichen Europa*, Schriften des Archäologischen Landesmuseums, 8 (Neumünster), pp 83–105.

Clarke, H. & B. Ambrosiani. 1991. *Towns in the Viking Age* (Leicester & London).

Crumlin-Pedersen, O. 1997. *Viking-Age ships and shipbuilding in Hedeby/Haithabu and Schleswig*, Ships and Boats of the North, 2 (Schleswig & Roskilde).

Eckstein, D. 1976. 'Absolute datierung der wikingerzeitlichen Siedlung Haithabu/Schleswig mit hilfe der dendrochronologie', *Naturwissenschaftliche Rundschau*, 29:3, 81–4.

Eckstein, D. & Schietzel, K. 1977. 'Zur dendrochronologischen gliederung und datierung der baubefunde von Haithabu' in K. Schietzel (ed.), *Berichte über die Ausgrabungen in Haithabu*, 11 (Neumünster), pp 141–64.

Eckstein, D. & K. Schietzel. 1984. 'Dendrochronologische gliederung der baubefunde von Haithabu' in H. Jankuhn et al. (eds), *Archäologische und naturwissenschaftliche untersuchungen an ländlichen und frühstädtischen siedlungen im deutschen Küstengebiet vom 5. Jahrhundert v. Chr. bis zum 11. Jahrhundert n. Chr. 2: handelsplätze des frühen und hohen Mittelalters* (Weinheim), 171–84.

Eisenschmidt, S. 1994. *Kammergräber der Wikingerzeit in Altdänemark*, Universitätsforschungen zur prähistorischen Archäologie, 25 (Bonn).

Eisenschmidt, S. 2004. *Grabfunde des 8. bis 11. jahrhunderts zwischen Kongeå und Eider*, Studien zur Siedlungsgeschichte und Archäologie der Ostseegebiete, 5 (Neumünster).

Hilberg, V. 2007. 'Haithabu im 11. jahrhundert: auf der suche nach dem Niedergang eines dänischen *emporiums* der Wikingerzeit' in C. Dobiat et al. (eds), *Geophysik und ausgrabung: einsatz und auswertung zerstörungsfreier prospektion in der archäologie*, Internationale Archäologie – Naturwissenschaft und Technologie, 6 (Rahden) 187–203.

Hilberg, V. 2009. 'Hedeby in Wulfstan's days', in A. Englert & A. Trakades (eds), *Wulfstan's voyage: the Baltic Sea region in the early Viking Age as seen from shipboard. Maritime Culture of the North*, 2 (Roskilde).

Hill, D. 2001. 'A short gazetteer of postulated continental wics' in D. Hill & R. Cowie (eds), *Wics: the early mediaeval trading centres of Northern Europe*, Sheffield Archaeology Monograph, 14 (Sheffield), pp 104–10.

Hoffmann, D. 2001. 'Archäologische Beiträge zu Wasserstandsveränderungen der Ostsee. Eine kritische Betrachtung', *Archäologische Nachrichten Schleswig-Holstein*, 11, 125–37.

Jankuhn, H. 1936. 'Die ausgrabungen in Haithabu 1935/36', *Offa*, 1, 96–140.

Jankuhn, H. 1943. *Die ausgrabungen in Haithabu (1937–1939). Vorläufiger Grabungsbericht* (Berlin).

Jankuhn, H. 1944. 'Die bedeutung der gußformen von Haithabu' in H. Jankuhn (ed.), *Bericht über die Kieler Tagung 1939: jahrestagungen der forschungs- und lehrgemeinschaft „Das Ahnenerbe"* (Neumünster), pp 226–37.

Jankuhn, H. 1977. 'Das bronzegießerhandwerk in Haithabu' in L. Gerevich & D. Salamon (eds), *La formation et le développement des métiers au Moyen Age (Vê–XIVê siècles) [Congress Budapest 25.–27. Oktober 1973]*, Akadémiai Kiadó (Budapest), 27–40.

Jankuhn, H. 1986. *Haithabu: ein handelsplatz der Wikingerzeit*, 8th ed. (Neumünster).

Kalmring, S. 2003. 'Möglicheiten und grenzen der dendrochronologie für die Haithabu-Hafengrabung 1979/80', *Arkæologi i Slesvig – Archäologie in Schleswig*, 10, 175–85.

Kalmring, S. 2008. 'Neue ergebnisse zum hafen von Haithabu', *Arkæologi i Slesvig – Archäologie in Schleswig*, 12, 151–62.

Kalmring, S. in preperation. 'Der hafen von Haithabu'. Ausgrabungen in Haithabu 14 (Neumünster).

Kramer, W. 1998–9. 'Neue untersuchungen im hafen von Haithabu', *Archäologische Nachrichten aus Schleswig-Holstein*, 9:10, 90–118.

Müller, S. 1897. *Vor Oldtid: Danmarks forhistoriske archæologi* (Copenhagen).

Randsborg, K. 1980. *The Viking Age in Denmark* (London).

Rudolph, M. 1936a. 'Die grundlagen der holzbauweisen von Haithabu', *Offa*, 1, 141–9.

Rudolph, M. 1936b. 'Grundsätzliches von den holzbauten in Haithabu', Nachrichten-blatt für Deutsche Vorzeit 12, 1936, 248–54.

Schietzel, K. 1969. 'Die archäologischen befunde der ausgrabung Haithabu 1963–1964' in K. Schietzel (ed.), *Berichte über die Ausgrabungen in Haithabu*, 1 (Neumünster), 10–59.

Schietzel, K. 1981. 'Stand der siedlungsarchäologischen forschung in Haithabu – ergebnisse und probleme' in K. Schietzel (ed.), *Berichte über die ausgrabungen in Haithabu*, 16 (Neumünster), pp 7–123.

Schietzel, K. 1984a. 'Die topographie von Haithabu' in H. Jankuhn et al. (eds), *Archäologische und naturwissenschaftliche untersuchungen an ländlichen und frühstädtischen siedlungen im deutschen Küstengebiet vom 5. jahrhundert v. Chr. bis zum 11. Jahrhundert n. Chr. 2: handelsplätze des frühen und hohen Mittelalters* (Weinheim), pp 159–62.

Schietzel, K. 1984b. 'Hafenanlagen von Haithabu' in H. Jankuhn et al. (eds), *Archäologische und naturwissenschaftliche Untersuchungen an ländlichen und früh-städtischen Siedlungen im deutschen Küstengebiet vom 5. Jahrhundert v. Chr. bis zum 11. Jahrhundert n. Chr. 2. Handelsplätze des frühen und hohen Mittelalters* (Weinheim), 184–91.

Schietzel, K. 1984c. 'Die baubefunde in Haithabu' in H. Jankuhn et al. (eds), *Archäologische und naturwissenschaftliche Untersuchungen an ländlichen und frühstädtischen Siedlungen im deutschen Küstengebiet vom 5. Jahrhundert v. Chr. bis zum 11. Jahrhundert n. Chr. 2. Handelsplätze des frühen und hohen Mittelalters* (Weinheim), 135–58.

Schmidt, H. 1999. '*Vikingetidens byggeskik i Danmark*' (Højbjerg).

Schultze, J. 2005. 'Zur frage der entwicklung des zentralen Siedlungskernes von Haithabu' in C. Dobiat (ed.), *Reliquiae gentium. Festschrift für Horst Wolfgang Böhme zum 65. Geburtstag*, I, Studia honoraria, 23 (Rahden), 359–73.

Schultze, J. 2006. 'Methodische grundlagen und auswertungsmöglichkeiten einer archäologisch-dendrochronologischen strukturierung der siedlungsgrabung Haithabu' (PhD thesis, Kiel University).

Schultze, J. 2008. 'Die siedlungsgrabung I: methode und möglichkeiten der auswertung', Ausgrabungen in Haithabu 13 (Neumünster).

Steuer, H. 1984. 'Zur ethnischen gliederung der bevölkerung von Haithabu anhand der gräberfelder', *Offa*, 41, 189–212.

Stümpel, H. & B. Borth-Hoffmann. 1983. 'Seismische untersuchungen im hafen von Haithabu' in K. Schietzel (ed.), *Archäometrische Untersuchungen*, Berichte über die Ausgrabungen in Haithabu, 18 (Neumünster), 9–28.

Utecht, T. & H. Stümpel. 1983. 'Magnetische sondierungen in Haithabu' in K. Schietzel (ed.), *Archäometrische Untersuchungen*, Berichte über die Ausgrabungen in Haithabu, 18 (Neumünster), 29–38.

Vogel, V. 1992. 'Profaner Holzbau des 11. bis frühen 13. jahrhunderts in Schleswig' in H.W. Böhme (ed.), *Siedlungen und Landesausbau zur Salierzeit*, I, den nördlichen Landschaften des Reiches, RGZM Monographien 27² (Sigmaringen), 263–76.

Westphalen, P. 1989. 'Die eisenschlacken von Haithabu: ein beitrag zur geschichte des schmiedehandwerks in Nordeuropa', *Berichte über die Ausgrabungen in Haithabu*, 26 (Neumünster), 7–109.

Zippelius, A. 1969. 'Zur frage der dachkonstruktion bei den holzbauten von Haithabu' in K. Schietzel (ed.), *Berichte über die Ausgrabungen in Haithabu*, 1 (Neumünster), 61–72.

Plot-use and access in an eleventh-century Dublin building level

PATRICK F. WALLACE

INTRODUCTION

Thanks to more than twenty years of post-excavation focus on Dublin's archaeological archive, we now have a good idea of the main building types of the Hiberno-Norse town (Wallace 1992a) and of how these compare with those in Ireland's other Viking-Age towns (Wallace 1992b). We also have a first overview of town layout (Wallace 1987; 2002; 2004; 2006; Simpson 1999) and of the significance of the tenement or plot (Wallace 2000).

A number of conclusions are emerging about the Dublin property plots. While not all of their lines may be demonstrated to be exactly continuous, what appear to be blocks of plots demonstrate a rigidity in continuity and, in general, their lines conform to those of the preceding levels. These boundary plots and their shapes determined the locations of the buildings as well as determining the shapes of houses, not the other way round. The wider ends of the plots, which are generally of trapezoidal plan, contained the larger buildings with lesser buildings often occurring in the narrower areas behind. I realize that the concept 'behind' is subjective, but I consciously use the term in the belief that in the mindset of Viking-Age Dubliners the big buildings along, for instance, Fishamble Street, Castle Street and Essex Street West, had their 'fronts' facing onto the streets and that the other structures in the plots were therefore 'behind' them, at least in our sense of 'in front' and 'behind'. In late medieval Venice, for example, large buildings either have their 'fronts' to canals and 'backs' to streets or lanes or vice versa. In this paper, therefore, the use of the term 'front', in reference to a plot or building, refers to its streetside façade, while the terms 'back' or 'rear' refer to its opposite aspect.

It is hoped that the use of a contemporary building level across Fishamble Street will convey something of the content, congestion and layout of the individual plots at different building levels over the tenth and eleventh centuries. Something of the continuity of the positions of the main buildings and the apparent primacy of the pathways behind them above other subservient or secondary structures should also emerge. This look at content and access is offered along with a first tentative background impression of the relative proportions of the plots devoted to buildings and pathways, that is, to structures which persisted in the archaeological record. We can only guess at the real clutter of such spaces; foodstuffs, building materials, bedding (straw?), raw materials of craft, and waste would all have contributed to this.

In this paper, the focus on particular building levels and plots is intended as a preliminary introduction to what is a much fuller record. The intention here is to convey something of the relative completeness of the evidence and, in so doing, the potential for understanding the use of available plot space with the caveat that in the northern half of the site the eastern parts of the plots were outside the area of the excavation, while in the south the western ends of the plots were mechanically sheared off. Despite these circumstances, it would appear that most of the Fishamble Street plots were available for excavation, and because the plots tended to have similar layouts it is possible to extrapolate their general extent, and indeed those of nearby Castle Street and Essex Street West also.

Putting the evidence of the plots together – the front ends from the southern half of Fishamble Street and the back ends from its northern half – it appears that they had pathways from the main streets which gave access to the front entrances of the main buildings. The more formal, often lined, rubbish pits also tended to be located at this side of the property. The main house at the wider end of the plot did not always span its width, as sometimes there was a narrow pathway along its side which gave access to the rear of the plot. The evidence points to a control of access through the plots. The emphasis on the front entrance, with its well-built pathway accessed from the street, the narrow pathways along the sides, where these occurred at all, and the relative frequency with which the front house spanned the width of the plot, emphasizes the formality of the front entrance and of the control of access through the plot. In many cases, visitors to the back areas of the plots would have had to pass through, rather than around, the houses at the front.

The exceptional occurrence of a pair of narrow houses positioned side-by-side at the front of one of the Fishamble Street plots, to be discussed below, only emphasizes the general rule that this space was normally taken up by a single large building. Similarly, the exceptional discovery of a large Type 1 building behind another at the front end of a plot, also for consideration below, again only serves to emphasize that it was more usual to have a small Type 2 building in this position. In this case, the second or internal Type 1 building was linked by a formal wooden yard to the back door of the front building, as if to underline that it may have been the internal building that was, in this case, the main house. The fact that the latter building spanned the entire width of the plot, and that its counterpart in front did not, supports the case for the internally located house being the main building in the plot. The point is that the owner of the main building controlled access *through* if not *to* the plot.

It would seem on present evidence that the provision of access through the plots was of paramount importance. Normally, pathways were built down the length of the plot from the rear of the main building, either down the middle or

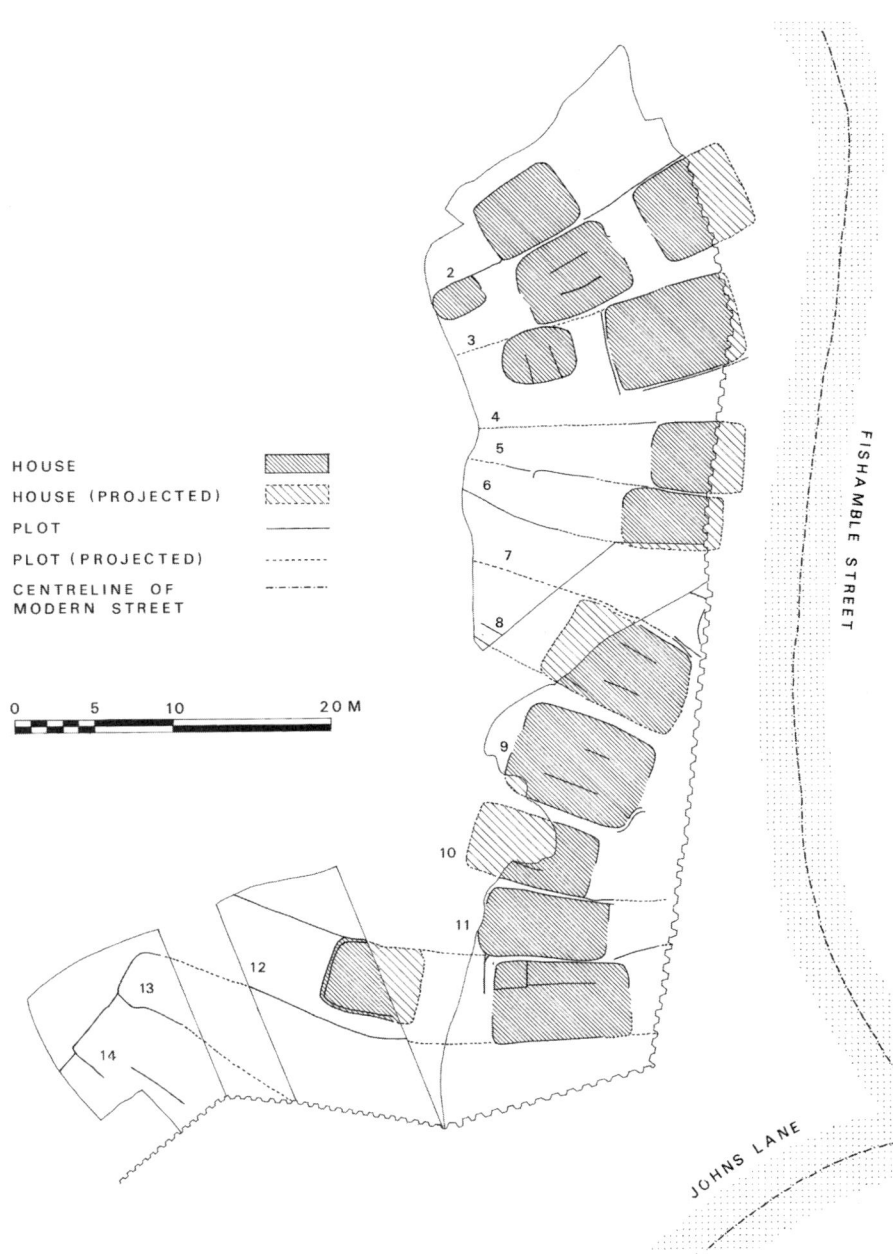

48.1 Simplified plan of Fishamble Street, Dublin (Building Level 10) showing overall relationship of buildings to plots. Plots are numbered from north to south.

along one of the boundary walls. The location of all other types of buildings and structures was secondary and subsidiary to the position of these pathways. Indeed, it seems to have been these pathways which determined not only the location but also the size and, possibly in some cases, the type of smaller buildings built inside the plot area. The attention that seems to have been lavished on internal pathways cannot be emphasized enough. In terms of the Fishamble Street evidence, it seems that the sequence of priorities within the plots began with the main building at the front of the site and the formal pathway that led to it from the street. The excavation and lining of the rubbish pits at the front may even belong to this part of prioritizing the uses of the plot areas. It was after this that a formal pathway was laid down from the back door of the main house; off and around this pathway were ranged the smaller buildings and huts.

There are, as has been noted, exceptions to all of this, but so as far the Fishamble Street evidence goes, such exceptions seem only to confirm the validity of the general impressions offered here. The extent to which there is chronological differentiation, if any, between this suggested order of building and layout priorities remains to be tested from existing site samples, and should perhaps be borne in mind for future excavation campaigns. The degree to which the Fishamble Street evidence is representative of the overall Dublin experience must also be constantly questioned, particularly in the light of fresh results from subsequent and future excavations.

FISHAMBLE STREET – LEVELS AND PROPERTIES

Including the lowest occupation level at ground or zero level, fifteen successive building levels have been identified on Fishamble Street, the best preserved and most extensive of the Dublin sites. Each level represents the use of the principal parts of twelve or thirteen contiguous plots over about two centuries (Fig. 48.1). Recent work by my associate, Adrienne Corless, has cast doubt on the existence of Plot 7, and this question will be resolved when the relevant stratigraphic report is completed.

Our evidence allows not only the comparison of various levels, but also comparison of the development and use of the plots represented on these different levels. By plotting the outlines of all the buildings from all the levels, for example, on one plan (Fig. 48.2), or all the boundary fences on another (Fig. 48.3), it is possible to see how plot areas were used over successive building levels, how restrictive the boundaries were and how buildings and fences tended to be located in more or less the same positions over more than a century and a half. While, logically, the larger buildings tend to be located in roughly the same spaces within the individual plots, the pattern with the succession of boundary fences is not as straightforward. With these, it seems that while some boundary

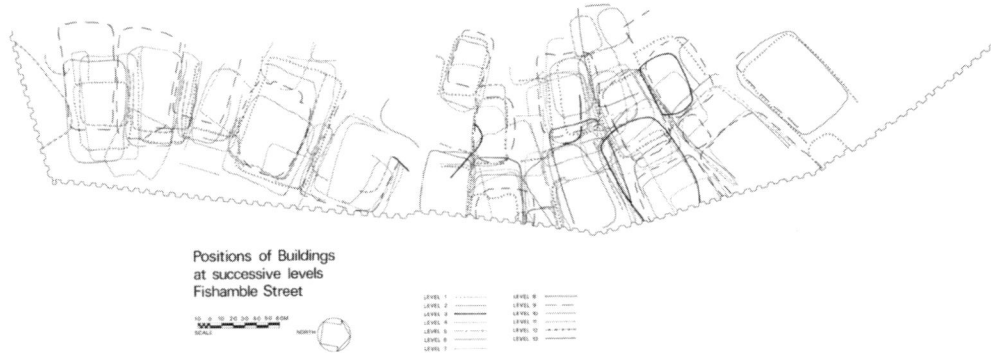

48.2 Positions of buildings at successive levels, Fishamble Street, Dublin.

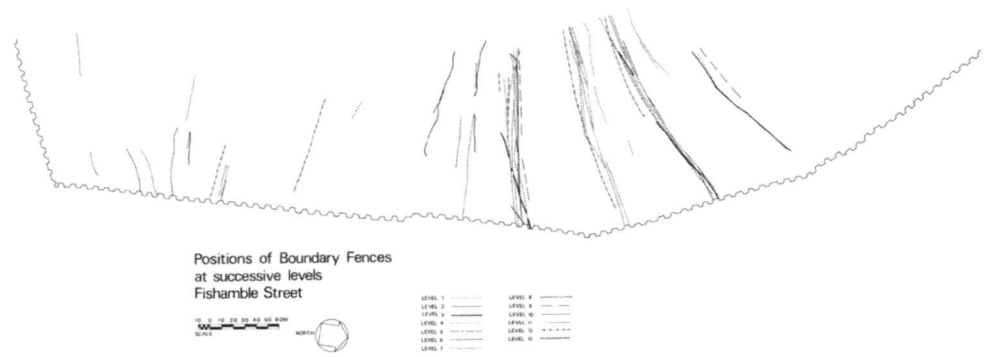

48.3 Positions of boundary fences at successive levels, Fishamble Street, Dublin.

lines offer clear evidence of continuity of position, others appear not to so do. It appears almost as if those boundary lines with demonstrable continuity may be the limits of inherited blocks of property rather than of less rigidly adhered to individual plot lines within blocks. Evidence for boundary fences was absent, for example, between Plots 8, 9 and 10 on Building Level 10.

The publication of the definitive report on the Fishamble Street building levels and the spatial implications of their successions, to be entitled *Plots, Pits and Paths* (Wallace & Corless, forthcoming), which will be combined with the site stratigraphical report, lies some way in the future. For the present, it suffices to say that there is a tendency for pits to be located near the pathways which led to the doorways of the main buildings located nearest the street (Fig. 48.4), and for the main pathways to lead to the presumed principal doorways. Pathways

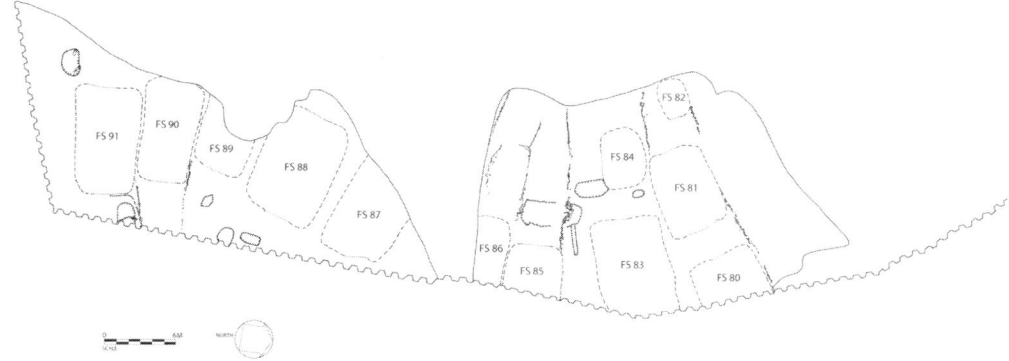

48.4 Positions of pits on Building Level 10, Fishamble Street, Dublin.

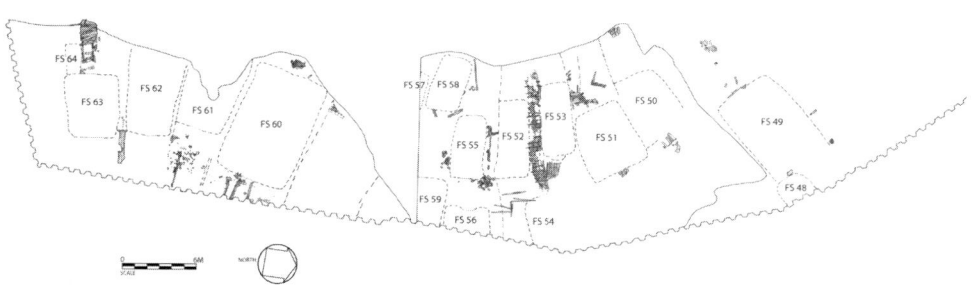

48.5 Positions of pathways on Building Level 8, Fishamble Street, Dublin.

48.6 Details of buildings, pits and pathways across Building Level 10, Fishamble Street, Dublin.

along the sides of the main buildings were of secondary importance, as were those leading rearwards from their back doors. A selection of pathways for Building Levels 8 (Fig. 48.5) and 10 (Fig. 48.6) are illustrated here to emphasize both the importance of access through the individual plots and the tendency to repeatedly locate them in the same positions over successive building levels.

The relative congestion of the individual plots becomes apparent when we sample the footprints of the houses on one of the building levels, Level 10. This apparent congestion becomes even more obvious when roofs are put on the buildings, and when other used surfaces are added – such as footpaths, working yard surfaces, unroofed pens and pits – an impression of congestion amounting to clutter is conjured up. This impression is best conveyed by the simplified plan of the main structural details discovered on Building Level 10 (Fig. 48.6) which, when read with the outline plan of the building footprints (Fig. 48.7), shows how much more than just buildings were constructed on the surfaces of these plots. The footprints of the buildings on Level 9 clearly show how Fishamble Street was excavated in two takes, which fortuitously combine to show the contrast between the fronts of the plots at the south or left of figure 48.8 and their middles and backs at the north or right-hand side.

Looking at the Fishamble Street properties over various building levels, it is possible to trace the use of the spaces and their boundary fences over successive generations for almost two centuries. At its developed stage in the tenth and eleventh centuries, twelve or thirteen adjoining plots were excavated along the western side of Fishamble Street. Of these, Plots 2, 3, 4, 5 and 6 were relatively intact for the dozen or so building levels in which foundation evidence survived, with fewer building levels being preserved in Plots 8, 9, 10, 11 and 12. There was a greater build-up of culture layers toward the north (i.e. the waterfront) end of the site, the settlement presumably developing from the waterfront backwards (i.e. southwards) up the hill. The topmost habitation layers of Plots 7, 8 and 10 were first tackled in small samples – A, B and C during preliminary excavation work on the site. Adrienne Corless has recently managed to reconcile the record of some features excavated in B and C in 1975–6 with what was subsequently recognized as Plot 8 in the more extensive excavations of 1980–1. Incidentally, only a few house foundations were ever identified on Plots 13 and 14.

Fishamble Street Plots 2 to 8 are widest at their east (or presumed streetward) ends, in contrast with 9 to 12, which are widest at their west ends. Plots 13 and 14 also appear to have been widest at their east ends. Only in Plot 13, which was delimited by a fence across its east end, was it possible to be certain of the position and width of any plot end. However, the original widths of the front and rear ends of many plots can be roughly estimated by projecting the lines of the plot sides to meet the line of the presumed street, on the one hand, and that of the waterfront embankments, on the other.

About 18m of Plot 2 survived and its average width was about 5.4m, with the available west and east ends respectively measuring 7.6m and about 4m. A

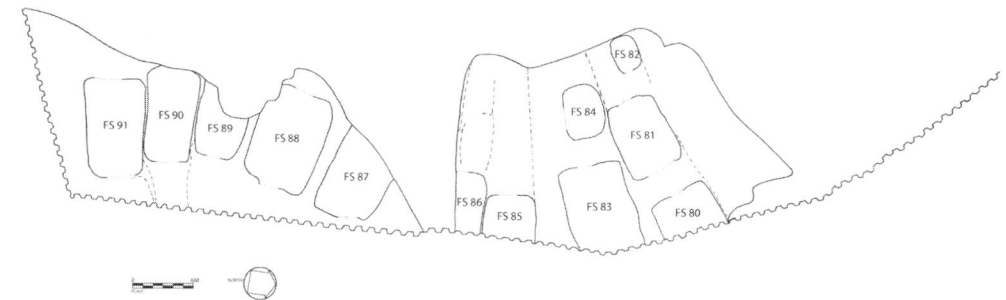

48.7 Positions of buildings on Building Level 10, Fishamble Street, Dublin.

similar length of Plot 3 was excavated and its east end was only about 2.5m wide
at some of the lowest (i.e. earliest) levels. The plot width at this end was gradually
increased in later levels at the expense of Plot 4, onto which it appears to have
encroached. Plot 4 in turn was also widened on its southern margin at the
expense of Plot 5 in a boundary change which may have been connected with a
realignment of plots possibly associated with the erection of one of the larger
earthen embankments. A 17m-length of Plot 4 was excavated, revealing widths
of 9.4m and 5m for the available east and west ends respectively. A similar stretch
of Plot 5 produced respective available east and west end widths of 4.6m and 3m.
A 17.6m-length of Plot 6 revealed east and west end widths of 5m and 2m
respectively, showing the relative equality of size of contiguous Plots 5 and 6 (the
latter may turn out to be much wider if Plot 7 comes to be rejected!). Plot 7, yet
to be confirmed as a separate plot, appears to have been wider with respective
available end widths of 5.4m and 4m in the 17.4m-length investigated. Plot 8 was
greater in size with respective end widths of 6m and 5m in the 17m which could
be measured.

Plot 9 was 7m wide at the available east end but was 9m at the west end of the
13m stretch that was excavated. 13.4m of Plot 10 showed that it was much
smaller than its northern neighbour, as available respective east and west end
widths of 4.6m and 5.5m were recorded. Plot 11 had even narrower east and west
ends widths of 3m and 5.2m respectively in the 12m-stretch which was
excavated. Plot 12 was at least 28m long and had respective west and east end
widths of 5.4m and 5.2m, showing that it was more rectangular in plan than any
other known Fishamble Street plot. Plot 13 measured 34m to the back of the plot
at its 3.2m wide east end and was 5.6m wide at the surviving west end. About
13m of Plot 14 was excavated and its respective east and west end available
widths were 5.4m and 4.4m.

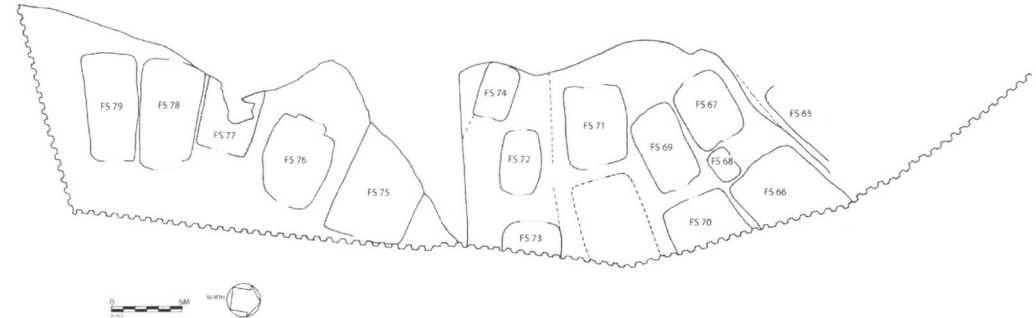

48.8 Positions of buildings on Building Level 9, Fishamble Street, Dublin.

The most extreme east and west plot end widths measurable show that the Dublin plots varied considerably in size. Some plots, especially 4 and 9, were relatively wide, while some, like the contiguous pair 5 and 6, were apparently narrow (that is if Plot 6 does not yet turn out to have actually originally incorporated what was originally thought to have been Plot 7). The discovery of relatively wide plots alongside narrower plots shows that properties of approximate size were not grouped together. Plots 5 and 6 are an exception to this and have a sequence of consistently narrow houses (Type 3, Wallace 1992a) seemingly specially designed to fit into relatively tiny plots, which may have resulted from the subdivision of a single plot at an early level.

Widths seem to be a more reliable indicator of plot area than lengths (although the latter also probably varied considerably in accordance with plot location). Not all properties can have been as long as Plot 13, which had a length in excess of 34m. The trapezoidal shape of the majority of the known Fishamble Street plots makes it difficult to assess the ratio between width and depth of plots, as is possible with certain English later medieval towns.

FISHAMBLE STREET, LEVEL 10

Level 10 is one of the best preserved of all building levels, not only in the remarkable Fishamble Street series but also in all of Dublin and, indeed, Europe for that matter. It will be discussed in a forthcoming general survey of the layout of the Viking age town (Wallace & Corless, forthcoming). Three of its properties have been chosen for detailed examination below, Plots 3, 4 and 9. Here, although little if anything survives in Plots 2 and 3 (Fig. 48.6), the quality of preservation of the two halves of the site enables us to appreciate the backyard

activity and the relative congestion in Plots 3 to 6 inclusive, where large
proportions of the plot areas were built over and there can be little question of
garden activity or indeed the housing of animals. By contrast, Plots 8 to 12 give
us a vivid view in foundation detail of what the interiors of the main buildings
were like, as well as details of the frontage of the plots where pathways led,
presumably from the street, to the doors. So good is the preservation here, and
so relatively different are the contributions of the two halves of the site to our
overall understanding of Dublin's plots, that one is tempted to use them with
one another to see how more extensive runs of plot might have looked. This can
be done by placing the streetward evidence from the south with the backyard
information from the north to get a better idea of what the overall plot evidence
might have been like had it been available for excavation in an open area site.

For present purposes, three plots from Building Level 10 have been chosen
for scrutiny – Plots 3, 4 and 9. Plot 3 (Fig. 48.9) contains three contemporary
buildings. Unusually, it has two Type 1 buildings (FS 80 & FS 81) and, at the
extreme west of the available area, a Type 5 building (FS 85). A major insight
into the property mindset of eleventh-century Dublin is provided by house FS 81,
because it spans the entire width of the plot (Fig. 48.10). There was, therefore,
no way anyone visiting either the front or back of the plot could conveniently do
so without going through FS 81, thereby implying that this could not be done
without the owner's or occupier's knowledge and/or consent. This provides
physical evidence for what is implied on other plots at other building levels,
where the surviving evidence is less direct and more implicit in nature.

Progressing from plot to plot southwards and starting at Plot 3 (Figs 48.9 and
48.10), at the street or wide end, we find a Type 1 house which does not straddle
the width of the plot, but has a woven wattle pathway curling around its south
wall between the house and the boundary fence. This pathway leads to a square
wooden pavement that links the back door of the main house with the east
entrance of a second Type 1 building (which does straddle the width of the
narrowing plot). Beyond the west doorway of this second house, a pathway leads
by FS 82, a small Type 5 hut (perhaps a privy), to the north and just inside the
boundary fence between Plots 2 and 3. Next door in Plot 4 (Fig. 48.11), a huge
Type 1 house also features a pathway between its south sidewall and the
boundary fence. This leads to a cobbled yard, to the west of which is a Type 2
house and, beyond that, a pathway which trails westwards beyond the site
margin. Next to the wide Plot 4, the narrow Plot 5 also has a Type 1 house at its
east end, this time straddling the width of the plot. Beyond this and trailing
alongside the north boundary fence is a solid timber pathway. Plot 6 presents a
complex of stone yards beyond the main house at its east end. The house, like its
neighbour in Plot 5, has a wooden drain exiting out its west doorway. However,
it is the two sub-rectangular post-and-wattle kerbed stone yards, one behind the
other, beyond and aligned with FS 86, that are the most intriguing features on

this plot. We can only guess at what such (quasi industrial?) surfaces may have been used for.

Beyond Plot 6 lay the woven wattle remains of a pathway at the rear of the missing Plot 7 (in this case the alignment and the relative amount of space argue for this not being an extension of Plot 8). Plots 9, 10 and 11 each had an extensive log pathway leading to their front entrances. The remains of the actual door survived in the case of FS 87 in Plot 9, while a really long stretch of pathway survived leading to FS 89 in Plot 10. A very wide pathway-cum-yard arrangement survived in front of FS 90 in Plot 11, where the planks of a dismembered wooden boat formed a drain under a log pathway laid on branches and runners which formed a wooden yard stretching across the width of the plot. The west or back doors of FS 88 in Plot 9 and FS 91 in Plot 12 had stone pathways leading from them. There is evidence for boundary fences on Plot 11 at either side of the wooden yard, just described, and some evidence also for pits at the ends of the main houses in Plots 9, 10 and 12; a pit also lay at the west side of Plot 13.

Before finishing with a closer look at the physical evidence for layout and content within this plot at this level, the apparent care that the builders lavished on the small rectangular wooden yard which linked the walking space between the end walls of the two Type 1 buildings on this level is intriguing. If this is a genuinely unusual detail, and not just an accident of survival from a norm which does not usually survive, it raises questions about why the builders or owners went to so much trouble with a linking yard between this pair of buildings. Could it, in some way, be representative of an attempt to create or suggest a parity or equality of status between the two buildings?

For the record, the little wooden yard consisted of a series of chopped up timbers fitted together on a bed of gravel to form a rectangle between the west doorway of FS 80 and the east doorway of FS 81. Amusingly, a thin stone sliver which cracked into two halves, presumably from use, had to make up the mosaic when the timbers ran out! The discovery of high-status artefacts, including coins, in these houses may be indicative of the owners' status.

Whatever about its status, the common sense rôle of the small yard was to keep dry the feet of the pedestrians who passed between this pair of homes. That this failed when the wooden paving planks were pressed into the soft gravel and the damp ground of Dublin is evident from the presence of a woven wattle mat which had to be placed on top. The mat linked with a woven wattle pathway which was laid along the south side of FS 80. This shows, incidentally, that while it may have been possible to walk between this building and the south wall of the plot, visitors (from the main street?) would have had to come to the little yard to pass through to the other end of the plot. Can it be that because visitors were funnelled or channelled in this direction that the second (interior) house (FS 81) was the main building on this plot and that the other Type 1 building at the streetward side of it functioned more as a business-cum-workshop?

48.9 Plan of excavated remains of Building Level 10, Plot 3, Fishamble Street, Dublin.

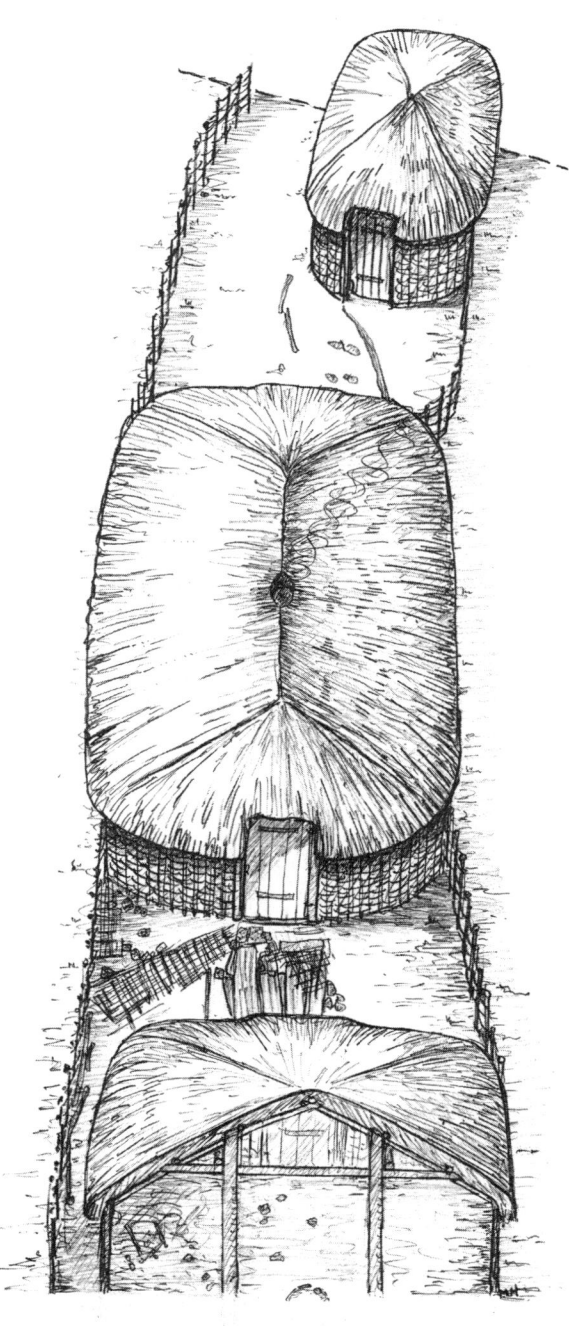

48.10 Reconstruction of Building Level 10, Plot 3, Fishamble Street, Dublin.

Incidentally, beyond FS 81 and outside its west end doorway, going towards the end of the area of the plot available for excavation, were the remnants of the runners of a pathway leading towards the east endwall entrance of a flimsy Type 5 building, a hut. This was without internal roof supports and was characterized by having a flat pole at the west end of its floor, which I interpret as a revetment for heaped dung.

Plot 4, wider than Plot 3, featured a pair of buildings. These comprised a large Type 1 example, FS 83, located at the wide end of the plot area available for excavation and, set well back from it, west of centre in the available area, a Type 2 building, FS 84 (Fig. 48.11). Both buildings were located right up against the north boundary of Plot 4, and a wide strip with the remnants of a woven wattle pathway occurred between the south sidewall of the Type 1 house and the boundary fence. A stone pavement covered the yard space between the west endwall of this house and the east end of the Type 2 building behind it. The latter building had the typical sidewall entrance, with the doorway in the south wall. In this particular case, part of the door itself actually survived. It was a woven wattle door of which the framing lath at the base survived along with the vertical rods which were alternately pinned at either side of it to make up the body of the door. Lucas (1956) has shown that doors of this type survived in use in Ireland until recent centuries. In plan, this building featured a low U- or apron-shaped post-and-wattle arc inside the entrance. Much of the original woven wattle matting, which presumably covered the floor, had disappeared.

The partial survival of a narrow line of a woven wattle pathway outside the southwest corner of FS 84, around which it originally was meant to skirt, recalls the outdoor access arrangement noted in the other plots at the various building levels. Presumably this surviving section of pathway originally linked to the fragments of a pathway discovered south of the main house, noted above, and linked to the small stone pavement between the two buildings. If this is the case and there was such a continuous pathway running east–west through Plot 4 at this level, it demonstrates the primacy of access with the buildings being constructed around and offset from the main pathway.

The last plot on this building level to be considered here is Plot 11 (Fig. 48.12). As with my other selections of plots, I am prompted to include it because of the quality of its preservation and the light it sheds on building evidence, urban layout, plot content and use. In this particular case, the main house (FS 90) and the elaborate entrance to it, presumably accessed from the original main street, are all that survived for excavation, as the west end of the plot – with whatever buildings and structures it may have contained – was cleared off mechanically before the archaeological excavation began.

The building spans the entire width of the plot and fits so tightly between the boundary fences that its plan reflects the oblong trapezoidal shape of the plot at this point. This recalls a phenomenon already noted with FS 81, where what was arguably the main house spanned the entire width of the plot, thereby implying that visitors intending to traverse the plot had to pass through the house, presumably with the owner's fore knowledge and, possibly, permission. This suggests that visitors *to* or, more properly perhaps, *through* plots were controlled.

Apart from the quality of preservation of building FS 90 itself, including its evidence for built-in furniture, which has been described elsewhere (Wallace 1992a), the main point of interest about this house concerns how it linked (possibly) to the main street, which lay in the area unavailable for excavation. It looks as though the whole area in front of the house's east entrance was given over to a very elaborate pathway-cum-drainage arrangement. A V-shaped wooden drain, built from the dismembered planks of a clinker-built vessel, was laid down in a wide setting of dressed and rough timbers. The drain's function was clearly to take water from the area of the front door while that of the timber setting was to provide a reinforcement raft for a series of wide timbers that were laid transversely on the drain to form an elaborate entrance pathway. Presumably the intention, or hope, was that any surplus water would filter through the timbers into the drain beneath. It probably worked for a time, at least based on the experience on the excavation a thousand years later when the drain still continued to convey water from our working area!

BUILDING AND PATHWAY FOOTPRINTS AS PROPORTIONS OF PLOT USE

Although it is possible, by reference especially to the evidence from Fishamble Street and Essex Street West, to know what the complete Dublin Viking-Age plot looked like and how its buildings, pits and pathways were arranged, no actual complete plot has been unearthed. By judicious use of the excavated evidence from all the sites, it is possible to reconstruct the average complete plot, a task to which I hope to return. Meanwhile, some interesting pointers in this direction emerge from measurement of the building footprints and pathway areas of the plots in question.

Bearing in mind that smaller areas of the total plots in Fishamble Street were available for excavation in the south (Plots 8 to 13 inclusive) than in the north (Plots 1 to 6) and that earlier building levels were not evident in the southern half of the site, a number of interesting points emerge in respect of the chosen plots and levels. Of the available area for excavation, for instance, of Plot 9 at Level 10, some 42.75m^2, or 89 per cent of it (38.13m^2) was occupied by building FS 90. As much as 95 per cent of the area was taken up when the pathway area is added.

Plot 3, another late Viking-Age eleventh-century plot, had an area of 97.37m^2 available for excavation. Here, three buildings (FS 80, 81 and 82) had a combined footprint of 66.26m^2, representing 68 per cent of the available area,

48.11 Plan of excavated remains of Building Level 10, Plot 4, Fishamble Street, Dublin.

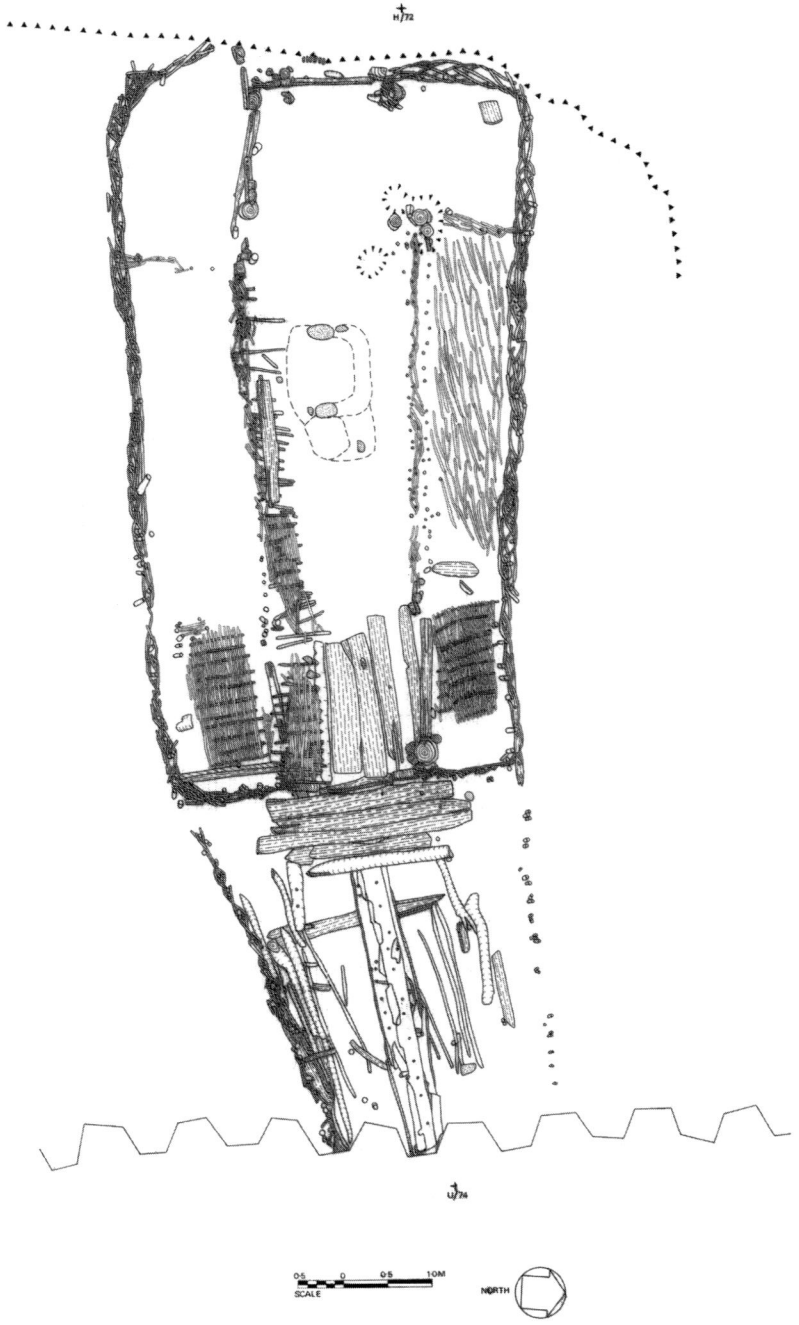

48.12 Plan of excavated remains of Building Level 10, Plot 9, Fishamble Street, Dublin.

but this figure rises to 80 per cent when the path area of 18.98m² is added. A great deal less of the wider Plot 4, which amounted to 127.5m² at this level, seems to have been occupied. Here, buildings FS 83 and 84 came to a total of 64.38m², or 50.5 per cent of the area of the plot, increasing to 59 per cent when the pathway area of 11.29m² is added.

There may be a greater usage of plot areas in Dublin as one progresses later into the Viking Age. Plots 11 and 4 at Level 10 may be the two most congested of the present sample. To demonstrate the difficulty of generalizations like this, however, Plot 4 on the same level is only the seventh highest in the congestion stakes. Two earlier plots, however, were used to explore the hypothesis further (Plot 2 on Level 7 and Plot 3 on Level 5). In the first of these, which had an available area of 97.85m², two houses (FS 37 and FS 38) had a combined footprint of 39.3m² or only 40 per cent of the plot, but 36.49m² of pathway use, while in its earlier neighbour, which had an available area of 100.8m², featured two houses (FS 21 and FS 22) which had a combined footprint of 54.7m² representing some 54 per cent of the area, there being only an extra 10.24m² of surviving pathway! It should be noted that the relatively large area of 'pathway' in Plot 2 at Level 7 includes one if not two areas which, as has been noted already, may have been roofed originally.

Plot 4 at Level 10 has already been noted as having a 59 per cent use of the available space. The same plot had a 56 per cent usage at the much earlier Level 4 and, perhaps significantly, only a 51 per cent usage at Level 7. The much higher usage of the available area of Plot 3 at Level 10 (80 per cent) has already been noted.

It is difficult to find patterns in terms of the relative proportions of plot spaces which were roofed and/or otherwise used in the nine plots which have been discussed. Two plots are not included in the overall discussion because, in contrast to the others selected, their widths are poorly understood. These are Plot 5, Level 8, with its two buildings (FS 56 & FS 58) which, with a small associated run of surviving pathway, accounted for 68 per cent usage of the available area, and Plot 6, at the same level which had a single building (FS 55) and a tiny pathway area accounting for 23 per cent of the available plot area. The southern boundary line was missing in the case of Plot 5 at this level and disrupted beyond retrieval in the case of Plot 6, the area of which, as has been remarked already, may include the area of what heretofore has been regarded as Plot 7.

For what it is worth, the two plots with a very high percentage of built use are Plots 3 and 11 from Level 10, dating from the early to middle eleventh century, well into the mature phase of Hiberno-Norse Dublin. It is also interesting that these plots belong with the northern and southern parts of the of the Fishamble Street site respectively, the latter in which the front entrance and main Type 1 house belonged and the former the middle or back parts of the plot in which only parts of the front or principal Type 1 house was preserved. Against the ready acceptance of this generalization is the fact that the next two plots with the highest proportion of built use are Plots 3 and 2 at the earlier Levels 5 and 7 respectively, of later tenth-century date.

Our conclusion must be that the plots were highly developed spaces. This is based solely on the surviving archaeological remains of building footprints and pathways, not on the uses of the plots and their buildings (such as, for instance, the storage of commodities), which would not normally have left recognizable archaeological traces. The actual proportions of built over or roofed space are obviously considerably less when the areas of pathway are not allowed for. All of this underlines the relative importance of pathways in the contemporary mindset.

ACKNOWLEDGMENTS

My thanks as ever to Michael Heffernan of the National Museum of Ireland's Design Department for the drawings and reconstructions used here and to Sinéad Lawlor, also of the National Museum of Ireland, for her help in the preparation of the essay for publication. I am also grateful for the observations of my colleague, Adrienne Corless, who measured the respective areas of the buildings and pathways in the selected plots and placed them at my disposal.

BIBLIOGRAPHY

Lucas, A.T. 1956. 'Wattle and straw mat doors in Ireland', *Arctica: Studia Ethnographica Upsaliensia*, 11, 16–25.

Simpson, L. 1999. *Directors findings – Temple Bar West: archaeology in Temple Bar* (Archaeological Report No. 5), Dublin.

Wallace, P.F. 1987. 'The layout of later Viking-Age Dublin: indications of its regulation and problems of continuity' in J.E. Knirk (ed.), *Proceedings of the Tenth Viking Congress, Larkollen 1985*, Oslo, pp 271–85.

Wallace, P.F. 1992a. *The Viking-Age buildings of Dublin: Medieval Dublin excavations 1962–81, Series A, Vol. 1*, Dublin.

Wallace, P.F. 1992b. 'The archaeological identity of the Hiberno-Norse town', *Journal of the Royal Society of Antiquaries of Ireland*, 122, 35–66.

Wallace, P.F. 2000. '*Garrda* and *airbeada*: the plot thickens in Viking Dublin' in A.P. Smyth (ed.), *Seanchas: essays in early and medieval Irish archaeology, history and literature in Honour of F.J. Byrne*, Dublin, pp 261–74.

Wallace, P.F. 2002. Artist's impression of Dublin (drawn by Simon Dick) and note. Pl. 1 in A. Simms, H.B. Clarke & R. Gillespie (eds.), *Dublin Part 1, to 1610* (Irish Historic Towns Atlas no. 11), Dublin.

Wallace, P.F. 2004. 'The big picture: mapping Hiberno-Norse Dublin' in H.B. Clarke, J. Prunty & M. Hennessy (eds), *Surveying Ireland's past: multidisciplinary essays in honour of Anngret Simms*, Dublin, pp 13–40.

Wallace, P.F. 2006. The bigger picture: reconstructing Hiberno-Norse Dublin' in H.B. Clarke & J.R.S. Phillips (eds), *Ireland, England and the Continent in the Middle Ages and beyond*, Dublin, pp 11–28.

Wallace, P.F. & A. Corless, with A. Halpin, forthcoming. Plots, pits and paths: Fishamble Street, a stratigraphic report.

On *eið*-names in Orkney and other
North Atlantic islands

DOREEN WAUGH

INTRODUCTION

At the Fourteenth Viking Congress held in Tórshavn in the Faroe Islands, I spoke about *nes*-names (Waugh 2005a, 250–6) and made the point that, in my opinion, place-names which on first consideration appear to be purely topographical in reference, and by implication on the part of some scholars somehow less significant and informative than habitative place-names, deserve much closer attention than they have sometimes received from toponymists. In this paper, I shall pursue that theme again in talking about *eið*-names (Old Norse [ON] *eið* n. 'an isthmus'). These are certainly topographical in reference in that, with a few exceptions which will be mentioned in the next paragraph, they refer to easily identifiable necks of land, but it is my firm belief that they also have much to tell us about patterns of movement of goods and people around the landscape in early Viking times and later centuries in the Northern Isles. I first spoke on this topic at a conference on portages in Norway in 2005 (Waugh 2006, 239–49) and subsequently wrote an article on Shetland *eið*-names for the summer edition of the *New Shetlander* (Waugh 2005b, 33–8), and I shall use this present opportunity to focus on Orkney *eið*-names, briefly comparing the number of such names in Orkney with numbers of similar names in Shetland and the Faroes.

EID-NAMES IN GENERAL

The fundamental question is 'when is an isthmus solely a topographical feature and when is it part of the economic landscape, used as a route for the movement of goods and/or boats from one coast to another?' The answer really is 'when *eið* forms all or part of the place-name which describes the location, there is good reason to conclude that the isthmus in question is part of the Norse economic landscape'. There are, of course, many isthmuses which do not have *eið* as part of their names and I would argue that these stretches of land were not regularly used for portage of goods or movement of people. *Eið* is also applied to stretches of land which were probably used as portage routes between two endpoints but which cannot be seen as isthmuses in the usual sense of the word. For instance, the 'isthmus' can be a stretch of four to five miles of raised ground intervening between one inlet of the sea and another, as from Aith to Effirth in Shetland (Waugh 2005b, 36–7). Documentary evidence to prove that an *eið* was used in the past as a portage route is regrettably insubstantial for both Orkney and Shetland but, in spite of the lack of documentary evidence, I have become convinced that *eið* is always used in the sense of a place where either portage of boats or movement of people and goods took place. Barbara Crawford stated in her book entitled *Scandinavian Scotland* that:

> The Vikings' ability to use narrow necks of land over which they dragged their boats in order to circumvent long sea routes is not to be under-estimated. Wherever the Old Norse element *eið* can be traced in a place name it is certain that the isthmus would have been used as a portage (Crawford 1987, 24).

I completely agree with the final sentence of this statement but do not believe that some of the *eið*-locations in the Northern Isles could have been regularly used for portage purely in the sense of 'places where boats could be dragged across land from one inlet of the sea to another'. That may have happened when the Vikings first arrived because, having sent runners on ahead to check the feasibility of dragging their boats across land at a particular location, they may have wished to explore the crossing further without abandoning their boats at one end of it. For the most part, however, *eið*-names indicate permanent settlement in their vicinity and functional use of the land between two expanses of sea.

Dragging of boats did, of course, sometimes happen in very unlikely places, and I have elsewhere cited the example of the late eighteenth-century dragging of a sixareen or six-oared boat from one part of Nesting in Shetland to another (Waugh 2005b, 34). The distance by land, in this instance, was not much shorter than the distance by sea, but presumably the dragging of the boat was dictated by a common-sense approach to the coastal maritime environment. Alternatively, one wonders if the boat was perhaps unseaworthy and was being taken to a place where it could be repaired, although there is no indication of that in the historical record:

> Beyond the township the landscape must have appeared open (due to lack of dykes). In fact the late Geordie Gair (local historian) spoke of John Sutherland of Gletness and his four sons dragging a large sixareen from the North Voe of Gletness to the Hame Ayre of South Gletness in 1776, unhindered by dykes, a feat which would not have been possible at the end of the nineteenth century (Leask, Bradley & Bradley 1998, 85).

Generally speaking, many toponymic parallels can be found by researchers who compare place-names in the North Atlantic islands of Orkney, Shetland, the Faroes and Iceland (also in the Hebrides but not discussed here). I certainly expected to find those *eið*-names which are recorded in *Orkney Farm-Names* (Marwick 1952) following the same toponymic patterns as the *eið*-names in its closest neighbour, Shetland, and that is generally true. Shetland, however, has more surviving *eið*-names than Orkney and, as can be seen from the collection of place-names listed in the Appendix, the Faroe Islands have a particularly large number of *eið*-names. It is, of course, possible that more *eið*-names could be collected locally in both Orkney and Iceland to tilt the numerical balance in their favour.

The element *eið* occurs in all of the North Atlantic islands, but it is only in the Shetland and Faroese names listed in the Appendix that it is demonstrably compounded with habitative elements such as *setr* and *garðr*, which refer directly to human habitation and clearly suggest a history of human activity in the area. Such secondary place-names would, most probably, have been coined after the creation of any simplex *eið*-name in the vicinity. Hugh Marwick does record one example of Aithstoun (now lost) from Sandwick in Orkney, dated 1595 (Marwick 1952, 148). Whether this is a different name from Aith, Sandwick, itself, however, is very debatable. Only one place is recorded as Aiths Town on an eighteenth-century chart of the area (Thomson 1996, 28) and in the *Rental Orchade, pro Rege et Episcopo 1595* as Aithston (Peterkin 1820, 46) but two names – *Aith* and *Upsale* – are listed together in Lord Henry Sinclair's 1492 Rental of Orkney (Peterkin 1820, 56). All the simplex *Aith*-names in Orkney are now associated with areas in which settlement has taken place and some refer to townships of significant size and longevity as farmed land. The farm at *Bu of Aith* in Walls is a particularly notable example, although the construction 'Bu *of* Aith' suggests a later analogical coinage in which the earlier Norse words, anglicized to 'Bu' (ON *bær* m. 'a farm': see also Thomson 2001, 51–4; Marwick 1952, 240–8) and 'Aith' are employed in an English language formation (cf. Nicolaisen 1983, 78). Hugh Marwick notes that Aith, Walls, appears in the '1492 and all later rentals', and goes on to comment that 'The head-house of this tunship was (and is) called The Bu of Aith' (Marwick 1952, 182) but there is no reference to the 'Bu' in the earliest rental; only a reference to Aith itself (Peterkin 1820, 27; Thomson 1996, 64).

Although *eið* is not a particularly common place-name element in either Orkney or Shetland, the fact that it occurs more frequently in Shetland than in Orkney, could suggest that, if portage was taking place, it was, surprisingly, more often practised in hilly Shetland than in the flatter terrain in many parts of Orkney. The relative numbers of place-names listed in the Appendix would, in fact, suggest that the archipelago where portage was most commonly practised was the Faroes, where the land is even more steep and difficult to cross in places. Presumably, as I have said elsewhere (Waugh 2005b, 34), the roughness of the surrounding sea, the distance round the headland which was being by-passed and the possible danger from coastal rocks or tidal swirls were the deciding factors that persuaded people to carry boats or goods across land. This opinion has been substantiated by Louise Hollinrake's observations about sea conditions and tides in Orkney, backed up by her interesting maps of tidal flow in the waters of the Pentland Firth (Hollinrake 2003).

One observation, with regard to all North Atlantic island *eið*-names, is that, although the land-crossings may appear to offer huge physical challenges, the place-names occur in convincingly strategic locations for crossing points. It is easy to understand why the places which do have *eið*-names were selected for use either as the starting points of portage routes or as necks of land across which boats or goods needed be transferred; sometimes, as in Iceland, because the neighbouring water would be frozen at certain times of the year and movement across land would be the only option. In fact, it is possible to take the next imaginative step and to envisage a network of interconnected, criss-crossing portage routes, particularly in Orkney, Shetland and the Faroes. The crossing points would have been important meeting places in the past.

The Orkney locations are spread across the Orkney archipelago from Eday to South Ronaldsay. The isthmuses which they describe on the smaller islands of Eday, Stronsay, Walls and South Ronaldsay could certainly have been used as route ways for local transport of goods or people. Aith, on the west mainland of Orkney, is in an interesting location because, like Aith in west Shetland, there is no obvious coastal neck of land to which it could apply. The current name, referred to as West Aith, lies on the eastern side of the Loch of Skaill. It seems likely that it may refer to one or both of the two stretches of land lying between the Loch of Skaill and the Lochs of Harray and Stenness respectively, which could have been regular routes for the transfer of goods into the heart of mainland Orkney and thence across to Kirkwall via the Bay of Firth or north to Dounby market using pack horses or some other means of travel across land. Alternatively, the portage could have been used to give a more sheltered approach for boats wishing to enter Scapa Flow coming from the north-west, or wishing to leave Scapa Flow with goods for the north-west mainland. This route, if it existed, must have been from the Bay of Skaill, through Skaill Loch, across the *eið* into the Loch of Stenness. It should be remembered that it is very likely that the surrounding area of flat land would have been much more waterlogged in the past than now, prior to the extensive drainage associated with agricultural improvement of the land (cf. Crawford 2006, 30). It may not have been all that difficult in the early Norse period, and for several ensuing centuries, to traverse the land in the west mainland of Orkney from waterway to waterway by boat.

The name Scapa itself is an *eið* name, recorded definitively in *Orkneyinga saga* as *Skálpeið* (*Orkneyinga saga*, 66). Marwick comments as follows:

> ON *skálpr* was a poetic term for a ship, but its more prosaic sense was that of a sword-sheath [...] and it could be used in place names for 'a long hollow or depression in the terrain'. That is exactly what there is between Scapa and the sea to the north, and the name might be understood as 'long valley isthmus'. On the other hand, if the original idea of 'something cleft in two' survived in the term *skálpr*, Scapa might be interpreted as the isthmus cleaving the Orkney Mainland in two (Marwick 1952, 100).

Whether the specific in the name Scapa refers to a ship or to a topographical feature, there can be little doubt that Scapa was used as a location for portage, giving access from the sea to the north into Scapa Flow, which became particularly well known as a sheltered anchorage for much larger ships during the last century. Traffic would, of course, have been two-way, with transfer of goods from the south through Scapa Flow to the various islands of Orkney lying to the north.

In general, the Orkney *eið*-names have not expanded into local clusters of names, based on the central *eið*-name with the addition of other elements such as ON *nes*, *vík* etc, to quite the same extent as the Shetland and Faroese *eið*-names have done. Aith in Stronsay has been used in the much later English construction, Bight of Aith, describing the wide bay. From Aith in South Walls a few more subsidiary names have developed: Aith Hope, Aith Head and Aithsdale and, as already noted, the 'Bu of Aith'. Aith Head is, of course, a later English construction and Aith Hope and Aithsdale are, at the very least, Anglicized from ON *hóp* (n. 'a small, land-locked bay') and *dalr* (m. 'a valley'); it is, in fact, perfectly possible that the latter two place-names were created by English or Scots speakers who used the words *hope* and *dale* in their form of the local Orkney dialect of English. The same comment has already been made with regard to the Bu of Aith. Whatever its exact date of origin, Aith in South Walls was evidently an important local crossing place for several centuries, created by the Norse and still being used by later English speakers.

Hoxa, on South Ronaldsay, is very usefully recorded in *Orkneyinga saga* as 'Haugaeið' (*Orkneyinga saga*, 8). In other words, it is the isthmus on which there is more than one mound, from ON *haugr* (m. 'a how, mound') which is a relatively common element in Northern Isles' place-names. Marwick comments about Hoxa that 'there are actually two mounds' and one of them is 'a large broch-mound prominent from afar'. He goes on to speculate that 'Here it probably was that Earl Thorfinn Skull-cleaver was *howe-laid*' (Marwick 1952, 172). What a perfect meeting place this must have been for people coming from various directions to congregate on the *eið* with its prominent landmark to guide them to the correct spot. It is very tempting to think of the implications of the place-name Hoxa (*Haugaeið*) in the same context as *Hauga-þing* (n. 'an assembly in Norway' (Cleasby & Gudbrand Vigfusson 1957, 241).

The question mark in the Appendix beside Doomy on Eday – itself an island which is defined by the *eið* at its centre – flags up that, while there is no uncertainty about the etymology of Eday (*eið*-island), there is considerable uncertainty about the etymology of Doomy. I think, however, that Doomy is worth including as a putative *eið*-name, in spite of the total lack of supportive early documentary references. I have placed it deliberately next to Hoxa in this discussion for reasons which should become apparent. Doomy forms the west part of the *eið* at Eday and the name itself appears to refer to a mound. Derivative names are all later topographical references (Bay of […], Sands of […], Loch of Doomy) and Doomy has not gone on to become a farm name. To speculate, however, could it have been an *eið* where people regularly congregated to discuss the meting out of justice (ON *dómr* m. 'doom, judgment, sentence; cf. also *dóm-hús* n. the 'house of doom' court-house; *dóm-kirkja* n. 'a cathedral'; *dóm-leggja* 'to lay before a court'; *dóm-nefna* f. 'the nomination of judges' in the Icelandic court)? Is **dóm-eið* possible in this context? Like Hoxa, Doomy is in a location which could easily have been approached from various directions by boat. As far as I am aware, there are no other place-names with this particular combination of elements and that does give rise to a considerable degree of doubt about this hypothetical etymology, but common sense and the topography both support the suggestion that Doomy might have been an important meeting place and I shall leave the question open.

Many *eið*-names do refer to places which are associated with administrative activities of one kind or another, often to do with the imposition of law. For example, there are *þing*-names, or sites where local assemblies were held, such as Aithsting and Lunnasting in Shetland: Aith on the Westside of Shetland has given rise to the *þing*-name Aithsting, now part of the conjoint parishes of Sandsting and Aithsting, with the head church in the village of Twatt which is situated half-way between Aith and Effirth (*eið-fjörðr*), both definitely *eið*-names with attested early forms; Lunna is a name in its own right and it is also the specific in Lunnasting, which is identified by Jakobsen as '**lund-eiðs-þing*' (Jakobsen 1993, 125). Incidentally, the first element in Lunnasting (ON *hlunnr* m. 'piece(s) of wood put under the keel of ships to be dragged') appears to be the only instance in either Shetland or Orkney of reference to actual dragging of boats across an isthmus.

CONCLUSION

In some ways, it is unfortunate to end with the debatable example of Doomy, but my study of *eið*-names is, in fact, a research project which is very far from ended and there are many questions still to be considered. The subsequent inclusion of examples of *eið*-names from the Western Isles will be particularly important in the Scottish context. In addition, I have not paused for discussion of the element *eið* in the present dialects of Orkney and Shetland, but the fact is that *eið* did not survive in regular use in the Orkney or Shetland dialects into the twentieth century, which suggests that it was no longer an active name-forming element by that time. Jakobsen, who collected evidence for his *Etymological Dictionary of the Norn Language in Shetland* between 1893 and 1895, records *ed* as a word which 'is still remembered in South Shetland, in its original meaning, but is elsewhere quite obsolete' (Jakobsen 1985, 139), but other nineteenth-century collectors of Shetland dialect do not record the word (Barclay 1862; Edmonston 1866). Marwick does not include any variant spelling of the word in his dictionary of *The Orkney Norn* (Marwick 1929). This is not conclusive proof that the practice of portage had ceased in Shetland and Orkney, because there are English words which convey exactly the same information. As far as I am aware, however, there is no Scots or Scottish English word in the local dialects which refers precisely to the act of portage or to the isthmuses across which boats were dragged in the past, which suggests to me that the practice had gradually dwindled in the centuries preceding the death of Norn *c.*1800 in Shetland and about half a century earlier in Orkney (Barnes 1998, 26). There is a Gaelic word *tairbeart* (f. 'an isthmus') which appears, in addition to ON *eið*, in place-names in the Western Isles and on the western coast of the Scottish mainland. It provides linguistic evidence of an ongoing post-Norse tradition of hauling boats and goods across land.

It was a privilege to attend the conference on 'The significance of portages' in Lyngdal, Vest Agder, Norway in 2004 and to be given an opportunity to speak on the topic in Cork. I hope that further meetings of like minds will take place in future to consider the very real importance of *eið*-names as indicators of movement of people and goods in the early Norse period and later centuries in the North Atlantic islands.

APPENDIX

Orkney
Eday (itself an island): Doomy, Bay of Doomy, Loch of Doomy, Sands of Doomy (?)
Aith (Stronsay): Bight of Aith
Scapa (parish of St Ola, in the heart of which lies the main town of Kirkwall) (*Skálpeið:*
    Orkneyinga saga, 66)
Aith (west mainland): *Aithstoun (a lost name)
Aith (Walls): Aithsdale, Aith Hope, Aith Head, Bu of Aith
Hoxa (South Ronaldsay) (*Haugaeið: Orkneyinga saga*, 8)

Shetland
Aith (Fetlar): Burn of Aith, Aith Ness, Wick of Aith, Aiths Lee, Aithbank

Aiths Hamar (Yell)
Mavis Grind (Northmaven, northern part of mainland)
Brae (north mainland)
Aith (west mainland): Aithsting (parish name), Aithsness, Loch of Aithsness, Stead of
    Aithsness, Aith Ness, Aith Voe
Effirth (west mainland)
Lunnasting (north-east mainland): ('i luneidestingom' 1490) (ON *hlunnr*; Shet. dialect
    linn = 'piece of wood laid on beach to facilitate drawing up or down of boat')
Dury Voe (east mainland): possibly, the narrow place where animals were driven across at
    the head of the voe or inlet of the sea
*Aith (Whalsay): a lost name (Jakobsen 1993, 36).
Eswick (Nesting): sixteenth-century references suggest *eið* for the specific
Aith (Bressay): Aithness, Loch of Aithness, Aith Voe, Loch of Aith, Brecks of Aith, Leir
    Wick of Aith, Minni of Aith
Aith (Cunningsburgh, south mainland): Aithsetter, Aithsness, Aith Voe, Aith Wick, Burn
    of Aith
Brae (Foula)

Faroes
Eiðsvík (Hattarvík, Fugloy)
Viðareiði (Viðoy): Eiðsvík
Eiðið (Klaksvík, Borðoy)
Eiðið or Svínoyareið (Svínoy): Eiðisá, Við Eiðið
Eiðið or Húsaeið(i) (Húsar, Kalsoy): Undir Eiðinum, Eiðisgjógv, Eiðisrætt
Eiði (Eysturoy): Eiðisflógvi, Eiðiskollur, Eiðisskarð, Eiðisvatn, Eiðisbotnur
Inni á Eiði (Norðragøta, Eysturoy): Høgeið, Eiðisá, Fyri innan Eið
Gøtueið (Syðrugøta, Eysturoy): Undir Gøtueiði, Eiðisá, Eiðisbrekka, Fyri handan Eið
Lambareiði (Eysturoy): Eiðisá, Kongseið
Eiðið (Kvívík, Streymoy): Eiðismúli
Uttan fyri Eið or Fyri uttan Eið: (Miðvágur, Vágar)
Eiðið (Koltur)
Eiðið (Hestur)
Eiðið (Nólsoy)
Eiðið (Sandur, Sandoy); Eiðiskeldur (Skálavík, Sandoy)
Eiðið (Stóra Dímun)
Eiðið (Sandvík, Suðuroy)
Norðbergseiði (Hvalba, Suðuroy)
Hvalbiareiði (Hvalba, Suðuroy): Eiðishamar
Eiðið (Trongisvágur, Suðuroy)
Vágseið(i) or Eiðið (Vágur, Suðuroy)
Lopranseið(i) (Lopra-Vágur, Suðuroy): Eiðisgarður, Eiðishamar (Lopra), Eiðishamar
    (Vágur)

Iceland
Eiðar (Suður-Múlasýsla): Eiðavatn, Eiðahólmar
Eiði (Seltjarnarnes)

Eiði (Eyrarsveit)
Eiði (Mosfellssveit): Eiðsvík
Eiði (Langanes): Eiðisvík, Eiðisvatn, Eiðishyrna
Eiðisvatn (Skilmannahreppur)

ACKNOWLEDGMENTS

I owe thanks to both Eivind Weyhe and Svavar Sigmundsson respectively for their help in providing me with information about the Faroese and Icelandic *eið*-names. Also thanks to Marilyn Amedro for her help with collecting Faroese place-names. Louise Hollinrake is an Orcadian who has considered portages from a practical point of view while canoeing around the islands and I am very grateful for her illuminating comments. I owe thanks to Peter Mason of Eday for information concerning Doomy.

BIBLIOGRAPHY

Barclay, T. 1862. 'Glossary of Shetland words prepared for Dr Jamieson', National Library of Scotland, Adv. MS 22.5.2.

Barnes, M.P. 1998. *The Norn language of Orkney and Shetland* (Lerwick).

Cleasby, R. & Gudbrand Vigfusson, G. 1957. *An Icelandic-English dictionary*, 2nd ed. (Oxford).

Crawford, B.E. 1987. *Scandinavian Scotland* (Leicester).

Crawford, B.E. 2006. '*Houseby*, *Harray* and *Knarston* in the West Mainland of Orkney: toponymic indicators of administrative authority?' in P. Gammeltoft & B. Jørgensen (eds), *Names through the looking-glass* (Copenhagen), pp 21–44.

Edmonston, T. 1866. *An etymological glossary of the Shetland and Orkney dialect* (London).

Fritzner, J. 1972. *Ordbog over det Gamle Norske Sprog* (Oslo).

Hollinrake, L. 2003. 'An investigation of the traces of Norse mariners in the seascape of Orkney' (unpublished coursework, Orkney College, Kirkwall).

Jakobsen, J. 1985. *An etymological dictionary of the Norn language in Shetland*, vols 1–2 (Lerwick).

Jakobsen, J. 1993. *The place names of Shetland* (Lerwick).

Leask, R., A. Bradley & J. Bradley. 1998. 'Landscape and life in Gletness and Railsbrough, South Nesting' in V. Turner (ed.), *The shaping of Shetland* (Lerwick), pp 83–94.

Marwick, H. 1929. *The Orkney Norn* (Oxford).

Marwick, H. 1952. *Orkney farm-names* (Kirkwall).

Nicolaisen, W.F.H. 1983. 'The post-Norse place names of Shetland' in D.J. Withrington (ed.), *Shetland and the outside world, 1469–1969* (Oxford), pp 69–85.

Orkneyinga Saga = Hermann Pálsson & P. Edwards (trans). 1978. *Orkneyinga Saga: the history of the earls of Orkney* (London).

Peterkin, A. 1820. *Rentals of the ancient earldom and Bishoprick of Orkney* (Edinburgh).

Thomson, W.P.L. 1996. *Lord Henry Sinclair's 1492 rental of Orkney* (Kirkwall).

Thomson, W.P.L. 2001. *The new history of Orkney* (Edinburgh).

Waugh, D. 2005a. 'From Hermaness to Dunrossness: some Shetland ness-names' in A. Mortensen & S. Arge (eds), *Viking and Norse in the North Atlantic* (Tórshavn), pp 250–6.

Waugh, D. 2005b. 'What is an *aith*? Place name evidence for portages in Shetland' in L. Johnson & B. Smith (eds), *The New Shetlander* (Lerwick), pp 33–8.

Waugh, D. 2006. 'Place name evidence for portages in Orkney and Shetland' in C. Westerdahl (ed.), *The significance of portages*, British Archaeological Reports, International Series, 1499 (Oxford), pp 239–50.

Textiles that work for their living: a late eleventh-century cloth from Cork, Ireland

ELIZABETH WINCOTT HECKETT

INTRODUCTION

The use of cloth, clothing and self decoration is behaviour exclusive to the human species, so it is an essential component of archaeological studies. Perhaps the greater part of textile research has been taken up with our use of clothing as a denominator of culture, identity, gender and status, as well of the practicalities of the demands of specific climatic and working conditions. However, right from the earliest days, the utility of plant fibres and textiles for practical purposes has been well understood. Yarn, ropes and netting, all made by twisting and plying fibres into load-bearing tools, are essential basics for pulling and hauling, making ladders, bridges, carrying bags and packaging, fishing and trapping nets and many other tasks. At some point, people realized that woven textiles, by trapping the wind, could create energy that empowered boats to move fast without the tremendous effort human bodies must exert to row or paddle them. In the European context, heavy, coarse-weave cloth made from sheep's wool or goat hair was used for packaging and other purposes at least from the eleventh century AD, and probably from many centuries earlier.

It is the general category of such textiles 'that work for a living' that is the subject of this paper and, in particular, the example of a late eleventh-century cloth from a Hiberno-Norse site at 35–39 South Main Street, Cork (Fig. 50.1). It was excavated by Hillary Kelleher of the Archaeological Services Unit, Department of Archaeology, University College Cork in the summer of 2005.

ANALYSIS OF CLOTH

The excavation, which was very close to the River Lee, uncovered what seems to be the heart of the Viking and Hiberno-Norse settlement. It appears that the early part of the site near to the river was built up with clay brought from elsewhere to make a knoll upon which a house was built. There was possibly an inlet of the river beneath the wooden trackway running beside one of the houses.

The textile discussed here was found under the trackway, and comes from late eleventh-century levels. It is woven from wool and is within the family of coarse tabby weaves described later in the paper, but has several unusual features.

Analysis showed interesting details, unlike many other coarse tabbies, that raise questions as to its function. It is closely woven with Z-spun yarn about 1mm in diameter in the warp system and about 2mm in the weft. The number of threads to the centimetre in each system is of medium density for this category of cloth, with 3–4 warp ends and 4–5 weft picks. The cloth smells strongly of tar or pitch; it is only the second medieval cloth known to the author with this particular characteristic. One part is black and seems to have blackened deposits through it. The cloth is stiffer to the touch in some parts in a way that is unusual. There is also certainly a visible yellowish-white residue that is not earth. It could be clay but it does not dissolve. The cloth thickness is about 4mm, and where it is stiffened, over 6mm, a high measurement for this type of cloth.

Another unusual feature is the way in which the yarn that is either the starting or finishing borders is worked. They are the warp threads that were either stretched over the beam at the top of the loom, or left unwoven at the end of the cloth piece. In this case, they are particularly long and have been carefully plaited together which, in the author's experience, is unique for this type of coarse cloth. One surviving complete plait is 110mm long. It seems unlikely that the weaver would go to the trouble of plaiting threads on such coarse industrial cloth unless there was a practical reason; for example, if the cloth needed to be tied into place. There are a variety of fancy tassels made up at the ends of light silk scarves dating from tenth- and eleventh-century Dublin, but no work of this sort has been noted on other basic coarse-weave cloths (Wincott Heckett 2003, 9–35).

COMPARANDA

Excavations were carried out in Grand Parade, Cork City, in 1984 at thirteenth-century levels, close to the South Main Street site. Seven quite substantial pieces of coarse tabby woven wool cloth were discarded alongside the wooden walkways leading from houses to the river banks where it would be logical to find the remains of wrapping materials associated with the transport and unloading of goods (Wincott Heckett 1990, 81–3).

Another very large cloth, with only a general medieval date, now in three pieces and probably originally over a metre in length, was retrieved nearby in the earlier Christ Church excavations (Wincott Heckett & Janaway 1997, 340–5). Janaway reported that originally the tabby weave textile was in a large ball enclosed in a solid matrix of soil and resin, with quite large quantities of an undissolved material (possibly resin) remaining. Indeed, even years later the cloth still smelt of resin. At the time, this suggested an industrial use perhaps to rub the resin into the caulking material used between planks in clinker built ships or in the construction of wooden jetties. It is very likely that such a large piece had a primary use as packaging before the later recycling. This wool cloth has two

50.1 Tabby wool cloth, South Main Street, Cork (photo: Elizabeth Wincott Heckett).

warp yarns, and two weft yarns per centimetre, and was therefore a very coarse weave. Both warp and weft were made from S-spun yarn that had been Z-plied.

Another eight pieces of tabby weave cloth, all S/S spun, and Z/Z plied with low counts of 1.5 to 3.5 threads to the centimetre were also recovered. One was made from animal hair, five from wool and three could not be identified.

Similar remains of coarse tabby weave cloth were found in Dublin in the 1969–71 National Museum of Ireland excavations in Winetavern Street near the River Liffey. From Lund, Sweden there are eleventh- and twelfth-century examples as there are also four eleventh-century pieces from London, two of which come from the settlement where Saxon merchants lived (Wincott Heckett 1990, 81–3).

No plain tabby sheep's wool cloth of the coarse 'packaging' type, like the Cork cloths, was found at Bryggen, although a similar cloth made from goats' hair was excavated in small numbers from the earliest late twelfth-century levels. The Bryggen cloth is a tabby weave, S-spun, Z 2ply, with a mean thread count per centimetre of 2.5 warp ends and 2.8 weft picks (Scholberg 1984, 79–88).

This general category of an 'invisible' coarse cloth, so often found near rivers or the sea, is likely to have been an all-purpose material, since medieval society had no access to the types of modern packaging we take for granted. Bales of cloth were traditionally sewn into an outer layer of sacking, and this practice persisted well into the twentieth century. For example, in the 1970s carpets were rolled up and sewn in a packaging cloth when being despatched abroad from the *souks* of North Africa.

POSSIBLE FUNCTIONS OF THE CORK CLOTH

There are at least three different possibilities for the original function of the Cork cloth. The first to be considered is whether it was part of a sail; the second is that it was associated with caulking activities: and the third is that it was part of a tarpaulin, or packaging for merchandise. The properties required from a particular cloth to fulfil these functions are now explored.

1) Sailcloth types and their properties
Although the importance of ships to the Vikings has always been clear, it has, perhaps, been only relatively recently that attention has focused on that essential component for the success of any Viking expedition – a well woven and well finished sail. For the last twenty years or so, experimental work has been under-taken by the Roskilde Museum, in collaboration with Norwegian colleagues, on the construction of the type of sails originally used. Three papers were published in *Northern Archaeological Textiles – NESAT VII* (2005) on this topic (Jørgensen 2005; Cooke & Christiansen 2005; Möller-Wierung 2005). These papers provide a solid foundation of contemporary scholarship on the topic of Viking sails.

Lise Bender Jørgensen describes the production of the wool sail for the SS *Sara Kjerstine* in 1992 by the Tømmervik Textile Trust at Hitra, Norway. Wool from 2,000 fleeces of the traditional *villsau* sheep, the Norwegian short-tailed wild sheep, was needed to weave the 100m² provided (Anderson 1995, 249). A choice was made to sort the wool from the fleeces into long hairs and soft bottom wool. The long hairs were combed and spun by hand into the 100km of strong, load-bearing yarn needed for the warp system, and the soft wool became a further 80km of weft thread. 164m of web were woven and fulled. The cloth was transformed into a sail by being smeared with tallow, tar and fish oil, and was most successful in its purpose. It took three years to complete the sail. Jørgensen quotes from the poem *Hǫfuðlausn*, written *c.*1023 by Ottar svarti, which contains the phrase 'The sail spun by women played at the ship's mast', thus emphasizing the crucial role played by women in ensuring successful expeditions for the whole community.

Research was undertaken in 1997 by Cooke and Christiansen at the University of Manchester's Institute of Technology using modern methods of analyzing the properties of cloth on the construction of textiles used at sea, and, in particular, sails, during the expanding maritime culture of Viking-Age and medieval

Scandinavia. They carried out yarn and fabric cross-section analysis, twist-testing for optimal tensile performance and effectiveness of the cloth fulling process, air permeability testing, and fabric tensile testing. Their major conclusion was that *smørring*, the process of applying the dressing of hard and soft tallow and ochre, was essential to the success of a sail. The weaver had to provide a web with the correct tensile properties to resist the force of the wind, and the correct extension and recovery properties to ensure an appropriate air foil shape in use.

Anna Nørgaard, who is a distinguished Danish weaver and expert in the reconstruction of ancient textiles, undertook the experiments in the dressing of the cloth. She used horse fat taken from the neck roll stored by well-fed horses, since this was written about in early sources (Nørgaard, pers. comm.). In her research into possible remains of sails, Möller-Wiering suggests a check list of possible and typical characteristics of woollen square sails and sails in general:

> The sail cloth should be tightly woven: fabrics and trimmings must be laid out to withstand severe weather; the leeward side should be smooth, while the windward side may be uneven; the surface will probably be finished with some greasy material e.g. with a mixture of tallow and tar (Möller-Wiering 2005, 75–6).

The evidence for sails of the Viking period and up into the eleventh century is that, in the main, sails were made from wool cloth in a 2/2 diagonal twill and some in 1/1 tabby. Plain tabby weave cloth was used for sails in the Faroe Islands and in Iceland, although with a higher and therefore denser thread count than the Cork textile. 2/1 twill began to be used in the eleventh century, certainly in Norway (Andersen 1995, 258–61).

2) The process of caulking
What were the materials used for caulking in the eleventh and twelfth centuries in Ireland and northern Europe? In Fishamble Street, Dublin, excavations where caulking was found on some of the ships planking in groups TG10, TG9, TG6 and TG3 the materials used were mainly sheep and cattle hair with some horse hair, matted together with tar. This was found within the overlaps of the planks, having been placed there before the planks were fastened together. Similar caulking was found on keels T56 (AD1180–1225), T381 (955–1000) and T383 (AD905–75: McGrail 1993, 44–5). Oak planks from Skuldelev 3 (early eleventh century), Lynaes (mid-twelfth century), Fishamble Street TG6 and TG9 (1180–1225) and TG3 (1230–75) all had caulking of tarred animal hair in their joints, as did an oak plank (DST354 Fishamble Street), within the overlap (McGrail 1993, Table 29, 91, 145).

Ole Crumlin-Pedersen (1988, 530–63) has demonstrated that there was probably an eastern Baltic or Slav variant tradition, where the basic caulking material was moss rather than animal hair. Confirmation that cloth was sometimes used for repairing ships' planks is provided by the 2/1 twill wool cloth used for this purpose on the twelfth-century ship from Karschau, Denmark. Also in the twelfth century, woven cloth used for caulking repairs was noted from ships Roskilde 2 (2/1, 2/2 wool twill), Roskilde 5 and Lynaes 1 (2/1 wool twill) (Möller-Wierung 2004, 115–16).

At Bryggen in Bergen, numerous animal-skin fibre products were found, most of which relate to caulking and marine activities. For the period AD1170–1198, fifty items of caulking cords are listed, the majority of which were pure sheep wool cords, a smaller number were hair cords, and even fewer of mixed hair and sheep's wool. Some had clearly been used for caulking. In the earliest time, all fifteen finds were made of sheep's wool. These earlier cords are finely spun in comparison to those of the later medieval periods. Schølberg interprets this as showing that the earlier caulking cords were more likely to be a traditional domestic craft (Schølberg 1984, 76–7).

Also from Bryggen are some finds of scraps of sheepskins or fells. Number 38996 consisted of a little bundle of such pieces, 8cm in diameter tied around with a leather strip. Two others (24690 & 25781) may have served as early work brushes, since they have tar in between the hairs that at the time of analysis was still black and sticky. Eleven of the fourteen finds are goatskin and goatskin scrapings (Schølberg 1984, 75).

Similar evidence has come from somewhat later English sites at Newcastle and Doncaster, with the earlier prevalence of wool 'rolag' type caulking rolls. The term *rolag* is used for loosely rolled bundles of spun wool fibres (Walton Rogers 1996, Introduction).

3) Tarpaulins and packaging
It is possible that the remaining piece of cloth was originally larger and was used as packaging that could protect its contents, a necessary function over many centuries. In relation to the deposits on the Cork cloth under discussion, it is of particular interest that McGrail records a yellowish-white deposit on the outboard face of planking in TG9 in his analysis of the marine wood from Viking-Age Dublin. This proved on analysis to be a mixture of calcium carbonate and pine resin, which he understood probably to be the remains of a waterproof coating (McGrail 1993, 56). He notes that 'paint' coatings were found on the Skuldelev (3) planking (Crumlin-Pedersen 1986b, 149), and that preservative treatments with pine tar were widely used in early medieval Scandinavia (Christensen 1985, 213). There is some specific evidence about the use of tar made from pine resin.

The only example of such finds from recent Dublin excavations (apart from tools) is a pot sherd, associated with TG3.2/3.3, which had a tarry deposit on its inner face. On examination, the deposit proved to be wood tar with rosin, which

50.2 Oakum being applied during caulking process
(from *The Useful Arts of the Pictorial Gallery of Arts*, 1847).

was shown by gas liquid chromatography (BM 6170/1) to be similar to the tar used in the caulking in TG3 seams (McGrail 1993, 87).

It seems likely therefore that a similar mixture was in use in Hiberno-Norse Cork, whether for caulking animal hair or small pieces of woven cloth between planks, or for weatherproofing large pieces of cloth as tarpaulins.

The 1911 edition of the *Encyclopaedia Britannica* (XXVI: 430), which mainly describes nineteenth-century knowledge and usage, defines the semantic origins of the word *tarpaulin* as a combination of *tar* and *palling*, a covering (Lat. *palla*, 'a mantle'). It is described as: 'A heavy, well-made, double warp plain fabric, of various materials [...] and for protecting goods on wharves, quays etc. To make it proof against rain and other atmospheric influences it is generally treated with tar'. It seems that even in the nineteenth century, the type of cloth used for tarpaulins is not too far removed in its manufacture from the medieval prototype.

An interesting description and illustrations of early nineteenth-century caulking is given in an 1847 reference book on skilled trades and manufacturing techniques (*The Useful Arts of The Pictorial Gallery of Arts*, 1847):

As a means of preventing water from entering between the planks, the seams are 'caulked,' or filled up by strings of 'oakum'. This oakum consists of old cables and ropes cut into pieces and picked asunder so as to form a mass of fibres; these fibres are rolled together as a kind of rude substitute for string, by means of the hand and a board placed in a sloping position [...]. The threads of oakum thus rolled are made up into bundles, and taken to the ship's side, where the caulker proceeds to use them. He drives in the threads by means of a hammer and an instrument called a 'caulking-iron' [...], filling up every seam so densely that it not only prevents the entrance of water, but also strengthens the framework generally. Any little rents, holes or fissures that may appear in the woodwork are similarly filled up with oakum. After this, the whole is coated with a hot mixture of pitch and resin' (Fig. 50.2).

The description of the oakum and the process of making it sounds very close to the 'rolags', or loosely rolled bundles of sheep's wool described by Schølberg and Walton Rogers (1984, 75–7; 1996, 78–9).

CONCLUSION

Although we do not know what kind of sails were used in Cork at the time, it is unlikely that the Cork textile is part of a sail since it is not densely woven and firm enough. Although it has a tar/pitch content, it does not appear to fulfil the requirements set out by Möller-Wiering (2005, 75–9). However, its unusual features strongly suggest a maritime function. Hillary Kelleher has emphasized the riverine character of the site, with its many islets and channels that would have been navigated in small open boats and ships (Fig. 50.3). The seamen would have used textiles in many capacities, and the Cork piece may have started its working life as packaging for merchandise. It seems that from early times, treatment with waterproofing materials like tar and calcium produced the specialized covering later known as tarpaulin. In addition, the cloth may have been 'recycled' as a work-cloth in the process of ship repair, being applied to damaged planking with a tar covering.

The strong smell of the resin, from which medieval tar was most likely extracted, can be accounted for by its use in the process of secondary repairs and caulking of ships' timbers. Alternatively, when the cloth was newly made, it was first treated with resin tar and perhaps a calcium component like chalk, before being used as a tarpaulin to protect merchandise being transported by land and sea.

50.3 Carving on wood of ship, masts and sailor, E122:16078, eleventh century, Christchurch Place, Dublin (© Royal Irish Academy/National Museum of Ireland).

BIBLIOGRAPHY

Andersen, E. 1995. 'Square sails of wool' in O. Olsen, J. Skamby Madsen & F. Rieck (eds), *Shipshape: essays for Ole Crumlin-Pedersen* (Roskilde), pp 249–60.

Bender Jørgensen, L. 2005. 'Textiles of seafaring: an introduction to an interdisciplinary research project' in F. Pritchard & J.P. Wild (eds), *Northern archaeological textiles*, North-European Symposium for Archaeological Textiles, 7 (Oxford), pp 65–9.

Cooke, W. & C. Christiansen. 2005. 'What makes a Viking sail' in F. Pritchard & J.P. Wild (eds), *Northern archaeological textiles*, North-European Symposium for Archaeological Textiles, 7 (Oxford), pp 70–4.

Christensen, A.-E. 1985. 'Boat finds from Bryggen', *Bryggen Papers*, 1, 47–280.

Crumlin-Pedersen, O. 1986. 'Aspects of wood technology in medieval shipbuilding' in O. Crumlin-Pedersen & M. Vinner (eds), *Sailing into the past* (Roskilde), pp 138–49.

Crumlin-Pedersen, O. 1988. 'Schiff und schiffahrtswege im Ostseeraum wahrend des 9–12 jahrhunderts' in M. Müller-Wille (ed.), *Oldenburg, Wolin, Staraja Ladoga, Novgorod, Kiev* (Mainz), pp 530–63.

Encyclopaedia Britannica. 1911. 11th ed., 26 (New York).

McGrail, S. 1993. *Medieval boat and ship timbers from Dublin*, Medieval Dublin Excavations, Series B, 3, 1962–81 (Dublin).

Möller-Wierung, S. 2004. 'Schiffbau und textil: ansatze zu einer systematischen untersuchung von Kalfat' in J. Maik (ed.), *Priceless invention of humanity – textiles*, North-European Symposium for Archaeological Textiles, 8, (Łødz), pp 113–19.

Möller-Wierung, S. 2005. 'Textiles for transport' in F. Pritchard & J.P. Wild (eds), *Northern archaeological textiles*, North-European Symposium for Archaeological Textiles, 7 (Oxford), pp 75–9.

Schølberg, E. 1984. 'The hair products', *Bryggen Papers*, 1 (Oslo), 73–91.

*The useful arts of the pictorial gallery of arts. c.*1847. 1 (London).

Walton Rogers, P. 1996. *Caulking, cordage and textiles from medieval ports of the North-East* (York).

Wincott Heckett, E. 1990. 'The textiles' in M. Hurley, 'Excavations at Grand Parade Cork II (part 2)', *Journal of the Cork Historical and Archaeological Society*, 95:254, 81–6.

Wincott Heckett, E. 2003. *Viking-Age headcoverings from Dublin*, Medieval Dublin Excavation, Series B, 6, 1962–81 (Dublin).

Wincott Heckett, E. & R. Janaway. 1997. 'The textiles: animal hair and yarn' in R. Cleary, M. Hurley & E. Shee Twohig (eds), *Excavations by D.C. Twohig at Skiddy's Castle and Christ Church, Cork 1974–77* (Cork), 340–8.

Index